TEACHING SECONDARY SCHOOL MATHEMATICS

Techniques and Enrichment Units

4th Edition

Alfred S. Posamentier
Professor of Mathematics Education
Associate Dean, School of Education
The City College
The City University of New York
New York, New York

Jay Stepelman
Supervisor of Mathematics Department (retired)
George Washington High School
New York, New York

Merrill, an imprint of
Prentice Hall

Englewood Cliffs, New Jersey   Columbus, Ohio

Library of Congress Cataloging-in-Publication Data

Posamentier, Alfred S.
    Teaching secondary school mathematics:
techniques and enrichment units/Alfred S. Posamentier,
Jay Stepelman,—4th ed.
        p.   cm.
    Includes bibliographical references and index.
    ISBN 0-02-396262-3
    1. Mathematics—Study and teaching
(Secondary) I. Stepelman, Jay. II. Title.
    QA11.P6175   1995
    510′.71′2—dc20
                                    94-44736
                                    CIP

Editor: Linda James Scharp
Production Editor: Rex Davidson
Production Management: Spectrum Publisher Services
Cover Art: Copyright Gregory Sams/Photo
    Researchers, Inc.
Cover Designer: Proof Positive/Farrowlyne Assoc., Inc.
Production Buyer: Laura Messerly

This book was set in Times Roman and Helvetica by
Bi-Comp, Inc. and was printed and bound by Courier/
Kendallville, Inc. The cover was printed by Phoenix
Color Corp.

Printed in the United States of America

10 9 8 7 6 5 4 3 2 1

ISBN: 0-02-396262-3

Prentice-Hall International (UK) Limited, *London*
Prentice-Hall of Australia Pty. Limited, *Sydney*
Prentice-Hall Canada Inc., *Toronto*
Prentice-Hall Hispanoamericana, S. A., *Mexico*
Prentice-Hall of India Private Limited, *New Delhi*
Prentice-Hall of Japan, Inc., *Tokyo*
Simon & Schuster Asia Pte. Ltd., *Singapore*
Editora Prentice-Hall do Brasil, Ltda., *Rio de Janeiro*

CONTENTS

PREFACE

The 21st century for school mathematics in the United States began in 1986 with the establishment of the Commission on Standards for School Mathematics. Two years later a document known as the *Curriculum and Evaluation Standards for School Mathematics* was issued. A second document, *Professional Standards for Teaching Mathematics,* made its appearance in 1990 after consideration and analysis by educators, mathematicians, teachers, and supervisors, followed by a third document, *Assessment Standards for School Mathematics* (1995).

These documents, created under the auspices of the National Council of Teachers of Mathematics, established a framework to guide reform in school mathematics in the coming decade. This fourth edition is a practical text on how to teach the mathematics curriculum of the *Standards.* It contains some of the same advice to new teachers that was so well received in earlier editions. In fact, how to teach secondary school mathematics well is what this book is all about. It is specifically written for preservice mathematics teachers and for in-service junior and senior high school teachers as well.

The fact is, there is no dearth of books on virtually every aspect of education. The education section may even be one of the largest in a college library. We believe this text offers an alternative to others available with respect to both style and coverage. The style is direct and to the point, with a minimum of theory and a maximum of practical information from experienced teachers.

This book has four parts. Part 1 consists of preparatory chapters that help teachers understand the basis for the most suitable approach for each type of lesson. Part 2 is in effect a handbook for teachers on how to determine which topics are best taught in small and which in large group lessons, how to develop challenging tasks, how to create a sound learning environment, ways to allow students time to reflect, how to encourage students to participate in discourse, how to make appropriate connections with other branches of mathematics or other subject areas, and how to improve a student's disposition toward mathematics. It considers alternative problem-solving strategies, the role of scientific and graphics calculators and computers, and extracurricular activities, where students will learn to value mathematics while developing confidence in their own mathematical ability.

Professional development of teachers is discussed in Part 3. This includes both self-evaluation and collegial interaction processes.

Part 4 is a unique section containing a wealth of enrichment ideas designed to be used by both junior and senior high school mathematics classes. Each enrichment unit is self-contained and includes performance objectives, preassessments, motivation ideas, teaching strategies, and postassessments. A cross-reference table relating the enrichment units to the appropriate topic, grade level, and ability level is provided at the start of Part 4. This table will facilitate the selection of an enrichment activity appropriate for a particular class.

With this fourth edition we have recognized a new audience of *Standards*-literate mathematics teachers. Not only must they be capable of teaching and enriching mathematics, but they must be mindful of their changing roles, as facilitators, questioners, encouragers, and role models. This awareness will ultimately bring school mathematics into the 21st century.

The book may be used as a text for both undergraduate and graduate courses in the teaching of secondary school mathematics as well as for an in-service course on topics in mathematics for secondary school teachers. The inclusion of the enrichment units (Part 4) makes this a valuable source of special topics and ideas for enriching mathematics instruction. The book is thus designed to play an active role in the mathematics teacher's professional library for many years to come.

ACKNOWLEDGMENTS

A book of this scope requires input from a wide variety of professionals. Many secondary school teachers participated in the preparation of the enrichment units, a majority of which were originally published by Croft-NEI Publications (Waterford, Connecticut). We extend our sincere gratitude to these teachers: Renee E. Baxter, Peter Catranides, Beatrice F. Cohen, Steven Colello, Joyce A. Dato, James DeMetro, Benito Gomez, Adele Hayda, Cynthia Horvath, Howard Kale, Gladys Kornfield, Arlene Kuperberg, Susan Loeb, David Martinez, Robert Parisi, Patricia Pearson, Steven Pottash, Soraida Rivera, Amelia O. Roges, Howard Sardis, Verna Segarra, Max Sharf, Malcolm Singer, Joseph Skittone, Jon Sontz, Daniel Stolnitz, Richard A. Vitulli, Stanley Weinstein, Barbara Winters, and Betty York.

In particular we thank Professor Brigitte Rollett, head of the Psychological Institute at the University of Vienna (Austria) for her valuable and insightful contribution to the chapter on teacher sensitivity. We also wish to thank Professor Alfred Weiss, formerly of the City College of the City University of New York, who contributed "A Psychological View of Problem Solving" in Chapter 9, as well as the section on "Creativity in Problem Solving," also in that chapter.

We also received some expert criticism and input for two specialized chapters. Dr. Gerald H. Elgarten, former Director of Mathematics at the New York City Board of Education, and Associate Professor of Mathematics Education at the City College of the City University of New York, made some valuable contributions on computers in Chapter 10. Steven Conrad, a well-known problem-solving expert, a leader in national and local mathematics contests, and a mathematics teacher at Roslyn High School (New York State), offered some valuable comments on Chapter 9, "Problem Solving." Both have our thanks for their assistance.

Special thanks are offered to Jacob Cohen, former Assistant Principal in Charge of Mathematics at Theodore Roosevelt High School (New York City), for his careful reading of the entire manuscript and for the very insightful comments he offered throughout. In particular, his work on Chapter 11, "Assessing, Evaluating, and Grading Students," and contributions to Part 2 were greatly appreciated. Thanks are also extended to the late Peter Catranides, former teacher of mathematics at George Washington High School (New York City), for drawing some of the more complex geometric figures in Part 4.

Many of the revisions in the Second Edition resulted from comments generously offered by Professor Miriam E. Connellan (Marquette University), Professor William M. Waters, Jr. (North Carolina State University), Professor Emeritus Claire M. Newman (Queens College, CUNY), and Professor Max Sobel (Montclair State College). We are grateful to these mathematics education experts for reviewing the text and providing their insights. The Third Edition had the valuable input of Professor Hope Hartman of The City College of the City university of New York; Dr. Harry Ruderman, former chairman of the mathematics department of Hunter College High School/CUNY; and Arlene Zimny, former Deputy Executive Director of the High School Division and of the Division of Curriculum and Instruction of the New York City Board of Education.

We would be remiss if we did not acknowledge the quiet, unassuming role of Deborah J. Stepelman, computer/mathematics teacher at the Bronx High School of Science for her constant encouragement, critical reading and proofreading of manuscripts, and her contribution of the section "Computer Classroom Management" in Chapter 10, "Enriching Mathematics Instruction."

To Jeff Daube and Barbara Rockow we owe many thanks for sharing with us their vast knowledge of computers and manipulatives, respectively.

We appreciate and truly regret the delay in acknowledging the permission granted by The National Council of Teachers of Mathematics and author Arthur A. Hiatt to reproduce significant portions of his "Activities for Calculators," which appeared in *Arithmetic Teacher* 34, no. 6 (February 1987): 38–42.

We are indebted to Kraus International Publications for permission to use portions of their Curriculum Resource Handbook, 1993 edition— *Current Trends in Mathematics* and *State Mathematics Frameworks*, by Jay Stepelman.

The Fourth Edition was strongly enhanced by contributions of Dr. Alice Artzt (Queens College, CUNY) and Dr. Claire Newman, who embellished the section on teaching sensitivity and contributed the unit on cooperative learning.

In addition, we thank reviewers William S. Bush, Jay Graening, Mark Klespis, Nancy A. Minix, and Ken Stilwell.

We are also grateful to our editor, Linda James Scharp, for providing valuable support services and generally allowing us to work in a pressure-free atmosphere.

PART 1
PREPARING TO TEACH MATHEMATICS

Before presenting material in Parts 2 and 3 to serve as a guide for budding mathematics teachers to reach full flower and bloom under the influence of the National Council of Teachers of Mathematics' (NCTM) *Curriculum and Evaluation Standards for School Mathematics* (or *Standards*), Part I offers three preliminary yet relevant chapters that consider small learning groups, writing in the mathematics classroom, and teacher sensitivity. Our goal is to create an environment in which new teachers will teach with enthusiasm and commitment, and experienced teachers will reconsider ways to help each student attain a significant degree of mathematical power. Knowledge of students' understandings and ways of thinking can guide teachers in creating stimulating and challenging tasks. New teachers must discard preconceived notions about the teaching profession. It is no longer sufficient for a teacher to be skilled only at producing well-polished lessons. New teacher roles now involve coordinating the activities of groups of students who are functioning simultaneously in different parts of the same classroom, encouraging all students to be effective mathematics communicators, and lessening student anxieties about mathematics. The *Standards* has moved teaching school mathematics into a "new era."

The influence of the *Standards* is evident in each of the three chapters. The teacher's role in small group management and the incorporation of such learning groups into the mathematics class are discussed at length in Chapter 1.

Chapter 2 addresses communication in the mathematics classroom, including speaking, listening, and writing. The chapter analyzes the purpose of student logs and journals, expository writing, items to consider in student writing samples, and the benefits of writing assignments.

Chapter 3 discusses the need for teacher sensitivity, open-ended questioning, and equal treatment of all students in the learning process. The purpose of these activities is to reduce math anxiety, which causes many students, particularly female and minority students, to avoid math.

CHAPTER 1
SMALL GROUP LEARNING

Small group learning is an approach that involves learners working together as a team to solve a problem, complete a task, or accomplish a common goal. Group members are part of the team, and the success or failure of the group is shared by all members of the group. Support for this kind of learning experience comes from the National Council of Teachers of Mathematics' (NCTM) *Curriculum and Evaluation Standards for School Mathematics* (or *Standards*). The *Standards* recommends that teachers provide opportunities for students to work together in small groups to solve problems. In this way, students can talk about the problem under consideration, discuss solution strategies, relate the problem to others that have previously been solved, resolve difficulties, and think about the entire problem-solving process. According to the *Standards,* "Small groups provide a forum in which students ask questions, discuss ideas, make mistakes, learn to listen to others' ideas, offer constructive criticism, and summarize their discoveries in writing" (p. 79). Group assignments enable learners to work together, helping one another to integrate new knowledge with prior knowledge and to discover their own meanings as they explore, discuss, explain, and question new ideas that arise in the group.

WHAT IS COOPERATIVE LEARNING?

Cooperative learning goes beyond merely putting students together in small groups and giving them an assignment. Certain elements are necessary to ensure that when students *do* work in groups, they work cooperatively. First, the members of a group must perceive that they are part of a team and that they all have a common goal. Second, group members must realize that the problem they are to solve is a group problem and that the success or failure of the group will be shared by all the members of the group. Third, to accomplish the group's goal, all students must talk with one another—engage in discussion of all problems. Finally, it must be clear that each member's individual work has a direct effect on the group's success. Teamwork is of utmost importance.

It is *not* a cooperative environment if students sit together in groups and work on problems individually or let one person do all the work. True cooperation in the learning process requires the guidance of a teacher who can help students understand group dynamics, develop the cooperative skills they need, and learn mathematics by working in groups.

True cooperative learning capitalizes on the presence of student peers, encourages student-to-student interaction, and establishes a symbiotic relationship among team members. Students in effective groups learn to listen to others' ideas, to discuss and disagree, to offer and accept constructive criticism from their peers, and to be comfortable about making mistakes.

HOW TO STRUCTURE SMALL LEARNING GROUPS

Small learning groups can be structured in many ways. The literature sets forth many techniques that researchers and teachers have developed and studied. Each of these methods is designed to ensure that within each group there is positive interdependence, individual accountability, face-to-face verbal communication, and positive social interaction. The techniques address four essential areas: group formation, task designs, reward structures, and group processing.

Group Formation

Those who are experienced in the field of small learning groups recognize that group formation is critical to its effectiveness—to maximize the benefits of small learning groups, the membership should be heterogeneous in ability and personal characteristics. The group must stay together long enough for cohesiveness to develop. A

successful group will be small enough for everyone to be needed but large enough to permit a diversity of ideas and skills.

The most effective way of ensuring heterogeneity is for the teacher to organize the groups. Teachers know their own students best and can see to it that they place readers with nonreaders, task-oriented students with non-task-oriented students, high-ability students with medium- and low-ability students, minority students with majority students, non-English-speaking students with those who speak English, students who have disabilities with nondisabled students, and females with males. Students can be asked to indicate which peers they would like to work with, and the teacher can consider their wishes when groups are being formed. It is important that students be happy in their groups if they are to work well.

One of the criteria for group success is the durability of the group. It takes time for group cohesiveness to develop. When students know that their group will be together for some time, they realize that they must improve their interpersonal skills so that they can function effectively. Small learning groups may stay together during a unit of work, a semester, or a year. Although it is important that groups stay together and learn how to work productively and harmoniously, if some groups are not working out well, changes should be made. When students are dissatisfied with fellow group members, it is unlikely that they can engage in the free expression and exploration of ideas. It is, therefore, important that the teacher keep informed about the attitudes and behavior of each group member. One way teachers do this is by observing how students interact with one another within the group. A group may seem to be functioning well, but sometimes observations are deceiving; a group may not be functioning as well as it seems to be. Students can be asked to use journals to communicate their feelings about their groups and the way that they function within the group. They should comment on the help they have given or received within the group. Together, the students and the teacher should decide when and if group arrangements should be changed.

The size of a group affects its ability to be productive. Experience has shown that groups of three to five students work well. A learning group should not be too large. If a group has too many students, it becomes very difficult for the group to function effectively. The most vocal students tend to take over, and the quiet ones recede into the background. In a large group it is difficult for everybody to air their ideas. Furthermore, it is difficult for a large group to get organized, to coordinate the work of its members, and to reach agreement.

To add to the feeling of camaraderie, each group might agree on a name for itself. In cases in which the groups have stabilized, the teacher may wish to take a picture of each group, have the students mount them on group-designed construction paper, and then post them on the bulletin board. This can add to the warmth and enjoyment of being part of a learning group.

Task Designs

For small group learning to succeed, the students must perceive themselves as being dependent on one another, they must communicate with one another, and they must be individually accountable for the work. To maximize the changes for these conditions to exist, group tasks must be designed thoughtfully.

One way to ensure that each student participates in the group assignment is to have each student prepare the work prior to the group's meeting. This work can be homework or it can be an in-class assignment. The important idea is that each student is required to do individual work on the task before the group meets to compare and agree on solutions.

For small group learning to succeed, there must be individual accountability. Responsibility for each person's learning is shared by other group members. Group members are expected to help and encourage one another. The emphasis is on working and learning together. Nevertheless, individual students are held accountable for their own learning and for their individual contributions to the group. Each member of the group is responsible for mastering the material. Each student is expected to bring assigned work to the group so that the group can complete its task. The group holds its members individually accountable for such assignments. Individuals may not sit back and defer to others in the group. They are expected to learn and to participate in the group's work.

Another way to ensure that each student participates in the group assignment is to divide the task in such a way that each student is responsible for doing one part of the work. That is, the group assignment cannot be completed unless each student in the group contributes his or her own piece of the work.

To achieve the group's goal or to complete the group's task, each member of a group expects each of the others to make a contribution. Cooperation is based on reciprocity. Maintaining effective working relationships among group members requires each student to appreciate the value of reciprocation. Each student must be prepared to give as well as receive.

Reward Structures

A well-designed reward structure gives added incentives for small group learning behavior among students. For example, after the groups have submitted an assignment, each group's products are evaluated by both the teacher and the students, and each group's score is recorded on a chart that is accessible to all the students. To ensure individual accountability, a group gets full credit for its results only if a randomly selected student in the group can adequately explain the solutions. There are many ways to score group products, depending on the nature of the assignments. Scoring may involve counting the number of correct solutions, qualitatively evaluating a solution strategy with a letter grade, or ranking the work from each group. Groups may compete with one another or strive to meet certain preestablished criteria. Care must be taken that this competition does not drive the weaker members into passive "backseat" roles. Rather, they must be as active as the more involved students.

Students working within such a reward structure are eager to check with one another to be sure that each person in the group understands the material, agrees with the results or conclusions, and is able to represent the group as a spokesperson. Students ask one another for help or clarification, they ask questions, and they answer questions. The quality of the verbal interaction is an important factor in the group's success.

Another motivating strategy is Student Teams-Achievement Divisions (STAD) (Slavin, 1984). The teacher presents a lesson, and then the students meet in teams of four or five to complete a set of worksheets on the lesson. Each student then takes an exam on the material, and the scores the students contribute to their teams are based on the degree to which they have improved over their individual past averages. Another method, Teams-Games-Tournament (TGT), is similar to STAD, but instead of taking quizzes the students play mathematics games as representatives of their teams. They compete with other students having similar achievement levels.

With these types of reward structures, students are encouraged to be concerned not only about themselves but also about the other members of the group. Students engage in peer teaching because they acknowledge that each group member must understand the material. Each student recognizes that group members expect him or her to complete the assigned work and to make a contribution to the group. Students help one another. One student explains a difficult concept to another in his or her own words. Group members share resources, act as resources for one another, and encourage one another to participate. Even those who are usually silent are made to feel that the group relies on them to participate in the group's activities. It is "all for one and one for all" because that is what makes group success possible.

In addition to the intrinsic rewards experienced by members of successful cooperative groups, additional incentives may be offered. Members of successful groups may be presented with certificates. Names of successful groups for the month may be listed on the bulletin board. Students are always motivated to improve their grades, but rewarding students in this way must be done very carefully. One valid technique is to count "cooperation" as a percentage of their final grade. Members of successful teams may then be given extra "cooperation" points.

Group Processing

The teacher must help students realize that for a group to function well, members must feel free to express their ideas, ask questions, and clarify differences. Thus, each person must be patient and exert self-control. Once all ideas have been discussed, group members must be willing to compromise—to integrate different perspectives into a single group solution that is acceptable to all. This may be difficult and not always achievable because of the students' prior educational experiences.

It is not unusual for differences and disagreements to arise even though the group is working cooperatively. Group members need the skills to manage such controversies. Teachers must help students realize that group members should be critical of ideas but not of people. They should understand that controversy strengthens understanding and helps the group reach consensus. They must learn how important it is for each student to listen carefully to what other group members are saying and to try to understand ideas with which he or she disagrees. Such skills of conflict management are essential to any group's functioning.

Teachers must monitor the groups while they are in progress and provide assistance as it is needed. When a group is functioning poorly, the teacher will want to intervene to help students with the skills they need. Once these skills have been identified and discussed, the teacher will want to see how well the group is practicing them and whether it is functioning more effectively. The teacher should provide feedback so that students know how well they are doing. The teacher may ask the groups to monitor their own performance by answering questions about the group's behavior and functioning. Is each person participating? Are students helping one another? Are they handling conflicts well?

THE TEACHER'S ROLE IN MANAGING SMALL GROUP LEARNING

The teacher plays a vital role in the implementation of effective small group learning. Before students are asked to work in groups, the teacher should give an explanation of the assignment, the time allowed for the activity, the academic expectations for the group, the expected collaborative behaviors, the procedures to follow, and the definition of group success.

The teacher, as class manager, must see to it that the room is organized in such a way that the members of a group are close enough to one another to work together comfortably and talk with one another quietly. The groups must be separated so that they do not interfere with one another.

During group work it is often difficult to get the attention of students. An effective technique that does not entail raising one's voice is for the teacher simply to raise a hand and require that each student who sees the hand raised do the same and stop talking. Then each student who sees another student's hand raised must do the same. This chain reaction stops when everyone has his hand raised, and the class is quiet and ready to pay attention to the teacher. This procedure must be implemented with care and forethought so that it may not appear too childish for the higher secondary grades.

As teachers become comfortable with the small group learning approach, they will decide for themselves how best to facilitate the process. A few suggestions follow for simple ways of getting started.

HOW TO INCORPORATE SMALL GROUP LEARNING INTO MATHEMATICS CLASS

Homework Review

The efficiency and enjoyment of homework review can be enhanced by using a small group learning approach. By having group members meet in their groups to check a homework assignment, students are able to discuss their problems with one another, iron out difficulties, and come to an agreement on the best solutions. Each group submits one set of solutions and advises the teacher of the difficulties that students have experienced. The teacher may call on any student in the group to explain the group's solution to the class. Since the teacher chooses the spokesperson, and group members have no idea who that will be, each student must be prepared to be that spokesperson.

Test Preview/Review

The group structure makes it convenient for students to help one another in preparing for a test. A sample test can be assigned for homework. The students then meet in groups to discuss the sample test and to deepen their understanding of the concepts and techniques that will be tested. By working on the sample test individually, each student comes to the group discussion with an accurate picture of his or her understanding. Students are able to prepare themselves and other group members for the forthcoming test. Once again, each group agrees on the solutions to the problems and hands in one group paper.

The teacher allows time for the whole class to discuss those areas that need clarification.

It is also important for learning to take place after a test has been returned! Members of a group can help one another understand and correct their errors. Students might even be given the opportunity to resubmit the problems they got wrong, provided that they do each problem correctly, explain why their original solution was incorrect, and justify their new solution by giving a written explanation of the thought processes they used. This can counterbalance the natural reaction of many students, which is to accept past failure only to move on to the next task, where a "clean slate" awaits them. The tests can then be regraded and a final grade can be formed taking a weighted average of the first and second test grades, perhaps using the first test as one-third of the grade and the second test as two-thirds of the grade.

The Task-Oriented Lesson

In a task-oriented lesson new concepts, techniques, or generalizations evolve during the course of preassigned tasks (the lesson). Typically, the teacher makes the connection (or presentation) and then asks the class to apply their new knowledge by trying similar applications on their own. This task lends itself to small group work. The teacher assigns the applications in the usual manner, allowing the students time to work on them individually. Instead of being called together for a whole class review of what they have done, the students meet in groups to discuss and agree on the assigned work. Each group is responsible for handing in one copy of the agreed-upon solutions. After the work has been submitted, the teacher leads a discussion of those applications that need clarification.

As an added assignment, the group may be asked to respond to two questions: "What have we learned today that we didn't know before?" and "What would we like to know as a result of today's work?" The two suggested questions provide each group with an opportunity to summarize the lesson and provide the teacher with feedback for future planning. Asking the groups to write a sentence or two about what they have learned on a particular day gives the students the opportunity to reflect, while the teacher has an opportunity to assess the impact of the lesson.

Enrichment

Group work is an excellent way of incorporating enrichment experiences in the mathematics class (see Chapter 12 for activity ideas). To spark student interest in a new topic, small learning groups can investigate the historical development of the topic. The members of the group should divide the work among themselves. One student should look up the dateline in the development of the topic. Another student should be responsible for uncovering the mathematicians who were instrumental in the development of the topic. The group also will want to have a person look for anecdotes and events related to the topic. Finally, it will be of interest for a group member to investigate how knowledge of this topic has affected the world as it is today. This group project might culminate in a bulletin board display or a report.

Small learning groups can engage in recreational mathematics that challenge the students to do creative problem solving (see Chapter 9 for problem solving). For example, the work can be organized in different ways, or the groups can be given a problem that is to be solved by the end of the week. At the end of the week, those groups that claim to have solved the problem present their solutions. The teacher chooses a spokesperson for each group. The spokesperson must present the group's solution satisfactorily before the group can get credit for having solved the problem.

Group problem solving has many advantages. Members of the group engage in brainstorming, an activity that enables all members to participate in a free flow of ideas. The student who is poor at solving problems has the opportunity to engage in the problem-solving process along with peers who are more able. Not only do all students learn how to solve problems, but they also share in the excitement the group experiences when the problem has been solved.

SUMMARY

There are many reasons for allowing students the opportunity to work and learn together in groups. Most important are the intrinsic rewards to be gained. The social aspects of group work are enjoyable. Students form new friendships and learn to appreciate differences in ability, in personal characteristics, and in opinion. Students find that learning together is fun and that being part of a group is exciting. Students who help other students experience gratification in giving. Students who know that they can depend on other group members for help and support are relieved of the anxiety often experienced by those who do not understand the work. There is a real sense of satisfaction in learning, achieving, and solving problems together.

Small group learning is a teaching strategy that holds promise for improving mathematical skills and attitudes of students. Teachers can create effective learning environments in their own special ways. Certain topics work better than others for this purpose. Each class is different, and what works for one may not work for another.

EXERCISES

1. A teacher notices that in some of the cooperative learning groups in her class the brightest student is doing all the work. What are some techniques that she can use to keep this from happening?

2. You receive an angry phone call from a parent of one of the brightest students in your class. The parent complains that his child is being held back by having to help the weaker students in his group. How would you respond to this parent?

3. The teacher notices that one of the lower-ability students is not participating in her group. How should the teacher handle this situation?

4. Design a cooperative learning discovery lesson that will enable students to make a conjecture regarding the relationship of the three angles of a triangle.

5. The teacher, realizing that many of the cooperative groups in his class are not functioning effectively, decides to change the group formations at the end of the unit. What procedures can he use to rearrange the groups in the best possible manner?

6. Describe three student characteristics that the teacher should consider when forming heterogeneous groups.

7. Why are conflict management skills needed by members of an effective cooperative learning group?

8. A student reports that her group is operating very well; there are no conflicts or disagreements. How would you handle this situation?

9. Describe some ways that a teacher can monitor the progress of cooperative learning groups.

10. Design a lesson that will enable members of cooperative learning groups to discover that the sum of the roots of an equation of the form $ax^2 + bx + c = 0$ is $-b/a$ and that the product of the roots is c/a. Assume that students can solve such a quadratic equation by factoring or by formula.

REFERENCES

Artzt, Alice F., and Newman, Clare M. "Cooperative Learning." *Mathematics Teacher* 83 (1990): 448–452.

Artzt, Alice F., and Newman, Claire M. *How to Use Cooperative Learning in the Mathematics Class.* Reston, VA: National Council of Teachers of Mathematics, 1990.

Davidson, Neil, ed. *Cooperative Learning in Mathematics: A Handbook for Teachers.* Menlo Park, CA: Addison-Wesley Publishing Co., 1990.

Gilbert-Macmillan, Kathleen, and Leitz, Steven. "Cooperative Small Groups: A Method for Teaching Problem Solving." *Arithmetic Teacher* 33 (1986): 9–11.

Johnson, David W., and Johnson, Roger. *Learning Together and Alone: Cooperation, Competition, and Individualistic Learning,* 2d ed. Englewood Cliffs, NJ: Prentice Hall, 1987.

Johnson, David W., and Johnson, Roger T. *Cooperation and Competition: Theory and Research.* Edina, MN: Interaction Book Co., 1989.

Kroll, Diana Lambdin, Masingila, Joanne A., and Mau, Sue Tinsley. "Grading Cooperative Problem Solving." *Mathematics Teacher* 85 (1992): 619–627.

National Council of Teachers of Mathematics. *Curriculum and Evaluation Standards for School Mathematics.* Reston, VA: National Council of Teachers of Mathematics, 1989.

Rosenbaum, Linda, Behounek, Karla J., Brown, L., and Burcalow, Janet V. "Step into Problem Solving with Cooperative Learning." *Arithmetic Teacher* 36 (1989): 7–11.

Slavin, Robert E. "Cooperative Learning and Individualized Instruction." *Arithmetic Teacher* 35 (1987): 7–13.

Slavin, Robert E., Leavey, Marshall, and Madden, Nancy. "Combining Cooperative Learning and Individualized Instruction: Effects on Student Mathematics Achievement, Attitudes, and Behaviors." *Elementary School Journal* 84 (1984): 7–13.

Sutton, Gail Oberholtzer. "Cooperative Learning Works in Mathematics." *Mathematics Teacher* 85 (1992): 63–66.

CHAPTER 2
WRITING IN THE MATHEMATICS CLASSROOM

The average mathematics teacher usually responds to the suggestion of incorporating writing assignments into the classroom with astonishment, claiming that there is hardly enough time to do the mathematics, let alone additional work with writing. The advantage of writing is that it allows students to reflect on their ideas, since the process requires a slower form of thinking than does oral expression.

Much psychological literature indicates that students who verbalize their learning have a far better recall of that learning, and students who write these newly learned concepts have a far more precise recall of that learning, than students who do neither. Therefore, writing would appear to be a strengthening factor in the learning process. This chapter explores a variety of ways in which writing can be incorporated into the mathematics classroom. Illustrative examples provide further clarification of these suggestions.

There are various formats in which writing can be utilized in the mathematics classroom. One such format is the *student log*. Such logs summarize either a class activity (usually done on a regular basis) or students' experiences when working on their homework assignments. A second type of writing is the *student journal.* A journal differs from a log in that the journal is more informal and includes perceptions and student opinions about the material that has been covered, whereas a log is merely a report of material covered. A rather broad form of writing is *exposition,* in which students write about assigned mathematical topics or themes. This activity can include explorations as well as merely reporting.

STUDENT LOGS

A student log, the more formal reporting of a learning activity, can be a highly structured instrument with several subtitles for easy entry. Students might be given sheets listing categories such as date, title, new relationships learned, new definitions, how to do something new, and important things to remember, and all they need do is respond to each category. In all writing assignments, students should be urged to write complete sentences rather than just key words. These writing assignments force them to verbalize, thereby further strengthening their understanding.

STUDENT JOURNALS

A journal can become the students' most direct form of communication with the teacher. It may be a daily, less formal form of reporting than the log. Students are urged to write about what they have just learned, to note any important facts, and to comment on this recent learning experience.

It is desirable for teachers to read the journals daily and to respond to students, also in writing, about what they read. Besides benefiting the students, who are allowed to less formally verbalize their understanding of the new mathematics presented, the journal writing assignments also provide the teacher with an excellent opportunity to assess the students' understanding of the concepts being presented to them. Students will find their own learning enhanced, and they will have a complete record of what they have learned. The students may begin to realize that they are now involved in a direct daily communication with the teacher. The extra work that journal writing requires is more than offset by the insights that it gives the teacher into the students and their learning habits.

EXPOSITION

Expository writing is an activity used to explore further the material presented in the classroom, to help the students better understand material presented in the classroom, or to expand or to extend the material considered in the classroom (see Chapter 10 on enrichment for the distinction between ''expand'' and ''extend'').

Some examples of the ways in which expository writing may be used in the context of mathematics instruction follow.

Explaining a Concept. Students might be asked to explain a concept in their own words, such as ''In what instances is multiplication used in calculating probability, and in what instances is addition used in calculating probability?'' Another possible topic for an expository writing assignment might be ''Connect the concept of locus with its use in everyday life,'' or ''Explain the significance of the Pythagorean theorem in trigonometry.''

Explaining an Algorithm (or Describing a Process). Students might be asked to present a written explanation of how an arithmetic operation, such as division of fractions, is performed or how a particular algebraic expression can be simplified. This type of activity entices students to inventory their thinking and formulate it in a logical way to make it intelligible to someone else.

Explaining a Theorem. Here students would be asked not only to explain a particular theorem but also to justify it and thereby give a paragraph proof. It could be a simple theorem or a complex one, such as ''The line segment joining the midpoints of two sides of a triangle is parallel to and one-half the length of the third side.'' The students should be encouraged to explain the theorem in their own words, not merely to paraphrase it.

Describing or Interpreting a Graph. The students might be given a mathematical curve and asked to try to explain curve inflection, turning point(s), slope, or any other features that can be described about it. Alternatively, students might be shown a descriptive graph, such as a statistical one from a newspaper, and be asked to explain what the graph tells the reader. Not only should the students read the graph and explain directly what they see, but they should also be encouraged to interpret what is being presented. A graphics calculator might be helpful for interpreting the graph of a polynomial or transcendental function.

Discussing the Solution to a Problem. After having solved a problem, students might be asked to write an explanation of the solution. Not only does this activity give them, or their group, a chance to bask in the success of having solved the problem, but it also forces them to reinforce that success by verbalizing it! This verbalization will help further reinforce their understanding of the solution.

Writing a Problem. Composing a problem, particularly a word problem, can be a very challenging activity for most students; however, they should be encouraged to do that and, of course, to provide a solution. The problem can be on something very simple, drawing on examples in everyday life, or it can cover topics previously presented in the classroom. Students should be encouraged not merely to change numbers and repeat a textbook problem but rather to pull a problem out of their everyday experiences that relates to the techniques learned in the mathematics classroom.

Connecting the Mathematical Significance with a Particular Newspaper Article.

Either the students might be asked to find an article that uses some mathematics to describe a situation, or the teacher might select a few representative articles from local newspapers and have the students write about the mathematics in them. There are advantages to both tasks. Students should be encouraged to feel free about their interpretations and about where they see mathematics applied. Thus, their work is open ended, which makes the assignment that much more exciting.

Rewriting an "Unclear" Textbook Explanation.

It can happen that a textbook explanation of a concept is not particularly clear to a student using the book. When a teacher senses that that may be the case, he might suggest to the students that they rewrite that explanation in their own words and in a way that will benefit the next class using the textbook. Thus, the students not only have to make sure they understand the concept, but they also have the opportunity to verbalize it, thereby further strengthening their understanding.

Describing a Geometric Figure.

Perhaps the best way to develop a writing assignment describing a geometric figure is to have the students imagine that they are about to describe that figure to a friend on the telephone. They should then be asked to verbalize their descriptions of that geometric figure. This activity requires students to think logically and thoroughly and sorts out a lot of untidy thinking.

Generalizing a Concept.

Very often, a concept is presented and kept in a concise form. Frequently, generalizations are limited because of classroom time constraints. A teacher might challenge the class to consider the day's topic (e.g., the factoring of a trinomial) and ask students to generalize that factoring. Or students might be asked to consider the Pythagorean theorem and see if it can be generalized to a power higher than two (Fermat's last theorem), or whether a consideration of three dimensions might prove enlightening, or whether it can be generalized to triangles other than right triangles (law of cosines). In any case, the challenge should be an open-ended one, and the generalizations should be the students' personal choice. These generalizations may sometimes be correct, and sometimes incorrect. Occasionally, students' generalizations will be unanticipated by the teacher (and yet prove to be pleasantly surprising for the teacher). These

kinds of open-ended assignments have led to some very interesting student investigations that provided the entire class with the benefit of an individual student's imagination.

The Mathematics Report.

There are a host of activities that can be reported on. Students might discuss topics from the history of mathematics, such as the development of a particular branch of mathematics (e.g., coordinate geometry or non-Euclidian geometry), or trace the history of the refinement of a value such as π. Students might also investigate the history of mathematical notation. There are nice surprises embedded in this topic, which makes it appealing.

A natural topic in the history of mathematics is the presentation of a brief study of the life of a famous mathematician. Biographical sketches can include some mathematics as well as a life story. Students might discuss controversies that occurred in the development of mathematics. For example, a number of theorems are named for people who did not invent them—Simson's theorem in geometry was actually not known to Robert Simson, an important geometer of the seventeenth century, but rather was developed by William Wallace in 1797, long after Simson's death. Another colorful controversy centers on the true developer of a solution to a nonfactorable cubic equation: Cardano or Tartaglia? Students might also report on new findings in mathematics, such as the recent solution of the Four Color Map Problem or the proof of Fermat's last theorem.

The history of mathematics offers perhaps one of the richest areas for exploration and for expository writing, and should be used for that purpose.

EVALUATION CRITERIA FOR STUDENT WRITING SAMPLES

1. Students may be a bit too brief, and in their brevity be either ambiguous or imprecise. Students' brevity is caused by a concern that too much detail will insult the reader who already knows the material anyway.
2. Students may not realize the difference between necessary and sufficient conditions in describing something.
3. Students may take an implication for granted without proper justification.
4. Students may be unaware of what actually constitutes a proper proof.
5. Students may make inaccurate diagrams that are too small to work with or that are inappropriately or incompletely labeled.

The foregoing are merely some of the things to look for in student writing. There are many other potential shortcomings in beginning written assignments. Teachers must assist the student in writing as soon as they detect weaknesses.

The question of whether writing should be assessed from a grammatical standpoint is an open one. For years, school classrooms exhibited the sign *Every Class Is an English Class,* and there are many teachers who still subscribe to that philosophy. There are others in the mathematics teacher community who feel that their concern with grammar would distract students from the content, and so they ignore any grammatical, style, or form weaknesses in the students' writing. If the latter is the case, the teacher should make it very clear that a lack of comments about grammar, style, and form does not imply that they are correct but rather that they still need to be addressed. In this case, the teacher would mention that these factors were intentionally overlooked in order to concentrate comments solely on the content.

BENEFITS OF WRITING ACTIVITIES IN THE MATHEMATICS CLASSROOM

Writing can be a catalyst for generating classroom discourse that might otherwise not take place. Consistent with the NCTM's *Standards,* writing assignments can be the kickoff for this kind of activity. The mathematics classroom environment could become less formal and, with the increased communication between student and teacher, far better tuned to the needs of the student. Thus, the student could enjoy a much more closely tailored mathematics presentation, and the instructor would be more aware of the students' learning, their needs and personalities, and their perceptions. Review of previously taught material can be far better handled in an atmosphere where writing activities in the form of logs or journals have been used, thus keeping current the review of concepts taught.

Peer evaluation may also be used when written assignments, whether they be expository or logs, are exchanged among students. Although this activity may create another level of anxiety—typical for teenagers—if handled properly, it can also establish a rather refreshingly enlightened classroom.

SUMMARY

Writing in the mathematics classroom has been gaining popularity in recent years. It is supported in the psychological literature as an excellent way of putting metacognition into the hands of the learner. That is, the learner is forced to analyze not only *what* he or she is learning but also, in many cases, *how* he or she is learning it. This comes as a very subtle byproduct of the writing process.

Furthermore, a not-to-be-neglected asset of the writing process in the classroom is the feedback the teachers get from students in all forms of the writing experience. Teachers have a marvelous opportunity here to generate a regular form of communication with their students.

EXERCISES

1. How would you respond to the following comment, made by a student in one of your mathematics classes: "We don't do any math in my English class. Why do we have to do writing in our math class?"

2. Select a topic that you presented while teaching one of your mathematics classes. Compare and contrast the entry a student might make in a log with that which he might make in a journal on this topic.

3. One of your students asks for help in planning a piece of expository writing on either the Fibonacci sequence or Pascal's triangle. She hopes to submit her paper to the school's mathematics journal for possible publication. What suggestions might you offer?

4. You have assigned the writing of an expository paper in one of your mathematics classes, consisting of average to better students. Some of the papers submitted are very poor, written in a perfunctory fashion and clearly showing a lack of sincere effort. What action would you take?

5. A student whose native language is not English submits an expository paper whose content is of high quality but that contains numerous errors in grammar, spelling, syntax, and the like. Would you correct his English? Why?

REFERENCES

Azzolino, Aggie. "Writing As a Tool for Teaching Mathematics: The Silent Revolution." *1990 Yearbook,* Reston, VA: NCTM.

Britton, James N. "Writing to Learn and Learning to Write." In *The Humanity of English.* Urbana, IL: National Council of Teachers of English, 1972.

Countryman, Joan. "Writing to Learn Mathematics." In *Functions.* Princeton, NJ: Woodrow Wilson National Fellowship Foundation, 1985.

Davison, David M., and Pearce, Daniel L. "Using Writing Activities to Reinforce Mathematics Instruction." *Arithmetic Teacher* 36 (1988): 42–45.

Evans, Christine Sobray. "Writing to Learn Math." *Language Arts* 61 (December 1984): 828–835.

Geeslin, William E. "Using Writing about Mathematics As a Teaching Technique." *Mathematics Teacher* (February 1977): 112–151.

Goldberg, Dorothy. "Integrating Writing into the Mathematics Curriculum." *The Two-Year College Mathematics Journal* (November 1983): 421–424.

Hayes, Lynn. "Writing to Enhance Learning in General Mathematics." *Mathematics Teacher* (October 1989): 551–554.

Hurwitz, Marsha. "Student-Authored Manuals As Semester Projects." *Mathematics Teacher* (December 1990): 701–703.

Johnson, Marvin L. "Writing in Mathematics Classes: A Valuable Tool for Learning." *Mathematics Teacher* (February 1983): 117–119.

Keith, Sandra. "Exploratory Writing and Learning Mathematics Classroom." *Mathematics Teacher* (December 1988): 714–719.

Le Gere, Adele. "Collaboration and Writing in the Mathematics Classroom." *Mathematics Teacher* (March 1991): 166–171.

Macintosh, Margaret E. "No Time for Writing in Your Class?" *Mathematics Teacher* (September 1991): 423–433.

Mett, Coreen L. "Writing As a Learning Device in Calculus." *Mathematics Teacher* (October 1987): 534–537.

Nahrgang, Cynthia L., and Peterson, Bruce T. "Using Writing to Learn Mathematics." *Mathematics Teacher* (September 1986): 461–465.

Schmidt, Don. "Writing in Math Class." In *Roots in the Sawdust: Writing to Learn across the Disciplines,* Anne Ruggles Gere (ed.), 104–116. Urbana, IL: National Council of Teachers of English, 1985.

Socha, Susan C. "Math Class Logs." *Mathematics Teacher* (October 1989): 511–513.

Watson, Margaret. "Writing Has a Place in a Mathematics Class." *Mathematics Teacher* (October 1980): 518–519.

CHAPTER 3
TEACHER SENSITIVITY

A teacher's lack of sensitivity to learners' feelings may contribute to an atmosphere of anxiety in the classroom. Hearing a teacher say "It's easy," for example, may produce unanticipated negative feelings. If students accept the teacher's word that "It's easy" when they don't understand a concept, they may question their own competence and feel *less* rather than *more* adequate to the task at hand. It is far more helpful for the teacher to say "It's difficult, but you can do it. I'll help you! After all, learning isn't supposed to be easy."

The teacher's position of authority may have behavioral and intellectual consequences for students. Students' strivings for independence are thwarted by learning experiences in which teacher authority is paramount. If teachers believe that there is a single best way of solving a mathematics problem, they are unwittingly participating in an authority struggle with students. Furthermore, they may be arousing feelings of anxiety among students.

CONCRETIZING MATHEMATICS

A teacher's belief that mathematical models and activities are appropriate for young children but should be abandoned as soon as possible predisposes a teacher to plan lessons and units without considering the possible contribution of these manipulatives and related activities. Concrete representations of abstract ideas not only make a significant contribution to the learning process but they provide the opportunity for restless learners to interact with the materials in an enjoyable way. Youngsters who are confronted with pencil-and-paper tasks much of the time can be expected to characterize math as ''boring'' and ''uninteresting.'' Such characterizations may, in reality, be a reaction to feelings of frustration and anxiety.

COMPETITION IN MATHEMATICS CLASS

Competition, which is energizing for some students, sets up conditions under which other students may feel vulnerable and exposed. In a competitive situation in which someone must be slower in order for another to win, students risk losing face among their peers. Speed-related tasks and the competition they demand may arouse feelings of anxiety. Tests also may engender anxiety in students who feel threatened by them. Students may be uncertain about their ability to handle the material, and they may fear that there will be questions that require formulas and rules unlike those they have studied. They anticipate that they will have to face questions far more difficult than any that were in the book or that were discussed during class sessions. Speed tests and short-answer tests are particularly threatening. Students can panic because of the fear that they cannot complete the test on time or that they will lose complete credit for a short-answer question because of a minor error in arithmetic. Even high-achieving mathematics students may be anxious about tests. Such students have an ''image'' to protect, and they are fearful that test results may not conform to standards set by teachers, parents, peers, or themselves.

CREATING A POSITIVE LEARNING CLIMATE FOR ALL STUDENTS

It is important for the teacher to help all students feel confident about their ability to learn mathematics. This does not call for making fewer demands, modifying the curriculum, or setting lower standards for students' performance. Instead, mathematics teachers need to have a variety of strategies at hand for meeting the challenges of students' learning.

Problem Solving

A classroom in which problem solving plays a central role can provide a good environment for mathematics learning to flourish. When confronted with an appropriately challenging and interesting problem, students feel both the urge to solve that problem and the concomitant tension that it arouses. It is this state of arousal that facilitates the process of solution.

Providing problems and activities on appropriate levels ensures that learners will experience the challenge and success that promote a positive sense of self while learning mathematics. The development and maintenance of a problem-solving, task-oriented, emotionally supportive classroom environment can be achieved through classroom strategies that stress understanding rather than rote memory. The teacher should provide open-ended problems that have more than one solution and problems that can be solved in more than one way. It is important to provide problems that ensure success.

Small Group Learning

Small learning groups minimize competition and allow students to work together in a nonthreatening environment. Group members learn to help one another in a comfortable setting. Mathematics understanding and learning thrives on the discussion and disagreements that take place within the group, and the communication of ideas helps clarify them. The opportunity to share solution strategies through discussion with peers may help students appreciate multiple problem-solving strategies and attempt to use more than one approach. Friendly relationships among group members make it possible for students to be willing to give a wrong answer without feeling ashamed or embarrassed. The teacher should help students develop the skills they need to be successful as a team.

Assessment Strategies

Written tests provide only one evaluation measure. Portfolios, projects, logs, journals, and expository and creative writing are all excellent alternatives that enable the teacher to assess mathematics learning.

Equal Treatment of Boys and Girls

Teachers should urge both girls and boys to enroll in mathematics classes and to pursue careers that use mathematics. Parents should also be involved in supporting mathematics for daughters as well as sons. The teacher should encourage girls' active participation in class, use classroom activities that appeal to both girls and boys, and give equitable amounts of attention to each. Discussion groups can be used to allow female students to air their concerns about mathematics within the context of popularity and competition with male friends.

Sensitivity to Students' Feelings

In the classroom everyone's contribution should be valued, sarcasm must be avoided, and praise and encouragement should be used generously. Students can perceive a teacher's comment as a lack of regard for their ability, thereby confirming doubts about their personal adequacy as mathematics learners. A student must not be made to appear foolish in front of his or her peers. When a student gives an incorrect response, much is at stake for the learner. A student who feels incapable, inadequate, or embarrassed may give attention and energy to defending sense of self rather than the mathematics at hand. This action takes a learner farther away from the task and increases negative feelings toward mathematics. The teacher who is comfortable in saying, "I don't know. Can we try to work this out together?" in answer to a student's question, tells the student *by actions* that it is all right not to know. Sensitive teachers who make use of a wide variety of interesting materials and approaches within an emotionally supportive classroom environment foster positive mathematics attitudes. Such teachers can modify the effects of earlier negative experiences by providing appropriate learning experiences and challenges and by recognizing the feelings of their students.

Providing Time For Thoughtful Questioning

Students sometimes give quick answers and jump to conclusions to "get it over with." The teacher should recognize this impulse and should pose questions that elicit thought rather than answers, to encourage students to deliberate and to understand the problem. A sequence of good questions can break a complex problem into simpler, manageable parts. The questions should be similar to those that students can ask themselves when they are solving problems on their own. Many artful teachers do much of their teaching by asking questions, beginning with those they know their students can answer. This approach tends to reduce anxiety and build up the confidence that students need to improve their performance. (see Chapter 6, Classroom Questioning).

SUMMARY

The long-term effect of mathematics anxiety is to create adults who cannot function effectively in a technological society. The inability of students (and, in some cases, their parents) to see the relevance of mathematics to their current and future interests may result in a mathematics education that seriously limits students' career opportunities.

The mathematics teacher can encourage student participation by building a classroom environment that increases students' confidence in their ability to learn mathematics. By being sensitive to each student's feelings, by valuing everyone's contribution, by recognizing students' needs for success, by involving students in their own learning, and by making mathematics exciting and interesting, teachers can help their students develop positive attitudes.

EXERCISES

1. Explain what is meant by "math serves as an invisible filter to students' access to careers."
2. Why is it important for teachers to encourage students to solve problems using various approaches and strategies?
3. Describe some factors that may make females more susceptible to mathematics anxiety than males.
4. Describe three student behaviors that may be symptomatic of mathematics anxiety.
5. Describe three ways in which anxiety can interfere with the learning of mathematics.
6. How can small, cooperative learning groups reduce competition and increase student participation?
7. Explain why it is important for the teacher to provide students with experiences of success.
8. Give two reasons for not using a speed test to evaluate a student's knowledge of mathematics.
9. Interview three adults who work in nonscientific careers. Ask them how they use mathematics in their work. Describe how you can use their responses to help your students appreciate the importance of mathematics in their lives.
10. Why is it a poor idea to give extra mathematics assignments as a form of punishment?

PART 2
CLASSROOM STRATEGIES

The establishment of a curriculum designed for *all* students is a fundamental recommendation of the *Standards* and as such is supported by this text. The core curriculum proposes three years of required mathematics that is "differentiated by the depth and breadth of treatment of topics and by the nature of applications" (*Curriculum Standards*, p. 129). Our discussion of the teaching of core mathematics focuses on a wide range of strategies, including problem-solving tasks, active involvement of students, effective questioning, a variety of instructional formats, the use of calculators and computers, communication of ideas, applications, review, and assessment.

All students will experience the full range of topics in the core curriculum. Because today's students will be confronting interesting and important mathematics regularly, they should not be subjected to the demeaning process of frequent repetition of the same topics that their younger siblings are studying. This text reflects those considerations.

The core lessons demonstrated in Part 2 are differentiated by levels of difficulty, activities, and applications. The sample *Standards* lessons offer a "no-nonsense" approach to covering the entire range of classroom activities: creating challenging tasks, leading discussions, making mathematical connections, and improving students' disposition towards mathematics.

One of the most essential skills in teaching is lesson planning. Following a detailed overview of that skill, we consider its "nuts and bolts." Specifically, we demonstrate the characteristics of alternative lesson formats, discourse, homework, assessment, communication, and classroom management. In addition, we discuss extracurricular activities.

A level 1 core lesson indicates one that is basic in both content and tasks. Level 2 includes justifications and proofs of the basic concepts that were developed in the level 1 lesson, but with more challenging tasks and applications. Level 3 includes earlier concepts, enhanced with alternative justifications and still more challenging tasks. Levels 4 and 5 are geared toward enrichment that will be of value to college-bound students.

CHAPTER 4
PLANNING A LESSON

A successful teacher is willing to take risks but must also possess certain traits, namely, the capability to make simple and clear that which is complex and clouded. The teacher must enjoy teaching the material and be an inspiration to students in addition to acquiring certain specialized skills with training—for example, the ability to plan, organize, and present any type of lesson to a class of young people.

Just as an actor focuses on his script and a musician on his score, so must a teacher focus on a lesson plan. Every teacher is expected to be fully prepared for each lesson, for his/her entering a classroom without a planned lesson will not be a gratifying experience for either teacher or student. In fact, it may become grounds for severe warning, reprimand, or dismissal if the pattern becomes a regular one. The teacher who walks into a classroom and begins a lesson with "Where did we end yesterday?" or who begins a lesson by taking out the text and merely reading from it to the class, or who teaches "off the cuff" from memory performs a gross disservice to the young people in his charge. Such actions show that the teacher has a lack of concern, perhaps even disdain, for them that might easily be construed as unprofessional conduct.

THE UNIT PLAN

While movement, flexibility, and changes are the hallmarks of *daily* classroom activities, lessons may be planned *long range* around an entire unit of work. Of course, the likelihood that any individual lesson will follow the script exactly as written is small, so when long-range plans are written, adjustments must be made on a daily basis. Teachers should not be reluctant to make modifications just because it is easier to leave the original plan as written.

No single lesson can be prepared in a vacuum, for the whole unit of work is the sum of its specific lessons. Each daily lesson should be viewed as part of a broader picture with the intent of meeting long-range expectations. Suppose you are teaching the topic of "radicals" in algebra. After reading the official course of study and appropriate material in texts, and seeking guidance from experienced colleagues, you must decide on a sequence of logically arranged lessons that will include all relevant topics as well as review and assessment lessons. Following is a sample of a possible unit:

SAMPLE UNIT: RADICALS

Suggested Daily Lessons

1. Powers and roots; evaluating radicals using the scientific calculator
2. Pythagorean theorem; solving quadratic equations of the form $x^2 = k$, where k may or may not be a perfect square integer
3. Rounding decimals
4. Square root algorithm, for college-bound students
5. Estimating the value of, simplifying, and combining radicals
6. Multiplying and dividing radicals
7. Rationalizing binomial denominators
8. Radical equations
9. Whole class review
10. Small group examination (for assessment purposes)
11. Written student evaluations of the unit (for assessment purposes)

We will complete this unit on radicals with an example of a mathematics writing test (p. 37).

LONG-RANGE PLANNING

If you become aware as much as a year or a full semester in advance that you will be teaching a particular course, some or all of the following steps are recommended to help you begin preparing yourself. If, however, you are aware of the situation for only a few days to a few hours, modifications of the listed suggestions must be made. These modifications will vary, depending on the amount of time available as well as your own "drive" and ambition toward a goal of excellence in your classroom.

Observe an Experienced Teacher

There is no step you can take that is more useful, practical, or helpful than your daily observation of an experienced, competent teacher who is presently teaching the course you expect to teach. First, obtain the teacher's consent, to observe her teaching, then if she agrees, observe regularly and take careful notes on what you see and hear. Copy the questions, the remarks, even the jokes for possible future use. Note the handling of homework, testing procedures, and classroom management. Especially note motivational techniques and clever ways of developing a topic. Even if you ultimately decide to "improve" on her style, at least you have a basis for your judgment.

It will be helpful if the teacher you are observing can meet with you regularly to discuss the course and reasons why she used certain teaching techniques.

Obtain Several Course Outlines

Your supervisor may have given you the official school outline or course of study or the appropriate state curriculum. You can and should secure similar outlines from other schools or state education departments simply by sending away for them. In addition to providing you with a suggested order of topics in the course, a good course outline will also provide you with guidance regarding the approximate amount of time to be devoted to each topic in the course.

Some state or local curriculum guides even offer a series of lesson plans for use in regular (standard) courses. These should be consulted and used sparingly so that your style is not "cramped" by these plans, written by someone else and not necessarily designed for your needs. What is important is that you gather as much curriculum information as possible about the course you are about to teach.

Examine Various Textbooks

Texts are a rich source of information and enrichment you can bring with you to the classroom. You will discover new approaches to certain topics and you will have a large source of problems from which to draw. Publishers are often pleased to send copies of their books to teachers for possible classroom adoption. You might even convince the school authorities to purchase a text you believe particularly suitable.

It is useful to obtain teachers' manuals or teacher editions of textbooks you will be using and to read the preface of each of your textbooks to determine the author's approach and viewpoint. Since the order in which topics are presented in a course often depends heavily on the order in which they appear in the textbook, caution must be exercised in using supplementary books in which the order differs from that of the textbook. Naturally, there are some topics whose development is independent of the order, yet caution should still be used.

Prepare Lessons in Advance

Based on the knowledge you are beginning to accumulate, prepare in advance several specific lessons, especially the early ones. But first, plan outlines for broad, larger units of work. You will be happy you did. Perhaps you can map out the entire course and then prepare some unit plans. This will give you some idea about properly anticipating the time factor involved.

As part of lesson planning, prepare solutions to as many exercises as possible prior to their consideration in class. This will provide many valuable insights into difficulties your students may encounter, and it will make you much more comfortable standing before the class with the full knowledge that you have complete mastery of the subject matter. This is especially important in subjects such as geometry where proofs may often be done in a variety of ways.

Observe Additional Teachers

Observe several teachers if you have the time, mainly to get different perspectives. You may be surprised at the differences you see. Follow similar procedures with each observation. Your supervisor can make valuable suggestions about which teachers it would be most useful to observe.

Familiarize Yourself with the Library or Media Center

The school and/or department library may have many books you and your more talented students will find useful. While becoming familiar with the school library, begin to build your own personal collection. In addition to *The Mathematics Teacher, Mathematics Teaching in the Middle School, Teaching Children Mathematics* (formerly *The Arithmetic Teacher*), and yearbooks of the National Council of Teachers of Mathematics (NCTM), the bibliographies in Chapter 7 and Chapter 10 provide a useful list of books with which to start. Many of these books can be obtained used in bookstores, or from the book publishers. You can also obtain free and inexpensive materials. Publications of such lists is yet another service of the NCTM.

Learn Pupils' Backgrounds

What types of youngsters will you be teaching? Try to obtain information from guidance counselors about your pupils' backgrounds before walking into the classroom, for it will be helpful to know in advance who is a weak student and who is strong. Although this is generally helpful, try not to prejudice your assessments before giving students a chance to prove themselves. You may also be alerted to potential discipline problems and you will be aware of who is repeating the course because of past failure or poor attendance.

On the other hand, some teachers prefer not to investigate the backgrounds of new students first so that they can form their own judgments without prejudice.

If it happens that your class will consist of youngsters from a particular ethnic background, you might find it helpful to learn about their language, culture, habits, and behavior patterns.

Obtain Supplies

Besides the usual "tools of the teaching trade," you might need board compasses, protractor, graph chart, geometric models, "flexible" quadrilaterals and other polygons, overhead projector, or graph paper. Try to secure these well before they will actually be needed.

SHORT-RANGE PLANNING

If you are made aware a few weeks, a few days, or even a few hours in advance that you will be teaching a particular course that you have never taught before, read the steps listed above for the long-range preparation program, but take the following preliminary actions so you can begin in an orderly manner. However, as the term progresses, begin to implement as many of the long-range steps as possible.

1. *Study the course outline.* Your supervisor will provide you with this so that you can at least begin with something tangible.
2. *Get the textbook.* Take it home and read it, always keeping the course outline in mind.

3. *Prepare initial lesson plans.* Prepare both daily plans for the opening days and longer-range unit plans.
4. *Arrange to observe a teacher.* Try to observe an experienced teacher who is teaching the same subject during the same term as you are. This is perhaps the most valuable action you can take.
5. *Pray for the best!*

The Daily Plan

Every detail of your classroom activities should be planned. The amount of written detail compared with the detail kept in the teacher's memory will vary with the number of years of experience as well as with the number of times the particular course has been taught. But the plan must include what you are going to do and what you expect to have your students do throughout the classroom period. You must think through the format of the lesson you plan, the relevant tasks in which students will be engaged, and difficulties you might encounter. Try to anticipate the unexpected, for that might easily upset your plans for the entire class. The beginning teacher, in particular, should include the precise wording of activities in the lesson plan, for it is so easy to forget details while facing the class despite having known them earlier.

A lesson may not turn out as planned for reasons you could not foresee. When this happens once in a while, there is no harm done. It merely supports the contention that every lesson must be carefully thought through.

Just as a successful performer spends a lot of time rehearsing a performance, a teacher needs to rehearse a lesson. But the practical way for a teacher to rehearse is mentally, by planning your ''performance'' (lesson) on paper. Writing a good lesson plan will force you to go through a detailed ''mental dry run'' of the lesson. This activity allows you not only to crystallize your thoughts but also to anticipate possible pitfalls in the actual lesson.

Lessons should be written in a *plan book* so you will have an organized daily record of the work your classes have done every day of the term. This book can be used as a guide for you in the future, or as a record for your supervisors or the parents, and as an aid to a substitute. Yet, it is advisable to write new plans each time you teach a course. Not only will this allow you to tailor each lesson to the specific class being taught, but it should go far in keeping your mind continuously stimulated.

The script that an actor uses follows a certain format, with appropriate variations determined by the nature of the performance itself, whether comedy, tragedy, or musical. Similarly, the teacher's lesson plan follows a certain basic format. These plans will also vary somewhat, depending on the nature of the lesson being planned.

Following is the basic format of a lesson plan. Not all parts of this suggested arrangement need be included in every lesson. Following the chart are details and explanations of specific items.

Topic

By stating the topic at the beginning of each lesson plan you make your focus clear when you are planning the lesson as well as when you are simply filing it or looking for it.

Prior Knowledge

This section calls for a listing of the previously learned material that is required for the present lesson and for which the students are responsible. Although the experienced teacher may frequently omit this section, it is useful for the starting teacher.

Instructional Format

Instructional format refers to small or large group instruction, peer instruction, whole class discussions, individual explorations, project work, independent research, and assessment of learning. Small group lessons may include homework review and analysis, discussion of in-class assigned tasks, and medial and final summaries. A group representative is usually designated to report back to the whole class. Also, tests or quizzes may be answered cooperatively by small groups of students, with each student expected to participate fully in the process.

Large groups are most suited for presentations that include videos or films, guest speakers, unique demonstrations, or mathematics assemblies. Prepared acetates with charts and diagrams make the overhead projector an ideal means of communication here.

Motivational Activity (see Chapter 10)

The initial motivational activity for the lesson may also be known as the ''do-now'' exercise. It should be written in the same section of the chalkboard every day, preferably *before* the official start of the lesson. It helps pupils settle down at the beginning of the period by assigning them a task to do on entering the room. It may indeed set the behavior and learning tone for the period regardless of instructional format and is therefore most crucial.

1. It could consist of an example made up by the teacher or taken from a text. It could be a brief selection to be studied silently before any large or small group analysis.

SUGGESTED OUTLINE FOR DAILY LESSON PLAN

Class: _____   Date: _____

TOPIC:

PRIOR KNOWLEDGE:

INSTRUCTIONAL FORMAT:

MOTIVATIONAL ACTIVITY:

Usually combined

EXPLORATION:

PRACTICE ACTIVITIES:

MEDIAL SUMMARY:

CONNECTIONS:

FINAL SUMMARY:

ASSESSMENT:

HOMEWORK ASSIGNMENT:

Same Weets

SPECIAL EQUIPMENT TO BE USED:

SPECIAL TASKS or PROJECTS:

IF TIME:

2. It might be the assignment of pupils to specified areas of the room. For example, small groups might be asked to report to their designated areas and continue working on previously assigned tasks, review an assignment, or discuss a challenging example.
3. It might serve as a managerial device, allowing the teacher or assistant a few minutes to perform the multitude of little chores at the beginning of the period (e.g., open or shut windows, clean boards, check attendance, return graded papers, or have students write and verify homework solutions).

Exploration

The ability of the teacher to create an effective learning environment that encourages students to explore, investigate, hypothesize, and draw conclusions is crucial in lesson development. Just as in formal painting classes one can learn techniques and styles of painting, so in education courses one can learn techniques and styles of teaching. In neither case will you learn to be an ''artist,'' for it is only after the training received in these courses that your talent takes over. After all, your first two or three years as a teacher are the formative ones in your professional growth.

Exploratory tasks should be viewed as your personal, creative inventions that will promote new concepts, skills, knowledge, and positive attitudes among your students. Suggestions from other teachers, a variety of textbooks, and the NCTM journals, *The Mathematics Teacher, Mathematics Teaching in the Middle School,* and *Teaching Children Mathematics* (formerly *The Arithmetic Teacher*) will all be invaluable in helping you create appropriate class activities. In addition, a sense of excitement and challenge will set the tone for your own performance and the positive results you hope to attain in the years ahead.

Exploration of ideas will occur when you initiate open-ended, stimulating comments that cause pupils to think and talk, agree and disagree, thirst for more knowledge, and make conjectures. You may utilize diagrams, graphs, sketches, physical models, and analogies to develop appropriate exploratory tasks. Further exploration of ideas will occur when you provide students with opportunities to record their mathematical thoughts in logs and journals.

An advantage of the give and take of class discussion is that it offers the teacher an opportunity to interject historical background, anecdotes, and connections with other topics.

1. Major questions and statements should be recorded. These should be written in the order they will be asked, at the appropriate points in the lesson plan. You may refer to the plan book on your desk, or hold it, if you wish, as you walk about the room. (Although holding the plan may indicate some insecurity on your part, if you, as a new teacher, feel that it will provide you with some confidence during a particularly difficult development that you want to do ''just right,'' you should not hesitate to do so.)
2. Board work should be planned so there will be no crowding and ample room is available to write all elements of the lesson. You ought to know such details as where the do-now will be written, where the development will take place, where the previous day's homework will be written, whether solutions to certain algebraic problems should be arranged horizontally or vertically, and finally, which practice exercises students will be asked to write on the board.

The board work serves as a model for students. If you are neat, write legibly, are well organized, and use a straightedge and compasses for diagrams, the chances are they will, too. This is an opportunity to help students develop work habits that will benefit them (as well as you, when you mark their test papers) for the remainder of their lives.

Practice Activities

Practice activities, coming after class explorations, are where theory yields to practice. The lessons are clinched at this point. Model problems/solutions are formulated, and individual or small collaborative group practice follows. Initial practice exercises should be limited to newly considered concepts or topics. Later exercises, which connect with other branches of mathematics, may include a wide range of mathematics topics and subject areas.

Medial Summary

The medial summary is an intermediate, brief summary of the salient features in the topic that have been developed thus far. It may occur at any point, or points, during the lesson, but before its conclusion. Among the many functions this medial summary can serve is to allow a student who is not sure about the aim of the lesson, or the nature of what was developed and its significance, or who may have simply daydreamed for some key moments at the early part of the lesson and is now lost, to catch up with the rest of the class and benefit from the remainder of the lesson.

Connections

Now that everyone, it is hoped, is caught up to the appropriate part of the lesson, and everyone has had an opportunity to practice using the new concept or topic in simple practice exercises, this section provides for applications and practice that connects the new concept or topic with other previously learned concepts or topics. These applications or practice exercises will be more complicated and more embedded in other topics than the first set of practice exercises. Naturally, the specific nature of the topic under consideration will determine the type of problems included in this or the other practice section.

Final Summary and Conclusion

The final summary is a brief review of the highlights of the lesson. Here the teacher should tie together all the parts of the lesson. This summary, as is the case with prior summaries as well, may be formulated by the students as they answer pointed questions or it may be in the form of simple statements, or a combination of both. Sometimes a simple question to the class such as ''Suppose your classmate was absent and called you on the phone to ask what today's lesson was about. What would you tell him or her about the lesson so that he or she would get a clear idea of the topics missed?'' will elicit a summary.

Assessment

Confidence building need not be limited to pupils. Teachers, too, must be assured that whatever the instructional format, the goals of arousing curiosity and having students understand and master the lesson were achieved. This assurance is gained by such lesson evaluation techniques as observing class interaction, orchestrating and participating in discussions, evaluating students through multiple strategies, considering written opinions, conducting conferences with pupils, and giving individual or collective written tests. During these assessments the teacher must be perceptive, sensitive, and understanding of students' diverse backgrounds and attitudes. Reactions may at times be unexpected, especially as the teacher challenges and provokes.

Homework Assignment

Since most mathematics lessons require follow-up by students to refine and sharpen their newly acquired skills, it is advisable that the homework assignment be carefully planned and included in the lesson plan. A second reason for assigning homework is to promote independence and to develop reflection and creative thinking skills. As means to those ends, each assignment completed by students is expected to be neat, organized, accurate, and as complete as possible.

Homework should be discussed in class the next day and usually reviewed as part of a small or large group activity. It might even be collected occasionally for the teacher's perusal and analysis. Small group or whole class analyses are appropriate for different types of assignments, and the teacher must make that determination—there is no formula for a best strategy. Chapter 8 is devoted entirely to the nature of homework assignments.

Weekly or long-range assignments often involve projects that require special formats determined by the teacher. Daily assignment sheets that are distributed in advance of the lesson require much planning and will very likely need some adjustment during the course of the semester.

Special Equipment to be Used

Special equipment to be used may be listed. These include items such as board compasses, graph chart, geometric models, overhead projector, etc. This list serves the purpose of reminding you what you must order from the supply room before the lesson. The special equipment to be used need not always be listed as part of the teacher's actual lesson plan. It might be listed, however, if one desires to present to an outside observer a complete picture of the lesson planned.

Special Tasks or Projects

The current lesson, or one in the not-too-distant future, may be strongly embellished by some preparatory work done either individually or in groups by the students. This may be in the form of an investigation, a data-collection exercise, historial report, or simply an independent study of a related topic. Such activities may appear as a report, a short paper, a poster, a group oral report, or a combination of these.

If Time

Every lesson plan should end with an ''if time'' section, which may include additional practice exercises, or enrichment, or any other useful time filler. Also, you should plan to cover more than can be done in one period rather than find yourself with everything done several minutes before the bell is to ring. Those moments can be horribly long and uncomfortable!

SAMPLE CORE LESSONS

We now investigate three sample core lessons with differentiated content that progress from the concrete level 1 to the more abstract thinking of levels 4 and 5. These are followed by five before-*Standards* lessons that are to be restructured until they become *Standards* ready.

In terms of the *Standards*, the core curriculum consists of three years of required mathematical study that demonstrates variations in depth and breadth of the treatment of topics and applications (*Curriculum and Evaluation Standards*, p. 129). Accordingly, all students, regardless of ability level, will experience the entire range of topics in the curriculum. Thus, students who might previously have been selected for a general or business track, with its own specialized curriculum, will now be exposed to the same subject matter as the college bound, even though they are at different levels of preparedness. The following core lessons illustrate how the same content may be presented at different levels of abstraction, even though teaching strategies will vary in accordance with students' levels of interest, skills, and goals.

First Sample Core Lesson

Consider the graph of the parabola $y = x^2 + x - 6$.

First Level. Students should already have developed skills in evaluating algebraic expressions containing exponents for both positive and negative values of x. They should also be prepared to plot points in a rectangular coordinate system. All students should complete the following table, plot the points on a coordinate grid, and connect them with a smoothly drawn continuous curve (Figure 1).

x	y
-4	6
-3	0
-2	-4
-1	-6
0	-6
1	-4
2	0
3	6

The reflective properties of a parabola (Figure 2) should be mentioned, including its uses in antennae and headlights.

Second Level. Students will use a graphics calculator to graph $y = x^2 + x - 6$ and to determine its zeros. The parabola will appear as in Figure 1, and its zeros will be the intersections with the x-axis, at -3 and 2.

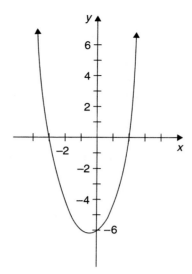

Figure 1. $y = x^2 + x - 6$.

Third Level. Students will draw a line of symmetry in the graph developed for levels 1 and 2. They will realize that this line of symmetry, which is also known as the *axis of symmetry*, falls midway between the zeros of the function, -3 and 2. They will then generalize that the axis of symmetry passes through the midpoint of the segment on the x-axis that joins the two zeros. For this example, the equation of the axis of symmetry is seen to be $x = -\frac{1}{2}$. They will further generalize when they realize that the midpoint is the mean value between the two zeros. From a previously learned formula for the sum of the roots of a quadratic equation, sum $= \frac{-b}{a}$, the equation of the axis of symmetry for the general function $y = ax^2 + bx + c$ must therefore be $x = \frac{-b}{2a}$. Students can then easily generate symmetrically arranged tables that will yield "symmetric" parabolas, beginning with the axis of symmetry and then selecting the same number of points on both sides.

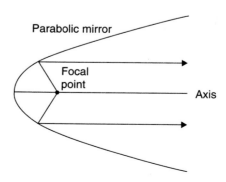

Figure 2. A parabolic mirror.

Fourth Level. After completing the first three levels, students will use the locus approach to sketch a parabola. This locus definition of a parabola should be introduced: *A parabola is the set of all points in a plane equidistant from a fixed line (the directrix) and a fixed point (the focus) not on the fixed line.* A general drawing should then be made illustrating this locus definition, together with specific examples of parabolas of the form $y = ax^2$ or $x = ay^2$. Students should be asked to determine the coordinates of the focus and the equation of its associated directrix. A manipulative consisting of a fixed point (nail) and a piece of string may be used to demonstrate the definition (Figure 3).

Figure 4 describes the parabola formed from the envelope created by tangent folds of a piece of waxed paper. (The basis of this construction is the definition of the parabola given earlier. This rather clever paper-folding technique is done as follows: Take a large piece of waxed paper, mark a point on it for the focus, and draw a line for the directrix. Fold the waxed paper several times so as to place the focus on the directrix each time, and crease each fold. The creases will form an envelope for the parabola.) Envelopes for the remaining conic sections may now be demonstrated, with an introduction to "string" art. The string art may be appropriate at other levels also (see Chapter 5 for reference to string art constructions).

Practice exercises may involve parabolas symmetric with respect to the y- or x-axes, or with axes that are rotated through any angle.

Fifth Level. At this level, college-bound students will learn that a parabola is a section of a cone formed from a "slice" that is parallel to one of its elements. This model will then be expanded to include proofs that "slicing" a cone in other directions will produce a circle, if it is a circular cone, or an ellipse, hyperbola, or even two intersecting lines (Figure 5).

A challenging enrichment exercise for the fifth level might be to prove the following: A uniform cable that

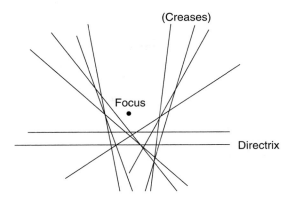

Figure 4. Parabolic envelope.

hangs freely under its own weight takes the shape of a catenary. However, it will hang in the shape of a parabola when it is weighted in such a way that the net weight per horizontal foot is constant. College-bound students with superior mathematical ability will be able to use vector geometry to prove these facts.

Second Sample Core Lesson

In postulational geometry, consider this definition: *The area of any plane surface is the number of square units it contains.*

First Level. The teacher will define and illustrate unfamiliar terms in the following four statements in conjunction with drawing, cutting, and rearranging concrete objects. (Arithmetic numbers used to represent dimensions may be whole, fractional, or decimal, as appropriate for the class.) Applications may include circles for the first level, but they will be irrelevant and superfluous for higher levels, because they do not fit into the upcoming postulational treatment. The value of π will be estimated as 3.14 or $\frac{22}{7}$. For more advanced students the teacher may illustrate the four statements by representing the dimensions with algebraic expressions instead of arithmetic numbers.

1. The area of a rectangle is equal to the product of its base and altitude.
2. The area of a parallelogram is equal to the product of one side and the altitude drawn to that side.
3. The area of a triangle is equal to one-half the product of a side and the altitude drawn to that side.
4. The area of a trapezoid is equal to one-half the product of the altitude and the sum of the bases.

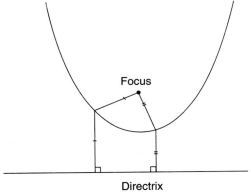

Directrix
Figure 3. The parabola as a locus.

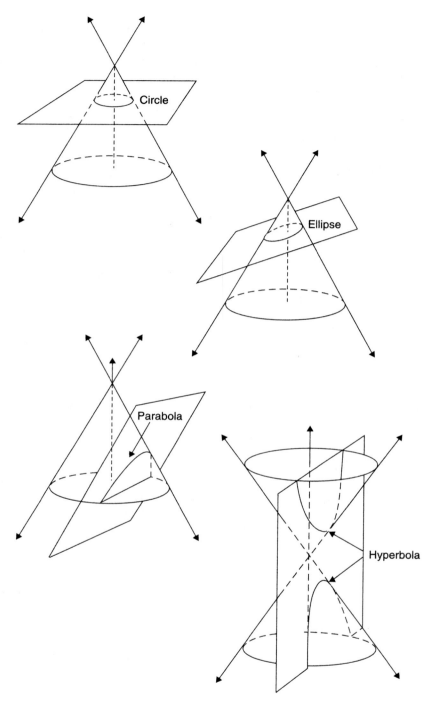

Figure 5. The conic sections.

Second Level. The teacher will postulate statement (1) above and follow with geometric proofs of the following sequence of theorems, where each proof is based on preceding theorems:

$$(2) \rightarrow (3) \rightarrow (4)$$

Note: Numbers used to represent the dimensions of the figures may be rational or irrational.

Third Level. Students will gain a historical perspective of the development of postulational systems by referring to Euclid's *Elements* and his five postulates of geometry. A discussion of Euclid's fifth postulate, Playfair's postulate, and the Saccheri quadrilateral are additional extensions that lead to the development of non-Euclidean geometry, a significant breakthrough in the history of mathematics.

Recommended enrichment includes studying the spherical, elliptic, and hyperbolic non-Euclidean geometries. Compass and straightedge constructions, constructions with other tools, trisecting an angle, and "duplicating the cube," may be discussed as well, leading to a discussion of Galois and the theory of groups.

Fourth Level. Students will be asked to create their own minipostulational systems from any other area of mathematics or from any real-life situation. The study of symbolic logic, syllogisms, and truth tables will assist students in their efforts to create consistent systems.

Third Sample Core Lesson

Pythagoras's well-known theorem for right triangle *ABC*, $a^2 + b^2 = c^2$, is the foundation of linear measurement in geometry. In both two- and three-dimensional geometric situations the impact of the Pythagorean theorem has been major. But linear measure is certainly not the only significance of the Pythagorean theorem. A generalization of this theorem, known as Fermat's last theorem, has also left an indelible mark on the theory of numbers.

First Level. The teacher will display a manipulative model of a 3-4-5 right triangle with plastic square units that can be arranged to form a square on each side to demonstrate that the sum of the areas of the squares on the legs is equal to the area of the square on the hypotenuse (Figure 6).

The more well known Pythagorean triples, besides 3-4-5, are 5-12-13, 8-15-17, and 7-24-25, as well as multiples and fractional parts of these. They will be used in real-life practical problem situations.

Students will learn algebraic techniques for determining the third side of any right triangle given the dimensions of the other two sides. Students will, in effect, be learning to solve equations of the form $x^2 = k$. This will involve the use of calculators, rational and irrational numbers, extraneous answers, rounding, and estimating.

Second Level. After developing the three mean proportional theorems that result from drawing an altitude to the hypotenuse of a right triangle, students will be prepared to fill in the blank spaces on their duplicated work sheets to answer the seven questions in the model lesson plan that follows on pp. 32–34.

Seven practice and challenge questions follow. It would be advisable for these to be solved as part of a small group discussion. After the class reassembles as a large group, they may be asked to discuss the final summary questions. At this point homework should be assigned. If desirable, the indicated challenge problem may be added to the homework assignment. Both the assignment and the challenge may be discussed in small groups the following day.

Right triangle trigonometry may be introduced here, with calculators being used to determine the values of trigonometric functions of any acute angle.

Third Level. Students will use coordinate geometry to plot points that form various right triangles in a variety of plane figures. They will derive the distance formula for two- and three-dimensional figures. Applications in plane or coordinate geometry are also appropriate, such as finding the diagonal of a cube of side 2 or of a rectangular prism with dimensions 2, 3, and 4. Also appropriate for this level is a discussion of indirect proofs in mathematics, such as for proving the converse of the Pythagorean theorem.

The law of cosines and the law of sines for any triangle may also be developed in both synthetic and coordinate geometry formats at this level. Extensive problem-solving applications, using calculators, as they relate to the solution of triangles are appropriate here. Solutions of these problems will lead to the development of definitions of inverse trigonometric functions.

Fourth Level. Students will now be prepared to understand spherical geometry and to define right angles on a sphere. An introductory lesson in non-Euclidean geometry will result in an informative diversion into the history of geometry, specifically, the consequences and implications of considering variations of Euclid's fifth postulate. Topological properties of non-Euclidean models such as the sphere and hyperbolic paraboloid may be presented alongside the transformations of rubber-sheet geometry.

On the heels of the Pythagorean theorem comes what is known as Fermat's last theorem. In the margin of one

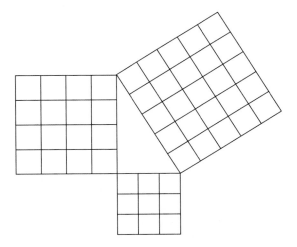

Figure 6. Plastic 3-4-5 Pythagorean triple model.

Model Lesson Plan

TOPIC: Lesson on the Pythagorean theorem.

*For the high school
geometry course.*

AIM: To introduce, prove, and apply the Pythagorean theorem.

MOTIVATIONAL ACTIVITY:

In the figure below, $\overline{CD}$ is an altitude of right $\triangle ABC$ with right angle at C. The lengths of the segments are marked. Referring to the figure, complete each of the following:

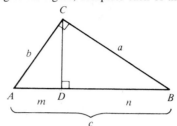

*This set of exercises will be
duplicated and distributed to
the class.*

1. AC is the mean proportional between $\boxed{AB}$ and $\boxed{AD}$.

2. Therefore $\dfrac{c}{\boxed{b}} = \dfrac{b}{\boxed{m}}$, or $b^2 = \boxed{cm}$. Why?

*Notice also that these
exercises review the mean
proportional theorems while
at the same time permitting
the student actually to prove
the Pythagorean theorem.
Although students may not
realize this at first, they will
be led to see this during the
development of the lesson.*

3. $\boxed{BC}$ is the mean proportional between AB and BD.

4. Therefore $\dfrac{\boxed{c}}{a} = \dfrac{\boxed{a}}{n}$; or $a^2 = \boxed{cn}$. Why?

5. Adding the results of Exercises 2 and 4, we get $a^2 + b^2 = \boxed{cm} + \boxed{cn} = \boxed{c}\,(m + n)$.

6. But $m + n = \boxed{c}$.

7. Therefore $a^2 + \boxed{b^2} = \boxed{c^2}$.

N. B. Circles indicate correct answers, which are obviously not included on actual answer sheets.

EXPLORATION:

1. Ask the class (make up a story) if they can get a 10 ft. diameter circular table top through a door that is only 8 ft. high and 6 ft. wide.

*Do not rush through your
story in an effort to get to
the "meat" of the lesson.
This will diminish the
effectiveness of this
approach.*

2. Use the prepared overhead transparency to review the do-now exercise with the class.

*This prepared transparency
should be just like the copy
of the do-now exercise given
to the class.*

3. Indicate to the class the significance of the do-now exercise. That is, *they* have just *proved* the Pythagorean theorem.

*This must be carefully
presented so as to reap the
full impact intended from
these exercises.*

4. Ask the class what Euclid and President James A. Garfield had in common. Now give the class some historical notes about the Pythagorean theorem (such as the Egyptian "rope stretchers," or the 360+ proofs).

*Both proved the
Pythagorean theorem.*

*This brief discussion should
generate some extra interest
for this topic.*

Model Lesson Plan (*Continued*)   Comments

5. Discuss an application of the Pythagorean theorem with the class.

Visual aids would be quite helpful here.

6. Find the length of the hypotenuse of the right triangle shown below:

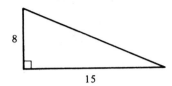

This is a very simple application and should be done together with the class.

PRACTICE:
Find *x* in each of the following (send students to chalkboard):

1.

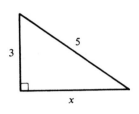

2.

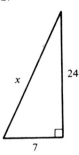

3.

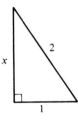

These are simple exercises that apply only the Pythagorean theorem and require no other prior knowledge.

Students will be asked to place their correct solutions on the chalkboard. These correct solutions will be detected by the teacher during his walk throughout the classroom while the students are working on these exercises.

MEDIAL SUMMARY (ask the following questions):

1. State the Pythagorean theorem.
2. For what can we use the Pythagorean theorem?
3. Can the Pythagorean theorem be applied to any triangle for which the lengths of two sides are given?

These questions should elicit the key points of the previous part of the lesson and thus serve as a summary up to this point in the lesson.

CHALLENGE:
Find *x* in each of the following (send students to the chalkboard when assigning the problems to the class):

1.

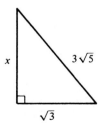

2.

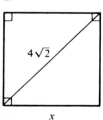

3.

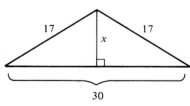

Students should be assigned to do their work on the chalkboard immediately, rather than first to work the problems at their seats and then just to copy them onto the board. The class can learn from classmates' errors, as well as from correct solutions.

4. *Given:* $\overline{PS}$ is an altitude of $\triangle PQR$
   Prove: $PQ^2 - RP^2 = QS^2 - SR^2$

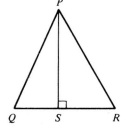

Model Lesson Plan (Continued)   Comments

FINAL SUMMARY (ask the following questions):   *This summary is intended to*
                                                                     review the topic of this
1. State in words the Pythagorean theorem.   *lesson and allow students to*
2. How can the Pythagorean theorem help us find the length of a diagonal of a rectangle *show that they really*
   when we are given the lengths of the sides of the rectangle?   *understand what it is and*
3. What would you guess to be true about a triangle whose sides have lengths 3, 4, and 5? *how it can be used.*
4. State the converse of the Pythagorean theorem.   *Questions 3–5 foreshadow*
5. Is it true?   *the next lesson on the*
                                                                     converse of the Pythagorean
                                                                     theorem.

HOMEWORK ASSIGNMENT: *This homework assignment*
                                                                     is a spiralled assignment
1. Four exercises similar to those in the application section of the lesson plan. *that reviews previously*
2. One proof involving the Pythagorean theorem.   *learned material as well as*
3. One exercise using the mean proportional theorems.   *the newly presented topic.*
4. One exercise on similar triangles.   *(See Chapter 8 on homework*
                                                                     assignments.)

IF TIME (discuss the following challenge problem with the class):   *This problem involves*
                                                                     numerous applications of the
In the figure, $\overline{PC} \perp \overline{BD}$ at C and $\overline{PB} \perp \overline{AB}$. $AP = 17$, $AB = 8$, $BC = 9$, and $CD = 3\frac{1}{2}$. Find PD. *Pythagorean theorem. It is a*
                                                                     departure from the
                                                                     previously simpler
                                                                     applications.

$\left(12\frac{1}{2}\right)$

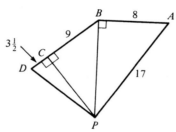

SPECIAL EQUIPMENT:
Copies of the Motivational Activity as well as a transparency of it, an overhead projector, colored
chalk, and ruler (or some sort of chalkboard straightedge).

---

of the books in his library, Fermat wrote that the equation $x^n + y^n = z^n$ cannot be solved in positive integers x, y, z for $n = 3, 4, 5, \ldots$.

Fruitless attempts to prove this conjecture produced much good mathematics for a period of more than 350 years, but no proof that was able to stand up to scrutiny by the mathematics community. The search for a valid proof culminated with a proof by Dr. Andrew Wiles of Princeton University in June 1993.

Further analysis of Fermat's theorem should evolve into discussions of finding solutions of Diophantine equations, especially of the first degree, (i.e., of finding all pairs of integers x, y that satisfy the equation $ax + by = n$, where a, b, and n are given integers).

Students at this level will learn the meaning of "relatively prime" and may be led to discover a method for generating primitive Pythagorean triples.

SAMPLE *STANDARDS* LESSONS

Lessons prepared for small or large group instruction that involve the use of manipulatives, calculators and computers, open-ended questions, challenging tasks, portfolios of sample student classwork, and other classroom activities recommended by the *Standards* will be designated as *Standards* lessons. Although the outline for a daily lesson plan (p. 25) was the basis on which the four sample *Standards* lessons were selected for this section, you should be aware of the following facts.

1. The daily lesson plan outline is merely a *recommended format* and is not meant to be the only possible lesson-plan outline.
2. Your analysis of before-*Standards* lessons (pp. 38—44) will serve you well in better under-

standing what is expected in lessons that use *Standards* strategies.

3. The reading lesson referred to later (p. 36) presents a formal geometry proof that is written in paragraph format and is based on a *Standards* recommendation that mathematical proofs be written that way, rather than in the two-column format that is now in common use.

Sample *Standards* Practice Lesson

Practice by repetition is an important technique in the teaching of mathematics. It reinforces previously learned skills while developing new ones via the nuances that are bound to arise from doing a large selection of varied examples. It may well lead to a better understanding of the underlying theory.

Both large and small group practice lessons may last the entire period, or they may be an adjunct to a task-oriented lesson for a portion of the period. To illustrate, we present an algebra lesson on factoring trinomials into a product of binomials that alternates between large and small group formats. Patterns developed and practiced in each small group may be reconsidered within a large group format, but with additional insights from other students and the teacher. The teacher facilitates student movement, coordinates summaries, assigns homework, and guides lesson assessments.

Sample Standards Practice Lesson

TOPIC: Introductory lesson on factoring a trinomial of the form $ax^2 + bx + c$ into a product of two binomials

PRIOR KNOWLEDGE: Pupils can multiply binomials by inspection.

INSTRUCTIONAL FORMAT: Both small and large groups.

MOTIVATIONAL ACTIVITY: (Assign small groups of students to determine the answers for each set below and suggest that each select a representative to report their proposals to the whole class after it reconvenes.)

Set 1	*Set 2*	*Set 3*	*Set 4*
$(x + 3)(x + 2)$	$(x + 5)(x - 2)$	$(x - 3)(x + 2)$	$(x - 3)(x - 5)$
$(x + 1)(x + 7)$	$(x - 3)(x + 5)$	$(x + 1)(x - 6)$	$(x - 1)(x - 8)$
$(x + 4)(x + 3)$	$(x + 5)(x + 1)$	$(x - 4)(x + 2)$	$(x - 7)(x - 2)$

EXPLORATION: After the whole class reconvenes, ask each group representative to

1. Discuss patterns for each set that were discovered by the group.
2. Demonstrate how the patterns can be used to work back to factors, using the product $x^2 + 8x + 15$ to illustrate. Then change "+" to "−" in front of $8x$ and follow the same procedure for each group.
   a. Teacher emphasizes: Always begin with parentheses ( )( ).
   b. Teacher notes: Factor the constant term so that the sum of the factors is equal to the coefficient of the middle term.

PRACTICE: (Return to small groups with duplicated or textbook assigned practice exercises)

1. $x^2 + 7x + 10$	5. $x^2 + 5x - 14$	9. $x^2 - 64$
2. $x^2 - 5x + 6$	6. $x^2 - x - 20$	10. $x^2 + 4x - 12$
3. $x^2 - 7x + 6$	7. $x^2 + 3x - 40$	11. $x^2 - 81$
4. $x^2 - 2x + 15$	8. $x^2 - 6x + 9$	12. $49 - x^2$
		13. $x^2 - \dfrac{25}{36}$

FINAL SUMMARY: (Each small group summarizes its own conclusions after having communicated with and received input from the other groups)

HOMEWORK ASSIGNMENT: Distribute additional sheets of practice exercises for all students.

Discuss the homework solutions in small groups in class the next day. Continue to assign daily additional homework on the same topic, including expansions to include trinomials with initial coefficient >1.

ASSESSMENT: After several days, collect and evaluate portfolios that will include homework solutions, quizzes, and tests.

Sample *Standards* Mathematics
Reading Lesson

Individual exploration may take a variety of forms. This
lesson employs a ''mathematics through reading'' approach.

Sample Standards Mathematics Reading Lesson

TOPIC: Prove the proposition: *If the diameter of a circle is perpendicular to a chord, it bisects the chord and its arc.*

PRIOR KNOWLEDGE: Students have sufficient background knowledge to prove the theorem.

INSTRUCTIONAL FORMAT: Individual exploration through reading mathematics.

MOTIVATIONAL ACTIVITY: Read the proof of the proposition and write it in paragraph form. Be prepared to answer questions
based on that reading. Also, be prepared to propose your own questions.

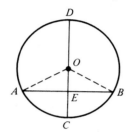

HYPOTHESES: In circle O, diameter $\overline{CD} \perp \overline{AB}$ at E.
CONCLUSION: $\overline{AE} \cong \overline{EB}$;
$\qquad\qquad\quad \overset{\frown}{AC} \cong \overset{\frown}{CB}$
$\qquad\qquad\quad \overset{\frown}{AD} \cong \overset{\frown}{DB}$

To prove $\overline{AE} \cong \overline{EB}$, we must first prove that $\triangle OAE \cong \triangle OBE$. Since radii $\overline{OA}$ and $\overline{OB}$ are congruent, and $\overline{OE}$ is a common leg
of right triangles OAE and OBE, it follows that the two triangles are congruent by the hypotenuse-leg $\cong$ hypotenuse-leg theorem.
    Because the triangles are congruent, it follows that the corresponding angles AOE and BOE are also congruent. However, angles
AOE and BOE are central angles of the circle, so they intercept congruent arcs.
    We know that a diamaeter of a circle divides it into two congruent arcs, so that arc $CAD \cong$ arc CBD. It follows by subtraction
that arcs AD and DB are congruent.
    After the students have read and studied the proof of the theorem, elicit their answers to these questions.

1. When this diagram was drawn, what was drawn first?
2. What was drawn next?
3. What else was drawn?
4. How was the diameter drawn?
5. Then what was drawn?
6. Why are radii $\overline{OA}$ and $\overline{OB}$ needed in the diagram?
7. What information can we get from the two triangles?
8. Why are arcs AC and CB congruent?
9. What follows from the fact that arc$CAD \cong$ arcCBD?

CONNECTIONS: Mathematical symbols and expressions are used in a reading exercise to assess comprehension. The discourse
continues as pupils probe with additional questions and responses. Questions such as how to find the center of a broken wheel
connect this topic with locus in geometry.

FINAL SUMMARY: It is appropriate to ask the old standby question, How would you explain over the telephone what you learned
in class to a friend who has no text?

ASSESSMENT: Ask pupils to formulate their opinions of reading lessons in mathematics class. Prepare or obtain a programmed
learning text that will guide pupils to learn some new knowledge or acquire a new skill.

HOMEWORK: Algebraic and geometric textbook applications.

Sample *Standards* Mathematics Writing Lesson

At the bottom of this page is an unusual method of assessing pupils' understanding of a unit on radicals. The technique is appropriate for other topics as well. If handled as a small cooperative group lesson, the assessment can also serve as a review lesson for the text. If handled as an individual examination, it will serve to expose those students who always claim to make excessive mistakes on traditional tests.

Sample *Standards* Mathematics Lecture Lesson

The lecture technique is most suited to a mature audience, one with a reasonably long attention span. College students, as well as those in the more advanced high school mathematics classes, are most often exposed to this type of lesson.

Although active pupil involvement is usually sought in most lessons, pupils who rarely interrupt the lesson are the "ideal" participants in a lecture. In fact, the active student in a lecture situation, one who constantly questions and probes, is often viewed by both lecturer and fellow students as an irritant who delays the lecture and prevents the teacher from delivering the planned lesson fully.

The lecture approach is probably the most efficient one when a complex body of material requiring pupil thought and concentration is to be presented. For example, the epsilon-delta method of finding limits, the "fundamental theorem of integral calculus," and the theory behind mathematical induction might very well lend themselves to the lecture approach. But it is most appropriate when

a special skill is being demonstrated, such as how to operate an abacus, slide rule, or some other uncommon manipulative.

Many of the formal features listed in a task-oriented lesson plan might also appear in a lecture, namely, the aim, motivational activity, connections, homework, summaries, and assessment. The difference is in the actual development of the new material—*lecture* versus *exploration*. Thus, *unless it is clear where the emphasis lies,* it may not be possible to determine the instructional format of the lesson by merely studying its plan.

SAMPLE BEFORE *STANDARDS* LESSONS

The five before-*Standards* plans that follow describe actual lessons from different teachers' records.

1. The versions you will see may be more neatly arranged than the teachers' written plans. (In the haste of lesson preparation, and in the course of developing a lesson, deletions and insertions may tend to make the handwritten plan a bit sloppy.)
2. Whenever the writer of the lesson refers to specific examples in a text, the examples and page numbers listed in the illustrations are fictitious; they are listed for illustrative purposes only.
3. A "comments" column appears on the right side of each plan. These are *our* comments on the plans being exhibited.

If you study, analyze, discuss, and comment on these lessons, you can learn what is right from the strong ones as well as what is wrong from the weak ones.

Sample Standards Mathematics Writing Lesson

TOPIC: A mathematics writing test for the radicals unit (see p. 22).

PRIOR KNOWLEDGE: Students know to use calculators to find powers and roots; they know the Pythagorean theorem; they also know how to solve equations of the form $x^2 = k$, where k may or may not be a perfect square; to round a decimal to any desired degree of accuracy; add, subtract, multiply, and divide radicals; rationalize a denominator; solve and check radical equations.

INSTRUCTIONAL FORMAT: Small cooperative group or independent work (teacher's decision).

MOTIVATIONAL ACTIVITY: Write for a full period all you have learned about four topics in the unit on radicals.

EXPLORATIONS: Students will consider answers to the following questions:

1. Explain concepts so that a new student will be able to do a homework assignment.
2. Write and solve sample problems.
3. Make sure that the mathematics is accurate and that explanations are clear. (You will be graded on these criteria.)

HOMEWORK ASSIGNMENT: Optional.

Newly trained teachers will be inspired by the *Standards* philosophy. However, since most new teachers will very likely have been taught during their own high school days by formerly acceptable methods, and since these may still be remembered, we present five plans from past years for those presently in teacher training courses to update to the *Standards*. We believe this to be an ideal way for new teachers to start their careers with a fresh slate.

As you read the following sample lessons, consider the following tasks and questions:

1. Use specific activities to show how a task-oriented development differs from the one presented.
2. Indicate the places in the lesson where communication activities could be enhanced.
3. How would you improve understanding through connections with other mathematics or with other subject areas?

Before-*Standards* Lesson Plan 1

Comments

AIM: To recognize quadratic equations and to learn how to solve them by factoring.

DO-NOW: When a number is multiplied by 3 more than itself, the result is 0. Find the number.

$$x = \text{the number}$$

$$x + 3 = 3 \text{ more than the number}$$

$$x(x + 3) = 0$$

These are the answers the teacher expects to elicit when reviewing the do-now.

Let's stop for a moment and see if we can discover something that will help us solve this equation.
Everybody, think of two numbers whose product is 0. (Write answers on board.)
What do you notice about each pair of numbers?
Who can say in words what we just noticed? (Write on board: If $ab = 0$, then $a = 0$ or $b = 0$.)
Now, let's use this fact to solve our equation:

These are the major questions and comments, written in the same order they were asked by the teacher.

x	$(x + 3)$
$x = 0$	$x + 3 = 0$
	$x = -3$

How would you use this same fact to solve: $x(x + 4) = 0$?
How would you solve $x^2 + 4x = 0$? (Elicit "factoring.")
What about this one: $x^2 + 5x + 6 = 0$?
How would you solve this: $x^2 - 4 = 0$?

This question was not asked because the teacher saw that the lesson was running too long and wanted to begin to cut out some parts of the prepared lesson.

Looking back at the equations we've just solved, who can tell us the steps we used? (Elicit the following.)
(Write on board)

Developing steps used in solving a quadratic serves as a medial summary.

1. Factor.
2. Set each factor $= 0$.
3. Solve each linear equation.
   Now use these steps to solve the following:
   (a) $x^2 = 0$ (b) $x^2 + 6x + 8 = 0$ (c) $x^2 - 16 = 0$
   (Go over solutions.)

Example (c) was cut out of the class presentation to save time.

How are these equations different from the ones you've learned to solve before today? ("degree 2," "two answers," etc.)

A pivotal question comparing students' new knowledge with previous knowledge.

These equations are called QUADRATIC EQUATIONS.

Which of the following are quadratic equations?
(a) $x^2 + 7x + 12 = 0$ (b) $x^2 - 2x = 0$ (c) $x^2 = 2x$ (d) $x^2 + 7x = -12$
(e) $x + 3 = 0$

Compare (a) and (d); (b) and (c).
Who can summarize for us how we go about solving quadratic equations? (*Note:* Extra step of gathering all terms on one side in descending powers.)

HOMEWORK ASSIGNMENT: Study pages 157 and 158.
                                          Do examples 3, 5, 7, 11, 13, 17, 19.

Go over homework today. Page 140/ 2, 3, 4, 6.

IF TIME: Solve each quadratic equation:

   (a) $x^2 + 8x + 15 = 0$ (b) $x^2 - 64 = 0$ (c) $a^2 = 7a$ (d) $b^2 + 6b = -8$

Boardwork (front):

PANEL I	PANEL II	PANEL III
DN	(1) If $ab = 0$, $a = 0$ or $b = 0$	Solve: $x^2 + 5x = 0$
$x(x + 3) = 0$	(2) Steps to solve (quadratics)	$x^2 + 6x + 8 = 0$
$x(x + 4) = 0$	a) Collect terms on one side.	$x^2 - 16 = 0$
$x^2 + 4x = 0$	Set = 0.	Which are quadratics?
$x^2 + 5x + 6 = 0$	b) Factor	$x^2 + 7x + 12 = 0$
$x^2 - 4 = 0$	c) Set each factor = 0	$x^2 - 2x = 0$
	d) Solve linear equations	$x^2 = 2x$
	(3) Facts about equations:	$x^2 + 7x = -12$
	a) degree 2	$x + 3 = 0$
	b) two answers	
	Note: Homework on side boards.	

Comments

The teacher wrote on the board the aim of the lesson: How to solve quadratic equations.

Students were asked to read the text explanation of the same topic and to do practice examples.
NOTE 1: The homework assignment was not spiral.
NOTE 2: Although the assignment was written last in the plan, it was written on the board FIRST by the teacher. At the end of the period, the teacher changed the assignment by eliminating the types of examples that were not discussed.

This was not done in class because of insufficient time.

This also was not done in class.

The classroom has three front board panels, and the teacher planned where everything was to be written.

---

4. How could calculators and computers play a more significant role in this lesson?
5. To what extent could a small group lesson be a useful strategy for this lesson? Same question for a large group lesson.
6. Where would manipulatives be useful or needed?
7. To what extent are questions provocative? Open ended?

8. What assessment strategies would you employ during the course of the lesson? At the conclusion of the lesson?

Remember, old lessons may have been taught by master teachers. Even though teacher roles have changed, their plans may still be informative with regard to style, technique, strategy, questioning, knowledge, and more. Let us now consider a second before-*Standards* lesson.

Before-*Standards* Lesson Plan 2

TOPIC: Introductory lesson on properties of the parallelogram.

AIM: (a) To learn and prove the properties of a parallelogram;
     (b) To do simple algebraic applications of these properties.

PREVIOUSLY LEARNED: (a) Properties of angles formed when parallel lines are cut by a transversal;
                                 (b) Methods of proving triangles congruent;
                                 (c) Definitions of quadrilateral and diagonal.

DO NOW:

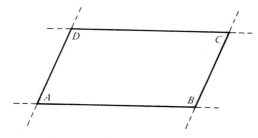

GIVEN: Quadrilateral *ABCD*
$\overleftrightarrow{AB} \parallel \overleftrightarrow{CD}$; $\overleftrightarrow{AD} \parallel \overleftrightarrow{BC}$

QUESTION: What relationship exists between $\angle A$ and $\angle B$? Why?

DEVELOPMENT AND METHODS:
(Students are not to write in their notebooks until told to do so by the teacher. All proofs of theorems that are elicited from the class will be done orally. Record all responses in tabular form as shown at the end of the plan.)

    1. Define "parallelogram." (Head the table "In a parallelogram:" and elicit the aim of the lesson.)
    2. Discuss the do-now. (Elicit: "Consecutive angles are supplementary," and prove.)
    3. Question: What must be true about $\angle A$ and $\angle C$? Why? (Elicit and prove: "Opposite angles are congruent.")
    4. Draw $\overline{BD}$.
    5. Question: What new things can you see in the diagram as a result of having drawn $\overline{BD}$? (Elicit and prove: "Two congruent triangles are formed, and opposite sides are congruent.")
    6. Erase $\overline{BD}$; Draw $\overline{AC}$.
    7. Question: Does drawing $\overline{AC}$ yield anything new that we can prove?
    8. Medial Summary: Have students read and explain the list developed so far and copy it into their notebooks.

DRILL:

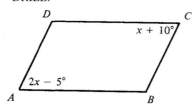

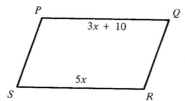

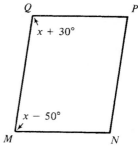

ABCD is a parallelogram.
Find *x*. (Reason?)

PQRS is a parallelogram.
Find *x*. (Reason?)

Parallelogram *MNPQ*.
Find m $\angle P$.

DEVELOPMENT (continued):

    9. Draw both diagonals;
   10. Question: State and prove a conclusion you might reach about the two diagonals that appear together in the diagram. (Answer: "Diagonals bisect each other.")

DRILL:

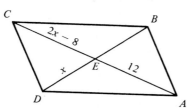

ABCD is a parallelogram
Find *DE*.

SUMMARY: Erase the table from the board and ask, "List in your own words the properties of a parallelogram that we discussed earlier."

HOMEWORK: (a) Six examples in textbook, similar to drill that was done in class;
(b) Several other examples from a previous topic.

IF TIME: As many examples as time permits on the same topic. (Specific examples should be listed here.)

Table (on side of front board:)

	IN A PARALLELOGRAM:
(Definition)	1. Opposite sides are parallel.
(Theorem)	2. Consecutive angles are supplementary.
(Theorem)	3. Opposite angles are congruent.
(Theorem)	4. Diagonal divides it into two congruent triangles.
(Theorem)	5. Opposite sides are congruent.
(Theorem)	6. Diagonals bisect each other.

Before-*Standards* Lesson Plan 3

Comments

TOPIC: Addition of simple arithmetic fractions.

APPERCEPTIVE BASIS:

1. Students are familiar with the basic concepts of fractions.
2. Students have studied multiplication and simplification of simple fractions.

This refers to previously learned material relevant to this lesson. It is usually one of those details kept in back of the teacher's mind rather than recorded in the plan.

DO-NOW:
Use this diagram:

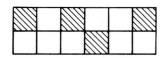

How many parts are shaded?   ④
Not shaded?   ⑧
What are the total number of parts?   ⑫

The expected answers are circled.

Write the following fractions:	Reduce each fraction to lowest terms:
$\dfrac{\text{shaded}}{\text{total}} = \left(\dfrac{4}{12}\right)$	$\dfrac{4}{12} = \left(\dfrac{1}{3}\right)$
$\dfrac{\text{not shaded}}{\text{total}} = \left(\dfrac{8}{12}\right)$	$\dfrac{8}{12} = \left(\dfrac{2}{3}\right)$

Review procedure for simplifying fractions:

$$\frac{4}{12} = \frac{\cancel{2} \times \cancel{2}}{\cancel{2} \times \cancel{2} \times 3} = \frac{1}{3}$$

$$\frac{8}{12} = \frac{\cancel{2} \times \cancel{2} \times 2}{\cancel{2} \times \cancel{2} \times 3} = \frac{2}{3}$$

CHALLENGE: What must $\dfrac{4}{12} + \dfrac{8}{12} = ?$ Why?

Use diagram to illustrate answer.

What must $\dfrac{1}{3} + \dfrac{2}{3} = ?$ Why?

Look at next diagram:

Name the fraction in each diagram:

$$\frac{\text{shaded}}{\text{total}} = \left(\frac{1}{4}\right) \qquad \left(\frac{2}{4}\right)$$

$$\frac{1}{4} + \frac{2}{4} = \frac{3}{4} \qquad\qquad \text{Simplify} \qquad \frac{2}{4} \left(\frac{1}{2}\right)$$

$$\frac{1}{4} + \frac{1}{2} = \frac{3}{4}$$

What topic will we learn today?

Write: *Addition of Fractions* on board

The aim of the lesson is elicited here. It was written on the board well into the lesson.

CHALLENGE:

(1).   (2).   Name the fraction in each diagram.

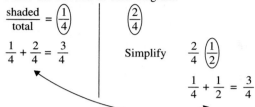 $\left(\frac{3}{9}\right)$ and $\left(\frac{1}{9}\right)$

Simplify $\frac{3}{9}$ $\left(\frac{1}{3}\right)$

$$\frac{3}{9} + \frac{1}{9} = ? \quad \left(\frac{4}{9}\right) \qquad\qquad \frac{1}{3} + \frac{1}{9} = \frac{4}{9}$$

Look at the two examples:

$$\frac{1}{4} + \frac{1}{2} = \frac{3}{4} \Longleftrightarrow \frac{1}{4} + \frac{2}{4} = \frac{3}{4}$$

$$\frac{1}{3} + \frac{1}{9} = \frac{4}{9} \Longleftrightarrow \frac{3}{9} + \frac{1}{9} = \frac{4}{9}$$

What must be true about the denominators of fractions when we add?   ⟨Same⟩

PRACTICE:

$$\frac{3}{5} + \frac{1}{10} \qquad \text{Are the denominators the same or different?}$$

Name the common denominator.   ⑩

The teacher demonstrated the addition in a vertical as well as in a horizontal arrangement.

$$\frac{3}{5} = \frac{6}{10} \quad \text{Why?} \quad \left(\frac{3 \times 2}{5 \times 2} = \frac{6}{10}\right)$$

$$\frac{6}{10} + \frac{1}{10} = \frac{7}{10}$$

MORE PRACTICE:

$$\frac{4}{7} + \frac{1}{21} = ?$$

CHALLENGE QUESTIONS:

$\frac{3}{5} + \frac{2}{3}$ What is the common denominator?

$\frac{1}{2} + \frac{2}{3} + \frac{5}{6}$

$\frac{2}{5} + \frac{1}{2} + \frac{2}{3}$

These are really "if time" questions, and in fact only the first was done.

FINAL SUMMARY: What have we learned today?

HOMEWORK: Page 157. ex. 2, 3, 5, 7, 9, 11, 12, 13, 15, 18.

Before-*Standards* Lesson Plan 4

HOMEWORK: p. 212/ 2, 4, 7; p. 208/ 8, 11

DO-NOW:

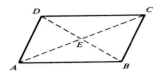

Rhombus *ABCD*
$AC = 10$
$BD = 8$
(1) What kind of angle is *AEB*? Why?
(2) Find area of $\triangle$ *AEB*
(3) Find area of entire rhombus.

Then: Let $AC = x$, $BD = y$

Show Area $= \dfrac{1}{2} xy$

DRILL: p. 212/ 3, 5, 6

Review homework.

The aim of the lesson was to derive the formula for the area of a rhombus in terms of its diagonals.

The do-now leads into the new work. This is the development.

The teacher demonstrated the first example on the board. The remaining two were done by students themselves at their seats and reviewed by the teacher.

Examples were assigned to be written on the board while class was working on the do-now.

"If time" is missing.

Before-*Standards* Lesson Plan 5

Comments

Return test.

The test had been reviewed previously.

Recall theorem about a line parallel to one side of triangle.

Students are reminded of previously learned relevant material.

Theorem: If a line parallel to one side of a triangle intersects the other two sides, then it cuts off segments proportional to those sides.

This is the theorem that was recalled.

Theorem: If a line intersects two sides of a triangle and cuts off segments proportional to those two sides, it is parallel to the third side.

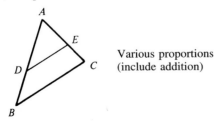

Various proportions
(include addition)

Teacher assigns 2 practice exercises.

Theorem: The bisector of an angle of a triangle separates the opposite side into segments whose lengths are proportional to the lengths of the adjacent sides.

The converse of the theorem above was discussed and explained but there is no indication in the plan how this was done.

"Addition" refers to
$\dfrac{AD}{DB} = \dfrac{AE}{EC}$ *and implies that*

$$\dfrac{AD + DB}{DB} = \dfrac{AE + EC}{EC}$$

Two algebraic applications.

The teacher knew the proof well and did not find it necessary to write it out in the plan.

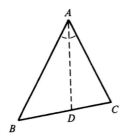

$$\frac{BD}{DC} = \frac{BA}{CA}$$

Page 193: ex. 1, 3, 4

Three drill examples, algebraic and geometric.

IF TIME: Page 192: ex. 17, 18

HOMEWORK: Page 192: ex. 11, 12, 15, 16
                 Page 193: ex. 5, 6

This one shows how, through a series of strategically placed (mostly oral) questions, all major properties of a parallelogram can be discovered and proved. Note that the style is somewhat different from the first. Remember, there is no one "perfect lesson plan." Each plan must conform to the personality and needs of the teacher using it.

The next before-*Standards* lesson is for middle school or junior high school pupils.

This next two plans are considerably less detailed than the previous ones. They were written by teachers of before-*Standards* experience having confidence in their ability to think on their feet while in front of a class.

CREATING CHALLENGING TASKS

Creating challenging tasks can indeed be a challenge for the teacher. You might begin by devising simple strategies for discovering generalizations. For example, you might ask a class to work out several numerical problems involving rate, time, and distance before the class concludes that rate × time = distance. Or you might have pupils toss coins before they conclude that there is a relationship between the coefficients of the terms of a binomial expansion and probability theory.

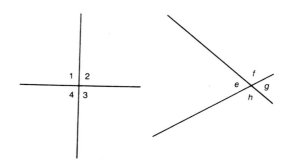

Comparing tables of values, studying graphs, using protractors and compasses, using calculators, or using your own imagination are all suitable tools for discovering generalizations. Here are two different strategies.

Illustration 1. Use your protractor to measure each angle in each diagram. What conclusions do you reach?

After appropriate class discussions, the following generalizations should come forward:

1. Vertical angles are congruent.
2. The sum of the measures of the angles about a point (in a plane) is 360°.
3. The sum of the measures of the angles about a point on one side of a straight line (in a half-plane) is 180°.

In junior high school, these generalizations need not be proved.

Illustration 2. To elicit properties of an indirect proof.

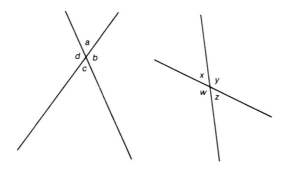

This notice was sent home to your parents near the beginning of the school year. It got torn in the mail. Which month is the meeting?

> 1. List the months ending in -*er* and the number of days of each:
>   September   30 days
>   October   31 days
>   November   30 days
>   December   New Year's eve
> 2. Eliminate all but one.
> 3. Therefore, the meeting is in October.

In each case, you must supplement your questions with diagrams, activities, historical embellishments, clarifications, and so forth, and these should all appear in your plans. Depending on the level and type of class, these generalizations sometimes must be proved after they are "discovered," whereas other times the mere discovery itself will suffice.

Yet, in spite of your best efforts in planning a good lesson, the words of the Scottish poet Robert Burns ring loud and clear, "the best laid plans o' mice an' men / Gang aft agley." Even after a defeat, and you will have them, you must study and analyze you plans so you will not repeat past mistakes.

SUMMARY

Just as no performer enjoys playing the same role day in and day out, so no student enjoys sitting for the same type of lesson every day. It kills initiative and dulls the imagination. So, too, it might affect a teacher who, for example, uses the small group instructional format every day. Variety is what makes the learning process, as well as the teaching aspect of that process, a pleasant one. Thus, the use of whole class discussions, peer instruction, individual exploration, guest lecturers, and video presentations must all become part of the mathematics teacher's repertoire.

Every lesson, however, ought to contain at least some task-oriented features such as challenging activities, use of calculators, computers, or manipulatives whenever appropriate, and stimulating, open-ended type questions *always*.

Whenever you plan a unit of work, a daily lesson, or an assessment strategy, do so carefully and imaginatively. You have a wide range of options to choose from, so choose wisely and try to use as many of them as possible throughout the semester.

EXERCISES

1. Select one of the topics from the unit plan on 'radicals' given on page 22 and write a lesson plan for it. What type of lesson plan did you write? Why did you choose that particular type for your topic?

2. a. What are the key features found in most lessons?
   b. What types of lessons lend themselves to the exploration technique?
   c. *True or false:* Every lesson can be exploratory. Discuss.

3. Select a topic from first year algebra and develop a small group lesson for it.

4. a. Find a section in a first year high school algerbra textbook to teach as a mathematics-through-reading lesson. Write a list of ten questions you plan to ask the class after they read the section.
   b. Do the same in a geometry text.
   c. Do the same in a second year algebra text.
   d. Do the same in an eighth grade mathematics text.

5. Write a lesson plan for the day before a long vacation, featuring mathematics puzzles and games.

6. Write a lesson plan for the first day of any mathematics class.

7. Select a topic from an advanced mathematics course and prepare a lecture on it.

8. Write a drill lesson plan for each of the following:
   a. fractional and negative exponents
   b. simple trigonometry (sin, cos, tan)
   c. the distance and midpoint formulas in coordinate geometry.
   d. the LCM and GCD in the eighth grade.

9. Prepare a series of review lessons for the topic "percent" in a core course.

10. What are the strengths and weaknesses of the following review lesson on congruent triangles?

    Do-Now: State the congruence postulate illustrated:

(1) 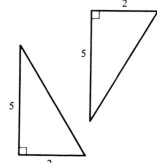   (2) 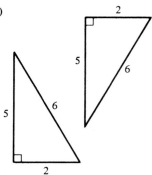   (3)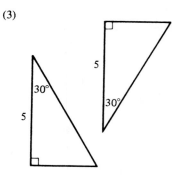

Then: Discuss with the class using AAA or SSA (explain ambiguity in using SSA).

Then: Do the following proofs:

Given: $\overline{BD} \perp \overline{AC}$
$\overline{AD} \cong \overline{DC}$
Prove: $\triangle ABD \cong \triangle CBD$

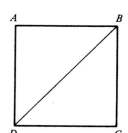

Given: $\angle ADB \cong \angle CDB$
$\angle ABD \cong \angle CBD$
Prove: $\triangle ABD \cong \triangle CBD$

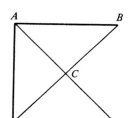

Given: $\overline{AB} \cong \overline{AD}$
$\overline{BC} \cong \overline{CD}$
Prove: $\triangle ABC \cong \triangle ADC$

11. Prepare a calculator lesson on:
   a. The first lesson on simultaneous equations for a first year algebra class.
   b. The first lesson on trigonometric curves.
   c. The first lesson on the law of sines.
   d. The first lesson on addition and subtraction of signed numbers in a middle school class.
   e. The first lesson on changing fractions to decimals in a high school core class.

12. Develop a series of eight ten-minute presentations on the following topics to be made to a class that does individualized work for most of the period:
   a. sequences
   b. history of mathematics
   c. patterns in mathematics
   d. recreational mathematics

13. How would you differentiate between a formal lesson plan one might discuss in a college methods course and a plan you might write for a secondary school class you are teaching?

14. Suppose you are asked to develop a long-range unit on truth tables for an eighth grade middle school mathematics class. Such concepts as negation, conjunction, disjunction, and truth values are to be included. Indicate
   a. What steps you would take to set up such a unit.
   b. The topics you would include.
   c. How many lessons this unit would require.

15. Select one topic from the truth-table unit you prepared for Exercise 14 and write a review lesson for it.

16. Prepare a lesson for a seventh grade mathematics class that develops the mean, median, and mode in one period. Allow sufficient time for practice exercises.

17. Find four mathematics teachers who are willing to cooperate with you on a small research project. Two teachers should be very experienced and two should be relatively inexperienced. Ask each to write a lesson plan on a topic in secondary school mathematics. If possible, have them all work on the same lesson and then observe each teaching that lesson, having the lesson plan in hand. Write a critique of both the lesson and the lesson plan based on information you learned in this chapter. (Promise each of the subjects that you will not share your critique with anyone and that it will be destroyed after use with this project.)

REFERENCES

Barnes, Susan. "Synthesis of Selected Research on Teaching Findings." Research and Development Center for Teacher Education. Austin: University of Texas, 1981.

Brissenden, T. H. F. *Teaching Mathematics: Theory Into Practice.* London: Harper & Row, 1980.

Brophy, Jere. "Research Linking Teacher Behavior to Student Achievement: Potential Implications for Instruction of Chapter 1 Students." *Educational Psychologist* 23, no. 3 (1988): 235–286.

Clarke, Christopher M., and Robert J. Yinger. "Teacher Planning." In *Exploring Teachers' Thinking.* Ed. James Calderhead. London: Cassell Educational Limited, 1987.

Costa, Arthur, ed. *Developing Minds: A Resource Book for Teaching Thinking.* Alexandria, VA: Association for Supervision and Curriculum Development, 1985.

Davidson, Neil. "A Demonstration of Terrible Teaching Techniques." *Mathematics Teacher* 70 (1977): 545.

Dessart, Donald J., and Marilyn M. Suydam. *Classroom Ideas from Research on Secondary School Mathematics.* Reston, VA: NCTM, 1983.

Ellis, Arthur K. "Planning For Mathematics Instruction." In *Teaching Mathematics in Grades K–8,* 2d ed. Ed. Thomas R. Post. Boston: Allyn & Bacon, 1992.

Henak, R. M. *Lesson Planning for Meaningful Variety in Teaching.* Washington, DC: National Education Association, 1984.

Henderson, Kenneth B. "Anent the Discovery Method." *Mathematics Teacher* 50 (1970): 287.

———. "A Model for Teaching Mathematical Concepts." *Mathematics Teacher* 60 (1967): 573.

Hiatt, Arthur A. "Discovering Mathematics." In *The Mathematics Teacher.* Reston, VA: NCTM, September 1987, 476–478.

Johnson, Donovan A., and Gerald R. Rising. *Guidelines for Teaching Mathematics.* Belmont, CA: Wadsworth Publishing, 1972.
   This text provides some interesting alternatives to this chapter.

Jones, Beau Fly, and Lawrence B. Friedman. "Active Instruction for Students at Risk: Remarks on Merging Process— Outcome and Cognitive Perspectives." *Educational Psychologist* 23, No. 2, 1988, 299–308.

Jones, Phillip S. "Discovery Teaching—from Socrates to Modernity." *Mathematics Teacher* 65 (1970): 501.

Kinney, Lucien B., and Dan J. Davison. "Mathematics in the Junior High School." *Mathematics Teacher* 49 (1956): 548.

Laing, Robert A., and John C. Peterson. "Assignments—Yesterday, Today, Tomorrow." *Mathematics Teacher* 66 (1973): 508.

Mathematics Teacher 69 (1976). Special Edition: Individualized Instruction.

Lefrancois, Guy R. *Psychology for Teaching,* 8th ed. Belmont, CA: Wadsworth, 1994.

Leinhardt, Gaea, C. Weldman, and K. M. Hammond. "Introduction and Integration of Classroom Routines by Expert Teachers." Paper presented at American Educational Research Association Conference, New Orleans, LA, April 1984.

National Council of Teachers of Mathematics. *Activities for Junior High School and Middle School Mathematics.* Reston, VA: NCTM, 1981.

National Council of Teachers of Mathematics. *The Learning of Mathematics, Its Theory and Practice,* Twenty-first Yearbook. Washington, DC: NCTM, 1953.

Although most of this book contains useful articles, the article by Irving Allen Dodes, Planned Instruction, *specifically addresses the topic of this chapter.*

National Council of Teachers of Mathematics. *The Teaching of Secondary School Mathematics,* Thirty-third Yearbook. Washington, DC: NCTM, 1970.

This book provides some outstanding discussions about teaching mathematics. Most articles are clear, crisp, and provide useful examples. Particularly appropriate is Part Three, Classroom Applications, *especially the lead article by F. Joe Crosswhite,* Implications for Teacher Planning.

Ortolan, Cathy, and Carol Camp. "Meet the Challenge: Individualize." *Mathematics Teacher* 73 (1980): 588.

Owens, Douglas T. *Research Ideas for the Classroom: Middle Grades Mathematics.* New York: Macmillan, 1993.

Rudnick, Jesse A., and Stephen Krulik. *A Guidebook for Teaching General Mathematics.* Boston: Allyn & Bacon, 1982.

This book discusses topics typically taught in general mathematics and provides insight into proper development of the topic and interesting applications.

Schmalz, Rosemary. "Categorization of Questions that Mathematics Teachers Ask." *Mathematics Teacher* 66 (1973): 619.

Schoen, Harold L. "A Plan to Combine Individualized Instruction with the Lecture Method." *Mathematics Teacher* 67 (1974): 647.

Smith, C. F., and H. S. Kepner. *Reading in the Mathematics Classroom.* Washington, DC: National Education Association, 1981.

Swireford, Edwin J. "Ninety Suggestions on the Teaching of Mathematics in Junior High School." *Mathematics Teacher* 54 (1961): 145.

Tobin, Kenneth, "The Role of Wait Time in Higher Cognitive Level Learning." *Review of Educational Research* 57, no. 1 (spring 1987) 69–95.

Van Patten, James, Chun-I Chao, and Charles M. Reigeluth. "A Review of Strategies for Sequencing and Synthesizing Instruction." *Review of Educational Research* 56, no. 4 (winter 1986) 437–471.

Wilkinson, Jack. "Teaching General Mathematics: A Semi-Laboratory Approach." *Mathematics Teacher* 63 (1970): 571.

Wilson, Patricia S. *Research Ideas for the Classroom: High School Mathematics.* New York: Macmillan, 1993.

CHAPTER 5
STRATEGIES FOR TEACHING MORE EFFECTIVE LESSONS

Effective teachers have available to them a broad range of specific teaching strategies, especially for pivotal lessons. Determining the best strategies for your lessons is an important aspect of your creative role in the classroom. Many of the strategies explained in the following pages will work equally well with examples other than those described. Furthermore, the illustrations shown certainly do not constitute an exhaustive set of either examples or strategies, for the number of strategies used by the creative teacher is endless.

The strategies listed include using tree diagrams or branching, paper folding or cutting, a picture is worth 1000 words, recognizing patterns, using mathematical models and manupulatives, using an overhead projector, and using a graphics calculator.

USING TREE DIAGRAMS OR BRANCHING

Tree diagrams or branching are often useful when a pupil faces a variety of choices and alternatives. They may provide insight into the overall view of a problem in question and may even offer direction as to decisions that must be considered in its solution. This strategy may arise in virtually any branch of mathematics, though not necessarily for every topic. Illustrations shown here represent topics in algebra, probability, permutations, set theory, and geometry.

EXAMPLE 1 (Algebra, Level 1 core): *Prime Factorization of Whole Numbers*

(A) Begin the lesson by defining and illustrating these three terms:

1. A *factor* of a given number is one of two or more numbers whose product is the given number. Thus, since the product of 2, 3, and 4 is 24, it follows that 2, 3, and 4 are factors of 24, i.e.,

$$24 = 2 \times 3 \times 4$$

Ask students to write 15 as the product of two factors. They will probably answer,

$$15 = 3 \times 5$$

However, they might answer $15 = 1 \times 15$. But you should point out that "1" is a special case because we could write *any* product with a whole string of 1's as factors, and that would not be very meaningful.

2. A *prime number* is a number whose *only* factors are 1 and itself. Thus, the only factors of 7 are 1 and 7, so that $7 = 1 \times 7$.

   Although it is true that $15 = 1 \times 15$, 1 and 15 are not the *only* factors, since it is also true that $15 = 3 \times 5$. So we see that 15 is *not* a prime number, while 7 *is* a prime number.

3. A number that is not prime is called *composite*.

(B) Point out that "2" is considered the smallest prime number. Ask students to list all numbers from 2 through 50 and to circle the primes.

ANSWER The circled numbers will be 2, 3, 5, 7, 11, 13, 17, 19, 23, 29, 31, 37, 41, 43, and 47. The remaining numbers are composite.

(C) Now, mention to the class that it is sometimes desirable to find only the *prime factors* of a number, for example, when you need to determine the least common denominator of several fractions. One strategy for finding prime factors is to use the *branching* method shown next. Whenever a prime number appears at the end of a branch, put a circle around it.

Students should now be shown how to use the branching method to express 12, 18, and 144 as the product of prime factors.

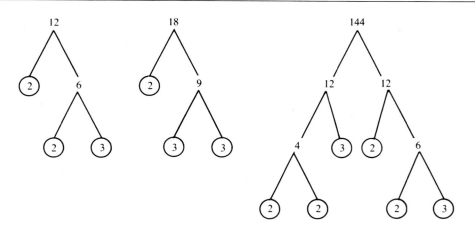

Here are the answers:

$$12 = 2 \times 2 \times 3 \qquad 18 = 2 \times 3 \times 3 \qquad 144 = 2 \times 2 \times 2 \times 2 \times 3 \times 3$$
$$\text{or} \qquad\qquad \text{or} \qquad\qquad\qquad \text{or}$$
$$12 = 2^2 \times 3 \qquad 18 = 2 \times 3^2 \qquad 144 = 2^4 \times 3^2$$

For practice, ask the class to use the branching method to express these numbers as the product of prime factors: 48; 36; 108; 72; 400; 125; 1024; 1215.

EXAMPLE 2   (Probability, Level 1 core): *Permutations*

Define a *permutation of a set of objects* as an ordered arrangement of all or some of the objects.

Ask the class: How many three-digit numbers can be formed with three discs marked, respectively, 1, 2, and 3? After listing their answers on the chalkboard in a random manner, show how to *organize* the arrangements of numbers with this tree diagram.

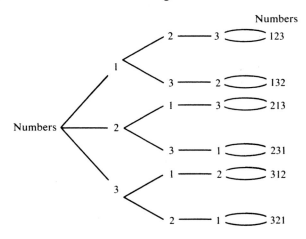

The equation $3 \times 2 \times 1 = 6$ suggests a rule for finding the number of permutations without drawing the tree.

As a second illustration, use a tree diagram to show that there are 24 ($4 \times 3 \times 2 \times 1$) permutations or arrangements of the letters of the word *five*.

For practice, ask the class to exhibit a tree arrangement to illustrate the permutations of 5 or 6 objects. Note that the numbers become quite large, so introduce factorial notation:

$$n! = 1 \times 2 \times 3 \times 4 \times 5 \times \ldots \times (n - 1) \times n$$

USING PAPER FOLDING OR CUTTING

Paper folding and cutting is a strategy often found in middle and junior high schools. It is used to demonstrate concepts or theorems that require a higher level of mathematical maturity than pupils of that age can be expected to have achieved. Nevertheless, a clever teacher will be alert to any situation, at any level of school, where cutting or folding paper may serve to enlighten, to clarify, to motivate. The following illustrations demonstrate these points.

EXAMPLE 1   (Geometry, Level 1 core): *Demonstrate the theorem, "The sum of the measures of the angles of a triangle is 180."*

1. Cut out a cardboard triangle *ABC*.

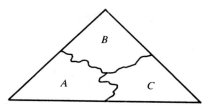

2. Cut off the three angles and rearrange along a straight line:

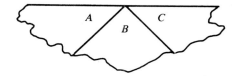

3. Remind students that the sum of measures of angles along a straight line is 180°, because a straight angle is formed by a straight line. This completes the demonstration.

EXAMPLE 2   (Geometry): *Prove the theorem, "If two sides of a triangle are congruent, the angles opposite these sides are congruent." (Also known as, "Base angles of an isosceles triangle are congruent.")*

This is usually the first lesson in which students are asked to write a formal proof from a verbal statement. Begin by reviewing the if-then form of a statement, with the phrase following the "then" known as the conclusion. Thus, the hypothesis in this example is "two sides of a triangle are congruent," and the conclusion is "the angles opposite these sides are congruent."

Draw and label a diagram and list what is "given" and what is "to be proved" based on the letters in the diagram. See illustration:

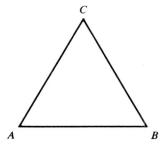

Given: $\triangle ABC$
$\overline{AC} \cong \overline{BC}$

Prove: $\angle A \cong \angle B$

Guide pupils to the need for using an auxiliary line in developing the formal proof as follows:

1. Cut out the isosceles triangle.
2. Hold the congruent sides together and fold down with a crease partway down, starting at the vertex (see Figure a).

(Note that the crease is in reality an angle bi-sector of the vertex angle.)

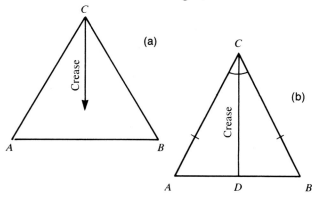

3. Extend the crease (angle bisector) until it hits the opposite side, forming two triangles (Figure b).
4. Prove the two triangles congruent by SAS, as illustrated (Figure b).
5. The two base angles are now congruent, which was to be proved.

EXAMPLE 3   (Sets, Level 1 core): *Subsets of a Given Set*

Set A is a *subset* of set B if every element of set A is also an element of set B.

This means that every set is a subset of itself.

Set A is a *proper subset* of set B if set A is a subset of set B and if there is at least one element in B that is not in A.

Note that all subsets of B, except set B itself, are proper subsets of set B.

The subsets of a given set may be arranged in a *tree diagram.*

At the top of the next column is a tree diagram exhibiting the subsets of $\{r, s, t, u\}$. We use x in the branches wherever one of the given elements is not to be included in a subset.

Note that the number of subsets of 4 elements is $2 \times 2 \times 2 \times 2 = 2^4 = 16$, provided that the given set is a subset of itself and that the null set is considered to be a subset of every set. After doing several examples you can generalize that the number of subsets of a set of n elements is 2^n.

Practice with these exercises: Make a subset tree for the set $S_1 = \{a\}$; $S_2 = \{a, b\}$; $S_3 = \{p, q, r\}$; Let $M = \{p, n, d, q\}$, where p = penny, n = nickel, d = dime, q = quarter. How many sums of money can be formed with none, one, more than one, or all the above coins?

EXAMPLE 4   (Geometry Level 1 core): *Quadrilaterals*

The following tree diagram can be used as the basis for a good summary lesson at the conclusion of the topic

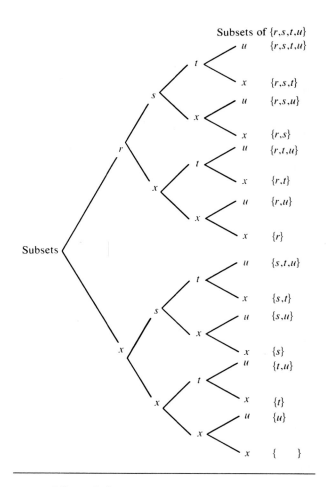

on quadrilaterals in geometry:

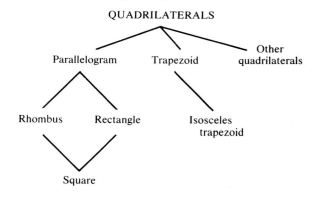

A PICTURE IS WORTH 1000 WORDS

This strategy is probably the most universally accepted by mathematicians at every level of achievement and sophistication. It guides students' thinking by suggesting insights toward solutions of problems, as well as toward generalizations of these problems. These ideas are represented here on a simple level with illustrations from mixture problems in algebra, probability, and Venn diagrams.

The value of "pictures" or diagrams in geometry is well known. Expanding these pictures from two to three dimensions has allowed mathematicians to even dare to think in terms of dimensions of higher order.

EXAMPLE 1   (Algebra): *Mixture Problem*

A 3-gallon, 20% alcohol-water mixture is to be upgraded by adding to it a certain amount of a 70% alcohol-water mixture. How many gallons of the 70% mixture must be added to make the new, enriched mixture a 40% alcohol-water mix?

SOLUTION

Picturing the containers that hold the mixture is a great aid and makes for a more real situation. Begin by drawing a diagram of the three containers: The amount of alcohol in each container can now be easily obtained:

A: $(0.20)(3)$ *B:* $(0.70)(x)$ *C:* $(0.40)(3 + x)$

Similarly, the amount of water in each container is

A: $(0.80)(3)$ *B:* $(0.30)(x)$ *C:* $(0.60)(3 + x)$

Since the amount of alcohol in container *C* is equal to the sum of the alcohol amounts in containers *A* and *B*, we get a

PURE ALCOHOL equation:
$$(0.20)(3) + (0.70)(x) = (0.40)(3 + x)$$

Also, since the amount of water in container *C* is equal to the sum of the water amounts in *A* and *B*, we get a

PURE WATER equation:
$$(0.80)(3) + (0.30)(x) = (0.60)(3 + x)$$

In either equation above we get $x = 2$.

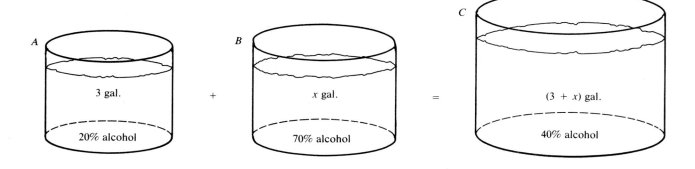

EXAMPLE 2   (Probability, Algebra): *Probability*

Consider the following problem. Although not the typical probability exercise, its solution involves a visualization principle that may be applicable to many areas in mathematics, such as coordinate geometry, statistics, topology, logic, and number theory as well as probability:

> A pair of dice (one red and one green) are rolled. What is the probability that the difference of the numbers coming up is less than or equal to 1?

The figure opposite shows the entire set of 36 possible outcomes. The dot with coordinates (5, 4) corresponds to the outcome: red die shows 5 while the green die shows 4. The favorable outcomes are indicated in the enclosed region and consist of a total of 16 events:

As all 36 outcomes are equally likely, each is given the probability of 1/36. The event has 16 outcomes, so its probability is $16(1/36) = 16/36$ or 4/9.

For this problem we could also have used the rule
$$\frac{\text{number of favorable outcomes}}{\text{total number of possible outcomes}} = \frac{16}{36} = \frac{4}{9}$$
as all the outcomes are equally likely.

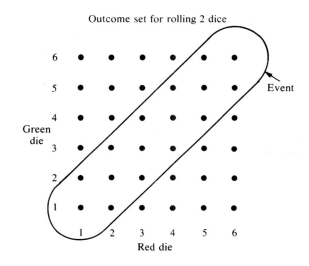

Outcome set for rolling 2 dice

EXAMPLE 3 (Algebra, Level 1 core): *Venn Diagrams*

Certain types of problems involving sets of elements and logical reasoning can best be solved with Venn diagrams, which are simply sets of overlapping circles. The intersection set is the smallest set of all common elements, and the union set is the smallest set of all different elements. Thus, in the diagram, if A and B are sets, $A \cap B$ represents the intersection set and $A \cup B$ the union:

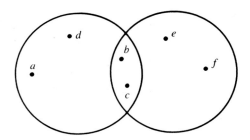

Illustration: Two sets are $\{a, b, c, d\}$ and $\{e, b, c, f\}$. Draw a Venn diagram for the two sets and indicate the union and intersection sets.

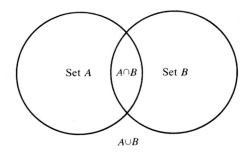

The union set $= \{a, b, c, d, e, f\}$

The intersection set $= \{b, c\}$

Now you can show your classes how to solve with relative ease "counting" problems like these:

PROBLEM   A pupil was paid 50 cents per person to ask how many liked Republican policies and how many Democratic. He reported that 27 liked Republicans, 31 liked Democrats, and 18 liked both. How much money did he earn?

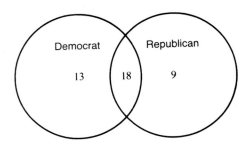

SOLUTION   The Venn diagram shows that there were only $13 + 18 + 9 = 40$ elements in the union set, giving him $20.00.

Here are some additional practice problems:

1. In a school newspaper poll, 110 pupils voted that they liked English, 150 voted that they liked mathematics, and 50 said they liked both. If everyone who was interviewed voted, how many pupils were actually interviewed?
2. An automobile survey showed that 19 people liked model X, 18 liked model Y, and 20 liked model Z. Five of these people liked X and Y, 8 liked Y and Z, and 7 liked X and Z. Two people liked all three. How many people were surveyed? *Hint:* Use this diagram:

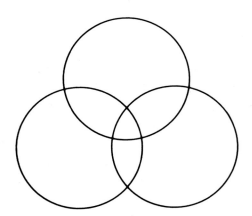

EXAMPLE 4 (Algebra): *Multiplying Binomials*

The visual demonstration that $(a + b)(a + b) = a^2 + 2ab + b^2$ starkly contrasts with the traditional proof that uses the distributive property. The demonstration follows:

Because the area of the square is both $(a + b)(a + b)$ *and* the sum of the areas of the four sections, $a^2 + ab + ab + b^2$, we have that $(a + b)^2 = a^2 + 2ab + b^2$.

	a	$+$	b
a	a^2		ab
$+$			
b	ab		b^2

RECOGNIZING PATTERNS

Recognizing and maintaining patterns is a powerful force in human behavior. It establishes the stability and routine that many people, especially youngsters, need. For the mathematician, it offers clues to the extension of ideas into new domains. The illustrations presented here appear simple and perhaps even trivial, yet their real purpose is to help germinate ideas for the teacher in order for him or her to think and plan along the lines suggested.

EXAMPLE 1 (Algebra): *Zero and Negative Exponents*

Have students study the pattern in this chart and replace the "?" with a number:

$$2^5 = 32 \qquad 3^5 = 243 \qquad 4^5 = 1024$$
$$2^4 = 16 \qquad 3^4 = 81 \qquad 4^4 = \,?$$
$$2^3 = 8 \qquad 3^3 = \,? \qquad 4^3 = \,?$$
$$2^2 = 4 \qquad 3^2 = \,? \qquad 4^2 = \,?$$
$$2^1 = 2 \qquad 3^1 = \,? \qquad 4^1 = \,?$$

The chart should be extended up a bit. When students attempt to extend it down to include the question marks, they will realize that each number is one-half, one-third, one-fourth, etc., of the number above it, depending on the column.

By following this pattern they will conclude:

$$2^0 = 1 \qquad 3^0 = 1 \qquad 4^0 = 1$$

Continuing to work down with the pattern, students will extend the chart until it looks like this:

$$2^{-1} = \frac{1}{2} \qquad 3^{-1} = \frac{1}{3} \qquad 4^{-1} = \frac{1}{4}$$
$$2^{-2} = \frac{1}{4} = \frac{1}{2^2} \qquad 3^{-2} = \frac{1}{9} = \frac{1}{3^2} \qquad 4^{-2} = \,?$$
$$2^{-3} = \frac{1}{8} = \frac{1}{2^3} \qquad 3^{-3} = \,? \qquad 4^{-3} = \,?$$
$$2^{-4} = \frac{1}{16} = \frac{1}{2^4} \qquad 3^{-4} = \,? \qquad 4^{-4} = \,?$$

Students can now generalize and establish these rules:

$$\text{If } x \neq 0, \; x^0 = 1 \text{ and } x^{-m} = \frac{1}{x^m}$$

EXAMPLE 2 (Geometry, Level 1 core): *The Sum of the Angles of a Polygon*

Have the class consider the question, "What is the sum of the measures of the angles of a polygon of any number of sides?"

By dividing these polygons into triangles, you can establish a pattern that will guide the class to the answer.

The class should, of course, be aware that a straight angle has the measure 180°.

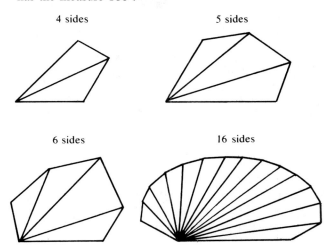

4 sides   5 sides   6 sides   16 sides

The sum of the angles of a polygon of 4 sides is 2 straight angles = 360 degrees.
The sum of the angles of a polygon of 5 sides is 3 straight angles = ? degrees.
The sum of the angles of a polygon of 6 sides is ? straight angles = ? degrees.

To find the sum of the angles of a polygon of 16 sides, we note that there will be 14 triangles. Hence, the sum of its angles is ? straight angles.

Pupils should be able to conclude that a polygon of n sides can be divided into $n - 2$ triangles, so that the sum of the measures of its angles is $n - 2$ straight angles or $(n - 2)$ 180 degrees.

EXAMPLE 3 (Algebra): *Product of Two Signed Numbers*

In mathematics, the desire to maintain patterns can provide the motivation for expanding and creating new mathematics, as illustrated in obtaining the rules for multiplying signed numbers.

Before beginning this topic, students must be familiar with the number line. They must also be aware that positive numbers may be written both with and without signs.

Have students study the pattern in the following chart and replace the "?" with a number:

FACTOR 1	×	FACTOR 2	=	PRODUCT
3	×	3	=	9
3	×	2	=	6
3	×	1	=	3
3	×	0	=	0
3	×	−1	=	?
3	×	−2	=	?
3	×	−3	=	?

When analyzing the pattern with the class, it would be informative to extend the chart up a bit as well as down. The pattern will suggest that we accept as a rule:

Positive number × negative number = negative number

The commutative property will then suggest that:

Negative number × positive number = negative number

Exactly the same kind of pattern recognition yields the usual rule for multiplying two negative numbers:

FACTOR 1 × FACTOR 2 = PRODUCT

3	×	−3	=	−9
2	×	−3	=	−6
1	×	−3	=	−3
0	×	−3	=	0
−1	×	−3	=	?
−2	×	−3	=	?
−3	×	−3	=	?

The suggested rule is thus:

Negative number × negative number = positive number

EXAMPLE 4 (Algebra): *Sum of an Arithmetic Progression*

When Carl Friedrich Gauss was a young boy, his propensity for mathematics became evident in a classroom incident that has since become a classic tale of budding genius. When his teacher asked the class to find the sum of all integers from 1 through 100, the class was struggling with their slates and writing implements while young Carl observed a pattern that could produce the answer rather simply and quickly.

Carl observed that if he paired the terms of the sequence of numbers from 1 through 100 as shown below, and added them, he would get 50 pairs of 101. The sum would thus be $50 \times 101 = 5050$.

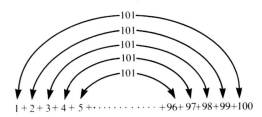

$$1 + 2 + 3 + 4 + 5 + \cdots\cdots\cdots + 96 + 97 + 98 + 99 + 100$$

Now generalize the technique Gauss used to determine a formula for the sum of the first n terms of an arithmetic progression. Let a be the first term and d be the common difference between terms. Thus, the sum of these n terms is

$$a + [a + d] + [a + 2d] + [a + 3d] + \ldots$$
$$+ [a + (n - 2)d] + [a + (n - 1)d]$$

Adding the first and nth terms gives

$$a + [a + (n - 1)d] = 2a + (n - 1)d$$

and adding the second and $(n - 1)$th term gives

$$[a + d] + [a + (n - 2)d] = 2a + (n - 1)d$$

and adding the third and $(n - 2)$th term gives

$$[a + 2d] + [a + (n - 3)d] = 2a + (n - 1)d$$

Continue this process until all pairs have been added. If there are $n/2$ such pairs, the sum of the terms is

$$S = n/2[2a + (n - 1)d]$$

which is the required formula.

Ask your students how this procedure accounts for the middle term of a series of an odd number of terms.

EXAMPLE 5 (Topology, Geometry, Level 1 core): *Polyhedra*

Leonhard Euler (1707–1783) discovered an interesting relationship among the vertices, faces, and edges of ordinary polyhedra. He said that if you take regular or nonregular polyhedra and let

$$V = \text{number of vertices};$$
$$E = \text{number of edges};$$
$$F = \text{number of faces};$$

then for every such solid, $V - E + F = $ a constant.

Use the figures on page 57 to help you visualize patterns among these quantities for the five regular polyhedra and verify the formula $V - E + F = 2$ for each case.

V	E	F	NAME
		4	Tetrahedron
		6	Cube
		8	Octahedron
		12	Dodecahedron
		20	Icosahedron

FIVE REGULAR POLYHEDRA

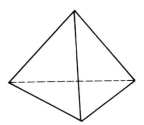

Tetrahedron
(4 equilateral triangles)

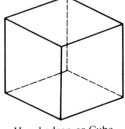

Hexahedron or Cube
(6 squares)

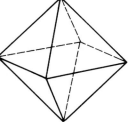

Octahedron
(8 equilateral triangles)

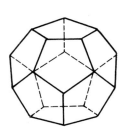

Dodecahedron
(12 regular pentagons)

Icosahedron
(20 equilateral triangles)

USING MATHEMATICAL MODELS AND MANIPULATIVES

Mathematicians and artists continue their attempts to produce physical models that simulate the abstract models that come from the mind. Students and teachers can also try their hand at homemade models such as the five regular polyhedra, string art, roulette wheels, transits, and whatever else the imagination conjures up. Even routinely used items such as rulers, compasses, and protractors are examples of mathematical models.

EXAMPLE 1 (Probability, Level 1 core, Algebra): *Probability Models*

Among the commonly used models to demonstrate the concept of probability are dice, spinners, playing cards, and a jar filled with marbles of different colors. All are relatively easy to obtain for classroom demonstration purposes.

Although the concept ''the probability that an event will occur'' appears to be intuitive among many youngsters, this would seem to be not universal and so must be formally defined at the outset.

The probability P that an event will occur is:

$$P = \frac{\text{number of favorable ways}}{\text{total number of possible ways}}$$

The teacher can use the models mentioned above to illustrate and amplify the definition.

A *die* is well known as a six-sided solid object, called a *cube*. Each side or face of the cube is a *square*. The sides are numbered 1, 2, 3, 4, 5, 6 with dots as shown. The plural of *die* is *dice*.

In rolling a die, find the probability of getting a 5.

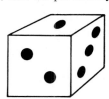

ANSWER $P(5) = 1/6$

A spinner is a simulated roulette wheel. It might contain, for example, eight regions, all of equal size, numbered 1 through 8. The arrow has an equally likely chance of landing on any of the eight regions. Assuming the arrow does not land on a line, what is the probability that it will land on 3?

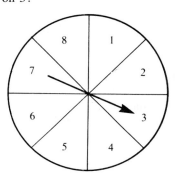

ANSWER $P(3) = 1/8$

A standard deck of playing cards contains 52 cards. There are 4 suits: spades, diamonds, hearts, and clubs. Each suit contains 13 cards: 2, 3, 4, 5, 6, 7, 8, 9, 10, jack, queen, king, ace. Spades and clubs are black, diamonds and hearts are red.

In picking a card at random, explain why the probability of drawing (a) the two of diamonds, (b) a two, (c) a diamond is

(a) P (two of diamonds) = 1/52
(b) P (two) = 4/52 = 1/13
(c) P (diamond) = 13/52 = 1/4

A jar contains 8 marbles: 3 are red and 5 are white. A marble is selected at random. What is the probability that it is red?

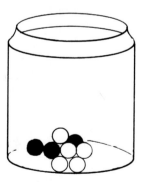

ANSWER P(red) = 3/8

Note that many variations and extensions of these problems can be developed with classes at many levels—from junior to senior high school and from basic math classes to advanced ones. Each class will, of course, have its own level of sophistication.

EXAMPLE 2 (Geometry, Level 1 core): *Linkages*

Commercially produced models of high-quality metal or transparent plastic are commonly available and can be used by the classroom teacher with or without an overhead projector to demonstrate the following theorems:

- Alternate interior angles of two parallel lines are congruent.
- Opposite sides of a parallelogram are parallel and congruent to each other.
- Diagonals of a parallelogram bisect each other.
- Opposite angles of a parallelogram are congruent to each other.
- Consecutive angles of a parallelogram are supplementary.

The quadrilateral is also known as a ''flexible quadrilateral'' and provides a beautiful, clear, dramatic model that the teacher can hold up in front of a class, moving sides in and out while at the same time changing angle size.

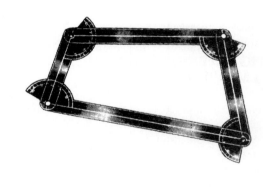

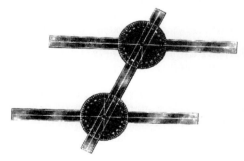

EXAMPLE 3 (Geometry, Level 1 core): *String Designs*

The straight-line segments that appear in the diagrams on page 60 suggest curves known as ''envelopes.'' An envelope is a curve that is tangent to every member of a family of straight lines. Strings of several colors can be used to represent the straight lines, and these can create a variety of envelope patterns that are both colorful and beautiful. These could serve as enrichment or motivation to study geometry, especially at the junior high school level—grades 7 and 8. Class projects could be proposed that might encompass a unit in geometric designs for a mathematics class. The following vocabulary and concepts are just some of the items that might be discussed and illustrated: circle, tangent, pentagon, hexagon, rhombus, and parabolic curve (see the diagrams on page 60).

How To Enrich Geometry Using String Diagrams by Victoria Pohl (NCTM, 1986) contains a variety of two- and three-dimensional string diagram instructions with illustrations.

As part of any project, you might also want to involve an art teacher to assist in technical matters as well as an English teacher to guide the students in reading and following very detailed directions about the design constructions.

EXAMPLE 4 (Geometry): *Finding the relationship between the measure of an angle and the arcs it intercepts on a circle.*

It is assumed that students have already learned that the measure of an inscribed angle of a circle is one-half the measure of its intercepted arc.

Begin by cutting out an appropriately large rectangular piece of cardboard and a cardboard circle. Staple two pieces of string to the rectangular cardboard, forming a convenient angle near the middle, and draw an angle of the same measure (as the angle formed by the two pieces of string) as an inscribed angle of the circle.

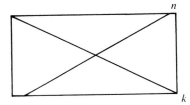

By moving the circle into various positions relative to the rectangle, all the theorems relating the circle to the different types of angles can be easily developed (and proved!).

1. An angle formed by two chords intersecting inside the circle has measure equal to one-half the sum of the intercepted arcs.

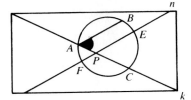

Place the circle so that $\overline{AB} \parallel n$ and $\overline{AC}$ is on k as in the figure above.

$$m\angle A = \tfrac{1}{2}m\widehat{BEC}$$

$$m\angle A = m\angle P$$

Therefore, $m\angle P = \tfrac{1}{2}m\widehat{BEC} = \tfrac{1}{2}(m\widehat{BE} + m\widehat{EC})$. But $m\widehat{BE} = m\widehat{AF}$, therefore,

$$m\angle P = \tfrac{1}{2}(m\widehat{AF} + m\widehat{EC})$$

2. An angle formed by two secants intersecting outside the circle has measure equal to one-half the difference of the intercepted arcs.

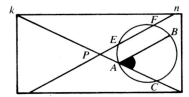

Place the circle so that $\overline{AB} \parallel n$ and $\overline{AC}$ is on k as in the preceding figure.

$$m\angle A = \tfrac{1}{2}\widehat{BC}$$

$$m\angle A = m\angle P$$

Therefore, $m\angle P = \tfrac{1}{2}m\widehat{BC} = \tfrac{1}{2}(m\widehat{FBC} - m\widehat{FB})$. But $m\widehat{FB} = m\widehat{AE}$; therefore,

$$m\angle P = \tfrac{1}{2}(m\widehat{FBC} - m\widehat{AE})$$

A similar argument can be made for

3. An angle formed by two tangents:

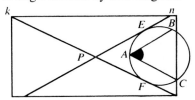

4. An angle formed by a tangent and a secant:

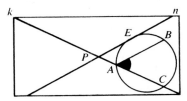

5. An angle formed by a tangent and a chord:

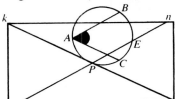

Circle in a square

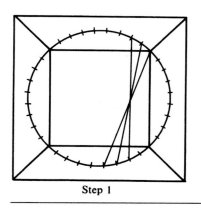

Step 1

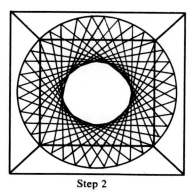

Step 2

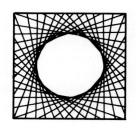

Step 3

Parabola

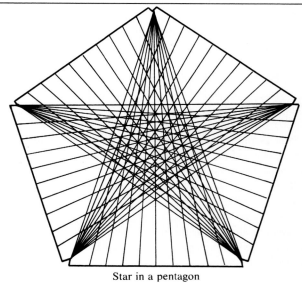

Star in a pentagon

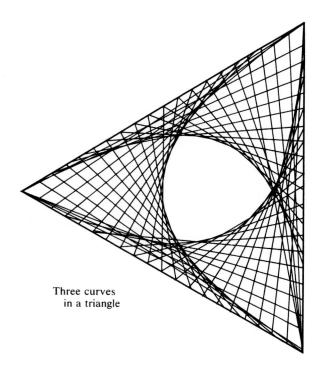

Three curves
in a triangle

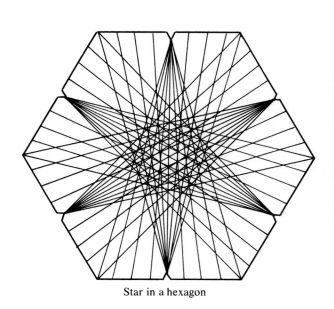

Star in a hexagon

The development of each of these is very similar and allows fast proofs of all these theorems in the same lesson! An important part of this type of development is to let students anticipate each succeeding circle placement and consequent argument.

EXAMPLE 5 (Trigonometry): *Angles of Elevation and Depression*

Before beginning this lesson, pupils should be made aware of the definition of *angle of elevation* and *angle of depression.*

Definition: If an object *A* is observed from point *O*, the angle of elevation or depression is the angle that the line segment $\overline{OA}$ from the eye of the observer to the object makes with a horizontal line in the same plane.

If the object lies higher than the observer, the angle is an angle of elevation; if lower, it is an angle of depression. See the illustrations:

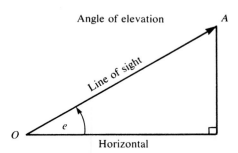

Angle of depression

Angle of elevation

A *transit* is a device used by many engineers for measuring angles of elevation and depression. It can be acquired for use in trigonometry lessons but is rather expensive. Students can learn to construct an alternate means of determining either of these angles with only a standard pupil's protractor, a piece of string, and some chalk to provide weight at the end of the string.

Guide pupils to prove that the angle of elevation *e* of an object may be measured as follows:

Fix a protractor in a vertical position as shown in the diagram on page 62 so that the prolongation of $\overline{BO}$ passes through *A*. Your eye must guide you here as accurately as possible. You might try gluing an ordinary drinking straw along $\overline{BO}$ and looking through it as a "sight."

A plumb bob (string with a weight attached to one end), held by a tack or nail at point *O*, intersects arc *BC* at *E*. The angle of elevation is measured by arc *EC* on the protractor (see the figure at the top of page 62).

Similarly, arc *C'E'* measures the angle of depression *d*. Also, develop a proof for the angle of depression.

In both proofs, you must use the theorem "Complements of the same angle are congruent." Students will have no difficulty "seeing" the proofs (see the figure at the top of page 62.

EXAMPLE 6 (Intuitive Geometry, Level 1 core): *Volumes*

Remind students that just as surface area is measured in square units, so is volume measured in cubic units such as cubic centimeters and cubic inches. Thus, if the dimensions of this box (rectangular prism) are 2 × 3 × 4 centimeters, the box contains 24 cubic centimeters, as shown in the diagram.

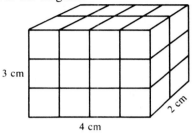

3 cm

4 cm

2 cm

Students will readily agree that practical experience as well as some physical models will lead to the reasonable conclusion that *for a rectangular solid, the volume is equal to the product of its three dimensions (V = lwh),* or *the volume is equal to the product of the area of its base and its altitude. (V = Bh)*

Another volume relationship can be demonstrated with the solids shown in the figure. The pyramid and the prism have equal bases and equal heights. When the pyramid is filled with liquid and emptied into the prism, the prism fills up just one-third of the way.

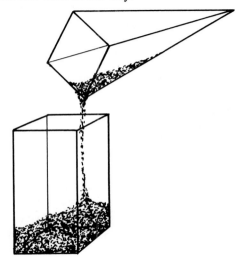

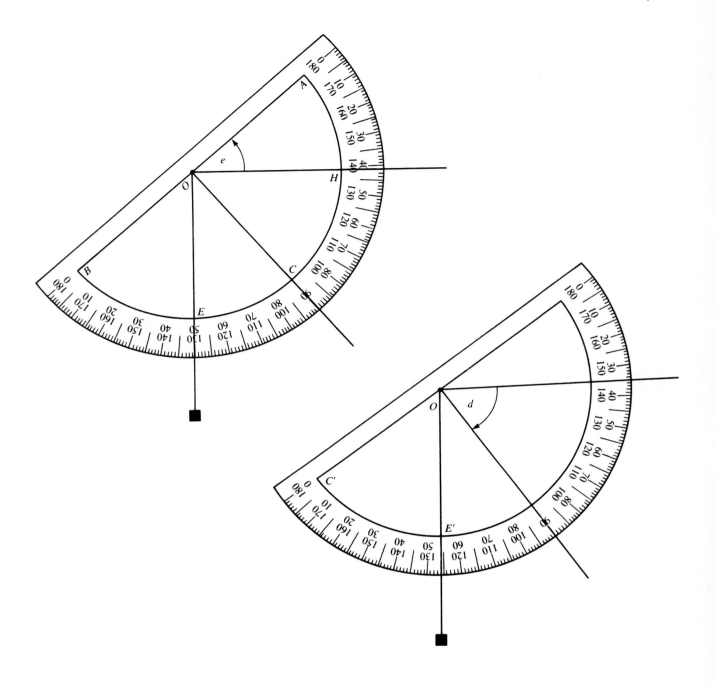

Here, too, students will agree after some additional experimentation, that *the volume of a prism is equal to the product of the area of its base and its altitude* ($V = Bh$).

They will also agree that *the volume of a pyramid is equal to one-third the product of the area of its base and its altitude* ($V = 1/3 \, Bh$).

The preceding formulas are valid even when the pyramids and prisms are oblique, as shown to the right.

In fact, they are valid even if the base is not a polygon but a curve such as a circle. Thus, in addition to the prism

we can also discuss the right circular cylinder and cone. The same formulas apply. These can, however, be adjusted by using the formula $B = \pi r^2$. In these cases *the*

Right prism   Oblique prism   Square pyramid   Regular pyramid *volume of a right circular cylinder is* $V = \pi r^2 h$ *and for a right circular cone it is* $V = 1/3\ \pi r^2 h$. See the diagrams.

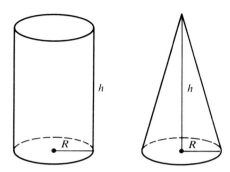

USING AN OVERHEAD PROJECTOR

An overhead projector can be especially effective for specifically mathematical purposes, such as demonstrating congruence for overlapping triangles and rotations and translations. In addition it gives the teacher the advantages of being able to note errors and corrections directly on the screen, of having students write their homework assignments directly on an acetate sheet for quick review, and of preparing in advance complicated diagrams and tables.

EXAMPLE 1 (Geometry, Level 2 core): *Overlapping Triangles*

Prove the perpendiculars from the ends of the base of an isosceles triangle to the legs are congruent.

You will need a supply of acetate sheets and grease pencils (china markers) of different colors to produce the overlays needed.

After students have read the problem, use the overhead projector to flash on the screen Figure 1. Students will not realize at first that the overlay displaying the figure is in reality composed of two overlays, Figures 1a and 1b *or* Figures 1c and 1d. These sets of acetates should be carefully prepared in advance, so that when one is superimposed on the other, the lineup is accurate.

Now begin the analysis of the problem with the class. They will suggest using $\triangle ACE$ and $\triangle BCD$ or $\triangle ABD$ and $\triangle ABE$. If students suggest using the first pair of triangles, use the Figure 1 display on the projector that is composed of Figure 1a with Figure 1b superimposed on it. At this point, as part of your continuing analysis with the class, you may display these acetates separately while you elicit and mark the congruent parts of the triangles.

If, however, students suggest the second pair of triangles, use the Figure 1 that is composed of Figures 1c and 1d. Elicit and mark the congruent parts for these triangles, as for the first pair.

The advantage of using the overhead projector in this type of problem is that since some pupils have difficulty visualizing the pairs of overlapping triangles to be proved congruent, you can now easily demonstrate a visual separation of the triangles.

The first proof will ultimately end up with these statements:

$$\overline{AC} \cong \overline{BC}$$

$$\angle\ CDB \cong \angle\ CEA$$

$$\angle\ C \cong \angle\ C$$

Therefore, $\triangle ACE \cong \triangle BCD$ by SAA.

The second proof ends up with these statements:

$$\overline{AC} \cong \overline{BC}$$

$$\angle\ CAB \cong \angle\ CBA$$

$$\angle\ ADB \cong \angle\ BEA$$

$$\overline{AB} \cong \overline{AB}$$

Therefore, $\triangle BDA \cong \triangle AEB$ by SAA.

Students usually find these proofs quite difficult, so practice exercises should be given. Any geometry textbook will have many examples from which to choose (see top of page 64.

EXAMPLE 2 (Trigonometry): *Inverse Sine Graph*

The overhead projector is a powerful tool for demonstrating inverse trigonometric graphs, such as the inverse sine graph.

Background knowledge for students must include an understanding of the following areas:

1. Writing the inverse of a given function, y of x. The following example illustrates the technique of replacing x with y, and y with x.

Let $y = 2x + 8$ be the given function. Then $x = 2y + 8$ represents the inverse, and $2y = x - 8$ by subtraction. So that $y = \frac{1}{2}x - 4$ is the inverse function of $y = 2x + 8$.

2. Counterclockwise rotation of 90° about the origin, so that $(x, y) \rightarrow (-y, x)$
3. Reflection through the y-axis, so that $(x, y) \rightarrow (-x, y)$.
4. Reflection through the line $y = x$, so that $(x, y) \rightarrow (y, x)$.

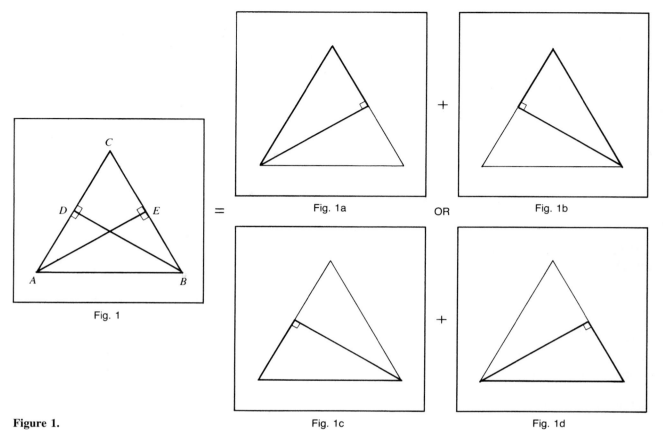

Figure 1.   Fig. 1c   Fig. 1d

Pose the following question to the class: How can we get the inverse graph of $y = \sin x$?

Students should already know that in order to get an inverse they must have a reflection through the line $y = x$. When points on the graph of $y = \sin x$ are reflected through the line $y = x$, the images are sets of inverse points called by a *new* name, $y = $ arc sin x. To understand the meaning of $y = $ arc sin x, we first replace x with y, and y with x, in the equation $y = \sin x$. When we now attempt to "solve" for y in the new equation, $x = \sin y$, the result is that $y = $ the angle whose sine is x, or, as mathematicians say, $y = $ arc sin x.

Now study the graph of $y = \sin x$ on the overhead projector (Figure 2). Take the acetate on which the graph is drawn and rotate it counterclockwise 90° around the origin. (This means that $(x, y) \rightarrow (-y, x)$.)

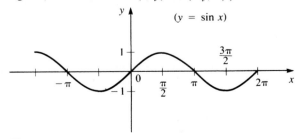

Figure 2.

Lift the acetate off the overhead projector plate. Rotate it once around the y-axis and place it back down on the plate, showing a new picture. (This is equivalent to a reflection through the y-axis, where $(x, y) \rightarrow (-x, y)$.)

The new picture on the screen, which is a result of a rotation and a reflection, is thus seen to represent the reflection $(x, y) \rightarrow (y, x)$. This is precisely the inverse transformation we seek, since it is equivalent to a reflection through the line $y = x$ (see Figure 3).

STRATEGY: EXTENDING FAMILIAR CONCEPTS

EXAMPLE 1 (Trigonometry, Level 2 core): *Functions of an Obtuse Angle*

Before beginning this lesson, students must be familiar with the three basic trigonometric functions of an acute angle in a right triangle. These functions will be extended to an obtuse angle.

Students must also be familiar with the properties of the 30-60-90 and 45-45-90 triangles.

Consider an angle in "standard position," where the initial ray is on the x-axis and the vertex is at the origin. Let the intersection of the terminal ray and a circle of

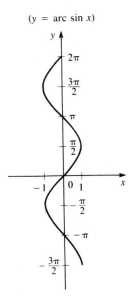

$(y = \text{arc sin } x)$

Figure 3.

radius r centered at the origin be the point (x, y) (see the following diagram). Using the traditional definitions for the functions of an acute angle:

$$\sin \theta = \text{opposite leg/hypotenuse} = y/r$$

$$\cos \theta = \text{adjacent leg/hypotenuse} = x/r$$

$$\tan \theta = \text{opposite leg/adjacent leg} = y/x$$

Note that r is always considered to be positive.

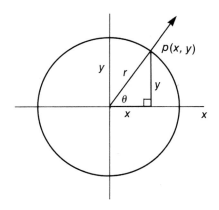

These definitions were based on the definitions for functions of an acute angle of a right triangle. If, however, we allow the terminal side to rotate in a direction such that the angle θ becomes right, obtuse, straight, or even negative, and if we further agree to *extend* the same definitions to these new angles, we will arrive at some very "unusual" results.

After studying the following diagrams, students should easily see that:

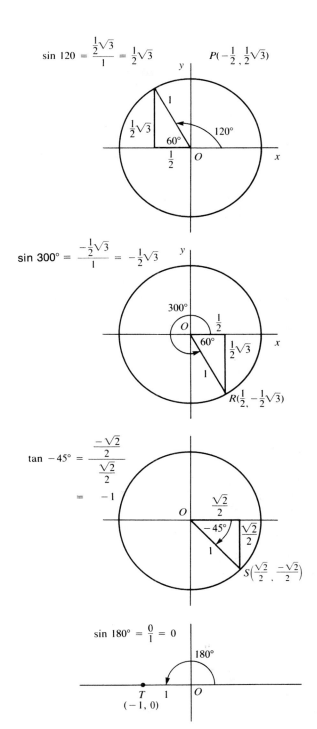

Additional practice examples must be given to reinforce these concepts.

EXAMPLE 2 (Trigonometry, Geometry): *Law of Cosines*

A traditional and simple method for introducing the law of cosines is a direct extension of the Pythagorean theorem.

Consider the acute $\triangle ABC$ (with altitude $\overline{CD}$)

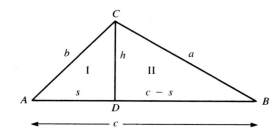

Using the Pythagorean theorem in $\triangle$II we get

$$a^2 = h^2 + (c - s)^2$$

Then

$$a^2 = h^2 + c^2 - 2cs + s^2$$

$$a^2 = (h^2 + s^2) + c^2 - 2cs \qquad [1]$$

However, using the Pythagorean theorem again, in $\triangle$I, we get

$$h^2 + s^s = b^2 \qquad [2]$$

Also,
$$s/b = \cos A \text{ or } s = b \cos A \qquad [3]$$

Now substituting [2] and [3] into [1] we get

$$a^2 = b^2 + c^2 - 2bc \cos A$$

This is the law of cosines for an acute triangle. Continue this extension by drawing an obtuse triangle, obtuse angle C. This time, the altitude will fall outside the triangle, but the development is similar to the one just demonstrated.

EXAMPLE 3 (Algebra, Level 1 core): *Distributivity*

In this lesson, students will extend their familiarity with arithmetic to conclude that multiplication and division are distributed over addition and subtraction, and that powers and roots may be distributed over multiplication and division.

The conclusions will be arrived at as conjectures after the teacher reviews order of operations and symbols of grouping, followed by these arithmetic illustrations:

(I) $3(4 + 5) = 3 \cdot 4 + 3 \cdot 5$?

Answer: YES (Multiplication may be distributed over addition.)

$5(3 - 2) = 5 \cdot 3 - 5 \cdot 2$?

Answer: YES (Multiplication may be distributed over subtraction.)

(II) $\dfrac{36 - 4}{4} = \dfrac{36}{4} - \dfrac{4}{4}$?

Answer: YES (Division may be distributed over subtraction.)

$\dfrac{40 + 15}{5} = \dfrac{40}{5} + \dfrac{15}{5}$?

Answer: YES (Division may be distributed over addition.)

(III) $(2 + 3)^2 = 2^2 + 3^2$?

Answer: NO (Powers are *not* distributed over addition.)

$(2 \cdot 3)^2 = 2^2 \cdot 3^2$?

Answer: YES (Powers may be distributed over multiplication.)

(IV) $\sqrt{4 + 9} = 2 + 3$?

Answer: NO (Roots are *not* distributed over addition.)

$\sqrt{4 \cdot 9} = 2 \cdot 3$?

Answer: YES (Roots may be distributed over multiplication.)

$\sqrt{\dfrac{4}{9}} = \dfrac{2}{3}$?

Answer: YES (Roots may be distributed over division.)

(V) Challenge: $\dfrac{3 \cdot 5 + 2}{3} = 5 + 2$?

Answer: NO

The teacher should illustrate amply with examples and counterexamples, such as $2(3 \times 4)$ is *not* equal to 2×3 times 2×4. Likewise, when multiplying $.03(2000 - x)$ by 100, only one of the factors is multiplied by 100, *not* both.

EXAMPLE 4 (Algebra): *Dividing Polynomials*

To divide one polynomial by another, we first recall how to divide two numbers in arithmetic. When we divide 806 by 26, we are really discovering how many times

26 is contained in 806 by using repeated subtraction. Using the same procedure and the same reasoning, when $x^2 + 5x + 6$ is divided by $x + 3$, we find by repeated subtraction that $x + 3$ is contained in $x^2 + 5x + 6$, $x + 2$ times.

We can thus extend the familiar arithmetic division algorithm to the algebraic division of polynomials.

A side-by-side comparison will be helpful for students.

Students should be familiar with the terms *dividend, divisor,* and *quotient.*

1. Usual long division:

$$26\overline{)806} \qquad x + 3\overline{)x^2 + 5x + 6}$$

2. Divide left number of dividend by left number of divisor to get first number of quotient.

$$\overset{3}{26\overline{)806}} \qquad x + 3\overline{)\overset{x}{x^2 + 5x + 6}}$$

3. Multiply entire divisor by first number of quotient.

$$\begin{array}{r} 3 \\ 26\overline{)806} \\ 78 \end{array} \qquad \begin{array}{r} x \\ x + 3\overline{)x^2 + 5x + 6} \\ x^2 + 3x \end{array}$$

4. Subtract this answer from dividend. Bring down next number of dividend to get new dividend.

$$\begin{array}{r} 3 \\ 26\overline{)806} \\ 78 \\ \hline 26 \end{array} \qquad \begin{array}{r} x \\ x + 3\overline{)x^2 + 5x + 6} \\ x^2 + 3x \\ \hline 2x + 6 \end{array}$$

5. Divide left number of new dividend by left number of divisor. Get next number of quotient.

$$\begin{array}{r} 31 \\ 26\overline{)806} \\ 78 \\ \hline 26 \end{array} \qquad \begin{array}{r} x + 2 \\ x + 3\overline{)x^2 + 5x + 6} \\ x^2 + 3x \\ \hline 2x + 6 \end{array}$$

6. Repeat steps 3 and 4 by multiplying whole divisor by second number of quotient. Subtract result from new dividend. Last remainder in this case is zero.

$$\begin{array}{r} 31 \\ 26\overline{)806} \\ 78 \\ \hline 26 \\ 26 \\ \hline 0 \end{array} \qquad \begin{array}{r} x + 2 \\ x + 3\overline{)x^2 + 5x + 6} \\ x^2 + 3x \\ \hline 2x + 6 \\ 2x + 6 \\ \hline 0 \end{array}$$

Answer: 31   *Answer:* $x + 2$

The division process for arithmetic comes to an end when the remainder is zero; for algebra it ends when the remainder is less than the divisor.

EXAMPLE 5 (Algebra): *Solving Digit Problems*

Students must be reminded of the meaning of hundreds(h), tens(t), and units(u) digits and should then be shown how to express two- and three-digit numbers in terms of these letters. Assign drill and practice.

Ask students to select any three-digit number with all digits different.

Let us select 365.

Have students write all possible two-digit numbers using the digits 3, 6, and 5. Now find the sum of these numbers:

$$\begin{array}{r} 36 \\ 35 \\ 63 \\ 53 \\ 65 \\ \underline{56} \\ 308 \end{array}$$

Now divide this sum by the sum of these digits, $3 + 6 + 5 = 14$:

$308/14 = 22$. Students will wonder why everyone gets 22 as the answer regardless of which number was selected at the start. The justification for this can lead to a discussion of what are traditionally known as "digit problems."

Justification: Let the three-digit number be represented by $100h + 10t + u$. The six possible numbers are:

$$\begin{array}{l} 10h + t \\ 10t + h \\ 10h + u \\ 10u + h \\ 10t + u \\ 10u + t \end{array}$$

The sum is $20(h + t + u) + 2(h + t + u) = 22(h + t + u)$. Now we are asked to divide by the sum of the digits, $(h + t + u)$, so that $22(h + t + u)/(h + t + u) = 22$.

When using this type of development, you must keep a clear focus on the purpose of this "trick."

EXAMPLE 6 (Geometry): *Use methods of coordinate geometry to prove that the diagonals of a parallelogram bisect each other.*

Many exercises of plane geometry can be proved more easily by methods of coordinate geometry than by those of Euclidean plane geometry.

When solving an exercise by means of coordinate geometry, half the battle in finding a proof is often won by setting it up well. It is frequently helpful to use the origin and one of the axes as vertex and side, respectively.

In the first column of the next page are some sample useful placements of quadrilaterals.

For this exercise, students must be familiar with simple coordinate geometry principles such as plotting points on

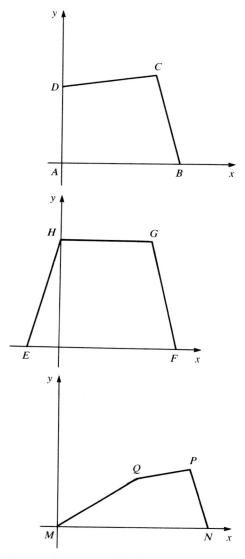

a coordinate axis system, midpoint formula, and definition and properties of a parallelogram.

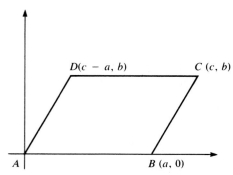

SOLUTION Place vertex A of parallelogram $ABCD$ on the origin and one side along the x-axis. Use $(a, 0)$ as the coordinates of B, and (c, b) for C. The coordinates of D will be $(c - a, b)$. From the midpoint formula, the midpoint of $\overline{AC}$ is

$\left(\dfrac{c}{2}, \dfrac{b}{2}\right)$, and the midpoint of $\overline{BD}$ is

$$\left(\frac{a + c - a}{2}, \frac{b}{2}\right) = \left(\frac{c}{2}, \frac{b}{2}\right)$$

Since the diagonals have the same midpoint, they bisect each other.

EXAMPLE 7 (Calculus, Level 3 core): *Use a graphics calculator to investigate the number of relative maximum and minimum points in a polynomial function of order n.*

Before beginning the investigation, students should draw the graph of a straight line, $y = ax + b$. They should know that this is a function of the first degree, which may look something like this:

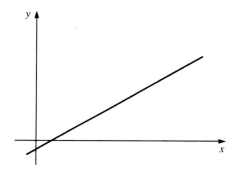

Next, draw a function of the second degree. The equation has the general form

$$y = ax^2 + bx + c$$

and looks something like this (a parabola):
(Note the possible positions)

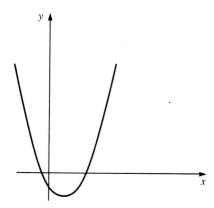

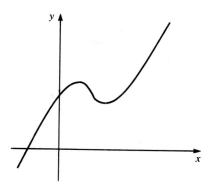

Finally, a picture of a fourth-degree polynomial function (a quartic function):

$$y = ax^4 + bx^3 + cx^2 + dx + e$$

(Note possible positions)

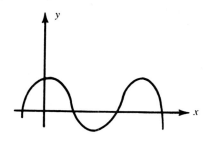

Next, obtain a picture of a third-degree polynomial function (a cubic function):

$$y = ax^3 + bx^2 + cx + d$$

(Note possible positions)

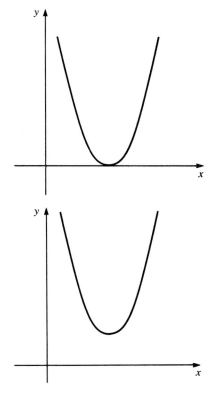

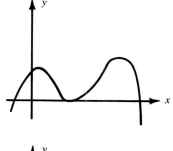

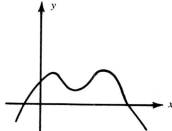

Study all the diagrams to conclude that

- 1st-degree function has 0 relative maximum or minimum points;
- 2nd-degree function has 1 relative maximum or minimum point;
- 3rd-degree function has at most 2 maximum or minimum points;

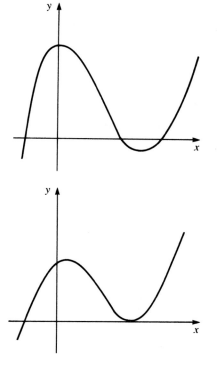

• 4th-degree function has at most 3 maximum or minimum points;

Students should now be able to generalize, on an informal level only, the maximum number of relative maximum and minimum points for a polynomial function of order n.

Further analysis with calculus would be in order at this time.

USING A GRAPHICS CALCULATOR

EXAMPLE 1 (Calculus, Level 3 core): *Use a graphics calculator to find the real positive root of the equation $x^3 - 2x - 5 = 0$ correct to three decimal places.*

After the graph appears on the screen, the root of the equation (i.e., the zero of the function) is obtained by

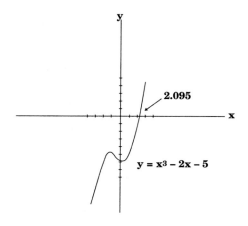

finding its intersection with the x-axis. The zero may be determined to any reasonable degree of precision by placing the cursor as near as possible to the intersection with the x-axis, then repeating the process on a magnification of the graph until desired accuracy is achieved. The approximate value of the root, 2.095, will appear on the screen (see figure in previous column).

SUMMARY

It was said in a past era that a chalkboard and a piece of chalk are the only tools a teacher needs to present a good lesson. This is not true any longer, especially because we are all accustomed to viewing "perfect" performances on our television and movie screens regularly.

If teachers hope to attract students' attention, they must compete with the image of the professional, highly paid actor or actress. Thus, a teacher now needs those tools and skills that may be used in each "performance," such as the ability to respond on the spot to clear up a youngster's confusion about difficult mathematics concepts. A teacher also needs to be sensitive and understanding when noticing confusion in a student's eyes in addition to being a skilled mathematician who is at ease with mathematics and its history and who can respond to any related questions. The creative teacher can also design and produce overhead projector acetates, string art, models, and appropriate graphics problems. This chapter illustrated some strategies and tools teachers can use to produce more effective lessons.

The interaction among students sitting together in a small or large room, under a teacher's guidance, also produces mental stimulation and challenge not produced by sitting alone in front of a screen.

EXERCISES

1. Write a whole class trigonometry lesson that introduces graphs of trigonometric functions. (*Suggestion:* Use a graphics calculator.)

2. Prepare a small group lesson introducing solution of systems of equations by the substitution method; by the addition method; by the graphing method. (*Suggestion:* Use a graphics calculator and an overhead projector.)

3. Write three open-ended questions in a lesson that derives the quadratic formula in a second year algebra class. (*Suggestion:* Use an overhead projector and a scientific calculator.)

4. a. Prepare a lesson with three word problems to be solved in a first year algebra class. (*Suggestion:* Use an overhead projector and a graphics calculator.)
   b. Ask students to use your word problems in (a) as a basis for creating five new, similar problems.

5. Describe three tasks that may be used as practice exercises for the lessons described in Exercises 1, 2, and 4a.

6. Prepare a lesson on "The sum of the angles of a triangle, quadrilateral, pentagon, etc., is a constant (for each type of polygon)" using paper folding and/or physical models.

7. Develop a geometry lesson that uses string art.

REFERENCES

Bidwell, James K. "Humanizing Your Classroom with History of Mathematics." *Mathematics Teacher* 86, no. 6 (Sept. 1993): 461–464.

Brandon, Paul R., Barbara J. Newton, and Ormrod W. Hammond. "Children's Mathematics Achievement in Hawaii: Sex Differences Favoring Girls." *American Educational Research Journal* 24, no. 3 (fall 1987): 437–461.

Crowley, Mary L. "Student Mathematics Portfolio: More Than a Display Case." *Mathematics Teacher* 86, no. 7 (October 1993): 544–547.

Davis, Robert, Elizabeth Jocksuch, and Curtis McKnight. "Cognitive Processes in Learning Algebra." *Journal of Children's Mathematical Behavior* 2, no. 1 (Spring 1978).

Educational Psychologist 23 no. 2 (Spring 1988).

Ellis, Arthur K. "Planning for Mathematics Instruction." *Teaching Mathematics in Grades K–8,* 2d ed. Ed. Thomas R. Post. Boston: Allyn & Bacon, 1992.

Lefrancois, Guy R. *Psychology for Teaching,* 8th ed. Belmont, CA: Wadsworth, 1994.

Leinhardt, Gaea, and Ralph T. Putnam. "The Skill of Learning from Classroom Lessons." *American Educational Research Journal* 24, no. 4 (winter 1987): 557–587.

Matz, M. "Toward a Process Model for High School Algebra Errors." In *Intelligent Tutoring Systems.* D. Sleeman and Brown, J. S., Eds. London: Academic Press, 1982.

Mayer, Richard. "Different Problem Solving Strategies for Algebra, Word and Equation Problems." *Journal of Experimental Psychology: Learning, Memory and Cognition* 8 (1982): 448–462.

National Institute of Education. Conference on Basic Mathematical Skills and Learning. Vol. 1, Contributed Position Papers. Euclid, Ohio, 1977.

Owens, Douglas T. *Research Ideas for the Classroom: Middle Grades Mathematics.* New York: Macmillan, 1993.

Reed, Stephan K., and Michael Ettinger. "Usefulness of Tables for Solving Word Problems." *Cognition and Instruction* 4, no. 1 (1987): 43–59.

Riley, Mary S., and James G. Greeno. "Developmental Analysis of Understanding Language about Quantities and of Solving Problems." *Cognition and Instruction* 5, no. 1 (1988): 49–101.

Simon, Martin A. "The Teacher's Role in Increasing Student Understanding of Mathematics." *Educational Leadership* 43, no. 7 (April 1986): 40–43.

Swing, Susan R., Karen C. Stoiber, and Penelope L. Peterson. "Thinking Skills Versus Learning Time: Effects of Alternative Classroom-Based Interventions on Students' Mathematics Problem Solving." *Cognition and Instruction* 5, no. 2 (1988): 123–191.

Vochko, L. E. *Manipulative Activities and Games in the Mathematics Classroom.* Washington, DC: National Education Association, 1979.

Wilson, Patricia S. *Research Ideas for the Classroom: High School Mathematics.* New York: Macmillan, 1993.

Zhu, Xinming, and Herbert A. Simon. "Learning Mathematics from Examples and By Doing." *Cognition and Instruction* 4, no. 3 (1987): 137–166.

CHAPTER 6
CLASSROOM QUESTIONING

Every teacher is a resource person who determines which classroom teaching strategies will be most effective. The good teacher strives to make the classroom a place where students will enjoy the learning process. Active student learning is usually a concomitant goal. Certainly, the manner in which new material is presented to a class will determine the true learning atmosphere. If students are *told* all the information they are required to know about a topic, they will inevitably become bored, lose interest and ultimately "tune out." Thus, the teacher must constantly try to promote an exciting learning atmosphere in the classroom. One way of achieving this is to set a tone of constant mental stimulation throughout the lesson. This can be done regularly by offering moderate mental challenges (in either the small or large group settings) in the form of carefully thought out questions presented in a nonthreatening manner.

By asking a class well-constructed questions, the teacher encourages active learning on the part of the students. What should the goal of such questioning be? Classroom questioning should elicit student responses consisting of information that would otherwise have been presented by the teacher. (Sometimes some valuable "original" comments are also received!) Although this is, in fact, quite difficult to fully achieve, it is a goal for which to strive.

To begin, consideration must be given to the construction of good questions which are not sexually or culturally biased. Good questioning is an art and is one of the most important elements of good teaching. As a result, it is either a great strength or a serious weakness in classroom work. Questions must be conscientiously prepared and patiently practiced. There are a number of pitfalls to avoid in asking classroom questions. We begin by considering these pitfalls, then examine some guidelines to follow.

TEN TYPES OF QUESTIONS
TO AVOID

In any sequence of questioning a few weak questions may be asked without harm, but many poor questions will weaken a lesson. Following are ten types of questions a teacher should consciously avoid, for they may be counterproductive.

Overlaid Question

Often teachers, in the midst of asking their classes a question, find that the question is not specific enough to elicit the desired response. Rather than let the original question ride on its merits and give students a chance to answer it, the teacher may augment the question before students have even had a chance to answer the original question. When this happens, students who may have understood the original question may now hesitate to answer, since they are uncertain about their understanding of the entire question. Thus, by elaborating on a question she felt was unclear, the teacher may have caused confusion by tagging on an additional thought.

> **EXAMPLE** What method shall we use to solve this problem, and that will make our solution elegant?

Even if a student knows which method to use to solve the problem in question, he may avoid answering the question because of uncertainty about the second part of the question, namely, whether his method will produce an ''elegant solution.'' An improved way to ask this question is: ''What method shall we use to solve this problem (pause) Noreen?'' ''Is this the most efficient way to solve this problem (pause) Yolanda?''

> **EXAMPLE** Which two triangles are congruent and also share a common angle?

Students might be ready to answer the first part of the question but then may hesitate on hearing the second part, for an inspection of the ''common angle'' would require further thought. Furthermore, some students may simply be overwhelmed by the question and shy away from it. This question may be asked as: ''Which two triangles sharing a common angle are congruent (pause) Mabel?'' You may also choose to ask the question as two separate questions.

In each of the two examples of an overlaid question, an elaboration of an original question was tagged on. This had exactly the opposite effect of what was intended.

Multiple Question

A multiple question is formed by asking two related questions in sequence without allowing for a student response until both parts of the question have been asked.

> **EXAMPLE** Which triangles should we prove congruent, and how will they help us prove $\overline{AB}$ parallel to $\overline{CD}$?

Although a student may know which triangles need to be proved congruent, he may not know how congruent triangles will help prove $\overline{AB} \parallel \overline{CD}$. This student will probably not answer the question. However, if the question is asked in two parts, allowing for an answer to the first part before the second part is asked, then more students will be likely to respond. This may be done as follows: ''Which triangles should we prove congruent (pause) Henry?'' ''How will these congruent triangles enable us to prove $\overline{AB} \parallel \overline{CD}$ (pause) Evelyn?''

This type of question is similar to the overlaid question in that it also has two parts. It differs from the overlaid question by being two questions that could actually stand separately. Teachers often resort to multiple questions when they feel that the time remaining for a lesson is too short, or when they get somewhat impatient and want the lesson to move along more rapidly. As before, students can easily be discouraged from answering this type of question. To provide a correct response, a student must be able to answer correctly *both* parts of the question. Thus, a student who can correctly answer only one part of the question will not volunteer to respond. By reducing the pool of students who will respond to questions, the teacher diminishes active learning throughout the class.

> **EXAMPLE** What is the discriminant of this equation (pointing to a quadratic equation), and what type of roots does it have?

The multiple question above could stand as separate questions, but in its present format it will most likely discourage students from responding. The same information can be elicited by asking: ''What is the discriminant of this equation (pointing to a quadratic equation) (pause) Alice?'' and ''Based on the value of the discriminant, what type of roots does this equation have (pause) Jordan?'' By stifling student responses, multiple questions reduce the effectiveness of a lesson and should therefore be avoided.

Factual Questions

There is certainly nothing wrong with asking a question that has a simple factual response if the question is part of a buildup of a series of sequential facts necessary for the solution to the problem under consideration. Otherwise, isolated factual questions do little to stimulate student thinking.

> **EXAMPLE** What is the Pythagorean theorem?

Not much thought is required to respond to this question. A student either knows the answer or does not know it. If we agree with our original premise regarding classroom questioning, then aside from being a part of a sequence of questions, factual questions contribute little to an active learning environment in the classroom.

Elliptical Questions

Questions that are unclear because the teacher has omitted specifics offer nothing to a lesson. Although not particularly harmful to a lesson, an elliptical question is simply an unnecessary waste of time.

EXAMPLE   How about these two angles?

Teachers frequently have a habit of thinking aloud. They may be looking at a pair of angles and thinking of what to ask about them, such as "What is their relationship?" or "Which angle has the greater measure?" In either case, the teacher may instead first voice the thought: "How about these two angles?" Verbalizing this thought into a question that has no answer wastes classroom time. The teacher might have asked, "What is the relationship between these two angles (pause) Gil?" where a definite answer was required.

Had the teacher wanted to say something (so as to avoid a lull in the lesson) when he was thinking about the two angles, he could have said, "Consider these two angles." This would have served the intended purpose and not wasted classroom time with possible student wisecrack answers such as, "How about them!"

EXAMPLE   What about these two parallel lines?

As before, this elliptical question asks for either nothing or more than most students are prepared to offer. At any rate, because of the omission of specifics, it leaves itself open to wisecrack responses. The teacher may wish to say something such as, "Which angles can we prove congruent using these parallel lines (pause) Laura?"

The teacher does not have to overreact to avoid lulls. Instead, she should stop and give some thought to a question rather than ask it in a form that has no clear response.

Yes-No or Guessing Questions

For the most part there is little value in a yes-no or guessing question. With few exceptions a yes-no question can easily be transformed into a good thought question.

EXAMPLE   Is $\overline{AB}$ perpendicular to $\overline{CD}$?

A student attempting to answer this question takes a very small risk. His chances of being correct are actually better than 50 percent. The teacher asking the question more often than not is seeking a positive response. In addition, the diagram to which this question relates should also offer assistance. Thus, the question becomes somewhat rhetorical. This question might be transformed to

read, "What is the relationship between $\overline{AB}$ and $\overline{CD}$ (pause) Stephanie?" This would require the student to scan the possible relationships that two line segments may have and then choose the one she feels is appropriate. In its transformed state, the question provokes active learning among the students.

EXAMPLE   Is triangle *ABC* isosceles?

Why would a teacher ask this question if the triangle were, in fact, not isosceles? Unless the teacher were set to trick the class, students would be correct in assuming that the teacher is simply seeking an affirmative response. Why then ask the question? The question will be far more productive when asked as, "What type of triangle is $\triangle ABC$ (pause) Ernie?" It is therefore a good practice to avoid yes-no or guessing questions whenever possible.

Ambiguous Questions

Occasionally, a teacher may seek a response that requires a specific interpretation of a situation. Here the questioner, trying to get the desired response with one question, may likely ask an ambiguous question, one that can have a variety of different, yet correct, answers. The desired response would be more easily attained by asking a series of short sequential questions.

EXAMPLE   How does the law of sines differ from the law of cosines?

Many different correct answers to this question can be given. Certainly the context in which this question is asked will help narrow the choices among the correct responses. Students will tend to shy away from responding to this question, however, out of obvious confusion caused by its ambiguity. Students may wonder if the question refers to the difference in appearance of the two laws, the difference in application, the difference in derivation, and so on. One possible form in which this question may be asked is, "Under what different circumstances are the laws of sines and cosines used (pause) Lynn?" Because such confusion is obviously counterproductive, ambiguous questions should be consciously avoided in classroom questioning.

EXAMPLE   What is the relationship between the area of a circle and the circumference of a circle?

Once again this question has many correct answers. Is the questioner concerned about the numerical relationship, the physical relationship, the dimensional relationship, or some other less obvious relationship? Although the context in which the question is asked will assist students in responding to the question, confusion is rarely avoided when an ambiguous question is asked. One specific way of asking this question is, "What is the numerical ratio between the area and circumference of a circle (pause) Carol?'' (*Note:* It is not necessarily a bad or undesirable feature to pose questions having several correct answers. We are considering the ''ambiguous question'' rather than this type of question here.)

Before asking a question that is likely to be ambiguous, set the specifics about the situation, then ask short simple questions to elicit the desired response.

Chorus Response Questions

Although a question calling for a chorus response may be good, the chorus response often provides little value to the lesson. When a class responds in chorus to a question, the teacher usually cannot determine which students are answering incorrectly and which students are not responding at all. Furthermore, a chorus response can become too unclear for students eager to learn from the answer to hear the answer correctly. By missing the answer to a question, a student could be missing an important link in a chain of reasoning, resulting in damage to the learning process for this student.

> **EXAMPLE** What type of quadrilateral is *ABCD*, class?

If we assume that not everyone in the class knows the correct answer to the question, some students will be shouting an incorrect answer while others will be answering correctly. Should one student not respond but instead listen for the correct answer, he may hear an incorrect answer (because a wrong response may have come from someone close by) and then try to learn a concept with an incorrect piece of information. The time lost in correcting this error is certainly undesirable.

A preponderance of chorus response questions will allow some students to glide through the lesson without actually learning the subject matter presented. The teacher in this situation will be unable to detect individual difficulties, since they are likely to be clouded by the chorus responses. This gives further reason to avoid the chorus response question as much as possible.

But an occasional use of this type of question may be acceptable if the response is not too crucial to a development and if it is necessary to involve the entire class, even for the sake of variety. A change of style, offering variety to the lesson, may be a healthy feature. When used for this purpose, however, the chorus response question should be used sparingly.

Whiplash Questions

A whiplash question usually is not planned by the teacher. It comes about when a teacher decides to make a question out of a statement midway through it.

> **EXAMPLE** The slope of this line is, what?

Aside from possibly frustrating students, little harm is caused by this type of question. Perhaps its greatest flaw is its uselessness. Not expecting a question, the students are caught off guard. They must first mentally rephrase the question before attempting an answer. Under normal circumstances the beginning key word of a question (e.g., why, when, what, how) puts the students in a psychological set, ready to receive and process a question. The whiplash question does not provide this readying process and thereby wastes time and loses much of the student audience. A more productive way to ask this question would be, ''What is the slope of this line (pause) Fred?''

> **EXAMPLE** We now have $\overline{AB}$ parallel to $\overline{CD}$ because of which theorem?

This question would have been much more effective had the key word announcing a question been at the beginning of the question. It would then read, ''Which theorem justifies the fact that $\overline{AB}$ is parallel to $\overline{CD}$ (pause) Edith?'' In this form, the students know from the first word that a question is being asked. The second word has them focus on the various theorems learned while they listen to the remainder of the question. At the completion of the question they are ready to respond without wasting time to rephrase the question. This latter form of the question is clearly more efficient than the whiplash format, and a teacher need not turn every statement into a question just for the sake of producing student participation. Such an attempt at increasing student participation could easily become counterproductive.

Leading Questions

A leading question is one that tugs the desired response from the student. This type of question serves no reasonable function.

> **EXAMPLE** Wouldn't you say that $\triangle ABC$ is equilateral?

Most students would be quite reluctant not to agree with the teacher asking such a question. Thus, the question does not provoke much thought, since the student is more than likely to simply respond in the affirmative.

> **EXAMPLE** Seven is a factor of 35, isn't it?

Again, there is no need to turn the statement ''Seven is a factor of 35'' into a question. The teacher would be better served either by leaving the statement stand as is, or by asking a question such as, ''What are the factors of 35 (pause) Walter?'' or ''By what number must 7 be multiplied to yield 35 (pause) Larry?'' Each of these questions requires some thought on the part of the students before they answer. In addition to replacing a time-wasting question, each induces active learning.

Teacher-centered Questions

It is generally desirable to have students consider the teacher as part of the class. Although students are well aware of the different roles of the teacher and the student, when addressing the class it is more effective for the teacher to use the first person plural (i.e., we and us) where appropriate. For example, saying "Let us consider the following. . ." rather than "I have the following. . ." would make the class feel that they are all part of one group working together on a common problem. They do not need a constant reminder that they are the students and the teacher is distinct from them. Regular use of the first person singular (i.e., I and me) could create an invisible shield between the teacher and the class, a possible detriment to a healthy active learning environment.

> **EXAMPLE** Give me the solution set of $3x - 5 = 2$.

A better way to ask this is: "Give us the solution set of $3x - 5 = 2$ (pause) Ellen."

> **EXAMPLE** What must I do next in solving this problem?

This question ought to be asked as: "What must we do next in solving this problem (pause) Jack?" Each of the preceding examples illustrates the sort of teacher comment that seeks to set apart (albeit subconsciously) the teacher from the students, which is not particularly conducive to a good classroom learning situation.

CLASSROOM QUESTIONING FEATURES TO DEVELOP

Besides avoiding the pitfalls of poor classroom questions, teachers must consciously develop habits of questioning that will strengthen their teaching performance. Each of the following suggestions for developing an effective style of classroom questioning should be carefully practiced, for their benefits extend beyond classroom questioning and can have a substantial impact on the teaching-learning process.

Direct and Simple Language

Classroom questions should be direct and simple in language. The student focus on a question should be on its content, not on the language used in its delivery. That is, if the language distracts students from the content, either by being too complex, or perhaps too humorous, the potential effectiveness of a question may be lost. By using direct and simple language (i.e., appropriate for the level of the intended class) a teacher can use classroom questions to fulfill their desired function.

Definite and Clear Meaning

Classroom questions should be definite and clear in meaning. If a question lends itself to various interpretations, students may be reluctant to respond. To maximize the number of volunteer respondents, ambiguities should be avoided. Often, shorter questions are less confusing.

A question should call for only one or two points in a line of reasoning. A teacher should ask more questions rather than try to limit the number of questions and lengthen each one. By trying to ask too much in a single question, the teacher may become prone to asking multiple or overlaid questions (see page 74).

Logical Sequence

Questioning should develop a train of thought in logical sequence. An inexperienced teacher's impatience with the developmental process may cause him to rush to the pivotal (or prime) question of a lesson without spending enough time leading up to it with shorter preparatory questions. This impatience often diminishes the ultimate effectiveness of the pivotal question. Since the pivotal question generally elicits a highlight of the lesson, its effectiveness should not be weakened. Thus, teachers should give special attention to all parts of a line of questioning that develops a train of thought in logical sequence. This means that the same care should be given to the early, perhaps almost trivial (or review), questions as is given to the pivotal and culminating questions. Remember, the pivotal question is rarely effective if it is not properly built up through a carefully developed sequence of subordinate questions in predetermined order.

Questions Keyed to Class Ability

The level of ability of a class should determine the language and complexity of the classroom questions used. It is easy for a teacher to use the same questions during two consecutive class periods, especially when the same lesson is being used. Yet if the ability levels of the two classes are different, this practice should be consciously avoided. For the slower or perhaps less sophisticated class, simpler language might be used than with a class comprising more able students. Teachers should be careful not to use condescending language, but at the same time they should not conduct the class with language beyond the students' ability to grasp the content comfortably. By asking questions properly suited for the intended audience, teachers will improve communication with classes at all levels.

Questions that Stimulate Effort

Questions should arouse an effort. While gearing the phrasing of a question to the appropriate level for a class teachers must make a special effort to prepare questions that are sufficiently difficult to arouse an effort yet not too difficult to stifle the class. Good classroom questioning should create a moderately challenging atmosphere throughout the lesson. Classroom questions should be short and crisp and arranged in a logical sequence building up to the desired point. A sequence of questions might well consist of a blend of factual and thought questions, with a majority of the latter kind. Included would be a balanced mixture of some short, yet challenging questions along with other review or connecting questions. Such a blend should go far to stimulate active learning.

Open-Ended Questions

Open-ended questions allow students to reach conclusions and make mathematical decisions consistent with their understanding and development. On a class examination, students can demonstrate the kind of depth that is impossible to determine on the basis of choosing one of several multiple-choice items or writing a single-number response. Open-ended questions also permit pupils to arrive at many possible ''correct'' answers.

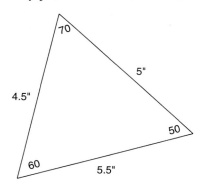

EXAMPLE Your friend shows you the examples $\frac{16}{64} = \frac{1}{4}$ by canceling the 6s, $\frac{26}{65} = \frac{2}{5}$ also by canceling the 6s, $\frac{19}{95} = \frac{1}{5}$ by canceling the 9s, and $\frac{49}{98} = \frac{1}{2}$ also by canceling the 9s. Using the same logic, he claims, the following must also be valid. Explain why his logic is incorrect.

$$\frac{12}{23} = \frac{1}{3} \text{ (cancel the 2s)}$$

$$\frac{15}{55} = \frac{1}{5} \text{ (cancel the 5s)}$$

$$\frac{28}{81} = \frac{2}{1} \text{ (cancel the 8s)}$$

Maintaining Student Interest

Classroom questioning should hold student interest throughout a lesson. A few important points should be included regularly.

Every effort should be made to call on as many different students throughout a lesson as possible and to try to avoid predictability in calling on students. Mixing calling on nonvolunteers with calling on volunteers will keep everyone attentive. Beginning a course by requiring students to give complete answers to classroom questions will help to ensure that such a practice will eventually become habitual in the class.

It is a good habit to praise students (with tact) for correctly answering a question. It is equally important, however, for a teacher to handle incorrect answers properly.

The best treatment for an incorrect answer depends on the type of class and the time available in the lesson. Under no circumstances should the teacher be abrupt to or scold a student for giving an incorrect answer. This would likely have an adverse effect on the student's learning and inhibit future willingness to respond to the teacher's questions.

With classroom time permitting, the teacher may guide the student to realize an error through a series of questions specially tailored to this discovery. Alternatively, the teacher may choose to refer the question to the rest of the class.

Student questions may also be answered by other students. The teacher should not feel that only she should provide the answers. Peer interaction can produce interesting results. For example, by answering another student's question, the first student can better learn the concepts under consideration. Teaching usually allows the teacher to better understand the subtleties of subject matter being taught. The same can be true when one student explains a concept to a classmate.

When students are expected to respond to one another's questions, there is a greater degree of alertness throughout the classroom, since students cannot predict precisely when they will be called on to correct or answer another student. This alertness should go far to enliven the class.

Avoiding Repetition

The teacher's question should generally not be repeated. Naturally, if for some unusual reason the question was inaudible, repetition may be necessary. Variety can be provided by having a student repeat a question when it was not heard by some students. Habitually repeating a question can make the class inattentive, however, since they can rely on the question being repeated. Students also may continually call for the repetition of a question to waste class time, but if they know that the repetition of a question is not easily obtained, this scheme will not work. The result will be an attentive class, with no time wasted.

Sometimes a teacher, having asked a question of the class, may repeat the question in perhaps a rephrased form before the class has even had a chance to respond to the question. An uncertainty on the part of the teacher about the clarity of the question will provoke this immediate repetition of the question. Very often only the teacher finds the question unclear. The class may have been ready to respond to the original question, but after hearing the rephrased question may be somewhat confused. The teacher should let the original question stand, give students sufficient time to respond, and rephrase the question only if no correct response is forthcoming. Students often have an unsuspected ability to properly interpret a teacher's question, even if it is a bit unclear. At such times teachers should not be overly critical of their own questions. Proper questioning preparation could prevent this entire situation.

Avoiding Repetition of Student Answers

The teacher should not repeat student responses, for reasons similar to those discussed above. If students can rely on the teacher to repeat most of the more important student responses to teacher questions, they may eventually not even listen to their classmates. This will greatly inhibit active student interaction throughout a lesson. If, in the teacher's judgment, a student's response is inaudible, then the teacher should have the student or another student repeat the response. Consistency with this procedure will eventually cause students automatically to speak loudly and clearly just to avoid having to repeat their responses (or hear other students do so).

Some teachers have a habit of "mentally processing" a student's response aloud. This results in a repetition of the student's response. Most teachers, when made aware of this habit, can curtail it. Tape recording a teacher's lesson will be helpful in demonstrating this flaw in a teacher's performance. A teacher who cannot avoid such repetitions, however, should at least try to incorporate this repetition into the next statement or question. This way it may not appear as a simple repetition of what has already been said.

Teacher repetitions of student responses are also caused by the teacher's fear that unless a substantive statement is made by the teacher, the class will not note it properly. This, too, will only be so if the teacher allows it to happen. The teacher sets the class tone and routines and the man-

ner in which classroom questioning and the resulting student responses are handled.

Calling on Students

Another way to generate constant student attention is to call on a particular student for a response after a pause at the end of a question.

> **EXAMPLE** Why is $\overline{AB}$ the perpendicular bisector of $\overline{CD}$ (pause) David?

If the class is accustomed to having the teacher call on a student to respond to a question after it has been asked, each student will be attentive just in case he or she is the one selected by the teacher to respond. On the other hand, if a teacher addresses David before asking the question, perhaps only David will be attentive, since the rest of the class will know they are not being asked the question. This latter situation does not promote an active involvement in the learning process. Thus, the teacher should address particular students at the end of the question and thereby assure student attention throughout the lesson.

It is sometimes helpful to discover which students in the class are trying to avoid being called on. There are times when it may be wise to call on them or simply meet with these students after class to discuss their apparent avoidance. The question is, How can the teacher discover which students are trying to avoid being called upon? Experience has shown that if after the teacher asks a question of the class and pauses to look around for a student to call on for a response, a student appears to make a conscious effort to avoid eye contact with the teacher, the teacher can assume that student does not want to be called upon. This avoidance sometimes manifests itself in the student appearing to be very "busy," and the teacher calling on him would be seen as interfering in his "concentration." Sometimes the teacher can discourage this by making a general statement to the class about this type of avoidance. Done properly, the class may find this humorous (since many of the students may have been guilty of this type of behavior at one time or another) and realize that this teacher must be very clever and not easily fooled. However, the teacher then must be watchful for other, perhaps more creative, techniques that some students may use to avoid questions (especially when they feel they cannot properly answer them).

Wait-Time After Asking a Question

Allowing students sufficient time to think about a teacher-posed question is a very important aspect of classroom questioning. One of the leading researchers in the area of the questioning behavior of teachers is Mary Budd Rowe. Her findings over the years have had a significant impact on teacher performance in the classroom. In her extensive analysis of classroom performances, she has found that most teachers, on average, wait less than one second for students to respond to their questions. On the other hand, some teachers wait an average of three seconds for students to reply. When she compared student responses with different wait-times, she found that the longer wait-times (three seconds or more) produced more thoughtful responses, increased classroom discussion, and enabled students to analyze a situation more critically than did the shorter wait-times following the teacher's questions. Dr. Rowe also found that teachers who waited an average of more than three seconds before calling for a response enjoyed the following results:

- the length of student responses increased 400%–800%
- the number of voluntary, yet appropriate, responses increased
- failure to respond decreased
- student confidence increased
- students asked more unsolicited questions
- weaker students contributed more (increases ranged from 1.5% to 37% more)
- there was a greater variety of student responses. Creative thinking increased!
- discipline problems decreased

One effective technique to determine the wait-time following your class questions is to make a tape-recording of your lesson and then during the playback, time the periods of pause following each question. Try increasing your wait-time if it is too short and again tape the lesson to inspect for an increase of wait-time. Such an exercise ought to produce favorable results.

Once you have succeeded in increasing the wait-time following your classroom questions, you might try to pause briefly after a student has responded to allow for reflection or to permit a student to add more information to his first response. This second type of wait-time has similar effects on the learning environment as the first

type of wait-time. This has been shown by an analysis conducted by Dr. Rowe of more than 800 tape recordings of lessons in urban, suburban, and rural schools.

Variety in Questioning

Perhaps one of the most important elements in good classroom questioning, as in most aspects of good teaching, is variety. Variety can refer to the types of questions asked, to the manner in which questions are asked, to the way students (volunteers and nonvolunteers) are called on to respond to questions, and to the procedure by which responses are handled. Variety reduces predictability, which in turn ought to promote continuous stimulation. When teachers vary the type of questions asked, students are constantly required to be alert to more than simply the content of the questions. This additional alertness should have a refreshing spin-off toward improved learning. In addition to providing students with a more interesting experience, teachers also are more apt to be aroused by the challenge of creating continuous variety in their questioning.

SUMMARY

In this chapter we considered one of the important elements of classroom teaching: questioning. Ten types of questions to avoid were presented and analyzed, after which numerous suggestions for effective classroom questioning were discussed. Although many points were made in this chapter, you should practice them in small doses, for considering them all at once could become overwhelming and as a result not very useful. Remember, when asking a classroom question, *listen to your own question* with a critical ear. You may be one of your own best critics. Should more careful self-analysis be desired, a videotape recording would be helpful. Constant self-assessment of one's teaching performance should have rewarding results.

EXERCISES

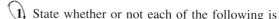

1. State whether or not each of the following is a good classroom question; if it is not, explain why.
   a. "What is the solution set for the equation $3x - 5 = 8$, and how will it help us solve the problem (discussed earlier with the class), Lisa?
   b. "How about this set of numbers . . . Daniel?"
   c. "Why is $\triangle ABC$ isosceles, Noreen?"
   d. "Yolanda, wouldn't you say these triangles are congruent?"
   e. "Class, is this curve a parabola?"
   f. "The discriminant of this equation is what?"
   g. "What is my next step in solving this problem?"

h. "What is the greatest common factor of these two numbers and how can we be sure that there is no greater common factor, Joshua?"

i. "How can we change this equation $\frac{x}{3} + \frac{5x}{7} = 2$ to one without fractions, Henry?"

j. "For what conditions will the roots of this equation (pointing at the chalkboard) be imaginary; and how will this help solve our problem, Evelyn?"

k. "Who can tell me what the solution to this equation (pointing to the chalkboard) is?"

l. "Which is the longest side of this triangle (pointing to right $\triangle ABC$), class?"

m. "How does solving a linear equation differ from solving a quadratic equation, Lynn?"

n. "Am I correct in dividing both sides of this equation (at chalkboard) by five, . . . Sue?"

o. "What is $\sqrt{196}$, class?"

p. "If we apply the Pythagorean theorem to this triangle we find AB equals what, Alice?"

q. "Why is there only one acceptable answer to this problem, Fred?"

2. Rephrase each question in Exercise 1 that is not a good classroom question.

3. Explain why it is more desirable to call on a student after the question has been asked rather than before.

4. Explain how you would react to the following student responses to your question.
   a. "I didn't hear the question."
   b. "I was absent yesterday."
   c. "I don't know."
   d. silence

5. Choose a short topic from the secondary school mathematics curriculum. Prepare a series of questions that you may use to develop this topic (through guided discovery) with your class.

6. What are some of the changes you can make in your questioning technique if you find that you have few volunteers responding to your questions?

7. Have a videotape made of one of your lessons (an audio tape will suffice if a videotape is impractical).
   a. Write an analysis of your classroom questioning by categorizing each of your questions according to the types of questions indicated in this chapter.
   b. Analyze the students' response patterns. That is, were you calling only on volunteers, only on nonvolunteers? What percentage of the students used simple yes-no answers, etc.?

8. Ask an experienced mathematics teacher if he or she would be willing to have you audiotape or videotape one lesson. Take this tape and perform the same analysis required for Question 7.

9. Review the tapes made for Questions 7 and 8 and gauge the wait-time after each question. Analyze and compare your results with the findings of Mary Budd Rowe.

REFERENCES

Bell, Frederick H. *Teaching and Learning Mathematics in Secondary Schools.* Dubuque, Iowa: William C. Brown Company, 1978.

Cangelosi, James S. "Increasing Student Engagement during Questioning Strategy Sessions." *Mathematics Teacher* 77 (1984): 470.

Costa, Arthur. "Teacher Behaviors That Enable Student Thinking." In *Developing Minds: A Resource Book for Teaching Thinking.* Ed. Arthur Costa. Alexandria, VA: Association for Supervision and Curriculum Development, 1985, pp. 125–137.

Davidson, Neil. "A Demonstration of Terrible Teaching Techniques." *Mathematics Teacher* 70 (1977): 545.

Dillon, J. T. "Cognitive Correspondence between Question/Statement and Response." *American Educational Research Journal* 19, no. 4 (winter 1982): 540–551.

Gall, Meredith D. "The Use of Questions in Teaching." *Review of Educational Research* 40 (1970): 707–721.

Gavelek, James, and Taffy Raphael. "Metacognition, Instruction, and the Role of Questioning Activities." Chap. 3 of *Instructional Practices.* Vol. 2 of *Metacognition, Cognition, and Human Performance.* Ed. D. L. Forrest-Pressley, G. E. MacKinnon, and T. Gary Waller. Orlando, FL: Academic Press, 1985.

Henderson, Kenneth B. "Anent the Discovery Method." *Mathematics Teacher* 50 (1970): 287.

Hunkins, Francis P. *Questioning Strategies and Techniques.* Boston: Allyn and Bacon, 1972.

Jones, Phillip S. "Discovery Teaching—from Socrates to Modernity." *Mathematics Teacher* 65 (1970): 501.

Kilpatrick, Jeremy. "Inquiry in the Mathematics Classroom." *Academic Connections.* New York: The College Board, Summer 1987.

Orlich, Donald C., et al. *Teaching Strategies: A Guide to Better Instruction.* Lexington, MA: DC Heath & Co., 1985, pp. 161–200.

Redfield, Doris, and Elaine Rousseau. "A Meta-analysis of Experimental Research on Teacher Questioning Behavior." *Review of Educational Research* 51, no. 2 (1981): 237–245.

Rowe, Mary Budd. *Teaching Science as a Continuous Inquiry: A Basic.* New York: McGraw-Hill, 1978.

Schmalz, Rosemary. "Categorization of Questions That Mathematics Teachers Ask." *Mathematics Teacher* 66 (1973): 619.

Swing, Susan, and Penelope Peterson. "Elaborative and Integrative Thought Problems in Mathematics Learning." *Journal of Educational Psychology* 80, no. 1 (1988) 54–66.

Swireford, Edwin J. "Ninety Suggestions on the Teaching of Mathematics in Junior High School." *Mathematics Teacher* 54 (1961): 145.

Walsh, Debbie. "Socrates in the Classroom." *American Educator* (Summer 1985): 20–25.

Wilen, W. W. *Questioning Skills, for Teachers.* Washington, DC: National Education Association, 1987.

———. *Questions, Questioning Techniques, and Effective Teaching.* Washington, DC: National Education Association, 1987.

Wolf, Dennis Palmer. "The Art of Questioning." *Academic Connections.* New York: The College Board, Winter 1987.

Wong, Bernice. "Self-Questioning Instructional Research: A Review." *Review of Educational Research* 55, no. 2 (Summer 1985) 227–268.

CHAPTER 7
MOTIVATIONAL TECHNIQUES

One of the more difficult tasks teachers of mathematics face is that of motivating students for a particular lesson. Planning motivation requires creativity and imagination. The needs and interests of students must be carefully considered. This will naturally vary with the many student characteristics found in today's schools.

It would appear that geometry, because of its visual nature, would readily generate interest among students. Unfortunately, this is not always the case. Much of the course deals with proving theorems and then applying these theorems to artificial problems. Interested mathematics students will be excited by this as they will be by almost any other mathematical activity. The teacher must focus attention on less interested students, however, in planning appropriate motivation, since they will not be enchanted with such concepts as the postulational nature of geometry.

To motivate students is to channel their interests to the specific topic to be learned. In this chapter we consider some techniques that can be used to motivate secondary school students in mathematics. Specifically, eight different techniques are presented, and a number of examples from algebra and geometry are provided for each. (Note that the technique is the important part to remember. The examples are provided merely to help understand the technique.)

WHAT IS MOTIVATION?

How to motivate students to learn is at the crux of one's concerns when preparing to teach a lesson, for if students can be made to be delightfully receptive learners, then the rest of the teaching process becomes significantly easier and profoundly more effective.

Naturally, when thinking of how to "make a student want to learn" what you are about to teach, certain *extrinsic* methods of motivation may come to mind. These may include token economic rewards for good performance, peer acceptance of good performance, avoidance of "punishment" by performing well, praise for good work, and so on. Extrinsic methods are applicable to students in varying forms. Their earlier rearing and environment has much to do with their adaptation of the commonly accepted extrinsic motivators. However, many students show intrinsic goals to understand a topic or concept (task-related), to outperform others (ego-related), or to impress others (social-related). The latter goal straddles the fence between being an intrinsic or extrinsic goal.

In a more structured form *intrinsic motivators* can be seen to adhere to the following basic types:

The learner wants to develop competencies. Students are often much more eager to do a challenging problem than one that is routine. It is not uncommon to see students beginning their homework assignment with the "challenge for experts" problem even if the time spent on this prevents them from completing their routine work.

The learner is curious about novel events and activities. It is a natural human trait to seek out unusual situations or challenges that can be conquered by existing skills and knowledge and then obtain a feeling of competence. Thus, the learner's curiosity about unusual stimuli is peaked and becomes a form of motivation.

The learner has a need to feel autonomous. The desire to act on something as a result of one's own volition is often a motivating factor in the general learning process. To determine for one's self what is to be learned, rather than to feel learning is being done to satisfy someone else, or to get some sort of extrinsic reward, is another basic human need.

The learner reacts with some internalized social values. Not to be overlooked when trying to simplify (and catalog) human needs and motives is the notion that all learners have certain moral values that have been internalized through years of social reinforcement—most often in the home environment. For example, if a parent constantly tells the child that hard work is good, then that value is manifested in the child and becomes a part of the motives that make him or her function.

The teacher's task is to understand the basic motives already present in the learners and to capitalize on the best knowledge of these. The teacher can then manipulate this knowledge to maximize the effectiveness of the teaching process. Oftentimes this manipulation can result in some rather artificial situations, specifically contrived to exploit a learner's motives for generating a genuine interest in a topic. This is eminently fair and highly desirable!

With these basic concepts in mind, we now explore how they can be used to motivate mathematics instruction. Naturally these specific techniques should be expanded, embellished, adapted to the teacher's personality, and, above all, made appropriate for the learner's level of ability and environment.

MOTIVATING STUDENTS

Indicate a Void in Students' Knowledge. Students usually have a natural desire to complete their knowledge of a topic. This motivational technique involves making students aware of a void in their knowledge and capitalizes on their desire to learn more. For instance, you may present a few simple exercises involving familiar situations followed by exercises involving unfamiliar situations on the same topic. Or you may mention (or demonstrate) to your class how the topic to be presented will complete their knowledge about a particular part of mathematics. The more dramatically you do this, the more effective the motivation. Often, guiding students to discover this void in their knowledge is effective. Following are some examples of how this technique may be used.

> **EXAMPLE** (Introducing the general angle—second year algebra.) Present the following questions to your students:

Find the value of each without the aid of a scientific calculator:

1. Sin 30° = ?
2. Cos 60° = ?
3. Cos 120° = ?

Students familiar with the 30-60-90 triangle ought to be able to answer the first two questions easily. The third question will cause students some discomfort, since students are unfamiliar with trigonometric functions of angles whose measure is greater than 90°. You should now have students realizing that there is a void in their knowledge. They are now motivated to learn how to find the values of trigonometric functions of angles greater than 90°.

> **EXAMPLE** (Introducing the measures of angles with their vertices outside a given circle—geometry.) Suppose students have learned the relationships between the measures of arcs of a circle and

the measure of an angle (whose rays subtend these arcs) with its vertex *in* or *on* the circle but not *outside* the circle. A possible set of exercises is shown below.

Find the value of *x* in each of the following:

1.   2.   3.

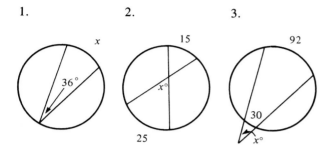

After completing the first two exercises, students should *want* to learn the relationship exhibited in the third exercise. This should serve as a good springboard into the lesson. (For an interesting alternative to teaching this unit, see Enrichment Unit 56, "Angle Measurement with a Circle.")

Show a Sequential Achievement. Closely related to the preceding technique is that of having students appreciate a logical sequence of concepts. This differs from the previous method in that it depends on students' desire to increase, but not complete, their knowledge. A chart may be useful in applying this method of motivation.

EXAMPLE (Quadrilaterals—geometry.) In the development of the properties of quadrilaterals, a chart such as the following may be developed.

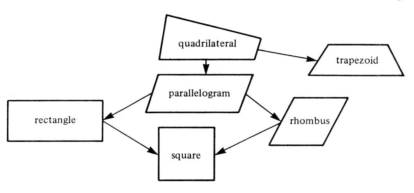

Students could be led to want to reach, sequentially, various levels of this diagramed development. The chart must be developed carefully with its intended purpose clearly in focus.

Present a Challenge. When students are challenged intellectually, they react with enthusiasm. Great care must be taken in selecting the challenge. The problem (if that is the type of challenge used) must not only definitely lead into the lesson but it must also be within reach of the students' ability. A challenge should be short and not complex. It should not be so engrossing that it may detract from the intended lesson. This would certainly defeat the purpose for which this challenge was intended. Thus, challenges providing motivation for one class may not do so for another. Teacher judgment is most important here.

EXAMPLE (Properties of tangents—geometry.) Suppose you wish to motivate your students to learn a lesson on tangents to a circle. Have students consider the following problem:

Given: $\overline{AQP}$, $\overline{BRP}$, and $\overline{QTR}$ tangent to circle *O* at
A, B, and *T,* respectively. *AP = 18.*
Find: The perimeter of $\triangle PQR$.

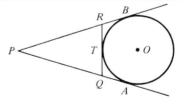

Students may feel that insufficient information was supplied. To solve this problem, they need know only the relationship between the lengths of two tangent segments to a circle from a common external point. Once the need for this theorem has been established (via this little challenge), students ought to be able to solve the problem by noting the equalities *AP = BP, AQ = TQ,* and *BR = TR.* That is, the perimeter of $\triangle PQR = PR + PQ + TR + TQ = PR + PQ + BR + AQ.$ Also, $AQ + PQ = AP = 18,$ and $BR + PR = BP = 18.$ Therefore the perimeter of $\triangle PQR = 36.$

EXAMPLE (Concurrency of angle bisectors of a triangle—geometry.) Another possible challenge may be used when introducing the idea of concurrency of the angle bisectors of a triangle. The student is asked to determine (or draw) the angle bisector of an angle whose vertex is located within an inaccessible area. Students should be familiar with constructions that require the use of straight-edge and compasses.

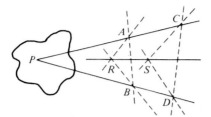

One desired solution requires drawing any lines $\overleftrightarrow{AB}$ and $\overleftrightarrow{CD}$ intersecting the rays of the angle, which is inaccessibly located at P. Angle bisectors of the four angles (as shown above) are drawn, and points R and S determine the desired angle bisector. Students should notice that since the bisectors of the angles of a triangle are concurrent (here considering $\triangle APB$ and $\triangle CPD$ separately), both points R and S *must* be contained in the bisector of the inaccessible angle. After witnessing this solution, students should want to prove the concurrency of the angle bisectors of a triangle. (For a more in-depth consideration of this problem see Enrichment Unit 37, ''The Inaccessible Angle.'')

EXAMPLE   (Introducing the sum of a geometric series—second year algebra.) Present the following challenge to your students:

What would you rather have:

   A. $100,000 per day for 31 days; or
   B. 1¢ the first day
        2¢ the second day
        4¢ the third day
        8¢ the fourth day
        16¢ the fifth day
        . . . and so on for 31 days?

   Most students will opt for choice A, since that seems like a lot of money; after 31 days, $3,100,000 will have been attained. The job of adding the 31 terms in B will be somewhat exhausting. Students should now be motivated for a shortcut for this addition. After they have developed the formula for the sum of a geometric series, the students can apply it to this problem. They may be surprised to discover the large number resulting: $21,474,836.47.

Indicate the Usefulness of a Topic.   Here a practical application is introduced at the beginning of a lesson. The applications selected should be of genuine interest to the class. Once again the applications chosen should be brief and not too complicated so that they motivate the lesson rather than detract from it. Student interest must be considered carefully when selecting an application.

Remember *usefulness* is appropriate only when a student has a prior knowledge of the topic involving the application. The following examples are offered to illustrate this technique.

EXAMPLE   (Properties of a line perpendicular to a plane—geometry.) In erecting a flagpole, students will be interested in knowing how to ensure perpendicularity—hence, a natural motivation for the theorem: ''If a line is perpendicular to each of two intersecting lines at their point of intersection, then the line is perpendicular to the plane determined by them.'' Further elaboration on the flagpole problem depends on the ability level and interest level of the class. (This is true with all methods of motivation presented here.)

EXAMPLE   (Relationship between the segments of two intersecting chords of a circle—geometry.) Finding the size of a cracked plate in which the largest remaining piece is a small segment of the original circle is an application in which students are required to find the diameter of the circle of which $\overset{\frown}{ACB}$ is a minor arc. Perhaps couching this problem in a story might be even more motivating.

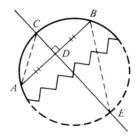

   Draw any chord $\overline{AB}$ of the arc and the perpendicular bisector $\overline{CDE}$ of that chord (where C is on the arc). Measure $\overline{AD}$ and $\overline{CD}$. Then use similarity to establish the proportion $DE/AD = BD/CD$. Thus DE and then CE, the desired diameter, may be found easily. This problem can serve as motivation for the theorem that states, ''If two chords intersect in the interior of a circle, thus determining two segments in each chord, the product of the lengths of the segments of one chord equals the product of the lengths of the segments of the other chord.'' Although students may be able to solve the problem in the manner shown above, they would welcome a shorter method. Hence, the problem has created a need for establishing the relationship $AD \cdot BD = DE \cdot CD$. The proof of the theorem is embedded in the solution above.

EXAMPLE   (Properties of similar triangles—geometry.) When introducing properties of similar triangles, ask the class how the ''cross-legs'' of an airplane service truck have to be positioned so that the plane of the box will be parallel to the plane of the truck.

As the cross-legs shift position, it should be noticed that the legs must always partition each other proportionally if the plane of the box is to remain parallel to the plane of the truck. This ought to motivate students to prove this fact.

Use Recreational Mathematics.

Recreational motivation consists of puzzles, games, paradoxes, or facilities. In addition to being selected for their specific motivational gain, these devices must be brief and simple. A student should realize the "recreation" without much effort in order for this technique to be effective.

EXAMPLE (Area of a circle—geometry.) When beginning the study of the area of a circle, students may be presented with five concentric circles (the smallest has radius one unit) whose radii differ by one unit, respectively, and asked to compare *intuitively* the areas of the two shaded regions (see diagram).

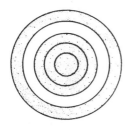

Most students conclude that the "inner region" has a greater area than the region of the "outer ring." Consideration of the area of a circle yields the true relationship. Students are generally astonished to find that the two regions have equal areas.

EXAMPLE (General.) Such topics as division by zero, betweenness, definitions such as $\sqrt{ab} = \sqrt{a} \cdot \sqrt{b}$ when a and b are nonnegative, and the existence of reflex angles are often dramatically presented via mathematical fallacies. Many books describe fallacies that involve these topics as well as many others. Four of these are listed below.

Ball, W. W. Rouse. *Mathematical Recreations and Essays.* Revised by H. S. M. Coxeter. New York: Macmillan, 1960.

Dubnov, Ya. S. *Mistakes in Geometric Proofs.* Translated by A. K. Henn and O. A. Titelbaum. Boston: Heath, 1963.

Maxwell, E. A. *Fallacies in Mathematics.* London, England: Cambridge University Press, 1959.

Northrup, E. P. *Riddles in Mathematics.* Princeton: Van Nostrand, 1944.

EXAMPLE (Introduction to digit problems—algebra.) Begin your presentation by asking your students to select any three-digit number in which the hundreds digit and units digit are unequal. Then have them write the number whose digits are in the reverse order from the selected number. Now tell them to subtract these two numbers (the smaller number from the larger one). Once again tell them to take this difference, reverse its digits and add the "new" number to the *original difference*. They *all* should end up with 1089.

For example, suppose a student selected the number 934. The number with the digits reversed is 439. Her computation would appear as:

$$
\begin{array}{rl}
934 & \\
\underline{439} & \\
495 & \text{(difference)} \\
\underline{594} & \text{(reversed digits)} \\
1089 & \text{(sum)}
\end{array}
$$

When students compare results they will be amazed to discover the uniformity in their answers. At this point they should be quite eager to find out *why* they all came up with the same result. A detailed discussion of this unusual number property is presented in Enrichment Unit 75, "Digit Problems Revisited."

Tell a pertinent story.

A story of a historical event or of a contrived situation can motivate students. All too often teachers, already knowing the story they are about to tell and eager to get into the "meat" of the lesson, rush through the story. Such a hurried presentation minimizes the potential effectiveness the story may have as a motivational device. Thus, a carefully prepared method of presentation of a story for motivating a lesson is almost as important as the content of the story itself.

EXAMPLE (Introducing the sum of an arithmetic series—algebra.) Tell your students about young Carl Friedrich Gauss, who at age 10 was in a class that was asked by its instructor to add the numbers from 1 to 100. Much to the astonishment of the instructor, young Gauss produced the correct answer immediately. When asked how he arrived at the answer so quickly, he explained that

$$1 + 100 = 101$$

$$2 + 99 = 101$$
$$3 + 98 = 101$$
and so on.

Since there are 50 such pairs, the answer is $50 \times 101 =$ 5050.

This scheme can be used to develop the formula for the sum of an arithmetic series.

> **EXAMPLE** (Various topics—geometry.) For the study of parallel lines, the story of Eratosthenes measuring the circumference of the earth might be appropriate (see Posamentier, Banks, and Bannister. *Geometry: Its Elements and Structure.* New York: McGraw-Hill, 1977, p. 226).

Before proving that the base angles of an isosceles triangle are congruent, the teacher may find a brief discussion of *Pons Asinorum* appropriate. Telling students that during the Middle Ages this proof separated weak students from better students should provoke attempts toward solution by all students.

An endless number of stories, historical and otherwise, can be used for motivational purposes. Some of these include the following topics. (After each we offer references.) Many other references can be found in *A Bibliography of Recreational Mathematics* (4 vols.) by William L. Schaaf (Washington, D.C.: National Council of Teachers of Mathematics, 1970(2), 1973, 1978):

1. The origin of certain symbols or terms to be introduced
   Cajori, Florian. *A History of Mathematical Notations* (2 vols.). La Salle, IL: Open Court, 1952.
2. The history of π
   Beckmann, Petr. *A History of π.* New York: St. Martin's Press, 1971.
3. The Golden Rectangle
   Posamentier, Alfred S. *Excursions in Advanced Euclidean Geometry.* Menlo Park, CA: Addison-Wesley, 1984.
   Runion, Garth E. *The Golden Section and Related Curiosa.* Glenview, IL: Scott, Foresman, 1972.
4. Ancient measuring devices
   Kline, Morris. *Mathematics: A Cultural Approach.* Reading, MA: Addison-Wesley, 1962.

   Polya, George. *Mathematical Methods in Science.* Washington, DC: Mathematical Association of America, 1977.
5. Major breakthroughs in mathematics
   Smith, David E. *A Source Book in Mathematics,* New York: McGraw-Hill, 1929.

   Newman, James R. *The World of Mathematics* (4 vols.). New York: Simon and Schuster, 1956.

   Bunt, L., P. Jones, and J. Bedient. *The Historical Roots of Elementary Mathematics.* Englewood Cliffs, NJ: Prentice-Hall, 1976.
6. Pertinent biographical notes
   Bell, E. T. *Men of Mathematics.* New York: Simon and Schuster, 1937.

   Coolidge, Julian L. *The Mathematics of Great Amateurs.* New York: Dover, 1963.

   Schmalz, Rosemary. *Out of the Mouths of Mathematicians.* Washington, DC: Mathematical Association of America, 1993.

   Turnbull, Herbert W. *The Great Mathematicians.* New York: New York University Press, 1961.
7. Pertinent anecdotes
   Aaboe, Asger. *Episodes from the Early History of Mathematics.* Washington, DC: Mathematical Association of America, 1964.

   Devlin, Keith. *All the Math That's Fit to Print.* Washington, DC: Mathematical Association of America, 1994.

   Eves, Howard. *In Mathematical Circles* (2 vols.). Boston: Prindle Weber and Schmidt, 1969.

   Eves, Howard. *Mathematical Circles Revisited.* Boston: Prindle Weber and Schmidt, 1971.

Get students actively involved in justifying mathematical curiosities. One of the more effective techniques for motivating students is to attempt actively to justify a pertinent mathematical curiosity. The students should be comfortably familiar with the mathematical curiosity before you "challenge" them to justify it. Although this could consume more time than may be normally allotted for a motivational activity, to proceed with a justification before sufficient exposure has been achieved would be counterproductive.

> **EXAMPLE** (Introducing the midline of a triangle—geometry.) Suppose students are about to

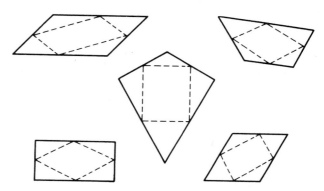

study the properties of a midline of a triangle. As motivation, they may be asked to draw any five quadrilaterals and then in each quadrilateral to join the midpoints of the adjacent sides with line segments. Much to their amazement, they will find that they have drawn five parallelograms.

A request for a proof of this can be expected from the class. One of the more elegant proofs is based on the properties of a midline of a triangle. Thus, the teacher has an excellent opportunity to introduce the midline and its properties.

> **EXAMPLE** (Similarity—geometry.) Another geometric curiosity is the *pantograph*, an instrument used for drawing similar plane figures. Students can construct this instrument at home. At the beginning of the lesson in which similarity is to be considered, the operation of the pantograph can be justified.

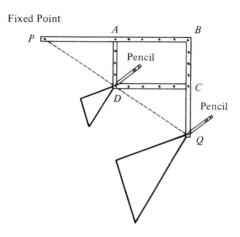

The pantograph consists of four bars hinged at points *A*, *B*, *C*, and *D*. Point *P* is fixed, and pencils are inserted in holes at *D* and *Q*. Various holes may be provided on the bars for other ratios of similitude, *BC/BQ*.

Use teacher-made or commercially prepared materials. Here motivation can be achieved by presenting the class with material of an unusual nature. This may include teacher-made materials such as models of geometric shapes, or specifically prepared overhead transparencies, or practical "tools" that illustrate a specific geometric principle. Some fine commercially prepared materials are available, ranging from geometric models to films of various kinds. Materials selected should be reviewed carefully and their presentation carefully planned so as to motivate students for the lesson and not to detract attention from it.

SUMMARY

Remembering a few general rules for using these eight motivational techniques will make them more effective.

1. The motivation should be brief.
2. The motivation should not be overemphasized. It should be a means to an end, not an end in itself.
3. The motivation should elicit the aim of the lesson from the class. This is a fine way of determining how effective the motivation actually is.
4. The motivation should be appropriate for the class's level of ability and interest.
5. The motivation should draw on motives actually present in the learner.

Although planning the motivation for a lesson is challenging, and at times difficult, the rewards are immeasurable. The higher degree of student learning resulting from a well-planned and well-executed activity will make this additional work worthwhile.

EXERCISES

1. How can you determine whether your motivational activity was successful?

2. For each of the following topics, prepare a motivational activity using one of the techniques presented in this chapter.
   a. The introductory lesson on area (geometry).
   b. The introductory lesson on solving factorable quadratic equations.
   c. The introductory lesson on reducing fractions (arithmetic).
   d. The introductory lesson on multiplication of signed numbers.
   e. The introductory lesson on mathematical induction.
   f. The introductory lesson on solving simultaneous equations algebraically (addition method).
   g. The introductory lesson on locus.
   h. The introductory lesson on truth tables (tautologies).
   i. The introductory lesson on parallelograms.
   j. The introductory lesson on proving trigonometric identities.

    k. The introductory lesson to bases of other than 10.
    l. The introductory lesson to the metric system.
    m. The introductory lesson on measurement.

3. Prepare a second motivational activity for each of the topics in Exercise 2.

4. Suppose you prepared a motivational activity that so captured the class interest that they did not want to leave the topic. What would you do to make this activity serve its intended purpose, that is, to excite students about the topic of the lesson? Justify your answer.

5. Select a topic in the secondary school mathematics curriculum and prepare two different motivational activities using the techniques presented in this chapter.

6. Repeat Exercise 5 using another topic from the secondary school mathematics curriculum.

7. Prepare three motivational activities for the same topic in the secondary school mathematics curriculum. After incorporating these motivational activities into the same lesson plan, teach this lesson (each of course with a different motivational activity at the beginning) to three different classes. If you cannot videotape these three lessons, have an experienced mathematics teacher observe the three classes. At the completion of this activity, analyze the three lessons with an experienced mathematics teacher and determine which of the three motivational devices worked best and why it worked best. Such factors as the appropriateness of the technique, the type of class it was used with, and the personality of the teacher using the technique should be addressed in the analysis.

8. Repeat Exercise 7. This time the teacher of the three lessons should be a volunteer, an experienced teacher of mathematics. However, the planning of the motivational devices can be done cooperatively.

REFERENCES

Brown, Lynn H. ''Motivating Students to Make Conjectures and Proofs in Secondary School Geometry.'' *Mathematics Teacher* 75 (1982): 447.

Gibson, Janice. ''Motivating the Student in the Classroom.'' *Psychology for the Classroom.* Englewood Cliffs, NJ: Prentice-Hall, 1976, chap. 6, 184–222.

Henson, Kenneth T. *Secondary Teaching Methods.* Lexington, MA: DC Heath, 1981, 165–167.

Kolesnick, Walter B. *Motivation, Understanding, and Influencing Human Behavior.* Boston: Allyn and Bacon, 1978.

LaConte, R. T. *Homework as a Learning Experience.* Washington, DC: National Education Association, 1986.

McCombs, Barbara. ''Processes and Skills Underlying Continuing Intrinsic Motivation to Learn: Toward a Definition of Motivational Skills Training Interventions.'' *Educational Psychologist* 19, no. 4 (1984) 199–218.

McEntire, Arnold, and Anita Narvarte Kitchens. ''A New Focus for Educational Improvement through Cognitive and Other Structuring of Subconscious Personal Axioms.'' *Education* 105, no. 2 (winter 1984).

Orlich, Donald C., et al. *Teaching Strategies: A Guide to Better Instruction.* Lexington, MA: D. C. Heath, 1985, chap. 6.

Sobel, M. A., and E. M. Maletsky. *Teaching Mathematics, A Sourcebook of Aids, Activities, and Strategies,* 2d ed. Englewood Cliffs, NJ: Prentice-Hall, 1988.

Stipek, Deborah J. *Motivation to Learn: From Theory to Practice.* Englewood Cliffs, NJ: Prentice-Hall, 1988.

Swireford, Edwin J. ''Ninety Suggestions on the Teaching of Mathematics in Junior High School.'' *Mathematics Teacher* 54 (1961): 145.

Weinert, Franz, and Rainer Kluwe, eds. *Metacognition, Motivation, and Understanding.* Hillsdale, NJ: Lawrence Erlbaum Associates, 1987.

Wlodkowski, Raymond J. *Motivation and Teaching: A Practice Guide.* Washington, DC: National Educational Association, 1978.

Wlodkowski, R. J. *Motivation.* Washington, DC: National Education Association, 1986.

CHAPTER 8
HOMEWORK

The regular assignment of homework for a mathematics class is accepted almost universally among mathematics teachers. Many teachers consider the homework assignment as important as, if not more important than, the classwork. Unfortunately, some teachers lose sight of the purpose for which homework is assigned. When this happens, all aspects of the homework assignment are weakened.

After a brief discussion of the purpose for which homework is assigned, we consider the many questions a new teacher is likely to have about homework assignments. Some of these questions are,

Why assign homework?
What should be involved in preparing the homework assignment?
What should be the nature of the homework assignment?
How much work should each assignment require?
Should all students be assigned the same work?
How frequently should homework be assigned?
When in the lesson should homework be assigned?
How should its assignment be made?
How should long term assignments be given?
How should the homework be arranged?
Where should the homework be written?
When should the homework be reviewed?
How should the homework assignment be reviewed?
Is there a role for collaborative homework assignments?
How much of the homework assignment should be reviewed?
How frequently should the homework assignment be reviewed?
Should homework be collected?
How should the homework assignment be collected?
What should be done with the collected homework assignments?
How should the teacher deal with students who copy homework from others?
Should quizzes be used to check if homework assignments have been mastered?

We do not pretend to provide all the answers to these questions; however, we present some possible responses with the hope that others might be generated by the reader. Our intention is to provide the reader with enough information to formulate his or her own strategies for providing classes with meaningful and effective homework assignments. Remember, there is no one correct answer to these questions. Since teaching is generally tailored to the particular personality of the teacher and the type of class being taught, so too must a homework assignment strategy be somewhat consistent with the teacher's style and the class's needs.

ASSIGNING HOMEWORK

Questions About Homework Assignments

Why Assign Homework? Many reasons exist for assigning homework regularly to a mathematics class. Perhaps the most important reason is to provide all students an active role in the learning process. Some educators think that although the classroom may provide an active learning environment, the "real learning" takes place when the student works alone at his or her own pace outside the classroom. This is not meant to minimize the importance of the classroom teaching process but to accentuate that of the assigned homework. In the classroom, the teacher generally paces the instruction for the average student, with some accommodation for the weaker and stronger students, but there still may be many students for whom the instruction was not precisely paced. For these students the classroom instruction may serve as a forum for exposure to new material, while the time spent on homework will provide the genuine learning experience.

Homework assignments provide the students an opportunity to gain a broader understanding of topics and concepts taught in class and also provide them a structure for deeper analysis of the subject matter. This is rarely possible in the classroom where the teacher is moving along at a predetermined pace. The homework assignment allows time for students to reflect on the work at their own pace, so that creative work can germinate through individual projects and independent study.

Another important reason for assigning homework is to motivate students for further learning. By being allowed to expand on what has been taught in class, students may be inspired to extend their knowledge. Occasionally a teacher may choose to foreshadow the next day's classroom lesson. By having students work on this type of carefully prepared assignment at home, where they can work alone, a real desire to move ahead in the subject area can be developed.

Perhaps one of the most common reasons for assigning homework is to provide practice in a newly developed skill. If planned properly, such drill of necessary skills can be quite effective. Unfortunately, this type of assignment is often abused. When used as punishment for some disciplinary reason, such a homework assignment not only becomes ineffective but may become counterproductive. A well-planned and effective teaching performance usually requires no special consideration of discipline. Weak teaching, however, which often promotes discipline problems, is damaged further by a punitive homework assignment given to solve these discipline problems.

The homework assignment is an integral part of the entire learning process and consequently must be handled properly. The remainder of this chapter is designed to allow the teacher to focus on the key aspects of homework assignments and then to formulate a personalized plan.

What Should be Involved in Preparing the Homework Assignment? It is helpful for both the teacher and the students to anticipate the homework assignment. The teacher, as part of the preparation of the lesson and homework assignment, should work out all the exercises being assigned to the students for homework. Not only will this be useful in more accurately determining the time required for a student to complete the assignment, but it will also enable the teacher to alert students about potential trouble spots in the homework assignment before they encounter them at home. By telling the class beforehand what is expected of them with regard to the homework assignment, the teacher makes the assignment a more meaningful part of the total learning process.

What Should be the Nature of the Homework Assignment? Many types of homework assignments are possible in a mathematics class. No one is necessarily better than another. The content of the lesson and the nature of the class should determine the type of homework. Perhaps the key thought to keep in mind when preparing a homework assignment is *variety*. Monotony is likely to be the chief factor influencing students to abandon their homework assignment.

Teachers should try to provide different kinds of exercises. For example, some of the types of exercises from which to choose would include drill exercises, verbal problems, proofs, construction exercises, thought questions, applications of newly taught principles, and reading assignments. Particularly in a mathematics class, a reading assignment needs a lot of student motivation, since a nonwritten assignment is likely to be omitted, being deemed unnecessary by the students.

In addition to varying in types of exercises offered, assignments may also vary in nature. For example, one assignment may be intended entirely for review of previously studied material, while another may include some discovery questions. Included in a review assignment may be a variety of different kinds of exercises. The assignment may simply offer exercises that review the previous lesson's work, or it may provide exercises that will assist the student to review for a test on an entire unit's work.

Another type of homework assignment may involve a discovery approach. Here the student is given a series of exercises that foreshadow the ensuing lesson. The questions are usually arranged in an order that will permit the student to discover a new idea after completing the sequence of questions. A few examples of this type of exercise follow.

EXAMPLE The homework assignment just prior to a discussion on the slope relationship between two parallel and two perpendicular lines might include the following:

1. Use the slope-intercept form of the equation of a straight line to determine the slope of each line and then use a graphics calculator to graph each pair of functions

   a. $y = 2x + 1$ and $y = -\frac{1}{2}x + 3$

   b. $y = \frac{3}{5}x + 2$ and $y = \frac{3}{5}x - 2$

   c. $y = -\frac{5}{3}x + 2$ and $y = \frac{3}{5}x + 1$

   d. $5x + 3y = 5$ and $5x + 3y = 15$

2. Which lines appear perpendicular? What is the relationship of their slopes?
3. Which lines appear parallel? What is the relationship of their slopes?
4. Make a generalized statement regarding the slopes of parallel or perpendicular lines (based on the above exercises).

This set of exercises provides review of a skill learned earlier, then requires the student to make some simple generalizations from the specifics presented.

EXAMPLE The homework assignment the day before introducing the Pythagorean identity to a trigonometry class might include the following: Use a scientific calculator to complete the following chart. Use the radical relationships when possible.

θ	Sin θ	Cos θ	Sin² θ	Cos² θ	Sin² θ + Cos² θ
30					
45					
60					
50					

What generalization seems to be true about $\sin^2 \theta + \cos^2 \theta$?

Although completing the chart ought to be relatively simple for students, it should lead them to discover an interesting relationship.

EXAMPLE The homework assignment immediately preceding the lesson that will introduce the topic of angle measurement with a circle to a geometry class might include the following set of exercises.

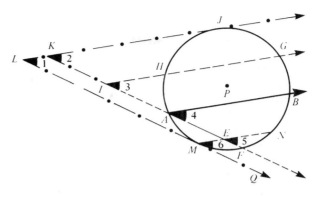

In the figure, consider all lines parallel that appear to be so. The answers to questions 2 through 8 are arcs.

1. Why are angles 1–6 congruent?

2. $m\angle BAF = \frac{1}{2} m\,\widehat{BF}$

3. $m\widehat{BN} = m\,\widehat{AM} = m\,\widehat{MF}$

4. $m\angle NMQ = m\angle BAF = \frac{1}{2}(m\widehat{BN} + m\,\widehat{NF}) =$

   $\frac{1}{2}(m\widehat{MF} + m\,\widehat{NF}) = \frac{1}{2} m\,\widehat{NM}$

5. $m\angle NEF = m\angle BAF = \frac{1}{2}(m\widehat{BN} + m\,\widehat{NF}) =$

   $\frac{1}{2}(m\widehat{AM} + m\,\widehat{NF})$

6. $m\angle GIF = m\angle BAF = \frac{1}{2} m\,\widehat{BF} =$

   $\frac{1}{2}(m\,\widehat{BF} + m\widehat{BG} - m\widehat{BG}) = \frac{1}{2}(m\,\widehat{BF}$

   $+ m\widehat{BG} - m\,\widehat{HA}) = \frac{1}{2}(m\widehat{GBF} - m\,\widehat{HA})$

7. $m\angle JKF = m\angle BAF = \frac{1}{2} m\,\widehat{BF} =$

   $\frac{1}{2}(m\,\widehat{BF} + m\widehat{JB} - m\widehat{JB}) = \frac{1}{2}(m\,\widehat{BF}$

   $+ m\widehat{JB} - m\,\widehat{JA}) = \frac{1}{2}(m\widehat{JBF} - m\,\widehat{JA})$

8. $m\angle JLM = m\angle NMQ = \frac{1}{2} m\,\widehat{NM} =$

   $\frac{1}{2}(m\,\widehat{NM} + m\widehat{JN} - m\widehat{JN}) = \frac{1}{2}(m\,\widehat{NM}$

   $+ m\widehat{JN} - m\,\widehat{JM}) = \frac{1}{2}(m\widehat{JNM} - m\,\widehat{JM})$

9. Express verbally the bold-printed relationships in Exercises 4–8.

These exercises succinctly develop all the angle measurement theorems related to the circle that are generally taught in the high school geometry class. Students are led through a series of simple questions that, because of their structure, essentially prove the sought-after relationships. Discovery here should be a natural result. We suggest interspersing discovery exercises with others, since their function satisfies only some of the purposes for assigning homework.

One of the more popular types of homework assignment is often called a *spiraled* assignment, since it spirals back over previously learned material. Perhaps it owes its popularity to its ability to satisfy two homework assignment functions. In addition to enabling students to reinforce the current classroom instruction, a spiraled assignment provides review of previously taught topics. For example, suppose you are assigning homework after a lesson on ''angle measurement with a circle'' in high school geometry. As part of this assignment, you might include one exercise reviewing similarity, one proof involving a parallelogram, and one construction. Regardless of which previous topics are selected for inclusion in a particular assignment, the selection ought to be done in an organized and orderly fashion.

One convenient method for spiraling the homework assignments is to mark dates of assignment in the margin next to the exercises in the teacher's copy of the textbook. This will assist in keeping a record of which items have or have not been assigned. The extent and degree of the spiral depends on each individual class's needs. This further reinforces the idea that lesson plans (including homework assignments) should not be used from one year to the next without making substantial adjustments for each class.

Many other types of homework assignments may be used for a mathematics class. These may include home experiments of some mathematical principle (e.g., coin tossing to compute probabilities empirically); short essays on famous mathematicians or some other vignette out of the history of mathematics (e.g., how Eratosthenes measured the circumference of the earth); library assignments (e.g., to find the origin of the $\sqrt{}$ symbol or the first use of the letter π to represent the ratio of the circumference of a circle to its diameter); and brief papers on some topics related to, but not included in, the curriculum (e.g., a paper on applications of parabolas and parabolic surfaces).

Whichever assignment a teacher chooses to use for a particular situation, the key to success is variety. Not only should the types of exercises be varied, but also the types of assignments should be dictated by the subject matter and therefore should change as needed. Although some teachers assign homework that consists of mixtures of the types of assignments described here, others exhibit no creativity in their homework assignments. Such teach-

ers' assignments simply read ''Do page 353, ex. 1–29, odd numbers only.'' It does not take long for students to react in kind to this type of homework assignment. The result is a lost opportunity to achieve meaningful learning in mathematics outside the classroom. Remember, the needs of the class determine the type of homework to be assigned.

How Much Work Should Each Assignment Require? The answer to this question must vary with each intended audience. We can answer this question only by providing guidelines for setting the proper assignment length for a particular class.

Each homework assignment will have specific objectives based on the needs of the class. The knack for preparing an appropriate assignment is to accomplish the objectives with the least amount of student work time. Unnecessary repetition should be eliminated, or at least minimized. The exercises should be carefully selected so that each one is highly effective in meeting the objectives of the particular homework assignment.

Students are quick to realize when an assignment is time-efficient and when it is loaded with superfluous material. When the exercises are largely repetitive, students can easily get bored and distracted. As a result, they may either do the work ''just to get it done,'' or they may copy the work from a classmate and submit that. Naturally this results in a waste of student time with little or no learning being accomplished. Therefore, the homework assignments should be succinct, properly covering the intended content in the minimum time.

It is difficult to specify a time limit to a mathematics homework assignment. The mathematics teacher obviously would prefer giving the class a longer homework assignment just to make sure everything is thoroughly covered. But she or he must remember that mathematics is only one of several courses each student must take. Therefore, the time allotted to mathematics homework should generally be kept to at most about one-half hour per assignment. (This is merely a guide and can vary with individual circumstances.)

Should All Students be Assigned the Same Work? Once again (and at the risk of repetition) the answer to this question depends on the type of class for which the homework assignment is intended. If the class is homogeneous with respect to student mathematical ability and achievement, then perhaps a uniform homework assignment for the entire class is appropriate. In reality, classes generally do not have this sort of uniform composition. Therefore an alternative to uniform assignments may be sought.

The best instruction is tailored to each student's individual needs. Unfortunately, it is not always practicable to satisfy such a desirable objective in the regular secondary school classroom. Perhaps one of the few ways of approaching such a goal is through the homework assignment. The homework assignment provides a useful means for adjusting class instruction to meet students' individual needs.

Special enrichment assignments can be provided for the more able students, and they can be excused from some drill or review exercises. On the other hand, students needing more drill and review of some necessary skills can be given exercises designed for this purpose. The mathematics teacher should not neglect this fine opportunity to individualize at least a part of the learning process.

How Frequently Should Homework be Assigned? Since one of the basic functions of the homework assignment is to reinforce the classroom instruction, a homework assignment should follow each classroom lesson. Naturally, some lessons may not require a follow-up homework assignment. Then either no assignment or a review assignment may be made.

Some teachers feel that no homework assignments should be given on the weekends. Others feel that homework should be assigned only four out of every five days, but the one day on which no homework is assigned should vary according to the class's instructional needs. Both of these two rather liberal plans have pitfalls. It is usually better to start a course with a stringent attitude regarding the frequency of the homework assignments, and then later make some adjustments where appropriate, than it is to begin with a ''promise'' to provide no-homework days and then have to renege on this ''promise'' when instructional considerations demand a change to more frequent homework assignments. Students will always welcome a change to a more relaxed pace rather than the reverse.

The question regarding frequency of homework assignments also can refer to the frequency with which assignments are presented to the class. Should they be given to the class on a daily, weekly, biweekly, or monthly basis? Once again, each teacher must decide which strategy (or combination of strategies) is best suited for his or her classes or teaching style. There are probably equally good arguments for many plans.

Those who favor assigning homework on a daily basis would probably argue that this is the only way in which the homework can be regularly tailored to instructional needs. Each day when a new lesson is planned (based on the experience of the previous lesson) a homework assignment is prepared based on the immediate needs of the students. Such precisely fitted assignments are far more difficult (if at all possible) to achieve when assignments are given a week at a time. For one thing, teachers who have planned a week's assignments and have given them to the students may find altering them inconvenient and may therefore not only be reluctant to make changes

based on instructional needs but also may try to pace their lessons (to a degree) to this predetermined plan. Consider the case in which a teacher finds that, midway through a week's assignments, a class needs some drill on a particular skill. The class may be resentful of a last-minute augmentation of the assignments. This negative student attitude could adversely affect the educational benefits that were intended by this additional work. Even if some previously assigned work is deleted from the assignment to accommodate the additional work, the resulting assignment may still not be as effective as if it were planned on a daily basis to meet the ongoing needs of the class. Thus, a daily planned assignment has as its chief advantage the ability to meet the regularly assessed needs of the students based on classroom experiences and previous homework performance.

Seemingly equally convincing arguments support weekly planned homework assignments. Here teachers will argue that by assigning homework a week (or more) at a time, they can better plan and spiral their homework assignments. They would also point out that by making the assignments only once every several days, they save classroom time otherwise taken up by giving out new assignments. In addition, proponents of weekly homework assignments would indicate that by having a week's assignments in their possession, students who are absent from school could without much inconvenience try to keep up with the rest of the class.

The weekly assignment also enables a student to accelerate his homework by going ahead of the class (if he is able to). This has both advantages and disadvantages. For example, if a student finds that, say on a Wednesday, he will not have time to do his homework assignment, he might complete (if capable) this assignment on Tuesday. Although this is not an ideal practice, it is better than coming in to his Thursday class unprepared. The disadvantage to knowing future assignments is that the surprise factor is gone. There is some motivational advantage to having students discover new concepts. By knowing what future assignments are planned, students also know which topics are going to be studied and when. The removal of this element of discovery could be a weakness for the instructional plan.

The question of frequency of assignments, like many others in this chapter, is one that can be answered only by the individual teacher. We present the chief arguments for the various positions and leave the choice to the reader. Whatever the choice, substantial justification should be consistent with a teacher's personality, teaching style, and educational philosophy, and with the nature of the class.

When Should Homework be Assigned? Perhaps an ideal time to give a homework assignment is at the point in the lesson that naturally leads up to the work to be assigned. For example, a teacher may say, ''Now that you know how to solve a quadratic equation, try the following for homework.'' It can be argued, however, that this approach breaks the continuity of the lesson and for this reason should be avoided.

Once again, for the teacher who elects to assign homework daily, there is probably no single ''right time'' to assign the homework. Those who argue for assigning the homework at the beginning of the lesson may say that asking students to write their assignment when they enter the room assures that they are occupied as soon as they enter and that they will not forget to write their assignment.

Others may argue that by assigning the homework at the beginning of the lesson, the teacher may reveal the topic of the ensuing lesson and thereby eliminate the effect or impact of a discovery approach. It is also possible that when an assignment is given out at the beginning of the lesson, some students may begin to work on it *during* the lesson just to ''get it over with early'' and as a result miss the new work presented during the lesson. This should certainly be discouraged.

Opponents may respond that a teacher could become so involved in the lesson that she might forget to assign the homework, or possibly give it to the students when the period-ending bell sounds and students are in the process of leaving the room. This would not give the teacher an opportunity to explain the homework assignment to the class. In addition, some students might miss receiving the assignment by exiting too quickly. At any rate, a rushed assignment is not desirable.

In response, the proponents of the end-of-lesson assignment would argue that by assigning homework at the end of the lesson, the teacher would be able to make adjustments in the originally planned assignment based on the class performance during the lesson without the class's knowing it. This way no ill feeling on the part of the class can result.

Many more arguments can be offered for the ''best time'' to assign homework. We have simply presented a sample of the options available so that the reader can make a decision. Whichever time the teacher finds best suited for both himself and the class, he must carefully review the assignment with the class. Ambiguous parts should be clearly explained and potential tough spots anticipated. This should also make students aware of the purpose of the particular homework assignment.

How Should the Assignment be Made?   This will depend on the way in which the homework is being assigned. If the homework is being assigned on a weekly basis, then the assignments ought to be written and duplicated and passed out to the class. A typical assignment sheet might include the assignment number, the topic of the lesson, the date, the actual assignment, and some of the highlights of the lesson that ought to be studied. One possible arrangement is shown in the sample Weekly Homework Assignment Sheet.

For the student, such a homework assignment sheet can also serve the function of reinforcing the objectives of the lesson. In addition, this sheet can serve as an ongoing form of communication with the parents. It will allow them to be aware of the direction of the course and where possible offer some assistance to their children. The direction of the course will also become more clearly focused for the students as a result of using these homework assignment sheets.

A small, but potentially important, benefit of using homework assignment sheets is that it avoids the possibility of students accidentally writing a wrong assignment. Such can be the case if they must copy it from the chalkboard or from teacher dictation.

Homework assignment sheets may also be used by a teacher giving out the assignments on a daily basis, in which case the sheets will probably be cut into individual assignments or run off daily. A difficulty with using any assignment sheet for daily assignments is that any adjustments in the assignment must involve the class in making the change. This procedure could have a negative effect among the students, although if handled properly, the negative effect could be minimized or even eliminated.

A popular way of giving out homework in the mathematics class is on the chalkboard. Teachers fortunate enough to have their own classroom may write the assignments for all their classes on the chalkboard, so that when each class enters the room, the students may simply copy the assignment into their notebooks. In this case it is possibly better to use the side chalkboard (if one is available) rather than the front chalkboard, reserving the front chalkboard for the regular classwork.

The teacher who assigns homework at the end of the lesson can use the chalkboard for this purpose. In this case, the front chalkboard is more desirable since it is no longer needed for classwork. The assignment is better seen at the front chalkboard and therefore less apt to be overlooked by the students.

Assignments may also be given orally, but this is usually not the most effective way. A student can miss hearing a portion of the assignment or possibly hear a part of the assignment incorrectly. The result may have negative effects on the learning process. Giving a homework assignment orally could require several repetitions and still cause confusion. When handled improperly, the oral assignment could leave students with the impression that the assignment is either optional or not too important.

Regardless of the manner in which the homework is assigned, the teacher should make every effort to be certain that there are no ambiguities. For example, if there are similarly numbered exercises at the top and bottom of a given textbook page, the location, top or bottom,

Weekly Homework Assignment Sheet

_____
(Class)

_____   _____   _____
(Assignment No.)   (Topic)   (Date)

Book / Page / Exercises
"   "   "
"   "   "

Concepts and Relationships to Remember:

_____   _____   _____
(Assignment No.)   (Topic)   (Date)

Book / Page / Exercises
"   "   "
"   "   "

Concepts and Relationships to Remember:

_____   _____   _____
(Assignment No.)   (Topic)   (Date)

Book / Page / Exercises
"   "   "
"   "   "

Concepts and Relationships to Remember:

_____   _____   _____
(Assignment No.)   (Topic)   (Date)

Book / Page / Exercises
"   "   "
"   "   "

Concepts and Relationships to Remember:

_____   _____   _____
(Assignment No.)   (Topic)   (Date)

Book / Page / Exercises
"   "   "
"   "   "

Concepts and Relationships to Remember:

should be specified in the assignment. Each assignment should be properly identified by class, date, and topic, as well as by any other relevant information. Above all, the manner in which the homework assignments are presented should be consistent with the teacher's instructional style and properly suited for the type of class. Some teachers feel that a weaker mathematics class is more apt to require homework assignments presented on sheets because they may copy their assignment incorrectly or simply forget to copy it. Thus, the type of class may well be an important consideration in selecting the best format in which to present the homework assignment.

How Should Long-term Assignments be Given?

Occasionally a long-term assignment may be appropriate for a mathematics class. A teacher may decide to assign a report on a famous mathematician, or students may be assigned a geometric construction project or a statistical experiment. For any of these long-term assignments, the manner in which the assignment is presented to the class is important.

The possibility of a long-term assignment should be announced to the class at the beginning of the course. When the teacher is ready to formally assign this project to the class, he or she must be sure to include the following:

> The extent of the work that will be required (specific topics should be listed);
> The specific guidelines for choosing a topic (if a choice is called for);
> The scope and limitations of the project;
> The format for submission of the work;
> The timetable for the assignment;
> Available resources (e.g., school, department or public library).

After a reasonable period of time, the teacher should monitor the students' progress. Those students who are floundering should be assisted and encouraged, while those students who are working in the wrong direction should be redirected. At this time the teacher may discuss with the class difficulties some students may have encountered in the process of working on the assignment, possibly helping others facing similar problems.

Midway through the project, the assignment format should be reviewed with the class. Students should be reminded about resources available (e.g., mathematics department library or school library).

To make a long-term assignment as meaningful as possible, students should be scheduled for individual conferences with the teacher to get ongoing assistance. This not only provides a necessary input for direction but also a usually much needed stimulus for further work.

Unlike the regular homework assignment, the long-term assignment requires continuous monitoring, guidance, assistance, and assessment. Unless special care is taken to prepare and assist students in these endeavors, such an assignment is likely to be ineffective.

FORMAT OF THE HOMEWORK ASSIGNMENT

Much to the amazement of the beginning teacher, students seek out direction from the teacher in almost every aspect of school work. This certainly includes direction regarding the format of the homework assignment. Two basic questions come up in this respect: How should it be arranged? and Where should it be written? Although the responses to these two questions are closely related, we discuss them separately.

Questions about Arrangement of Homework

The format of the homework, if uniform among the students, is useful to the teacher when reading individual assignments. Endless options exist for selecting a convenient format for students to follow when writing their homework. We indicate some, with the hope that this discussion will generate other, perhaps more useful, ideas for the reader. In deciding on a format to have your students follow, you ought to consider *your* work with these homework assignments as well as the students' eventual use for them.

Both Sides of Paper?   Perhaps one place to begin is by asking yourself if you find it more convenient to have students write their work on only one side of the paper or on both sides. Except for special situations (e.g., an unusual proof, problem or report to be submitted), requiring students to write on only one side of a sheet of paper is perhaps wasteful and costly. Yet some teachers may prefer to do so, and with adequate justification.

Identifying Information?   The teacher should specify what information should be written on the homework paper. In addition to the student's name, should the subject class, homework assignment number, the date, etc. be included? Should each assignment be numbered in a particular way? Whatever the teacher chooses to require should be uniform throughout the class.

Writing the Questions?   Another issue the teacher must decide is whether students should copy a homework question before answering it. Many teachers consider this a poor use of a student's time, while others feel that if students have the questions before them, the homework assignment papers become a better source from which to study.

Margins?   Any teacher who has gotten a homework assignment paper from a student who left no margins on the paper will appreciate having students leave sufficient margins for teacher comments. Students may also like to use this space to make necessary corrections after listening to a class review of the homework assignment.

Framing Answers?   Some teachers require students to frame in (with a rectangle) their answers to a question to separate them from the rest of the work. This makes the teacher's work easier when reading many papers. An extra benefit derived from this practice is that it requires students to identify the answer to a question, a skill often taken for granted but sometimes not so trivial. After working a problem, students sometimes lose sight of what exactly was being asked and, having worked the problem correctly, do not submit the proper answer.

Format of the Paper?   For some short problems in algebra or arithmetic, a teacher might want the students to fold a sheet of paper into a specific number of rectangles. This not only may result in a neater paper, but it also allows the student to get more work onto a sheet of paper. A similar effect can be obtained by ruling lines on the paper instead of folding it.

Teachers often insist on a format for working particular types of problems. For example, for solving equations it is desirable to have students line up the equal signs vertically. Students may simplify radicals by working horizontally. Special directions may be given when the homework assignment involves graphing functions or proving geometric theorems. Since both of these latter types of exercises usually require using a full page for each problem, a more efficient format would involve folding a piece of 8½″ × 11″ paper in half to form a ''booklet'' (5½″ × 8½″) of four pages, each of which can accommodate one problem (see figure at the top of the next column). This format allows a student to place four, instead of two, longer problems (such as a geometric proof or a graph of a function) on a sheet of paper. Teacher handling of the paper also should be easier.

Regardless of which format a teacher chooses to use, uniformity among the students serves two useful functions: It gives the students the direction they desire, and it makes the teacher's job of reading the papers much easier.

Where Should the Homework be Written?   Depending on the type of class involved and the subject matter being taught, a uniform arrangement should be worked out for the class. For example, for high school geometry, the teacher may require a loose-leaf or spiral notebook (8½″ × 11″) with a clip or large envelope

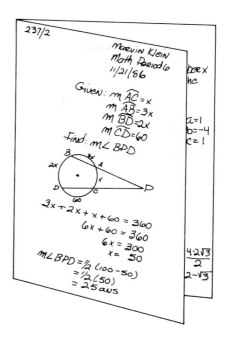

fastened to the inside back cover. This will enable the students to keep their notes and their homework in folded booklets together.

Teachers may instead ask students to keep a separate homework section in their loose-leaf notebook (of a specified size) so that after it is collected by the teacher it can be reinserted in the notebook or placed in the students' portfolio.

There are many useful ways to have students keep their homework. The exact manner should be determined by the teacher and may vary with each class, considering such things as subject matter, class discipline, student work habits, and so on.

REVIEWING THE HOMEWORK ASSIGNMENT

A teacher must answer several questions about the review of homework. The teacher must decide when and how to review the homework, whether to go over the homework with the class, and how much of it to discuss. That is, should every exercise be reviewed before the whole class or only a representative few? We discuss these questions in this section.

Questions about Reviewing Homework Assignments

When Should the Homework Assignment be Reviewed?   There is probably no ''best time'' during a lesson for discussing the previous night's homework. Some teachers feel that every lesson must begin with a review of the previous lesson's homework assignment.

They argue that new work should not be presented until the previous work (in the form of the homework assignment) has first been mastered.

Other teachers review the previous lesson's homework at the end of the lesson so as to allow the new lesson to get off to a crisp and motivating start. These teachers prefer to begin the lesson with a motivating activity leading into the development of the lesson. Only after the new topic has been completely discussed do they want to go over the past homework assignment.

A teacher certainly could adopt both systems and even include one that calls for a review of the previous homework assignment at a point in the class period at which it most naturally fits! In the case of a discovery-type homework assignment, it might be appropriate to discuss the homework just before introducing a concept or relationship that might come up in the middle of the lesson. Here the homework would be useful to elicit from students the desired mathematical relationship. When used in this way, various parts of the homework might well be reviewed at different times throughout the class period. Although this variety is nice, the final determination should be based on the individual class's needs and the appropriateness for the lesson.

How Should a Whole Class Homework Assignment be Reviewed?

Different kinds of homework exercises require different methods of review with the class. Some homework exercises can be gone over orally—for example, exercises that call for single-word (or short phrase) answers.

Using the chalkboard is one of the most popular methods of reviewing homework in a mathematics class. The chalkboard can be used in a number of different ways. The teacher may write correct solutions on the chalkboard, or students may be assigned to write particular problems from the homework on the chalkboard. One popular way to review homework at the chalkboard is to assign students to write the solution to a particular homework problem at the side chalkboard when they enter the room. It is usually better to make these chalkboard assignments as students walk in rather than when the homework is first assigned, so that, while doing their homework, students do not concentrate only on the chalkboard-assigned problem at the expense of the rest. At the appropriate time in the lesson, these students should explain their work to the rest of the class and answer any questions their classmates might have. Occasionally it may suffice simply to have the class read the chalkboard work and ask the writer questions if something is not clear. This should not be done on a regular basis unless the teacher feels sure that no student lets a problem's solution go by without question when it is still unclear to him or her. Oftentimes, some teacher questions regarding the homework exercises will help determine the extent to which students understand the work. Only in special circum-

stances, such as when there is little remaining time in a lesson, should the teacher explain the students' chalkboard work. Students may at first show reluctance at having to explain their own chalkboard work to the rest of the class, but after a while they will begin to enjoy it, taking pride in their own work. This sort of procedure goes far to promote an active learning environment for the class.

Another way of reviewing homework is to have previously selected students prepare model solutions. At some time before the mathematics class, these students make enough copies for the rest of the class. These sheets are then passed out to the class at the appropriate time in the lesson. The main advantage to this procedure is that no students are taken away from classwork at the beginning of the class period to write solutions to a part of the previous homework assignment on the chalkboard. All necessary corrections on these papers would be made when reviewing the work with the class. This procedure is costly and inconvenient, since it requires a substantial amount of extra time to make duplicates; however, it allows students to leave the class with a correct copy of the homework and with a minimum of writing when the problems are being reviewed in class.

One way of avoiding the inconvenience mentioned above, but still deriving many of the advantages this scheme has to offer, is to have the specially selected students write their work on overhead projector transparencies. Then when the teacher is ready to have the class review the previous day's homework, these specially selected students simply exhibit their work on an overhead projector. For this system, each student in the class has a supply of reusable acetate transparencies, so that when assigned specific problems from the homework for the next day's review, these students merely copy the solutions to the selected problems on the transparencies after they have completed their entire homework assignment. This method includes many of the desirable features of the other methods described and in a rather efficient manner. The only difficulty with this method is the continuous need for an overhead projector and the comparatively short time that the class sees the work flashed on the screen.

Certainly there are other methods for reviewing homework assignments that were not discussed here. We simply chose a few proven methods to give the reader some ideas. An imaginative teacher will develop numerous variations.

Small Group Homework Assignments

Part of every homework assignment should be a determination by the teacher of whether it is a small group or a whole class assignment. Review and drill assignments may best be accomplished in small groups; assignments in preparation for introductory lessons are best done in large groups.

Reviewing homework in small groups is an effective way to accomplish the goal of assigning responsibility to do homework. It becomes the group's responsibility to ensure mastery of the assignment by each member of that group. Students know that in the event someone who is unsure about a problem is selected to represent the group when it reports back to the entire class, it becomes a poor reflection on all. An advantage of this approach is subtle peer pressure to master the material adequately. In addition, explanations by one's peers in small group settings may offer insights that were overlooked in the teacher's original presentation. The teacher can clarify what may still be unclear after each group's report is presented.

This technique is also time efficient, allowing the focus of reviewing homework to be concentrated on the problem or problems of particular students. Thus, the remainder of the class is not burdened or bored with a repetition of material they may have already mastered.

The problem of copying homework for fear of being ''caught'' without it is eliminated, since homework has now become a group responsibility. Another situation reduced in significance is that of collecting and grading large numbers of individual homework assignments. Papers may still be collected, but they become the *group's* responsibility as to accuracy and completeness.

Absent pupils will also find value in the peer-directed explanations of small groups. Reviewing missed material for absent pupils in front of the entire class is unfair to the class, for it may be repetitive and not an efficient use of time. Thus, small group assignments are ideal.

How Much of the Homework Assignment Should be Reviewed?

Teacher judgment is probably the only way to determine how much of the homework assignment should be reviewed. The teacher must consider the subject matter involved, the class level and their ability to learn the particular topic, the type of students, and their achievement. If the class is a high-ability mathematics class, then perhaps only a representative sample of the homework needs to be reviewed. If the teacher can ascertain that no one in the class had any difficulty with the assignment, then perhaps no review may be necessary, although in this case the teacher might just spotcheck with some pointed questions to see if, in fact, the entire class really did have no difficulty with the homework.

On the other hand, a low-ability mathematics class could very likely require a complete review of the homework assignment, possibly in small groups. Many of the students might have missed some of the homework questions and would greatly benefit from a comprehensive review of the homework.

How Frequently Should the Homework Assignment be Reviewed?

In most cases, the homework assignment should be gone over with the class during the lesson following the assignment. Naturally, there are exceptions to this. For example, if a homework assignment has nothing to do with the succeeding lesson but does relate to a lesson a few days in the future, it might be more advisable to defer a discussion of this homework assignment until the later lesson.

The ability level (or achievement level) of a class can also be a determining factor in the frequency of a homework review. A gifted class may not require a daily review; here it might be done only on request. A teacher should be cautious about not reviewing homework daily. Students could give a teacher a false sense of security, saying they do not need to discuss the homework when, in fact, such a review might help them.

Generally, it is best to review a homework assignment immediately after it has been done by the students, for this ensures that it is still fresh in their minds and remains part of the total learning process.

CHECKING HOMEWORK ASSIGNMENTS

Once the homework has been assigned and completed according to a prescribed format, the teacher should direct a review of this work. At the same time, the teacher must grapple with the issue of collecting and checking each individual's homework. The following questions arise: Should the homework be collected? From whom? How regularly? Should it be graded? Aside from reading a student's homework, how can the teacher determine the level of student mastery of the homework? We now consider these and other questions about checking homework assignments.

Questions on Checking Homework Assignments

Should Homework be Collected? Although some teachers collect homework daily, it is quite a chore for the teacher carrying a full teaching load to read so many papers. Suppose a teacher has five classes, each consisting of thirty students. If this teacher were to collect each student's paper daily, she would have to read 750 papers per week! If she spent just one minute on each paper (far too little time to offer meaningful comments), she would be spending 12½ hours per week reading homework assignments. This is an inordinate amount of work, especially when coupled with the chores of planning lessons, preparing tests, and caring for other school-related matters. Unless a teacher is willing to devote these vast amounts of time to reading students' homework papers, it is probably better to collect fewer papers but to read them more carefully.

If the homework is important enough to assign, then it is important enough to check. Therefore, whatever homework is assigned should also be checked. Since there is a gargantuan chore involved in reading and making meaningful comments on each student's homework paper every day, it would be advisable to collect only a small portion of the class's homework daily and enter these into the students' portfolio for future reference. By reading a different sample of student homework papers each day, the teacher ought to get a reasonably good feeling for the progress of all the students in the class.

For some classes, it may not be necessary to actually collect homework papers for some topics. The teacher may walk about the room during the lesson, when students are working on a classwork problem, and quickly check some of the students' homework papers. This sort of homework reading might be possible when the assignment involves graphing some functions, which can be checked quickly by inspection.

Constructive criticism as well as complimentary remarks should be made to the students on the papers which are looked over. Remember, this process is part of the learning process.

The following discussions may appear to be somewhat punitive but should still be brought to the attention of the teacher.

How Should the Homework Assignment be Collected? Students should not be able to predict when their homework papers will be collected by the teacher. Otherwise they may avoid doing their homework on days when they feel reasonably sure their homework papers will not be collected. The teacher should set up a random selection, noting in his record book when each student's work was read.

The teacher might collect one row's homework on one day, then a diagonal the next day, then perhaps a column of students the following day. Such a system would allow the teacher to collect the homework from one particular student in need of extra help on two or three consecutive days without embarrassment before the class. This would be the student who could be made to be at the intersection of a row, column, and diagonal of students in the room. The student might just view his multiple collections as "bad luck" when, in fact, it was deliberately planned. The teacher then has the opportunity to give this student extra help with the homework.

What Should be Done with the Collected Homework Assignments? There is a wide range of choices of what might be done with collected homework assignments. One option is for a teacher to do nothing with the collected work; another is to do an in-depth evaluation of every homework paper with comments and a grade. Neither extreme is very advisable. Doing nothing with the homework collected is dishonest to the students. If homework is collected, the student expects that it will at least be looked at, and rightly so.

The other extreme is ill-advised from the point of view of the workload consideration discussed earlier. In addition, this extreme also introduces the question of grading homework papers. This is generally a bad practice to follow, since it brings a potential punitive aspect to the homework assignment. When homework papers are graded, students are likely to go out of their way to get the right answers. They may go to classmates, parents, friends, or even other teachers and have these people do the homework assignment for them. Although this sometimes has educational value (such as when students actually learn the material as a result of seeing it done correctly by others), the concern usually lies with getting the correct answer down on paper to show to the teacher rather than learning how to correctly solve the problem.

Those homework papers that have been collected should be read for completeness and accuracy. Where appropriate, detailed comments should be made and complimentary remarks should be offered for encouragement. Having read some sample homework assignments, the teacher is far better equipped to teach the class, for she will now know more precisely the weaknesses and strengths of the students. Such information can improve the learning process significantly.

There may be situations when the teacher wishes to check a class's homework in detail. He may want to determine whether a particular difficult point was properly mastered, or whether the students are preparing themselves for an upcoming examination (such as the Advanced Placement Examination given by the Educational Testing Service). Generally, however, one would not check all homework daily and in great detail, since this would be too time-consuming.

Remember, the primary value of a homework assignment is the students' work on it. The teacher checking the homework serves as motivation for the student for the next lesson. This ought to be kept clearly in mind when offering comments on the students' papers.

How Should the Teacher Deal with Students Who Copy Homework from Others? Traditionally the student who copied the homework (if this can be proved) is penalized in some manner. If desperate, the student may try again at some future date, taking a chance copying it from a classmate's work rather than be penalized for not having done the homework assignment. An effective way to deal with this problem is to "dry up the source." Penalizing the student who *gave* the homework assignment to the other student to copy will make the giver far more reluctant to repeat this incident. Thus, attacking the source may eliminate the problem of copied assignments.

Another effective way to handle this problem is to speak to both students involved. Confront them with the "evidence" and discuss the virtues of honesty. After a second occurrence, parents of the copier should be notified. A warning to the class of this plan at the beginning of the course could prevent the problem entirely.

Should Quizzes be Used to Check if Homework Assignments Have Been Mastered?

As long as a quiz is not given for primarily punitive reasons, it may be sparingly used to determine the true level of mastery of the class on a particular homework assignment. The quiz should be brief and should consist of material covered in the homework (if that is the area of concern). The questions on the quiz should be simply stated with no complications so as to avoid confusion. The extrinsic motivation presented by the expectation of a quiz could also be a useful factor in the total learning process.

SUMMARY

This discussion on homework assignments is not intended to be all-inclusive. It should serve as a guide to the various aspects of assigning homework. To keep some basic principles as a ready reference, consider the following brief review of the chapter:

1. Homework should be assigned daily, with adjustments in this routine made only after the daily pattern has been well established.
2. All homework should conform to a uniform format.
3. The homework assignment should be planned so that students do not have to work more than thirty minutes on mathematics each evening. (Occasional exceptions are acceptable.)
4. Homework assignments may be varied for a single class to meet individual student needs.
5. The homework assignment should be properly motivated, making the class aware of its purpose.
6. The homework assignment should be clear and unambiguous.
7. The content of the homework assignment should be revised as needed, based on classroom experiences, and made meaningful to the students.
8. Attempts should be made to vary the type of homework assignments.
9. Homework should never be considered as punishment.
10. Homework should be reviewed daily, using any of a variety of techniques.
11. A system should be established to select a sample of different students (daily) to submit their homework for teacher reading and comments.
12. Grading homework assignments could be counterproductive.
13. Short quizzes might be used to measure mastery of homework assignments.

EXERCISES

1. For each of the following topics write a homework assignment for an average-ability class. You may use any appropriate mathematics textbook to assist you. Try to make a provision for both ends of the ability spectrum in this class.
   a. The first lesson on the quadratic formula.
   b. The last lesson before a test on special parallelograms.
   c. The first lesson on multiplying signed numbers.
   d. The first lesson on the law of sines.
   e. A lesson on the greatest common factor (eighth grade).
   f. The first lesson on the Pythagorean theorem (high school geometry).
   g. The first lesson on metric measures (seventh grade).

2. Suppose you are teaching a mathematics class at the high school level. The principal asks the faculty to assign a short-term project to each class. Describe the project you would have your students do in each of the following courses. Then discuss how you would handle this project with the class. Include in your discussion the amount of class time you would devote to it, credit allotted, penalties for failure to do a creditable job or failure to do it at all, and uses to which student research would be put (follow-up activities).
   a. Elementary algebra.
   b. Second year algebra.
   c. Trigonometry.
   d. Geometry.
   e. Level 1 core mathematics.

    f. Senior mathematics.

    g. Advanced placement mathematics

3. React to the following student reasons for not doing homework:

    a. "I did not have time last night, since I had too much homework in my other subjects."

    b. "I work after school and do not have much time to do homework."

    c. "I have to do various housework chores and care for my younger brothers and sisters after school and have no time for my homework."

    d. "I didn't understand the homework."

    e. "I forgot to copy my homework assignment yesterday."

    f. "I lost my (1) assignment pad, (2) textbook, (3) completed homework."

    g. "I didn't do my homework."

    h. "I left my homework home."

    i. "I did the wrong assignment and threw it away this morning when a classmate told me I did the wrong work."

    j. "I forgot I had homework last night."

4. Select a unit of study in the secondary school curriculum and prepare a review homework assignment.

5. Prepare three different discovery homework assignments. You may choose any three topics from the secondary school mathematics curriculum.

6. Indicate the topics that would be useful to review through "spiraling" in a homework assignment in each of the following areas:

    a. A first lesson in factoring polynomials.

    b. A lesson on the area of a trapezoid.

    c. A lesson on the reduction formulas (the general angle) in trigonometry.

    d. A lesson on solving third- and fourth-degree equations having rational and irrational roots.

    e. An introductory lesson on irrational numbers in elementary algebra.

7. Prepare one enrichment problem for inclusion in a homework assignment on each of the following topics:

    a. Multiplication and division of monomials in elementary algebra.

    b. Operations with complex numbers in second year algebra.

    c. Proving triangles congruent in plane geometry.

8. Select any topic from secondary school mathematics and show how the homework assigned to prepare the class for a unit test differs from the homework assigned elsewhere in the unit.

9. React to the following student complaints:

    a. "You give too much homework."

    b. "The homework is too hard."

    c. "My other teachers don't give homework on weekends."

    d. "You collected my homework assignment three times this week and you didn't collect Jay's homework even once!"

    e. "I do my homework in a hardcover (bound) notebook and having to tear it out to hand it in is messing up my whole notebook!"

    f. "You didn't go over the problems in class which I didn't understand."

    g. "You don't *look* at the homework I hand in. All you do is place a check mark on it."

10. Develop a questionnaire to be administered to at least twelve mathematics teachers that asks the following questions.

    a. How frequently are students required to do homework?

    b. What type of assignments are required? What kind of questions are asked? How long are the assignments?

    c. Are assignments made on a daily, weekly, or monthly basis?

    d. How are assignments checked by the teacher or by other students?

    e. How are assignments reviewed for quality and completeness?

    f. What is the required format for these assignments?

    g. Does the respondent ever assign research projects or term papers in the mathematics class?

After you collect the completed questionnaires, analyze the responses to see if there is agreement among the respondents on any of the issues or if there is total disagreement on some of the issues raised in the questionnaire. What can you conclude from this analysis?

REFERENCES

Cangelosi, James S. *Teaching Mathematics in Secondary and Middle School,* New York: Macmillan, 1992.

Henson, Kenneth T. *Secondary Teaching Methods.* Lexington, MA: D.C. Heath, 1981, pp. 165–167.

LaConte, R. T. *Homework as a Learning Experience.* Washington, DC: National Education Association, 1986.

Swireford, Edwin J. ''Ninety Suggestions on the Teaching of Mathematics in Junior High School.'' *Mathematics Teacher* 54 (1961): 145.

CHAPTER 9
PROBLEM SOLVING

Learning to solve problems is the principal reason for studying mathematics. Problem solving is the process of applying previously acquired knowledge to new and unfamiliar situations. Solving word problems in texts is one form of problem solving, but students also should be faced with non-text problems. Problem-solving strategies involve posing questions, analyzing situations, translating results, illustrating results, drawing diagrams, and using trial and error. Students should see alternate solutions to problems; they should experience problems with more than a single solution.

We present here both routine and nonroutine problems together with their solutions. The teacher should use these with the students to help create an intellectual atmosphere that fosters curiosity, questioning, and creativity. Students must be encouraged to take risks and question what appears to be absurd. They must study problems together with their solutions from past eras but yet not allow their reasoning to become so clouded as to stifle new thinking. They will achieve the goal of mathematical power through problem solving by suggesting alternative solutions, creating a variety of techniques that include the use of calculators and computers, and even altering the problems themselves.

In its *Curriculum and Evaluation Standards for School Mathematics* (1989), the NCTM lists as its first standard for secondary school mathematics the following:

> STANDARD 1. MATHEMATICS AS PROBLEM SOLVING
> In grades 9–12, the mathematics curriculum should include refinement and extension of methods of mathematical problem solving so that all students can:
>
> • use with increasing confidence problem-solving approaches to investigate and understand mathematical content;
> • apply integrated mathematical problem-solving strategies to solve problems within and outside of mathematics;
> • recognize and formulate problems within and outside of mathematics;
> • apply the process of mathematical modeling to real-world problem situations. (p. 137)

NCTM then continues to stress that mathematical problem solving, in its broadest sense, is nearly synonymous with doing mathematics.

Before exploring problem solving in mathematics, we discuss the general topic of problem solving from a psychological standpoint.

The National Council of Supervisors of Mathematics (NCSM), in a position paper *Essential Mathematics for the 21st Century* (NCSM Newsletter, June 1988, Vol. XVII, No. 4), lists problem solving as its first component of essential mathematics:

A PSYCHOLOGICAL VIEW OF PROBLEM SOLVING

All problem solving involves some form of information (perceptual, physiological, sensory) and use of that information to reach a solution. Given the individual differences we find on a developmental level as well as the varieties of content and levels of complexity of problem situations, a single, simple approach to problem solving would be difficult to discover (let alone implement).

As far back as 1910, John Dewey, in his book *How We Think* (Boston: D.C. Heath), outlined five steps for problem solving. They were presented in the following order.

1. Recognizing that a problem exists—an awareness of a difficulty, a sense of frustration, wondering or doubt.
2. Identifying the problem—clarification and definition, including designation of the goal to be sought, as defined by the situation which poses the problem.
3. Employing previous experiences, such as relevant information, former solutions, or ideas to formulate hypotheses and problem-solving propositions.
4. Testing, successively, hypotheses or possible solutions. If necessary, the problem may be reformulated.
5. Evaluating the solutions and drawing a conclusion based on the evidence. This involves incorporating the successful solution into one's existing understanding and applying it to other instances of the same problem.

While not all problem solving will necessarily follow this order, Dewey's analysis of the thinking process in problem solving has not been improved on yet. Note that it involves both the intake or reception of information and discovery learning in an interrelated process—one in which the learner is an active participant in his own learning.

In terms of mathematics, the work of George Polya in *How To Solve It* (Princeton, N.J.: Princeton Univ. Press, 1945) presents techniques for problem solving that not only are interesting but are also meant to ensure that principles learned in mathematics will transfer as widely as possible. His techniques are called *heuristics* (serving to discover), strategies that aid in solving problems. He says that there is a "grain of discovery" in the solution of any problem. "Your problem may be modest; but if it challenges your curiosity and brings into play your inventive facilities, and if you solve it by your own means, you may experience the tension and enjoy the triumph of discovery."

He suggests the following heuristic methods.

1. Understand the problem. What is the unknown? What are the data? What is the condition? Draw a figure, introduce suitable notation. Separate the various parts of the condition.
2. Devise a plan: Find the connection between the data and the unknown. Have you seen it before? Do you know a related problem?
3. Carry out the plan. Check each step. Can you see that each step is correct? Can you prove that it is correct?
4. Look back. Examine the solution obtained. Can you check the result? Can you check the argument? Can you derive the result differently? Can you see it at a glance? Can you use the result, or method, for some other problem?

In 1974, a study revealed that teachers asked for rote responses in all but 5 percent of classrooms observed. Such teaching methods tend to promote habitual, rigid thinking. Such "set" thinking interferes with more effective problem-solving techniques.

As an example, examine this series of problems presented by Luchins and Luchins in their book, *Rigidity of Behavior* (Eugene, Oregon: Univ. of Oregon Press, 1959). Pupils were given the following chart and asked to solve each problem regarding water jars. Given three jars with listed capacities, they were asked to measure the amount of water requested in a fourth column. (Only three of the seven problems will be listed here.)

Problem Number	Jar Capacity (quarts)			Quarts Needed
	A	B	C	
1	29	3	0	20
4	18	43	10	5
7	23	49	3	20

In each of the first six cases, the largest jar is filled first and emptied into the smaller jars until the required amount is obtained. Most pupils attempt to solve the seventh problem in the same way, even when they are cautioned to "look carefully."

Polya presents many aspects of mathematical problem solving—from induction to working backward. Let us illustrate his approach with a problem similar to the one above that he presents to illustrate working backward.

1. Let us try to find an answer to the following tricky question: *How can you bring up from the river exactly six quarts of water when you have only two containers, a four-quart pail and a nine-quart pail, with which to measure?*
   [He proceeds immediately to visualize the pails with no scale markings (what is given).]

[Then] We do not know yet how to measure exactly six quarts; but could we measure something else? (If you cannot solve the proposed problem, try to solve first some related problem. Could you derive something useful from the data?) [He notes that most people, when confronted with a puzzle, work forward, trying this or that, and goes on to say:]

2. But exceptionally able people, or people who had the chance to learn in their mathematics classes something more than mere routine operations, do not spend too much time in such trials but turn around, and start working backward. [Polya notes that the Greek mathematician Pappus gave an important description of this method. See Enrichment Unit 93, "Problem Solving—A Reverse Strategy."]

What are we required to do? (What is the unknown?) Let us visualize the final solution as clearly as possible. Let us imagine that we have here before us exactly six quarts in the larger container and the smaller container is empty. (Let us start from what is required and assume what is sought as already found, says Pappus) (pp. 198–199).

Polya goes on to demonstrate the subsequent steps in solving the problem. He asks, "From what antecedent could the desired result be derived?" and notes that if the larger container were filled and exactly three quarts poured out we would achieve the result. How to do that? Well, if only one quart were left in the smaller container, then we could pour out exactly three ("let us inquire into what could be the antecedent of the antecedent"). He notes that this may be encountered accidentally, possibly seen before. Certainly by pouring four quarts from the larger container twice in succession, "we come eventually upon something already known (these are Pappus's words) and following the method of analysis, working backward, we have discovered the appropriate sequence of operations."

As the fine teacher he is, Polya uses problem-solving techniques that include both associative and insightful learning. He adds an ingredient of personal enthusiasm for his subject and a respect for the capacities of his students. One could ask little more of a teacher in any subject—that he be informed, use his information in a skillful manner in sharing with students, and provide them an opportunity to explore, analyze, and demonstrate their own skills.

PROBLEM-SOLVING PRELIMINARIES

As we begin our discussion of problem solving in the classroom, we need to consider some basic "ground rules."

Students often form a psychological set when they approach a problem. For one thing they expect numerical answers to a problem to be simple, and when something complex emerges as a possible answer, students doubt their work and try again. A student's psychological set can also manifest itself in a more dramatic way. Consider the following examples.

PROBLEM   As quickly as you can, point to each of the numbers on the chart below in consecutive order beginning with 1.*

15	13	26	34	11		23	38
	28			16	9		2
4	30	39	22		3	18	
17			36				
6	32	24	8	37	20	7	33	25	5
					29	1			
10	19	35	31	14	40	12
	21		27			

As students take on this seemingly easy challenge, they find frustration setting in very early. It is not as easy as expected to move along quickly because a psychological set develops that has students looking for each successor number to be of the same size as its predecessor. Only after students become aware of this psychological set and consciously avoid looking for numbers of the same size can they count the numbers more rapidly.

A similar syndrome is established with the following problem.

PROBLEM   Using only four straight lines, connect the nine dots below, without lifting your pencil off the paper and without retracing a line.

* This problem was contributed by Professor Brigitte Rollett of the University of Vienna (Austria).

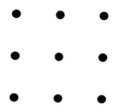

Most students will begin with one of the following attempts:

Other similar tries usually will be equally unsuccessful. To break this psychological set, students should be encouraged to *negate unsuccessful attempts.*

They see that beginning at one dot and staying within the matrix of nine dots does not work. To *negate* this is to say, "Do *not* be restricted by the matrix; instead consider a straight line that is partially *outside* the matrix." This will lead to a solution such as the one below.

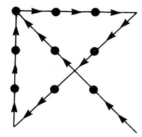

Another problem that dramatizes the problem-solving technique of negating an unsuccessful attempt follows.

PROBLEM   Given four separate pieces of chain (each three links long), show how to join these four pieces into a single circle by opening and closing *at most* three links.

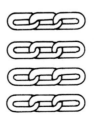 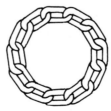

A typical first attempt is to cut an end link of each of the first three pieces. Negating this can be "do *not* cut one link in each piece," or "cut *all* links in *one* piece." This leads to a solution directly, since the three cut links can be used to join the remaining pieces of chain to form the desired circle.

Another basic tenet of problem solving is to have students list all the information given (or implied) by the problem. Consider the following problem.

PROBLEM   Given a checkerboard and 32 dominoes (each of which covers exactly two squares of the checkerboard), show how 31 of these dominoes can cover the checkerboard with a pair of opposite corner squares deleted.

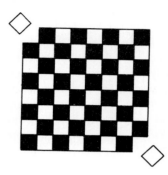

Experience shows that most students will immediately begin to start shading pairs of squares in order to establish a pattern for the solution of the problem. This will not work. Furthermore, it will result in a rather messy situation, especially if a student uses ink, rather than pencil, to do mathematics. Students should be encouraged to list all the facts they are given:

- There are 64 squares on the checkerboard.
- There are 32 dominoes, each the size of exactly two squares.
- Two white squares are deleted.
- There are only 62 squares remaining on the truncated checkerboard.
- There are 32 black and 30 white squares.
- The number of black squares is not equal to the number of white squares.
- Each domino must cover a black and a white square.

Therefore, since the number of black and white squares is not the same, it *is impossible* to cover the truncated checkerboard with the 31 dominoes as requested, and the problem *is solved.* Teachers should stress the importance of recognizing that this is now a solved problem, even though what was requested in the problem led to a disappointing solution.

An analogous situation in the history of mathematics is Leonhard Euler's solution of the famous "trisection problem." He proved that trisecting any angle with straightedge and compasses *cannot* be done. The discussion of such a solution is a worthwhile investment of time.

Perhaps the best way to prepare students to be effective problem solvers is to provide them with many examples covering a variety of problem-solving techniques. Naturally it is helpful at the beginning to classify the techniques shown, although over time it is wise to have students discover the appropriate technique (of course, not problem specific) for the solution to a particular problem, since that is an important part of the problem-solving process.

Self-awareness, especially with regard to learning habits, is helpful to the learning process. Metacognition, which refers to a knowledge (and belief) of the cognitive process, leads to an eventual control of the regulation and control of the cognitive actions.

When a problem situation is presented, the raw information must be processed and refined to an acceptable answer. The processing is usually a multistep operation, in which each step feeds off the results of the preceding one, using whatever available equipment is stored in the problem solver's arsenal of skills and knowledge. The planning step is the development of a processing schedule, designed for the specific problem being considered.

Successful conception of a good plan is the primary achievement in the problem-solving process. It is also the most difficult part of the process to teach. In his article ''Metacognitive Aspects of Problem Solving'' (in *The Nature of Intelligence,* Resnick, Lauren, Hillsdale, NJ: Erlbaum, 1976), John Flavell states that metacognition is an essential element in a student's development of a solution plan. According to Flavell, ''Metacognition refers to one's own cognitive processes or anything related to them. It refers not only to one's awareness of cognitive processes but also to the self-monitoring, regulation, evaluation, and direction of cognitive activity.''

These metacognitive activities involve making connections between the problem statement, broken down into its intelligible parts, and the students' previous knowledge and experiences. This process continues until the problem can be classified into some already familiar group ready for solution. The ability to classify and to have groups of problem types available is crucial to the process. Sometimes this may require breaking down a problem into smaller parts that are simpler to classify. Monitoring this process by the problem solver is essential. This self-awareness produces *control* of the processing.

The key to successful problem solving is to be in *control* of the process. It is perfectly normal, moreover even desirable, to ''talk to yourself'' (subvocally) when working on a mathematics problem. This is a way of trying to control the problem-solving process. To be in control is to have a mastery of the necessary heuristics and then to select and pursue the correct approach for the solution. By ''talking to yourself,'' you are monitoring the problem-solving process, which is key to enabling control.

There are a number of possible control decisions that ought to be considered:

- **Thoughtless decisions** move the process in scattered directions and do not build on any previous experiences or knowledge.
- **Impatient decisions** either stop the process entirely or keep the problem solver moving directionless in quest of a solution, without even seeing a path to a conclusion, either successful or unsuccessful.
- **Constructive decisions** involve carefully monitoring control while employing knowledge and skills in a meaningful way, using proper solution paths and abandoning unsuccessful ones.
- **Immediate procedure decisions** require no control since they simply access the appropriate solution path stored in long-term memory.
- **Nondecision** results when the statement of the problem is so perplexing that no knowledge or prior experience is helpful in the solution and the problem solver gives up.

An awareness of the problem-solving process is the first step for attaining control. This control enables the learner to find a proper solution path.

PROBLEM SOLVING IN MATHEMATICS

A mathematical problem may be described as ''challenging'' if its solution requires creativity, insight, original thinking, or imagination. To each person, some problems are found to be considerably more challenging than others. In fact, what may be challenging for one person may be quite routine to another. Thus, consider this problem:

> **PROBLEM** If it takes Big Ben 5 seconds to strike 6 o'clock, how many seconds will it take to strike 12 o'clock?

If you present this problem to a group of people you will undoubtedly find that some will ''see'' the answer immediately, while many others will ''struggle'' for a while before arriving at a solution, if they ever do. (Ten seconds is NOT the correct answer.*)

On the other hand, the problem:

> **PROBLEM** If 5 is subtracted from three times a number the result is 8. Find the number.

may be a bit challenging to the uninitiated student in first year algebra, but is trivial to anyone versed in even the most elementary aspects of the subject.

Another facet of problem solving is that the challenge that may be inherent in solving a problem may not be

---

* Since it takes 5 seconds for 6 strikes, 5 seconds are required for 5 intervals (assuming no time for a strike). Therefore each interval between strikes is one second. Thus, at 12 o'clock there are 11 intervals for the 12 strikes, which require a total of 11 seconds to be completed.

apparent at the outset. The following problem appears to be harmless enough, but turns out to be one of the most complex in elementary Euclidean geometry! It is called a "classic" problem and is often named "The Internal Bisectors Problem." It has been discussed in *Scientific American*'s "Mathematical Games" section. To see how difficult this problem is, try it! The problem may be stated as follows:

PROBLEM

Given: $\overline{AE}$ bisects $\angle BAC$
$\overline{BD}$ bisects $\angle ABC$
$\overline{AE} \cong \overline{BD}$
Prove: $\triangle ABC$ is isosceles

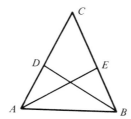

SOLUTION
Here's one solution
of this problem:

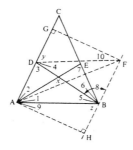

$\overline{AE}$ and $\overline{BD}$ are angle bisectors, and $AE = BD$. Draw $\angle DBF \cong \angle AEB$ so that $\overline{BF} \cong \overline{BE}$; draw $\overline{DF}$. Also draw $\overline{FG} \perp \overline{AC}$, and $\overline{AH} \perp \overline{FH}$. By hypothesis, $\overline{AE} \cong \overline{DB}$, $\overline{FB} \cong \overline{EB}$, and $\angle 8 \cong \angle 7$. Therefore $\triangle AEB \cong \triangle DBF$, $DF = AB$, and $m\angle 1 = m\angle 4$.

$m\angle x = m\angle 2 + m\angle 3$

$m\angle x = m\angle 1 + m\angle 3$

$m\angle x = m\angle 4 + m\angle 3$

$m\angle x = m\angle 7 + m\angle 6$

$m\angle x = m\angle 7 + m\angle 5$

$m\angle x = m\angle 8 + m\angle 5$

Therefore, $m\angle 4 + m\angle 3 = m\angle 8 + m\angle 5$
Thus, $m\angle z = m\angle y$,
Right $\triangle FDG \cong$ right $\triangle ABH$, $DG = BH$, and $FG = AH$.
Right $\triangle AFG \cong$ right $\triangle FAH$, and $AG = FH$.
Therefore, $GFHA$ is a parallelogram.

$m\angle 9 = m\angle 10$ (from $\triangle ABH$ and $\triangle FDG$)

$m\angle DAB = m\angle DFB$

$m\angle DFB = m\angle EBA$ (from $\triangle DBF$ and $\triangle AEB$)

Therefore, $m\angle DAB = m\angle EBA$, and $\triangle ABC$ is isosceles.

Textbook problems, especially algebraic ones, are normally routine and repetitive. Their greatest challenge of-

ten lies in the attempt to unravel the wording of the problem so that it may be made to fit a predetermined "mold" that will then lead to the solution.

Here is a typical digit-problem like so many hundreds of others found in algebra textbooks.

PROBLEM The sum of the digits of a two-digit number is 7. If 9 is added to the number, the result is a number with the digits of the original number reversed. Find the original number.

The predetermined mold is *always* to begin a digit problem this way.

Let $t =$ tens' digit

$u =$ units' digit

$10t + u =$ original number

$10u + t =$ original number reversed

This is followed by the appropriate pair of simultaneous equations to solve the problem.

Another standard type is this uniform-motion ("upstream-downstream") problem.

PROBLEM A boat travels 16 miles downstream in 2 hours. It then travels the same distance upstream in 8 hours. What is the rate of the boat in still water, and what is the rate of the current?

Another favored type of predetermined mold is this table, which is set up to help solve uniform-motion problems:

Let $x =$ rate of current

$y =$ rate in still water

	RATE	$\times$ TIME	$=$ DISTANCE
Upstream	$y - x$	8	16
Downstream	$y + x$	2	16

This is followed by the appropriate pair of simultaneous equations to solve the problem.

These problems are so typical of all others of the same type that if a pupil studies the solution of only one or two of them she should be able to devise a similar solution for all of them. The challenge (if any) exists only in the formulation of the solution to the first problem of the type with which the student is confronted. One mark of a good textbook is that it offers a reasonable number of "nonroutine" problems in addition to the standard ones.

Next, we discuss why problem solving should be taught and offer some guidelines for teaching problem solving. We also show how mathematics problems may be created by pupils. Finally, we present some "nonroutine" problems that, over the years, have been shown to possess sufficient challenge and interest to be worthy of being called "classics." Their solution usually carries a useful message about problem solving.

Why Teach Problem Solving?

Students need to know how to solve problems for the future—whether in mathematics or in life applications. There are other useful byproducts to learning problem solving.

Students Will Learn to Read Mathematics. In order for students to handle problems effectively, they must be taught how to read mathematics well. They must learn that even a single phrase or sentence may contain a great deal of significant information. Even a student who may be a rapid reader in other areas should read mathematics slowly. Specifically, the student must read the problem slowly, pausing at commas or at the end of an idea. The student must reflect on what has been read, must determine what it means, and must reread and reexamine the problem as often as necessary. Skimming has little value in reading a mathematics problem. Many teachers and textbook authors agree that standard textbook problems may be less than challenging. They rarely lead to discovery of new generalizations or unusual insights, due to their repetitive nature. However, when standard type problems are organized heterogeneously rather than by type, and when they are treated as a collection of random word puzzles, students will be eager to solve them by any means possible—arithmetic, algebra, geometry, intuition, calculator, or computer. With this open-ended approach, "solutions" may come via many routes. An acceptable "solution" to a mathematical problem may be a single number, an alternative problem, a challenging question, an intelligently presented opinion, or some variation of these.

Students Will Develop a Sense of Pride. They will be enthusiastic, seeing how their skills have grown and developed over the years of mathematical training.

Situations often arise in which students face the same problems in their later secondary school years as in their earlier ones. The approaches used in solutions should prove enlightening to both pupil and teacher and serve as an indicator of the student's growth and increased mathematical maturity over the period of years they spend in secondary school. Students will also recognize that as their knowledge of mathematics expands, so does their ability to devise problem-solving strategies.

To better understand this point, consider the following examples.

PROBLEM Find the number of diagonals in a convex polygon of *n* sides.

The advanced eleventh or twelfth grade secondary student might determine the number of diago-

nals, *d*, the following way:

SOLUTION

$$d = {}_nC_2 - n \quad \text{or} \quad \binom{n}{2} - n$$

$$= \frac{n!}{2!\,(n-2)!} - n$$

$$= \frac{n(n-1)}{2} - n$$

$$= \frac{n^2 - 3n}{2}$$

$$= \frac{n(n-3)}{2}$$

However, the geometry student, usually a tenth grader, might use a diagram and might realize that $n - 3$ diagonals can be drawn from each of the *n* vertices. Since each diagonal passes through two vertices, the number of diagonals is $\frac{n(n-3)}{2}$.

The arithmetic or algebra student, at eighth or ninth grade level, might first prepare the table of values

n	3	4	5	6	$\cdots$
d	0	2	5	9	$\cdots$

She would then spend some time "guessing" a formula relationship between *n* and *d* until she "struck" on $d = \frac{n(n-3)}{2}$ or some variation thereof. A proof of the formula might not be her major concern at this point but she would "feel" sure that was correct!

A second situation in which students can appreciate how their increased knowledge has improved their problem-solving skills is when they are asked to do the following problem.

PROBLEM Show that $\sin(x + y) = \sin x \cos y + \cos x \sin y$, for appropriate *x, y,* and $x + y$.

Students with some knowledge of elementary trigonometry will appreciate this solution for acute angles *x, y,* and $x + y$. (An outline of the derivation is shown.)

SOLUTION

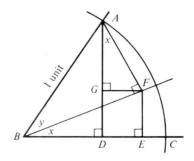

B is the center of a circle with radii $\overline{AB}$ and $\overline{BC}$.

I

In $\triangle ABD$

$$\sin(x + y) = EF + AG$$

II

In $\triangle AGF$
  m∠*GAF* = *x*
  AG = (cos *x*) (*AF*)

In $\triangle BAF$
  AF = sin *y*
  AG = (cos *x*)(sin *y*)

III

In $\triangle BFE$
  EF = (sin *x*) (*BF*)

In $\triangle ABF$
  BF = cos *y*
  EF = (sin *x*)(cos *y*)

Incorporating the results of Part II and Part III into Part I, we get the required formula.

By eleventh or twelfth grade, the same formula can be derived for *x, y,* and *x* + *y* in any quadrant (i.e., any size, as opposed to the restriction of an acute angle of the earlier derivation) by using the law of cosines, and identities for functions of negative angles. (This derivation is lengthy, but may be found in any trigonometry textbook.)

In a twelfth grade mathematics class the Euler relationship

$$e^{i\theta} = \cos \theta + i \sin \theta$$

may be used to derive the same formula in this manner:

For any *x, y:*

$$e^{ix} = \cos x + i \sin x$$

$$e^{iy} = \cos y + i \sin y$$

(I) $e^{i(x+y)} = \cos (x + y) + i \sin (x + y)$

But also

$e^{i(x+y)} = e^{ix}e^{iy}$

(II) $= (\cos x + i \sin x)(\cos y + i \sin y)$

  $= (\cos x \cos y - \sin x \sin y)$

   $+ i(\sin x \cos y + \cos x \sin y)$

Comparing the real and imaginary parts of (I) and (II), we get two formulas, one of which is

$$\sin (x + y) = \sin x \cos y + \cos x \sin y$$

Thus, we see that if the same set of problems were presented to a freshman class and to an advanced mathematics senior class, the solutions suggested by the more mathematically mature group might readily reflect their additional knowledge, training, and experience. At least, the teacher could direct the lesson so that this would be the likely outcome.

This problem demonstrates how the content of the core curriculum of the *Standards* can be differentiated according to students' varying abilities and levels of interest. The teacher will begin at the elementary trigonometry level before reaching the higher levels of abstraction shown in the problem.

Students Will Learn to be Critical of and Analytical with the Problems Presented to Them.   Problems "with a twist" may be made to contain either insufficient or excessive information or may be made to have no solution at all. Students should always be alerted to anticipate these possibilities.

Consider these three problems "with a twist."

1. The sum of 3 consecutive even integers is 26. What are the integers?
2. Find the area of a right triangle whose sides are 8, 15, and 17.
3. Two trains start from the same point at the same time. The first train travels 60 mph and the second, 80 mph. In how many hours will they be 500 miles apart?

Each of these problems has something "wrong" with it. After students attempt to solve them, they should be analyzed for their specific pitfalls. This will inevitably lead to productive discussions and generalizations should significantly improve the students' problem-solving skills by alerting them to be more critical. Thus, in problem 1, the attempted solution might produce:

For *x* = first even integer

x + 2 = second consecutive even integer

x + 4 = third consecutive even integer

Then 3*x* + 6 = 26

3*x* = 20

$$x = 6\frac{2}{3}$$

x turns out to be nonintegral, which is impossible.

An analysis and discussion would lead to the conclusion that the sum of three consecutive even integers must always be divisible by 3.

Problem 2 has a superfluous term, "right," since an 8-15-17 triangle is automatically right by virtue of the converse of the Pythagorean theorem. However, further investigation by the class might lead to the possibility of encountering a similar problem type in which the sides have dimensions 8, 15, and 18, for example (a non-right triangle). Under proper guidance by the teacher, this could lead to a derivation of the general area formula of a triangle in terms of the lengths of the three given sides, *a, b, c* (this is known as Heron's formula).

$$\text{Area} = \sqrt{s(s - a)(s - b)(s - c)}$$

$$\text{for } s = \frac{1}{2}(a + b + c)$$

Problem 3 contains insufficient data. There is no indication of the paths taken by the trains. Thus, if the two trains travel in opposite directions, we get

For x = number of hours the trains travel

60x miles   80x miles

500 miles

$$60x + 80x = 500$$

However, if the trains travel at right angles to each other, we conclude that

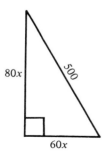

so that $100x = 500$ (Pythagorean theorem). The paths of the trains may in fact make any other angle with each other, in which case the law of cosines would be needed to obtain a solution.

It therefore seems to be clear that problems that have "something wrong" with them may lead to challenging situations with fruitful results. A skilled teacher can use this technique to develop exciting mathematics.

Non-college-bound Students Will Learn to Solve Problems. Simple games of strategy are uniquely suited to develop problem-solving skills among general students. Most students are familiar with and enjoy participating in games of all types. They have been exposed to them regularly from early childhood. They know that there are rules to be followed, that there is usually a winner, and they know, furthermore, that if they develop a proper strategy for a particular game they could become a consistent winner. Checkers, chess, tic-tac-toe, backgammon, and electronic games are some of the more

obvious ones. Although mathematics students do not always have the verbal ability to deal with word problems, they can nevertheless learn subconsciously how to develop winning strategies. These turn out to be similar to the strategies needed to solve verbal problems:

ANALOGY	
GAME STRATEGY	**PROBLEM STRATEGY**
1. Read the rules.	1. Read the problem.
2. Understand the rules.	2. What is given and what are you looking for?
3. Develop a plan.	3. Write an equation.
4. Carry out the plan.	4. Solve the equation.
5. If you win, smile. Otherwise, figure out why you lost.	5. Check your answer.

Games alone might not be sufficient to develop the problem-solving skills of mathematics students. In fact, many students may not be interested in "playing" games of strategy at all. Other activities that could develop analytical and critical skills in such students at their level might include the following:

1. Ask the students, in a motivating manner (and that is possible!) to state the characteristics of objects. For example: How long is a line? Say everything you can about a cube. Will a three-legged stool ever wobble?
2. Have the pupils list (in a challenging way) similarities and differences between squares, and rectangles, circles and spheres, points, and lines.

While some mathematics students have difficulty functioning at the level of problem solving that college oriented students can handle with relative ease, exposure to the ideas just mentioned will prove beneficial to all and can improve facility with many of the skills involved in problem solving.

STRATEGIES FOR SOLVING PROBLEMS

Planning to Solve a Problem

The number of strategies that can be developed to solve problems are probably as many and varied as the problems themselves. Some of the more common strategies are listed:

1. Making a picture
2. Working backward
3. Guessing and testing
4. Finding a pattern
5. Making a table
6. Collecting data

7. Using a computer or calculator
8. Using deductive reasoning
9. Solving a simpler analogous problem
10. Approximating
11. Determining necessary and sufficient conditions
12. Determining characteristics of objects

We now pose some problems together with sample suggested strategies for their solution. The reader may find other and better strategies and should indeed be encouraged to do so.

Making a Picture. Pictures, or diagrams, are a "must" in most geometric problems, but they are also useful in motion problems, mixture problems, and many others that have no "type" classification. Here is an example of a well-known problem, which clearly demonstrates why "a picture is worth a thousand words."

> **PROBLEM** A frog is at the bottom of a 10-foot well. Each day it crawls up 3 feet and at night it slips back 2 feet. In how many days will the frog get out of the well?

> **SOLUTION** Make the following picture of a well and mark the position of the frog at the end of each day, and again at the end of each night. The frog will reach the top of the well on the eighth day, at which time it escapes and does not fall back.

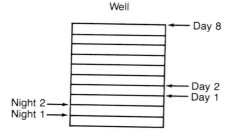

Well

Day 8

Day 2
Day 1

Night 2
Night 1

Working Backward.* Many proofs in geometry can be written by first assuming the conclusion and then determining which step must have preceded the last. Use the same reasoning for the penultimate step. Continue in this manner until the proof begins to unravel. One illustration of the application of this technique in a nongeometric setting is after a student has learned to solve a quadratic equation by factoring.

> **PROBLEM** Write a quadratic equation whose roots are 2 and -3.

> **SOLUTION** Proceed in reverse order as follows:

Roots: $x = 2$ and $x = -3$

_____
* See "The Analytic Method" (page 121).

Previous line must have been: $x - 2 = 0$ and $x + 3 = 0$

Previous line must have been: $(x - 2)(x + 3) = 0$

The answer must therefore be: $x^2 + x - 6 = 0$

Finding a Pattern. Finding a pattern among a sequence of numbers may be quite challenging. No single rule can be applied to all cases.

We present several sequences of six numbers and in each case "discover" a pattern among them that will then yield the next three numbers in the sequence. Patterns in sequences are often not unique. It is highly recommended that students make up their own sequences of six numbers and suggest different patterns that might be used to generate the next three terms.

> **PROBLEM** Find the next three terms in the sequence 2, 4, 6, 8, 10, 12.

> **SOLUTION** The pattern is

$$2 + 2 = 4$$
$$4 + 2 = 6$$
$$6 + 2 = 8$$
$$. . . . .$$

So that the answer is

$$12 + 2 = 14$$
$$14 + 2 = 16$$
$$16 + 2 = 18$$

> **PROBLEM** Find the next three terms in the sequence 3, 6, 12, 24, 48, 96.

> **SOLUTION** The pattern is

$$3(2) = 6$$
$$6(2) = 12$$
$$12(2) = 24$$
$$. . . . .$$

So that the answer is

$$96(2) = 192$$
$$192(2) = 384$$
$$384(2) = 768$$

> **PROBLEM** Find the next three terms in the sequence 3, 7, 15, 31, 63, 127.

SOLUTION   The pattern is

$$2(3) + 1 = 7$$

$$2(7) + 1 = 15$$

$$2(15) + 1 = 31$$

· · · · · · ·

So that the answer is

$$2(127) + 1 = 255$$

$$2(255) + 1 = 511$$

$$2(511) + 1 = 1023$$

PROBLEM   Find the next three terms in the sequence 2, 4, 8, 24, 72, 144, 288.

SOLUTION   The pattern is

$$2(2) = 4$$

$$2(4) = 8$$

$$3(8) = 24$$

$$3(24) = 72$$

$$2(72) = 144$$

$$2(144) = 288$$

So that the answer is

$$3(288) = 864$$

$$3(864) = 2592$$

$$2(2592) = 5184$$

PROBLEM   Find the next number in the sequence: 2, 4, 8, 16, 31, __, (there is no misprint here; the last given number *is* 31).

SOLUTION   Set up a table of successive differences:

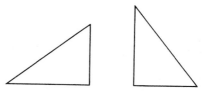

This is no accident. If you consider the maximum number of regions formed by drawing straight lines through given points on a circle, you will notice the following pattern.

NUMBER OF POINTS ON A CIRCLE	NUMBER OF REGIONS FORMED
2	2
3	4
4	8
5	16
6	31
7	57

Determining Characteristics of Objects.   Activities requiring seventh or eighth grade students to create geometric shapes enable them to understand the properties of polygons.

PROBLEM   Here are two triangles:

How many figures can be formed by arranging these triangles in different ways? Do these figures share any common properties, such as shape, area, perimeter, number of vertices, and number of sides?

SOLUTION

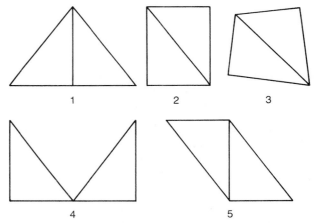

Organizing Data.   While it is often desirable to approximate answers, there are occasions when exact answers are required. We present some strategies for organizing data that may be used when exact sums are requested.

PROBLEM   A $20.00 bill may not go very far in a variety store where you may see items with the following prices:

A: $ 0.38

B: $ 8.57

C: $ 3.00

D: $ 0.62

E: $11.43

F: $ 8.64

G: $16.00

H: $ 8.05

I: $18.68

J: $15.33

K: $ 7.95

L: $ 1.32

What combinations of items would cost exactly $20.00? Assume no tax is added.

SOLUTION   The strategy to solve this type of problem is to discover the proper combination of items. For example, first try to combine items whose units digits add up to 10. However, you must also try to find combinations of cents that have a sum of $1.00. Several correct answers are:

1. B, E

2. A, B, C, H

3. A, C, D, G

4. A, C, D, H, K

Using Computers to Solve Problems.   Computers may often be used as tools to assist pupils in solving problems whose solutions might be suggested by the results of time-consuming calculations. These calculations would be of a repetitive nature, which is perfect for computer solution.

PROBLEM   A rectangular piece of cardboard measures 36 inches × 44 inches. Suppose a box is to be made by cutting equal-size squares from each corner and folding up the sides (see the figure). What is the maximum volume of the boxes formed when

a. 1-inch squares are cut out?

b. 2-inch squares are cut out?

c. 3-inch squares are cut out?

.

.

.

q. 17-inch squares are cut out?

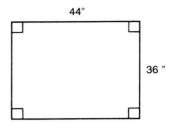

SOLUTION   RUN this program to compute the dimensions corresponding to the 17 volumes.

```
10 PRINT "HEIGHT", "VOLUME"

20 for H = 1 to 17

30 LET L = 44 − 2 * H

40 LET W = 36 − 2 * H

50 LET V = L * W * H

60 PRINT H, V

70 NEXT H

80 END
```

Next, study the following data to determine the box of largest volume.

Height	Volume
1	1428
2	1560
3	3420
4	4032
5	4420
6	4608
7	4620
8	4480
9	4212
10	3840
11	3388
12	2880
13	2340
14	1792
15	1260
16	768
17	340

Trial and Error.   No matter how clever your strategy for solving a problem, you may still have to resort to a "trial and error" scheme as part of a solution. This can at times be quite subtle.

PROBLEM   Find the replacement numerals that will make this addition correct:

$$\begin{array}{r} XY \\ \underline{YZ} \\ YZY \end{array}$$

SOLUTION   We begin with an inspection of the unit's digit addition. Which number when added to Y will leave it unchanged? Only zero has this property! Therefore, $Z = 0$. We have the following so far:

$$\begin{array}{r} XY \\ \underline{Y0} \\ Y0Y \end{array}$$

We must now find numbers whose sum is a number with a unit's digit of 0. Since the sum of two single-digit numbers cannot be 20, the sum we seek for $X + Y$ must be 10. Let us "try" some of the possible combinations:

$$5 + 5$$
$$4 + 6$$
$$3 + 7$$
$$2 + 8$$
$$1 + 9$$

Each trial will give us a different value for Y. However, Y must be 1 (in the sum); therefore, $X = 9$. The correct addition problem is

$$\begin{array}{r} 91 \\ \underline{10} \\ 101 \end{array}$$

STANDARD ALGEBRAIC PROBLEMS

Before students can be expected to develop facility in solving verbal problems algebraically, they must have considerable practice expressing English phrases and sentences in terms of their algebraic counterparts. (Newton compared the setting up of an equation in problem solving to "translating" from one language to another, and in fact we now use the word "translate" to direct pupils to rewrite the English "longhand" into its equivalent algebraic "shorthand.")

While many students find problem solving painful no matter how much assistance they get from the teacher, a set of strategies developed over the course of time can ease the "pain" of problem solving. For the simpler problems, one strategy is to start by selecting key phrases and sentences, determining the variables and algebraic expressions that would represent them, and finally formulating a relationship of equality that would make an equation (called the "key" equation) emerge. The solution to this "key" equation should yield a solution to the problem.

In more complicated problems, the teacher may resort to charts, diagrams, and tables. Estimates, guesses, demonstrations, and models all have a value in helping students see the problem more clearly. Underlying all these schemes is a relationship formula that will ultimately be used in the formulation of the key equation. It may be helpful for students to know that even with the large variety of standard-type problems such as uniform motion, investment, coin, mixture, and others, there is a unifying form for each formula:

$$A \times B = C$$

Thus,

for motion problems:
RATE $\times$ TIME = DISTANCE

for investment problems:
PRINCIPAL $\times$ RATE = INTEREST

for coin problems:
NUMBER OF COINS $\times$ VALUE OF EACH COIN = TOTAL VALUE

for mixture problems:
NUMBER OF POUNDS $\times$ PRICE PER POUND = TOTAL COST

Whatever the strategy used, whether selecting key phrases, drawing boxes, diagrams, or any other aid, the pupil should use the appropriate formula as a guide to setting up the key equation. Key equations can occasionally be elusive, however, for certain useful facts in verbal problems are sometimes obscure or implied and not explicitly stated. In many situations "subtle" equalities that are not explicitly stated lead to the key equation. For example, consider the following from a typical uniform-motion problem.

PROBLEM   If two trains start from the same station, one earlier and the other later, and travel in the same direction along parallel tracks, so that the faster (second) train overtakes the slower train, then. . . .

The students should be led to realize that the key equation will emerge from the implied fact that the distances that the two trains travel are equal at the instant the second train overtakes the first.

A similar situation exists in the following mixture problem.

PROBLEM   How many liters of water must be added to 8 liters of pure alcohol to make a mixture containing 35% alcohol?

Here the point that needs to be highlighted is that adding water to pure alcohol does not change the *amount* of alcohol. Therefore, the key equation can be obtained from this equality of the amount of alcohol before and after the mixture with water.

We now demonstrate some specific methods of solving verbal problems, using techniques discussed above.

PROBLEM Part of $10,000 is invested at 12% per year and the remainder at 8% per year. The total income from both investments is $920.00 per year. Find the amount invested at each rate.

SOLUTION 1 (Selecting and translating key phrases)

Let x = number of dollars invested at 12%
(*This comes from the phrase, "Part of the $10,000 is invested at 12%."*)

$10,000 - x$ = the number of dollars invested at 8%
(*This comes from the phrase, "The remainder is invested at 8%."*)

$0.12x$ = amount of yearly income from the 12% investment
$0.08(10,000 - x)$ = amount of yearly income from the 8% investment
(*These came from the formula PRINCIPAL × RATE = INTEREST.*)

Sentence leading to the key equation:

The total income from both investments is
$920.00 per year.

Key equation:

$$0.12x + 0.08(10,000 - x) = 920$$

SOLUTION 2 (Using a table or boxes)

	PRINCIPAL	× RATE	= INTEREST*
FIRST Investment	x	0.12	$0.12x$
SECOND Investment	$10,000 - x$	0.08	$0.08(10,000 - x)$

* (Income from each investment)

The key equation is usually obtained from the column whose boxes are filled in by multiplication (or, in some cases, division). Here the key equation (obtained from the third column) is

$$0.12x + 0.08(10,000 - x) = 920$$

The value of x would then be found and checked in the *statement* of the problem. The solution may be written

and labeled as

Answer: $3000 was invested at 12%

$7000 was invested at 8%

PROBLEM Yolanda has $1.35 in nickels and dimes. She has a total of 15 coins. How many of each kind of coin are there?

SOLUTION 1 Most students can guess the answer to this question with little difficulty before ever attempting to use a formal approach. They should be encouraged to do so where possible; as every mathematician knows, intelligent guessing is a skill worth developing (provided teacher guidance is used at the outset, since students generally need instruction in guessing).

SOLUTION 2 (Selecting and translating phrases and sentences)

Let y = number of dimes

$15 - y$ = number of nickels

$0.10y$ = total value of dimes

$0.05(15 - y)$ = total value of nickels

Total value of all coins is $1.35.

Therefore, the key equation is

$$0.10y + 0.05(15 - y) = 1.35$$

SOLUTION 3 (Using a table or boxes)

	NUMBER OF COINS	× VALUE OF EACH COIN	= TOTAL VALUE
DIMES	y	0.10	$0.10y$
NICKELS	$15 - y$	0.05	$0.05(15 - y)$

The key equation is usually obtained from the column whose boxes are filled in by multiplication (or, in some cases, division). Here the key equation is

$$0.10y + 0.05(15 - y) = 1.35$$

SOLUTION 4 This method of solution would be similar to 2 but would involve using two variables and then solving the resulting simultaneous equations.

Answer: There are 12 dimes and 3 nickels.
(*Note:* The answer should be checked in the *statement* of the problem.)

As a general rule, we suggest that students be trained to take the following steps in the solution of verbal problems.

1. Read the problem carefully. If you are able to restate it in your own words, no matter how simply, you are well on your way toward understanding the problem.
2. Determine the formula (if any) for the type of problem under consideration.
3. If possible, estimate your answer and jot it down somewhere on your paper. If the solution to your key equation is not reasonably similar to your estimate, check your work.
4. Select a variable that can be used, such as, "Let $x = \ldots$" and express key phrases in terms of that variable.
5. Determine the subtle or explicit statement and write the key equation.
6. Solve the key equation.
7. Label answers correctly, in terms of the units stated in the problem.
8. Reread the problem and see if your answer makes sense. This is called, "checking your answer."

A word of advice to the teacher: *Do not do* the problem for your students. Once you have given them initial guidelines in solving problems, the most you ought to do is provide hints, clues, or leading questions. And remind students that "neatness counts." Neat work can be helpful in developing a solution to a given problem, while sloppy work can be a hindrance.

STANDARD GEOMETRIC PROBLEMS

Problems in geometry usually include:

Proving theorems synthetically (using methods of Euclidean geometry);
Solving construction exercises with compasses and straightedge;
Proving geometric theorems using algebra, arithmetic, coordinate geometry, or vectors;
Determining the measure of some part of a given geometric figure.

One aspect of geometric problem solving that is different from algebraic problem solving is that each problem requiring a proof, *with few exceptions*, is an "original" in the sense that there are no types one can follow to

virtually guarantee a solution every time as in algebra. This is not to say that there are no similar approaches among such geometric proofs.

We offer three general suggestions to be considered in the process of proving theorems in geometry:

1. *Analyze the hypothesis.* Draw a neat, relatively accurate diagram and mark it, indicating segments, angles, etc. that are known to be congruent. Mark all parallel lines. A well-drawn figure frequently suggests a productive line of reasoning.
2. *Analyze the conclusion.* Consider the conclusion and how it may be reached. It is often wise to consider how similar conclusions have been reached in the past. Be certain that you clearly understand the desired conclusion before proceeding.
3. *Find the connection between hypothesis and conclusion.* In order to do this you must have, at your fingertips, all appropriate postulates, definitions, previously proved theorems, and common techniques. In addition, the experience you have acquired in solving other problems, your intuition, and your imagination must all be synthesized in an effort to prove a theorem or perform a construction.

Finally, subscribe to the motto "If at first you don't succeed, try again," but give the problem time to "ferment." Often, not thinking about a problem for a while provides the needed mental rest to spark the creative fires.

The Analytic Method

Some have found a technique, known as the *analytic method,* helpful in bridging the gap between hypothesis and conclusion in geometry. This method consists of a series of retrogressive steps that start with the conclusion and end with the hypothesis. In other words, the entire proof may be constructed by starting with the conclusion and asking yourself, "What step must have immediately preceded this step?" After deciding on the answer, you ask the same question about that answer, until the entire logical sequence is uncovered in reverse. After the hypothesis is reached, the proof is written by simply reversing these steps. This method of working backward was discussed earlier in this chapter as one of Polya's suggested techniques of problem solving. (For a detailed discussion of this technique see Enrichment Unit 93, "Problem Solving—A Reverse Strategy.")

Following is an illustration of how the analytic method may be used in proving a geometric theorem.

PROBLEM

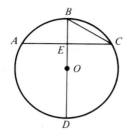

Given: O is the center of the circle;
$\overline{AC} \perp \overline{BD}$
Prove: $BE \times BD = (BC)^2$
Analysis:

1. $BE \times BD = (BC)^2$ can be proved if we can show that $\dfrac{BE}{BC} = \dfrac{BC}{BD}$

2. $\dfrac{BE}{BC} = \dfrac{BC}{BD}$ can be proved if we can show that $\triangle BEC \sim \triangle BCD$ (an auxiliary line segment, $\overline{CD}$, must be drawn).

3. $\triangle BEC$ can be proved similar to $\triangle BCD$ if we can show that two angles of one are congruent to two angles of the other (or possibly one of the other similarity theorems).

4. $\angle B$ is common to both triangles.

5. $\angle BEC$ and $\angle BCD$ are right angles ($\angle BCD$ is inscribed in a semicircle). Therefore, $\triangle BEC \sim \triangle BCD$.

A synthetic proof now can be written by reversing the arguments in the analysis.

The analytic approach also may be used to solve construction problems. Following are two illustrations of this procedure:

PROBLEM Construct a triangle, given the lengths of a side and the altitude and median to that side.

Analysis:

1. Sketch the picture of the final step of the construction, where the lengths of the given segments are as follows

altitude $\overline{AH}$: A ——————— H
median $\overline{AM}$: A ——————— M
side $\overline{BC}$: B ————————— C

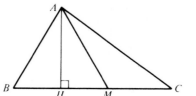

2. Construct right triangle *AHM,* using the lengths of given leg $\overline{AH}$ and the hypotenuse $\overline{AM}$. (This can be done in a number of ways.)

3. Draw $\overleftrightarrow{HM}$. Locate the midpoint M of $\overline{BC}$. On $\overleftrightarrow{HM}$, mark off $\overline{BM}$ and $\overline{MC}$ as shown in the diagram.

4. Complete the triangle *ABC* by drawing $\overline{AB}$ and $\overline{AC}$. This construction problem was solved by working in reverse. An inspection of the end product showed a need to establish some "structure," here in the form of a triangle ($\triangle AHM$). Once this structure provided rigidity to the figure, the rest was completed simply.

Another illustration of the analytic approach can be seen in the following more difficult problem.

PROBLEM Construct a $\triangle ABC$ given only the lengths of the three medians, $\overline{AM}$, $\overline{BN}$, and $\overline{CK}$.

Analysis:
Begin by drawing the completed figure.

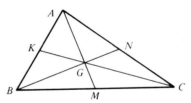

There is a need to establish some rigidity to the figure (by construction). With only the lengths of the medians given and no angles established we must seek out a way of constructing either an angle or a triangle.

Consider extending $\overline{GM}$ to P so that $GM = MP$.

Drawing $\triangle BGP$ gives us a triangle that is fully determined, since the lengths of its sides are each two-thirds the length of a median of $\triangle ABC$.

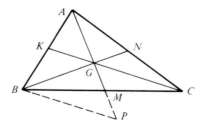

Since the point of intersection of the medians (the centroid) trisects each median, $GM = \dfrac{1}{3} AM$. Therefore, $GP = \dfrac{2}{3} AM$. Also, $BG = \dfrac{2}{3} BN$. Since $\overline{GK}$ is a midline of $\triangle ABP$, it is half the length of $\overline{BP}$. But $GK = \dfrac{1}{3} CK$.

Therefore, $BP = \dfrac{2}{3} CK$.

Now having determined the lengths of the sides of $\triangle BGP$, we can construct it (with straightedge and compasses).

The remainder of the construction problem continues in the same reverse procedure. That is, we now ask how C may be found. This can be done by locating the midpoint, M, of $\overline{GP}$ and extending $\overline{BM}$ to C so that $BM = MC$. In a similar way N can be located. Then the intersection of $\overline{CN}$ and $\overline{PG}$ will determine point A.

The analysis is complete and all that remains is the actual construction that follows these designated steps.

Using "Brute Force"

Some problems are best solved by "brute force" methods. The example that follows illustrates such a problem. There are no shortcuts, and the analytic method does not properly apply. What does apply is some powerful geometric thinking.

A second solution of the same problem, this time using coordinate geometry, follows the first solution. The beauty of the second proof is that it illustrates how coordinate geometry techniques get about as close as one can to a methodical approach in the solution of geometric problems, as opposed to the often hit-or-miss synthetic method.

> **PROBLEM** In a parallelogram, the sum of the squares of the lengths of the diagonals is equal to twice the sum of the squares of the lengths of any two adjacent sides.

Proof 1:

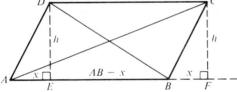

Given: ▱ *ABCD*
Prove: $(AC)^2 + (BD)^2 = 2[(AB)^2 + (AD)^2]$

1. Draw perpendiculars $\overleftrightarrow{DE}$ and $\overleftrightarrow{CF}$ as in the diagram.
2. $AE = BF = x$ and $DE = CF = h$ (since $\triangle ADE \cong \triangle BCF$)
3. In right triangles BDE and ADE,
   $(BD)^2 = h^2 + (AB - x)^2 = h^2 + x^2 + (AB)^2 - 2x(AB)$ and $h^2 + x^2 = (AD)^2$
4. $\therefore (BD)^2 = (AD)^2 + (AB)^2 - 2x(AB)$
5. In right $\triangle ACF$,
   $(AC)^2 = h^2 + (AB + x)^2 = h^2 + x^2 + (AB)^2 + 2x(AB)$
6. $\therefore (AC)^2 = (AD)^2 + (AB)^2 + 2x(AB)$
7. From steps 4 and 6,
   $(AC)^2 + (BD)^2 = 2[(AB)^2 + (AD)^2]$

Proof 2:

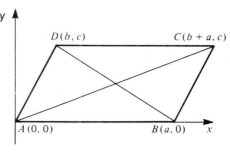

Given: ▱ *ABCD*
Prove: $(AC)^2 + (BD)^2 = 2[(AB)^2 + (AD)^2]$

1. $(AC)^2 = (c - 0)^2 + (b + a - 0)^2 = c^2 + b^2 + 2ba + a^2$
2. $(BD)^2 = (b - a)^2 + (c - 0)^2 = b^2 - 2ab + a^2 + c^2$
3. $\therefore (AC)^2 + (BD)^2 = 2(a^2 + b^2 + c^2)$
4. $AB = a$, so that $(AB)^2 = a^2$
5. $(AD)^2 = (b - 0)^2 + (c - 0)^2 = b^2 + c^2$
6. $\therefore (AB)^2 + (AD)^2 = a^2 + b^2 + c^2$
7. $\therefore$ From steps 3 and 6, $(AC)^2 + (BD)^2 = 2[(AB)^2 + (AD)^2]$

The Algebraic Method

Algebraic methods are often used when solving geometric problems, especially when synthetic techniques become cumbersome. A prime example of this is the synthetic proof of the Pythagorean theorem, which the average geometry student usually finds somewhat difficult to follow. Compare this with a considerably simpler algebraic proof (of which there are many variations). You can appreciate the contrast if you study the outlines of these two proofs.

> **PROBLEM** Prove the Pythagorean theorem.

> **SOLUTION**

Version 1 (synthetic method):
The area of the square on the hypotenuse of a right triangle is equal to the sum of the areas of the squares on the legs.

Given: Right $\triangle ABC$;
Squares *ACHK*,
BCGF, and *BAED*

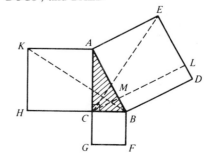

1. Construct $\overline{CL}$ perpendicular to $\overline{DE}$; draw the other lines as shown.
2. $\triangle CAE \cong \triangle BAK$
3. Area $\triangle CAE = \dfrac{1}{2}$ (area $MLEA$)
4. Area $\triangle BAK = \dfrac{1}{2}$ (area $ACHK$)
5. Area $ACHK$ = area $MLEA$
6. In a similar manner, show that area $BCGF$ = area $MLDB$
7. Area $ACHK$ + area $BCGF$ = area $BAED$

Version 2 (algebraic method):

The square of the hypotenuse of a right triangle is equal to the sum of the squares of the legs.

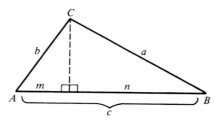

1. Since similar triangles are formed by constructing the altitude, then

$$\frac{c}{a} = \frac{a}{n} \quad \text{and} \quad \frac{c}{b} = \frac{b}{m}$$

or $\qquad a^2 = cn \quad \text{and} \quad b^2 = cm$

2. Therefore, $a^2 + b^2 = cn + cm$
$$= c(n + m)$$
$$= c \cdot c = c^2$$

We cannot conclude a discussion on geometric proofs without mentioning the indirect method of reasoning (*reductio ad absurdum*) that is used extensively in higher mathematics.

PROBLEM   Prove by indirect reasoning that if two angles of a triangle are congruent, the sides opposite them are congruent.

A sketch of the proof follows. Incidentally, this is the proof found in Euclid's *Elements*. Current textbooks usually prove this theorem directly.

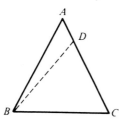

SOLUTION

Given $\triangle ABC$, where $\angle B \cong \angle C$. If $\overline{AB} \not\cong \overline{AC}$, then assume $AC > AB$. Mark off point D in $\overline{AC}$ such that $\overline{DC} \cong \overline{AB}$. Then $\triangle DCB \cong \triangle ABC$. This is impossible, so $\overline{AB} \cong \overline{AC}$.

NONROUTINE PROBLEMS

Solving a problem is like inventing something new, and there are no set rules that inventors follow. The best way to learn to solve mathematical problems is by solving more problems. Experience is often the best teacher. There is simply no substitute for building up a reservoir of experience, "tricks," or strategies (such as the analytic method, indirect proofs, estimating results, or guessing).

For some, many of the problems described earlier would be "child's play." For them, the challenge comes with problems where nonroutine, or novel, approaches are needed. We present several such problems together with their solutions, which, incidentally, you can best appreciate only after you attempt the problems yourself. These problems are not arranged in any special order; however, the first three appear in many forms, and knowledge of the basic versions should enable you to handle variations.

The problems illustrated here all exhibit some use of an unusual approach. A keen awareness might be developed by reading these and others similar to them.

PROBLEM   If the sum of two numbers is 12 and their product is 4, find the sum of their reciprocals.

The following solutions demonstrate the power of intuition, insight, and some experience in problem solving—compare solution 1 with solution 2. You can easily see which is more elegant!

SOLUTION 1   Let x = first number
y = second number

Key equations: $\qquad x + y = 12$
$$xy = 4$$

By substitution:

$$x(12 - x) = 4$$
$$x^2 - 12x + 4 = 0$$

Using the quadratic formula we get

$$x = 6 \pm 4\sqrt{2}$$

By substituting for x we get values for y:

x	$6 + 4\sqrt{2}$	$6 - 4\sqrt{2}$
y	$6 - 4\sqrt{2}$	$6 + 4\sqrt{2}$

By rationalizing denominators and simplifying:

$$\frac{1}{x} = \frac{1}{6 + 4\sqrt{2}} = \frac{3 - 2\sqrt{2}}{2}$$

$$\frac{1}{y} = \frac{1}{6 - 4\sqrt{2}} = \frac{3 + 2\sqrt{2}}{2}$$

so that

$$\frac{1}{x} + \frac{1}{y} = \frac{3 - 2\sqrt{2}}{2} + \frac{3 + 2\sqrt{2}}{2} = \frac{6}{2} = 3 \quad (Answer)$$

SOLUTION 2

$$\frac{1}{x} + \frac{1}{y} = \frac{x + y}{xy} = \frac{12}{4} = 3 \quad (Answer)$$

This solution illustrates the value of using a "reverse strategy." For more on this strategy in problem solving, see Enrichment Unit 93.

PROBLEM   Find the sum of the coefficients in the binomial expansion of $(x + y)^8$.

(The solutions of this problem also demonstrate the power of intuition, insight, and experience.)

SOLUTION 1

$$(x + y)^8 = \binom{8}{0}x^8 + \binom{8}{1}x^7y + \binom{8}{2}x^6y^2 + \binom{8}{3}x^5y^3 +$$

$$\binom{8}{4}x^4y^4 + \binom{8}{5}x^3y^5 + \binom{8}{6}x^2y^6 + \binom{8}{7}xy^7 + \binom{8}{8}y^8$$

$$\text{Sum of the coefficients} = \binom{8}{0} + \binom{8}{1} + \binom{8}{2} + \binom{8}{3} + \binom{8}{4}$$

$$+ \binom{8}{5} + \binom{8}{6} + \binom{8}{7} + \binom{8}{8}$$

$$= 1 + 8 + 28 + 56 + 70 + 56 + 28$$

$$+ 8 + 1$$

$$= 256 \quad (Answer)$$

SOLUTION 2

Let $x = y = 1$ in the first equation of solution 1.
Then

$$(x + y)^8 = (1 + 1)^8 = \binom{8}{0} + \binom{8}{1} + \binom{8}{2} + \binom{8}{3} + \binom{8}{4} +$$

$$\binom{8}{5} + \binom{8}{6} + \binom{8}{7} + \binom{8}{8}$$

So that the sum of the coefficients is

$$(1 + 1)^8 = 2^8 = 256$$

PROBLEM   A bug perched on corner B of a solid box chooses to reach the diagonally opposite corner H by the shortest route. What path does it take?

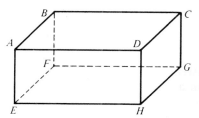

(The solution to this problem demonstrates the role that imagination as well as insight plays in problem solving.)

SOLUTION   Open the box along several edges to flatten it out. The illustration below is one possibility. $\overline{BH}$ is the shortest path between B and H.

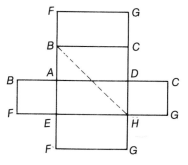

PROBLEM   As shown in the following figure, E is on $\overline{AB}$ and C is on $\overline{FG}$. Prove that parallelogram $ABCD$ is equal in area to parallelogram $EFGD$.

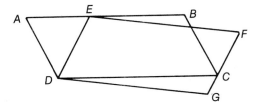

Although the solution is an easy one (once one knows it), the solution is invariably evasive, even for bright high school students who have some experience in solving difficult mathematics problems.

SOLUTION   Draw $\overline{EC}$ (see next figure). Since $\triangle EDC$ and $\square ABCD$ share the same base ($\overline{DC}$) and a common altitude (from E to $\overleftrightarrow{DC}$) the area of $\triangle EDC$ is equal to one-half the area of $\square ABCD$.

Similarly, $\triangle EDC$ and $\square EFGD$ share the same base ($\overline{ED}$), and the same altitude to that base; thus, the area of $\triangle EDC$ is equal to one-half the area of $\square EFGD$.

Since the area of $\triangle EDC$ is equal to one-half the area of each parallelogram, the parallelograms are equal in area.

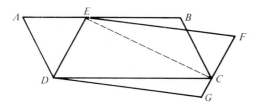

Sometimes the obvious solution is just overlooked because of prior training. That is, students often react to a problem in the manner in which similar problems have been done (this is not necessarily a bad idea). This oversight could lead the student to go awry, as illustrated with the preceding problems. Sometimes an alternative solution, albeit long and cumbersome, may not be possible or may be vastly out of a student's reach, as illustrated by the following problem:

> **PROBLEM** Two trains, each traveling at a uniform speed, start toward each other at the same time along a straight track. One train is traveling at 60 mph and the other at 90 mph. At the start, with the trains 150 miles apart, a bee travels from one train to the other at the rate of 200 mph. When the bee reaches the second train, it immediately returns to the first train. This continues until the trains meet (and the bee is crushed by the impact). How many miles did the bee travel?

> **SOLUTION** Don't be distracted by trying to track the path of the bee! Instead, simply calculate the bee's distance by multiplying its rate of speed by the time it traveled. The latter is obtained from calculating the time it took the trains to meet.

$$\text{Let } t = \text{the number of hours}$$
$$\text{the trains traveled}$$
$$\text{before meeting.}$$

$$60t + 90t = 150$$

$$150t = 150$$

$$t = 1$$

In one hour the bee traveled a total of 200 miles.

> **PROBLEM** *Monkey on a rope*
> Suppose there was a rope hanging over a pulley with a weight on one end of the rope. Suppose also that at the other end was a monkey who weighed the same as the weight. Assume that the rope weighed 4 ounces for every foot, and the age of the monkey and the monkey's mother was 4 years, and the weight of the monkey was as many pounds as the mother was years old. The monkey's mother was twice as old as the monkey was when the monkey's mother was half as old as the monkey will be when the monkey's mother was three times as old as the

monkey, and the weight of the weight and the weight of the rope was half as much again as the difference between the weight of the weight and the weight of the weight and the weight of the monkey. What was the length of the rope?

SOLUTION

Let L = length of rope, in feet

$\quad W$ = weight of rope, in ounces

$\quad A$ = age of mother, in years

$\quad a$ = age of monkey, in years

$\quad m$ = weight of monkey, in ounces

$\quad w$ = weight of weight, in ounces

$\quad x$ = number of years ago when monkey was . . .

$\quad y$ = number of years later when monkey will be . . .

$\quad z$ = number of years ago when mother was . . .

Solve these nine equations simultaneously.

1. $m = w$
2. $W = 4L$
3. $a + A = 4$
4. $\dfrac{m}{16} = A$
5. $A = 2(a - x)$
6. $A - x = \dfrac{(a + y)}{2}$
7. $a + y = 3(A - z)$
8. $A - z = 3(a - z)$
9. $w + W = \dfrac{3}{2}\left| w - (w + m) \right|$

Answer: Length of rope is 5 feet.

> **PROBLEM** A quality control worker is told to make sure that all metal plates being manufactured with a vowel printed on one side have an even number printed on the other. Which of the following plates *must* the worker turn over to make sure the rule is being followed?

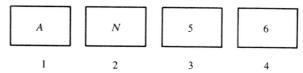

> **SOLUTION** He must only turn over plates 1 and 3. Plate 1 must be inspected to make sure there is an even number on the reverse side. Plate 3 must be turned over to be sure that there isn't a vowel on the reverse side (or else the rule has been violated). Plate 2 does not have a vowel printed; there-

fore it is not covered by the rule. Plate 4 has an even number printed, so if it has a vowel on the other side then the rule is adhered to, while if the reverse side has a consonant then the rule does not apply. Therefore it does not have to be turned over.

An analogous problem, which appears to be different, uses the same reasoning.

PROBLEM   A store manager is required to initial for approval any check over $600.00. Which of the checks shown in the first column *must* be turned over to see if the manager followed the rule?

SOLUTION   Check 1 must be turned over, since it is over $600.00. Check 2 must also be turned over to make sure that the uninitialed check is not over $600.00. Check 3 is under $600.00 and therefore does not have to be initialed, while check 4 was initialed and therefore would not be violating the rule if the check was more than $600.00.

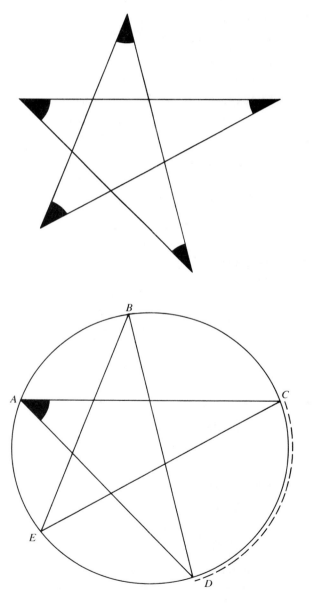

1.

Manager's approval _____

2.

3.

Manager's approval _____

4.

PROBLEM   Find the sum of the measures of the vertex angles of any pentagram.

SOLUTION   Since the type of pentagram was not specified, we can assume the pentagram is either regular or one that is merely inscribable in a circle (i.e., all the vertices lie on a circle).

In the latter case, we notice that each of the angles is now an inscribed angle of the circle and so has half the measure of the intercepted arc. Consequently we get the following:

$$\angle A = \tfrac{1}{2}\widehat{CD}; \quad \angle B = \tfrac{1}{2}\widehat{ED}; \quad \angle C = \tfrac{1}{2}\widehat{AE};$$

$$\angle D = \tfrac{1}{2}\widehat{AB}; \quad \angle E = \tfrac{1}{2}\widehat{BC}$$

$$\angle A + \angle B + \angle C + \angle D + \angle E =$$

$$\tfrac{1}{2}(\widehat{CD} + \widehat{ED} + \widehat{AE} + \widehat{AB} + \widehat{BC})$$

That is, the sum of the vertices is one half the circumference of the circumcircle.

PROBLEM   Find the rational value of:

$$\cos 20 \cdot \cos 40 \cdot \cos 80$$

SOLUTION

(Remember: $\sin 2\theta = 2 \sin \theta \cdot \cos \theta$)

$$\text{Multiply by} \quad \frac{2 \sin 20}{2 \sin 20}$$

$$\frac{(2 \sin 20 \cdot \cos 20) \cdot \cos 40 \cdot \cos 80}{2 \sin 20}$$

$$\frac{2}{2} \cdot \frac{\sin 40 \cdot \cos 40 \cdot \cos 80}{2 \sin 20}$$

$$\frac{2}{2} \cdot \frac{\sin 80 \cdot \cos 80}{2 \cdot 2 \cdot \sin 20}$$

$$\frac{\sin 160}{2 \cdot 2 \cdot 2 \cdot \sin 20} = \frac{\sin 20}{8 \cdot \sin 20} = \frac{1}{8}$$

What originally seemed to be a difficult problem was reduced to a rather simple one.

Another example of simplifying a problem by using a "bit of insight" is the following.

PROBLEM   The tangent $\overline{AB}$ of the smaller of the two concentric circles is a chord of the larger circle. Find the area of the shaded region, if $AB = 8$.

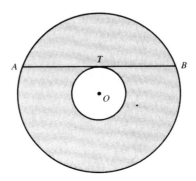

SOLUTION 1   A rather straightforward solution, which, although it uses traditional methods, becomes quite streamlined, follows.

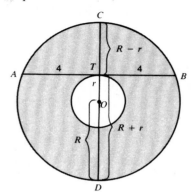

Area of shade $= \pi R^2 - \pi r^2 = \pi(R^2 - r^2)$

"product of chords":

$$(R - r)(R + r) = 4 \cdot 4 = 16$$

$$R^2 - r^2 = 16$$

Therefore, area of shade $= 16\pi$.

The following solution is quite novel and provides a useful procedure for other appropriate problem situations.

SOLUTION 2   Assume the smaller circle is reduced to a point; then $\overline{AB}$ becomes the diameter of the larger circle. The area of the shaded region (larger circle) $= \pi R^2 = 16\pi$.

PROBLEM   Point P is in the interior of equilateral triangle ABC, such that $AP = 5$, $BP = 3$, and $CP = 4$.

Find the area of triangle ABC.

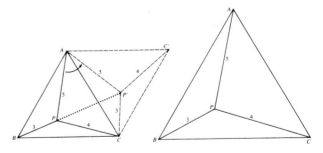

SOLUTION   Rotate $\triangle ABC$ on point A for 60°. It now assumes the position of $\triangle AC'C$. Point P now goes to point P'. $m\angle PAP' = 60$. Therefore, $\triangle APP'$ is equilateral and $PP' = 5$. By the Pythagorean theorem applied to $\triangle PCP'$, $m\angle PCP' = 90$. [$\mathscr{A}$ means area]

$$\mathscr{A} \,\triangle APB + \mathscr{A}\triangle APC =$$

$$\mathscr{A}\triangle AP'C + \mathscr{A}\triangle APC =$$

$$\mathscr{A}\triangle APP' + \mathscr{A}\triangle CPP' =$$

$$\frac{25\sqrt{3}}{4} + 6$$

To find $\mathscr{A}\triangle BPC$:

$$m\angle BCC' = 120; \ m\angle BCP + m\angle P'CC' = 30$$

But, $m\angle PBC = m\angle P'CC'$.
Therefore, $m\angle BCP + m\angle PBC = 30$, and $m\angle BPC = 150$.

$$\mathscr{A}\triangle BPC = \tfrac{1}{2}BP \cdot PC \cdot \sin\angle BPC$$

$$\mathscr{A}\triangle BPC = \tfrac{1}{2} \cdot 3 \cdot 4 \cdot \tfrac{1}{2} = 3$$

Thus, $\mathscr{A}\triangle ABC = \dfrac{25\sqrt{3}}{4} + 9$.

PROBLEM In the adjoining square *ABCD,* arc *DXB* is part of a circle with center at *C*, and arc *DYB* is part of a circle with center at *A*. The area of square *ABCD* is 4 square units. Find the area between the arcs (i.e., the shaded region).

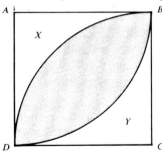

SOLUTION This solution demonstrates a rather unusual procedure for solving a straightforward problem.

Add the areas of sectors *ABD* and *CBD. The result is 2π.*

Subtract the area of square *ABCD* from this sum. The resulting area is that of *BXDY*, since the area of *BXDY* was used twice in the addition of the areas of the sectors. The result is $2\pi - 4$.

Naturally, there are many other nonroutine problems, each with a different "message." Some books where these can be found are listed at the end of this chapter, but you may wish to be adventurous and create your own problems.

CREATING MATHEMATICAL PROBLEMS

The changes made in two of Euclid's five postulates (the Parallel Postulate and the Infinitude of a Line) led to a revolution in mathematics—the development of non-Euclidean geometries. The technique of making minor or major adjustments in the given conditions of a mathematics problem "just for the fun of it" has a long tradition among mathematicians and students of mathematics. The results have, on occasion, proved startling to say the least—as evidenced by the example just cited. Another example is an extension of the fact that there exist Pythagorean triples (x, y, z) that satisfy $x^2 + y^2 = z^2$. However, one would not have such an easy time trying to find integers x, y, and z that satisfy $x^n + y^n = z^n$ for integral $n > 2$. In fact this leads to the well-known "Fermat's last theorem," (proved by A. Wiles in June 1993 and corrected in October 1994).

Students can be trained to develop and solve their own, self-made problems by making changes in existing ones, even simple changes. When students are developing their own problems they may occasionally create problems that are beyond their ability or capacity to solve, however. Some may even be unsolvable.

Every problem that is posed can have some conditions changed to produce a new problem or variation of the original problem. Thus, the teacher should determine some alternative assessment scheme for giving credit to students not only for solving problems correctly, as is traditionally the case, but also for creating problems. Through this creative effort students begin to really understand what problems are all about.

As an aid to teachers and prospective teachers, we offer some suggestions on how specific problems may be changed to produce new ones. These can be used to demonstrate to students the types of variations that might be made. The real creativity, however, will come from students' own variations of problems.

PROBLEM David has 45 coins, consisting of nickels and dimes. The total value is $3.50. How many coins of each kind does he have?

POSSIBLE VARIATIONS

1. What is the largest number of nickels and dimes he could have that would total $3.50?
2. What is the smallest number?
3. How would the problem change if it included quarters as well as nickels and dimes?
4. Is it possible to have only dimes and quarters instead of nickels and dimes?
5. In how many ways could $3.50 be represented in nickels and dimes?

PROBLEM By construction (using straightedge and compasses), locate the midpoint of segment *AB:*

A —————————————————— *B*

POSSIBLE VARIATIONS

1. Are there any other ways of locating the midpoint of a segment?
2. Suppose a pupil forgot to bring a straightedge to school. Is it possible to locate the midpoint with compasses alone?
3. With straightedge alone?
4. Suppose a student had a pair of compasses that were rusted and could not be adjusted. Can the segment $\overline{AB}$ be bisected with unadjustable compasses?

PROBLEM At a point on level ground 100 feet from the foot of a flagpole, the angle of elevation of the top of the pole is 31°. Find the height of the flagpole to the nearest foot.

POSSIBLE VARIATIONS

1. Suppose the same pole had a 15° tilt. How would you then compute the length of the pole?
2. Suppose the original flagpole is standing vertically on a hill that has a 15° rise. How would you compute the height of the pole?

PROBLEM Prove that in a circle, chords are congruent if they are equidistant from the center.

POSSIBLE VARIATIONS

1. State and prove the inverse of the problem.
2. State and prove the converse of the problem.
3. State and prove the contrapositive of the problem.
4. Are there any other variations?

CREATIVITY IN PROBLEM SOLVING

If there is difficulty in teaching effective ways of using the techniques of problem solving, there is, perhaps, greater difficulty in teaching for "creativity." One of the major difficulties is in defining the term itself. At one time, it was thought that creativity was a genetic capacity granted to the fortunate few, but now a number of psychologists have attempted to demonstrate that processes associated with creativity are teachable (or, at least, encourageable). For our purposes, we may define creativity as the ability to evolve unusual, highly useful, or unique solutions to problems. (Remember that such solutions do not necessarily occur quickly. It took Johannes Kepler almost

twenty years to develop his three laws of planetary motion—one of the most creative performances in scientific history.)

While there is continuing investigation into the relationship between creativity and intelligence, preliminary findings indicate that the domains are not identical. Highly creative students are not necessarily those with the highest I.Q. Different tests of creativity may, of course, be responsible for some of the differences in findings, but some psychologists seem to agree that intelligence tests do not measure the same operations as found in creativity.

Following are some suggestions for encouraging creativity in the classroom.

1. Provide a classroom atmosphere that encourages freedom of expression.
2. Respect unusual questions, and set an example by your own inquiry and creativity.
3. Respect and reward unusual ideas.
4. Provide opportunities for learning that involve searching for students' own solutions without being graded.
5. Do not discourage controversy.
6. Encourage students to value their own ideas and to record them in concrete form whenever possible.
7. Share examples of the efforts of famous creative people—and their difficulties.
8. Encourage the acquisition of knowledge in a variety of fields.
9. When giving assignments, provide opportunities for originality and exploration.
10. Encourage cooperative learning efforts in developing creative problems.

SUMMARY

The one statement that best summarizes this chapter is, "We learn best how to solve problems by solving them." This is the case whether the problems are of the standard textbook varieties found in algebra or geometry textbooks, or any of the challenging types one finds in some textbooks as well as special puzzle or problem books (see list on p. 132). It is impossible to include in any chapter on the subject a sampling of every solution type. Rather, we have tried to impart a feeling or sensitivity toward the whole area of problem solving that establishes it as an interesting, challenging, and fruitful branch of mathematics.

Problem solving, perhaps more than any other branch of mathematics, sharpens a student's analytical and critical powers. At the same time, it may help develop a sense of accomplishment and achievement in students. As a matter of fact, the discovery (or development) of many areas of mathematics is a direct result of problem solving. Much of probability theory results from the solution of posed problems and challenges.

Whatever one can say about the achievement of mathematical power through problem solving applies to both the college-bound and the non-college-bound student. Teaching the fine art of problem solving to all students is indeed a challenge—to students and teachers alike.

EXERCISES

1. Write lesson plans for small groups to create and solve problems dealing with uniform motion, coins, mixture, and investment.
   a. Recommend the incorporation of calculators, computers, diagrams, and tables.
   b. Suggest presentation of each group's results to the entire class by a group representative.

2. Prepare a lesson on how you would teach students to create new problems by changing part of the hypothesis or given conditions for
   a. algebraic problems.
   b. geometric problems.

3. Write any two verbal problems in algebra and one geometric "proof" that have
   a. insufficient data.
   b. excessive data.

   Write a lesson plan indicating how you would introduce this type of problem to an algebra (or geometry) class.

4. Look in some of the books listed in the references (see below) and select five challenging problems and their solutions that are appropriate for a middle school or high school mathematics class (you select the level). Indicate how you would use these problems in your classes.

5. List five activities that can be described as problem solving for a level 1 core class.

6. Consider the following challenging problems. In which types of classes would you present them? Indicate the benefits you think your pupils could derive from these problems.
   a. One method of obtaining the product of two numbers, say 43 and 75, is illustrated by the following:

   $$
   \begin{array}{cc}
   43 & 75 \\
   21 & 150 \\
   (10) & (300) \\
   5 & 600 \\
   (2) & (1200) \\
   1 & 2400
   \end{array}
   $$

   from which

   $$43 \times 75 = 75 + 150 + 600 + 2400 = 3225$$

   (i) Use this method to multiply 73×120.
   (ii) Explain why the method is valid.
   b. Find to the nearest hundredth, the value of

   $$1 + \cfrac{1}{1 + \cfrac{1}{1 + \cfrac{1}{1 + \cfrac{1}{1 + \ldots}}}}$$

   c. Solve: $x + y = 5xy$
   $$y + z = 7yz$$
   $$z + x = 6xz$$

    d. If $3^{2x} + 9 = 10(3^x)$, solve for x.

    e. Determine which is larger: $\sqrt[9]{9!}$ or $\sqrt[10]{10!}$

    f. How many positive integers less than or equal to 1 million are squares or cubes of integers?

7. Read *How To Solve It* by George Polya (Princeton University Press), then discuss how some of Polya's heuristic strategies can be applied to the secondary school mathematics curriculum. Consider at least three strategies in your response to this exercise.

8. Read *How To Solve Problems* by Wayne A. Wickelgren (San Francisco: W. H. Freeman & Co., 1974), then discuss how Wickelgren's heuristic strategies can be applied to the secondary school mathematics curriculum. Consider at least three strategies in your response to this exercise.

9. Read the 1980 Yearbook of the National Council of Teachers of Mathematics, *Problem Solving in School Mathematics*. In particular, prepare a report on Chapter 3, "Heuristics in the Classroom" by Alan R. Schoenfeld.

10. Select one of the challenging problems from *Mathematics As Problem Solving* by Alexander Soifer (Colorado Springs: Center for Excellence in Mathematics Education, 1987), then take the problem you have selected and show how the unusual nature of the problem or the solutions given by the author can serve to model skills students ought to incorporate into their problem-solving activities. Repeat this exercise for two other problems in the book.

SOURCES FOR PROBLEMS

Alexanderson, G. L., A. P. Hillman, L. F. Klosinski, and D. Logothetti. *The Santa Clara Silver Anniversary Contest Book,* Palo Alto, CA: Dale Seymour Publications, 1985.

ApSimon, H., *Mathematical Byways.* New York: Oxford University Press, 1984.

Aref, M. N., and W. Wernick. *Problems and Solutions in Euclidean Geometry.* New York: Dover, 1968.

Barbeau, E., M. Klamkin, and W. Moser. *1001 Problems in High School Mathematics.* Montreal: Canadian Mathematical Congress, 1976, 1978.

Artino, R. A., A. N. Gaglione, and N. Shell. *The Contest Problem Book IV.* Washington, DC: Mathematical Association of America, 1982.

Barry, D. T., and J. R. Lux. *The Philips Academy Prize Examination in Mathematics.* Palo Alto, CA: Dale Seymour Publications, 1984.

Bates, N. B., and S. M. Smith. *101 Puzzle Problems.* Concord, MA: Bates Publishing Co., 1980.

Bolt, B. *The Mathematical Funfair.* New York: Cambridge University Press, 1990.

Brousseau, Bro. A. *Saint Mary's College Mathematics Contest Problems.* Palo Alto, CA: Creative Publications, 1972.

Bryant, S. J., G. E. Graham, and K. G. Wiley. *Nonroutine Problems in Algebra, Geometry, and Trigonometry.* New York: McGraw-Hill, 1965.

Burkill, J. C., and H. M. Kundy. *Mathematical Scholarship Problems.* London: Cambridge University Press, 1961.

Butts, T. *Problem Solving in Mathematics.* Glenview, IL: Scott, Foresman, 1973.

CEMREL. *Elements of Mathematics. Book B, Problem Book,* vols. 1 and 2. St. Louis, MO: CEMREL, 1975.

Charosh, M. *Mathematical Challenges.* Washington, DC: National Council of Teachers of Mathematics, 1965.

Dorofeev, G., M. Potapov, and N. Rozov. *Elementary Mathematics: Selected Topics and Problem Solving.* Moscow: Mir Publishers, 1973.

Dorrie, H. *100 Great Problems of Elementary Mathematics.* New York: Dover, 1965.

Dowlen, N., S. Powers, and H. Florence. *College of Charleston Mathematics Contest Book.* Palo Alto, CA: Dale Seymour Publications, 1987.

Dudney, H. E. *The Canterbury Puzzles.* New York: Dover Publications, 1958.

————. *Amusements in Mathematics.* New York: Dover Publications, 1970.

Dunn, A. *Mathematical Bafflers.* New York: McGraw-Hill, 1964.

Dunn, A. F. *Second Book of Mathematical Bafflers.* New York: Dover Publications, 1983.

Edwards, J. D., D. J. King, and P. J. O'Halloran. *All the Best from the Australian Mathematics Competition.* Melbourne, Australia: Ruskin Press, 1986.

Filipiak, A. S. *Mathematical Puzzles.* New York: Bell Publishing, 1942.

Fisher, L. *Super Problems,* Palo Alto, CA: Dale Seymour Publications, 1981.

Fisher, L., and W. Medigovich. *Problem of the Week,* Palo Alto, CA: Dale Seymour Publications, 1981.

Fisher, L., and B. Kennedy. *Brother Alfred Brousseau Problem Solving and Mathematics Competition, Introductory Division.* Palo Alto, CA: Dale Seymour Publications, 1984.

Fisher, L., and W. Medigovich. *Brother Alfred Brousseau Problem Solving and Mathematics Competition, Senior Division.* Palo Alto, CA: Dale Seymour Publications, 1984.

Garvin, A. D. *Discovery Problems for Better Students.* Portland, ME: J. Weston Walch, 1975.

Gilbert, G. T., M. I. Krusemeyer, and L. C. Larson. *The Wohascum County Problem Book,* Washington, DC: Mathematical Association of America, 1993.

Goebel, J. A. *Contest Problem Book,* Palo Alto, CA: Dale Seymour Publications, 1992.

Graham, L. A. *Ingenious Mathematical Problems and Methods.* New York: Dover, 1959.

———. *The Surprise Attack in Mathematical Problems.* New York: Dover, 1968.

Grietzer, S. L. *International Mathematical Olympiads 1959–1977.* Washington, DC: Mathematical Association of America, 1978.

Halmos, P. *Problems for Mathematicians, Young and Old,* Washington, DC: Mathematical Association of America, 1991.

Higgins, A. M. *Geometry Problems.* Portland, ME: J. Weston Walch, 1971.

Hill, T. J. *Mathematical Challenges II—Plus Six.* Washington, DC: National Council of Teachers of Mathematics, 1974.

Honsberger, R. *Mathematical Morsels.* Washington, DC: Mathematical Association of America, 1978.

Honsberger, R. *More Mathematical Morsels.* University of Waterloo, Washington, DC: Mathematical Association of America, 1991.

Hunter, J. A. H. *Challenging Mathematical Teasers.* New York: Dover Publications, 1979.

Jamski, W. D. *Mathematical Challenges for the Middle Grades.* Reston, VA: NCTM, 1990.

Kessler, G., and L. Zimmerman. *NYSML-ARML Contest 1983–1988,* Reston, VA: NCTM 1989.

Klamkin, M. S. *International Mathematical Olympiads, 1979–1985.* Washington, DC: Mathematical Association of America, 1986.

Kordemsky, Boris A. *The Moscow Puzzles,* New York: Charles Scribner's Sons, 1972.

Krechmer, V. A. *A Problem Book in Algebra.* Trans. V. Shiffer. Moscow: Mir Publishers, 1974.

Krulick, S., and J. A. Rudnick. *Problem Solving: A Handbook for Teachers.* Boston: Allyn and Bacon, 1980.

Kutepov, A., and A. Rubanov. *Problems in Geometry.* Trans. O. Meshkov. Moscow: Mir Publisher, 1975.

———. *Problem Book: Algebra and Elementary Function.* Trans. L. Levant. Moscow: Mir Publisher, 1978.

Larson, L. C. *Problem Solving Through Problems.* New York: Springer-Verlag, 1983.

Lenchner, G. *Creative Problem Solving in School Mathematics.* Boston: Houghton Mifflin Co., 1983.

Moser, W., and E. Barbeau. *The Canadian Mathematics Olympiads 1969, 1975.* Montreal: Canadian Mathematical Congress, 1976.

Mosteller, F. *Fifty Challenging Problems in Probability.* New York: Dover, 1965.

Mott-Smith, G. *Mathematical Puzzles for Beginners and Enthusiasts.* New York: Dover, 1954.

Newton, D. E. *One Hundred Quickies for Math Classes.* Portland, ME: J. Weston Walch, 1972.

Phillips, H., S. T. Shovelton, and G. S. Marshal. *Caliban's Problem Book.* New York: Dover, 1961.

Polya, G., and J. Kilpatrick. *The Stanford Mathematics Book.* New York: Teachers College Press, 1974.

Posamentier, A. S. *A Study Guide for the Mathematics Section of the Scholastic Aptitude Test.* Boston: Allyn and Bacon, 1983.

Posamentier, A. S., and C. T. Salkind. *Challenging Problems in Algebra.* Palo Alto, CA: Dale Seymour Publications, 1988.

———. *Challenging Problems in Geometry.* Palo Alto, CA: Dale Seymour Publications, 1988.

Posamentier, A. S., and W. Wernick. *Advanced Geometric Constructions.* Palo Alto, CA: Dale Seymour Publications, 1988.

Ransom, W. R. *One Hundred Mathematical Curiosities.* Portland, ME: J. Weston Walch, 1955.

Rapaport, E. *Hungarian Problem Book,* vols. 1 and 2. New York: Random House, 1963.

Ruderman, H. D. *NYSML-ARML Contests 1973–1982.* Norman, OK: Mu Alpha Theta, 1983.

Salkind, C. T. *The Contest Problem Book.* New York: Random House, 1961.

———. *The MAA Problem Book II.* New York: Random House, 1966.

Salkind, C. T., and J. M. Earl. *The MAA Problem Book III.* New York: Random House, 1973.

Saul, M. E., G. W. Kessler, S. Krilov, and L. Zimmerman. *The New York City Contest Problem Book.* Palo Alto, CA: Dale Seymour Publications, 1986.

Shklarsky, D. O., N. N. Chentzov, and I. M. Yaglom. *The USSR Olympiad Problem Book.* San Francisco: W. H. Freeman, 1962.

————. *Selected Problems and Theorems in Elementary Mathematics.* Trans. V. M. Volosov, and I. G. Volosova, Moscow: Mir Publisher, 1979.

Sitomer, H. *The New Mathlete Problems Book.* Valley Stream, NY: Nassau County Interscholastic Mathematics League, 1974.

Soifer, Alexander. *Mathematics As Problem Solving.* Colorado Springs, CO: Center for Excellence in Mathematics Education, 1987.

Soifer, Alexander. *How Does One Cut a Triangle?* Colorado Springs, CO: Center for Excellence in Mathematics Education, 1990.

Steinhaus, H. *One Hundred Problems in Elementary Mathematics.* New York: Pergamon Press, 1963.

Straszewicz, S. *Mathematical Problems and Puzzles from the Polish Mathematical Olympiads.* Trans. J. Smolska. New York: Pergamon Press, 1965.

Trigg, C. W. *Mathematical Quickies.* New York: McGraw-Hill, 1967.

Ulam, S. M. *Problems in Modern Mathematics.* New York: John Wiley, 1960.

Waterloo Mathematics Foundation, *Canadian Mathematics Competition Problems, Problems, Problems,* vols. 1–5. University of Waterloo, Waterloo, Ontario, Canada, 1988–1992.

Wells, D. *Can You Solve These?* Stradbroke, Diss, Norfolk, England, 1982.

Whimbey, A., and J. Lochhead. *Problem Solving & Comprehension.* Hillsdale, NJ: Lawrence Erlbaum Associates, Inc., 1986.

Yaglom, A. M., and I. M. Yaglom. *Challenging Mathematical Problems with Elementary Solutions,* vols. 1 and 2. San Francisco: Holden-Day, 1964, 1967.

REFERENCES

Adams, James L. *Conceptual Blockbusting,* 2d ed. New York: W. W. Norton & Co., 1979.

Andre, Thomas. ''Problem Solving and Education.'' In *Cognitive Classroom Learning.* Ed. Gary Phye & Thomas Andre. Orlando, FL: Academic Press, 1986, ch. 7.

Arnold, William R. ''Students Can Pose and Solve Original Problems.'' *Mathematics Teacher* 64 (1971): 325.

Baron, Joan Boykoff, and Robert J. Sternberg. *Teaching Thinking Skills: Theory and Practice,* New York: W. H. Freeman and Co., 1987.

Bransford, John D., and Barry S. Stein. *The Ideal Problem Solver.* New York: W. H. Freeman, 1984.

Brown, Stephen I., and Marion I. Walter. *The Art of Problem Posing.* Hillsdale, NJ: Lawrence Erlbaum Assoc., 1983.

Butts, T. ''In Praise of Trial and Error.'' *Mathematics Teacher* 78 (1985): 167.

Charles, R., and F. Lester. *Teaching Problem Solving, What, Why, and How.* Palo Alto, CA: Dale Seymour Publications, 1982.

Charles, Randall, I., and Edward A. Silver. *The Teaching and Assessing of Mathematical Problem Solving,* vol. 3. Reston, VA: NCTM, 1989.

Chipman, Susan, Judith Segal, and Robert Glaser. *Thinking and Learning Skills.* Vol. 2, *Research and Open Questions.* Hillsdale, NJ: Erlbaum, 1985.

Costa, Art. ''Mediating the Metacognitive.'' *Educational Leadership* (November 1984): 57–62.

Curcio, Frances, ed. *Teaching and Learning: A Problem-Solving Focus.* Reston, VA: NCTM, 1987.

Davis, Robert, Elizabeth Jockusch, and Curtis McKnight. ''Cognitive Processes in Learning Algebra.'' *Journal of Children's Mathematical Behavior* 2, no. 1 (spring 1978).

Derry, Sharon J., and Debra A. Murphy. ''Designing Systems That Train Learning Ability: From Theory to Practice.'' *Review of Educational Research* 56, no. 1 (spring 1986): 1–39.

Dolan, Stan, Tim Everton, Ron Haydock, Tom Patton, and Jeff Searle. *Problem Solving.* New York: Cambridge University Press, 1991.

Frederiksen, Norman. ''Implications of Cognitive Theory for Instruction on Problem Solving.'' *Review of Educational Research* 54, no. 3 (fall 1984): 363–407.

Gallo, Delores. ''Think Metric.'' In *Thinking Skills Instruction: Concepts and Techniques.* Ed. Marcia Heiman & Joshua Slomianko. National Education Association, 1987, pp. 284–303.

Greenes, Carole, Linda Schulman, Rika Spungin, Suzanne Chapin, Carol Findell. *Mathletics: Gold Medal Problems.* Providence, RI: Janson Publications, 1990.

Hayes, John R. *The Complete Problem Solver,* 2d ed. Hillsdale, NJ: Lawrence Erlbaum Associates, Publishers, 1989.

Heiman, M., R. Narode, J. Slomianko, and J. Lochhead. *Thinking Skills: Mathematics, Teaching.* Washington, DC: National Education Association, 1987.

Hough, Julia S., ed. *Problem Solving.* Newsletter, vols. 1–5. Philadelphia, PA: Franklin Institute Press, 1984.

Hudgins, Bryce B. *Problem Solving in the Classroom,* New York: Macmillan, 1967.

Jensen, R. J. "Stuck? Don't Give Up! Subgoal-Generation Strategies in Problem Solving." *Mathematics Teacher* 80 (1987): 614.

Karmos, Joseph, and Ann Karmos. "Strategies for Active Involvement in Problem Solving." In *Thinking Skills Instruction: Concepts and Techniques.* Ed. Marcia Heiman and Joshua Slomianko. National Education Association, 1987, pp. 99–110.

Kauke, Marion. *Spielintelligenz.* Heidelberg: Spektrum Akademischer Verlag 1992.

Kluwe, Rainer. "Executive Decisions and Regulation of Problem Solving Behavior." In *Metacognition, Motivation and Understanding.* Ed. Franz Weinert & Rainer Kluwe. Hillsdale, NJ: Lawrence Erlbaum Associates, 1987, ch. 2.

Krulik, S., ed. *Problem Solving in School Mathematics, 1980 Yearbook.* Reston, VA: National Council of Teachers of Mathematics, 1980.

Mathematics Teacher 76 (1983). Special Issue—Gifted Students.

Mayer, Richard. "Mathematics." In *Cognition and Instruction.* Ed. Ronna Dillon and Robert Sternberg. Orlando, FL: Academic Press, 1986, ch. 5.

Mayer, Richard, J. Larkin, and J. Kadane. "A Cognitive Analysis of Mathematical Problem Solving Ability." In *Advances in the Psychology of Human Intelligence,* vol. 2. Ed. R. Sternberg. Hillsdale, NJ: Erlbaum, pp. 231–273, 1984.

Nickerson, Raymond. "Thoughts on Teaching Thinking." *Educational Leadership* (October 1981): 21–24.

Nickerson, Raymond, David Perkins, and Edward Smith. *The Teaching of Thinking.* Hillsdale, NJ: Lawrence Erlbaum Associates, 1985.

Polya, G. *How To Solve It.* Princeton, NJ: Princeton University Press, 1945.

———. *Patterns of Plausible Inference.* Princeton, NJ: Princeton University Press, 1954.

———. *Introduction and Analogy in Mathematics.* Princeton, NJ: Princeton University Press, 1954.

Reeves, C. A. *Problem Solving Techniques Helpful in Mathematics and Science.* Reston, VA: National Council of Teachers of Mathematics, 1987.

Schoenfeld, A. H. *Mathematical Problem Solving.* Orlando, FL: Academic Press, 1985.

———. *Problem Solving in the Mathematics Curriculum.* Washington, DC: Mathematical Association of America, 1983.

Segal, Judith, Susan Chipman, and Robert Glaser, eds. *Thinking and Learning Skills.* Vol. 1, *Relating Instruction to Research.* Hillsdale, NJ: Lawrence Erlbaum Associates, 1985.

Silver, E. A., ed. *Teaching and Learning Mathematical Problem Solving.* Hillsdale, NJ: Lawrence Erlbaum, 1985.

Simon, Martin A. "The Teacher's Role in Increasing Student Understanding of Mathematics." *Educational Leadership* 43, no. 7 (April 1986): 40–43.

Skemp, Richard R. *The Psychology of Learning Mathematics.* Baltimore: Penguin Books, 1971.

Soifer, Alexander. *Mathematics As Problem Solving.* Colorado Springs, CO: Center for Excellence in Mathematics Education, 1987.

Topoly, William. "An Introduction to Solving Problems." *Mathematics Teacher* 58 (1965): 48.

Troutman, Andrea, and Betty P. Lichtenberg. "Problem Solving in the General Mathematics Classroom." *Mathematics Teacher* 67 (1974): 590.

Walter, Marion I., and Stephen I. Brown. "Problem Posing and Problem Solving." *Mathematics Teacher* 70 (1977): 4.

Whirl, Robert J. "Problem Solving—Solution or Technique?" *Mathematics Teacher* 66 (1973): 551.

Winckelgren, W. A. *How To Solve Problems.* San Francisco: W. H. Freeman, 1974.

CHAPTER 10
ENRICHING MATHEMATICS INSTRUCTION

Enriching mathematics instruction requires a multifaceted effort. We discuss a three-pronged approach utilizing challenging and historical perspectives, the technology of calculators and computers, and manipulatives in the classroom.

Mathematics can be enriched in ways that are appropriate for all students, even those with different levels of ability. The *Standards* makes recommendations regarding topics that ought to receive increased attention and emphasis in secondary schools. One of these recommendations is that historical topics be integrated into the curriculum across all grade and ability levels. Certain topics are illustrated in this chapter because of their motivational value. These illustrations are merely representative, for every teacher can relate some favorite tales, perhaps even a few "spicy" ones, from the rich lore of mathematics history.

A second recommendation is that the technology of calculators and computers be utilized in every classroom. Scientific calculators are especially valuable in evaluating radicals, trigonometric functions, logarithms, and inverse functions. They show quite easily relationships among the right-triangle ratios, and the circular functions, and are helpful in solving triangles.

The versatile graphics calculator quickly draws any graph; it indicates solutions of equations by locating real roots on coordinate axes and can thus guide the student in determining the existence of extraneous roots. It can graph inequalities and perform matrix and statistics calculations. Graphics calculators can also be used to solve word problems by setting up appropriate functions.

Scientific and graphics calculators should have been part of your professional development, be it in mathematics or school mathematics. If they have not, there are several types of calculators available, and they are not prohibitively expensive. Many of the problems we present in this chapter require scientific and graphics calculator skills. We suspect that many students already possess such skills. If you do not, several lessons guided by your calculator's operational manual should suffice.

Manipulatives in the mathematics classroom, for all grade levels and for all levels of ability, are the third path to enrichment. We present a more "modern" set of manipulatives than the "ancient" abacus, Napier's rods, or slide rule, although the importance of these and other tools in the development of mathematics should not be overlooked.

ENRICHING MATHEMATICS INSTRUCTION WITH A HISTORICAL APPROACH

It is a popular myth that a mathematics class is lifeless and dull. Unfortunately, that myth is too often true—though it need not be so! We frequently find ourselves concentrating on the teaching of mathematics to reach a deadline such as giving a test or completing a course of study. The luxury of teaching what mathematics is all about seems to be beyond our grasp. But is it really? We can easily teach where mathematics comes from, who first thought of it, and who later developed and refined it. In short, we can use the history of the subject, including the lives, loves, successes, and failures of the people who created it to breathe life into what might otherwise be a rather drab experience. There are times when history should be integrated into the subject matter in a light and lively way.

The sections that follow provide a small sample of how such integration might be accomplished for certain topics in secondary school mathematics. A carefully selected bibliography appears at the end of the chapter that can help you develop the background needed to use the ''historical'' approach when teaching mathematics.

Geometry: In the Beginning

The original development of geometry in Egypt and Babylonia was a result of the desire of priests to construct temples and of kings to survey land for tax purposes. The techniques were crude and intuitive but sufficiently accurate for the needs. We have evidence of some of these techniques in the Ahmes Papyrus, which was written about 1650 B.C. and discovered in the nineteenth century. Portions of it are preserved in museums in London and New York. The papyrus contains formulas to calculate areas of rectangles, right triangles, and trapezoids that have one leg perpendicular to the bases, and to approximate the area of a circle. The Egyptians apparently developed these formulas from their experience with area of land.

The first mathematician who appeared to be dissatisfied with methods based solely on experience was Thales (ca. 640–546 B.C.). We honor him today as the man who always said, ''Prove it!'' And he frequently did. Among the better known theorems first proved by Thales are:

> The base angles of an isosceles triangle are congruent.
> Vertical angles are congruent.
> An angle inscribed in a semicircle is a right angle.

Pythagoras (ca. 582–507 B.C.) and his followers, the Order of the Pythagoreans, followed in the footsteps of Thales. They used his method of proof to develop not only the Pythagorean theorem but also theorems concerning the sum of the measures of the angles of a polygon, the properties of parallel lines, the five regular solids, and incommensurable quantities.

It was Thales' work, however, that marked the beginning of an era of mathematical development in which deductive proof became the accepted method of logical reasoning. This method is used to derive theorems from postulates and, in this way to develop a system of logically arranged statements. This era reached its apex with Euclid's *Elements,* 300 years after Thales.

In the *Elements,* Euclid unified the work of the scholars who had preceded him by presenting all the mathematics known in his day in a systematic manner—a truly stupendous achievement. Much of his work was also original, for by means of the deductive method he demonstrated the vast amount of knowledge that can be acquired through reasoning alone. Euclid included algebra and number theory as well as geometry in his writings.

The *Elements* turned out to be a work of major importance in the history of the civilized world. In later years it was translated from Greek to Arabic (ca. 800) and from Arabic to Latin (ca. 1120). The first printed edition appeared in Latin (1482), and many other editions followed. Next to the Bible, the *Elements* has been published in more editions and in more languages than any other book.

The original work was written in thirteen separate parchment scrolls, or ''books.'' The fifth theorem in Book I is the familiar ''Base angles of an isosceles triangle are congruent.'' (''Isosceles'' is derived from the Greek words ''isos,'' meaning equal, and ''skelos,'' meaning legs.) The method now most frequently used to prove this theorem requires the construction of an angle bisector through the vertex angle. This process has been disputed by ''purists,'' since it prematurely introduces the angle bisector. Euclid, however, demonstrated it differently. A sketch of his proof follows:

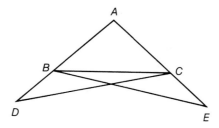

Given $\triangle ABC$ with $\overline{AB} \cong \overline{AC}$. Extend $\overline{AB}$ and $\overline{AC}$ through B and C, respectively, to points D and E, so that $\overline{BD} \cong \overline{CE}$. Therefore, $\triangle ADC \cong \triangle AEB$, so that $\angle D \cong \angle E$ and $\overline{DC} \cong \overline{EB}$. Then $\triangle BDC \cong \triangle CEB$, so that $\angle DBC \cong \angle ECB$. Therefore, $\angle ABC \cong \angle ACB$. Q.E.D.[1]

---

[1] Q.E.D. is an abbreviation for ''quod erat demonstrandum,'' which means ''that which was to be demonstrated.'' It is sometimes written after the conclusion of a proof in mathematics.

The theorem just proved was known as the "pons asinorum," or "bridge of asses (fools)" in the Middle Ages. The implication was that certain students had difficulty "crossing" this bridge in order to proceed further in their study of geometry. Euclid proved the converse of this theorem by the indirect method (reductio ad absurdum.):

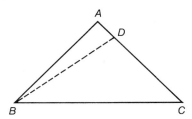

Given $\triangle ABC$, where $\angle B \cong \angle C$. If $\overline{AB} \not\cong \overline{AC}$, then assume $AC > AB$. Mark off point D in $\overline{AC}$ such that $\overline{DC} \cong \overline{AB}$. Then $\triangle DCB \cong \triangle ABC$. This is impossible, so $\overline{AB} \cong \overline{AC}$.

Throughout the course of history, but especially during the last four centuries, Euclid's *Elements* has endured unimaginable "torture." It has been simplified, complicated, projected, distorted, deformed, and sometimes changed beyond recognition. The result?—analytic geometry, projective geometry, topology, non-Euclidean geometry, logic, and even calculus and modern theoretical physics. The end is not yet in sight!

Constructions: Compasses and Straightedge

Whenever constructions are required in geometry, the tools to be used, unless otherwise noted, consist of the ordinary compasses and an unmarked straightedge only.[2] The justification for the employment of these instruments rests on the following three postulates mentioned at the beginning of Euclid's *Elements:*

Let it be granted

1. That a straight line may be drawn from any one point to any other point; [straightedge]
2. That a line segment may be extended to any length along a straight line; [straightedge]
3. That a circle may be drawn from any center at any distance from that center; [compasses].

Euclid worked with rather crude collapsible compasses. The ones we use today can be used only with the preceding postulates, and they have the advantage of making the constructions somewhat simpler than they were for Euclid.

It is possible to perform the familiar constructions of

Euclidean geometry with compasses alone. In 1797, Lorenzo Mascheroni, an Italian mathematician, wrote *The Geometry of Compasses,* in which he proved that all construction problems that can be solved by the use of straightedge and compasses can be solved by compasses alone.[3] These are known as *Mascheroni Constructions.*

Here is an example of a simple Mascheroni construction:

Given a line segment $\overline{AB}$. Determine with compasses alone the midpoint, M, of $\overline{AB}$.

The following sequence of diagrams utilizes the popular compasses of today and demonstrates the solution to the problem just posed.

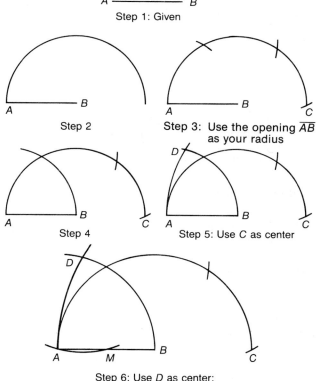

Here is an outline of the proof that the construction is correct.

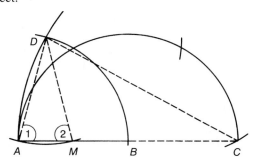

[2] The word *compasses* is a plural noun, as are the words *pants* and *scissors,* because each has two branches. Although the word "compass" is often used to denote "compasses," a compass is, strictly speaking, an instrument for determining direction.

[3] For a proof that the straightedge alone can replace the straightedge and compasses see *Advanced Geometric Constructions* by A. S. Posamentier and W. Wernick. (Palo Alto: Dale Seymour, 1988.)

Draw the construction lines as indicated. Note that $\overleftrightarrow{ABC}$ is a straight line.

1. Since ΔACD is isosceles, $\angle CDA \cong \angle 1$.
2. Since ΔDAM is isosceles, $\angle 1 \cong \angle 2$.
3. Therefore, $\Delta ACD \sim \Delta DAM$
4. Therefore, $\dfrac{AM}{AD} = \dfrac{AD}{AC}$ or $AM = \dfrac{(AD)^2}{AC}$.
5. But $AD = AB$ and $AC = 2(AB)$.
6. Therefore, $AM = \dfrac{(AB)^2}{2(AB)}$ or $AM = \dfrac{AB}{2}$.

Bisecting a line segment or an angle with compasses and straightedge is a simple matter. Trisecting a line segment is a bit more complicated but clearly possible. Early Greek geometers must have been quite puzzled when they were unsuccessful in all attempts to trisect an angle with straightedge and compasses alone. (We are speaking here of a general angle, not the special ones like right angles, which can be trisected by constructing a 60° angle and then a 30° angle.)

One of the most productive techniques in mathematics is that of changing the regulations under which you operate, if these regulations tie your hands. Thus, if the restriction to use traditional construction tools leads to failure in seeking a solution for the trisection problem, perhaps other tools will do the trick. This means, of course, that Euclid's construction postulates must be altered.

Archimedes suggested that he could trisect an angle with compasses and a straightedge that had only two marks on it. Here is a description of Archimedes' construction. The proof follows.

Let the distance between the markings be d

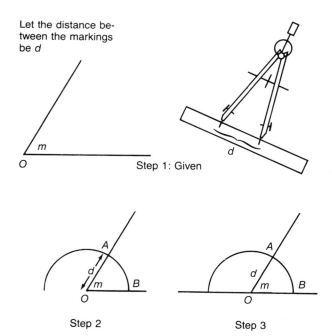

Step 1: Given

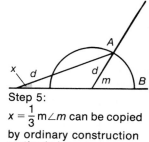

Step 4

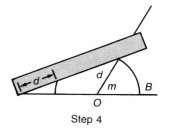

Step 5:
$x = \frac{1}{3}\text{m}\angle m$ can be copied by ordinary construction methods into $\angle m$

PROOF

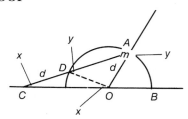

1. $\overline{OD}$ is drawn. $OD = d$.
2. Isosceles ΔDCO has congruent base angles. Isosceles ΔADO has congruent base angles.
3. In ΔDCO, $y = x + x = 2x$.
4. In ΔACO, $m = y + x$.
5. Therefore, $m = 2x + x$ or $x = \dfrac{m}{3}$.

This construction was made possible because the rules of the game (the postulates) were changed. Other mathematicians in ancient as well as modern times have changed the rules even more dramatically and have produced ingenious and elegant procedures for trisecting an angle.

The French mathematician Blaise Pascal invented an unusual instrument to trisect an angle. Here the rods represented by $\overline{PQ}$, $\overline{QO}$, and $\overline{OR}$ are equal in length. Q and O are movable pivots, and R moves along the slot.

You can easily prove that:

$$x = \frac{1}{3}\,\text{m}\angle AOB$$

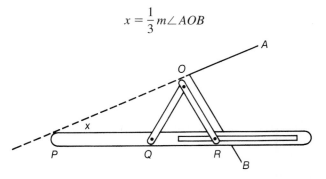

Still other constructions baffled the Greeks and later mathematicians for more than 2000 years. One of these, "squaring the circle," requires the construction of a square whose area is equal to that of a given circle.

Another, "duplication of the cube" (doubling the volume), requires the construction of a cube whose volume is to be twice that of a given cube. These, like the trisection problem, were proved only in modern times to be incapable of construction with compasses and straightedge alone.[4]

Other constructions also eluded the capabilities of the best mathematicians for centuries. While certain polygons could be constructed with ease, using the traditional tools of geometry, others such as the regular seven-sided polygon (heptagon, or 7-gon) or regular 17-gon seemed to be beyond their reach. In 1796, a nineteen-year-old youth, Carl Friedrich Gauss, proved that it was possible to construct a regular seventeen-sided polygon with compasses and straightedge only and that certain others, such as the regular 7-gon, could not.

What Gauss proved is that a regular polygon with an odd number of sides can be constructed if either of the following two conditions is satisfied:

CONDITION 1   The number of sides is equal to $2^{2^n} + 1$, where n is a whole number and $2^{2^n} + 1$ is a prime number; examples can be found in the following chart.

n	$2^{2^n} + 1$	Can a polygon be constructed?	Number of sides
0	3	Yes	3
1	5	Yes	5
2	17	Yes	17
3	257	Yes	257
4	65537	Yes	65537
5	Not prime	No	—

CONDITION 2   The number of sides is the product of two or more different numbers obtained in Condition 1. (You can construct a regular polygon of, say, fifteen sides, because $15 = 5 \times 3$, and 5 and 3 are numbers derived from the rule in Condition 1.)

The discovery of this remarkable theorem convinced Gauss to enter into the field of mathematics for his life's work, instead of linguistics, in which he also excelled. A monument erected to him in Brunswick, Germany, at the place of his birth consists merely of a regular 17-gon, the symbol of his great achievement.

Practical Trigonometry: The Original Sin

Although Euclid showed in his *Elements* that two triangles that agree with respect to two sides and an included

angle are congruent (SAS), in other words, that the size of the triangle is fixed when the measures S, A, and S are given in that order, he did not indicate any particular concern about finding the specific measures of the remaining three parts of the triangles. Similarly for ASA and SSS. The Greek mathematician-philosophers of Euclid's day did not consider "practical" or "applied" geometry to be worthy of any serious consideration. This view slowed the development of that branch of mathematics known as trigonometry.[5]

Regardless of popular opinion against any serious study of the subject, trigonometry managed to get itself born among the Greeks. Its inventor, Hipparchus (ca. 140 B.C.), developed the need for triangle measurements in connection with his work in astronomy, and he developed techniques for determining the measures of the dimensions of a fixed triangle. Menelaus (ca. A.D. 100) also contributed knowledge to this field by developing "spherical trigonometry," the measurement of triangles on a spherical surface, which he needed in connection with his work in astronomy. However, it remained for Ptolemy (ca. A.D. 150), the great astronomer and mathematician who lived in Alexandria, to produce the first major contribution in the field of trigonometry (also in connection with astronomy) in his book *The Almagest*. In this work, whose title means "the greatest," the first extensive trigonometric tables appeared.

Trigonometry remained a servant of astronomy until 1464 when the German mathematician Johann Müller (also known as Regiomontanus) wrote a book that treated trigonometry as a purely mathematical subject, an outgrowth of geometry, which stood on its own merits. Today it is an important tool in mathematics because the nature of the trigonometric functions is such that they are appropriate for use in analyzing physical phenomena that occur with periodic regularity, such as electricity, music, and light.

We say that "a triangle is solved" when the measures of its six dimensions (three angles and three sides) have been determined. The four major tools used to solve triangles are

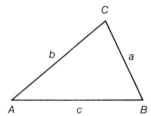

1. The Pythagorean theorem
2. The sum of the measures of the angles of a triangle is 180°

---

[4] For a proof of the impossibility of the angle trisection see *Geometry: Its Elements and Structure* by A. S. Posamentier, J. H. Banks, and R. Bannister. (New York, McGraw-Hill, 1977)

[5] Trigonometry is derived from the Greek words "trigonon," meaning triangle, and "metria," meaning measurement.

3. The law of sines:
   For any triangle *ABC*,

$$\frac{a}{\sin A} = \frac{b}{\sin B} = \frac{c}{\sin C}$$

4. The law of cosines:
   For any triangle *ABC*,

$$c^2 = a^2 + b^2 - 2ab \cos C$$

$$\text{or} \quad b^2 = a^2 + c^2 - 2ac \cos B$$

$$\text{or} \quad a^2 = b^2 + c^2 - 2bc \cos A$$

The trigonometric tables we now use to solve triangles had as their forerunner a table invented by Ptolemy. We now present a general idea of how the trigonometric table was developed by Ptolemy, except that we will use modern notation and symbols. (Ptolemy used the sexigesimal, base 60, number system.) First, we give some background material.

I   Trigonometric functions may be represented as line segments:
    In a unit circle, *O*,

$$\sin x = \frac{AD}{OD}; \cos x = \frac{OA}{OD}; \tan x = \frac{BC}{OB}$$

Since $OD = OB = 1$, then

$$AD = \sin x$$

$$OA = \cos x$$

$$BC = \tan x$$

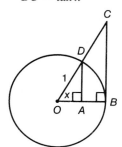

II Derivation of the word "sine": The segment $\overline{AD}$ in the diagram is a "half-chord" known as a "jiva" in Sanskrit. This word was first found in Hindu writings in the year 510. Translators mistakenly wrote this as "jaiv" in Arabic, meaning "pocket" or "cavity." This was eventually translated into the Latin word for "cavity"— "sinus." Thus, the half-chord, "jiva," became "sine," or "sin" in abbreviated form.

III Certain formulas used to develop the trigonometry table appeared in the *Almagest*. Several of these follow:

1. $\sin^2 x + \cos^2 x = 1$
2. $\sin (x - y) = \sin x \cos y - \cos x \sin y$
3. $\sin (x + y) = \sin x \cos y + \cos x \sin y$
4. $\sin 2x = 2\sin x \cos x$
5. $\sin \frac{1}{2}x = \sqrt{\dfrac{1 - \cos x}{2}}$
6. $\tan x = \dfrac{\sin x}{\cos x}$

The sixth formula, for tan *x*, was used by the Arab mathematician el-Hasib in the year 860 to produce the first table of tangents. (Derivations of these formulas can be found in any standard trigonometry textbook.)

IV Ptolemy computed a table of lengths of chords for arcs from 0° to 180° in steps of ½°, in a circle whose radius equals 60 units. Thus, his table gives the measure of chord $\overline{ED}$, which cuts off an arc of *x*°, for 0° < *x*° < 180°.

Part of the table, translated into notation we can follow easily, is reproduced below. The lengths of the chords are stated in sexigesimal notation. For example, 2, 5, 40 in sexigesimal becomes

$$2 + \frac{5}{60} + \frac{40}{60^2} = 0.0350 \text{ in decimal}$$

Arcs	Chords
½°	0, 31, 25
1°	1, 21, 50
1½°	1, 34, 15
2°	2, 5, 40
2½°	2, 37, 4
3°	3, 8, 28
3½°	3, 39, 52

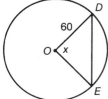

Modern trigonometric tables give the length of the half-chord $\overline{AD}$ (= sin *y*) for the corresponding angle 2*y* in the circle of unit radius.

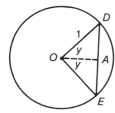

Thus, if you look up the value of sin 45° in your trigonometric table, you will find it to be .7071, whereas the corresponding notation in Ptolemy's table, after appropriate conversions, will tell you that an arc of 90° cuts off a chord of length 1.4142. In this way one can convert from Ptolemy's table of chords to the "modern" sine function.

The cosine and tangent can then be computed from the formulas

$$\sin^2 x + \cos^2 x = 1 \qquad \text{and} \qquad \tan x = \frac{\sin x}{\cos x}$$

The following is an outline of a proof known as Ptolemy's theorem, from which he derived many of the formulas he needed to construct tables such as sin $(x - y)$ and sin $(x + y)$.

THEOREM If *ABCD* is a quadrilateral inscribed in a circle, then the sum of the products of the opposite sides equals the product of the diagonals.

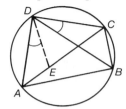

GIVEN: Quad. *ABCD* inscribed in a circle; diagonals $\overline{AC}$ and $\overline{BD}$.

PROVE: $AB \times CD + BC \times AD = DB \times AC$

1. Construct $\angle ADE \cong \angle BDC$
2. $\angle CDE \cong \angle ADB$
3. $\angle ACD \cong \angle ABD$
4. $\therefore \triangle ADB \sim \triangle CDE$
5. $\therefore \dfrac{CD}{DB} = \dfrac{CE}{AB}$ or $AB \times CD = CE \times DB$
6. Show that $\triangle ADE \sim \triangle CDB$
7. $\therefore \dfrac{AD}{DB} = \dfrac{AE}{BC}$ or $BC \times AD = DB \times AE$
8. From steps 5 and 7:

$$AB \times CD + BC \times AD = CE \times DB + DB \times AE$$

$$= DB(CE + AE)$$

$$= DB \times AC \qquad \text{Q.E.D.}$$

EXERCISE Use Ptolemy's theorem to derive the formula

$$\sin (x - y) = \sin x \cos y - \cos x \sin y$$

An outline of the proof follows:

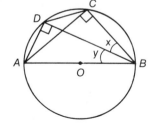

In a circle of unit diameter *AB*,

1. $AB \times CD + BC \times AD = DB \times AC$
2. In right $\triangle BDA$, $AD = \sin y$ and $DB = \cos y$
3. In right $\triangle BCA$, $BC = \cos x$ and $AC = \sin x$
4. In $\triangle DCB$, $\dfrac{CD}{\sin(x - y)} = \dfrac{BC}{\sin \angle CDB}$
5. But since $\angle CDB = \angle CAB$, then

$$\sin \angle CDB = \sin \angle CAB = \frac{BC}{AB} = \frac{BC}{1} = BC$$

6. From steps 4 and 5, $\dfrac{CD}{\sin(x - y)} = \dfrac{BC}{BC} = 1$

$$\text{or } CD = \sin(x - y)$$

7. Now verify, by substituting the results of steps 2–6 into step 1, that sin $(x - y) = \sin x \cos y - \cos x \sin y$.   Q.E.D.

EXERCISE Use this diagram and Ptolemy's theorem to derive the formula

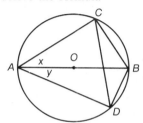

$$\sin (x + y) = \sin x \cos y + \cos x \sin y$$

Most of the material needed to solve a triangle was developed prior to the year 1600. Further refinements came about as a result of work with logarithms and calculus.

DeMoivre's theorem (ca. 1722) demonstrated a relationship between the trig functions and the imaginary *i* in the formula

$$(\cos A + i \sin A)^n = \cos nA + i \sin nA$$

By the end of the seventeenth century the infinite series for sin *x* and cos *x* were known.

$$\sin x = x - \frac{x^3}{3!} + \frac{x^5}{5!} - \frac{x^7}{7!} + \dots$$

$$\cos x = 1 - \frac{x^2}{2!} + \frac{x^4}{4!} - \frac{x^6}{6!} + \dots$$

Today's scientific calculators take advantage of the convergence of these series to determine the values of sine and cosine of any angle whose measure is in radians. The number of displayed decimal places is limited only by the size of the calculator.

So, while trigonometry began as a tool to solve triangles in geometry, it is thought of today as a periodic relationship of complex numbers—quite different from its "practical" beginnings.

Algebra: Mathematical Shorthand

The algebra that is traditionally taught to our secondary school pupils came about as a result of independent developments by mathematicians of ancient Greece as well as those of the Hindu and Arab worlds.

The treatment of algebra by the Greeks was geometric. A large portion of Euclid's *Elements* is in fact devoted to finding solutions, geometrically, to what we call today ''algebraic'' equations. An illustration of this is shown later in this section.

Thus, what we write as

$$(a + b)^2 = a^2 + 2ab + b^2$$

was thought of by the Greeks in terms of this diagram:

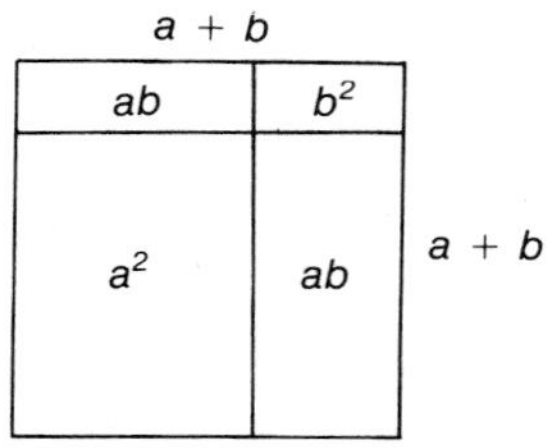

a + b

ab	b^2	
a^2	ab	a + b

Much of the algebraic knowledge of the Greeks was brought together by Diophantus (ca. 275), a prominent mathematician whose work on integral solutions to certain types of equations is still studied today. Incidentally, the first woman mathematician we hear of in ancient times is Hypatia (ca. 410), who wrote commentaries on the work of Diophantus.

In another part of the world, Hindu mathematicians were also concerned with methods for solving equations, especially the quadratic. One of their more interesting contributions to the subject is that they enjoyed posing problems in a colorful way. Here is one example: (Many more can be found in books on the history of algebra that are listed in the bibliography at the end of this section.) ''Of a collection of mango fruits, the king took ⅙, the queen took ⅕ of the remainder, and the three chief princes took ¼, ⅓, and ⅐ of that same remainder, and the youngest child took the remaining 3 mangoes. Oh, you who are clever in problems on fractions, give out the number of mangoes in that collection.''

Arab writers dominated the scene of algebraists in ancient times for many centuries. The greatest Arab writer on algebra was Mohammed ibn Musa al-Khowarizmi (ca. 825), from whose book *Al-Jabr W'al Mukabala* the name ''algebra'' is derived. His major contribution was the introduction of the use of algorithms as a mathematical tool. Incidentally, the word *algorithm* is derived from the name ''al-Khowarizmi.''

Al-Khowarizmi's work became known in Europe in the twelfth century. By the sixteenth century, the symbols we now use in algebra had already been, for the most part, slowly and painstakingly developed. Here are two examples of how equations were written in the years indicated. Just imagine how cumbersome they were to work with. (The modern notation is given in parentheses.)

1545: cubus p 6 rebus aequalis 20. ($x^3 + 6x = 20$)

1631: $xxx + 3bbx = 2ccc$. ($x^3 + 3b^2x = 2c^3$)

The ''='' sign was first introduced by Robert Recorde in his book *The Whetstone of Witte* in 1557.

In 1637, René Descartes introduced the exponent notation that we take for granted today.

Quadratic equations and their solutions played a special role in the history of algebra. The Babylonians first solved certain forms of quadratic equations 3600 years ago, as found in tablets that are now in a collection, YBC 6967, at Yale University. A translation of the problem on these tablets is equivalent to ''Find the dimensions of a rectangle whose length exceeds its width by 7, and whose area is 60.'' The Babylonian solution uses no algebraic notation but serves as a prototype for similar problems. Thus, the solution to the Babylonian quadratic

$$x^2 + px = q, \ q > 0$$

is shown in the tablet to be

$$x = \sqrt{\left(\frac{p}{2}\right)^2 + q} - \frac{p}{2}$$

So that for $y =$ length and $x =$ width, the equations $y = x + 7$ and $xy = 60$ reduce, after appropriate substitution, to the Babylonian type $x^2 + 7x = 60$. Thus the solution to the problem posed is

$$x = \sqrt{\left(\frac{7}{2}\right)^2 + 60} - \frac{7}{2} = 5$$

Compare this solution with the quadratic formula solution used today.

Another famous quadratic is solved geometrically by Euclid in position 11, Book 2 of *Elements:*

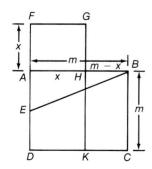

PROPOSITION To divide a given straight line into two segments such that the rectangle contained by the whole line and one of its segments is equal to the square on the remaining segment; [i.e., to divide a line ($AB = m$) into two parts x and $m - x$, such that $m(m - x) = x^2$].

SOLUTION

1. On $\overline{AB}$ construct a square $ABCD$
2. Bisect $\overline{AD}$ at E and draw $\overline{EB}$
3. Extend $\overline{AD}$ through A to F so that $\overline{EF} \cong \overline{EB}$
4. On $\overline{AF}$ construct a square, $AFGH$
5. Extend $\overline{GH}$ to intersect $\overline{DC}$ at K
6. Therefore rectangle $HBCK$ equals, in area, the square $AHGF$

PROOF

1. $\overline{AE} \cong \overline{ED}$ (because E is a midpoint)
2. Area of rectangle $FGKD =$
   $(EF + ED)(EF - ED)$
3. Area of rectangle $FGKD = EF^2 - ED^2$
4. Area of rectangle $FGKD = EF^2 - AE^2$
5. $\therefore FGKD + AE^2 = EF^2$
6. $AB^2 + AE^2 = EB^2 = EF^2$ (because $EF = EB$ and AEB is a right triangle)
7. $\therefore AB^2 + AE^2 = FGKD + AE^2$ or $AB^2 = FGKD$
8. $\therefore AH^2 = HBCK$ (by subtracting $AHKD$ from both sides)   Q.E.D.

What Euclid did here, translated into algebraic symbolism, is show how to divide the given line segment AB into segments x and $m - x$ such that $m(m - x) = x^2$, and segment AH, or x, is the required number. We now know by the quadratic formula that

$$x = \frac{m(\sqrt{5} - 1)}{2}$$

Those who delve beyond secondary school mathematics know that algebra has become a powerful tool to solve problems via group theory and linear algebra.

Historical Notes

The embellishment resulting from the inclusion of historical notes in a mathematics lesson may be considered enrichment. Students usually get a more complete appreciation of a topic if they can relate to its origin. Any book on the history of mathematics can provide useful ideas for enriching your instruction by the inclusion of short anecdotes from the history of mathematics. The following references are of particular value for this use.

Beckmann, Petr. *A History of π*. New York: St. Martin's Press, 1971.

Bell, E. T. *Men of Mathematics*. New York: Simon and Schuster, 1937.

Burton, David M. *The History of Mathematics, An Introduction*. Boston: Allyn and Bacon, 1985.

Dunham, William. *Journey Through Genius*. New York: John Wiley, 1990.

Eves, Howard W. *An Introduction to the History of Mathematics*. New York: Saunders College Publishing, 1983.

————*The Other Side of the Equation*. Boston: Prindle, Weber, and Schmidt, 1971.

————. *In Mathematical Circles*. Vols. 1 and 2. Boston: Prindle, Weber, and Schmidt, 1969.

————. *Mathematical Circles Revisited*. Boston: Prindle, Weber, and Schmidt, 1971.

Gamon, George. *One, Two, Three . . . Infinity*. New York: Viking Press, 1947.

National Council of Teachers of Mathematics, *Historical Topics for the Mathematics Classroom*, 31st Yearbook, Reston, Virginia: NCTM, 1969.

Kasner, E., and J. Newman, *Mathematics and the Imagination*. New York: Simon and Schuster, 1940.

Moritz, R. E. *On Mathematics: A Collection of Witty, Profound, Amusing Passages about Mathematics and Mathematicians*. New York: Dover, 1958.

Schaaf, William L., ed. *Our Mathematical Heritage*. New York: Macmillan, 1963.

Stillwell, John. *Mathematics and its History*. New York: Springer-Verlag, 1989.

Turnbull, H. W. *The Great Mathematicians*. New York: New York University Press, 1961.

Willerding, Margaret. *Mathematical Concepts, A Historical Approach*. Boston: Prindle, Weber, and Schmidt, 1967.

Some of these books will lend themselves better to quick extraction of anecdotes for classroom use, while others will require a somewhat more thorough reading. These books should provide you with ample resources for enrichment through historical anecdotes.

ENRICHMENT TECHNIQUES FOR ALL LEVELS

The core curriculum of the *Standards* proposes that all students be exposed to the same mathematics, though differentiated by levels of abstraction of tasks and concepts. Opportunities for enrichment of instruction exist at every level, particularly when integrated with real-life applications.

The teacher will determine the extent of movement from concrete to abstract for each student, the utilization of small or large groups of students, project work, or lectures. Flexibility is the key to productive enrichment.

When enrichment activities are reserved for small groups, each particular group can move at its own pace. Students will delve into ideas with classmates who may be interested in similar ideas. They will have an opportunity to look more deeply into and even beyond those ideas developed during regular class sessions. Thus, they will make more challenging explorations and broader connections within and outside of mathematics.

Relevant Applications

Realistic and relevant *applications* of the mathematics being studied generally can provide an excellent source for enrichment, as illustrated by the following examples.

TOPIC   Addition and multiplication of fractions

ENRICHMENT   Computing simple probabilities after developing some class-made probability games (e.g., selecting cards from a deck, tossing a coin or die). The teacher's creativity is very important in making this a success.

TOPIC   Percentage

ENRICHMENT   Computation of and verification of newspaper advertisements involving percentages (e.g., sales, bank advertisements). Handled properly, these investigations can be both motivating and revealing. Some astonishing results often appear.

TOPIC   Using formulas

ENRICHMENT   Have students compute the areas of real floor plans, or compute bank interest, or compute the volume of real, but irregular, shapes. When possible, these computations should take place in a realistic setting so as to take on more meaning for the students.

TOPIC   Reading tables

ENRICHMENT   Provide students with realistic problems using mileage charts, postal rate schedules, telephone rate schedules, bus schedules, income tax schedules, etc. Where possible, these should relate to local situations.

TOPIC   Basic concepts of geometry

ENRICHMENT   Direct and indirect measurement of local structures. Students should then be asked to compute areas, volume, etc., from the data gathered.

Recreational Mathematics

Another form of enrichment is *recreational mathematics.* Anything ''recreational'' is generally of interest to students. Therefore, mathematics topics being studied can be reinforced enthusiastically under the guise of recreation.

TOPIC   Reducing fractions

ENRICHMENT   Introduce some divisibility rules for easier recognition of common factors (see Enrichment Unit 84).

TOPIC   Practice with addition

ENRICHMENT   Magic squares of various kinds (see Enrichment units 1 and 2) can be used to reinforce addition facts through an unusual drill.

TOPIC   Miscellaneous computation drill

ENRICHMENT   Various games and puzzles that require students to do computations as part of the activity can enrich an otherwise boring topic. These may be competitive games or puzzles that are individual activities. Here the enrichment activity can be very instrumental in the class's ultimate success with the regular work, since a motivated student should perform better than a student ''turned off'' to mathematics.

TOPIC   Miscellaneous calculator activities

ENRICHMENT   Games and puzzles with a hand-held calculator (see Enrichment Unit 11). These must be carefully selected (and planned).

It is easy to fall into a trap of letting the recreational aspects of a lesson dominate the session. When taken to this extreme, the introduction of recreational topics can become counterproductive, so that any attempt to return to the intended curriculum will be viewed by the students with displeasure. Remember, the recreational aspect of a lesson is merely designed to enrich, not to replace, the regular curriculum.

Field Trips

Although perhaps less directly, some class trips can be used fruitfully to enrich the instruction of mathematics students. Similarly, films and video tapes are available that, if properly introduced and carefully reviewed, can be effective in enriching the teaching of mathematics.

The imaginative teacher will certainly add much to these suggestions for enriching mathematics instruction. Concerned teachers are constantly seeking new ways of enriching their teaching.

THE GIFTED STUDENT

Gifted students in mathematics are usually described as exhibiting ingenuity, intellectual curiosity, creative talent, an ability to assimilate and generalize, and a high level of mathematical achievement. Gifted students usually will participate in many extracurricular activities in mathematics. They are also more apt to read mathematics books, periodicals, and pamphlets. These independent activities may lead the more motivated among them to pursue a study of topics in mathematics that are either "off the beaten path" or are a part of some more advanced course (likely to be studied at a later date). Perhaps one of the more rewarding experiences for a teacher of gifted students is to observe a student making a discovery or developing an unusual approach to a topic or problem. This rare insight possessed by the gifted should be nurtured by the teacher through appropriately selected enrichment activities.

Enrichment activities for gifted students can be categorized into three types: *acceleration, expansion,* and *digression.*

Acceleration

Acceleration usually involves moving gifted students along at a faster than usual pace. This might mean starting a student's study of elementary algebra earlier and then enabling her to reach calculus (and sometimes beyond) while still in high school. It could also mean that full-year courses would be covered in less time, making room for a study of more advanced topics earlier. Perhaps the main advantage of this practice is that it allows the gifted student to remain appropriately challenged and thereby prevents loss of interest resulting from an otherwise lock-step curriculum geared to the average-ability student.

But there are also possible dangers to watch for when accelerating gifted students. If the acceleration is too rapid, the student may be asked to work with too much abstraction too quickly or too soon, that is, before he is actually "ready" for it. This sort of experience could be counterproductive, with long lasting effects. Not only must the teacher look for student readiness, but he or she must also never lose sight of the motivation that any student needs, regardless of ability. A student, after having been identified as gifted, should not merely be *pushed* along a predetermined track. If a proper balance between interest and ability is not achieved, there exists a likelihood that this gifted student could be "turned off" to mathematics.

Regardless of the form and degree of the acceleration, careful monitoring of the student both academically and socially is of paramount importance. The teacher must be sensitive to signs that may indicate that a student is perhaps mathematically overextended, generally overworked, or improperly placed socially. With this prescribed care, the acceleration process can be worthwhile; without such care it could be irreparably harmful.

Expansion

Expansion refers to that form of enrichment that allows students to delve more deeply into the topics being studied. Such expansion of the regular mathematics curriculum would take place primarily as part of the classroom mathematics instruction, but it might be a part of an extracurricular program as well. Let us look at some examples.

TOPIC　The Pythagorean theorem (high school geometry course)

ENRICHMENT　Expansion would allow the students to study any or all of the following:

1. Investigate a variety of proofs of the Pythagorean theorem.
2. Investigate the expansion of the Pythagorean theorem to acute and obtuse triangles (i.e., for acute triangles: $a^2 + b^2 > c^2$ and for obtuse triangles: $a^2 + b^2 < c^2$).
3. Study some of the properties of Pythagorean triples beginning with the formulas for generating these triples:

$$a = m^2 - n^2$$

$$b = 2mn$$

$$c = m^2 + n^2, \text{ where } m > n$$

4. Classify various types of Pythagorean triples, for example, by discovering the generating values of m and n that produce triples where $|a - b| = 1$ or where $|b - c| = 1$, and so on.
5. Consider the relationship of the Pythagorean theorem to other topics in mathematics (e.g., trigonometry, Ptolemy's Theorem and Diophantine equations).
6. Generalize the Pythagorean theorem to the law of cosines.

TOPIC　Factoring

ENRICHMENT　From the usual factoring techniques (such as factoring the difference of two squares) an expansion might have students consider some "special factorings" such as:

$$a^3 - b^3 = (a - b)(a^2 + ab + b^2)$$

$$a^3 + b^3 = (a + b)(a^2 - ab + b^2)$$

For very gifted students the general case might be very rewarding:

1. For *odd n:* $x^n + y^n = (x + y)(x^{n-1} - x^{n-2} y + x^{n-3}y^2 - \ldots + y^{n-1})$
2. For *all n:* $x^n - y^n = (x - y)(x^{n-1} + x^{n-2} y + x^{n-3} y^2 + \ldots + y^{n-1})$
3. For *even n:* $x^n - y^n = (x^{\frac{n}{2}} + y^{\frac{n}{2}}) (x^{\frac{n}{2}} - y^{\frac{n}{2}})$

In addition, some more intricate factoring examples might be provided for students to work on, such as:

$$y(y - 1)x^2 + (2y^2 - 1)x + y (y + 1)$$

which can be factored as:

$$(xy + y + 1) (xy - x + y)$$

A good source for some of these more unusual factoring examples is

Hall, H. S., and S. R. Knight. Revised by F. L. Sevenoak. *Algebra for Colleges and Schools.* New York: Macmillan, 1941.

Other older algebra texts generally have similar material.

TOPIC   Trigonometry

ENRICHMENT   Here the teacher might lead students to expand the law of sines to the law of tangents.

After the law of cosines has been developed, some more complicated triangle solution problems might be presented as an expansion of the usual problems found in current textbooks.

Once again, older textbooks provide an excellent source for expansion of a topic. One such book on trigonometry is

Kells, L. M., F. K. Willis, J. R. Bland, and J. B. Orleans. *Elements of Trigonometry.* New York: McGraw-Hill, 1943.

TOPIC   The geometry of the circle

ENRICHMENT   One possible expansion of this topic might involve a discussion of the definition and history of π, beginning with its reference in the Bible (I Kings 7:23)[6] and tracing its development to the modern computer methods of computation. A

discussion of the calculation of π can lead to some very interesting investigations (e.g., see "Constructing π," Enrichment Unit 59.)

TOPIC   Probability

ENRICHMENT   As easy as it is to state the Birthday Problem, that is how difficult it is to comprehend this unusual phenomenon. The development of the various probabilities makes a nice expansion of elementary probability and can lead the student to other related investigations (see "The Birthday Problem," Enrichment Unit 31).

TOPIC   Triangle constructions

ENRICHMENT   Usually the only geometric constructions (using straightedge and compasses) of triangles in high school geometry are those made from given measures of sides and angles. The expansion of the database to include the measures of any three of angle bisectors, medians, altitudes, or other triangle-related parts should lead the student to a more genuine understanding of triangle properties. You can begin to acquaint yourself with this topic by reading "Triangle Constructions," Enrichment Unit 38. A far more extensive treatment of this very rich topic can be found in *Advanced Geometric Constructions* by A. S. Posamentier and W. Wernick (Palo Alto: Dale Seymour, 1988).

In each of the preceding examples of enrichment through the expansion of a topic in the regular curriculum, you will notice that the discussion was always confined to an embellishment of the original topic and not a digression to another topic. This latter situation is our last form of enrichment to be discussed.

Digression

A popular form of enrichment generally results when the teacher digresses from a topic in the regular curriculum to consider another topic that is related to and generally an outgrowth of the first topic. Since a gifted class can usually master a topic more quickly than an average class, more time is available for discussion of another related topic before continuing with the regular prescribed curriculum. These digressions are usually rewarding and can last from a portion of a class session to several sessions. As with other enrichment activities discussed, digressions should be used to enrich the regular curriculum, not detract from it. Often these enrichment activities can be glamorous, which by contrast can make the regular curriculum appear somewhat less appealing. Therefore, the teacher, conscious of this possibility, should try to continuously relate a digression to the regular curriculum, so

---

[6] For an interesting interpretation of this reference see "An Astounding Revelation on the History of π" by A. S. Posamentier and N. Gordon. *The Mathematics Teacher.* (Reston, Virginia: January 1984.) National Council of Teachers of Mathematics.

that instead of detracting from it, the enrichment topic will in fact embellish it. The following examples should help provide a better understanding of what is meant by an enrichment activity that represents a digression from the regular curriculum.

TOPIC   Geometry (junior high or middle school)

ENRICHMENT   Treated appropriately, the topic of networks can be a worthwhile digression from the study of informal geometry. With the possible goal of investigating the Königsberg Bridge problem, the study of networks can be exciting and can lead to other related topological investigations (see ''Networks,'' Enrichment Unit 96).

TOPIC   Trigonometry (high school level)

ENRICHMENT   After a student has a good working knowledge of the trigonometry included in the regular curriculum, an interesting digression might be one that allows the student to study spherical trigonometry. Of course, this presupposes a knowledge of some spherical geometry. Yet, this sort of digression can lead to a more complete understanding of trigonometry.

TOPIC   Concurrency (high school geometry)

ENRICHMENT   Perhaps because the topics of concurrency and collinearity are often slighted in the high school geometry course, a digression to study these topics more fully might be worthwhile. Specifically, the development of the theorems of Giovanni Ceva (1647–1736) and Menelaus of Alexandria (ca. A.D. 100) can lead to many other interesting geometric phenomena. To begin to acquaint yourself with these topics, see ''Proving Lines Concurrent,'' Enrichment Unit 53 and ''Proving Points Collinear,'' Enrichment Unit 55. For further ideas you may wish to consult *Excursions in Advanced Euclidean Geometry* by A. S. Posamentier (Menlo Park, CA: Addison-Wesley Pub. Co., 1984).

TOPIC   Quadratic equations (algebra)

ENRICHMENT   After studying the various ways to solve quadratic equations, students may wish to learn how to solve other higher-degree equations. A consideration of some methods of solving cubic equations might be enlightening to gifted students. This sort of investigation will lead them to appreciate some of the work of the early mathematicians (e.g., Nicolo Tartaglia, 1506–1557). (See calculator section, this chapter.)

TOPIC   Conic sections (advanced high school level)

ENRICHMENT   The resourceful teacher certainly will discuss some of the many physical applications of conic sections, yet rarely will a teacher digress to discuss how conics can be constructed. This discussion should lead to envelopes of the conic curves. An enjoyable offshoot of this investigation is the topic of curve stitching (see ''Constructing Ellipses,'' Enrichment Unit 106, and ''Constructing the Parabola,'' Enrichment Unit 107).

The only restriction on the topics that make appropriate digressions for enrichment is the teacher's judgment. There are many possible topics from which to choose. The selected digression should be related to the topic in the curriculum that is to serve as the takeoff point and should be properly planned so as to have a clear beginning, a logical conclusion, and above all, a specific purpose.

USING TECHNOLOGY TO ENRICH INSTRUCTION

Integrating the latest technological advances in computers and calculators to enrich the curriculum must be an ongoing process for educators. Today, it means teaching the skills needed for effective use of scientific and graphics calculators. Tomorrow, who knows? Multimedia classroom lessons are already in the works for the available large monitors and screens, video projectors, flat panel displays, and a huge variety of audio equipment.

New visions of computer literacy include word processing, graphics, transformations and fractals, desktop publishing, database building, computer-constructed designs, spreadsheets, and programming.

Networks that utilize fiber optic technology already exist and connect different sites with a single master teacher. These are not just sit-and-stare setups; students respond to each other and to the teacher. Homework assignments, corrected papers, and exams are faxed for instant communication.

A branch of computer science devoted to simulating functions of the human brain is the growing field of artificial intelligence (AI). A course of study in AI has been proposed for the high school level, although the topic had been reserved for advanced graduate work in the past. Students who delve into this field will learn about problems that are not easily solved because they involve areas of ''uncertainty.''

The calculator industry began a process of significant advances in 1958 with the development of an integrated circuit. Thus, the need for many separate transistors and mechanical connections in the design of calculators was eliminated. In 1971, Texas Instruments' ''calculator-on-a-chip'' paved the way for the hand-held minicalculator.

In addition to being acquainted with the role of computers and calculators in society, most students will have obtained a working knowledge of how to use them well before taking this course. The availability of the technology has had an impact not only on the computational skills demanded by society but on such algebraic skills as solution of equations and graphing functions. The impact has also been felt through a diminished need for trigonometric and logarithmic tables and interpolation. Furthermore, the range of problems that can be readily solved has expanded dramatically. Each of these dimensions is demonstrated in the following pages.

The NCTM's *Standards* strongly endorses the availability of calculators for all students at all levels. The National Council of Supervisors of Mathematics, in its June 1988 newsletter, notes that, ''Teaching strategies that emphasize concept development rather than skill development need to be used. When calculators are used efficiently and appropriately, students become better problem solvers, their achievement level increases, and they will become more mathematically powerful.'' This is one of the anticipated goals of the mathematics of the *Standards*.

Calculators

The simplest and least expensive calculators usually contain the four basic operations, some memory capabilities, and, occasionally, square root and percent keys. Scientific calculators possess the same capabilities plus much more. They vary greatly as far as function capabilities, display panel, size, and ease of operation.

Advanced scientific calculators are usually calculators with graphing capabilities. These contain a small screen capable of indicating a line of numeric or alphabetic text, a graph in rectangular or polar coordinates, a matrix, bar graph, shaded regions, and more.

Calculators are available from several manufacturers, and although each has its own operating instructions, certain significant features remain constant. As a result, the suggested fundamental exercises apply to any calculator regardless of age or type. Any special feature required to produce the desired outcome are indicated in the activities that follow.

USING A CALCULATOR

A recommended beginning-of-the-term small group activity suitable for any level, geared to make students feel comfortable with one another, with the teacher, with a new group, or with the entire class, is a quick review of the calculator's memory and square root keys. This could

be followed by a speed and accuracy ''contest'' involving arithmetic operations.

Most calculators are equipped with memory keys that make possible a variety of challenging activities. These keys provide an efficient way to save intermediate results. They can also store a number that needs to be used several times during the course of an exercise.

The [M+] key adds the number displayed to the contents of the memory and stores the sum in the memory. The number displayed is not changed.

The [M−] key subtracts the number displayed from the contents of the memory and stores the difference in the memory. The number displayed is not changed.

The [MR] key recalls the contents of the memory, which replaces the contents of the display.

EXAMPLE   Find the value of $5 \times 12 + 13 \times 16$.

SOLUTION   Press:

$$5 \times 12 = [M+]13 \times 16 = +[MR] =$$
The display will read 268.

Now challenge your students to use the memory keys when finding the values in exercises such as these:

1. $15 \times 13 + 18 \times 32$
2. $-15 \times 13 + 226 - 81$
3. $(253/11) + (-23)$
4. $(335 - 281) \times (-81 + 37)$

The following examples illustrate additional exercises. Their number and type should be increased if they are being used for any sort of contest.

5. Evaluate $\dfrac{23.4 \times 17.6}{50 \times 8}$ to the nearest tenth

or even

6. Evaluate $\dfrac{2}{\sqrt{2} - 1}$ to the nearest hundredth

When preparing the class for such contests, much excitement can be generated while good arithmetic is being taught.

A Device for Better Understanding Mathematics Concepts

By experimenting with calculators, students can see various relationships between numbers evolve. For example, they can discover what type of divisors will generate repeating or terminating decimals. They can discover ways of detecting prime numbers. They may discover unusual number patterns. They can dissect the common arithmetic computational algorithms and perhaps devise others. All these activities can lead to creative work. Yet, most important is proper teacher guidance, for without this the student could end up losing the educational benefits of this attractive and useful device.

An Aid to Learning Problem Solving

A common complaint among teachers is that "students have great difficulty with computation and, what is worse, they are very weak in problem solving." This is unfortunately a self-perpetuating ill. Students who cannot succeed with arithmetic computation are constantly told to drill these skills and are rarely allowed to practice any problem-solving skills. Those who do go on to working on some elementary problems often do not get near an answer because of computational deficiencies. Their only exposure to problem solving is one of frustration, and they never realize success because of computational obstacles. Here the calculator can be of significant assistance. Selective use of the calculator to bypass potential computational barriers will allow students to concentrate on problem-solving skills without fear of meeting frustration previously caused by their computational difficulties. Such activities should be carefully designed and monitored to be effective. After realizing success in problem solving, students should then be intrinsically motivated to conquer their computational deficiencies.

Making Mathematics Problem Solving More Realistic

Although continuously nurtured on the typical textbook problems, students usually find them boring and unrealistic. Traditionally, textbook authors design the problems in a way that will make the arithmetic computations as simple as possible so as not to detract from the problem. Real-life situations frequently are quite different. The numbers used are generally not simple. With the aid of a calculator, a teacher can provide realistic situations for problem solving and not worry about computational distractions. A uniform-motion problem, for example, can involve fractional quantities and yield an answer that is not an integer and cause no displeasure for the student who has a calculator available. Furthermore, students using a calculator can be encouraged to create problems based on their own experiences (e.g., calculating their average speed walking to school). New vistas are opened up when a calculator is used to assist in problem solving.

Investigating Unusual Curiosities

With the aid of a calculator, many interesting (and often unquestioned) mathematical curiosities that appear in the average citizen's everyday experiences can serve as excellent applications of high school mathematics. For example, bank advertisements highlight the *effective annual yield* after stating their annual interest rate. A recent inspection turned up the following effective annual yields for a 5¼% annual interest rate compounded daily: 5.35%, 5.38%, 5.39%, and 5.46%. Legally inserting a varying number of days (in a year), n, at different parts of the formula $I = \left(1 + \dfrac{r}{n}\right)^n - 1$, creates a variety of answers. Availability of a calculator encourages this sort of investigation. Another possible investigation might involve determining the effect of tax-exempt income on individuals in various income tax brackets.

An example in the *Standards* (p. 132–136) illustrates how the same content may be presented at different levels even though teaching strategies will vary in accordance with levels of interest, skills, and goals. A brief description of the example follows.

Consider the problem of finding the amount of money that will be in a savings account at the end of ten years given the amount of the original deposit ($100) and an interest rate compounded annually (6%).

At Level 1 in the core curriculum, students use calculators to solve the problem by determining the amount after each successive year. They might also use a computer spreadsheet. Students are encouraged to find an underlying pattern, for example:

$$\text{Amount at the end of 1 year} = 100(1.06)^1$$

$$\text{Amount at the end of 10 years} = 100(1.06)^{10}$$

At Level 2, students generalize this problem in stages, finally arriving at the formula $A_n = A_0(1 + r)^n$, where A_n is the amount after n years, A_0 is the amount of the original deposit, and r is the annual interest rate.

At Level 3, students further generalize the formula so that they can explore problems in which the rate is compounded semiannually, quarterly, monthly, or daily.

At Level 4, students should be able to solve the formula given by Level 2 for any of the variables.

Possible extensions of the topic include

- solving problems in which compound growth in biology and rate of decay in chemistry provide appropriate applications;
- proving the results using mathematical induction;
- making a connection between this topic and the irrational number e.

Many other real-life problems (such as loans, taxes, and installment purchases) can be investigated with the aid of a calculator. Such investigations can serve as excellent sources of applications for the regular secondary school curriculum. There are many ideas for problems in the NCTM's 1979 Yearbook, *Applications in School Mathematics.*

Classroom Calculator Activities

Teachers ought to take advantage of the fact that calculators can generate data accurately and rapidly. The student is thus allowed the "luxury" of exploring mathematics and making observations and conjectures without being burdened with tedious and difficult calculations. A class can now have the opportunity to explore problems that would otherwise remain within the realm of the staggering or possibly even discouraging. Problems that would *never* be considered are now candidates for solution by students with only marginal arithmetic ability. It is hoped that the result will be a sharpening of thinking and analytical skill.

Preliminary activities such as gathering or estimating appropriate data will make these problems far more realistic and enjoyable than the traditional ones with their plug-in solution techniques. Here are some examples of the types of problems that might be considered, depending on the grade level, ability, and maturity of the class:

1. How many drops of water are contained in an ordinary drinking glass?
2. How many hairs are on the heads of all pupils in the class?
3. What is the number of grains of sand in a box whose dimensions are 12 inches $\times$ 4 inches $\times$ 6 inches?
4. Estimate the area of a circle whose radius is 5 inches. Find the dimensions of a rectangle whose area is approximately that of the circle.
5. How many minutes, or hours, or days do you spend watching television each month? Each year? Compare this number with the amount of time you spend in school.
6. How many feet are there in the circumference of the earth? How many inches? How many meters?

There is an unlimited variety of problems that a creative teacher can encourage pupils to both *write* and *solve* with a calculator. See Enrichment Unit 11, Enrichment with a Hand-Held Calculator.

Following are six additional calculator activities that could serve as special challenges for students in grades 7–9:

Conjecturing Rules

Complete the chart:

List 50 random whole numbers	(1) Multiply by 2	(2) Multiply by 10	(3) Multiply by 100	(4) Multiply by 1000
1				
2				
17				
23				
107				
113				
⋮				

Now answer these questions:

1. What do you notice about the last digit of each number in column 1? Make a conjecture.
2. Compare columns 2, 3, and 4. What do you notice? Make a conjecture.
3. Complete the chart for 50 random decimals. Make some conjectures and test them. Can you prove your conjectures?
4. Complete the chart for 50 random decimals but divide in columns 2, 3, and 4. Make and test some conjectures. Can you prove them?

Four Magic Digits

1. Choose any four different digits, such as 2, 3, 4, and 5.
   Follow these steps:
   (a) Form the largest number you can: 5 4 3 2
       Form the smallest number: − 2 3 4 5

       Subtract: 3 0 8 7
   (b) With the digits 3, 0, 7, and 8, from the difference, follow these steps:
       Form the largest number: 8 7 3 0
       Form the smallest number: − 3 7 8

       Subtract: 8 3 5 2
   (c) With 8, 3, 5, and 2, follow these steps:
       Form the largest number: 8 5 3 2
       Form the smallest number: − 2 3 5 8

       Subtract: 6 1 7 4
   After three subtractions you have a number with the magic digits 1, 4, 6, 7.
2. Repeat exercise 1 with 1, 5, 6, and 8. You will find the magic digits 1, 4, 6, 7 in some order after three subtractions. Write your solution as in exercise 1.

3. With four different digits, it is always possible to reach a four-digit number having 1, 4, 6, and 7 in some order. Start with the digits 9, 8, 7, and 6. See if you can reach 6174 after three subtractions.

4. Study your solution for exercise 2. Starting with four digits obtain a number with 1, 4, 6, and 7 in it after these numbers of subtractions: 1, 2, 4, 5, 6.

Magic Squares

1. This magic square has four rows, four columns, and two diagonals. Find the sum of each. If the eight sums are not the same, check your work.

16	2	3	13
5	11	10	8
9	7	6	12
4	14	15	1

2. Find sets of four numbers in a pattern whose sum is 34. Here are three examples. Find twelve more examples. Draw 4-by-4 squares to show your solutions.

Strange Products

1. Find the product of each of the following:

(a)   68   86   (b)   63   36
     × 43   × 34   × 24   × 42

(c)   93   39
     × 13   × 31

2. (a) Are the two products in exercise 1 equal in (a), (b), and (c)?
   (b) Are the digits in the factors reversed in exercise 1(a), 1(b), and 1(c)?

3. Find the product of each of the following:

(a)   84   48   (b)   64   46
     × 12   × 21   × 23   × 32

(c)   82   28   (d)   56   65
     × 14   × 41   × 21   × 12

(e)   49   94   (f)   75   57
     × 63   × 36   × 68   × 86

4. (a) Are the digits in exercise 3 reversed in each factor?
   (b) In which pairs of exercise 3 are the products equal?
   (c) Try to write examples such as exercise 3(a) to 3(c) where the products are equal.

5. Check to make sure the products are equal in each of the following:

(a)   96   69   (b)   84   48
     × 23   × 32   × 36   × 63

(c)   93   39
     × 26   × 62

6. Make up some examples like those in exercises 1 and 5.

7. Write the rule you used for making up the examples in exercise 6.

Surprises

1. (a) Choose a three-digit number, for example, 295.
   (b) Make a six-digit number by repeating the 295. The number is now 295 295.
   (c) Divide 295 295 by 13. The quotient is _____.
   (d) Divide that quotient by 11. The quotient is _____.
   (e) Divide that quotient by 7. The quotient is _____.

2. Repeat exercise 1 with the numbers 347 347, 921 921, and 164 164.

Social Chains

Two numbers are amicable (or friendly) if each is the sum of the proper divisors of the other. For example:

284 and 220 are amicable.

The proper factors of 220 are 1, 2, 4, 5, 10, 11, 20, 22, 44, 55, and 110. The sum is 284.

The proper factors of 284 are 1, 2, 4, 71, and 142. The sum is 220. (220 and 284 were known to Pythagoras about 500 B.C.)

No new pair of amicable numbers was discovered until 1636 when the French number theorist Fermat announced 17 296 and 18 416 as another pair. In about 1760, after searching systematically, Euler discovered over sixty pairs. A small pair that he overlooked (1184 and 1210) was discovered by Nicolo Paganini, a sixteen-year-old boy, in 1886. Today about 1000 pairs of amicable numbers are known. The last pair was discovered in 1976. One number in this pair is 5 070 746 263 958 274 212 545 800 175 616.

    a. Prove that 17 296 and 18 416 are amicable.
    b. Prove that 1184 and 1210 are amicable.
    c. Can you prove that both numbers must be even or odd?

Aids in Advanced Mathematics Courses

Problems in advanced secondary school mathematics courses can often involve extensive calculations. It is not many years ago that the slide rule or logarithms were used to solve such problems. Even Napier's rods and the abacus played a role at one point in the history of people's attempt to be free of the burden of onerous manual calculations. The abacus is still used in some parts of the less technologically advanced world. Today, the logical method of computation at this level is the calculator. A scientific calculator (i.e., one that, among other features, includes trigonometric functions) and a graphics calculator are very useful aids.

The Scientific Calculator

With the increased availability of, and student familiarity with, scientific calculators, there is less need for trigonometric tables, logarithmic tables or linear interpolation techniques. This is not to be interpreted as meaning that these skills should not be studied by students.

In addition to the trig and log functions, most scientific calculators also include the $\sqrt{\ }$ key for square roots, a y^x key for powers, and often a $\sqrt[x]{y}$ key that can be used to calculate cube roots, fourth roots, fifth roots, and so on.

Compound interest or exponential decay problems connect mathematics with real-life situations as well as with scientific and mathematics applications. After developing the compound interest formula (page 151), students will be ready to consider this problem:

> **PROBLEM** What is the resulting amount if $1000 is invested for 10 years at 11% compounded annually?

CALCULATOR SOLUTION (use the power key)

$$A_n = \$1000(1.11)^{10} = \$2839.42$$

The half-life of a substance is defined to be the amount of time it takes for half of an initial amount to disappear as a result of decay. For example, suppose you have 100 grams of a substance that has a half-life of 5 days. This means that after 5 days, $100\left(\dfrac{1}{2}\right) = 50$ grams remain. After 10 days, $100\left(\dfrac{1}{2}\right)^2 = 25$ grams remain. After 15 days, $100\left(\dfrac{1}{2}\right)^3 = 12.5$ grams remain, and so forth. Ask the class to generalize the formula that describes exponential decay for such a substance: $A_n = A_0\left(\dfrac{1}{2}\right)^{\frac{n}{5}}$, where A_n is the amount of this substance remaining after n days, A_0 is the initial amount, n is the number of days the substance was subjected to decay. Ask the class to use a calculator when they consider these problems:

> **PROBLEM** How many grams of 100 grams of a substance with a half-life of 5 days will remain after 30 days? After 60 days?

CALCULATOR SOLUTION

$$A_{30} = 100\left(\frac{1}{2}\right)^6 = 1.5625 \text{ grams}$$

$$A_{60} = 0.0244 \text{ grams}$$

A general formula for substances with other rates of decay should now be considered, and a calculator should be used to solve problems involving them.

The law of sines in trigonometry is another area where complex manual or logarithmic calculations may be bypassed with a calculator, after some initial preparation. Consider the following exercise:

> **PROBLEM** In $\triangle ABC$, $m\angle A = 35.1°$, $a = 24.7$ cm, $b = 38.2$ cm. Use a calculator to determine $m\angle B$ to the nearest $0.1°$.

Initial equation: $\sin B = \dfrac{38.2 \sin 35.1°}{24.7}$

CALCULATOR SOLUTION (use the arc or inverse function to find $m\angle B$)

$$m\angle B = 62.8° \text{ or } 117.2°$$

Although many scientific calculators do not have secant, cosecant, or cotangent keys, they may have inverse or $\dfrac{1}{x}$ keys, so that those three functions can still be evaluated for any positive or negative angles.

Inverse trig, various statistics functions, random numbers, exponential and hyperbolic functions, and an assortment of miscellaneous capabilities usually round out the scientific calculator's available keys. Most of these are more than sufficient for regular or extracurricular use by students, whether college bound or not. Guide your pupils, if they have not already done so, to invest in a scientific calculator that will be suitable for both their present and future needs.

The Graphics Calculator

A significant advance in miniaturization has been achieved in the pocket or pocketbook size graphics calculator. Containing all the power of a scientific calculator, it has the additional capability of displaying graphs of algebraic or trigonometric functions, continuous or discontinuous, in either rectangular or polar coordinates. It can indicate shaded regions determined by linear and/or quadratic inequalities, solve systems of first-degree equations using matrix operations, solve higher order equations of any reasonable degree to any reasonable degree of accuracy, and do an assortment of statistical calculations. The ''reasonable'' limitations of the graphics calculator are usually due to its physical design and are indicated in the operator's manual.

Some of the capabilities of the graphics calculator are best described through the illustrations and demonstrations that follow. Although many types of graphics calculators are produced, their operating variations are not significant. Each is packaged with an operator's manual that specifies details about that particular machine. For purposes of this text, two calculators widely used by students and schools, Texas Instruments' TI-81 Graphics Calculator and Casio's fx-115M scientific calculator, are utilized. However, all students will adapt themselves to their chosen calculator once they establish a degree of comfort with that machine through its operator's manual.

Activities for the Graphics Calculator (Grades 9–12)

PROBLEM Use a graphics calculator to find the real positive root of the equation $x^3 - 2x - 5 = 0$, correct to three decimal places.

After you enter the graph of the function $y = x^3 - 2x - 5$ on the screen, obtain the roots of the equation by determining its intersection(s) with the x-axis. Roots may be determined to any degree of precision by placing the cursor as close as possible to the intersection of the graph with the x-axis, reading the x-intercept as indicated

on the graphics calculator, and repeating this process on a magnification of the graph until the desired accuracy is obtained.

Specific instructions for the TI-81 follow: After turning the calculator on, press the keys of the letters, numbers, symbols, or words in the order indicated:

1. $\boxed{\text{y} =}$
2. $\boxed{\text{x} \, \text{t}}$ $\boxed{\land}$ $\boxed{3}$ $\boxed{-}$ $\boxed{2}$ $\boxed{\text{x} \, \text{t}}$ $\boxed{-}$ $\boxed{5}$ $\boxed{\text{enter}}$ $\boxed{\text{graph}}$ (see figure)
3. $\boxed{\text{trace}}$ (this places a flashing cursor on the graph)
4. Move the cursor to the left or right with the appropriate ◄ or ► key,
5. After setting the cursor as close as possible to the root (note that the coordinates of the cursor appear on the screen), you can get a more precise estimate after you press the sequence $\boxed{\text{zoom}}$ $\boxed{2}$ $\boxed{\text{enter}}$ several times, readjusting the cursor to the left, right, up, or down until it falls as close as possible to the intersection of the graph with the x-axis.

After pressing this sequence of keys four times and readjusting the cursor each time, you will see the approximate value of x, 2.095, on the screen. Thus, the root, correct to the nearest thousandth, is 2.095 (see figure).

Note that quadratic, linear, trigonometric, logarithmic, and exponential equations may be solved in a similar manner.

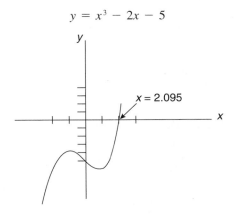

$$y = x^3 - 2x - 5$$

PROBLEM Use a graphics calculator to shade the region determined by the inequalities $y > x^2 - 2$ and $y < 2x + 1$.

After determining that the memory has been cleared, press $\boxed{\text{2nd}}$ $\boxed{\text{quit}}$ to begin on a clean blank line. Continue to press the keys sequentially as shown:

1. $\boxed{\text{2nd}}$ $\boxed{\text{Prgm}}$
2. $\boxed{7}$ (shade)
3. $\boxed{\text{x} \, \text{t}}$ $\boxed{\land}$ $\boxed{2}$ $\boxed{-}$ $\boxed{2}$

4. |alpha| |.|
5. |2| |x,t| |+| |1|
6. |)|
7. |enter|

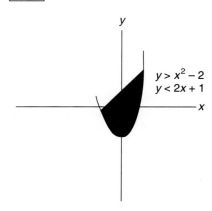

$y > x^2 - 2$
$y < 2x + 1$

PROBLEM Use the matrix capabilities of a graphics calculator to solve the system

$$2x - y + z = 5$$
$$x + 2y - z = 0$$
$$4x + 2y + 5z = 6$$

Use the calculator to create a 3 × 3 matrix [A] containing the coefficients of x, y, and z; a 3 × 1 matrix [X] containing the variables x, y, and z; and a 3 × 1 matrix [C] containing the constant terms in the equation. Then solve [A][X] = [C] for [X] by multiplying [C] by the inverse matrix $[A]^{-1}$, so that $[X] = [A]^{-1}[C]$.

After pressing |ON|, press the following sequence of keys:

1. |MATRIX| |▶|
2. |1| |3| |▶| |3|
3. Enter the elements by rows following each with a movement down |▼|:
   |2| |▼| |(−)| |1| |▼| |1| |▼|
   |1| |▼| |2| |▼| |(−)| |1| |▼|
   |4| |▼| |2| |▼| |5|
4. |MATRIX| |▶| |3|
5. To set dimensions of [C] to 3 × 1, press
   |3| |▶| |1|
6. To enter the elements into matrix [C], press
   |▼|
   |5| |▼|
   |0| |▼|
   |6|
7. Press |2nd| |QUIT|

8. Then press |2nd| |1| ([A]) |x⁻¹| |2nd| |3|([C])
   |ENTER| and obtain $x = 2$, $y = -1$, $z = 0$.

$$\begin{bmatrix} 2 & -1 & 1 \\ 1 & 2 & -1 \\ 4 & 2 & 5 \end{bmatrix} \begin{bmatrix} x \\ y \\ z \end{bmatrix} = \begin{bmatrix} 5 \\ 0 \\ 6 \end{bmatrix}$$

$$\Rightarrow \begin{bmatrix} x \\ y \\ z \end{bmatrix} = \begin{bmatrix} 2 & -1 & 1 \\ 1 & 2 & -1 \\ 4 & 2 & 5 \end{bmatrix}^{-1} \begin{bmatrix} 5 \\ 0 \\ 6 \end{bmatrix}$$

$$= \begin{bmatrix} 2 \\ -1 \\ 0 \end{bmatrix}$$

Answer: $x = 2$, $y = -1$, $z = 0$

PROBLEM Compare the graphic calculator solution with the identical problem solved algebraically. Use your graphics calculator to help you

a. sketch the shape of each graph;
b. determine its domain and range;
c. write the equation(s) of asymptotes (if any);
d. describe what happens as $x \to \pm \infty$;
e. find the intercepts.

(i) $y = \dfrac{8x + 1}{x^2 + 1}$

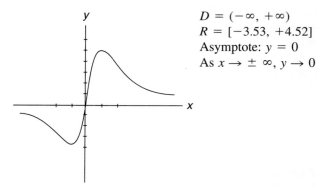

$D = (-\infty, +\infty)$
$R = [-3.53, +4.52]$
Asymptote: $y = 0$
As $x \to \pm \infty$, $y \to 0$

(ii) $y = \dfrac{x^2 - x - 6}{x^2 - 5x + 4}$ (see page 157)

$D = (-\infty, +\infty)$
$R = (-\infty, +\infty)$
Asymptotes $y = 1$, $x = 1$, $x = 4$
As $x \to +\infty$, $y \to 1^+$
As $x \to -\infty$, $y \to 1^-$

$$y = \frac{x^2 - x - 6}{x^2 - 5x + 4}$$

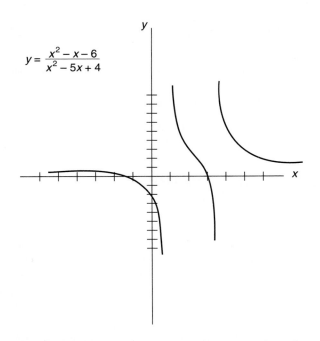

PROBLEM Solve each rational equation algebraically, then use the graphing methods outlined below to confirm your solution:

(a) $\dfrac{9}{2x + 1} = 3$

    Algebraic solution:

      $3(2x + 1) = 9$

        $6x + 3 = 9$

          $6x = 6$ and $x = 1$ (*Answer*)

Graphic solution: Graph $y = \dfrac{9}{2x + 1} - 3$ and determine the root (i.e., confirm your algebraic solution).

$$y = \frac{9}{2x + 1} - 3$$

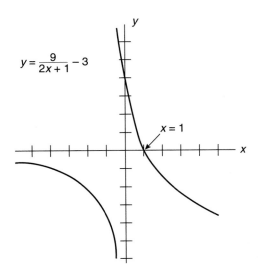

$x = 1$

(b) $\dfrac{4}{3} + \dfrac{x - 3}{4} - \dfrac{3x - 1}{6} = 0$

Algebraic solution:

$$12\left(\frac{4}{3} + \frac{x - 3}{4} - \frac{3x - 1}{6} = 0\right)$$

$$16 + 3(x - 3) - 2(3x - 1) = 0$$

$$16 + 3x - 9 - 6x + 2 = 0$$

$$-3x + 9 = 0$$

$$3x = 9$$

$$x = 3 \quad (\textit{Answer})$$

Graphic solution: Graph $y = \dfrac{4}{3} + \dfrac{x - 3}{4} - \dfrac{3x - 1}{6}$ and determine the root to confirm your algebraic solution.

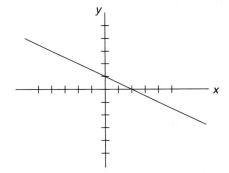

Note: The graphic solution is between

$$x = 2.842$$
and
$$x = 3.053$$

It is therefore reasonable to attempt $x = 3$ as the solution of

$$\frac{4}{3} + \frac{x - 3}{4} - \frac{3x - 1}{6} = 0$$

PROBLEM A riverboat can travel 5 miles per hour when there is no current. The captain takes some passengers up the river on a 6-mile round trip excursion, 3 miles each way. The total time for the trip is 7 hours. What is the rate of the current, x?

Algebraic solution: $\dfrac{3}{5 - x} + \dfrac{3}{5 + x} = 7$

$$30 = 175 - 7x^2$$

$$x = \sqrt{\frac{145}{7}}$$

$$x \approx 4.6 \text{ miles per hour}$$

Graphic solution: Use a calculator to graph the function.

Total time $T(x) = \dfrac{3}{5-x} + \dfrac{3}{5+x} - 7$, and find $x \approx 4.55$.

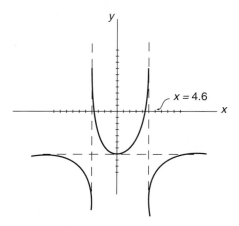

$x = 4.6$

PROBLEM An automobile mechanic can repair a carburetor in 2 hours less time than her assistant. After they work together for 3 hours, the mechanic leaves to do a brake job for another customer. Meanwhile, the assistant finishes the carburetor job in 1 more hour. How long would it have taken each to do the carburetor job alone?

SOLUTION The equation $\dfrac{4}{x} + \dfrac{3}{x-2} = 1$ yields $x = 1$ and $x = 8$. Reject the $x = 1$ as being meaningless for this problem. Use a calculator to find the root(s) of the function $T(x) = \dfrac{4}{x} + \dfrac{3}{x-2} - 1$ to verify the algebraic answer.

PROBLEM Find the first quadrant angle that satisfies the equation $\cos x + \sin x = \sqrt{2}$.

An algebraic solution produces $\cos x = \dfrac{\sqrt{2}}{2}$, so that $x = \dfrac{\pi}{4} \approx 0.8$ (see page 159).

Graphing the function $f(x) = \cos x + \sin x - \sqrt{2}$ produces the value $x \approx 0.8$.

ENRICHMENT IN THE 21ST CENTURY

Pages 160–162 contain charts of SAMPLE ENRICHMENT TOPICS for years 1, 2, and 3 of a model core curriculum as found in the ADDENDA SERIES, GRADE 9–12, of the *Standards* (pp. 68–71.) Contained in the chart are proposals for enrichment of school mathematics beyond the nineties. They provide gifted students with opportunities to achieve new perspectives and deeper explorations in mathematics—for example, studying paradoxes, exploring unsolved problems, constructibility of squares on a geoboard, generating random numbers, properties of combined functions such as $y = x \sin x$, DeMorgan's laws of logic—as well as innumerable calculator tasks. One such calculator task is this TI-81 program to plot a fractal using random numbers:

```
PrgmF:FRACTAL
2 → X
1.5 → Y
Lbl 4
(Int(Rand*3)+1) mod #4 → A
If A=0
Goto 4
```

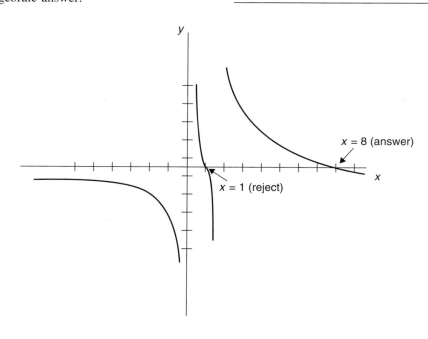

$x = 8$ (answer)

$x = 1$ (reject)

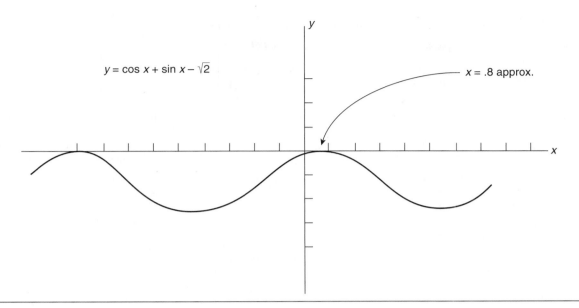

$y = \cos x + \sin x - \sqrt{2}$

$x = .8$ approx.

```
If A=1
Goto 1
If A=2
Goto 2
If A=3
Goto 3
Lbl 1
(X+1)/2 → X
(Y+1)/2 → Y
Pt-On[X,Y]
Goto 4
Lbl 2
(X+3)/2 → X
(Y+1)/2 → Y
Pt-On(X,Y)
Goto 4
Lbl 3
(X+2)/2 → X
(Y+(1+√3))/2 → Y
Pt-On(X,Y)
Goto 4
```

Note: Range of graphics screen should be set at [1, 3] ×[1, 3]. (Adapted and reprinted with permission from *A Core Curriculum: Making Mathematics Count for Everyone,* copyright 1992 by the National Council of Teachers of Mathematics.)

PSEUDO-CALCULATORS

Many pseudo-calculators currently on the market can provide students with preprogrammed drill or arithmetic exercises. These units range from small hand-held types, which *appear* to be calculators, to large desktop models, which provide a printout record. Each generates randomly selected exercises within a preselected skill area and reacts to a correct student response by offering another exercise or informing the student of an error if an incorrect response is given. Very often the printout provided by the desktop calculators will be particularly useful to the teacher who has to monitor numerous students working at different skills.

Some of the features of calculators produced today are programming capabilities, a useful constant feature that allows for repeated operations with the same number or expression, rounding and fraction capabilities, the ability to express division as a quotient with remainder, and printout capabilities when linked with a compatible computer. The Casio FX-7500G, and a series of Texas Instruments display calculators are among the brands that feature many of the qualities just described.

Calculators use the same kinds of components as computers and are, in fact, capable of many of the same kinds of operations. They can be considered a subset of the set of computers. Calculators are computers that process numerical data and perform mathematical operations. They are most efficient for routine computations. However, when the need for repetitive calculations arises, computers are the dominant tool.

COMPUTERS

The advances of the electronic computer, since the development of the ENIAC in 1946, have been dramatic. From the large, expensive computers known as mainframes, to minicomputers of moderate cost and size, to the smaller, quite versatile microcomputers that are relatively inexpensive, computer availability as well as accessibility has continued to increase for school as well as home use.

Microcomputers, which we will simply refer to as computers, began to be used seriously in the classroom in the early 1980s. Although the uses of the computer span the

SAMPLE ENRICHMENT TOPICS*
Year 1

UNIT	POSSIBLE ENRICHMENT TOPIC	RELATING TO ... IN UNIT	COMMENTS
Exploring [plane] geometric figures	Finite geometries	Basic vocabulary and concepts	Investigate concepts such as parallel lines in finite geometries, where the concepts will be analogous but will look different.
Exploring data	Representing geographic data by scale drawings; creating databases for future analysis	Representing data	A map of Africa can be redrawn to illustrate each country as a function of its population. If 1 cm^2 represents 1 million people, Nigeria would have an area of 115 cm^2 and Malawi an area of 8 cm^2.
Graphs	Finite graphs using modular numbers	Representations of solutions of open sentences	Relate the graphs of equations over the integers modulo 3. For example, the graph of $x + 2y = 1$ (mod 3) will consist of three points with coordinates (0, 2), (1, 0), and (2, 1), and the graphs of $x + 2y = 0$ and $x + 2y = 2$ will be ''lines'' that are ''parallel.''
Expressions, sentences	Tautologies and inconsistencies	Equivalent and non-equivalent expressions	Identify sentences that are always true and their proofs.
Models for operations	Geometric (length) models for sums, differences, products, and quotients	Models for operations	This could be done using geometric software (such as the Geometer's Sketchpad).
Linear situations, sentences, graphs	Diophantine equations	Solving linear equations	This could include problems like ''the chickens and cows have 50 legs and 16 heads'' problem. (How many of each are there?)
Special powers	Generating Pythagorean triples and Fermat's last theorem	Pythagorean theorem	
Properties of geometric figures	Fractals	Perimeter and area	Investigate fractal dimension using guess-and-check (e.g., to solve $3^D = 4$, use the calculator exponent key to estimate that D is about 1.26).
Measures in geometry	Archimedes' approach to area and volume, such as the area under a parabola	Areas of irregular figures	
Probability and simulation	Fractals	Simulation	See pages 158 and 159 for a program that generates random ordered pairs of numbers, which when plotted result in a fractal.
Functions	Graphing relations as unions of functions and solving problems about relations	Solving equations using a function grapher	For example, solve the system $x^2 + y^2 = 4$ and $y = x^3$ by graphing the circle as $y = \pm \sqrt{4 - x^2}$.

SAMPLE ENRICHMENT TOPICS*

Year 2

UNIT	POSSIBLE ENRICHMENT TOPIC	RELATING TO ... IN UNIT	COMMENTS
Variation and modeling	Chaos theory	Introduction to modeling	See the use of quadratic functions to model animal populations in *Chaos* by James Gleick.
Coordinate geometry	Constructibility of figures on a lattice (geoboard)	Proofs in coordinate geometry	For example, what size squares can be constructed on a geoboard?
Transformations and geometric figures	Symmetry groups, such as that of an equilateral triangle	Composition of transformations	Possibly include expressing translations and rotations as compositions of reflections.
Introduction to trigonometry	The historical perspective on the geometric interpretation of the names of the trigonometric functions	Definitions of trigonometric functions	For example, define the ''tangent'' as the length of a tangent segment to a unit circle, and the''cotangent'' as the length of a tangent generated by the complementary angle.
Functions	Functions of several variables	Functions of one variable	For example, find and optimize the volume of a box with dimensions l, w, and h under given constraints.
Lines, parabolas, and exponential curves	The role of e in mathematics, natural sciences, and business	Exponential functions	
Transformations of functions and data	Generalizing the effect of transformations on data, including proofs	Transformations of data	For example, replace x-values by $x + b$, ax, or $ax + b$ and investigate the effect on measures of central tendency and dispersion. This can be done more generally than in the regular material.
Systems	Graphing in three dimensions	Graphing systems	For example, what is the graph of $2x + 3y - z = 12$?
Matrices	Matrix representations for transformations and their products	Interpreting products of matrices	As the core treats matrices more informally, this ''traditional'' approach becomes enrichment.
Combinatorics and binomial distributions	Multinomial coefficients	Binomial coefficients and Pascal's triangle	For example, Pascal's triangle can be used to solve this problem: How many ways are there to pick a committee of 6, with at least one member from each high school grade?

Year 3

UNIT	POSSIBLE ENRICHMENT TOPIC	RELATING TO ... IN UNIT	COMMENTS
Fitting curves to data	Fitting reciprocals (and other functions)	Curve fitting	If the data seem to fit a curve of the form $y = k/x$, replace x by $X = 1/x$ in the data points and find a linear fit of these points, which can be used to find k in $y = k/x$. For example, this method can be used to find $k = 72$ in the rule of 72.
Circular functions and models	Graphs of sums and products of linear and trigonometric functions	Graphs of trigonometric functions	For example, graph $y = x + \sin x$ and $y = x \sin x$.

SAMPLE ENRICHMENT TOPICS*

Year 3 (Continued)

UNIT	POSSIBLE ENRICHMENT TOPIC	RELATING TO . . . IN UNIT	COMMENTS
Exponential and log functions	Curve fitting exponentials and log functions using log transformations	Log transformations (and chapter 1 curve fitting)	For example, fit $y = ab^x$, as $\ln y = \ln a + (\ln b) x$.
Logic	DeMorgan's laws (relating to sets)	Quantifiers and negations	
Reasoning in geometry	Fermat's optimization problem to find a point that minimizes the sum of the distances from three given vertices of an acute triangle.	Geometric models and transformations	This can be presented as "the cable TV problem," finding where to locate a cable TV station so that the sum of the distances from three cities is minimal. Have students find solutions by guess-and-check, using software such as the Geometer's Sketchpad. Then show a solution that has an elegant, yet accessible proof (which can be found in Coxeter's *Introduction to Geometry* [1969]) to illustrate the power of proof.
Reasoning in algebra	Further examples and generalizations of isomorphisms	Finite systems and isomorphisms	
Reasoning in intuitive calculus	Contrasting methods to find areas under curves (rectangles, trapezoids, Simpson's rule)	Area under curves	This unit makes ample use of technology.
Reasoning in discrete mathematics	Fibonacci searches	Systematic searches	
Reasoning in probability	Bayes' theorem	Conditional probability	
Reasoning in statistics	Paradoxes in statistics	Statistical reasoning	Investigate Simpson's paradox (e.g., a baseball player's average against right-handed pitchers and his average against left-handed pitchers are both higher than another player's, yet his overall average is lower).

*Reprinted with permission from *A Core Curriculum: Making Mathematics Count for Everyone,* copyright 1992 by the National Council of Teachers of Mathematics.

entire range of the secondary school curriculum, it often falls upon the mathematics teacher to assume the role of "expert." Somehow, it is he or she who is generally expected to teach programming, to run school computer programs, to know which computers the school should purchase, and to train the staff in its uses and versatility.

Even though computers can be used by business and vocational education teachers, as well as teachers of social studies, English, the sciences and foreign languages, it is nevertheless a fact that computers *are* mathematical machines—they can *do, learn,* and *teach* mathematics. They can, in fact, transform the nature of the secondary school mathematics curriculum from remedial arithmetic through calculus.

It is probably in mathematics classes that pupils will learn to become computer literate as well as computer confident.

Computer-Assisted Instruction

Although not intended to replace the teacher, the computer can guide a student through the development of a mathematics topic. This sort of activity, often called Computer-Assisted Instruction (CAI), must be carefully worked into the school curriculum. It should supplement, not supplant, the regular instruction. Using specially prepared programs, a teacher might have a student who missed a lesson (or topic) make up his or her work individually on the computer. This program would gently guide the student through the development and applications of the topic. Often such programs are purchased by the teacher to meet his or her specific needs. A similar arrangement can be used to accelerate a gifted student. This sort of instruction should be done in moderation, under the close monitoring of the teacher.

Commercially prepared programs may be wholly or partially appropriate for classroom use. Specifically, *Mathblaster Plus* (Davidson Associates) has already achieved the status of a classic in the field of drill and practice type programs.

Geometric Supposer and *Geometric Inventor* (Sunburst) or *Discovery Lessons in Trigonometry* (Conduit) are excellent aids for their respective subjects. These are "discovery" programs with an imaginative and creative approach. Not all software that is published is of such high quality.

Topics readily available from software dealers include

> problem solving strategies
> discrete mathematics
> fractals and transformations
> encoding and decoding
> logic
> sorting, grouping, and graphing
> probability and statistics
> vectors and matrices
> Scholastic Achievement Test preparation

At the end of this chapter are listed names, addresses, and phone numbers of computer software and calculator dealers. Most companies publish catalogs with descriptions of their wares that you will find informative.

Many of these programs have built-in management systems that maintain records of student progress and achievement. These systems are often arranged in such a way as to maintain the privacy of each pupil's records. Only the teacher will know the code and password needed to retrieve the information.

Tutorial Programs

Computer programs that provide students with selected topics in the secondary school curriculum can be developed or purchased. The computer can be programmed to provide drill in algebra, geometry, and trigonometry, as well as arithmetic. Moreover, the computer can do more than just acknowledge a correct answer and generate another problem (or indicate "error" and repeat the same problem). It can be programmed to indicate where an error was made or offer suggestions for reaching a correct answer based specifically on the student's incorrect answer.

There are a number of ways that computers can be used for tutorial, drill, and practice. The software should be adjustable in terms of level of difficulty, number of problems, and mastery level, and it should provide an easy "escape" for the pupil. The software should be "intelligent," i.e., it should sense when a student is having difficulty with a particular operation or concept and automatically branch to a tutorial with another set of problems. It would also be helpful if the software included a classroom management component and a record-keeping facility.

One of the major problems for a teacher in a large class is the constant tension of "being spread too thin," even with an aide or teacher's assistant. Weak students tend to be very needy and often require considerable attention. A computer with the right kind of software could help tremendously with the ongoing problems of logistics and resources. In addition, weak students usually have an acute awareness of their own deficiencies. The argument that computers are nonthreatening, noncritical, and nonjudgmental is certainly valid, especially if the software includes positive reinforcers.

Selecting Software

Guidelines for selecting software suitable for your specific needs are available from some publishers upon request. However, the very best guide of all is for you to personally view the software to see if it meets your needs. Indeed you may never find exactly what you would like, in which case you must settle for a compromise package or create your own. A checklist to guide you in selecting computer software wisely is shown on page 164.

It seems that there is a proliferation of new software and new catalogs weekly. As one who might be responsible for selecting appropriate programs, you will be faced with making choices from a wide variety of sources. These might include large or small software publishers, hardware manufacturers, computing magazines, distributors, salespeople, colleagues, and students. How do you systematically attack the selection problem?

Educators who are involved with computers in schools are suggesting that steps need to be taken to provide teachers with the means to solve this problem intelligently. One suggestion is the creation of electronic bulletin boards that contain descriptions of programs together with recommendations by those who have used them in classroom settings.

COMPUTER LITERACY

Departments of mathematics are often involved with teaching computer literacy courses. Following are some

---

Software Evaluation Criteria Form

Title: _____   Publisher: _____

Level: _____ J.H.S.   _____ Middle School   _____ High School

Application(s):   _____ Practice   _____ Problem Solving

                       _____ Tutorial   _____ Enrichment

                       _____ Simulation   _____ Other _____

Yes	No	Not Applicable	
_____	_____	_____	1. Content has clear instructional objectives.
_____	_____	_____	2. Content is accurate.
_____	_____	_____	3. Content is free of stereotypes.
_____	_____	_____	4. Objectives are related to the course of study.
_____	_____	_____	5. Program is appropriate for audience.
_____	_____	_____	6. Computer branches to appropriate difficulty.
_____	_____	_____	7. Graphics/sound/color enhance the instructional program.
_____	_____	_____	8. Programs are easily accessible to students.
_____	_____	_____	9. Teachers can utilize the program easily.
_____	_____	_____	10. Instructional manuals/guides are clearly written and organized.
_____	_____	_____	11. Computer is an appropriate tool for activity.
_____	_____	_____	12. User can control rate/sequence/directions.
_____	_____	_____	13. Feedback used is effective and appropriate.

---

types of software that might be needed for such courses:

    word processor programs
    spreadsheet programs
    transformations
    computer-constructed designs
    database management systems
    programming languages
    logic programs
    problem-solving packages
    graphics programs

In retrospect, it appears that many computer literacy classes evolved (or were spontaneously generated) because of an unfounded panic. They placed an emphasis on programming, possibly because there was virtually no applications software available. There was an implicit pressure, mostly from panic-stricken parents, to put computer literacy classes in place so that their children would not be lost in the "computer age."

With the realization that all our budding "prodigies" could not be expert programmers, that there were not going to be that many programming jobs available, and that there were now sophisticated applications being used by the business and scientific communities, there came the final (at least for the time being) metamorphosis in computer literacy curricula.

Programming has been the big loser in computer literacy. Despite the trend away from programming for the masses, it has found a comfortable niche in programs for the gifted and talented and in extracurricular programs. In addition, most computer literacy programs still devote some time to programming, if for no other reason than to familiarize students with the discipline.

Electronic Bulletin Boards

Telecommunications involves sending data over long distances from one computer to another via telephone lines. A computer, a modem, and communications software are needed.

The modem can be used to send information directly to another party. An innovative development along these lines is the creation of ''bulletin boards'' that can serve entire geographic areas. Local computer stores or school districts may have developed ''users' groups'' to create a bulletin board to which only subscribers have access via their modems and telephone lines. These bulletin boards may service teachers as well as pupils with specific problems, whether they be suggestions on how to teach a certain topic most effectively or what approach ought to be considered when solving a problem.

You may find commercial information services that can fulfill your needs. Some of these, for example, are COMPUSERVE, THE SOURCE, PRODIGY, and *Grolier's Electronic Encyclopedia,* which can make available the services of educators on a national scale—a situation that was not within the realm of reality or possibility just a few years ago. A growing number of school districts are also forming and using electronic bulletin boards.

In communications networks, individual computers can be used to send messages back and forth. Such networks provide classes of geographically separated students and teachers with the means of sharing ideas, programs, and problems. Networking is a development still in its infancy, with the potential to become a giant.

What is Hypercard? Are There Classroom Uses?

Hypercard, simply put, is a creative environment where even nonprogrammers can bring graphics, sound, and text together in an interactive and interconnected way. The Hypercard method uses the metaphor of index cards, on which can be placed graphics, text, etc. Buttons (visible or invisible) are then attached to the card and ''linked'' to other cards so that the user can move through the cards sequentially, in a lesson for example, or can move arbitrarily to any other card based on information in the current card.

Possible applications include such diverse things as a genealogy file, with pictures and voices of the family; a program with facts and sounds of animals of the world; an introduction to musical instruments; a controlled-path adventure story. This is an open-ended medium where the possibilities are truly limitless in all areas including the classroom, and mathematics in particular.

A Source for Recreational Mathematics

Many programs are available that allow students to play games with the computer. Carefully selected games can be effective in furthering the development of a student's skills in logic. The level and sophistication of the game must be selected by the teacher with the specific student user clearly in mind. A game that is not challenging enough may either bore the student or make for a silly experience. On the other hand, a program that generates a game beyond the level of the intended student user may frustrate the student and eventually turn him or her away from computers. Computer games are a fine source for developing logic skills as well as for motivating students to study programming.

An Integrated Part of the School Curriculum

What role should the computer play in the general education of students? One interesting suggestion is that students be taught how to use the computer as a tool for problem solving. This can be accomplished by infusing a computer component into various mathematics courses (algebra, geometry, and trigonometry) and/or offering elective courses in computer mathematics.

A computer mathematics curriculum should be designed to reinforce, enrich, and extend concepts that are taught in the school's regular program. With this in mind, students should be challenged to solve various mathematical problems and then analyze them with an eye toward computer solution. How to proceed from this point depends on the computer equipment available.

All the computer equipment that would constitute an ideal computer classroom model has been demonstrated in programs sponsored by IBM, TANDY, and APPLE. These classrooms are equipped with computers with disk drives, a hard drive, a file server, and printers—all hard-wired so that the teacher can constantly monitor the work and progress of each student. Of course, the vast majority of classrooms are not so equipped. Computer-assisted classroom management usually takes the form of software that can be customized and has a record-keeping feature. Classroom management is also facilitated by test-scoring optical scanners and card readers and by class attendance and grading software packages.

On a more practical level, however, management of a computer classroom will present you with new problems and challenges. The section that follows is a very detailed, carefully developed guide for computer classroom management. It is based on the experience of master teachers in the field.

COMPUTER CLASSROOM MANAGEMENT

When called on to teach a computer class, whether it be in programming or in computer literacy, you will be faced with classroom management decisions that differ from those of the traditional math classroom. Some of the things you will need to consider include:

1. Where to store class disks
2. Where to store student disks
3. How to distribute and collect class disks
4. How to distribute and collect student disks
5. How to assign ''hands on'' time for each student
6. How to ensure printer time for each student
7. What to do with students not working on the computer
8. What to do with the early finishers
9. How to minimize copying of files
10. Password protection
11. How to avoid injury to hardware, software, and data

Although your *particular* solutions to the problems posed will, of course, depend on the specific setup you face, we offer the following suggestions as to how to approach the management of a computer classroom.

Disks

If your computer lab has a network system, then working with disks will not be a major concern for you. A discussion of classroom management suggestions for networked rooms will follow shortly.

A. Storage. Ask your supervisor to supply secure storage facilities in the classroom. This might be a special disk library cabinet, a filing cabinet with room for disk storage, or, as a bare minimum, space in a desk drawer. Disks should usually be stored in molded plastic cases, which come in a multitude of sizes and shapes. They can be color-coded, as well. If no appropriate supplies are available to you, keep the disks in the box from which they came.

B. Distribution and Collection. You will find the beginning and end of the period to be extremely busy times for you to get through these tasks. It is advisable for each computer as well as each class disk in each set to be numbered. In this way you can tell at a glance which workstation has not returned the disk(s). You might find it helpful to appoint a student monitor in charge of each set of disks, responsible for collecting and ordering them. You yourself must, of course, check on each set before the end of each period to see that all class disks are there. Only *you* should go to the secure storage facility to retrieve and return the sets of class disks. Student disks should be handled in a similar manner. However, numbering the disks is not practical because students' seat assignments might be changed. A specific count is necessary here to check that you have them all.

Networked Computer Labs

As time passes, more and more computer classrooms will be networked; that is, all the computers will be connected to each other and to the teacher's file server. If you are operating on a network you could work in a diskless environment. However, it is wise to require all students to keep a backup of their work each day on their own disks. Since networks can and do very often ''go down,'' student backups are a prudent precaution.

Networking usually eliminates problems associated with printing. The printer queue is capable of storing students' work in the buffer and continuously printing the work of each student in the order it was received, even beyond the end of the period when necessary. In addition, students need not get out of their seats to print; it is all done from the workstation. This, of course, keeps the room more orderly.

The teacher has the capacity to distribute files to each member of the class. Using the network, it is relatively simple to have various students in the class working on different software or distinct projects. This is much easier than having to keep track of numerous disks for a variety of software.

However, there are some aspects of networking that demand caution and vigilance. Students must be urged to choose a password or a user identification code that they will never forget, as it is very time consuming to place a user back on the list during class if access is denied because an identification is forgotten. On the other hand, you must be alert to the possibility of students' ''stealing'' one another's IDs and manipulating files. Encourage students to change their password each month or two as some Internet providers do.

While the necessity to log on to a network is obvious, it is also crucial that each student log off properly. Failure to do so could cause the system to jam. Therefore, you must factor sufficient time into your lesson to allow for this at each student's turn.

Effective Use of Time

A. Student-to-Hardware Ratios. Optimally, the ratio of students to computers should be 1 : 1. But since most of us are not teaching in Utopia, we must solve the problems of handling more students than there are computers in the classroom. With the decline in the price of hardware over the course of time, and with increased funding earmarked for computer education on many state and local levels, many schools have been able to dramatically increase the number of computer workstations. It is no longer uncommon to have a student-to-computer ratio of 3 : 1 or 2 : 1, if 1 : 1 is not possible.

Students can learn a great deal from their peers by watching them work on the computer for several minutes. They can learn what to do and what *not* to do. It will be helpful if you have a kitchen-type timer at your desk. Divide the "hands on" part of the period into a number of equal parts, with enough time for each student to get one or two turns on the computer, depending on your particular situation and the particular day. Set the timer to help you keep track of "save and switch" time. You will be so busy helping students with problems that without a timer it will be extremely difficult for you to keep accurate track of the time elapsed for each turn. The students not actually working on the computer either may be allowed to do preparatory work for their upcoming turns or may be asked to watch their partners distinguish between the good and bad aspects of their work.

There are rarely enough printers for each computer. Ask your supervisor to purchase "printer switch boxes" that link one printer to two, three, or four computers. This increases printer usage dramatically at a very inexpensive cost. However, students should get your permission to use each printer, lest they cut off someone who is in the midst of printing but might have had to pause to retrieve a different file.

B. Early Finishers. As with any class, some students work faster and more efficiently than others. You will need to accommodate the early finishers without compromising the time needed by the other students. Here are some suggestions to handle this situation.

1. Have an extra credit project available that is appropriate to the current topic.
2. Have some extra credit projects available that are relevant and meaningful at any time.
3. Have a few software packages available that are both educational and fun. Some examples include typing programs, such as *Typing Tutor, Mavis Beacon Teaches Typing,* and *Type,* to improve keyboarding skills; SAT review programs; programs that are subject oriented but in game format, such as *Tic Tac Show, The Game Show,* or *Jeopardy.*
4. Have available applications software programs similar to ones you are using in class, such as a different wordprocessor or database or graphics program. The students should transfer their knowledge from class and try to work on these packages without being taught.
5. Avoid letting the early finishers either do nothing or do homework for a nonrelated course.

To free as many computers as possible for those still completing the projects, you might group several of these quicker students together.

Miscellaneous Concerns

A. Integrity of Work. It is considerably more difficult to monitor students' work in a computer classroom than in a regular mathematics classroom. The bulky machines obscure your view, and multiple students per workstation invite sharing of data and technical knowledge. Because of this, you have to be extremely alert and vigilant as to who is doing whose work.

B. Integrity of Hardware. Students of all ages tend to be fidgety in a computer classroom and seem to enjoy banging aimlessly on the keyboard. This is both a distraction to teaching and a potential source of damage to the computers. If your computers have keyboards that are separate from the CPU, insist that the keyboards be placed on top of the monitors while you are *teaching* the class and the computers are not in use. This minimizes the aforementioned problems and it frees up desk space for notebooks as well.

You must also be alert to potential mischievous vandalism in the classroom. Some problems include graffiti on computers, stuffing of disk drives with paper, and removal or interchanging of keys from the keyboard. Sometimes otherwise wholesome youngsters behave in strange ways in a computer classroom. A very strict set of rules is a must.

What Should Be Taught?

As mentioned earlier, computer problems should be designed to reinforce, enrich, or extend ideas taught in the regular program. This section contains several expanded lesson ideas around topics that appear in the middle/

junior and senior high school curriculum. It is intended to give you a feel for how a course in computer mathematics could unfold.

Before beginning, it must be noted that students should be permitted by school authorities to have access to computers whenever they are free to do so. Since most officials are usually cooperative in this area, there should be no problem arranging this, especially since it often involves a computer classroom or office housing the appropriate equipment. These rooms are frequently staffed all day.

The course should be project oriented. That is, students should be given a choice of several problems to solve, of varying difficulty, every few weeks. A completed project should include a description of the solution, including algorithm used, a flowchart, program listing, and sample output. Use of the printer to print out the program even before the project is complete will enable the student to spend more time debugging the program. This will allow for a more polished final product.

On the Middle/Junior High School Level

LESSON A   To develop a formula for finding the area of a triangle.

LESSON B   To develop a computer solution to find the area of a triangle.

PROBLEM   Find the area, *A,* of a triangle given the lengths of the base, *b,* and height, *h.*

1. Elicit from the class the following analysis:

ANALYSIS   In this problem we are to find the area of a triangle. We use the formula $A = \dfrac{b \cdot h}{2}$

2. Have class develop a plan. Review that developing a plan is to list the steps taken to use the formula $A = \dfrac{b \cdot h}{2}$ to find the area of a triangle.

   Plan: 1. Enter B,H
   2. $A = \dfrac{B*H}{2}$
   3. Print A
   4. End

3. Elicit from the class the following planned output:

   a. FINDING THE AREA OF A TRIANGLE
   b. ENTER THE BASE
      ?10
   c. ENTER THE HEIGHT
      ?6
   d. THE AREA is 30

4. Have class write the program.

THE PROGRAM

```
10 PRINT ''FINDING THE AREA
   OF A TRIANGLE''
20 PRINT ''ENTER THE BASE''
30 INPUT B
40 PRINT ''ENTER THE HEIGHT''
50 INPUT H
60 A = B * H/2
70 PRINT ''THE AREA IS'', A
80 END
```

On the High School Level

LESSON A   To review solving systems of equations in two variables. Students could be asked to solve equations such as

$$3x + 2y = 10$$
$$\underline{2x + 3y = 10}$$

LESSON B   To develop a technique for the solution of a system of equations. Students could be led through the solution of

$$ax + by = c$$
$$\underline{dx + ey = f}$$

Several systems that were solved in Lesson A could be solved using the new formula.

With a more gifted class, one might introduce a 2 × 2 determinant and then show Cramer's rule.

LESSON C   To develop a flowchart and write a program for the solution of a system of equations.

1. The flowchart might look like the following:

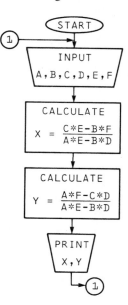

2. The program in BASIC (without any fancy print statements) would be:

```
10 INPUT A, B, C, D, E, F,
20 X = (C*E-B*F)/(A*E-B*D)
```

```
30 Y = (A*F-C*D)/(A*E-B*D)
40 PRINT X, Y
50 GOTO 10
60 END
```

REVISED FLOWCHART

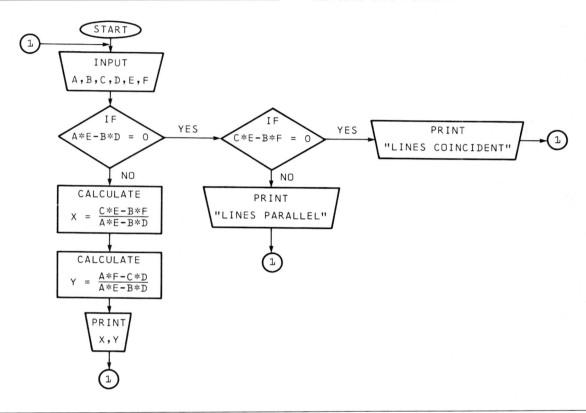

LESSON D To solve systems of equations graphically.

LESSON E To discuss the possible intersections of linear graphs (intersecting, parallel, and coincident).

LESSON F To revise the flowchart and program to allow for coincident, parallel, and intersecting lines.

Students will see that if $A*E - B*D = 0$, then the lines are parallel. If, in addition, $C*E - B*F = 0$ and $A*F - C*D = 0$, then the lines are coincident.

```
REVISED PROGRAM
10 INPUT A, B, C, D, E, F
20 IF A*E-B*D=0 THEN GOTO 70
30 X = (C*E-B*F)/(A*E-B*D)
40 Y = (A*F-C*D)/(A*E-B*D)
50 PRINT X, Y
60 GOTO 10
70 IF C*E-B*F=0 THEN PRINT
     ''LINES COINCIDENT'': GOTO 10
```

```
80 PRINT ''LINES PARALLEL'': GOTO 10
90 END
```

Since computer programming is a possible component of a modern mathematics curriculum, you may find yourself teaching the subject early in your career. While BASIC is in common use because it is both a powerful language and a relatively simple one, it also usually comes "free" with the computer and is thus the programming language of choice. PASCAL, FORTRAN, COBOL, C, and LOGO are other languages you may be asked to teach. Since many new teachers have at least some background in programming and computers, they will probably not find it too difficult to use a standard text and brush up on the language their school uses. Fortunately, computer manufacturers usually supply reference manuals that explain any differences between their version of the language and the standard version.

You may find that your school has a computer laboratory. This room may contain several computers, a terminal hookup to a larger facility, and some related supplies and equipment. You may even be asked to supervise this room at some time during the day in order to assist pupils who are using the facilities at that time.

Your teaching assignment may include a computer techniques class where pupils will be involved with special computer projects. Typical projects might include the following:

Generating a Fibonacci sequence
Generating relatively prime pairs
Finding the prime factors of a number
Evaluating factorial *n*
Finding the area under a curve
Sum of series
Computing sales tax, discount, etc.
Generating fractals

With a little creativity on your part, you can develop dozens of other projects.

There is a great deal of work involved in teaching such a course, such as checking each student's programs, helping them debug their programs and preparing lesson plans that will involve your own writing of programs—all very time-consuming tasks. But the satisfaction can be immense.

Remember, most of the classroom lessons will be developing mathematical ideas. The instructor must incorporate into the lessons the necessary programming concepts to enable the students to work on their projects and understand the lessons.

If you set up a project-oriented program, students may more readily accept having several classroom lessons to develop a mathematical topic that seems to be unrelated to programming, since *they* are always working on a computer project.

Usually at the beginning of a project-oriented course, students tend to wait for the last possible day to begin working on a project. This should not come as a surprise, since many of us may have been guilty of this same procrastination. Thus, the teacher must continually remind students to begin a new project the day they complete an earlier one. What can easily happen is that the day before a due date there can be long lines of students waiting to run projects on the computer. Students may ask to "skip a class" in order to run their programs. This should be discouraged, since every class session is important, as it is the only time new material is presented. Students simply must learn to better organize their time. Most students follow the teacher's advice and have no trouble completing projects. However, if there are several classes using the same equipment, the teachers might stagger the due dates for a more balanced use of "hands-on time" on the equipment. It might also be helpful to impose a "log-on sheet" two days before projects are due. Students can be given fifteen minutes each on the computer to provide hands-on time for more students.

The Computer as a Part of a Mathematics Class

Only a few programming concepts are needed to begin solving problems in mathematics. The INPUT, PRINT, IF-THEN and GOTO statements of the BASIC language are sufficient to solve many mathematics problems. But how can these statements be introduced in the secondary school mathematics curriculum? Use as an illustration the following method of introducing the concept of flowcharting and the computer statements above in the context of an elementary algebra class.

EXAMPLE   After solving equations of the form $ax + b = c$, students can be taught how to generalize the solution. Such generalizations are part of the curriculum and usually come under the title of *literal equations*. Once a student has solved the equations for x in terms of a, b and c, an algorithm has been developed for a computer solution to all linear equations of this form. Here we have a vehicle to introduce students to computer programming, following these five steps:

1. Show flowcharting as a means for planning computer solutions.

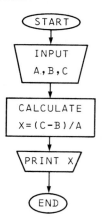

2. The program in BASIC is

```
10 INPUT A, B, C
20 X = (C-B)/A
30 PRINT X
40 END
```

3. Instead of having the program end we can have it start again, which introduces the GOTO statement.
   FLOWCHART (First Revision)

```
PROGRAM (First Revision)
10 INPUT A, B, C
20 X = (C-B)/A
```

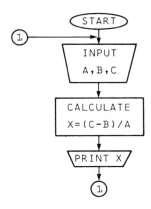

```
30  PRINT X
40  GOTO 10
50  END
```

4. What happens if $A = 0$? Students should realize that we cannot divide by zero. Therefore, an error will result. The IF-THEN statement can be introduced to avoid this problem. FLOWCHART (Second Revision)

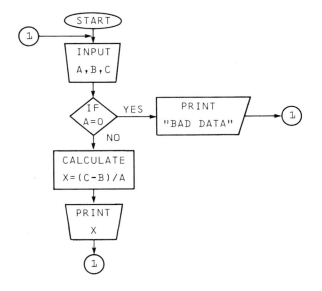

PROGRAM (Second Revision)
```
10  INPUT A, B, C
20  IF  A  =  0  THEN  PRINT  ''BAD
    DATA'': GOTO 10
30  X  =  (C-B)/A
40  PRINT X
50  GOTO 10
60  END
```

5. Time can be spent on how to make the output more readable by using the PRINT statement with quotation marks.

This same procedure could be used in other courses, such as geometry or second year algebra.

If you are going to introduce a computer component in all mathematics classes, you must consider the availability of equipment. It might be wise to introduce the computer in each class at a different point in the curriculum. This will help alleviate the overcrowding that might occur around the computers.

This scheme for introducing programming as an integrated part of the school curriculum allows students to develop a better understanding of mathematics. This usually results from the special analysis required in writing a computer program. Whether as part of regular mathematics courses or as elective courses, programming concepts should be developed within the context of secondary school mathematics. Although you may not be specifically training computer programmers, students will be knowledgeable about developing algorithms for computer solutions, which is one of the highest levels in the computer programming process.

A Source for Boundless Creativity

Once the more gifted (or the more motivated) students become reasonably familiar with computer programming, the computer can serve as a source for boundless creativity. There are almost no limits to what students will do with a computer. They may develop games (which they will certainly use), try to continuously improve earlier programs, derive numerical relationships, generate special numbers (such as amicable numbers, or Pythagorean triples), create fractal art, break codes, or simply attempt to solve problems (some teacher-generated, some self-composed, and even some classical problems). Remember, the famous Four-Color Map Problem was recently "solved" by computer!

A reasonable amount of computer time should be set aside for student use so they can work on these projects at their leisure.

MODELS AND MANIPULATIVES THAT ENRICH INSTRUCTION

"Explorations with models and manipulatives" is an alternative instructional method that bears consideration for some students, and for selected topics. Departing from traditional teacher-led discussions and demonstrations, small group and individual explorations of creative models or manipulatives can demonstrate underlying principles of algebraic processes or geometric relationships.

A winter 1993 survey, conducted by the Association of Mathematics Teachers of New York State, noted a dropoff in the use of manipulatives after the sixth grade. This study appeared to indicate that upper grade mathematics instruction was more traditional than the classroom activities of the lower grades. Nevertheless, a clever teacher will incorporate the best features of small group explorations into the study of advanced mathematics.

For those who utilize occasional manipulatives in the classroom, there is a wide selection of catalogs containing available materials that should be previewed before any are ordered. Catalogs are available from

> Creative Publications, 5040 West 111th Street, Oak Lawn, IL 60453
>
> Activity Resources, P.O. Box 4875, Hayward, CA 94540

Critical Thinking, P.O. Box 448, Pacific Grove, CA 93950

Wings/Sunburst, 1600 Green Hills Rd., Box 660002, Scotts Valley, CA 95067

Regular Polyhedra (Platonic Solids) Activities

Historical perspectives may surface in the process of using mathematical models, such as for the regular polyhedra shown below.

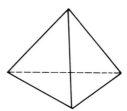

Tetrahedron
(4 equilateral triangles)

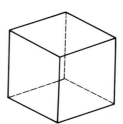

Hexahedron or Cube
(6 squares)

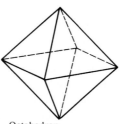

Octahedron
(8 equilateral triangles)

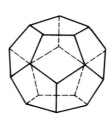

Dodecahedron
(12 regular pentagons)

Icosahedron
(20 equilateral triangles)

Arrange the class in groups of six students, working in pairs. Each group will make cardboard models of the regular polyhedra by constructing these patterns (see top of page 173), cutting them out, folding along the dotted lines and using tape to hold the edges together. *Note: Make each edge = 2 units.* Each group will report back to the entire class with the results of their investigations after they complete the chart and answer the questions.

Regular Polyhedra Patterns

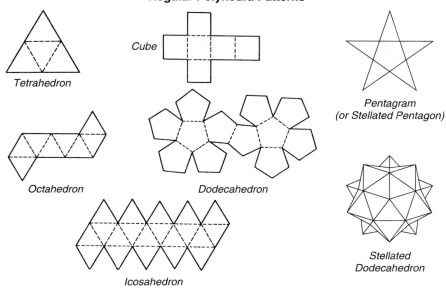

Tetrahedron

Cube

Pentagram
(or Stellated Pentagon)

Octahedron

Dodecahedron

Stellated
Dodecahedron

Icosahedron

Regular Polyhedra

Exploration	Regular tetrahedron	Regular hexahedron	Regular octahedron	Regular dodecahedron	Regular icosahedron
Number of faces					
Number of vertices					
Number of edges					

QUESTIONS

1. Suggest a formula that relates the number of vertices (V), the number of edges (E), and the number of faces (F) for each of the polyhedra.
2. Choose a face of each polyhedron. How many of the remaining faces (a) are parallel to your chosen face? (b) intersect your chosen face?
3. Choose an edge of each polyhedron. How many of the remaining edges (a) are parallel to your chosen edge? (b) intersect your chosen edge? (c) are skew to your chosen edge?
4. Find the total surface area of each polyhedron. Recall the formulas for the areas of an equilateral triangle, a square, and a pentagon.
5. Find the volume of the hexahedron, tetrahedron, and octahedron. Recall that the octahedron is composed of two pyramids, and the formula for the volume of a pyramid is $\frac{1}{3}$ (area of base) × (height).
6. Verify that the formula known as Euler's formula, $V - E + F = 2$, is valid for other than the regular solids, such as the parallelepiped, prism, and pyramid.
7. As a challenge exercise, prove Euler's formula.

Historical Comments. The regular polyhedra are also known as *Platonic bodies* in honor of Plato, who associated them with the spherical layers of earth, water, air, and fire. These were believed to be the fundamental elements that surrounded the universe. Euclid reserved the study of the regular polyhedra for the concluding topic in his geometry text, the *Elements,* believing, apparently, that the last was the best. Knowledge about the properties of polyhedra has expanded since the times of the ancient Greeks. Johannes Kepler (1571–1630) discovered a new type of regular polyhedron. He first noted that if the sides of a regular polygon are extended, a new regular polygon may be formed. Thus, a regular pentagon became the stellated pentagon, or pentagram shown above. Generalizing this technique, he could also construct such solids as the stellated dodecahedron. For additional investigations, see *Mathematical Recreations and Essays* by W. W. R. Ball (New York: Macmillan, 1962).

Geoboard (dot paper) Activities

Pick's formula states that the area of a triangle whose vertices are all on pegs of a geoboard, or on the dots of dot paper, is $\frac{b}{2} + i - 1$, where b is the number of dots on the boundary of the triangle, and i is the number of dots in the interior of the triangle. Thus, the area of $\triangle ABC$ is 7 square units.

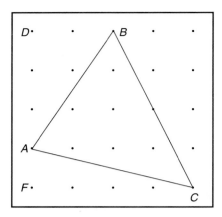

Exercises

a. Use 5 dot × 5 dot paper to construct a second triangle, *RST,* of area 7.

b. Circumscribe a square around triangle *RST*. If the distance between each pair of dots is 1 unit, find the number of square units in each right triangle in the picture of triangle *RST*. Add the areas of the right triangles and subtract the sum from the area of the square, 16, to verify the answer 7.

c. Use the Pythagorean theorem to find the length of $\overline{RS};$ of $\overline{ST};$ of $\overline{TR}.$

d. Use the area formula $\frac{1}{2}$ (base) × (height) to find the length of the altitude from *R*; from *S*; from *T*.

e. Construct a parallelogram on the geoboard and find its area; its sides; its altitudes.

Group Properties of Braids

The most useful models and manipulatives are often of the homemade variety. One such model that came to our attention uses braids to illustrate the properties of mathematical groups.

A braid of order 3 consists of two rods connected by three strands, as in Figure 1 below. The rods *P* and *Q,* holding the upper and lower strands, may be spread apart or moved together without changing the braid configuration. Thus, braids illustrated in Figures 1 and 2 are equivalent.

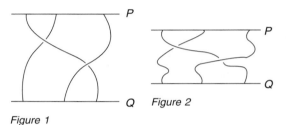

Figure 1   *Figure 2*

Operation: "addition" defined as follows: Place two braids, *A* and *B*, in the position indicated in Figure 3a, and after removing the rods *Q* and *R*, tie the corresponding strands together. The resulting braid is *A + B* (Figure 3b).

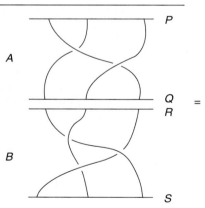

Figure 3a

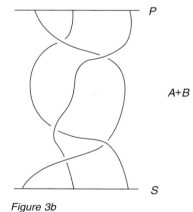

Figure 3b

The *closure* condition is satisfied, since the sum of two braids of order 3 is still a braid of order 3 and must be in the group.

The *associative law* is satisfied, since for braids *A, B,* and *C*, the result of first removing the rods between *A* and *B*, and then between *A + B* and *C*, is the same as of removing the rods between *B* and *C* first and then the rods between *A* and *B + C*. Thus, *(A + B) + C = A + (B + C)*.

Identity element: *I* (see Figure 4):

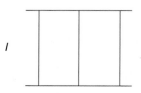

I

Figure 4

Clearly, $A + I = A$ (see Figure 5).

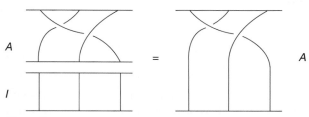

Figure 5

Inverse element of a braid, A, is its mirror image, $-A$.
Thus, $A + (-A) = I$ (Figure 6).

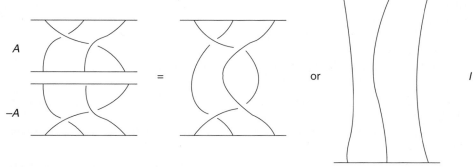

Figure 6

(*Note:* When the two braids are added, the result is obviously the identity braid, which is more easily recognized by spreading the upper and lower rods farther apart.)

The group is *not Abelian,* since, for any two braids A and B, $A + B$ is not necessarily equal to $B + A$.

SUMMARY

Teachers should be encouraged to constantly gather materials and ideas for enriching their teaching of mathematics. Regardless of the ability level of the students, appropriate enrichment activities can always be found. In some cases these enrichment activities may be harder to secure than in others, yet the process of searching for an appropriate topic can, in and of itself, prove to be of great benefit to the teacher.

Every teacher should make a genuine effort to enrich his or her instruction. Very often these motivating enrichment experiences go a long way toward developing a new appreciation for mathematics among the weaker or average students while being instrumental in encouraging further study in mathematics among the above average and gifted students.

The units offered in Part 4 of this book should provide you with many ideas for enriching your teaching of mathematics. Another fine source of ideas is *A Bibliography of Recreational Mathematics,* Vols. 1–4, by W.L . Schaaf (Washington, D.C.: National Council of Teachers of Mathematics, 1970, 1973, 1978). With these tools at your disposal, you are ready to enrich your students' knowledge and appreciation of mathematics.

EXERCISES

1. Select a topic for enriching your instruction of
   a. an average-ability eighth grade mathematics class.
   b. a gifted tenth grade class.
   c. a remedial ninth grade class.
   d. an average-ability eleventh grade class.
   e. a gifted seventh grade class.
   f. a gifted twelfth grade class (currently studying calculus).

Explain how you would treat each of the topics listed above. Specify how much material you would plan to cover.

2. For each of the following, select a grade level and ability level and provide an example of an enrichment topic that represents
   a. expansion.
   b. digression.

3. Suppose you are approached by the parents of one of your better-achieving students and asked to accelerate their son's mathematics instruction because they feel he is not being adequately challenged. Explain how you would deal with this request. Discuss your response to the parents and your actions before and after you give this response.

4. The parents of one of your deficient ninth grade students have come to ask why you occasionally spend time with the class on "peripheral matters" (i.e., enrichment) instead of spending all your instructional time with remedial work. Explain how you would answer these parents.

5. For a gifted class, prepare an outline for an enrichment unit for each of the following curriculum topics (specify whether it is an expansion or digression):
   a. Quadrilaterals (high school geometry course)
   b. Progressions (second year algebra course)
   c. Percentages (seventh grade mathematics class)
   d. Binomial theorem (eleventh or twelfth grade mathematics class)
   e. Angle measurement with a circle (high school geometry course)
   f. Systems of equations (first year algebra course); also do this with a graphics calculator
   g. Quadratic equations (first year algebra course)

6. Locate a secondary school mathematics textbook whose copyright date is earlier than 1950 and list the various types of enrichment activities included in this book. Repeat this for a textbook whose copyright date is later than 1980. Compare the two books with regard to their enrichment activities. How can you explain the differences in enrichment philosophies between the two books?

7. Choose a topic appropriate for the secondary school mathematics student that is not listed among the enrichment units in Part 4 of this book. Develop an enrichment activity based on your chosen topic in a style similar to that used in Part 4 of this book. This unit should be aimed at a gifted audience.

8. Choose a topic appropriate for the secondary school mathematics student that is not listed among the enrichment units in Part 4 of this book. Develop an enrichment activity based on your chosen topic in a style similar to that used in Part 4 of this book. This unit should be aimed at an average audience.

9. Choose a topic appropriate for the secondary school mathematics student that is not listed among the enrichment units in Part 4 of this book. Develop an enrichment activity based on your chosen topic in a style similar to that used in Part 4 of this book. This unit should be aimed at a lower-ability student.

REFERENCES

Billings, K., and D. Moursand. *Problem Solving with Calculators.* Salem, OR: Math Learning Center, University of Oregon, 1978.

Bitter, G. G., and J. L. Mikesell. *Activities Handbook for Teaching with the Hand-held Calculator.* Allyn and Bacon, 1980.

Bolt, B. *Mathematics Meets Technology.* New York: Cambridge University Press, 1991.

Bramble, W. J., and E. Mason. *Computers in Schools.* McGraw-Hill, 1985.

Chin, W. G., R. A. Dean, and T. N. Tracewell. *Arithmetic and Calculators.* W. H. Freeman, 1978.

Chrystal, G. *Algebra and Elementary Textbook,* 2 vols. New York: Chelsea, 1964.

Coburn, T. G. *How To Teach Mathematics Using a Calculator.* Reston, VA: NCTM, 1987.

Coburn, et al. *Practical Guide to Computers in Education.* Addison-Wesley, 1982.

Collis, B. *Computers, Curriculum, and Whole Class Instruction.* Wadsworth, 1988.

Court, N. A. *College Geometry.* New York: Barnes & Noble, 1952.

Coxeter, H. S. M. *Introduction to Geometry.* New York: John Wiley, 1969.

Day, R. P. "Solution Revolution." *Mathematics Teacher* 86 no. 1 (January 1993): 15–22.

Dolan, D. ed. *Mathematics Teacher Resource Handbook: A Practical Guide for K–12 Mathematics Curriculum.* Millwood, NY: Kraus International Publications, 1993.

Easterday, K. E., L. L. Henry, and F. M. Simpson. *Activities for Junior High School and Middle School Mathematics.* Reston, VA: NCTM, 1981.

Elgarten, G., and A. S. Posamentier. *Using Computers: Programming and Problem Solving.* Menlo Park, CA: Addison-Wesley, 1984.

Elgarten, G., A. S. Posamentier, and S. Moresh. *Using Computers in Mathematics,* 2d ed. Menlo Park, CA: Addison-Wesley, 1986.

Farrell, M. A. *Imaginative Ideas for the Teacher of Mathematics, Grades K–12.* Reston, VA: NCTM, 1988.

Farrell, M. A., ed. *Imaginative Ideas for the Teacher of Mathematics, Grades K–12. Ranucci's Reservoir.* Reston, VA: NCTM, 1988.

Flake, et al. *Classroom Activities for Computer Education.* Wadsworth, 1987.

Gleick, James. *Chaos: Making a New Science.* Viking Press, 1987.

Hall, H. S., and S. R. Knight. *Higher Algebra.* London: Macmillan, 1960.

Kastner, B. *Space Mathematics: A Resource for Secondary School Teachers.* Washington, DC: NASA, 1985.

Kelman, et al. *Computers in Teaching Mathematics.* Addison-Wesley, 1983.

Kenelly, J. W. *The Use of Calculators in the Standardized Testing of Mathematics.* New York: College Entrance Examination Board, 1989.

Kieren, T. E. ''Computer Programming for the Mathematics Laboratory.'' *Mathematics Teacher* 66 (1973): 9.

Klein, M. F. ''Mathematics as Current Events.'' *Mathematics Teacher* 86, no. 2 (February 1993).

Lockwood, E. H. *A Book of Curves.* London: Cambridge University Press, 1971.

Loomis, E. S. *The Pythagorean Proposition.* Reston, VA: NCTM, 1968.

Maor, Eli. ''The Pocket Calculator as a Teaching Aid.'' *Mathematics Teacher* 69 (1976): 471.

Mathematics Enrichment Program Grades 3–12, Richmond, VA: Department of Mathematics, 1986.

Mathematics Teacher 71 (May 1978). Special Issue: Computers and Calculators.

Mathematics Teacher 74 (November 1981) Special Issue: Microcomputers.

Mottershead, L. *A Source Book of Mathematical Discovery.* Palo Alto, CA: Dale Seymour Publications, 1977.

National Aeronautics and Space Administration. *Space Mathematics, A Resource for Teachers.* Washington, DC: January 1972.

National Council of Teachers of Mathematics. *Calculators: Readings from Arithmetic and Mathematics Teacher.* Bruce C. Burt. Reston, VA: NCTM, 1979.

———. *Enrichment Mathematics for the Grades.* Twenty-seventh Yearbook, 1963.

———. *Enrichment Mathematics for High School.* Twenty-eighth Yearbook, 1963.

———. *Topics in Mathematics for Elementary School Teachers.* Twenty-ninth Yearbook, 1964.

———. *Historical Topics for the Mathematics Classroom.* Thirty-first Yearbook, 1969.

———. *Geometry in the Mathematics Curriculum.* Thirty-sixth Yearbook, 1973.

———. *Applications in School Mathematics.* 1979 Yearbook.

———. *Problem Solving in School Mathematics.* 1980 Yearbook.

———. *Teaching Statistics and Probability.* 1981 Yearbook.

———. *Computers in Mathematics Education.* 1984 Yearbook.

———. *Secondary School Mathematics Curriculum.* 1985 Yearbook.

———. *Estimation and Mental Computation.* 1986 Yearbook.

———. *Learning and Teaching Geometry, K–12.* 1987 Yearbook.

———. *The Ideas of Algebra, K–12.* 1988. Yearbook.

———. *Calculators in Mathematics Education,* 1992 Yearbook.

Olson, Alton T. *Mathematics Through Paper Folding.* Reston, VA: NCTM, 1975.

Posamentier, A. S. *Excursions In Advanced Euclidean Geometry.* Menlo Park, CA: Addison-Wesley, 1984.

Posamentier, A. S., and G. Sheridan. *Math Motivators: Investigations in Pre-Algebra.* Menlo Park, CA: Addison-Wesley, 1982.

———. *Math Motivators: Investigations in Geometry.* Menlo Park, CA: Addison-Wesley, 1982.

———. *Math Motivators: Investigations in Algebra.* Menlo Park, CA: Addison-Wesley, 1983.

Posamentier, A. S., and W. Wernick. *Advanced Geometric Constructions.* Menlo Park, CA: Dale Seymour Publications, 1988.

Row, T. Sundara. *Geometric Exercises in Paper Folding.* New York: Dover, 1966.

Runion, G. E. *The Golden Section and Related Curiosa.* Glenview, IL: Scott, Foresman & Co., 1972.

Salem, L., F. Testard, and C. Salem. *The Most Beautiful Mathematical Formulas.* New York: John Wiley, 1992.

Schaaf, W. L. *A Bibliography of Recreational Mathematics,* Vols. 1–4. Washington, D.C.: National Council of Teachers of Mathematics, 1970, 1973, 1978.

Sloyer, C. *Fan-Tas-Tiks of Mathematiks.* Providence, RI: Janson Publications, 1986.

Sobel, M. A., and E. M. Maletsky. *Teaching Mathematics: A Source Book of Aids, Activities and Strategies.* Englewood Cliffs, NJ: Prentice Hall, 1988.

Suydam, M. N. *Using Calculators in Pre-College Ed.: Third State-of-Art Review.* Columbus, Ohio: Calculator Information Center, 1980.

Troputman, A. P., and J. A. White. *The Micro Goes to School.* Brooks/Cole, 1988.

Turner, S., and M. Land. *Tools for Schools.* Wadsworth, 1988.

Williams, D. E. "One Point of View: Remember the Calculator?" *Arithmetic Teacher* 30 (March 1983): 4.

Worth, J. "Let's Bring Calculators Out of the Closet." *Elements: A Journal for Elementary Educators* 17 (1985): 18–21.

Bibliography for the *History of Mathematics*

Aaboe, Asger. *Episodes from the Early History of Mathematics.* New York: Random House, 1964.

Ball, W. W. Rouse. *A Short Account of the History of Mathematics.* 4th ed. New York: Dover, 1960.

Bell, Eric Temple. *Men of Mathematics.* 6th paperback ed. New York: Simon & Schuster, 1937.

Bell, Eric T. *Mathematics: Queen and Servant of Science.* Washington, DC: Mathematical Association of America, 1987.

Beckmann, Petr. *A History of Pi.* St. Martins Press, New York, 1971.

Boyer, Carl B. *A History of Mathematics.* New York: John Wiley, 1968.

————. *The History of the Calculus and Its Conceptual Development.* New York: Dover, 1959.

Bunt, Lucas N. H., Jones, Philip S., and Bedient, Jack D. *The Historical Roots of Elementary Mathematics.* Englewood Cliffs, NJ: Prentice Hall, 1976.

Burton, David M. *The History of Mathematics and Introduction.* Boston, MA: Allyn & Bacon, 1985.

Cajori, Florian. *A History of Mathematics.* New York: Chelsea Publishing, 1985.

————. A History of Mathematical Notations, 2 vols. LaSalle, IL: Open Court, 1928.

Campbell, Douglas M., and Higgins, John C., ed. *Mathematics: People, Problems, Results.* 3 vols. Belmont, CA: Wadsworth, 1984.

Eves, Howard. *An Introduction to the History of Mathematics,* 5th ed. New York: W. B. Saunders College Publishing, 1983.

————. *Great Moments in Mathematics After 1650.* Washington, DC: Mathematical Association of America, 1981.

————. *Great Moments in Mathematics Before 1650.* Washington, DC: Mathematical Association of America, 1980.

Eves, Howard W. *In Mathematical Circles,* 2 vols. Boston, MA: Prindle, Weber, Schmidt, 1969.

————. *Mathematical Circles Revisited.* Boston, MA: Prindle, Weber, Schmidt, 1971.

Gittleman, Arthur. *History of Mathematics.* Columbus, Ohio: Charles E. Merrill Publishing Co., 1975.

Heath Thomas. *History of Greek Mathematics,* 2 vols. New York: Dover, 1981.

Hoffmann, Joseph E. *The History of Mathematics to 1800.* Totowa, NJ: Littlefield, Adams & Co., 1967.

Karpinski, Louis C. *The History of Arithmetic.* New York: Rand McNally, 1925.

National Council of Teachers of Mathematics. *Historical Topics for the Mathematical Classroom.* Thirty-first Yearbook. Reston, VA: NCTM, 1969.

Newman, James Roy, ed. *The World of Mathematics,* 4 vols. New York: Simon & Schuster, 1956; paperback, 1962.

Perl, Teri. *Math Equals: Biographies of Women Mathematicians and Related Activities.* Menlo Park, CA: Addison-Wesley, 1978.

Sanford, Vera. *A Short History of Mathematics.* Boston: Houghton Mifflin, 1958.

Smith, David E. *History of Mathematics,* 2 vols. New York: Dover, 1953.

Struik, Dirk J. *A Concise History of Mathematics,* 3rd rev. ed. New York: Dover, 1967.

Turnbull, Herbert W. *The Great Mathematicians.* New York: New York University Press, 1961.

van der Waerden B. L. *Science Awakening.* New York: John Wiley, 1963.

New Mathematics Library

Mathematical Association of America, New Mathematics Library. Over thirty titles on topics designed to enrich the mathematics curriculum. These can be ordered from the Mathematical Association of America, 1529 Eighteenth Street, N.W., Washington, DC 20036. A list of the first 31 titles follows:

1. *Numbers: Rational and Irrational* by Ivan Niven.
2. *What is Calculus About?* by W. W. Sawyer.
3. *An Introduction to Inequalities* by E. F. Beckenbach and R. Bellman.
4. *Geometric Inequalities* by N. D. Kazarinoff.
5. *The Contest Problem Book I.* Annual High School Mathematics Examinations 1950–1960. Compiled and with solutions by Charles T. Salkind.
6. *The Lore of Large Numbers* by P. J. Davis.
7. *Uses of Infinity* by Leo Zippin.
8. *Geometric Transformations I* by I. M. Yaglom, translated by A. Shields.
9. *Continued Fractions* by Carl D. Olds.
10. *Graphs and Their Uses* by Oystein Ore.
11. *Hungarian Problem Books I and II.* Based on the Eötvös.
12. Competitions 1894–1905 and 1906–1928, translated by E. Rapaport.
13. *Episodes from the Early History of Mathematics* by A. Aaboe.
14. *Groups and Their Graphs* by I. Grossman and W. Magnus.
15. *The Mathematics of Choice* by Ivan Niven.
16. *From Pythagoras to Einstein* by K. O. Friedrichs.
17. *The Contest Problem Book II.* Annual High School Mathematics Examinations 1961–1965. Compiled and with solutions by Charles T. Salkind.
18. *First Concepts of Topology* by W. G. Chinn and N. E. Steenrod.
19. *Geometry Revisited* by H. S. M. Coxeter and S. L. Greitzer.
20. *Invitation to Number Theory* by Oystein Ore.
21. *Geometric Transformations II* by I. M. Yaglom, translated by A. Shields.
22. *Elementary Cryptanalysis: A Mathematical Approach* by A. Sinkov.
23. *Ingenuity in Mathematics* by Ross Honsberger.
24. *Geometric Transformations III* by I. M. Yaglom, translated by A. Shenitzer.
25. *The Contest Problem Book III.* Annual High School Mathematics Examinations 1966–1972. Compiled and with solutions by C. T. Salkind and J. M. Earl.
26. *Mathematical Methods in Science* by George Polya.
27. *International Mathematical Olympiads 1959–1977.* Compiled and with solutions by S. L. Greitzer.
28. *The Mathematics of Games and Gambling* by Edward W. Packel.
29. *The Contest Problem Book IV.* Annual High School Mathematics Examinations 1973–1982. Compiled and with solutions by R. A. Artino, A. M. Gaglione, and N. Shell.
30. *The Role of Mathematics in Science* by M. M. Schiffer and L. Bowden.
31. International Mathematical Olympiads 1979–1985. Compiled and with solutions by Murray S. Klamkin.
32. *Riddles of the Sphinx* by Martin Gardner.
33. USA Math Olympiads 1972–1986, by Murray S. Klamkin.
34. *Graphs and Their Uses* by Oystein Ore.
35. *Exploring Math with Your Computer* by Engel.
36. *Game Theory and Strategy* by Straffin.

Other titles in preparation.

There are many additional ideas in Part 4 of this book.

SOFTWARE PUBLISHERS

Advanced Logic Systems
Alderwood Ave.
Sunnyvale, CA 95014
(408) 747-1988

Broderbund Software
17 Paul Drive
San Rafael, CA 94903
(415) 492-3500

The Cactusplot Company
4712 E. Osborn Road
Phoenix, AZ 85018
(602) 840-3811

Claris Corporation
5201 Patrick Henry Drive
Box 58168
Santa Clara, CA 95052-8168
(800)-3CLARIS

Computeach
78 Olive Street
New Haven, CT 06511
(203) 777-7738

Conduit
Oakdale Campus-U. of Iowa
Iowa City, IA 52242
(319) 335-4100

Davidson Associates
3135 Kashiwa Street
Terrance, CA 90505
(213) 534-4070

Edmark Corporation
PO Box 3218
Redmond, WA 98073
(800) 362-2890

Jostens Learning Corporation
4920 Pacific Heights Boulevard
San Diego, CA 92121
(800) 422-4339

MECC
6160 Summit Drive North
Minneapolis, MN 55430
(800) 685-6322, ext. 529

Microsoft Corp.
16011 NE 36th Way
Redmond, WA 98073
(206) 882-8080

Scholastic Software
730 Broadway
New York, NY 10023
(212) 505-3000

Styleware, Inc.
5250 Gulfton #2E
Houston, TX 77081
(713) 668-1360

Sunburst Communications
39 Washington Avenue
Pleasantville, NY 10570
(914) 769-5030

The Learning Company
6493 Kaiser Drive
Fremont, CA 94555
(415) 792-2101

Timeworks
444 Lake Cook Road
Deerfield, IL 60015
(312) 948-9200

CHAPTER 11
ASSESSING, EVALUATING, AND GRADING STUDENTS

The most effective teachers use multiple assessment strategies to determine their students' mathematical growth and power. Written tests play an important role in this evaluation process, as do quizzes, classwork, contributions to class discussions, small/large group work, projects, oral reports, homework, and evaluations of the student notebooks' completeness and neatness. Additional assessment strategies include take-home tests, standardized achievement tests, and the confidence and skill demonstrated by students in their use of calculators, computers, and manipulatives. Assessment should also reflect the diversity of teachers' instructional styles. Ultimately, the teacher will use these assessment strategies to arrive at a balanced and valid scheme for evaluating and grading students.

Teachers can design their own grading schemes, within the guidelines described in this chapter, to reflect the values they consider important and desirable. Each teacher's personal and ongoing experiences with different assessment techniques will aid him or her in arriving at the best balance of strategies. We suggest alternatives that ought to be considered in the evaluation process. Assigning a

numerical "grade" to each assessment strategy for evaluation purposes then becomes a professional judgment that each teacher will make and justify to students, parents, supervisors, and colleagues. No predetermined formula is suitable for all teachers, although the following scheme, with appropriate variations determined by each teacher, has been suggested by some for guidance in producing a balanced, overall assessment. Several of the following items require a teacher's subjective evaluation, and others, such as test grades, can be assigned specific number values more objectively. Since the final grade is a "sum" of each of its parts, the teacher should feel confident that the resultant grade is a valid reflection of his or her teaching style.

Assessment strategies which ought to be considered include:

- class tests and quizzes
- midsemester evaluation
- final examination grade
- standardized test results

Although the assessment strategies indicated above may be assigned unambiguous numerical grades, the following more subjective categories may be ranked by the teacher from 1 to 5, with the specific meaning of the rankings determined by the teacher.

- degree of student's acceptance by other group members
- "success" rate of the group in which student participated
- quality of the student's participation in large groups
- oral reports
- projects
- written comments and evaluations as found in portfolios
- attempts at solving enrichment exercises
- neatness, completeness, and overall quality of homework
- scientific and graphics calculator skills
- use of computer technology
- applications of prepared/self-generated manipulatives

Not all the assessment techniques indicated above need be used by each teacher all the time. Additional assessment techniques, such as observing student behavior in small and large group settings as well as noting the facility of calculator and computer use, have been discussed in previous chapters. We now discuss and illustrate the preparation, administration, grading, and interpretation of several types of written tests. We consider aspects of this testing process after presenting a variety of sample written quizzes and examinations.

CONSTRUCTING A CLASS TEST

The art of constructing a good class test is mastered over a period of time and with help from as many sources as possible. Beginning teachers can draw on the experience of others as well as on their own early ones, and they should not hesitate to do so. Teachers should consult with their supervisors and their colleagues, especially those who have taught or are teaching the same courses being taught by the new teacher, and they should check files of old examinations for style, content, format, and so on. Many department offices contain these files for reference, and the new teacher should not hesitate to use them. Other members of the mathematics department often will be happy to share their experiences with new colleagues. Their suggestions on the preparation of class tests are often most helpful, and the new teacher should draw on them to as great an extent as possible, thus avoiding making the same mistakes made by others in the past.

How to Begin

The first step in preparing a test, of course, is to determine what is to be tested. Every test has an objective, whether it be narrow or broad, and the teacher must have this purpose clearly in mind to prepare a test that is appropriate for the class.

A test may be very limited in scope, covering only one or two topics, and of short duration—perhaps five or ten minutes. Such tests are usually referred to as quizzes, and they often contain only a single question or perhaps a few simple ones. Quizzes are often designed to measure student understanding of a topic taught the previous day. Or they may be given to determine whether or not the students in a particular class have done their assigned homework for the day! In this case, the quiz question(s) will most likely be very similar to the ones assigned the day before for homework. A quiz is usually not announced in advance though you should remind the class early in the semester that they may use scientific or graphics calculators to solve any problem during regular classwork, homework, *a quiz, or a test* (unless directed by you to do otherwise). Samples 1–4 show some sample quizzes.

A more comprehensive examination would be designed to measure the extent of student mastery of several topics and would most likely be planned to require a full class period to complete. Such tests are generally administered on completion of a unit of work in the classroom. They should be announced several days in advance to enable students to prepare, through review of their text sections, notes, homework assignments, class exercises, etc. Topics should be listed on the board and typical test questions given the day before. Such tests carry much more weight in student evaluation than do single quizzes, and students may be expected to devote much effort to preparing for them. The scope of full-period tests is generally quite broad. Samples 5–7 are three more sample tests; two are actual full-period tests and one is a double-period (midyear) examination. Study carefully their layout of questions, point values, types of questions, use of extra credit, and so on. Note that collaboratively answered examinations will be most valuable as an instructional tool when the test contains topics suitable for small group discussions and when some members of each group are strong and others weak in their understanding of those topics. Collaboratively prepared answers may also serve as a review lesson for those topics that appear on the test and will be especially worthwhile for students who need the review most. Group responsibility for each student's understanding of every answer is reinforced when they are reminded that *any* student may be called upon to explain *any* solution that appears on the group's collaboratively prepared answer sheets and that the collective grade for the examination belongs to each.

Whether the examination is a short quiz or a lengthy midyear examination, certain procedures should be followed.

Sample 1. First Year Algebra Quiz (10 minutes)

SHOW ALL WORK

1. Express as a trinomial $(2a + 5)^2$.

2. For which value of the variable is the fraction $\dfrac{x + 2}{3 - x}$ meaningless:

   (a) 3 (b) 2 (c) −3 (d) −2

3. Express in lowest terms $\dfrac{x^2 - 4}{3x - 6}$.

4. Factor completely $3ax + 6a$.

5. The product of two factors is $2x^2 + x - 6$. One of the factors is $(x + 2)$. What is the other factor?

Name: _____

Answers

1. _____

2. _____

3. _____

4. _____

5. _____

Sample 2. Plane Geometry Quiz (5 minutes)

The measure of an exterior angle at the base of an isoceles triangle is 105°. Find the measure of the vertex angle of the triangle.

Sample 3. Second Year Algebra Quiz (8 minutes)

Given the equation $2x^2 - 3x - 7 = 0$

  1. Calculate the value of the discriminant.
  2. Describe the nature of the roots of the equation.

Sample 4. Eighth Grade Quiz (5 minutes)

---

  1. What is 20% of 40?
  2. Express 7% as a decimal.
  3. What percent is equivalent to $0.3\overline{3}$?

Sample 5. Collaborative Geometry Test—Parallelograms (full period)

Name: _____

I. Place the answer in the space provided (5 points each).

1–5. Indicate whether Always, Sometimes or Never true.

_____ 1. Diagonals of a rhombus bisect each other.

_____ 2. If two lines are perpendicular to the same line, they are parallel.

_____ 3. An equilateral quadrilateral is equiangular.

_____ 4. If the diagonals of a quadrilateral are $\perp$, it is a rhombus.

_____ 5. Opposite angles of a parallelogram are supplementary.

6–9. Choose the best answer.

_____ 6. An exterior angle at the base of an isosceles triangle is
          (a) acute (b) obtuse (c) right (d) dependent upon the type of triangle.

_____ 7. If the measures of the angles of a triangle are represented by x, y, and $x + y$, the triangle is
          (a) isosceles (b) equilateral (c) right (d) unknown—depends on x and y.

_____ 8. Which of the following is used to prove that the accompanying construction (of a line parallel to a given line through a given point) is correct: (a) Through a given outside point only one line can be constructed $\parallel$ to a given line. (b) If two lines are parallel their corresponding angles are congruent. (c) Two lines are $\parallel$ if their corresponding angles are congruent.

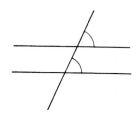

_____ 9. In $\triangle ABC$, $\overline{BC}$ is extended through C forming $\angle x$. Which of the following must be true?
(a) m $\angle x >$ m $\angle C$ (b) m $\angle x <$ m $\angle C$ (c) m $\angle x >$ m $\angle B$ (d) m $\angle x <$ m $\angle B$

10–13. If always true write TRUE, otherwise write FALSE.

_____ 10. Two lines are either parallel or intersecting.

_____ 11. If a diagonal divides a quadrilateral into two congruent triangles, it is a parallelogram.

_____ 12. The bisectors of a pair of opposite angles of a parallelogram coincide.

_____ 13. If the diagonals of a quadrilateral are both congruent and perpendicular, then the quadrilateral is a square.

14–16. Numericals

_____ 14. Find the perimeter of a triangle formed by joining the midpoints of the sides of a triangle with sides of lengths 5, 12, 13.

_____ 15. Given rhombus $ABCD$, $AB = 5$, m $\angle ABC = 120°$, find BD.

_____ 16. Given parallelogram $ABCD$, m $\angle A = 50$, m $\angle ABD = 75$, find m $\angle CBD$.

II. (20 points)   **Statements**   **Reasons**

Given: parallelogram *MOTE*
$\overline{HO} \cong \overline{AE}$ *Fold here and continue proof on other side.*
Prove: *MATH* is a parallelogram.

FOR EXTRA CREDIT *(show work on other side)*:
Prove: If the diagonals of a trapezoid are congruent, it is isosceles.

_____

In selecting topics and questions, the teacher should try to include a number of questions similar to those done in class or as part of homework assignments and should make the typical question moderately difficult. A test that is as important to most students as a full-period class test should not be filled with surprises (unexpected or novel questions). It should be designed so that a student who has conscientiously done the work and has a reasonably good grasp of the subject will pass.

A sample test might be presented and discussed the day before the real test so that the test format and type of questions do not come as a complete surprise, thus allowing students to focus on the content.

Test papers should be marked promptly by the teacher. Using student assistants as markers is dangerous because of errors they might make and because they might be partial to friends. Student markers should be used only when they can be supervised carefully. Furthermore, it is best for a teacher to mark the exams in order to become sensitive to the types of errors students are making. Ideally, the papers should be marked and returned to students the next day, while the test is still fresh in their minds.

If the tests are returned at the beginning of the period, the teacher should be prepared to review the test for most of that period (except for quizzes that might already have been reviewed immediately after they were given). If papers are returned at the end of the period, students can be assigned to correct their papers at home and thus be prepared for the in-class review of them the next day. An advantage of returning papers at the end of the period is that the commotion caused by returning tests at the beginning is avoided, as students are often more interested in what grades their classmates earned on the test than on why they themselves got something wrong.

Sample 6. Pre-Algebra Math Test—Fractions and Decimals (full period)

Name: _____   Date: _____

1. Find the area:

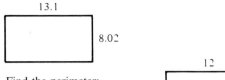

13.1

8.02

2. Find the perimeter:

12

8.03

3. From 269 subtract 0.33

4. Divide:
   (a) $7\overline{)14.35}$ (b) $0.5\overline{)51.510}$

5. Draw a circle around the fractions equivalent to the first fraction in each of the following:
   (a) $\dfrac{1}{2}$ $\left|\ \dfrac{3}{5},\ \dfrac{4}{8},\ \dfrac{5}{10},\ \dfrac{7}{15},\ \dfrac{20}{40}\right.$
   (b) $\dfrac{2}{5}$ $\left|\ \dfrac{4}{9},\ \dfrac{3}{8},\ \dfrac{8}{20},\ \dfrac{7}{15},\ \dfrac{14}{35}\right.$

6. Simplify:
   (a) $\dfrac{9}{24}$ (b) $\dfrac{8}{56}$ (c) $\dfrac{5}{45}$

7. Use the symbols $<$ and $>$ between the two given numbers:
   (a) 8   3   _____
   (b) $\dfrac{3}{5}$ $\dfrac{4}{7}$ _____
   (c) $\dfrac{1}{2}$ $\dfrac{2}{5}$ _____

8. Draw a diagram to illustrate the fraction $\dfrac{2}{3}$.

9. In the fraction $\dfrac{9}{4}$, the number 9 is the fraction part called a _____.

10. Find the missing number.
    (a) $\dfrac{2}{3} = \dfrac{\ \ }{12}$ (b) $\dfrac{4}{5} = \dfrac{\ \ }{100}$

11. Add (simplify your answers):
    (a) $\dfrac{2}{3}$ (b) $\dfrac{3}{10}$ (c) $\dfrac{1}{2}$
    $+\dfrac{1}{3}$ $+\dfrac{1}{10}$ $+\dfrac{3}{2}$

12. Find the missing number:
    (a) $\dfrac{13}{8} = 1\dfrac{?}{8}$ (b) $\dfrac{13}{4} = \,?\,\dfrac{1}{4}$

13. Add (simplify):
    (a) $2\dfrac{3}{8}$ (b) $5\dfrac{7}{10}$
    $+3\dfrac{5}{8}$ $+4\dfrac{9}{10}$

14. Change to a mixed number:
    (a) $\dfrac{38}{5}$ (b) $\dfrac{29}{4}$

15. Write equivalent fractions with the lowest common denominator for each pair:
    (a) $\dfrac{3}{8}$ (b) $\dfrac{1}{6}$
    (c) $\dfrac{3}{4}$ (d) $\dfrac{2}{9}$

Selecting Priorities Among Topics and Concepts Taught

No test, no matter how broad its scope, can test everything. When we remember that most tests administered by teachers during the course of a school term or year are limited to single class periods, we realize that priorities must be established. The teacher must select from among all the topics that have been taught in class in a given interval of time and determine which to include and which to omit on a given test. This does not mean that the latter topics will never be tested. They may be tested on a future class test, especially one of a cumulative nature, and they may certainly appear on midyear or final examinations, whether teacher prepared or uniform throughout a department. The teacher also must decide whether to "spiral" back to topics taught earlier in the term on a given test.

Types of Tests

The type of test presented to a mathematics class depends, of course, on the purpose for which the test is being given. Most often, the teacher will be seeking to measure student achievement. Achievement tests may range in scope and length from brief quizzes to comprehensive midyear and final examinations. A quiz may be prepared to test student understanding of just one or two concepts, or it may be designed to achieve a prompt start of a lesson, to check student comprehension of a homework assignment or of the work taught the previous day, or even to provide additional grades for students to assist the teacher in evaluating their work accurately.

Comprehensive tests of student achievement include full-period class tests on work covered over an extended period of time, perhaps two weeks or longer, unit examinations, midyear examinations, and final examinations.

Sample 7.   Second Year Algebra—Midyear Examination (80 minutes)

DO NOT WRITE ON THIS PAPER.   *SHOW ALL WORK ON YOUR ANSWER PAPER.*   *WRITE NEATLY.*

Part I: Answer all questions (5 points each).

1. Express in terms of i the sum of $5i$ and $3\sqrt{-100}$.

2. (a) If $93{,}000{,}000 = 9.3 \times 10^n$, find the value of n.
   (b) If $0.0000286 = 2.86 \times 10^k$, find the value of k.

3. Simplify: $\dfrac{\dfrac{a}{b} - 2}{4 - \dfrac{a^2}{b^2}}$

4. If $\log x = a$, $\log y = b$ and $\log z = c$, express $\log \dfrac{\sqrt{xy}}{z^3}$ in terms of a, b, and c.

5. Write the quadratic equation whose roots are $1 + i$ and $1 - i$.

6. If $\log x = 8.4365 - 10$, find x.

7. If $x = 7$, find the value of $3x^0 + (x + 2)^{1/2} - 49x^{-2}$.

8. If $R = \{(1,2),\ (-1,5),\ (6,2),\ (3,-7)\}$ find R^{-1} and state whether R and R^{-1} are functions, and why.

9. Solve for x: $3^x = 9^{x-1}$.

10. Find the value of k such that the following equation will have equal roots: $x^2 - 4x + k = 0$.

11. If $f(x) = x^2 - 4x + 1$, find the value of $f(\frac{1}{2})$.

Part II: Answer only three (3) questions (15 points each).

12. Find the roots correct to the nearest tenth: $2x^2 - 3x - 1 = 0$

13. Evaluate $\sqrt[3]{\dfrac{(67)(0.0973)}{100}}$.

14. Solve the following for a, b, and c and check in all three equations:
$$a + 3b - 4c = -13$$
$$2a - b + 2c = 4$$
$$4a - 6b + c = -1$$

15. Write an equation or system of equations that could be used to solve the following problems. In each case, state what the variable(s) represent. (*Solution of the equation(s) is not required.*)
    a. A motorboat travels 8 miles downstream in $\frac{1}{3}$ hour and then returns upstream to its starting point in $\frac{1}{2}$ hour. Find in miles per hour the rate of the boat in still water and the rate of the current.
    b. A two-digit number is 2 less than 5 times the sum of its digits. If the digits are reversed, the new number will be 9 more than the original number. Find the original number.

Final examinations may be prepared by individual teachers for administration in their own classes, or they may be prepared by committees of department members for uniform usage. In any case, they must be constructed carefully to measure the objectives of the unit or course and the extent to which students have mastered these objectives.

Teachers of mathematics are sometimes called on to prepare other types of tests. Diagnostic tests are used to identify student strengths and weaknesses in a particular area of mathematics so that the teacher may build on the strengths and plan remedial activities to overcome the weaknesses. Although many such tests are commercially prepared for computers, the teacher may wish to prepare his or her own test to measure some specific aspect of student background or to supplement the information provided by standardized tests.

Types of Questions

The types of questions to be included on any test are determined by a number of factors, including the ability level of the class, the nature of the material to be tested and the time available for the test. The following are illustrations of some types of questions commonly found on mathematics tests.

True-false questions may involve only a simple decision one way or the other. The teacher may require that an answer of "false" be accompanied by a correction of the statement offered.

Always-sometimes-never questions are modifications of true-false questions, since they require a determination as to whether a statement is always true (indicated by a response of "true" if in true-false form) or only sometimes true or never true (both of the latter require responses of "false" on true-false tests). A decision with two options now becomes a decision with three options.

Multiple choice questions are more challenging than either of the two types mentioned, since they require selection of a correct answer from four or five responses offered.

Enhanced multiple choice questions require students to make connections among several concepts before arriving at an answer that is the "best choice." They may also find it necessary to use more than one strategy to solve the problem and will thus require perhaps 2 or 3 additional minutes to answer the question. Students must briefly supply the reasons for selecting the best choice.

Completion questions reduce many aspects of guessing. They require a student to supply a correct response to an incomplete statement.

Matching questions permit some guessing, but this can be minimized by providing more choices in the column from which selections are being made than in the other column.

Numerical and algebraic exercises are objective questions that may be used to test understanding of principles, recall and application of formulas, and so on.

Types of questions mentioned thus far are essentially objective. *Geometric proofs* fall more into the subjective category, corresponding to essay questions in other subject areas. Like an essay question, a proof can often be done in a variety of ways and still be correct (i.e., there may not be only one correct solution). They require recall of postulates, definitions, and theorems proved in earlier work. They also may call for some degree of memorization, since some theorems are of such major importance that, although their proofs are included in the textbook, their recall may be expected of students. Other theorems whose proofs are called for on examinations may measure the ability to reason sequentially and logically better than those that are often memorized.

EXAMPLE (Geometry)

1. Prove that the sum of the measures of the angles of a triangle is 180°.
2. Given parallelogram $ABCD$, M is the midpoint of $\overline{AD}$, $\overline{BM}$ intersects diagonal $\overline{AC}$ at E.

   Prove: (a) $\triangle BEC \sim \triangle MEA$.
   (b) $AE \times BE = ME \times CE$
   (c) If $BE = 8$, what is the length of $\overline{ME}$?

The first example is a theorem whose proof is found in every textbook on plane geometry. The second example might be considered an "original" one. It challenges students to draw and label properly an appropriate diagram and to reason logically. The second part of the question asks for further recall of the properties of similar triangles and proportions, and the final part reviews the concept of ratio of similitude. Finally, the question combines geometry and algebra, as well as arithmetic.

Questions requiring sequential reasoning through several parts must be carefully constructed. If possible, the parts should be somewhat independent of each other. Otherwise, an early error in the work results in a string of errors and perhaps a situation in which it is impossible for a student to work subsequent parts of the question at all.

> **EXAMPLE** (trigonometry) A flagpole 40 feet high is anchored to the ground by a wire extending from the top of the pole to a point 30 feet from the base of the pole. The pole is perpendicular to the ground,
> (a) Find the measure of the angle made by the wire with the ground, to the nearest degree.
> (b) Find the length of the wire, to the nearest foot.

A student who uses the result of part (a) to answer part (b), using the sine or cosine function, gets a slightly different result from that obtained by the student who does part (b) independently, by the Pythagorean theorem. As a matter of fact, the latter may wonder why the specification "to the nearest foot" is made when she gets an answer of exactly 50. The other student accepts this specification as something to be expected and rounds off his answer to 50 also, unless he has made an error in part (a), in which case he will have an error in part (b) also. This difficulty could easily have been avoided by reversing parts (a) and (b) and phrasing the new part (a) unambiguously: (a) Find the length of the wire.

Writing a Good Question and Arranging Questions

Writing a good test is indeed an art. The questions must be prepared carefully and arranged on the test paper to enable students to achieve to the limit of their abilities. Before actually constructing the exam, the teacher should list the topics and concepts to be tested, including all major ideas, principles, and skills. Clear, concise, straightforward questions should then be prepared for each of these areas. Guidelines used in preparing good classroom questions apply in writing test questions as well. For example, test questions should be simple in structure and precisely phrased; if multiple concepts are involved in working particular questions, they should be included in separate parts of each question. Test items should test students' abilities to think as well as to merely recall information. Types of questions will vary with the content being tested and the ability of the class, but an effort should be made to include both objective questions and subjective ones, such as problems and proofs, utilizing graphics calculators. Examinations may be filed for future use in the teacher's personal file or in files maintained in the department office. New teachers are advised to have their tests critiqued in advance by more experienced colleagues and/or by their supervisors. In this way, unanticipated "traps," pitfalls, inconsistencies in questions, and the like can be caught before they reach the students. The new teacher will soon learn how often a question that appears straightforward to the teacher may seem ambiguous or unclear to a student.

> **EXAMPLE**   Find the slope of each of the lines whose equations follow: (a) $y = 3x - 5$
> (b) $2x + y = 3$ (c) $y = -7$ (d) $x = 2$

The question tests understanding and recognition of slopes of straight lines from their equations. However, the line whose equation is given in part (d) has no slope. From the wording of the question, however, students may feel that each of the lines given *must* have a slope and therefore may search fruitlessly or incorrectly for a number that does not exist for the slope of (d). Better wording of the question, which would avoid this problem, might be, "Find the slope of each of the lines whose equations follow. If no slope, write 'none'."

An effort should be made to arrange questions so as to proceed from the simple to the more complex. This helps to build student confidence and encourages poorer students to do their best, since they encounter the simpler questions first. Teachers sometimes wonder whether it is wise to provide students with a choice of questions on a test. Choices are most often found on final examinations, especially if they are uniform throughout a department. This provides students with some latitude to compensate for different depths of treatment of various topics by different teachers, different emphasis, different amounts of time spent, and so on. When these reasons are pertinent, choice of questions may be appropriate. For relatively short (one period or less) class tests, however, providing a choice of questions is not recommended, since students often waste inordinate amounts of time browsing among questions, making poor starts and then abandoning questions, and losing valuable time.

Assigning Point Values to Parts of the Test

Credit for each question should be determined by the teacher before the test is administered to a class. Students are always interested in knowing how much each question on a test is worth. This serves as somewhat of a guide to them as to how to apportion their time. Credit values should be assigned in proportion to a number of factors, including the relative importance and difficulty of each question and the time expected to be required by an average student to work each question. For a single-period test, less challenging questions requiring little time, such as objective questions of a factual or simple computational nature, true-false questions, and always-sometimes-never questions, should generally be assigned little credit, such as three to five points each. Fill-ins might be worth five or six points. More time-consuming numerical and/or algebraic exercises are generally weighted at perhaps ten to fifteen points. Geometric proofs and verbal problems may deserve fifteen or even twenty points.

The teacher should work the test in order to check its time requirements before administering it to his class. A test designed to be done by a class in a forty-minute period should not take the teacher more than seven or eight minutes to complete.

Presenting the Test

Tests may be written on the chalkboard or projected on a screen with the help of an overhead projector, or individual copies may be produced for each student on copier or duplicator machines. Most teachers prefer the latter method whenever possible, since it provides each student with a copy of the test. This minimizes (but does not eliminate altogether) errors in copying questions, reading symbols, reading directions, following instructions, etc. A single quiz exercise, however, might well simply be written on the board and students given a few minutes to write their responses on plain sheets of paper. The overhead projector might be used, for example, to project a partially completed geometric proof on a screen, and students could be asked to complete it on plain sheets of paper. If a teacher should work out the test from the original copy before administering it to the class to catch typographical errors—before students get frustrated trying to do impossible questions. Also, a test written on the board should be proofread.

ADMINISTERING A TEST

The primary concern of the teacher in administering a class test should be to provide optimum conditions so that the students may have the best opportunity to demonstrate their knowledge. To achieve this objective, the teacher can follow a number of simple principles in presenting any class test.

Alternatives for Administration

Every test should begin promptly so that students have the full time promised to them for working on the questions presented. A late start, for whatever reason, both upsets students and deprives them of working time. Whether a test is to be written on the chalkboard by the teacher (a slow, less desirable practice) or distributed to all students through duplicated sheets of questions, the questions should be made available to the students very soon after the period begins. This is particularly important if the test is scheduled for a full period, since time lost at the beginning of the period cannot be made up later.

The teacher must decide whether students are to answer questions and work problems directly on the question paper, in spaces provided, or on separate sheets of plain paper. Sufficient space must be provided for students to work each question and write an answer for it. If there are to be uniform formats for answer sheets, and if students must prepare these themselves, the time spent doing this must be considered when preparing the test. Also, students must be told in advance of any special equipment they are expected to bring to the test, such as rulers, compasses, calculators, or graph paper.

Classroom Arrangement

Teachers are often concerned with the problem of obtaining honest results when they give tests. Students who are unsure of themselves or who actually have little knowledge of the material being tested may be driven to desperate measures. Of course, it is better for the teacher to anticipate such problems and prevent them from happening than to deal with them after the fact. If the class is not too large and empty seats are available in the room, students can be separated from one another. An empty seat on each side of a student (and perhaps in front and behind) is clearly a good deterent to cheating during a test. Or, if classroom furniture is movable, it is easy to arrange the students so that they are reasonably well ''spread out.'' Every effort should be made to remove temptation from students. If they have no opportunity to cheat, their test results will be as representative of their abilities and achievements as possible.

Some teachers reorder questions on test papers so as to present students with what appear to be two different tests, and these are used in alternate rows to minimize cheating problems or with different classes in the same subject meeting at different times of the day. This procedure may be effective for a time, but students often become aware of what is being done and then they easily can defeat this technique. A somewhat better approach, especially for classes meeting at different times and being tested on the same material, is for the teacher to prepare alternate forms of each question and, in effect, prepare two different versions of the same test. This is only fair to the extent that the alternate forms of the questions are of equal difficulty and the tests are truly equivalent. Otherwise, the fate of a particular student is dictated by the seat he chooses or to which he is assigned in the classroom during the test. Clearly, this is grossly unfair to the remaining students!

Alertness During Proctoring

Even the most experienced and skilled teacher sometimes encounters the problem of cheating in spite of all precautions taken to prevent it. Presumably, the class members have been cautioned at the beginning of the testing period to do their own work and keep their eyes on their own papers. As long as this warning has been issued, what action should a teacher take when a violation occurs?

Most teachers who observe attempts at cheating on a test usually speak quietly to the offender first. She is warned, without making a scene that would disturb other students while they are trying to concentrate on their work, and perhaps her seat is changed. The teacher also may make a notation on her test paper to indicate at which point in the test the cheating occurred; presumably, work following that point may be considered the student's own (if no further attempts at cheating are observed). Penalties for cheating must be decided on by each teacher. It is a good idea to consult a supervisor on these matters. Experience will help the teacher to formulate his or her own philosophy and practices with regard to this problem and to refine these as circumstances change.

Cheating discovered only after a test is over, during the course of grading papers, is a different and more difficult problem with which to deal. Identical errors on papers of students who were seated adjacent to each other during a test suggest a lack of vigilance on the part of the teacher. Accusations at this point may accomplish little more than to build bad feelings; students will deny wrongdoing and one student actually may be innocent! It is possible for one student to copy from another without the latter's knowledge. Some teachers may be tempted to retest the suspected parties, but many will prefer just to minimize the significance of these particular grades for the students involved and to make a mental note to themselves to be more alert next time. In effect, the teacher learns from experiences as much as the students do, whether these experiences are good or bad.

Early Finishers

A test should be so constructed as to require the time *planned* for its completion from almost all the students in a given class. If a great many students finish early, the test was too short! Some students in every class, however, will work faster than their classmates and will, accordingly, finish a given test before the time allotted. Such students may be kept busy by being offered optional or honor problems for extra credit while their classmates are completing the required part of a test. These problems should be available to all students, of course, but the likelihood is that only the best students will have the time to attempt them or to complete them successfully. In any case, perfect papers with additional problems correctly completed may be given grades such as 100+ or grades based on more than 100 points or separate extra credits or any other credit allowance the teacher considers appropriate. Rewards for such credits presumably will include higher grades at the end of given rating periods or at the end of the school term.

Absentees

The problem of dealing with students absent from a test is a perennial one that has no simple or entirely satisfactory solution. The best advice to the beginning teacher simply is to evaluate each case on its own merits and discuss the situation with the supervisor. The primary concern is to be fair to all students involved.

GRADING A TEST

Marking test papers is a time-consuming task, but it is a most important one for the teacher. Not only does he arrive at an evaluation of the work of his students, but in a very large sense, he does so for his own work as well. By studying student techniques and errors, the teacher can measure the success of his own teaching program. He may also be in for a number of surprises, involving student misunderstandings, when he grades a set of test papers.

Assigning Partial Credit

Partial rather than full credit should be given for a student's answer that indicates some but not complete understanding of how to arrive at that answer. Also, a student who makes an obviously careless error fully deserves most of the credit the problem is worth. Many questions, indeed, do not lend themselves to the assignment of partial credit. Included in this category are true-false questions, always-sometimes-never questions, and factual questions (e.g., Write the quadratic formula). On the other hand, more lengthy problems that involve numerous calculations in sequence (any one of which a student might inadvertently perform incorrectly, leading to an incorrect final result) would certainly be deserving of partial credit.

Geometric proofs done with a substantial degree of accuracy and with only minor errors by a student also deserve some recognition. Experience and consultation with others will help the beginning teacher to formulate policies on partial credit and to modify these as circumstances dictate.

Students often have much correct work in connection with a test exercise, but a blunder somewhere along the way leads to an incorrect final result. On the other hand, students may have little, if any, correct work on a particular exercise, but they may have the correct final result. Consider the following examples.

EXAMPLE (Elementary algebra) Reduce the fraction

$$\frac{x^2 - 25}{x - 5}$$

Correct procedure: $\dfrac{(x + 5)(x - 5)}{(x - 5)} = x + 5$

Student's incorrect procedure:

$$\frac{\overset{x + 5}{\overline{x^2 - 25}}}{x - 5} = x + 5$$

Here the student has obtained the correct answer by an outrageous procedure.

Such a procedure, although it delivered the correct result, clearly shows no understanding of factoring of binomials or of reduction of algebraic fractions, and deserves no credit of any kind. In the normal course of grading, a teacher would see the answer, not the method, and give credit.

EXAMPLE (Trigonometry) Find the value of sin 75° in radical form.
Student response:

$$\begin{aligned}
\sin 75° &= \sin (45° + 30°) \\
&= \sin 45° \cos 30° + \cos 45° \sin 30° \\
&= \frac{\sqrt{3}}{2} \cdot \frac{1}{2} + \frac{\sqrt{3}}{2} \cdot \frac{\sqrt{2}}{2} \\
&= \frac{\sqrt{3} + \sqrt{6}}{4}
\end{aligned}$$

Here a student clearly deserves some partial credit, although he has confused the radical forms of the values of the trigonometric functions. Credit is deserved for realizing that sin 75° can be written as the sine of the sum of 45° and 30°, for knowing the correct expansion of sin $(A + B)$, and for knowing how to multiply and add fractions properly, albeit the wrong fractions. Thus, if the question were worth ten points, it might be given six points of credit.

In geometry, students are called on to write proofs of theorems on examinations. The teacher must first glance at the entire proof to see if it makes any sense at all. Many students make errors in some of the statements and/or reasons in these theorems. If the errors are so numerous and the reasoning so poor as to show little understanding on the part of the student, then perhaps no credit at all is deserved. When the student shows a good deal of knowledge, however, but perhaps she has an error here and there or some of her steps are not properly sequenced, then certainly, some partial credit is deserved. Generally speaking, a minor error of the mechanical type might be penalized to the extent of a ten percent deduction, while a major error in theory might result in deductions ranging from thirty to fifty percent of the credit value of a given problem, depending on its significance. These are only general guidelines; the beginning teacher will want to refine them as he gains experience.

Can a Wrong Answer Not Result in a Deduction?

Often, a student will obtain an incorrect answer to a problem by using a correct procedure and making no mechanical errors. How is this possible? Quite simply. The student is working on a problem involving sequential reasoning and several steps, some of which make use of answers obtained in earlier steps. The student should be penalized for the original error(s) only. Deductions should not be made twice because of the one, initial error.

> **EXAMPLE** (Trigonometry) In $\triangle ABC$, $\angle C$ is a right angle, m$\angle A = 37°$, $BC = 6$. Find, to the nearest integer, AC and AB.
> Student response:

$\tan 37° = \dfrac{6}{x}$ (Error: student read table or pressed the calculator key incorrectly—sin 37° instead of tan 37°)

$.6018 = \dfrac{6}{x}$

$x = 10$, to the nearest integer

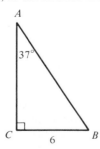

The student thinks she has found AC, but she has actually found AB. If she now tries to find AB by the Pythagorean theorem, obtaining an answer of 12, to the nearest integer,

she has made what is called a "consistent error." There should be only one deduction, since there was only one error.

Rounding off answers in early parts of a problem can lead to numerous errors later on in the same problem. Problems should be formulated so as to minimize the effects of such procedures. Alternative approaches to some problems (e.g., using the Pythagorean theorem or using trigonometry of the right triangle to find the lengths of the legs or the hypotenuse of the triangle) may result in slightly different results; if these results are then to be used in subsequent parts of the same problem, difficulties may arise. The teacher must be alert to all these possibilities.

What to Look for in Grading a Test

The teacher must make every effort to grade each test paper carefully and fairly. Students compare graded test papers with those of their peers and will be upset if they feel that they were not treated equitably. They also may compare their papers to tests they took earlier in the term to measure their own improvement.

Generally speaking, the teacher will examine test papers to determine the depth of student understanding of the concepts being tested, their ability to reason logically and sequentially and to solve problems, and their ability to carry out numerical calculations and algebraic procedures carefully and correctly. In grading papers, the teacher discovers the most common errors made by students and can then plan appropriate remedial or reteaching activities. These errors should be explored carefully with the class, to minimize the likelihood that they will be repeated on the next test. It is wise to review the entire test with the class after it has been returned to them, corrected and graded. Reviews may be accomplished by having students place their solutions to individual questions on the board and then explaining their procedures to their classmates and answering questions posed by the latter. When time is an important factor, a review may also be accomplished by the teacher distributing to all students copied or duplicated sheets containing correct and complete solutions to all test questions, and then answering student questions on these solutions after they have had some time to study them. Although this procedure does save some time, it also reduces student participation in the review (and the learning) process; thus, it is most suitable for a whole class review.

Small groups are often more effective for review lessons than larger groups, since pupils will have a greater opportunity to discuss, consider, and correct their own errors in this type of setting, as opposed to a larger, whole class setting. In either case, the teacher should prepare an answer sheet to guide the groups in their review. Teachers should also be available to answer further questions or make additional comments, as needed.

INTERPRETING TEST RESULTS

After a test has been given to a class, graded, and reviewed with the students, the teacher should examine the test closely to interpret the results. She can then plan the teaching of future units more carefully, plan for necessary remediation or complete reteaching of certain material, and plan for better construction of her next test if the present one contained surprises or unexpected problems (misunderstanding of questions by students, insufficient time).

What the Test Results Indicate

Tests are measurement devices. As such, they indicate the degree to which students understand the material being tested. A test may measure the amount of attention students paid, the degreee to which they grasped the concepts being taught, their ability to apply these concepts to solving problems of various types, and whether they did the assigned homework.

Tests also provide the teacher with information about himself and his teaching strategies. They often reflect the degree to which he was understood. The new teacher who feels most frustrated and concerned that students are not performing well enough is usually the one who ends up being a fine teacher, for he is constantly seeking the means to do better.

Analyzing Individual Items or Parts of a Test

Item analysis of test questions after the test has been marked is a valuable technique for improving construction of tests. It helps the teacher to determine which questions are too simple, too difficult for the average student but perhaps suitable as honor or extra credit questions, too difficult for almost all students, too short, too long, unclear, confusing, subject to misinterpretation because of the use of poor terminology or notation, and perhaps unfair as far as the assignment of appropriate credit is concerned.

It can help a teacher to determine which topics were best understood by the class and which were least understood. Item analysis is a question-by-question analysis of student responses. It will often lead to a conclusion concerning the significance of a particular question on this test. A good question is an effective discriminator between the more and less able students.

MULTIPLE CHOICE TESTS

With the ever-increasing availability of computers in schools, short-response tests are being used where in earlier years they may have been avoided. The most popular test is the multiple choice (or response) test. Computer use is most convenient here, since the respondent must give only one-letter answers. To make such an examination effective, care must be taken in preparing and interpreting these instruments.

When writing test items, the teacher must be careful (as always) to ensure against ambiguities. If one has the luxury of time, it is wise to write the test one day and then set it aside for a few days. A second reading of the items (after a period of time) usually will reveal any possible ambiguities.

The multiple choice item is not a particularly easy item to write, because part of its effectiveness rests on the writer's ability to construct good ''distractors''— incorrect responses to a multiple choice question. The test constructor should try to anticipate the kinds of errors students might commit in each item and derive these distractors from these incorrect procedures.

Naturally, if one has time available, an item analysis ought to be done for each item before the test is administered. This, however, requires administering the test to a representative student group and analyzing the effectiveness of each item as a discriminator between high-, average-, and low-achieving scorers. An item is deemed effective if the high scorers answer correctly and the low scorers do not. An item analysis is not usually practicable for regular classroom tests, since administering a test twice is usually not possible. For major schoolwide tests, such a procedure might be reasonable, especially if the test is to be used for more than one semester.

The question about how a multiple choice test should be scored is sometimes controversial. Some educators claim that the number of items answered correctly should determine the test score, whereas others hold that a multiple choice test should be ''corrected for guessing.'' That is, the test score (or raw score) should be obtained from the formula

$$\text{Raw score} = R - \frac{W}{n-1}$$

where R is the number of correct items, W is the number of incorrect items, and n is the number of choices provided for each item. The number of items omitted does not directly figure into the calculations.

Although multiple choice tests are easier to score (especially with the help of a computer) when properly prepared, they are much more difficult to construct, since there is more to writing the item than just constructing a question. Searching for good ''distractors'' can be quite time consuming.

STUDENT RESPONSIBILITIES

The impression that passing or failing a course depends only on the average of test marks, or on attendance in class, must be altered so that students realize that those are only *two* factors of several that help determine a final grade. The effort to have a student succeed in a course is a joint teacher-student-parent one. The teacher will try to live up to her end of the deal by presenting appropriate lessons, giving fair tests, assigning reasonable tasks and projects, and so on. The student must also live up to his responsibilities if he expects to succeed. But what exactly must the student do? Some of his responsibilities include the following.

1. *Homework assignments*
   Students are responsible for
   a. Getting the assignment accurately.
   b. Following directions in the homework examples.
   c. Working diligently and accurately.
   d. Doing every assignment completely.
   e. Making an effort to get assistance if it is needed.
   f. Doing assignments even on days when they are absent.
   g. Periodically reviewing previously done homework assignments (as required).
   (For more details, see Chapter 9, Assigning Homework.)

2. *Classroom Participation*
   In the classroom, students should always
   a. Get ready quickly at the start of the lesson.
   b. Have all necessary equipment: notebook, text, pencils, etc.
   c. Try to concentrate on the material being discussed.
   d. Ask pertinent questions to the day's lesson.
   e. Listen to the questions and answers of others.
   f. Be an active participant in all group and class discussions.
   g. Volunteer to do work at the board or answer questions at their seats.

3. *Tests*
   Test results can be maximized if students
   a. Review far enough in advance so they can do an unhurried, thorough job on the test to reflect their true ability.
   b. Read appropriate sections and model exercises in the textbook.
   c. Believe in their ability and remember that the final mark will be determined on the basis of an entire term's work and not only one test.
   d. Have all necessary equipment—pencils, compasses, etc.
   e. Follow directions and read instructions carefully.
   f. Show all work clearly.
   g. Make an all-out effort to prepare well for every exam.
   h. Do their homework regularly.

4. *Attendance in class*
   Students should be reminded that
   a. Each day's absence from a mathematics class is especially serious because it means a real loss of two days' work—the day they were absent as well as the day they return (since they may not have a full understanding of what the teacher will be doing on their return to class).
   b. Cutting a class is a breach of school discipline, besides the loss of a day of instruction.
   c. Coming late to class means loss of valuable time during which they might have learned something significant. In addition, lateness is disruptive to the class and teacher. Regular lateness reflects students' attitude towards the subject.

5. *Discipline*
   Improper behavior in the classroom is disruptive to everyone. It cannot help but influence the teacher and other pupils to develop a negative feeling toward the student.
   (For more details, see Chapter 14, Classroom Management.)

6. *Attitude and Effort*
   The student must show that she cares about doing well by seeking extra help when she needs it (from the teacher, from a classmate, or from a tutorial group in or out of school), by doing extra credit work when it is assigned, by not walking into the class late or with a preconceived negative attitude toward mathematics, and by living up to the responsibilities listed previously.

PARENTAL RESPONSIBILITIES

Every young person has two hands. The teacher ''holds'' one to help guide and direct the student in the educational process, as the teacher is trained to do. The other hand is ''held'' by the child's parents, who have the moral, as well as legal, obligation also to guide and direct, to the best of their ability. Thus, parents share the responsibility for a student's performance in class. Although parents' responsibilities may be fewer and somewhat different from those of the pupil and those of the teacher, they are no less important. In fact, the parents' responsibilities are more in the nature of being overseers, confidants, and encouragers.

Parental Responsibilities

1. Check that students do their homework completely and conscientiously whenever it is assigned.
2. Show a genuine concern in their child's test results, providing encouragement and support when appropriate.
3. Contact the teacher occasionally to check on the student's progress.
4. Discuss with their son or daughter problems that may be affecting the learning process.
5. Provide for additional assistance when needed.

DETERMINING THE COURSE GRADE

Your Grading Philosophy

Before you consider the question of determining grades, you ought to know your own philosophy about the grading of students. But you must realize that just as there is no point in trying to arrive at a "right" or "wrong" view in politics or religion, so, too, with marking philosophies.

Are you a "hard-nosed" type who will stick strictly to "averages" on tests with no room for emotionalism or feeling in determining a grade? Do you feel that this is the only way to "maintain standards" and raise the level of performance that has "dropped" so low in the public schools? If so, you will tend to give your students "low" grades.

On the other hand, are you a "bleeding-heart" type who feels that everyone's marks are affected by background as well as ability? Do you feel that those factors that are beyond the students' control and that they possess merely by accident of birth should not be used to determine grades that may affect their future—whether it be college or employment? If so, you will tend to give your students "high" grades.

While arguments can be presented for either point of view by adherents of those views, it is probably best to set for yourself a middle-of-the-road course. A balance should be sought in which sensitivity to students and their backgrounds as well as firmness in requiring evidence of satisfactory performance should be considered when determining students' grades.

Techniques for Determining Grades

Once the responsibilities of students, parents, and teachers in the educational process have been considered, both pupils and parents will be ready to understand how a teacher arrives at a report card grade. This report card rating, sent to students and parents several times a year, is the culmination of a process of evaluation. At these times, you examine your records of such items as the quality and quantity of the students' homework, every aspect of their classwork, their test marks, attendance, discipline in class, overall attitude, their contributions to small and large group discussions, projects, standardized test scores, portfolios of reports and other written work, and knowledge of calculators, computers, and appropriate manipulatives.

In other words, you will attempt to determine whether the student is fulfilling his responsibilities and how extensively he is doing so. You must examine each of his responsibilities and arrive at a judgment as to how successful the student is in fulfilling them. Finally, you arrive at a grade—either a letter:

A = outstanding level of performance
B = good level of performance
C = satisfactory level of performance
D = poor but minimally acceptable level of performance
F = failing level of performance

or a number:

91–100 = A
81–90 = B
71–80 = C
65–70 = D
Below 65 = F

The ways of arriving at a grade are often not understood by either student or parent. In addition, they have a degree of subjectivity and are sometimes arbitrary. Even test scores reflect a certain degree of subjectivity, since they often result from a teacher-made test, a somewhat subjective instrument itself. Although attempts have been made to determine a "scientific" or objective way of arriving at report card ratings, no one has ever succeeded in doing so. No one has succeeded in replacing the teacher's professional judgment with an objective formula.

Some of the ways of arriving at a grade, described more fully in the paragraphs that follow, include

1. Using a formula.
2. Making comparisons with other students in the class.

3. Determining the amount of improvement.
4. Using anecdotal record rather than a grade.
5. Assigning a ''Pass'' or ''Fail'' grade only.

Consider the following formula that assigns certain categories a percentage of the final grade:

Class test average	40%
Classwork and groupwork	20%
Portfolios (which include homework, projects, reports, etc.)	20%
Final exam	20%

You may feel that this is a reasonable rule or guideline for determining grades. In fact, a similar formula is used by many teachers. Yet, consider the subjectivity involved in such areas as preparation and grading of tests, as well as in the determination of the percentage values assigned. Furthermore, the nonincluded items of punctuality, attendance, attitude, and discipline ultimately must affect the teacher's decision in a subjective way, so that even after the formula has been applied the mark so determined may be adjusted up or down as the teacher sees fit.

A second technique for determining a rating for a student is comparing his actual performance with the performance of other students in his class. Thus, students doing best on test results, homework, etc., (as decided by the teacher) are rated A; the next category is rated B, and so on. This technique is best for ''honors'' or ''slow'' classes rather than ''average'' classes. A more extensive explanation of this technique follows later in this chapter.

A third technique used is that of determining the amount of improvement that has occurred during the period of time involved. For example, in a remedial class, where a student who began with a fifth grade equivalent arithmetic level (according to standardized tests) but ended the term with a seventh grade equivalent arithmetic level, gets a certain grade to reward the two years of growth in one semester. In this type of situation, school philosophy will determine whether such a student passes the course, even though the work is below the appropriate high school level. School policy will determine whether such a mark should be included in the student's overall high school average (on a par with courses such as English and social studies).

The anecdotal record type of report to students and parents has gained popularity in some school districts. The teacher is thereby relieved of determining a numerical or letter grade but instead submits a written description of the pupil's attitude, test results, homework, behavior, etc. This technique is sometimes combined with a numerical or letter grade at least once a year.

''Pass-Fail'' reports gained widespread popularity in the 1960s and early 1970s. This was merely a judgment by the teacher of whether the pupil should ''pass'' the course and receive credit for it or not. While many are vocal advocates of this system, only small pockets of school systems continue to use it. It was dropped mainly because it seemed to place academic mediocrity on the same level as real achievement. The lack of recognition of talent, ability, and scholarship was not acceptable to many people.

Assigning grades is one of the most difficult tasks confronting teachers, since so many subjective decisions must be made. How can a teacher determine objectively whether a student is working to capacity or what her attitude toward the subject is? Furthermore, the grade itself varies in meaning to a great degree. An ''A'' could mean ''genius at work'' or ''plugger at work.''

Yet, those of us who are products of our school systems, as well as those who are still involved in it, have learned, through some sort of ''sixth sense,'' what a grade means. If you were to ask a student in your class to rate herself before you did, she would likely do so with a grade reasonably similar to one you might expect to give her. Teachers who have asked for their students' own assessment of their progress and achievement in class at the end of the term know this. Things are not as haphazard as they might seem after all, for there appears to be an unwritten understanding among students and teachers regarding what mark a particular student ought to get for his work in a course.

Nevertheless, the grade a student is determined to have earned in a course may be unreliable as an indicator of ability and achievement. Yet, it is precisely this grade that is supposed to inform the student, parents, colleges, or employers of the student's success or failure in a course. It is even sometimes used to predict possible success or failure in a wide range of future activities. With such a large potential impact on a student's career, much care must be taken in preparing these student assessments.

OTHER GRADING SCHEMES

One simple technique that has been successfully used by some teachers involves several steps:

1. The concept of the traditional 100% as an indicator of a perfect test paper is discarded. In fact, some tests are more difficult, more comprehensive, or more mathematically significant than others. Thus, to rate all types of tests on the basis of 100% may be blatantly unreasonable, especially if all are equally weighted when they are averaged. Tests might be made to total *any* number of points, depending on the teacher's

judgment about the point value for each question.

2. At the end of the marking period, everyone's test points are totaled. In addition, a teacher-determined ''formula'' of the type described earlier that includes homework, class work, attitude, attendance, etc. also can be used to determine a ''grade'' for these nontest aspects of the pupil's total evaluation. A grand total of test and nontest scores is then calculated.

3. A list of pupils written in order of highest grand total first, down to lowest, is then made. Thus the student ranked first may receive a grade of 99% (or 100%, or 95% if the teacher so judges). Other grades will vary downward accordingly.

4. After the grading is completed, a final check by the teacher is necessary to determine if the scheme used produced any glaring inequities to any student, giving an unjustifiedly low grade, or one that is too high. Thus, for example, while a student might have performed poorly for the first half of the marking period, she might have performed superbly during the second, perhaps more important, half. The teacher might want this fact reflected in the student's final grade, and she would thus adjust the grade accordingly. This is another example of the subjective judgments used by teachers to determine grades.

Other types of grading systems are available for teacher use in some schools. For example, there is a criterion-referenced system (in contrast with the norm-referenced system described above) that allows the teacher to assess the extent to which the student has met specific objectives. These are usually itemized by skill or concept. The primary advantage to this system is that students (as well as their parents) are apprised of the student's particular strengths and weaknesses within a given course, as opposed to a ''blanket'' grade for the entire course. The latter does not provide any breakdown by skill, which

the former does. Unfortunately, the decision as to the type of grading system is not up to the teacher. Such decisions are generally made by the administration, yet a teacher's knowledge of the various options can be useful if he is called on by the administration for input into the decision-making process.

A draft of a new, alternative system of assessment standards is now in the process of being prepared by the National Council of Teachers of Mathematics. The focus of these standards will include items such as important mathematics, enhanced learning, valid inferences, and consistency.

SUMMARY

What does ''passing a course'' mean? It means that the student has fulfilled all his responsibilities concerning such items as homework, class participation, attitude, discipline, and satisfactory test results. Parents as well as teachers have a role to play in assisting the student to fulfill his responsibilities: the parent as an overseer, the teacher as a guide.

Similarly, ''failing a course'' means that the student's responsibilities have not been discharged, and certainly it is not the teacher alone who shoulders the responsibility for this occurrence.

The teacher evaluates a student on the fulfillment of these responsibilities several times a semester, rating her with a numerical or letter grade, or with a written report, depending on school policy. In spite of efforts to place grading of students on a scientific basis, the subjective judgment of the teacher is bound to play a decisive role in the evaluation process.

In the matter of grading, some have viewed the role of the teacher as that of a scribe who merely records the students' performance. This is a rather narrow view, for it limits the role that the professional judgment of the teacher must play in the process.

EXERCISES

1. Consider these ''special cases'' and determine the final rating you might make in each. Support your answer with appropriate reasons.
   a. Robert is a very bright boy in a high school first year algebra class who learns the mathematical material very well on his own. He was absent from class thirty days, has a 94% test average on the three tests he took, but was absent from three others. He is never a discipline problem, but rarely does his homework. At a meeting with his mother, she admitted that she is not capable of assisting or even speaking to him in a meaningful manner.
   b. Joanne's behavior in a mathematics class is very volatile. Her mother forces her to attend school, and she does so regularly. She has a 59% test average and behind her tough facade she seems to want to pass the subject and even studies at home, on occasion.

    c. Paula is an eighth grade student who does all the extra credit work she can, and seeks more. Her attendance and homework are excellent, though you have suspected for some time that she copies the homework from someone. Her test average is 52%. She always comes to you for help outside class and tells you how much she loves the subject.

    d. David is your best student in geometry and earned 100% on every exam throughout the term. Would you give David a 100 as a report card mark if his class work was also very good? Or would you assign him a 99 since ''no one is perfect'' enough to earn 100, a ''perfect'' mark? Would you do the same in any mathematics class?

2. Suppose you used the first scheme described in the section ''Other Grading Schemes.'' After giving the first test of the term to your honors class, you returned the papers and students found that their marks ranged to a maximum of 37 points for a perfect paper. How would you explain the rating scheme to the class? How would you overcome the tendency of students to ''convert'' their score to a ''mark'' on the basis of 37 points = 100%?

3. What grade would you give to a sixteen-year-old student who managed to raise his arithmetic grade equivalent level from sixth to seventh grade in six months? This increase was due to intensive remediation efforts on your part.

4. Suppose you were a parent who received an anecdotal type report card from your son's school, with this report from his teacher:

    ATTITUDE: Poor, lazy
    TEST RESULTS: 68%
    HOMEWORK: Incomplete
    BEHAVIOR: Needs improvement

    What could you learn from this report card? What more would you like to know? What additional details should the teacher have included?

5. Based on your own experience as a student and/or teacher, what method of determining grades would you like to have put into effect?

6. Earlier in this chapter, the ''Pass-Fail'' method of grading students was mentioned. What are some positive features of this method?

7. Prepare a well-structured interview guide that you will use to interview six mathematics teachers, three relatively inexperienced and three experienced teachers. Focus your interview on eliciting their methods of evaluating student performance. Write a short report to summarize your findings.

8. Prepare a five- to ten-minute quiz on each of the following topics:
    a. Converting from a base 10 number to one expressed in base 2; base 8.
    b. Using formulas for angle measurement with the circle for angles whose vertices are on the circumference of the circle.
    c. Recalling the values of the trigonometric functions of 30°, 45°, 60° in radical form (without the use of tables).
    d. Determining the sum and product of the roots of a quadratic equation.
    e. Determining the union and intersection of sets.
    f. Converting fractions to decimals (seventh grade).

9. Discuss the three tests shown earlier in this chapter (pp. 183, 185, 186) with respect to
    a. Variety of questions.
    b. Level of difficulty.
    c. Repetition of concepts.
    d. Format.
    e. Challenge.
    f. Point values.

10. Prepare a full-period test on each of the following topics:
    a. Area formulas for the rectangle, square, parallelogram, and triangle.
    b. Equilateral triangle, and trapezoid.
    c. Operations with radicals (simplification, four fundamental operations) in elementary algebra.
    d. The unit on trigonometric graphs, including amplitude and period.
    e. Metric measures.

11. Comment on the quality of each of the following test questions:
   a. *True or false:* tan 90° = ∞.
   b. *True or false:* $x^2 - 4x + 4 = 0$ has two roots.
   c. *Always, sometimes, or never:* If the opposite angles of a quadrilateral are supplementary, the quadrilateral is a parallelogram.
   d. Complete the following: A triangle is _____
   e. Simplify the expression $\dfrac{\frac{3x}{2}}{5}$.
   f. Find the measure of an angle whose supplement exceeds its complement by 90°.
   g. How does the measure of an inscribed angle of a circle compare with that of a central angle?
   h. Arrange in order so that each set of figures is a subset of the preceding set: rhombus, square, parallelogram, rectangle, quadrilateral.

12. React to the following comment made by a teacher of geometry: "My students always do much better with numerical and algebraic exercises than they do with proofs. They just don't know how to proceed with a proof after they write the hypotheses. I give as few proofs as possible on my tests."

13. On a test on the topic of areas and circumferences of circles, different students in a class obtained varying results to test questions by using different approximations of π, such as $\dfrac{22}{7}$, 3.14, 3.1416, or simply leaving their results in terms of π. How should the teacher grade these answers?

14. Some teachers like to "drop" students' lowest test grades when making their determinations of final course grades. Discuss the advantages and disadvantages of this policy and decide whether you favor the policy.

15. Discuss your feelings on the granting of partial credit in each of the following situations:
   a. When asked to solve a quadratic equation by the method of completing the square, the student merely used the quadratic formula.
   b. When asked to solve a system of simultaneous linear equations graphically, the student used algebraic techniques of substitution or addition-subtraction.

16. A student complains to you that you graded his test paper unfairly. He points out that on a particular question his neighbor had exactly the same errors as he had, but received more partial credit than he did. Discuss the implications of the complaint and your reactions to it.

17. Find a commercially prepared multiple choice test appropriate for the subject you are teaching (this need not be a standardized test, but can be one provided by a publisher as a supplementary item of a textbook series). Administer the test to about forty students, then analyze the responses as follows: tally the number of responses for each choice of each question, then determine whether the majority of students answered an item correctly, only the high scorers answered an item correctly, or only low scorers answered an item correctly. Draw conclusions from your analysis of the responses on each item as discussed in the chapter.

18. Write a ten-item, multiple choice test with five choices for each question. Pay particular attention to writing effective distractor choices. Administer this test to about forty students and then analyze the items in a way similar to that required for Exercise 17.

REFERENCES

Anrig, G. R., N. F. Daly, S. P. Robinson, L. J. Rubin and J. G. Weiss. *What is the Appropriate Role of Testing in the Teaching Profession?* Washington, DC: National Education Association, 1987.

Baron, Joan Boykoff. "Evaluating Thinking Skills in the Classroom." Chap. 11 in *Teaching Thinking Skills: Theory and Practice.* Ed. Joan Boykoff Baron and Robert Sternberg. New York: W. H. Freeman & Co., 1987.

"The Changing Face of Testing and Assessment: Problems and Solutions." 1991. Single copies are available. American Association of School Administrators (AASA), 1801 N. Moore Street, Arlington, VA 22209-9988; (703) 528-0700. (Stock number 021-003-00338) Discounts available for bulk orders.

Costa, Arthur, ed. *Developing Minds: A Resource Book for Teaching Thinking.* Alexandria, VA: Association for Supervision and Curriculum Development, 1985.

Educational Leadership 49, no. 8 (May 1992). Association for Supervision and Curriculum Development (ASCD), 1250 North Pitt Street, Alexandria, VA 22314-1403; (703) 549-9110.

Expanding Student Assessment, edited by Perrone, Vito, Association for Supervision and Curriculum Development (ASCD), 1250 North Pitt Street, Alexandria, VA 22314-1403; (703) 549-9110. (Stock number 611-91114)

Focus Issues on Assessment. *Arithmetic Teacher* (February 1992) and *Mathematics Teacher* (November 1992).

For Good Measure: Principles and Goals for Mathematics Assessment. 1991. Mathematical Sciences Education Board, 2101 Constitution Avenue NW, Harris 476, Washington, DC 20418; (202) 334-3294.

Gagné, Ellen D., Robert J. Crutcher, Joella Anzelc, Cynthia Geisman, Vicki D. Hoffman, Paul Schultz, and Lloy Lizcan. ''The Role of Student Processing of Feedback in Classroom Achievement.'' *Cognition and Instruction* 4, no. 3 (1987): 167–186.

George, W. C., and K. G. Bartkovich. *Teaching the Gifted and Talented in the Mathematics Classroom.* Washington, DC: National Education Association, 1980.

Grace, Cathy, and Elizabeth F. Shores. *The Portfolio and Its Use: Developmentally Appropriate Assessment of Young Children.* Southern Association on Children Under Six, P.O. Box 5403, Little Rock, AR 72215-5403. 1991. (ISBN 0-942338-05-4)

Guidelines for Assessment Systems. National Forum on Assessment, c/o Council for Basic Education Board, 725 15th Street NW, Washington, DC 20005; (205) 347-4171.

Hynes, Michael C. ''Alternative Assessment in Mathematics.'' 1991. Teacher Training Materials from University of Central Florida, Center for Education Research and Development, Orlando, FL 32816-0250; (407) 823-5228; Fax (407) 823-5135.

The Influence of Testing on Teaching Math and Science in Grades 4–12. A report of a study of the impact of standardized testing programs on curriculum and instruction. Request order form: NSF Study, CSTEEP, 323 Campion Hall, Boston College, Chestnut Hill, MA 02167.

International Mathematics and Science Assessments: What Have we Learend? New Orders, U.S. Government Bookstore, Room 118, Federal Building, 1000 Liberty Avenue, Pittsburgh, PA 15222. Stock # 065-000-00487-7.

It's Elementary! Bureau of Publications, Sales Unit, California Department of Education, P.O. Box 271, Sacramento, CA 95812-0271; (916) 445-1260.

Kilpatrick, Jeremy. ''Methods and Results of Evaluation with Respect to Mathematics Education.'' *New Trends in Mathematics Teaching,* Vol. 4. Paris: United Nations: UNESCO, 1979, pp. 162–178.

Kulm, Gerald. *Assessing Higher Order Thinking in Mathematics.* Washington, D.C.: American Association for the Advancement of Science, 1990.

Lester, Frank K., Jr., and Diana Lambdin Kroll. ''Evaluation: A New Vision.'' *Mathematics Teacher* (April 1991): 276–283.

Assessment of Authentic Performance in School Mathematics. Lesh, R. and S. J. Lamon, eds. 1992. AAAS Books, Dept. A62, PO Box 753, Waldorf, MD 20604: (301) 645-5643.

Linking Educational Assessments: Concepts, Issues, Methods, and Prospects. Educational Testing Service, Policy Information Center, 04-R, Princeton, NJ 08541.

Long, Lynette. ''Writing an Effective Arithmetic Test.'' *Arithmetic Teacher:* (March 1982): 16–18.

MCTP Assessment Kit. Mathematics Curriculum Teaching Program. Kit and videotapes. 1991. NCTM.

''Math Portfolios: A New Form of Assessment.'' *Teaching K–8* (September 1991): 62–68.

Mathematics Assessment: Alternative Approaches. 1992. Video and Guide. NCTM.

Mathematics Assessment: Myths, Models, Good Questions, and Practical Suggestions. Student Assessment Mathematics Project teacher resource book. Includes portfolio and other assessment techniques. 1992. NCTM.

Measuring UP: Prototypes for Mathematics Assessment. Mathematical Sciences Education Board. 1993. Single copies are available. National Academy Press, 2101 Constitution Avenue, Box 285, Washington, DC 20055. (800) 624-6242; (202) 334-3313. Discounts available for bulk orders.

Miederhoff, Jennifer W., and Judy W. Wood. ''Adapting Test Construction for Mainstreamed Mathematics Students.'' *Mathematics Teacher* 81 (1988): 388–392.

Miller, P. W., and H. E. Erickson. *Teacher-Written Student Tests.* Washington, DC: National Education Association, 1985.

Mumme, Judy. *Portfolio Assessment in Mathematics.* California Mathematics Project, University of California, Santa Barbara, CA, 1991.

———. *Curriculum and Evaluation Standards for School Mathematics.* NCTM, 1989.

National Council of Teachers of Mathematics. *Assessment in the Mathematics Classroom.* 1993 Yearbook. Reston, VA: NCTM.

———. *Professional Standards for Teaching Mathematics.* NCTM, 1991. (ISBN 087353-307-0)

————. *Teaching and Learning Mathematics in the 1990s.* 1990 Yearbook. Ed. Thomas J. Cooney. (ISBN 0-87353-285-6)

National Research Center on Assessment, Evaluation, and Testing. UCLA, Center for the Study of Evaluation, 145 Moore Hall, Los Angeles, CA 90024-1522; (213) 206-1530.

Nickerson, Raymond, David Perkins, and Edward Smith. "Evaluation." Chap. 11 in *The Teacher of Thinking.* Hillsdale, NJ: Lawrence Erlbaum Associates, 1985.

Pechman, Ellen, and Sigrid Wagner. "Mathematics Assessment Process for Middle Grades Pilot Project." 1990. Catalyst Project, Center for Research in Mathematics and Science Education, North Carolina State University, 315 Poe Hall, Raleigh, NC 27695-7801; (919) 515-2013.

On Their Own: Student Response to Open-Ended Tests in Mathematics. Massachusetts Department of Education, 1989.

Pandey, T. *A Sampler of Mathematics Assessment.* California Department of Education, Sacramento, CA, 1991.

Performance Assessment Sampler: A Workbook. 1993. A collection of reproduced excerpts from a range of alternative assessment projects. ETS Policy Information Center. Rosedale Road, Princeton, NJ 08541; (609) 734-5694.

Pilot Assessment of the Mathematical Sciences. Prepared for the House Committee on Science, Space, and Technology. Notices of the American Mathematical Society 39, no. 2 (February 1992): 101.

A Question of Thinking: A First Look at Students' Performance on Open-Ended Questions in Mathematics. California State Department of Education, Sacramento, CA, 1989.

Redesigning Assessment. Three videotapes. Association for Supervision and Curriculum Development, 1250 N. Pitt St., Alexandria, VA 22314; (703) 549-9110.

Romberg, Thomas A. "The Alignment of Six Standardized Tests with the NCTM Standards." Wisconsin Center for Education Research, 1025 W. Johnson Street, Madison, WI 53706.

Ronshausen, Nina L., ed. *Facilitating Evaluation: the Role of the Mathematics Supervisor.* Reston, VA: NCTM.

Spitze, H. T., and M. B. Griggs, *Choosing Evaluation Techniques.* Washington, DC: National Education Association, 1976.

Stenmark, Jean Kerr. Assessment Alternatives in Mathematics: An Overview of Assessment Techniques that Promote Learning. 1989. EQUALS, Lawrence Hall of Science, University of California, Berkeley, CA 94720, Attn: Assessment Booklet. (ISBN 0-912511-54-0)

————, ed. *Mathematics Assessment.* Reston, VA: NCTM, 1993.

Standardized Tests and Our Children: A Guide to Testing Reform. Booklet available from FairTest, 342 Broadway, Cambridge, MA 02139.

Standards, Not Standardization. With Grant Wiggins. Four-volume video and print. Center of Learning, Assessment, and School Structure (CLASS), 39 Main Street, Geneseo, NY 14454; (716) 243-5500, Fax (716) 243-5014.

Swadener, Marc, and Franklin Wright. "Testing in the Mathematics Classroom." *Mathematics Teacher* 68 (1975): 11.

Swireford, Edwin J. "Ninety Suggestions on the Teaching of Mathematics in Junior High School." *Mathematics Teacher* 54 (1961): 145.

Testing and Evaluation: Learning from the Projects We Fund. Council for Aid to Education, 51 Madison Ave., Suite 2200, New York, NY 10010.

Thompson, Alba G., and Diane J. Briars. "Assessing Students' Learning to Inform Teaching: The Message in NCTM's Evaluation Standards." *Arithmetic Teacher* (December 1989): 22–26.

Troutman, Andrea, and Betty P. Lichtenberg. "Problem Solving in the General Mathematics Classroom." *Mathematics Teacher* 67 (1974): 590.

Walter, Marion I., and Stephen I. Brown. "Problem Posing and Problem Solving." *Mathematics Teacher* 70 (1977): 4.

Williams, Irene S., and Chancey O. Jones. "Multiple Choice Mathematics Questions." *Mathematics Teacher* 67 (1974): 34.

CHAPTER 12
EXTRA-CURRICULAR ACTIVITIES IN MATHEMATICS

With the crowded mathematics curriculum at every level of the secondary school, teachers find extensive digressions from the sequential development of the mathematics course a hardship. Yet, there is great benefit to be derived from a consideration of mathematics outside the regular curriculum. Teachers must therefore seek ways of providing students with mathematics that is extracurricular. Many extracurricular activities in mathematics can be conducted through the structure of a mathematics club, as well as in the regular classroom.

THE MATHEMATICS CLUB

Although the mathematics club structure can facilitate many of the activities to be discussed in this chapter, it is not necessary to form a club in order to conduct any of these activities. Forming a mathematics club requires substantial planning, ranging from a selection of participants (both a faculty sponsor and student members) to a determination of an organization and purpose. The germination of a mathematics club can come from an administrator or an interested teacher, as well as from a group of students interested in participating in such a club. Whatever the origin of the mathematics club, the teacher who is chosen as faculty sponsor should realize that a sizable investment of time, work, and effort will be required to make the venture successful. Naturally, the rewards for this investment usually make it all worthwhile. Club activities frequently allow the faculty sponsor to grow both mathematically and experientially. Because a mathematics club permits unlimited investigation of mathematical topics and applications beyond the scope of the secondary school curriculum, all involved can feel a sense of fulfillment that comes from a genuine appreciation of mathematics, its development, and its role in society.

Establishing a Mathematics Club

Once chosen, the faculty sponsor should begin to familiarize himself or herself with the task by discussing the problem of getting started with colleagues, administrators, and a select group of interested students. It is particularly helpful to seek out a mathematics club faculty sponsor in another school who may already have undergone similar experiences. Suggestions based on first-hand experiences and materials that have proved successful will be helpful to the new mathematics club sponsor, who would probably otherwise grapple for workable ideas. (See references listed at the end of this chapter.)

After having received advice and suggestions from colleagues both in and outside school, and having gained the support of both the administration and a group of interested students, the teacher must tackle the job of recruiting. All paths of communication with the student body should be used. Announcements over the public address system, flyers sent to all homeroom sections, and student newspaper coverage of the new club should be included in the initial publicity. Especially important in the recruitment process is direct contact with mathematics classes that contain potential club members. This can be done by the class's teacher or by the faculty sponsor directly. The approach should be carefully planned so that the presentation about the club to these special classes is particularly attractive.

Part of the recruitment drive should involve inviting eligible students to an organizational meeting. It is important that this first meeting have a carefully planned and well-thought-out agenda. Student input should be welcomed, yet the faculty sponsor might present the plans that were prepared in consultation with the administration and colleagues, and have the group of interested students react. Although this prepared plan should be flexible and open for student suggestions, for the faculty advisor to come to the first meeting unprepared, without some sort of plan, would be ill-advised. The first meeting might also be used for the selection of club officers, who would in turn form a steering committee. Together with the faculty sponsor, this committee would decide on time and frequency of meetings, membership eligibility, and perhaps most important, the activities in which the club will engage. The rest of this chapter presents various extracurricular activities in mathematics that can be used with a mathematics club. However, a school may provide any of the activities without the structure of a mathematics club.

MATHEMATICS TEAMS

Most regions of the country have mathematics leagues organized for the competition of local secondary schools. These competitions are usually organized on three levels: middle/junior high school students; senior high school students in grades nine, ten, and eleven; and seniors in high school. The competition questions for each level are intended to be appropriately challenging yet within the scope of the student's knowledge of mathematics. Some mathematics leagues are organized so that schools compete directly against each other on a rotating basis; however, most leagues simply make an award to the team with the highest total score (e.g., number of correctly solved problems) at the end of the school year (or semester). Information about the mathematics leagues in your area can easily be obtained through local professional organizations or colleges.

It is likely that the school's mathematics team comprises students who are also members of the mathematics club. But recruiting should not by any means be limited to students in the mathematics club. There are likely to be some talented students in the school who, because of other commitments, were unable to join the mathematics club but might well join the mathematics team. In addition to obtaining teacher recommendations, the mathematics team coach should construct an entrance examination for all prospective candidates for the mathematics team. Such an examination should cover as wide a range of topics as possible, using the types of questions likely to come up at a mathematics team meet. In addition, a successful kind of item for this examination is one in which a new topic (or concept) is succinctly introduced and then a question about this new topic is asked. For such an examination for geometry students, one example might be to introduce Ptolemy's theorem and then ask a question that can be solved using that theorem.

EXAMPLE *Ptolemy's theorem:* In an inscribed quadrilateral, the product of the lengths of the diagonals equals the sum of the products of the lengths of the opposite sides.

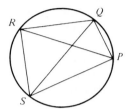

For the inscribed quadrilateral *PQRS*, Ptolemy's theorem gives us

$$(RP)(SQ) = (PQ)(RS) + (PS)(RQ)$$

Use Ptolemy's theorem to find the length of side $\overline{BC}$ of $\triangle ABC$, which is inscribed in a circle of radius of length 5. The lengths of $\overline{AB}$ and $\overline{AC}$ are 5 and 6, respectively.

The above-average mathematics student should correctly solve this problem with either answer: $3\sqrt{3} - 4$ or $3\sqrt{3} + 4$. The truly gifted mathematics student, however, will realize that there are *two* possible solutions, depending on whether $\angle A$ is acute or obtuse. A sample solution follows.

SOLUTION

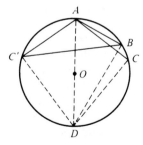

We notice that there are two possibilities to consider in this problem. Both $\triangle ABC$ and $\triangle ABC'$ are inscribed in circle *O*, with $AB = 5$ and $AC = AC' = 6$. We are to find BC and BC'.

Draw diameter $\overline{AOD}$, which measures 10, and draw $\overline{DC}, \overline{DB},$ and $\overline{DC'}$. $m\angle AC'D = m\angle ACD = m\angle ABD = 90°$.

Consider the case in which $\angle A$ in $\triangle ABC$ is acute. In right $\triangle ACD$, $DC = 8$, and in right $\triangle ABD$, $BD = 5\sqrt{3}$. By Ptolemy's theorem applied to quad-

rilateral *ABCD*,

$$(AC)(BD) = (AB)(DC) + (AD)(BC)$$

or

$$(6)(5\sqrt{3}) = (5)(8) + (10)(BC)$$

and

$$BC = 3\sqrt{3} - 4$$

Now consider the case in which $\angle A$ is obtuse, as in $\triangle ABC'$. In right $\triangle AC'D$, $DC' = 8$. By Ptolemy's theorem applied to quadrilateral $ABDC'$,

$$(AC')(BD) + (AB)(DC') = (AD)(BC')$$
$$(6)(5\sqrt{3}) + (5)(8) = (10)(BC'), \text{ and}$$
$$BC' = 3\sqrt{3} + 4$$

In addition to testing a student's ability to use a newly learned fact, this type of question permits the more able student to shine. She will discover the ambiguity in the question posed and offer a complete solution. Each question on this entrance test should serve a clearly defined function.

Once the mathematics team members have been selected, a time must be set for them to be trained. Mathematics teams have been known to meet before the school day begins, during the lunch hour (students can eat their lunch while working on mathematics team activities), during the regular school day, or after the last period of the day. In some instances, the mathematics team might meet as a class. Some schools have chosen to give students course credit for a course on problem solving and special topics in mathematics that is not part of the secondary school curriculum. A course of this kind also serves to train members of a mathematics team. In addition to using the mathematics team materials listed at the end of this chapter, the mathematics team coach would be wise to try to obtain questions used at previous mathematics team meets. This will give students an excellent idea as to what to expect at future mathematics team meets and how to prepare for them.

George Polya's classic book, *How To Solve It* (Princeton, N.J.: Princeton University Press, 1945), should serve as a good initial source for the mathematics team coach to use in preparing to train the mathematics team in problem-solving skills. Mathematics team training sessions provide an excellent opportunity to present topics normally not taught in the secondary school but useful for solving typical problems encountered at mathematics team meets.

The following list suggests some topics that might be useful to a mathematics team:

> Diophantine equations
> Means: arithmetic, geometric, and harmonic
> Modular arithmetic-algebraic applications
> Divisibility tests
> Geometry theorems of Ceva, Menelaus, Ptolemy, Stewart, Heron, etc.
> Techniques in problem solving
> Various algebraic relationships
> Topics in number theory
> Sequences and series
> Probability
> Inequalities
> Systems of equations
> Topics from theory of equations
> Maxima-minima problems in geometry and algebra

As an outgrowth of a discussion of these and many other appropriate mathematics topics, useful facts and relationships should be separately recorded by each student and kept available for ready reference. A student's collection of facts and relationships might include those listed at the end of this chapter.

Mathematics team coaching requires a total commitment from the faculty sponsor. In addition to preparing extensively and gathering previously used mathematics team questions (and other related materials), the faculty sponsor must be available for after-school mathematics team meets. This could likely involve traveling with the team to other schools. The work of the mathematics team coach requires much dedication, but the rewards are gratifying.

MATHEMATICS CONTESTS

Closely aligned with the activities of a mathematics team is the administration of various national, statewide, or local mathematics contests. These contests, including the American High School Mathematics Examination (AHSME) and the American Junior High School Mathematics Examination, which are chiefly sponsored by the Mathematical Association of America, are usually open to all students (not just those on the mathematics team). Extensive publicity in the school is required to attract as large a group for the contest as possible. Here students who may not be among the ten strongest mathematics students in the school can enter a contest for purely recreational reasons. Many of the questions on these mathematics contests are within reach of average mathematics students. Naturally, these contests also contain challenging questions to help select the superior students. Often, schoolwide awards are given as well as regional, state-

wide, and sometimes national awards. As they are usually set up, the mathematics contests can offer entertainment and enrichment to a reasonably large portion of the school's population. This is particularly so when the mathematics team coach reviews the contest questions with students after the contest has ended.

There are times when mathematics contests go beyond merely a test situation. A notable example is the American Regions Mathematics League (ARML). It involves an annual conference where teams of fifteen students, representing winners of various city, county, and state competitions, meet to hear lectures on mathematics, compete against one another in yet another contest, and socialize.

The League continues to grow, currently representing states from most regions of the country. To facilitate matters, regional centers are used for these annual conferences.

High school mathematics contests generally go far toward promoting an interest in mathematics throughout the school. The National Council of Teachers of Mathematics as well as local mathematics teacher organizations are excellent sources of information about which mathematics leagues or which mathematics contests are available to your students.

MATHEMATICS PROJECTS

Think of writing a term paper or doing a term project in your mathematics class. This activity has proved to be successful with groups of varying levels of ability. A mathematics project may take the form of a construction project such as curve stitching, special tool constructions, or construction of linkages. The term paper might involve an original investigation of some mathematics topic; it might report on an experiment that the student has conducted; it might be an exposition on some previously unfamiliar mathematics topic (this is best when not too broad in scope); or it might offer a discussion of a topic from the history of mathematics (e.g., involving the historical development of a topic or concept). On page 206 we list some possible topics that students might use for a term paper (or project). (This list is merely intended as a guide for generating additional topics.)

The topic for a mathematics project should be selected by the student, with the teacher serving as a facilitator by stimulating interest in various topics. Having selected a topic, the student should read as much about it as is available. Keeping accurate notes throughout this study period is essential for a successful project. Periodic conferences with the teacher will ensure that the student is kept properly on track. Careful notes taken during these sessions along with complete and accurate notes obtained from readings will make work on the written report simpler.

SAMPLE MATHEMATICS CONTEST QUESTIONS

1. If $1 - \dfrac{4}{x} + \dfrac{4}{x^2} = 0$, then $\dfrac{2}{x}$ equals

   (a) -1 (b) 1 (c) 2 (d) -1 or 2 (e) -1 or -2

2. If four times the reciprocal of the circumference of a circle equals the diameter of the circle, then the area of the circle is

   (a) $\dfrac{1}{\pi^2}$ (b) $\dfrac{1}{\pi}$ (c) 1 (d) π (e) π^2

3. For all non-zero numbers x and y such that $x = \dfrac{1}{y}$, $\left(x - \dfrac{1}{x}\right)\left(y + \dfrac{1}{y}\right)$ equals

   (a) $2x^2$ (b) $2y^2$ (c) $x^2 + y^2$ (d) $x^2 - y^2$ (e) $y^2 - x^2$

4. If $a = 1$, $b = 10$, $c = 100$ and $d = 1000$, then
   $(a + b + c - d) + (a + b - c + d) +$
   $(a - b + c + d) + (-a + b + c + d)$ is equal to

   (a) 1111 (b) 2222 (c) 3333 (d) 1212 (e) 4242

5. Four boys bought a boat for $60. The first boy paid one half of the sum of the amounts paid by the other boys; the second boy paid one third of the sum of the amounts paid by the other boys; and the third boy paid one fourth of the sum of the amounts paid by the other boys. How much did the fourth boy pay?

   (a) $10   (b) $12   (c) $13   (d) $14   (e) $15

6. The number of distinct pairs (x, y) of real numbers satisfying both of the following equations:

   $$x = x^2 + y^2$$
   $$y = 2xy$$

   is

   (a) 0 (b) 1 (c) 2 (d) 3 (e) 4

7. Opposite sides of a regular hexagon are 12 inches apart. The length of each side, in inches, is

   (a) 7.5 (b) $6\sqrt{2}$ (c) $5\sqrt{2}$ (d) $\dfrac{9}{2}\sqrt{3}$ (e) $4\sqrt{3}$

8. Al's age is 16 more than the sum of Bob's age and Carl's age, and the square of Al's age is 1632 more than the square of the sum of Bob's age and Carl's age. The sum of the ages of Al, Bob and Carl is

   (a) 64 (b) 94 (c) 96 (d) 102 (e) 140

9. How may pairs (m, n) of integers satisfy the equation $m + n = mn$?

   (a) 1 (b) 2 (c) 3 (d) 4 (e) more than 4

10. Each of the three circles in the adjoining figure is externally tangent to the other two, and each side of the triangle is tangent to two of the circles. If each circle has radius three, then the perimeter of the triangle is

    (a) $36 + 9\sqrt{2}$ (b) $36 + 6\sqrt{3}$
    (c) $36 + 9\sqrt{3}$ (d) $18 + 18\sqrt{3}$
    (e) 45

11. Three fair dice are tossed at random (i.e., all faces have the same probability of coming up). What is the probability that the three numbers turned up can be arranged to form an arithmetic progression with common difference one?

    (a) $\dfrac{1}{6}$ (b) $\dfrac{1}{9}$ (c) $\dfrac{1}{27}$ (d) $\dfrac{1}{54}$ (e) $\dfrac{7}{36}$

12. If $y = (\log_2 3)(\log_3 4) \ldots (\log_n [n + 1]) \ldots (\log_{31} 32)$ then

    (a) $4 < y < 5$ (b) $y = 5$ (c) $5 < y < 6$ (d) $y = 6$
    (e) $6 < y < 7$

13. Let E be the point of intersection of the diagonals of convex quadrilateral $ABCD$, and let P, Q, R and S be the centers of the circles circumscribing triangles ABE, BCE, CDE and ADE, respectively. Then

    (a) $PQRS$ is a parallelogram
    (b) $PQRS$ is a parallelogram if and only if $ABCD$ is a rhombus
    (c) $PQRS$ is a parallelogram if and only if $ABCD$ is a rectangle
    (d) $PQRS$ is a parallelogram if and only if $ABCD$ is a parallelogram
    (e) none of the above are true

14. For how many paths consisting of a sequence of horizontal and/or vertical line segments, with each segment connecting a pair of adjacent letters in the diagram below, is the word CONTEST spelled out as the path is traversed from beginning to end?

    (a) 63 (b) 128 (c) 129
    (d) 255 (e) none of these

    ```
              C
             COC
            CONOC
           CONTNOC
          CONTETNOC
         CONTESETNOC
        CONTESTSETNOC
    ```

Reprinted from the 1977 and 1978 Annual High School Mathematics Examinations with permission of the Mathematical Association of America, Committee on High School Contests.

TOPICS FOR MATHEMATICS PROJECTS

Advanced Euclidean Geometry
Algebraic Fallacies
Algebraic Models
Algebraic Recreations
Analog Computer
Ancient Number Systems and Algorithms
Arithmetic Fallacies
Arithmetic Recreations
Bases Other than Ten
Binary Computer
Boolean Algebra
Brocard Points
Calculating Shortcuts
Cavalieri's Theorem
Checking Arithmetic Operations
Conic Sections
Continued Fractions
Cryptography
Crystallography
Curves of Constant Breadth
Cylindrical Projections
Desargues' Theorem
Determinants
Diophantine Equations
Divisibility of Numbers
Duality
Dynamic Symmetry
Elementary Number Theory Applications
The Euler Line
Extension of Euler's Formula to N Dimensions
Extension of Pappus's Theorem
Fermat's Last Theorem
Fibonacci Numbers
Fields
Finite Differences
Finite Geometry
The Five Regular Polyhedra
Flexagons
The Four-Color Problem
The Fourth Dimension
Fractals
Game Theory
Gaussian Primes
Geodesics
Geometry Constructions (Euclid)
Geometric Dissections—Tangrams
Geometric Fallacies
Geometric Models
Geometric Stereograms
Geometric Transformations
Geometry of Bubbles and Liquid Film
Geometry of Catenary
Gergonne's Problem
The Golden Section
Graphical Representation of Complex
   Roots of Quadratic and Cubic Equations
Groups
Higher Algebra
Higher Order Curves
Hyperbolic Functions

The Hyperbolic Paraboloid
Hypercomplex Numbers
Intuitive Geometric Recreations
Investigating the Cycloid
The Law of Growth
Linear Programming
Linkages
Lissajou's Figures
Lobachevskian Geometry
Logarithms of Negative and Complex Numbers
Logic
Magic Square Construction
Map Projections
Mascheroni's Constructions
Mathematics and Art
Mathematics and Music
Mathematics of Life Insurance
Matrices
Maximum-Minimum in Geometry
Means
Methods of Least Squares
The Metric System
Minimal Surfaces
Modulo Arithmetic in Algebra
Monte Carlo Method of Number Approximation
Multinomial Theorem
Napier's Rods
Networks
The Nine Point Circle
Nomographs
The Number Pi, Phi, or e
Number Theory Proofs
Paper Folding
Partial Fractions
Pascal's Theorem
Polygonal Numbers
Perfect Numbers
Prime Numbers
Probability
Problem Solving in Algebra
Projective Geometry
Proofs of Algebraic Theorems
Properties of Pascal's Triangle
Pythagorean Theorem—Triples
Regular Polygons
The Regular Seventeen-Sided Polygon
Relativity and Mathematics
Riemannian Geometry
Special Factoring
Steiner Constructions
Solving Cubics and Quartics
Spherical Triangles
The Spiral
Statistics
Tesselations
Theory of Braids
Theory of Equations
Theory of Perspectives
Three-Dimensional Curves
The Three Famous Problems of Antiquity
Topology
Unsolved Problems
Vectors

Sometime during the early stages of the project, the teacher should specifically indicate what the written product should include. It is important that the teacher not fix the format and content so rigidly as to stifle creativity. The teacher might suggest individual conferences with students who find the suggested format inappropriate for their particular projects. Such features as a bibliography would probably be a part of all papers. Support of calculator and computer results should be encouraged, where appropriate.

MATHEMATICS FAIR

In many regions of the country, regular (annual, semiannual, etc.) exhibitions of student mathematics projects are held. These range from schoolwide to national in scope. Some are locally sponsored, while others may be sponsored by national organizations. Such information should be readily available from school administrators or local mathematics teacher organizations. The prospect of eventual exhibit at a mathematics fair could serve as additional motivation for students.

Naturally, when a student's project involves some physical model such as a linkage or a geometric construction, the mere exhibition may be meaningful; however, when a student's project is a mathematical development or a study of some concept, then a presentation is necessary. Most mathematics fairs are organized to allow students to present their papers (orally) before a group of judges. In progressive stages, winners are selected, usually from each grade level entered. Community members are often attracted to such events.

The learning experience involved in the process of preparing a project or writing a paper, and then presenting or even defending it, is very valuable. Whether a student wins this fair competition is not as important as the recognition offered for his or her work.

THE SCHOOL MATHEMATICS MAGAZINE

A common activity for a mathematics club is the publication of a school mathematics magazine. A school mathematics journal could consist of some of the better student term papers (or projects). Students' work (with some editorial refinements) could be easily disseminated by such a mathematics magazine. Typically such magazines are distributed (or sold) throughout the school and sent to other nearby schools, either to the students there or to the mathematics department head.

A project of this kind usually offers a productive activity for every member of the club. The more motivated mathematics students and the more advanced mathematics students might undertake writing the content of the prospective mathematics magazine, while the more artistic students might become involved in designing the layout, cover, and artwork. Others might be in charge of the ''business'' aspects of the project, such as publicity, circulation, or costs.

The role of the faculty sponsor is essentially that of a facilitator who defines the job and then allows students to adjust it to their needs and desires. As with any well-organized project, at least one person must be in charge of the entire project. Careful consideration to such things as organizational ability and leadership traits should be given before the student editor-in-chief is selected. The selection is most effective if it can come (at least in part) from the student group.

In addition to providing an outlet for exhibition of individual mathematics projects, a mathematics magazine will be a source of genuine pride on the part of all involved. Such an activity goes far in promoting an increased interest in mathematics while providing a good source for mathematics enrichment.

THE MATHEMATICS ASSEMBLY PROGRAM

Although less popular than a mathematics magazine, the mathematics assembly program may be an oral analog of the magazine. Students are provided an opportunity to exhibit some individual or group work to a larger audience. Most teachers' first reaction to the prospect of a mathematics assembly program is one of incredulity! The thought of presenting a program to a large heterogeneous group is overwhelming.

There are a variety of possibilities for such an assembly program. For example, a series of short skits could be used to dramatize some of the major breakthroughs in the history of mathematics. These might also include some light-hearted (yet instructive) skits such as the story of young Gauss, described in Chapter 7 (page 87). A skit could be written dramatizing a useful application of a topic in secondary school mathematics. Here caution must be exercised so that topics selected are appropriate for the majority of the intended audience.

Successful mathematics assembly programs have been produced that involved having individual or small groups of students present short and highly stimulating topics to a general audience. For example, short arithmetic tricks are usually simple enough to generate interest among students of all abilities in the audience. The presenter may show the audience a method of multiplying by 11 mentally. Multiplying 62 by 11 would simply involve adding 6 + 2 and inserting this sum between the 6 and the 2 to get 682. For a number like 75, the mental multiplication 75 × 11 would involve adding the tens digit of the sum 7 + 5 to the 7 after inserting the units digit between the 7 and 5; that is 75 × 11 = 825. For numbers of three or more digits, the rule involves adding every pair of digits starting from the right and each time successively inserting the units digit of the sum (carrying the tens digit) between the end digits. Thus, 3542 × 11 = 3(3 + 5)(5 + 4)(4 + 2)2, or 38,962.

Another exciting number "trick" might be the first example on page 87 in Chapter 7. Here the whole audience can become actively involved. Simply have each student select his or her own three-digit number and follow the specified steps to attain 1089. The unusual result that everyone, regardless of the number they selected (within the guidelines), gets the same answer should certainly arouse student interest.

In part because of its visual nature, geometry offers many topics that might be appropriate for this type of mathematics assembly program. Cutting a very large Möbius strip first half the width from the edge and then one-third the width from the edge should produce some excitement in the audience. To avoid a lull in the presentation, it would be advisable to perforate (i.e., partially cut) the Möbius strip before the program.

Many other topological concepts can intrigue a general audience. Such topics might include removing a vest without removing a covering jacket, untying two people joined by ropes tied to their wrists without removing the ropes, and others. A perusal of Part 4 of this book should enable you to come up with many additional ideas for a mathematics assembly program. Another fine source for such ideas is *Riddles in Mathematics* by E. P. Northrop (Princeton, N.J.: D. Van Nostrand, 1944).

It is sometimes educational as well as entertaining for an audience to watch a mathematics quiz show on stage. Two teams might be selected to compete before a general audience. As long as the questions are presented clearly for all to hear and see, this experience might be stimulating to the audience, who would likely work along with the contestants on stage. Where possible, the questions selected for use should be within the realm of understanding of most students in the audience. A large screen should be used to present the questions to the audience.

The suggestions offered for a mathematics assembly program could also be used for a television production, either taped for viewing by individual classes or presented live through a closed circuit television system (if available) within a school or district. It is hoped that the ideas for possible programs presented stimulate, and eventually generate, others that are appropriate to the intended audience.

GUEST SPEAKERS PROGRAM

In many areas throughout the country there are mathematics speakers bureaus available to secondary schools. They are often sponsored by local universities or professional organizations. Generally, a listing of speakers, their addresses and a list of topics on which they are prepared to speak is made available to all local schools. There is usually no cost to the host schools for this service. A customary activity for a mathematics club is to arrange the invitations for selected speakers and then to publicize each talk. Depending on the topic selected, the audience might be large or small, and it may be heterogeneous or homogeneous. It is probably most advisable to have students rather than a teacher select the speaker. Students will likely turn to the teacher for guidance and input. The teacher should be careful not to impose personal biases onto the speaker selection process, but merely provide guidance. The teacher might contact other secondary schools to find out which speakers were well received there and which were not. If properly planned, this activity should prove to be quite worthwhile.

CLASS TRIPS OF MATHEMATICAL SIGNIFICANCE

Large metropolitan areas offer many exciting examples of applications of mathematics. Teachers in these areas should occasionally avail themselves of these resources. For example, an engineering or research laboratory (such as Bell Laboratories or IBM Laboratory) might be of interest to students. Others may find a visit to a race track parimutuel installation interesting. There they can observe how betting odds are computed, a direct application of probability. There are occasionally special exhibits presented to motivate students toward further study in mathematics. These can also be used for an interesting mathematics class trip. A resourceful teacher will discover many other ideas for worthwhile mathematics class trips.

Proximity to a major metropolitan area is by no means necessary for a successful mathematics class trip. In every area there is industry that relies heavily on mathematics. For example, if a road is being constructed, a class can benefit from observing engineers and surveyors preparing maps and other plans. Even a police helicopter automobile speed surveillance offers some interesting mathematics applications. In some localities a teacher's initiative and creativity will be more necessary than in others. This is part of the challenge of being a mathematics teacher!

Perhaps most important in preparing a successful class trip is careful planning. This refers to more than merely planning the logistics of the trip. Certainly the travel and other arrangements are necessary; however, perhaps even more important is planning a proper class preparation for the trip. This means providing the class with the necessary mathematical and experiential background for a planned trip well before the departure dates. This might entail presenting a topic that might otherwise not be taught, presenting a topic sooner than it otherwise would be reached, or perhaps embellishing a topic to make the trip more appropriate. Under certain circumstances, it may be possible to bring a representative from the place to be visited to the school to motivate and prepare the students for the impending class trip. This extra dimension may help students get the most out of the planned trip. Planning a trip can be indispensable if it involves visiting a nearby museum with the purpose of seeking out only items of mathematical significance. These can range from paintings and architecture to ancient tools. Whatever type of activity is involved, planning (including a preliminary visit by the teacher to the destination of the class trip) is an essential step in making a mathematics class trip a success.

PEER TEACHING PROGRAM

A program of peer teaching can be conducted for all three levels of teaching: on-grade teaching, remediation, and enrichment. Perhaps it will be an activity that the mathematics club chooses to undertake or simply an activity initiated by a group of students along with a faculty advisor. Peer teaching can benefit the student doing the teaching as well as the student being taught. By teaching a concept or topic, one gains a much more comprehensive understanding of the topic. This is, in part, the result of having to organize the presentation in an intelligible manner, which in turn causes the teacher to crystallize his or her thoughts on the topic. Therefore, although this is usually not the primary reason for establishing a peer teaching program, it is an added benefit.

Before any peer teaching begins, time must be provided to train the students involved in teaching their peers. These students must be familiarized with basic teaching techniques and the resources available to them. It is natural to focus on the content when preparing peer teachers; however, a significant amount of time must be devoted to the actual teaching process.

Peer teaching can take various forms. It can be individualized tutoring, it can involve small groups of students, or it can supplement regular class instruction. Whichever format is used, substantial preparation must precede any peer teaching. Special skills are required for each type of instruction. If the peer teaching is to be for remedial purposes, then the peer teachers should be made aware of diagnostic procedures and trained to be sensitve to the needs of the slow learner. It is equally important for a peer teacher to know how to interest students considered average-ability learners. To ensure success with this activity, methods of instruction should be carefully developed.

When peer teaching is done by gifted students for the purpose of enriching others, a model can be established for involving a majority of the school population. For example, the faculty advisor may present enrichment topics to this select group of gifted peer teachers or he or she may set up a schedule of outside speakers to present various enrichment topics to these students. Once this has been done and the peer teachers feel reasonably comfortable with the new topic learned, they would convene under the guidance of a faculty member to set up a strategy for presenting this topic to various types of classes. The level of the intended audience should be considered carefully in the preparation of peer teaching. To the extent appropriate for varying ability levels, a majority of the students in the school can be offered enrichment in mathematics using this model.

Although we use the term ''peer teaching'' in the literal sense, the ideas presented here may easily be extended by having the ''peer teachers'' present material to younger students, either in the same school or in nearby lower schools. Under all circumstances, both content and methodology must be carefully planned before any peer teaching is attempted. Done properly, peer teaching can be rewarding for the peer teachers as well as the students being taught.

THE COMPUTER

After students have demonstrated an acceptable degree of computer confidence and literacy, they should be encouraged to work with the computer during their unassigned school time or after classes have ended for the day. Students may find it fascinating to extend extracurricular explorations to two- and three-dimensional figures, real-world applications and modeling, random numbers, Mandelbrot's fractals, or whatever else they might reasonably choose.

THE BULLETIN BOARD

Every school should have at least one large bulletin board exclusively for mathematics and placed near the mathematics department office or near the mathematics classrooms. This bulletin board can tie together all the extracurricular activities described in this chapter. Both as an aid in providing these activities and as a means for publicity, the mathematics bulletin board can become indispensable in any secondary school. Often the bulletin board sets the tone for the mathematics department.

Some suggested uses for the mathematics bulletin board follow:

1. The bulletin board can be used to stimulate interest in a mathematical topic or process. Similarly, it can be used to motivate students to further study in mathematics by providing only enough material on a certain topic or concept to get students interested enough to do some individual research. Such motivation might well be in the form of a challenge as well as an open-ended question.
2. The results (including questions and model answers) of mathematics team meets can be exhibited on the bulletin board.
3. Mathematics contests (open to all students) can be publicized on the bulletin board.
4. The bulletin board can be the focus for an ongoing weekly intraschool mathematics contest, with a "Problem of the Week" posted weekly. Every week the preceding week's problem is shown along with a model solution and a list of successful solvers. Properly publicized by an enthusiastic teacher, this activity can set a very healthy mathematics atmosphere.
5. Mathematics club activities, including special events for nonmembers (e.g., guest speakers), can be publicized on the bulletin board.
6. Various appealing mathematics projects can be exhibited on the bulletin board. In addition, such events as mathematics fairs might also be publicized there.
7. The bulletin board also can be used to facilitate a peer teaching program by offering publicity and helping with the organization of the program.

8. Career guidance in mathematics, often sought after by stronger mathematics students, may well be given a place on the mathematics bulletin board.
9. The bulletin board may also be used to coordinate computer activities as well as display some more exceptional student programs, such as fractal art. Done attractively, this can help to extend the use of the computer to other students.
10. Seasonal displays as they relate to mathematics can be set up to entice students to investigate some unusual applications of mathematics (e.g., a spring display might relate phyllotaxis to the Fibonacci numbers).
11. The bulletin board can be used to post announcements by colleges and universities concerning special mathematics programs that are offered during the summer and academic year.

SUMMARY

We have discussed many types of extracurricular activities in secondary school mathematics. Some of these activities are carried on outside of the mathematics class (such as clubs, teams, and contests), while others can supplement the regular instruction (such as mathematics projects, guest speakers, and class trips).

It is highly unlikely that a single school will offer all these activities, yet an awareness of some options for extracurricular activities in mathematics is essential for designing an extracurricular program in mathematics suitable for a particular school. A good program of extracurricular activities in mathematics can go a long way in strengthening the regular mathematics program in the school.

EXERCISES

1. Assume that you have volunteered to serve as faculty advisor to your school's mathematics club, which has been a department activity for some time. Your predecessor, who has just retired, was not very dynamic, and during his tenure the club membership declined sharply, and activities involving the club became few and far between. Explain the steps you would take to rejuvenate the club, increase its membership, and develop an attractive program of activities.

2. Assume that you have been coaching your school's mathematics team, which has been trained on a rather informal basis until now, mostly meeting during your spare time to work a few practice problems before each meet. Your supervisor advises you that next term the school is willing to make provision for scheduling the mathematics team as a formal class on your program. Indicate your plans for improving the training program for members of the team and the topics you would plan to teach during the regularly scheduled class period, and justify your decisions.

3. In what type of mathematics class do you feel that a term paper or other project might be appropriately assigned as a requirement of the course? How would you respond to a student who feels that such a "chore" is a waste of time?

4. What would you do to encourage students to enter papers in a mathematics fair if they do not object to doing the research and writing the paper, but they fear giving an oral presentation of their findings before a group of their peers and the judges?

5. Assume that you are the faculty advisor to the school's mathematics magazine. Address the following problems and propose tentative solutions for each.
   a. Very few students are willing to expend the effort needed to write quality papers worthy of inclusion in the magazine.
   b. Too many articles are submitted for inclusion in the magazine. The student editorial staff fears rejecting any material submitted lest the authors be offended and never submit material again.
   c. The magazine sells poorly and you are unable to meet the expenses of its production.
   d. Conflict develops among the members of the student editorial board, and the editor-in-chief resigns two weeks before the due date of publication.

6. Plan a forty-minute mathematics assembly whose primary purpose is to fascinate a general audience of students and attract as many of them as possible to elect mathematics courses next term.

7. As faculty advisor to the mathematics club, you arrange for a speaker to be invited to address a meeting of the club. How would you deal with each of the following situations?
   a. The speaker's presentation is far over the heads of his audience and students begin to leave before the talk is completed.
   b. The speaker is boring, talks down to the students, discusses trivia to a great extent, and begins to lose his audience.
   c. The speaker's presentation degenerates into a sales pitch to have students apply for admission to the college at which she is a faculty member.
   d. The speaker does not appear as scheduled.

8. The chapter discussed planning class trips and preparing students for the experiences they might have during the trip. What follow-up activities would be appropriate *after* the class has returned from a trip to make the trip a complete educational experience?

9. Assume that you are assigned to supervise a peer tutoring program operated by the mathematics department. Most of the tutors are members of the school's honor society and are in the highest mathematics classes in the department. However, students being tutored often complain that their tutors are haughty, impatient with their "slowness" in learning, and sometimes confusing. Peer tutoring is a compulsory activity for honor society members in order to maintain their standing therein. How would you handle this situation?

10. As a professional assignment, your supervisor asks you to maintain the department bulletin board in an attractive manner. You find it cluttered with class honor rolls, announcements of coming activities, team scores, computer schedules, the "Problem of the Week," and many other items. What steps would you take to bring order out of a chaotic arrangement and develop a bulletin board of which the mathematics department can be proud?

NOTES FOR THE MATHEMATICS TEAM

Triangle Properties

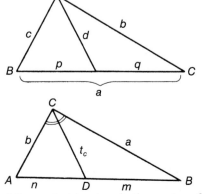

Stewart's Theorem:

$$pb^2 + qc^2 = a(d^2 + pq)$$

Angle Bisector Relationships:

1. $a:b = m:n$
2. $ab - mn = t_c^2$
3. $t_c = \dfrac{2\sqrt{abs(s-c)}}{a+b}$
4. The point of intersection of the angle bisectors is the center of the inscribed circle of the triangle.

Triangle Median Relationships:

1. $m_a = \frac{1}{2}\sqrt{2b^2 + 2c^2 - a^2}$

2. $m_a^2 + m_b^2 + m_c^2 = \frac{3}{4}(a^2 + b^2 + c^2)$

3. $(a + b + c) > (m_a + m_b + m_c) > \frac{3}{4}(a + b + c)$

4. The medians of a triangle are concurrent at a point that trisects each median.

5. The median partitions a triangle into two triangles of equal area.

6. In a right triangle, the median to the hypotenuse (a) divides the triangle into two isosceles triangles; (b) is one-half the length of the hypotenuse.

Triangle Altitude Relationships:

1. $ah_a = bh_b = ch_c = 2\mathcal{A}$ (Where $\mathcal{A}$ represents the area)

2. $a : \dfrac{1}{h_a} = b : \dfrac{1}{h_b} = c : \dfrac{1}{h_c} = 2\mathcal{A}$ or $h_a : h_b : h_c = \dfrac{1}{a} : \dfrac{1}{b} : \dfrac{1}{c} = bc : ac : ab$

3. $h_c = \dfrac{ab}{2R}$

Area of a Triangle:

1. $\mathcal{A} = \frac{1}{2}ah_a$

2. $\mathcal{A} = \frac{1}{2}ab \cdot \sin C$

3. $\mathcal{A} = \dfrac{abc}{4R}$

4. $\mathcal{A} = rs$

5. $\mathcal{A} = \sqrt{s(s - a)(s - b)(s - c)}$ (*Heron's formula*)

6. $\mathcal{A} = \dfrac{b^2 \sin A \cdot \sin C}{2 \sin(A + C)}$

7. For an equilateral triangle: $\mathcal{A} = \dfrac{S^2\sqrt{3}}{4} = \dfrac{h^2\sqrt{3}}{3}$

8. The ratio of the areas of two triangles having an angle of equal measure equals the ratio of the products of the lengths of the pairs of sides including the congruent angles.

Inscribed and Circumscribed Circles of a Triangle:

1. $r = \dfrac{a}{s}\sqrt{\dfrac{(s - a)(s - b)(s - c)}{s}}$

2. $R = \dfrac{abc}{4\mathcal{A}}$

3. $\dfrac{a}{\sin A} = \dfrac{b}{\sin B} = \dfrac{c}{\sin C} = 2R$

4. Radius of an *escribed circle:* $r_a = \sqrt{\dfrac{s(s - b)(s - c)}{s - a}}$

To Find the Measure of an Angle of a Triangle:

$\cos A = \dfrac{b^2 + c^2 - a^2}{2bc}$ (*law of cosines*)

Pythagorean Triples:

$a^2 + b^2 = c^2$, where $a = u^2 - v^2$; $b = 2uv$; $c = u^2 + v^2$ and $u > v$ for integers u and v.

Transversal Theorem:

1. In Figure 1, $\overline{AL}$, $\overline{BM}$, and $\overline{CN}$ are concurrent. Therefore, $AN \cdot BL \cdot CM = AM \cdot BN \cdot CL$

   Figure 1

   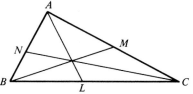

2. In Figure 2, points P, Q, and R are collinear. Therefore, $AP \cdot BR \cdot CQ = AQ \cdot BP \cdot CR$

   Figure 2

   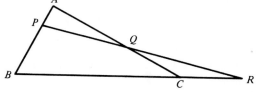

3. In Figure 3, lines a, b, and c are parallel. Therefore,

$$\frac{1}{a} + \frac{1}{b} = \frac{1}{c}; \frac{a}{x} = \frac{b}{y}$$

Figure 3

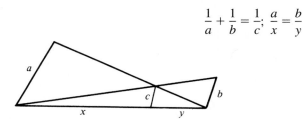

Properties of Polygons

1. The sum of the measures of the interior angles $= (n - 2)180°$ where $n = $ *number of sides.*
2. The sum of the measures of the exterior angles $= 360°$.
3. In an *equiangular polygon:* (a) the measure of each interior angle $= 180° - $ (measure of exterior angle)

   (b) the measure of each interior angle $= \dfrac{(n - 2)180°}{n}$

   (c) each exterior angle has measure $= \dfrac{360°}{n}$

Regular Polygons:

1. Triangle: $\mathcal{A} = \dfrac{S^2\sqrt{3}}{4} = \dfrac{h^2\sqrt{3}}{3} = \dfrac{3R^2\sqrt{3}}{4} = 3r^2\sqrt{3}$

2. Pentagon: $S = \sqrt{2r\sqrt{5} - 2\sqrt{5}} = \dfrac{1}{2}R\sqrt{10 - 2\sqrt{5}}$

3. Hexagon: $S = R$, and $\mathcal{A} = \dfrac{3}{2}R^2\sqrt{3} = 2r^2\sqrt{3}$

4. Octagon: $S = 2r(\sqrt{2} - 1) = R\sqrt{2 - \sqrt{2}}$

5. Decagon: $S = \dfrac{2}{5}(r\sqrt{25 - 10\sqrt{5}} = \dfrac{1}{2}R(\sqrt{5} - 1)$

6. Dodecagon: $\mathscr{A} = 3R^2$

7. General: $\mathscr{A} = \dfrac{1}{2}ap = \dfrac{1}{2}rp$ (a = apothem; p = perimeter)

Areas of Quadrilaterals:

1. Rectangle: $\mathscr{A} = bh$
2. Square: $\mathscr{A} = S^2 = \frac{1}{2}d^2 = 2R^2 = 4r^2$
3. Parallelogram: $\mathscr{A} = bh = ab \cdot \sin C$
4. Rhombus: $\mathscr{A} = bh = \frac{1}{2}d_1d_2 = ab \cdot \sin C$
5. Trapezoid: $\mathscr{A} = \frac{1}{2}h(b_1 + b_2)$

Miscellaneous Triangle and Quadrilateral Theorems:

1. The sum of the lengths of the perpendiculars on the legs of an isosceles triangle from any point on the base is equal to the length of an altitude on one of the legs.
2. In an equilateral triangle, the sum of the lengths of the perpendiculars from any point to the three sides is equal to the length of an altitude.
3. In a circumscribed quadrilateral, the sum of the lengths of the opposite sides are equal.
4. In an inscribed quadrilateral, the sum of the products of the lengths of the opposite sides equals the product of the lengths of the diagonals (*Ptolemy's theorem*).
5. The area of a *cyclic quadrilateral* (i.e., an inscribed quadrilateral) $= \sqrt{(s-a)(s-b)(s-c)(s-d)}$ (*Brahmagupta's formula*).
6. In any parallelogram the sum of the squares of the lengths of the diagonals equals the sum of the squares of all the lengths of the sides.
7. In a triangle whose sides are 13, 14, 15, h_{14} divides side 14 into segments 5 and 9, and h_{14} is 12.
8. In any triangle, the square of the length of a side opposite an acute angle is equal to the sum of the squares of the lengths of the other two sides diminished by twice the product of the length of one of those sides and the length of the projection of the other side upon it.

(For $\triangle ABC$: $a^2 = b^2 + c^2 - 2cp$.)

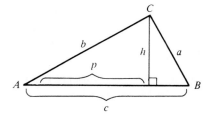   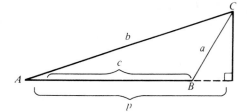

9. In any obtuse triangle, the square of the length of the side opposite the obtuse angle is equal to the sum of the squares of the lengths of the other two sides increased by twice the product of the length of one of these sides and the length of the projection of the other side upon it.

(For obtuse $\triangle ABC$: $a^2 = b^2 + c^2 + 2cp$.)

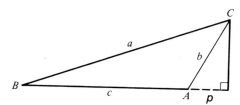

Miscellaneous Theorems on Perimeter and Area

1. Of all triangles having the same base and equal areas, the isosceles triangle has the minimum perimeter.
2. Of all triangles having the same base and equal perimeters, the triangle whose other two sides are congruent has the greatest area.
3. Of all polygons constructed with the same given sides in a given order, that which can be inscribed in a circle has the greatest area.
4. Of two regular polygons with equal perimeters, that which has the greater number of sides has the greater area.
5. If similar polygons are constructed on the three sides of a right triangle, the sum of the areas of the polygons on the legs is equal to the area of the polygon on the hypotenuse. (This is an extension of the Pythagorean theorem.)

Pappus's Theorem

A *volume* that is generated by the motion of a plane section through space equals the product of the area of the plane section and the length of the path of the center of gravity of the plane section.

Some Number Theory Facts

1. Divisibility by 2: last digit of number is even (or "0").
2. Divisibility by 3: sum of the digits is divisible by 3.
3. Divisibility by 4: last two digits when considered as a number are divisible by 4 (e.g., 7812).
4. Divisibility by 5: last digit 5 or 0.
5. Divisibility by 6: rules for divisibility by 2 and 3.
6. Divisibility by 8: last three digits when considered as a number are divisible by 8 (e.g., 57256).
7. Divisibility by 9: sum of the digits is divisible by 9.
8. Divisibility by 10: last digit is 0.
9. Divisibility by 11: the difference of the sums of alternate digits is divisible by 11.
10. Divisibility by 12: rules for divisibility by 3 and 4.
11. *Fermat's theorem:* $N^{p-1} - 1 =$ multiple of p, where p is prime and N is prime relative to p (e.g., $3^{7-1} - 1$ is a multiple of 7).

Factoring

1. For *odd e:* $x^e + y^e = (x + y)(x^{e-1} - x^{e-2}y + x^{e-3}y^2 - \ldots + y^{e-1})$
2. For *all e:* $x^e - y^e = (x - y)(x^{e-1} + x^{e-2}y + x^{e-3}y^2 + \ldots + y^{e-1})$
3. For *even e:* $x^e + y^e = (x^{e/2} + y^{e/2})(x^{e/2} - y^{e/2})$

Binomial Theorem

$$(a + b)^n = a^n + na^{n-1}b + \frac{n(n-1)}{1 \cdot 2} a^{n-2}b^2 + \frac{n(n-1)(n-2)}{1 \cdot 2 \cdot 3} a^{n-3}b^3 + \ldots + b^n$$

Logarithms

1. $\log_a b = x$ means $a^x = b$
2. $(\log_a b)(\log_b c) = \log_a c$

Inequalities

1. $a + \dfrac{1}{a} \geq 2$ 2. $\dfrac{a}{b} + \dfrac{b}{a} \geq 2$ 3. $\dfrac{a + b}{2} \geq \dfrac{2ab}{a + b}$

Means

Arithmetic Mean: (AM) $= \dfrac{a + b}{2}$ 1. AM $\geq$ GM $\geq$ HM

Geometric Mean: (GM) $= \sqrt{ab}$ 2. (AM) (HM) $=$ (GM)^2

Harmonic Mean: (HM) $= \dfrac{2ab}{a + b}$

REFERENCES

Altshiller-Court, Nathan A. *College Geometry*. New York: Barnes & Noble, 1952.

Barnett, I. A. *Elements of Number Theory*. Boston: Prindle, Weber & Schmidt, 1972.

Bruckheimer, Maxim, and Rina Hirshkowitz. "Mathematics Projects in Junior High School." *Mathematics Teacher* 70 (1977): 573.

Chrystal, G. *Textbook of Algebra*. 2 vols. New York: Chelsea, 1964.

Courant, Richard, and Herbert Robbins. *What Is Mathematics?* New York: Oxford University Press, 1941.

Coxeter, H. S. M., and S. L. Greitzer. *Geometry Revisited*. New York: Random House, 1967.

Davis, David R. *Modern College Geometry*. Reading, MA: Addison-Wesley, 1949.

Elgarten, Gerald H. "A Mathematics Intramurals Contest." *Mathematics Teacher* 69 (1976): 477.

Hall, H. S., and S. R. Knight. *Higher Algebra*. London: Macmillan, 1960.

Holmes, Joseph E. "Enrichment or Acceleration?" *Mathematics Teacher* 63 (1970): 471.

House, Peggy A. *Interactions of Science and Mathematics*. Columbus, OH: ERIC Clearing House for Science, Mathematics, and Environmental Education, 1980.

James, Robert C., and Glenn James, eds. *Mathematics Dictionary*, 4th ed. New York: Van Nostrand Reinhold, 1976.

Johnson, Roger A. *Modern Geometry*. Boston: Houghton Mifflin, 1929.

Jones, Mary H. "Mathcounts: A New Junior High School Mathematics Competition." *Mathematics Teacher* 76 (1983): 482.

Karush, William. *The Crescent Dictionary of Mathematics*. New York: Macmillan, 1962.

Leonard, William A. *No Upper Limit, The Challenge of the Teacher of Secondary Mathematics*. Fresno, CA: Creative Teaching Assoc., 1977.

Lichtenberg, Betty K. "Some Excellent Sources of Material for Mathematics Clubs." *Mathematics Teacher* 74 (1981): 284.

Newman, James R. *The World of Mathematics*. 4 vols. New York: Simon & Schuster, 1956.

Olds, C. D. *Continued Fractions*. New York: Random House, 1963.

Posamentier, Alfred S. *Excursions in Advanced Euclidean Geometry*. Menlo Park, CA: Addison-Wesley, 1984.

Schaaf, William L., ed. *A Bibliography of Recreational Mathematics*. 4 vols. Washington, DC: National Council of Teachers of Mathematics, 1978.

Smith, David E., ed. *Source Book in Mathematics*. New York: McGraw-Hill, 1929.

Wright, Frank. "Motivating Students With Projects and Teaching Aids." *Mathematics Teacher* 58 (1965): 47.

RESOURCES FOR EXTRACURRICULAR ACTIVITIES

History of Mathematics

Ball, W. W. Rouse. *A Short Account of the History of Mathematics*. New York: Dover, 1960.

Bell, E. T. *Men of Mathematics*. New York: Simon & Schuster, 1937.

Boyer, Carl B. *A History of Mathematics.* New York: John Wiley, 1968.

Bunt, Lucas N. H., Philip S. Jones, and Jack D. Bedient. *The Historical Roots of Elementary Mathematics.* Englewood Cliffs, NJ: Prentice Hall, 1976.

Cajori, Florian. *A History of Mathematic Notations.* 2 vols. LaSalle, IL: Open Court, 1928.

Eves, Howard. *An Introduction to the History of Mathematics,* 4th ed. New York: Holt, Rinehart & Winston, 1976.

Heath, Thomas L. *Greek Mathematics.* New York: Dover, 1963.

Smith, David E. *A Source Book in Mathematics.* New York: McGraw-Hill, 1929.

———. *History of Mathematics.* 2 vols. New York: Dover, 1953.

van der Waerden, B. L. *Science Awakening.* New York: John Wiley, 1963.

Mathematical Recreations

Ball, W. W. Rouse, and H. S. M. Coxeter. *Mathematical Recreations and Essays.* New York: Macmillan, 1960.

Benson, William, and Oswald Jacoby. *New Recreations with Magic Squares.* New York: Dover, 1976.

Caldwell, J. H. *Topics in Recreational Mathematics.* London: Cambridge University Press, 1966.

Cundy, H. Martyn, and A. P. Rollett. *Mathematical Models.* New York: Oxford University Press, 1961.

Honsberger, Ross. Mathematical Morsels. Washington, DC: Mathematics Association of America, 1978.

Kraitchik, Maurice. *Mathematical Recreations.* New York: Dover, 1942.

Madachy, Joseph. *Mathematics on Vacation.* New York: Charles Scribner's Sons, 1966.

Northrop, Eugene. *Riddles in Mathematics.* Princeton, NJ: D. Van Nostrand, 1944.

Ogilvy, C. Stanley. *Through the Mathescope.* New York: Oxford University Press, 1956.

Posamentier, Alfred S. *Excursions in Advanced Euclidean Geometry.* Menlo Park, CA: Addison-Wesley, 1984.

———. *Advanced Geometric Constructions.* Palo Alto, CA: Dale Seymour Publications, 1988.

Posamentier, Alfred S., and Gordon Sheridan. *Mathematics Motivators, Investigations in Pre-Algebra.* Menlo Park, CA: Addison-Wesley, 1982.

———. *Math Motivators, Investigations in Geometry.* Menlo Park, CA: Addison-Wesley, 1982.

———. *Math Motivators, Investigations in Algebra.* Menlo Park, CA: Addison-Wesley, 1983.

Schuh, Fred. *The Master Book of Mathematical Recreations.* New York: Dover, 1968.

Mathematics Clubs

Carnahan, Walter H., ed. *Mathematics Clubs in High Schools.* Washington, DC: National Council of Teachers of Mathematics, 1958.

Gruver, Howell L. *School Mathematics Contests: A Report.* Washington, DC: National Council of Teachers of Mathematics, 1968.

Hess, Adrien L. *Mathematics Projects Handbook.* Washington, DC: National Council of Teachers of Mathematics, 1977.

Mu Alpha Theta. *Handbook for Sponsors.* Norman, OK: University of Oklahoma, 1970.

Ransom, William R. *Thirty Projects for Mathematical Clubs and Exhibitions.* Portland, ME: J. Weston Walch, Publisher, 1961.

Problem Solving

The Conference Board of Mathematical Sciences. *The Role of Axiomatics and Problem Solving in Mathematics.* Boston: Ginn, 1966.

Hudgins, Bryce B. *Problem Solving in the Classroom.* New York: Macmillan, 1966.

Krulik, Stephen, and Jesse A. Rudnick. *Problem Solving, a Handbook for Teachers.* Boston: Allyn and Bacon, 1980.

Polya, George. *How to Solve It.* Princeton, NJ: Princeton University Press, 1945.

———. *Mathematics and Plausible Reasoning.* 2 vols. Princeton, NJ: Princeton University Press, 1954.

———. *Mathematical Discovery.* 2 vols. New York: John Wiley, 1962.

Whimbey, Arthur, and Jack Lochhead. *Problem Solving and Comprehension, A Short Course in Analytical Reasoning,* 2d ed. Philadelphia: Franklin Institute Press, 1980.

Wickelgren, Wayne A. *How To Solve Problems.* San Francisco: W. H. Freeman, 1974.

Sources for Mathematics Team Problems

Aref, M. N., and William Wernick. *Problems and Solutions in Euclidean Geometry.* New York: Dover, 1968.

Barbeau, E., M. Klamkin, and W. Moser. *1001 Problems in High School Mathematics.* Montreal, Canada: Canadian Mathematics Congress, 1978.

Barry, Donald T., and J. Richard Lux. *The Philips Academy Prize Examinations in Mathematics.* Palo Alto, CA: Dale Seymour Publications, 1984.

Brousseau, Brother Alfred, ed. *Mathematics Contest Problems.* Palo Alto, CA: Creative Publications, 1972.

Bryant, Steven J., George E. Graham, and Kenneth G. Wiley. *Nonroutine Problems in Algebra, Geometry, and Trigonometry.* New York: McGraw-Hill, 1965.

Butts, Thomas. *Problem Solving in Mathematics.* Glenview, IL: Scott, Foresman, 1973.

Charosh, Mannis, ed. *Mathematical Challenges.* Washington, DC: National Council of Teachers of Mathematics, 1965.

Comprehensive School Mathematics Program. *E. M. Problem Book.* 2 vols. St. Louis: CEMREL, 1975.

Dowlen, Mary, Sandra Powers, and Hope Florence. *College of Charleston Mathematics Contest Book.* Palo Alto, CA: Dale Seymour Publications, 1987.

Dunn, Angela, ed. *Mathematical Bafflers.* New York: McGraw-Hill, 1964.

———. *Second Book of Mathematical Bafflers.* New York: Dover, 1983.

Edwards, Josephine D., Declan J. King, and Peter J. O'Halloran. *All the Best From the Australian Mathematics Competition.* Canberra, Australia: The Australian Mathematics Competition, 1986.

Fisher, Lyle, and Bill Kennedy. *Brother Alfred Brousseau Problem Solving and Mathematics Competition.* Introductory Division. Palo Alto, CA: Dale Seymour Publications, 1984.

Fisher, Lyle, and William Medigovich. *Brother Alfred Brousseau Problem Solving and Mathematics Competition.* Palo Alto, CA: Dale Seymour Publications, 1984.

Greitzer, Samuel L. *International Mathematical Olympiads.* Washington, DC: Mathematical Association of America, 1978.

Hill, Thomas J., ed. *Mathematical Challenges II—Plus Six.* Washington, DC: National Council of Teachers of Mathematics, 1974.

Polya, George, and Jeremy Kilpatrick. *The Stanford Mathematics Book.* New York: Teachers College Press, 1974.

Posamentier, Alfred S., and Charles T. Salkind. *Challenging Problems in Algebra.* Palo Alto, CA: Dale Seymour Publications, 1988.

———. *Challenging Problems in Geometry.* Palo Alto, CA: Dale Seymour Publications, 1988.

Rapaport, Elvira, trans. *Hungarian Problem Book.* 2 vols. New York: Random House, 1963.

Salkind, Charles T., ed. *The Contest Problem Book.* New York: Random House, 1961.

———. *The MAA Problem Book II.* New York: Random House, 1966.

Salkind, Charles T., and James M. Earl, eds. *The MAA Problem Book III.* New York: Random House, 1973.

Saul, Mark E., G. W. Kessler, Sheila Krilov, and Lawrence Zimmerman. *The New York City Contest Problem Book.* Palo Alto, CA: Dale Seymour Publications, 1986.

Shklarsky, D. O., N. N. Chentzov, and I. M. Yaglom. *The U.S.S.R. Olympiad Problem Book.* San Francisco: W. H. Freeman, 1962.

Sitomer, Harry. *The New Mathlete Problem Book.* Nassau County, NY: Interscholastic Mathematics League, 1974.

Steinhaus, Hugo. *One Hundred Problems in Elementary Mathematics.* New York: Pergamon Press, 1963.

Straszewicz, S. *Mathematical Problems and Puzzles from the Polish Mathematical Olympiads.* New York: Pergamon Press, 1965.

Trigg, Charles W. *Mathematical Quickies.* New York: McGraw-Hill, 1967.

CHAPTER 13
MATHE-MATICALLY DEFICIENT STUDENTS

Our objective in this chapter is to offer various alternatives for students whose mathematical skills are deficient at the secondary level. The student who has somehow not developed the necessary skills in the early, formative years in school is usually the focus of considerable attention from teachers in class. The deficiency may have occurred in the past because of ineffective teaching, inadequate curriculum, repeated failure, poor work habits, dislike of school, slow maturation, oppressive or nonsupportive environment, or simply because the child may be a slow learner or one with emotional or physical problems.

The goal of any remediation program is, at the very least, to raise the student's mathematical performance to an "acceptable" level some time before he or she graduates from high school. This is a desirable goal because the student will then be employable as a mathematically literate high school graduate and may even be able to handle college preparatory work in mathematics.

For the readers of this book who are mathematically mature, an understanding of "acceptable" high school performance level might include, at the very least, algebra, geometry, and trigonometry, as well as the accompanying arithmetic skills. But realistically, this is not a universally attainable goal. If the students had mastered much of what they were taught through the eighth grade (before coming to high school), there would be no need for remediation programs, for everyone would be at the proper starting point for high school mathematics. However, many students reach middle school and high school already improperly prepared, which we define specifically as being two or more years below grade level in arithmetic skills and in general mathematical knowledge.

Students with mathematical deficiencies may have already experienced the boredom of repeated lessons, the embarrassment of studying the same topic as their younger brothers or sisters, the ridicule of insensitive teachers and friends, and the frustration of making little progress in their goal of graduating from high school and going to college. As teachers we must find ways to help these students.

Might it not be of value to attempt pedagogical techniques in a learning environment that conforms to the goal of the *Standards* to provide the same curriculum for all students, differing only by the depth and variety of classroom tasks?

BASIC MATHEMATICS CURRICULUM

What is an average pupil, on grade level, taught in elementary school and middle/junior high school before arriving at the senior high school? Although courses of study do vary in different parts of the country, basically you can expect a student's background through eighth grade to include exposure to many, if not all, of the following topics:

I. Sets
   A. Concept
   B. Notation
   C. Kinds (finite, null, etc.)
   D. Union, intersection, complement
II. Real numbers
   A. Integers
      1. Positive, negative
      2. Order of operations
      3. Properties (closure, commutative, associative, distributive, etc.)
      4. Prime and composite numbers
      5. Factors
      6. Linear open sentences
   B. Rationals
      1. Decimals
      2. Scientific notation
      3. Properties (commutative, identity, inverse, etc.)
      4. Simplifying expressions
      5. Terminating and repeating decimals
      6. Irrationals (square root)
III. Ratio, proportion, percent
IV. Geometry
   A. Point, line, plane
   B. Angles
   C. Polygons
   D. Perpendicular lines
   E. Parallel lines
   F. Congruence
   G. Similarity
   H. Polygons
      1. Triangle properties
      2. Quadrilateral properties
      3. Perimeter and area
   I. Circles
      1. Arc length and measure
      2. Circumference
      3. Area
   J. Solids
      1. Surface area
      2. Volume
V. Coordinate geometry
   A. Plotting points
   B. Pythagorean theorem

   C. Graphing
   D. Inequalities
VI. Statistics
   A. Interpretation of data (including graphing)
   B. Mean, median, mode
   C. Probability
VII. Technology
   A. Basic calculator skills
   B. Computer confidence

From ninth grade through twelfth grade the exposure to mathematics becomes much more specialized, to include algebra, geometry, trigonometry, possibly some calculus, computer programming, and more. While exposure to the mathematics of the early grades is universal, the remaining high school grades see fewer and fewer pupils electing to continue their mathematics studies.

MINIMUM COMPETENCY

Recent trends, which are perhaps more the result of public pressure than educational leadership, are in the direction of preventing a student from graduating from high school with a diploma if he or she has not mastered the basic mathematical skills and concepts that are usually taught through eighth grade (listed above). (Reading, writing and sometimes speaking are generally also included as the required basic skills for graduation.) Thus, many communities have established minimum competency or minimum proficiency requirements, usually at the eighth grade level of work, before the student can receive a high school diploma.

An understanding of what minimum competency or proficiency exams are like ought to prove helpful to teachers who are faced with the problem of providing remediation for students who must pass such an examination in order to graduate. Sample 1 (see page 223) is a partial set of questions one might find on a minimum competency test. A full examination may contain twice as many questions as this set. A student might need to answer 60% to 70% of the questions correctly to be considered as having "passed" the examination and thus be entitled to receive a high school diploma.

WHO NEEDS REMEDIATION?

Several categories of students, at some time in their secondary school careers, may need some form of remediation service. These are:

1. Students who are two or more years below grade level in mathematical skills (as determined by standardized tests).

2. Students who are chronic failures in mathematics.
3. Students who are unable to score a passing grade on a minimum competency or proficiency examination.
4. Pupils whose families, friends, neighborhoods, and cultures do not encourage success in school and who are therefore not succeeding in their mathematics work.
5. Students with interfering physical or learning disabilities.
6. Students who transfer from one school to another and who are having adjustment problems (perhaps because of poor coordination between the two schools involved).
7. Recent foreign immigrants who may be having language and other adjustment difficulties.

DIAGNOSTIC PROCEDURES

A guidance counselor may identify a student as belonging to one or more of the categories above by checking the previous records, interviewing the teachers, speaking to the child and the parents, and finally, by administering, or having the mathematics teacher administer and interpret, a diagnostic test. The results of some or all of these efforts will lead to a determination of whether or not placement in a remedial program is justified. This procedure may also help determine which program is most appropriate if several are available.

Several diagnostic procedures are available to the counselor or mathematics teacher.

Teacher-Made Materials

One appropriate type of examination may cover typical seventh or eighth grade topics similar to the sample minimum competency test shown in this chapter. Every well-managed mathematics department office has records of examinations of this type that may have been used in the past. A comprehensive examination, even though not scientifically prepared and tested for statistical validity, can provide the teacher and counselor with immediate and reasonable insight into the student's mathematical ability, as well as areas of strength and weakness.

Standardized Tests

The California Achievement Test (Level 5, Form B) is but one example of the type of standardized test that is not only easy to administer and interpret but also comprehensive, testing computation, understanding of mathematical concepts, and problem solving. Your supervisor should be able to provide you with a packet of this or some other standardized test that contains answer keys, grade equivalency conversion tables, and other pertinent analyses of the test. Ideally, someone has already selected the test deemed most appropriate for your district's students and provided you with the specific information required.

For example, after administering a standardized test as part of a diagnostic procedure, you may wish to be able to determine (easily!) the areas, if any, in which a student is deficient. Some such tests will provide you with an analysis of the student's strengths and weaknesses in the various key mathematical skills and concepts. Such an analysis can be extremely helpful in designing a remediation program for the individual student.

Thus, the standardized test can, and should, be used to identify candidates for mathematics remediation, as well as to design and prepare individual programs based on each student's needs.

Survey Tests

Survey tests are generally found in mathematics textbooks and workbooks that deal specifically with arithmetic skills. Although these tests do not give norm-referenced data, they may well provide you with a good idea of a student's mathematical strengths and weaknesses. In addition, the results of this type of test should guide you to the appropriate part of the textbook for each pupil tested.

Criterion-Referenced Tests

Criterion-referenced tests also provide a form of diagnosis. Here the diagnosis is more an assessment of specific previously taught skills and concepts than a general, all-encompassing, survey of abilities. Whereas the previously mentioned tests essentially inventory a student's general (and required) mathematical knowledge, the criterion-referenced test is an instrument designed to assess specific learning goals prescribed prior to instruction. Both types of tests play an important role in assessing student mathematical ability or achievement.

Attitudinal Assessment Instruments

Very often assessing a student's attitude toward mathematics, school, discipline, society, and so on can reveal some interesting notions about groups of students as well as about individual students. Information of this sort can have a profound effect on a remediation program. Although at first thought the extra work involved in either selecting an instrument or developing one might not appear to be worth the investment in time, teachers who have taken the time to inspect apparent remedial problems from the point of view of a student's attitude toward related factors have found such additional insights useful in preparing a remedial program.

Much time has been devoted to studying various aspects of attitude measurement. An excellent source from which a teacher can learn about the different kinds of attitude scales as well as ways to construct these instruments is *Scales for the Measurement of Attitudes* by M. E. Shaw and J. M. Wright (McGraw-Hill, 1967).

In addition to assessing attitude, teachers might also find it useful to determine their students' interests. For this purpose various interest inventories have been prepared and are readily available. Some of these inventories attempt to measure a student's tendency to like and choose from among some specific activities. Other inventories correlate a student's interests in school, recreation, and work. Much can be learned about a student's interests from such inventories. The teacher who takes the time to view how all possible factors (including attitude and interests) may affect student achievement in mathematics is probably most likely to design and prepare a meaningful program for her deficient students.

Mathematical Deficiency

Mathematical deficiency will probably manifest itself in any one of the diagnostic procedures just outlined. Although deficiency may be a result of environmental factors or inherited traits, these diagnostic testing procedures are usually not adequate to determine the specific causes of the slow learner's problems. Possible causes may range from limited manipulative abilities to sight and hearing disabilities, as well as other physical problems. Family-related educational pressures and other emotional problems may also adversely affect student achievement.

If the deficiency is innate or permanent, the student may never be able to reach the appropriate grade level in mathematics achievement, regardless of the intensity of remedial work being offered. If, however, the deficiency is related to external factors, it may be remediable. Thus, the curriculum and methods of instruction must be adapted to a level of achievement that is realistic for the individual. Every teacher of deficient students must be aware of the limitations of each child so that his or her expectations for that child's mathematical performance are consistent with the student's abilities and problems.

METHODS OF REMEDIATION

Individualization

Many individualized programs use a diagnostic-prescriptive approach for the remediation of skill deficiencies in mathematics. A standardized mathematics diagnostic test (such as the California Achievement Test mentioned earlier) may be administered at the beginning of the school year to determine each pupil's specific skill deficiencies and the areas that need work. In addition, the teacher may interview the pupil to further focus on areas of difficulty.

The teacher can then analyze the test results more carefully and prescribe remediation activities using workbooks, arithmetic skill kits, calculators, computers, and teacher-prepared materials. These materials are most efficiently organized in individual portfolios that contain a continuous record of each pupil's work. Such portfolios may include the diagnostic test results, the prescribed remediation plan, progress tests, and the student's actual work as each assignment is completed.

Each portfolio will be complete at the end of the term only when a posttest is given and its results compared with the pretest results to determine the progress made. Comparing the end-of-year results with those of the same diagnostic test given at the beginning of the year provides a sound basis for judgment of the overall success of the individualized remediation program for that pupil.

Mathematics Proficiency Test

A listing of remediation topics, for your information and guidance, is provided below. Students may use a scientific or graphics calculator to solve *any* problem on these tests after appropriate training with these instruments.

1. *Whole numbers*
   Place value: reading and writing whole
      numbers
   Rounding off
   Addition
   Subtraction
   Multiplication
   Order of operations
   Prime and composite numbers
   Division
   Exponents
2. *Fractions*
   Comparing fractions
   Reducing fractions
   Improper fractions and mixed numbers
   Ratio, proportion
   Least common multiple; lowest common
      denominator
   Adding and subtracting fractions
   Multiplication of fractions
   Reciprocals
   Division of fractions
3. *Decimals*
   (already listed previously)

Sample 1. Mathematics Competency Test (Use of calculators is permitted.)

---

1. Add:

   835
   218
   81

2. Subtract:

   3016
   − 259

3. Multiply:

   259
   × 63

4. Divide:

   34)2476

5. Reduce the fraction to lowest terms:

   $\dfrac{12}{16} =$

6. Express as an equivalent fraction:

   $\dfrac{3}{5} = \dfrac{}{15}$

7. Add:

   $\dfrac{1}{2}$
   $+ \dfrac{1}{3}$

8. Multiply:

   $\dfrac{2}{3} \times \dfrac{3}{5}$

9. What is $\dfrac{2}{3}$ of 24?

10. Multiply $3\dfrac{1}{3} \times 2\dfrac{1}{2}$.

11. Round 2.37 to the nearest tenth.

12. Divide $\dfrac{2}{3} \div \dfrac{1}{3}$.

13. Subtract 3.51 from 20.20.

14. Find 12% of 8.

15. Add −5 and −6

16. Divide .03)4.215

17. Solve for x: $2x + 4 = 10$

18. Find the average (mean) of 62, 70, 70, 88.

19. A woman buys an air conditioner for $500. The sales tax is 8%. How much sales tax must she pay?

20. What is the circumference of a circle whose radius is 10? (Use the formula $C = 2\pi r$. Use $\pi = 3.14$.)

21. What is the length of the line segment joining A and B?

22. On the graph below plot the point (2.3).

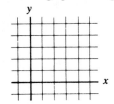

23. What is the perimeter of a triangle whose sides are 5, 12 and 13?

24. Which angle best approximates 30°?

  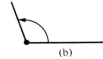

    (a)   (b)   (c)   (d)

25. What is the area of a rectangle whose length measures 10 m and whose width measures 8 m?

26. In the circle, what is the line segment AB called?

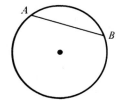

27. Write $\dfrac{3}{5}$ as a percent.

28. Express $\dfrac{3}{25}$ as a decimal.

29. Express $\dfrac{37}{7}$ as a mixed number.

30. José earns $4.50 per hour. How much does he earn for working 6 hours?

31. Solve for x: $\dfrac{4}{7} = \dfrac{x}{14}$

---

4. *Percent*
   Changing decimals and fractions greater than 100%; less than 1%
   Finding percent of a number
5. *Algebra*
   Signed numbers
   Evaluating formulas (including exponents)
   Solving simple equations
6. *Graphs*
   Plotting points
   Linear graphs
   Reading and interpreting graphs: bar graphs, line graphs, circle graphs and pictographs
7. *Geometry*
   Definitions
   Figures (recognition and parts)
   Area, perimeter
8. *Measurement*
   Ruler
   Time
   Conversion of units
   Metrics
   Scale drawings
9. *Statistics*
   Mean, median, mode
   Probability
10. *Problem Solving*
    Word problems
    Arithmetic
    Algebra
    Writing your own problems

Each pupil's progress should be tested frequently with a ten- to fifteen-minute quiz. These regular assessments can be incorporated into the individualized program in such a way as to enable the pupil to take this quiz and demonstrate some accomplishment of the unit tested before moving on to the next programmed item. If the pupil does not succeed, a second prescription may have to be written by the teacher for that particular topic. As an example, we show here Sample 2, a progress test.

Students may be held accountable for the quality as well as the quantity of work they do based on the teacher's determination. They might be asked to record satisfactorily completed assignments on a personal progress record such as Sample 3.

In a typical individualized remedial class, when a student walks into the room, she picks up her folder, returns to her seat, opens her folder, and checks the individualized prescription assigned, to see what she completed the day before, along with the teacher's comments or assessments of this work, and what she should be doing today. She

Sample 2.   Progress Test—Division of Fractions

---

1. Write the reciprocal of each
   $\dfrac{4}{7}$; $3\dfrac{1}{2}$;   2;

2. Divide each pair of numbers as indicated:
   $\dfrac{3}{5} \div \dfrac{9}{15}$; $\dfrac{1}{2} \div 3$; $20 \div \dfrac{5}{9}$; $3\dfrac{1}{2} \div 2\dfrac{3}{5}$;

3. $8\dfrac{1}{3}$ yards of cloth are divided into five equal pieces. How many yards long is each piece?

Sample 3.   Personal Progress Record

Student _____

Class _____

Unit	Date Started	Topic	Progress Test	
			Mark	Date
1		Whole numbers —place value —rounding off —addition —subtraction . . . etc.		

then determines the materials she needs for that session. After picking up that material from the appropriate place in the classroom (where it has already been laid out in advance by the teacher), she returns to her seat and begins working. The teacher and/or teacher's assistant in the room checks her progress regularly during the period and assists her when needed.

This "typical" day has many variations that the teacher will implement as required. Some of these are listed below and include a variety of activities that add many new dimensions to the individualized lesson.

Small Group and Whole Class Instruction

Even in the individualized type of class just described, some small group and whole class instruction may be conducted to teach specific skills when a general weakness is exhibited among a number of students.

If the remedial program in your school is not set up with individualized classes, you will find that students' abilities at that level vary so greatly that you will be forced to offer, at the very least, some form of small group instruction to young people with similar deficiencies. It is no simple matter to break up the class into several groups, each with similar skill deficiencies. While assignments are given to the rest of the class, a group you select to work with for a portion of the period may sit around you as you demonstrate a specific skill that the members of this group lack. An educational assistant would be helpful in such a class to check on others while you are busy with the one group. Such assistants are not always available, however, in which case you might have more capable mathematics students assigned to assist the poorer ones. These mathematics students might be taken from this or other groups.

Even if you are assigned a nonindividualized remedial mathematics class with a specific textbook that you are asked to use, you will find it beneficial and useful to administer some type of diagnostic test so you can at least determine the direction you will follow for the term. Appropriate topics in such a class would include the same ones listed previously for individualized classes. Activities such as mathematical games and use of calculators and computers, as well as some form of "camouflaged drill," can be used to motivate students and help them understand mathematical concepts. These activities are explained further in the following sections.

Student Projects

In any type of class, you may develop activities that will enable students to apply their skills in a variety of interesting and challenging ways. Project activities are generally long range, perhaps two or three months. They require planning by both pupils and teacher. In addition, regular meetings between individual pupils and the teacher must be arranged so that progress can be monitored and evaluated.

You may propose a list of topics for the class to consider and have them construct, build, draw, and/or write something on one topic they select. They must be encouraged to use mathematics books and encyclopedias from the school or public library.

Following are some ideas for possible topics for remedial mathematics class projects. The teacher's assistance is vital in having a student select the area of research most appropriate for him.

Abacus	Magic Squares
Altitude	Möbius Strip
Angles	Negative Numbers
Calendar	Parabola
Clocks	Pi (π)
Computer	Prime Numbers
History of Mathematics	Repeating Decimals
Hypotenuse	Square Root
Infinity	Volume

Mathematics Games and Puzzles

As a supplement to mathematics instruction, whether individualized, small group, or whole class, games and puzzles that challenge students and make them think are appropriate for periodic use in the class. A detailed listing and discussion of appropriate games appears on p. 229 of this chapter. Above all, remember that games should be selected to meet both the deficiency needs of the student and his or her recreational needs.

Field Trips

Field trips should relate directly to instruction in order to provide a challenge for learning and should be correlated with classroom learning activities. Planning a trip to such places as a computer center, a television or radio studio, a newspaper office, or a bank should always be done with an eye toward highlighting the mathematics applications appropriate for the remedial audience. Arithmetic computations may even be used by the class in preparing for the trip in such activities as calculating the cost per student and calculating the distance to be traveled. Scale maps may be drawn where appropriate. Letters, charts, and tables for every possible aspect of the trip should become a learning experience for the students. Above all, whatever experiences are encountered as part of the field trip should be used to motivate further instruction.

Camouflaged Drill

All too often deficient students are "turned off" to the instruction. Most often the reason is that they feel bored with learning the same mathematics topics year after year in a similar way each time. Sometimes students find instruction in arithmetic degrading and as a result avoid it in whatever way they can, leading to discipline problems or truancy.

One way of avoiding this dislike for remediation activities among students is to camouflage the drill work in a meaningful setting. There are countless ways to offer practice skills in such a way as to camouflage the intent of the exercise. Drills can be camouflaged by:

1. Having the student take an active role in planning a field trip. Here the arithmetic applications would have to be carefully planned and not appear to be artificial.
2. Requiring each student to bring to school a supermarket receipt, together with an analysis of the items purchased, price per item, total cost, change given, etc. Once again a specific plan must be in hand before this is tried with a class. All arithmetic applications would have to be anticipated and careful directions provided for the students.
3. Suggesting that pupils keep a record of daily Fahrenheit and Celsius temperature readings, comparing accuracy by using the appropriate conversion formula.
4. Computing the cost of maintaining a family car, including computing gas mileage, cost of gas, insurance, repairs, etc. Comparisons between this cost and the cost of public transportation also should be made.
5. Involving students in simple probability games such as computing probabilities that require the addition and multiplication of fractions. This provides a fine camouflage of these often "meaningless" arithmetic processes.
6. Allowing students free time to "play" with a calculator will enable them to discover number patterns, decimal equivalents, powers, and exponents. They should also be encouraged to create and solve simple verbal problems, which use nontrivial numbers. The purpose of this activity is to allow students to feel more comfortable when working with numbers.

The purpose of camouflaging drill is to generate a desire for learning some of the arithmetic skills that students have often shrugged off as boring or unattainable. Usually when the skills are placed in a real-world context, students are more apt to want to learn information that has evaded them for years.

Peer Group Tutoring

Tutoring by one's peers who are more mathematically advanced may be effective when a professional teacher's efforts may not be. Many schools have organized peer tutoring programs in which students receive remedial assistance that supplements the work they receive in their regular mathematics classes. This applies to remedial work at every level of secondary mathematics, and such a tutorial service is often available whether the remediation is needed in arithmetic, algebra, or geometry. The initial diagnostic testing, as well as progress and posttesting, is often supervised by a teacher-in-charge. The peer tutor is often directed to follow a particular course of action or plan with the pupil seeking assistance. Training of peer tutors is usually an integral part of such a program. Such training sessions involve discussing methods and techniques of presenting the material to be covered as well as alerting the tutors to the various resources available to them. This experience can be enlightening to the peer tutors. In addition to learning and developing "new" methods of communication, they are provided with an opportunity to better understand the mathematics they are assigned to teach, since teaching a topic provides the teacher with an opportunity to crystallize her thoughts on that topic, and as a result, she obtains a better grasp of the topic. Thus, a peer tutoring program benefits the tutor as well as the deficient student being tutored.

Relevant Applications

Mathematics may be made meaningful and relevant to the student when it is in some way tied to his own experiences, hobbies, and interests. Thus, for example, a youngster's interest in art might suggest that the teacher develop a program for that student and others like him, in the following areas:

1. Geometric patterns that may be created with compasses and straightedge. This might lead to measurement of segments and angles, properties of the circle and regular polygons, and much more, depending on the students' interests as well as the imagination of the teacher. The teacher must always remember the specific intent of the unit so that the art does not become an end in itself but remains a means to an end.
2. String designs that may be created by connecting appropriately located points (or holes in card-

board) such as the points A_1 and B_1, A_2 and B_2, etc.,

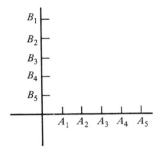

thereby forming an envelope for a parabola (see Enrichment Unit 91, ''The Parabolic Envelope''). Other conic sections may be similarly constructed (see Enrichment Unit 106, ''Constructing Ellipses''). Before advanced work can be done in this unit, students learn about measurement on a ruler (both inches and centimeters), acute, right and obtuse angles, names of conic sections, etc. Once again, this activity is limited only by the teacher's imagination and students' interest. While at first thought some of these examples may appear too ambitious, actual experience with them has proved otherwise.

An investigation of some relevant topic through arithmetic applications can be extremely fruitful in motivating students toward mathematics. Many possible topics are available, but the main criterion for this selection is the interests already present among the intended audience. A proper topic selection together with a creative and imaginative teacher should ensure success in this mathematical endeavor.

Computer Assisted Instruction (CAI)

The computer will probably prove to be the most revolutionary teaching aid ever. In the case of remedial instruction it is but one more tool to supplement individualized, small group, or large group lessons.

Well-written programs that result in a high degree of student interaction and involvement are becoming increasingly available for all the popular computers found in schools these days. It is not unusual to find a computer lab with students doing remedial work in arithmetic (any of the four operations), problem solving, and algebra (solving first- or second-degree equations, multiplying binomials, factoring, graphing, and so forth).

Programs are available to teach, reteach, reinforce, drill, and practice. Many also take into account such factors as learning rates and ability levels.

Frequently the software allows pupils to select the topic as well as the level of difficulty by themselves. Of course, the teacher might prefer to make that decision for the student.

One problem with CAI is that there is sometimes no place for a student to go after completing a unit of study. In other words, the structure of most curricula is such that it is difficult to individualize only the remediation aspect of a particular topic. If you have an opportunity to work with CAI, you will handle both fast and slow individuals, as well as those with needs that cannot be predicted.

Your mathematics department office is a good place to obtain catalogs, brochures, and other information regarding available software. Unfortunately, it is not always easy to check a software's quality before it is purchased. In any event, you must preview all software before you offer it for pupils to use.

The variety of topics and techniques is vast. One can easily obtain software dealing with:

> basic number facts
> whole numbers
> fractions
> decimals
> arithmetic drill and practice
> introduction to algebra
> learning first year algebra
> selected topics in algebra
> introductions to geometric concepts
> logic
> fundamental concepts in trigonometry
> introductory ideas in calculus
> reflections
> fractal programs
> random numbers

Computer games that reinforce specific skills are especially popular among pupils and make the business of learning mathematics a pleasant one.

CLASSROOM ARRANGEMENTS FOR REMEDIAL SKILLS INSTRUCTION

The Mathematics Skills Laboratory

Physical settings are important regardless of the educational objectives. This is particularly true for the remedial class. A room appropriate for and conducive to the intended instruction can be instrumental in the success of a remedial program.

Wherever possible, a *mathematics skills laboratory* room should be made available to serve as a resource center and exclusive classroom for students in remedial mathematics classes. The purpose of such a room is, first of all, to provide a pleasant atmosphere for the students, and second, to have readily available in one location all the software and hardware that may be needed for remedial instruction.

Following are suggested features that should be included in an effective mathematics skills laboratory. You may augment or delete from this list according to your needs. For the most part, remedial mathematics classes are wholly or partially individualized, and these features are suggested in that spirit.

Textbooks, Workbooks, and Kits. A display table containing available textbooks, workbooks and kits should be a prominent feature of this laboratory. The table should also contain recreational mathematics materials, such as puzzles and other manipulatives, challenging activities, and board and computer games, in addition to supplementary textbooks and skills kits from other mathematics department sources.

Calculators and Computers. A second display table (or tables) should contain calculators and computers. These might include:

> Electronic printing calculators (any simple types would be satisfactory)
> Display calculators (here, too, any simple types with at least the four basic operations would be satisfactory)
> The Apple II series, Macintosh, and IBM or IBM compatible computers offer a variety of basic skills programs that provide challenge, stimulation, and novelty to students required to do remedial work.

Videotapes and Cassettes. An additional table should be set aside for cassettes and videotapes. Many textbook publishers produce cassettes to accompany workbook exercises in order to direct students to alternative paths, depending on their success or lack of it, in strengthening their mathematics skills. In addition, a wide variety of suitable instructional videotapes are available for class use, although it is advisable to preview them first. Some interesting tapes include:

> *The Story of Pi and Theorem of Pythagoras* (California Institute of Technology's Project Mathematics series)
> *Teaching Math with Calculators* (National Workshop)
> *Let us Teach Guessing,* with George Polya
> *You're Gonna Need These Numbers* (MAA)

Television. An ordinary UHF/VHF television receiver is sometimes useful, especially if you live in an area that has an educational television station. Interesting mathematics programs are occasionally broadcast, and pupils should certainly be given the opportunity to view them as part of their remediation program.

Work Portfolios. Student portfolios containing all relevant data (such as diagnostic test results, teacher prepared prescriptions, progress reports, and student work) should be easily accessible. Here, too, laying them out on a table for individual student accessibility is probably best. However, storage in a file cabinet at other times is probably advisable.

Classroom Bulletin Boards. An ample number of classroom bulletin boards should be available in the room so that student work may be exhibited. These bulletin boards may also be used for weekly mathematics contests and for displaying the answers to past contests and the names of winners. Interesting commercial or student-made posters may also be exhibited here, along with announcements for the students.

Storage Facilities. It is essential that adequate storage facilities be available, such as supply cabinets, file cabinets, closets, and bookcases (for supplementary texts and workbooks, as well as for teacher resource materials).

Storage facilities are vital so that the room will not acquire the atmosphere of a storage room and so that the materials will be better protected from vandalism and theft. In addition, adequate storage facilities will encourage the teacher to gather as much useful material as possible without fear of becoming overcrowded and unable to make these materials easily accessible.

Chalkboard. A chalkboard must be available in the room for any work you may present to the entire class as well as for small group lessons, or to display the daily mathematics puzzle (if you want to have your class involved in this type of competitive activity). These puzzles can consist of relatively simple questions involving a bit of thought and leading to some discussions, such as:

> What is the next number in the series, 1, 1, 2, 3, 5, 8, 13, ___?
> What is the smallest number of coins you need to make 61¢?

The chalkboard can be used for many other functions and is therefore an indispensable part of a mathematics skills laboratory.

Cubicles or Carrels. Individual work cubicles (or carrels) are built into some laboratory-type classrooms to provide students with as much privacy as possible. Here they can listen to tapes or whatever individualized work has been assigned to them with minimum distraction. A disadvantage is that students may not feel that they are part of a class while secluded in their own cubicles. Teacher awareness of this possible problem usually rectifies any difficulties that may arise in this respect.

Games. No laboratory would be complete without a mathematics recreation section that may be accessible to students periodically (as determined by the teacher). Boardgames that might improve arithmetic skills or mathematical thinking include:

> Backgammon
> Chess
> Checkers
> Concentration
> Treasure Hunt
> (Many games are listed in the catalogs of Creative Publications and other similar companies)

Computer games and puzzles, such as the following, are also appropriate motivators for students with mathematics deficiencies:

> *Castle of Dr. Brain* (Sierra on Line)
> *Codes and Ciphers* (Optimum Resource)
> *Algeblaster Plus;* and *What's My Angle* (Davidson Associates)
> *Algebra Proposer* (True BASIC)
> *Geoart* (Ventura)
> *Math Exploration Tool Kit* (IBM)
> *Math Blaster Mystery* (Davidson)
> *Building on Word Problems* (Decision-Development)
> *Connections* (Society/Visual Education)
> *Geometric Golfer* (MECC)

If you are even a bit creative and imaginative, you will discover and devise additional appropriate recreational games.

Some teachers we know who use games that have a more or less mathematical content have found their value to lie in areas other than skill or concept building. The value seems to lie in providing a break in the daily class routine as well as in providing time for some students to "catch up" to others in the class or to do extra work if they desire. Yet, some positive spinoff always results from playing games involving strategy or other mathematical or logical skills.

Pupils should be allowed to select the games they prefer (dominoes and backgammon are two favorites in one school with which we are familiar). Other pupils will learn the games by asking those who are knowledgeable with the rules to teach them or by watching pupils play against each other. The interaction is often lively and tends to breathe some life into a class, which can leave a "halo" effect for several days afterward.

THE "TRADITIONAL" CLASSROOM

The traditional classroom is, of course, the "old reliable" standby if a laboratory room is not available. Nevertheless, even in this type of class setting, many of the features mentioned earlier may be employed, depending on the type of traditional classroom available (presumably containing built-in storage space, bulletin boards, and chalkboards). As in the mathematics skills laboratory, instruction can be individualized, in small groups, or as a whole class. Once again, a great deal depends on your creativity to develop a pleasant atmosphere conducive to learning and appropriate for the remedial program designed. Your supervisors and the school custodian may be helpful in arranging for any physical changes you believe to be reasonable and necessary.

A drawback of using such a classroom is that other classes may be likely to use it during the day, thus seriously limiting the amount of materials that can be on regular display and limiting any significant reconstruction.

INDIVIDUAL TUTORING

Individual tutoring is a commonly used method for remedial instruction, either by a teacher or by another student. The student in need of remediation receives one-to-one assistance based on the results of diagnostic examination and record of previous performance. Many of the materials used are the same as those used in the individualized approach. The advantage of such an approach is obvious—the student receives immediate corrective action in the event he or she makes a mistake while solving a problem. Perhaps the disadvantage (if any actually exists) is the large number of personnel required for an individualized tutoring program. The cost is high for what may perhaps be one of the best remedial approaches.

HANDICAPPED STUDENTS

Recent directives by federal authorities require schools to consider more carefully than ever before the individual strengths and weaknesses of students with handicapping conditions. Individualized programs for such students must be developed by the schools, and one aspect of such programs is to mainstream them into regular classes whenever it is deemed feasible by school personnel.

Thus, teachers will often find students with mild handicaps and special needs who have been programmed into their regular math classes. Such students often receive additional services such as mathematics remediation, psychological counseling, and so on. As the class teacher of one or more such pupils, you may be called upon to advise and assist the counselors in determining their mathematics programs.

As a consultant, you will attempt to draw on information from a variety of sources, including aptitude and achievement tests, teacher recommendations, and social or cultural background. You will be informed of the student's specific physical condition as well as adaptive behavior.

The disabilities you might encounter include poor health, poor vision, hearing loss, social and emotional maladjustment, low general intelligence, and communicative and motor disabilities. As the student's classroom teacher, you must learn to deal with his or her special needs within the context of a regular class. Some direction and guidance for teachers is usually provided within the school.

SUMMARY

The deficient student who is in need of remediation is most likely to be the pupil who is a chronic mathematics failure. Some success in mathematics is needed to reverse this syndrome so the student can see that failure is, indeed, not inevitable. Placement in appropriately designed programs may be just what is needed. The counselor and/or mathematics teacher may administer one or more diagnostic instruments (standardized tests and/or teacher-made tests) to determine correct placement in such a program.

Generally, students who are two or more years below their grade level are candidates for remedial instruction. Also, those students who are unable to pass a minimum competency examination in mathematics some time before graduation might well be potential members of such a program.

The most common type of skills program is the individualized approach. This usually consists of a "diagnostic-prescriptive" evaluation, where a student's weaknesses are first diagnosed, and then, for each deficiency detected by this diagnosis, an individualized "prescription" of corrective work is provided. However, small group instruction, formal classes, and peer-group tutoring are also frequently used methods of teaching remediation classes. Within these classes one can occasionally find in use such items as mathematical games, computers, calculators, and arithmetic kits when the necessary drill work may be camouflaged in a form that permits variety and sustains interest.

The physical setting in which remedial instruction can occur may vary from the regular classroom to the fully furnished mathematics laboratory that contains such items as calculators, preprogrammed computers, audiocassette activity kits, workbooks, reference books, mathematical games, and other related materials.

The basic idea behind this program is that secondary school remediation should generally not resemble the elementary school methods. Since these students obviously met with much frustration at the elementary levels, every effort should be made to provide a fresh, new start in attaining mastery of the basic mathematics skills.

EXERCISES

1. Suppose your mathematics skills class just completed the unit on all operations with fractions. Write a "camouflaged drill" lesson related to this topic while using
   a. Perimeter and area formulas.
   b. Calculators.
   c. Some aspect of probability.

2. In your mathematics skills class, you ask students to add $\frac{1}{2} + \frac{1}{3}$, and many of them write $\frac{1}{2} + \frac{1}{3} = \frac{2}{5}$. You then present the same problem vertically

$$\begin{array}{r} \frac{1}{2} \\ + \frac{1}{3} \\ \hline \end{array}$$

and most of those who did it incorrectly the first time write

$$\begin{aligned} \frac{1}{2} &= \frac{3}{6} \\ + \frac{1}{3} &= \frac{2}{6} \\ \hline & \frac{5}{6} \end{aligned}$$

Explain how this phenomenon will have an impact on your teaching this class.

3. Suppose you are teaching in a large urban high school and you find that most of the students in your skills class are from minority backgrounds (i.e., African Americans and Hispanics) with parents whose incomes are below the poverty level. How would the topics you present to this class differ from the topics you would present to a skills class composed primarily of middle-income white students?

4. Find some mathematically relevant recreational games, either those listed in this chapter or others, and determine how they can be effectively used in a skills class. State the specific topic with which they are to be used.

5. Determine a set of appropriate activities with which you would involve a mathematics skills class during the course of planning a trip to a local factory. Specify the destination of the trip.

6. Obtain three different sixth grade arithmetic textbooks or workbooks and use these (as well as a calculator) to write an individualized prescription for a student having trouble with any form of long division.

7. Develop ten brief, simple-challenge exercises that could be used in a "puzzle for the day" section of the chalkboard or bulletin board in your skills class. Indicate the particular benefit that may be derived from each exercise.

8. Describe an activity (besides a trip) that would fall into the category of "camouflaged drill."

9. Discuss how the attendance patterns of students in a mathematics skills class will very likely determine the methods of instruction used with this class. First specify the attendance in the hypothetical class.

10. A computer lab with one machine per student is available for your mathematics skills class one day each week. A sufficient amount of computer assisted instruction software is available. Prepare a long-range strategy for using this laboratory for your class.

11. Write a plan for a typical computer assisted instruction lesson in the computer lab described in Exercise 10. Assume a laboratory assistant is available to work with you.

12. Suppose you are a teacher in a high school assigned by your supervisor to teach a full program of mathematics skills classes. Since your school has no special mathematics laboratories, your supervisor asks you to redesign a conventional classroom to best suit your needs for a skills class. She further indicates that the school is prepared to obtain whatever furniture you may need and make whatever physical alterations you desire.

   Prepare a detailed plan for this mathematics skills laboratory. Include a floor plan, a list of materials and equipment (and furniture) to be purchased, and any other work that may be required (e.g., electrical alterations).

13. Visit three secondary schools and observe the skills program in each. Write a brief report on each program, pointing out what, in your judgment, are the strengths and weaknesses of each program. As a summary to this assignment, compare the three programs with regard to their similarities, differences, and highlights.

SUGGESTED READINGS

Beckmann, Milton W. "Teaching the Low Achiever in Mathematics." *Mathematics Teacher* 62 (1969): 443.

Boyer, Lee E. "Provisions for the Slow Learner." *Mathematics Teacher* 52 (1959): 56.

Brophy, Jere. "Research Linking Teacher Behavior to Student Achievement: Potential Implications for Instruction of Chapter 1 Students." *Educational Psychologist* 23, no. 3 (1988): 235–286.

Cohen, Peter, James Kulik, and Chen-Lin Kulik. "Educational Outcomes of Tutoring: A Meta-analysis of Findings." *American Educational Research Journal* 19, no. 2 (summer 1982): 237–248.

Fremont, Herbert, and Neal Ehrenberg. "The Hidden Potential of Low Achievers." *Mathematics Teacher* 59 (1966): 551.

Glennon, Vincent J. *The Mathematical Education of Exceptional Children and Youth.* Reston, VA: NCTM, 1981.

Haitt, Arthur A. "Basic Skills: What Are They?" *Mathematics Teacher* 72 (1979): 141.

Hedin, Diane. "Students as Teachers: A Tool for Improving School Climate and Productivity." *Social Policy* (winter 1987): 42–47.

Herman, Maureen L. "Hopeless in Mathematics? It's Too Soon to Say." *Mathematics Teacher* 76 (1983): 515.

Jenkins, Joseph, and Linda Jenkins. "Making Peer Tutoring Work." *Educational Leadership* (March 1987): 64–68.

Jones, Beau Fly, and Lawrence B. Friedman. "Active Instruction for Students at Risk: Remarks on Merging Process-Outcome and Cognitive Perspectives." *Educational Psychologist* 23, no. 2 (1988): 299–308.

Kenney, Robert. "Basic Competencies in Vermont." *Mathematics Teacher* 71 (1978): 702.

Levine, Marsha. "Docemur Docendo." *American Educator* (fall 1986): 22–48.

Maor, Eli. "The Pocket Calculator as a Teaching Aid." *Mathematics Teacher* 69 (1976): 471.

Mathematics Teacher 69 (May 1976). Special Issue—Individualized Instruction.

Mathematics Teacher 71 (February 1978). Special Issue—Minimum Competency.

Ortolan, Cathy, and Carol Camp. "Meet the Challenge—Individualize." *Mathematics Teacher* 73 (1980): 588.

Paul, Frederic. "New York Basic Competency Examination." *Mathematics Teacher* 71 (1978): 767.

Pope, Lillie. *Tutor!* Brooklyn, NY: Book-Lab, Inc. 1976.

Proctor, Amelia D. "A World of Hope—Helping Slow Learners Enjoy Mathematics." *Mathematics Teacher* 62 (1965): 118.

Putnam, Ralph. "Structuring and Adjusting Content for Students: A Study of Live and Simulated Tutoring of Addition." *American Educational Research Journal* 24, no. 1 (spring 1987): 13–48.

Rauff, James V. "Minimum Mathematical Skills." *Mathematics Teacher* 72 (1979): 50.

Sasse, Katherine J. S. "Mathematics for the Non-College Bound in Junior High School." *Mathematics Teacher* 58 (1965): 232.

Shaw, M. E., and J. M. Wright. *Scales for the Measurement of Attitudes.* New York: McGraw-Hill, 1967.

Slavin, Robert. "Learning Together." *American Educator* (summer 1986): 6–13.

Sleeman, D., and Brown, J. S., eds. *Intelligent Tutoring Systems.* London: Academic Press, 1982.

Turner, Linda M. "GCM + TC + PR—A Formula for Survival in a Non-Academic Mathematics Club." *Mathematics Teacher* 72 (1979): 580.

Vogel, James R., and Dale Gentry. "Remediation of Number Facts Using Finger Multiplication." *Mathematics Teacher* 73 (1980): 118.

Wilkinson, Jack. Teaching General Mathematics: A Semi-Laboratory Approach." *Mathematics Teacher* 63 (1970): 571.

CHAPTER 14
CLASSROOM MANAGEMENT

Paper planes? Spitballs? Tacks on the teacher's seat? All quaint relics of the past. What could you really expect to see today if you walked into any class at a random high school? Anything imaginable! The little red schoolhouse has yielded to the assembly-line secondary school whose population often numbers in the thousands and thus is a microcosm of society and all that is good and bad in it.

Many classrooms are managed well, and you would see an orderly, businesslike atmosphere where students are learning while teachers are teaching. Yet, the identical group of students could very well be raising havoc in another room while the teacher is wringing his hands in despair. Wherein lies the difference?

In this chapter we present three aspects of classroom management that affect, both directly and indirectly, the teaching-learning process: classroom practices, discipline, and administrative details.

CLASSROOM PRACTICES

The development of proper habits and attitudes concerning classroom practices, for pupils as well as the teacher, ought to begin on the first day that the class meets. From the moment the starting bell of the class sounds until the end of the class period, students should see in you an efficient, well-organized teacher who is aware of everyone and everything that is happening in the classroom. If this atmosphere is maintained in the succeeding days, the result will ultimately be a class where every minute of learning time is considered precious and where wasted moments are unacceptable. Following are some suggestions you may find helpful in the classroom.

Establish Routine

Accustom the pupils to sit down to work as soon as they enter the room. Loitering in the halls in the vicinity of the classroom while waiting for the starting bell to ring should not be permitted, for it is a distraction to those who do begin promptly or even early. You need only stand at the door for a moment to check outside the room and move students in. Students should be accustomed to then look for the homework and do-now exercise, or whatever activity you want them to work on, on the same corner of the board every day. As school policy, latecomers are usually expected to present a late pass, and you will find that if you adhere strictly to this policy, pupils will tend to arrive promptly to your class. Students should realize that their mathematics class *always* starts on time and with meaningful work. Remember that teachers have no right to expect of students what they do not demand of themselves. Arrive in class on time yourself, and always be prepared!

Start Out Strict!

As a new teacher you will find it helpful to be a bit more stern at the beginning of the term than you might generally like to be. Try not to engage in frivolous remarks or behavior; avoid smiling too much until you are certain that you are master of the situation. By starting off as a strict disciplinarian, you capture control. Then, when appropriate, you can relax this strictness. The reverse, that is, starting off in a relaxed fashion and then becoming stricter, is difficult, if not almost impossible! You will also find the initial strictness to be helpful in "nipping in the bud" the tendency of some students to call out answers and thus distract you as well as other students.

Learn Names

Learn students' names quickly. Most teachers prefer using first names but others prefer the more formal Mr. or Ms. Choose whichever you are more comfortable with and remain consistent. If your room has fixed furniture, you will find it helpful to keep a seating plan on your desk while you teach so you can learn the names quickly at the beginning of the term. If you have movable seats, best for arranging small group lessons, try to have the students return to the same location for their whole class session.

Distribute and Collect Materials Efficiently

Avoid wasting time when passing out or collecting papers, books, supplies, folders, etc. If your furniture is fixed in a "column" and "row" formation, this can be done most efficiently by passing and collecting either by column or row. The advantage of row passing is that it requires only a hand motion from side to side and avoids the confusion caused by pupils turning around and rising from their seats when papers are passed by column. When seats are not fixed, they may be arranged in various ways for the small learning groups. Nevertheless, make a conscious effort to determine the most efficient collection-distribution scheme for the prevailing conditions.

Keep the Classroom Tidy

Make yourself conscious of the physical condition of the room, such as ventilation, lighting, condition of floors, bulletin boards, and teacher's desk. Remind the class to treat school property, such as loaned textbooks, properly. When you erase board work from the previous class, be sure that you do it completely. Any stray marks left on the board can interfere with later board work. For example, a stray vertical line could later be interpreted as a "one" in a future problem. If the floor is littered with paper from the previous period, pupils can help you place the litter in wastebaskets. You are thereby training them in the virtue of cleanliness in a public area. Gum chewing disturbs many students as well as the teacher and should be curtailed.

Have Supplies on Hand

Plan to have all necessary supplies in the room before the lesson begins. Some of the items you may need might include overhead projectors, graph charts, calculators, or colored chalk. To send for them during the period, when the supply room might be locked, would cause a needless interruption in the lesson.

Insist on Neatness

Insist on neat written work both on the board and on paper. The students should understand that work written on the board is not only for themselves but for the entire class. It should be legible so that all may be able to read it easily.

Use Correct English

Pay particular attention to your own use of English and to the accuracy of your students' oral responses. Although, generally, students "understand" each other's careless and inaccurate responses to teacher questions, there may be a few students who may be confused or misled by such careless responses. Thus, it is the teacher's responsibility to ensure accuracy. Not all answers need to be given in complete sentence form, but whenever a response requires it, insist on correct English. In mathematics, more so than in other subjects, every word uttered is important and the pupils must say exactly what they mean and not leave it to the teacher to remedy the deficiencies.

Omit Reasons in Chalkboard Two-Column Proofs

When teaching geometry, some teachers feel that once the class has learned to write two-column proofs, theorems and proof exercises, written on the board, should show only the diagram, hypothesis, conclusion, and statements. Reasons need not appear on the board except in those instances when the teacher wants to demonstrate a model solution. They feel that there is little value in having pupils read aloud reasons from the board, for they can be done orally. Furthermore, the omission of the reasons eliminates the tendency toward crowded, illegible handwriting. You will, of course, eventually make your own judgment.

Keep Homework Relevant

Even though the homework assignment may have been put on the board at the beginning of the period, or discussed with other pupils in the students' learning groups, reference should be made to it during the period so that the pupils will see its connection to the work being done in class. It is not necessary to review every single homework exercise in class every day, since the purpose of the assignment is to enable the pupils to determine whether or not they have mastered the work that has been taught, and this can sometimes be done after reviewing only a few exercises. See Chapter 8, Homework, for a detailed analysis of the many methods of handling homework.

Prevent Cheating on Tests

Be vigilant while proctoring a test or quiz. Walk about the room constantly. Students can be very creative in devising schemes to obtain answers improperly. Proctoring is a full-time job and should not be shared with marking other tests or reading a newspaper.

Work the Entire Period

Give the classroom the atmosphere of a well-managed team. Be especially efficient by planning what students will be doing every moment of the period. Work up to the bell at the end of the period. Insist that students not stop working until you tell them that the lesson is over. If it should happen that there are a few minutes remaining, do *not* dismiss the class early, for they may disturb other classes. Keep them in their seats, either working on more "if time" exercises in your lesson plan or beginning their homework for the next day.

Don't Sit Down!

Some experienced, competent teachers believe that the purpose of the chair at the teacher's desk is to remind her of the one spot in the room where she should *never* be. Students can be best taught and supervised by a teacher who is constantly up and around the room. When a teacher is at the side of the room, the adjacent column of students is at the new "front of the room," and when a teacher is standing in the middle, the students there for that moment feel a sense of being "up front."

Check Attendance Daily

Attendance and tardiness should be recorded daily, usually during a moment of the lesson when students are working on their own at their seats. It is best done quietly and quickly by looking about the room, spotting the empty seats, checking the seating plan or class list, and recording the date of absence on the list, the seating plan, or other document provided by the school. In order to avoid forgetting to check attendance, routinize the procedure to occur at the same moment of the lesson every day if possible, usually during the do-now exercise. Some teachers allow students to assist them in this task, and if you do, remember that you are still responsible for errors.

Grouping Students by Ability

Some teachers find it helpful to arrange the class into ability groups so that special assignments can be made to meet the needs of each particular group of students. Also, the teacher can work with each group as the need arises during the course of the lesson, providing slow students with special remedial work, and bright pupils with enrichment. Grouping is especially valuable if a paraprofessional assistant to the teacher is available in the room. Teachers should be aware that, although the high ability level group clearly benefits from this special attention, the lower ability group might lose some motivation in this arrangement. Therefore, the teacher using this scheme must make a special effort to have high expectations and motivate this slower group appropriately.

Call on Every Student

Volunteers as well as nonvolunteers should be called on during the course of every lesson—whether it is to answer a question directed by the teacher or to write an exercise or homework example on the board or in a small-group arrangement, as the representative reporting back to the entire class. You must make every effort to call on every student at least once during the day, if possible, and be especially careful not to let the loud, aggressive student monopolize the responses.

Work that has been put on the chalkboard by one student might occasionally be explained by another student. To be able to explain what another student has written, or to locate an error, is almost as important as being able to do the exercise oneself. This method of dealing with class work (or homework review) tends to hold the attention of the class.

Adjust the Lesson Plan

Keep an eye on your lesson plan as well as on your watch throughout the period. There will be times when you will find it necessary to adjust your plans during the lesson to be able to end it on time and in a logical spot.

Develop Bulletin Boards

Well-maintained, informative, colorful bulletin boards are often a useful way to disseminate information as well as to provide a vehicle for displaying unusual student work—whether special projects or examinations. You may assign a pupil to be in charge of the care of the bulletin board, or you may prefer to maintain it entirely yourself (see Chapter 12).

Encourage Active Involvement

The ability to develop a teacher-pupil-pupil–pupil-teacher dialogue is one requiring skill and practice. This type of socialization can be the outgrowth of a skillfully placed question. For example, consider this conversation in a high school geometry class:

> Teacher: What is the locus of points 3 inches from a given line?

> Student 1: The locus consists of two lines parallel to the given line, on either side of it and 3 inches away.
> Student 2: Isn't it really a circular cylinder of radius 3 with the given line as an axis?
> Student 3: Student 1 is right because the course we're studying is called Plane Geometry.
> Teacher: The fault is really mine. What should my original question have been?
> Student 4: What is the locus of points in a plane that are 3 inches from a given line?

DISCIPLINE

Discipline problems, like accidents, may often be avoided with keen awareness and if proper precautions are taken. Poor classroom practices tend to promote an atmosphere that is ripe for potential troublemakers to fill the vacuum in class control with undesirable actions. Every dean of discipline and guidance counselor knows that there are some teachers who rarely if ever have discipline problems in their classrooms, while others have frequent flare-ups, often serious, with students. It would be foolish to say that, in general, discipline problems are caused by the teacher. No teacher seeks them. Yet there are days when a teacher may not be feeling well, or is particularly irritable for some personal reason, or has a real bias toward a student. The sensitive teacher may be able to understand and control these feelings, while another may not be capable of doing so. Thus, confrontations with students that might occur one day, might not come about on the next.

What are some disciplinary problems a teacher may encounter in the classroom? Different teachers have differing notions of what constitutes a breach of discipline, so the following list is by no means exhaustive. It is merely suggestive, to get you thinking in the right direction. Also, it is impossible to arrange the items in any order of seriousness, for out of context many of the items appear to be not worth fussing over. But in the setting of a classroom where effective control over a large number of students is needed, the teacher must often respond (either actively or passively) to save face. However, pupils must also save face before their peers. Thus, a confrontation over a seemingly insignificant matter may arise and may be blown entirely out of proportion. Some examples are breaches of class discipline by students include the following:

> Getting out of seat and walking around during the lesson
> Leaving the room without permission
> Excessive talking to neighbors
> Calling out answers in spite of the teacher's request not to do so

Not doing the assigned homework

Coming to class unprepared—no text, no notebook, etc.

Cheating on a test

Using improper language in class

Often arriving late to class

Chewing and cracking gum

Tossing paper across the room

Throwing paper on the floor

Doing work for another subject in the mathematics class

Laughing aloud, wisecracking

Fighting with another pupil

Excessive absence or cutting

Reading a newspaper in class

Daydreaming, staring out the window, and not paying attention to the lesson

Speaking to another pupil across the room in a foreign language

Threatening the teacher verbally or physically

Handling Discipline Problems

Suppose you are in your classroom and, for whatever reason, a disciplinary problem arises with a student. Will you feel intimidated by his or her aggressive behavior into doing nothing, waiting for the "storm" to pass, hoping that it will "go away by itself" soon? Or will you resolve the situation quickly? Instinct sometimes plays an uncontrollable role in a situation where tempers flare, but perhaps even certain instinctive behavior can be channeled into the proper direction. We therefore offer the following thoughts, as well as do's and don'ts, which might prove helpful in various situations.

Speak to the student involved in a loud, clear, firm voice. Do not shriek, or become hysterical. Remain calm. Do not show evidence of timidity or fear or uncertainty. Be polite!

Merely tell the student, "Please stop doing that" or "Cut it out!" or "Please see me after class" (this can be said to the pupil publicly or privately). Do not insult, embarrass, or curse at the pupil. More students will respond to a polite request than you might believe. It is often said, "You can catch more flies with honey than with vinegar."

Try to avoid making public demands that you cannot enforce and that might cause a confrontation. Thus, if a pupil is misbehaving and you tell her, "Change your seat," she may refuse to do so. At this point, you must weigh the effect on the class of either calling in a supervisor to assist you or merely backing off for the moment and ignoring her refusal to obey. The situation might have been avoided if you had approached the student quietly and asked her to behave and/or change her seat. In fact, quiet, "behind-the-scenes diplomacy" is often an effective discipline tool in every area of misbehavior.

Remember that there may be times when you will have to swallow your pride if you feel this will defuse the situation. Keep in mind that this is only a temporary action that may be the most expedient one for that moment.

You might, of course, try to speak to the student in an attempt to resolve the issue on a one-to-one level later.

In every case in which you want to pursue action against the student who has created a problem in class, *referral* can be made after class to the dean of discipline, guidance counselor, or other appropriate school official. They have several courses of action they might take, such as removal of a student from the class (permanently or temporarily), a class discussion led by the dean or a counselor (not necessarily in the presence of the teacher) on behavior in school, or automatic failure in the subject. The proper person to notify will vary with each school. A new teacher should become familiar with the organizational structure in the school.

The dean might notify the parents as a matter of course. However, you also might want to discuss the matter with them. A telephone call, rather than a parental visit, might be all that's needed. Just remember to make no threats. Simply inform them of their child's misconduct and the *possible* consequences of such behavior.

If you prefer to send a note, one that follows this format might be recommended:

Dear Mrs. Smith,

Suzanne has been disrupting her mathematics class with her behavior. Such behavior may adversely affect her course work and ultimately result in lower grades.

I would very much like to discuss this matter with you as soon as possible. Please call me at 567-7879 so that we may set up a conference to discuss ways in which we can solve this problem together.

Sincerely,

More Serious Problems

In most cases, discipline problems do *not* involve physical danger to anyone. However, if the discipline problem in question appears to be a direct or imminent threat to the physical well-being of one or more students, or yourself, such as when a fight breaks out between two students, you may (if you are capable of doing so) attempt to physically separate them to prevent the pupils from harming each other or you. Often, students themselves will break up fights among other students. In any event, aid must be summoned to keep the youngsters apart even if the fight has already been stopped, in order to escort the students involved in the fracas to the dean of discipline (if not already on the scene). Similarly, the dean or a supervisor should be summoned immediately if there is an immediate threat against you. A student in the class, or a neighboring teacher, can help in the situation by calling for additional help. After matters have calmed down in the classroom, continue the lesson. You will handle the necessary disciplinary details after class.

If you suspect a student in your class of using drugs, notify the guidance counselor or dean. You may be wrong, but allow experts to make that determination. If you are right, you may be instrumental in preventing the student from committing further harm to himself. In any event, the problem is out of your hands once you've reported it.

Student Responsibilities

Remind students early in the term of their duties and obligations in a classroom, and that infractions will inevitably lead to disciplinary action. In order to avoid problems in class, they will be expected to:

Arrive in class before the late bell sounds
Take their seats quickly and quietly
Get started on the do-now exercise immediately
Remain in their seats throughout the period
Leave the room only with permission of the teacher
Do homework regularly
Come to class fully prepared to do work—with pencil, notebook, textbook, etc.
Speak courteously
Keep a civil tongue
Refrain from shouting out answers or calling across the room
Keep the room clean
Refrain from fighting
Refrain from cutting class
Refrain from doing other than mathematics work in class

Unacceptable Teacher Practices

Below are some situations in which the teacher may have failed to use ordinary common sense or acceptable classroom practices, and that may have provoked either direct disciplinary eruptions or behavior leading to such eruptions:

Often arriving late to class
Walking out of the room during a lesson to talk to a colleague
Turning pages to look for suitable exercises while the class waits
Leaving the classroom to pick up supplies
Talking to a colleague who comes to the classroom
Giving examples that are too complicated, too trivial, or too repetitious
Teaching in a monotonous, dull manner
Offering no motivation for pupils to learn
Always embarrassing students
Often making mathematical errors
Not knowing students' names, and not looking at them when teaching the class
Making direct or indirect racial slurs
Showing no enthusiasm for teaching
Never praising pupils when they might deserve it
Spending excessive time discussing matters of little general interest or unrelated to the topic
Ignoring minor infractions
Erasing the chalkboard too soon
Rarely asking or answering questions
Irritating mannerisms—constantly looking at watch, pacing back and forth, etc.
Talking too quickly or too slowly
Carrying on private discussions or helping one or two students with class work while ignoring the rest of the class

Common sense dictates that the teacher will make every effort to avoid these situations. Sometimes it will require a supervisor's assistance. Other times it will require a greater awareness by the teacher in order to avoid them. Thus, while improved pupil motivation techniques can be suggested by the supervisor, *you* are the one who must implement the program of improvement. Do it eagerly and enthusiastically, for you will be the ultimate beneficiary with classes that are manageable and functioning properly.

Other causes of disciplinary eruptions in a classroom that are beyond the control of the teacher may be:

Flare-up of a disagreement between two students (perhaps carried over from another class)
Family or other personal problems affecting a student
Racial attitude of student
Aggressive behavior towards peers and/or adults
Mental or emotional problems resulting in anti-social behavior.

These problems are best left for the dean to handle.

ADMINISTRATIVE DETAILS

Most administrative aspects of classroom management (called "clerical work") affect the teaching process peripherally. They may be required for legal reasons, disciplinary purposes, or organizational needs. Most professionals who have secretarial services available need not be personally involved in them. However, teachers, generally, do not have such services available, or if they do, the services are minimal. Thus, some consider these chores onerous, performing them only perfunctorily, yet they are necessary for the smooth functioning of the classroom as well as the entire school. Some of these tasks are the following:

> Writing a test and making copies for the students
> Maintaining records of grades, attendance, lateness
> Calling or writing parents personally
> Distributing notices, announcements, information to pupils
> Completing governmental or board-of-education-mandated surveys
> Recording end-of-term grades and recommendations to counselors
> Maintaining records and files of parents' absence notes, book receipts, supervisors' notices, etc.
> Recording minutes of departmental meetings

Who has not seen the absent-minded-professor type walking down the hallway with books, papers, folders, and supplies flying about in disarray? Teachers are often inundated with paperwork, but if you have to do it, you might learn to at least do it well. Plan a schedule and stick to it!

If you make an effort to perform your clerical tasks well early in your teaching career, it will be to your advantage in the years to come, for it will become habit-forming. If you don't, you will find them to be a constant burden, and it need not be so!

SUMMARY

Proper classroom practices are most important in maintaining a refreshing teaching-learning atmosphere. These involve not only training students to respond positively to the teacher's efforts but having the teacher perform and behave in a responsible, professional manner. The teacher must always be fully prepared and knowledgeable in the lesson for the day and must at the same time maintain effective discipline as well as perform clerical chores satisfactorily.

A well-managed classroom is a pleasure to behold. To the uninformed it seems the "natural" way for a class to be conducted. The informed observer, however, is well aware of the effort and skill required to establish and maintain a viable classroom situation with a wholesome setting, where genuine and enthusiastic learning takes place.

Some consider the classroom to be the teacher's private domain. Others reject this description of the teacher's role in the classroom as implying a sort of dictatorial approach toward classroom management. Whatever your feelings, it is every teacher's desire to teach a class that is well behaved, attentive, and receptive. It is up to you to make that possible.

EXERCISES

1. Comment on the following note by a teacher to the dean of discipline: "I found Frank cheating on a test, so I tore up his paper. He cursed at me and threatened to 'get me,' then he ran out of the room in the middle of the period. I think he should be suspended from school."

2. A student receives his report card indicating 23 days' absence in his mathematics class, resulting in a failing mark, since a school rule mandates failure for pupils absent over 21 days. The student vehemently denies being absent that many days and claims that no other teacher recorded that many absences. How would you handle the situation?

3. A school guidance counselor informs you that three girls want to drop your class because there is too much noise in the room and they can't concentrate. What would be your reaction?

4. A note from the assistant principal summons you to her office to explain why your attendance records are often submitted late and why students from your homeroom class are often found wandering the hallways. What are some explanations that might be tenable?

5. A supervisor admonishes a teacher for regularly coming to class a little late. The teacher's response is, "The homework assignment and do-now are always up on the board (from my earlier class) before the period begins, the class knows which row is to put the homework up on the back chalkboard, and I have an excellent student monitor taking attendance, so it makes no difference whether or not I come in one or two minutes late." What is your reaction?

6. One of your students asks permission to leave the room. For some reason, you refuse his request. He insists he "must go" and, after an ensuing verbal battle, gets up and walks out. How would you handle the situation upon his return?

7. Several different teachers occasionally found one of their students repeatedly doing work for another subject during mathematics class, despite warnings not to do so. Following are the ways the situation was handled by the various teachers:
   a. Material was confiscated and destroyed.
   b. Situation was discussed with the teacher of the other subject.
   c. Parent was notified.
   d. Dean was notified.
   e. Student was sent out of the room.
   What are your reactions to these "solutions"?

8. A teacher has a preparation period immediately preceding his two consecutive first year algebra classes. Therefore, he always constructs and duplicates the tests and quizzes for these classes during this period. He feels that this increases the security of these exams. What are some arguments for and against this procedure?

9. Comment on the following solution to a discipline problem: If a student persists in disturbing your class, send her out of the room and into a nearby mathematics class functioning on a much lower level (with the other teacher's permission, of course).

10. Suppose a student in a ninth grade mathematics class is constantly inattentive and intentionally disturbs other students nearby. Frequent requests to curb this disruptive activity go unheeded. Explain some steps you may take to seek relief of this situation. Justify your responses.

11. Ask a mathematics department supervisor to discuss classroom management during a portion of a department conference. At this conference you serve as a recorder. Following this conference, write a report to summarize the conference highlights and contrast the different styles of classroom management as voiced by the teachers at the conference.

12. Arrange to have a videotape made of the mathematics lesson you would teach. Invite several teachers, both experienced and inexperienced, to view the videotape and comment on your classroom management techniques. Summarize the comments rendered during this videotape viewing.

REFERENCES

Cangelosi, James S. *Teaching Mathematics in Secondary and Middle School.* New York: Macmillan, 1992.

Copeland, Willis D. "Classroom Management and Student Teachers' Cognitive Abilities: A Relationship." *American Educational Research Journal* 24, no. 2 (summer 1987): 219–236.

Doyle, Walter. "Academic Work." *Review of Educational Research* 53, no. 2 (summer 1983): 159–199.

Emmer, Edmond T., et al. *Classroom Management for Secondary Teachers.* Englewood Cliffs, NJ: Prentice Hall, 1984.

Gnagey, William J. *Motivating Classroom Discipline.* New York: Macmillan, 1981.

Kohut, S., and D. R. Range. *Classroom Discipline: Case Studies and Viewpoints.* Washington, DC: National Education Association, 1986.

Martin, B. B., and J. I. Quilling. *Positive Approaches to Classroom Discipline.* Washington, DC: National Education Association, 1981.

Swick, K. J. *Discipline, A Proactive Approach.* Washington, DC: National Education Association, 1985.

————. *Disruptive Student Behavior in the Classroom.* Washington, DC: National Education Association, 1987.

————. *Student Stress: A Classroom Management System.* Washington, DC: National Education Association, 1987.

Wolfgang, Charles H., and Carl D. Glickman. *Solving Discipline Problems: Strategies for Classroom Teachers.* Boston: Allyn and Bacon, 1980.

CHAPTER 15
PERFOR-MANCE OBJECTIVES

As we discussed in previous chapters, part of your planning to teach a unit of work may involve assembling courses of study, reviewing textbooks and other relevant material, and then eventually developing a sequence of logically arranged lessons that cover the appropriate topics. You then get more specific and prepare daily lesson plans. Because of your efforts and careful planning, you expect to be able to teach successful developmental, review, drill, or other types of lessons.

But now we raise the question, "How do you measure a successful lesson?" One way is by observing the performance of the teacher. Another is by judging the performance exhibited by students after the lesson has been presented.

Some time ago during a snowstorm when few teachers and students arrived at school, one teacher, who apparently did not want to feel that his difficult trip was in vain, was seen presenting an elaborately prepared introductory lesson on drawing graphs of the trigonometric functions. The board work was well done and colorful, and the presentation was energetic and lively. The sight of all this was humorous, however, because only one pupil was in the room.

Had the aim of the lesson, so carefully planned by the teacher, been fulfilled? Was the lesson a successful one? If we answer these questions from the point of view of teacher performance, then we might have to answer yes. If, however, we consider the skills that students were expected to learn and perform as a result of this lesson, then the success of the lesson, at least for the one pupil involved, will be known only when that pupil is tested. Furthermore, one must determine what percentage of a class must show mastery of a topic for the lesson to be judged successful.

Some teachers believe that a properly planned lesson *must* include a set of student objectives, in addition to the traditional "aim." In other words, with every lesson the teacher should focus attention on the students and state objectives *they* will achieve by the end of the lesson. Furthermore, these objectives should be clearly stated at the beginning of the lesson in terms of expected student performance at the end of the lesson. Some argue rather forcefully that this ought *not* to be done. We do not resolve this controversy here; however, the pros and cons of this argument are presented later in this chapter. We begin our discussion of student objectives by considering how these objectives should be formulated and when they should be used, if the teacher chooses to use them.

PERFORMANCE OBJECTIVES

A statement specifying the particular capabilities of a learner (known as "observable student behavior") when he or she has reached the end of a specific learning activity, together with any given conditions or restrictions, as well as a statement of the evaluation process (known as "minimum level of acceptable performance") is known as a *performance objective* (or *behavioral objective*). To paraphrase the definition above, the statement of a performance objective must actually name the type of act a student will be observed performing successfully, under specific given conditions, at the completion of the activity.

Let us suppose, for example, that at the completion of a unit on conic sections in a second year algebra class you might expect that students will have acquired not only an appreciation of the practical applications and aesthetic aspects of the conic sections but also specific skills related to second-degree equations. With this in mind, we now formulate some typical performance objectives for this topic (see Sample). We analyze each from the point of view of given conditions, observable student behavior, and minimum level of acceptable performance. The reader should realize that these performance objectives are written in an ideal form. An individual teacher's objectives may likely vary with his or her needs and personality.

Performance Verbs

Let us now consider this statement of a performance objective written for the unit on conic sections just discussed:

> The student will appreciate the practical applications of conics.

Although some practical applications of conics might have been discussed in class, the verb "will appreciate" is so vague that the observable student behavior cannot be clearly determined in terms of it. How will the student show his appreciation? By presenting the teacher with a gift in appreciation of the knowledge imparted? By writing an essay on the subject? By thinking or dreaming about it? The answer here is obvious: the desired student behavior must be not only observable but also *measureable* to be useful in assessing the success of an instructional experience.

Similarly, consider this statement of a "performance objective":

> The student will know what conic sections are.

If the observable student behavior is to be determined, what will be observed? Does knowing the names of the conics indicate knowledge of the corresponding graphs? Does knowing how to draw the graphs indicate a knowledge of their names as well as their properties? Certainly "knowing" can take on a host of definitions, some of which are easily measurable, while others are not. At any rate more specificity is required, so you now see that the *key* to stating well-defined performance objectives is the verb. Verbs such as *understand, appreciate,* and *know* are open to a very wide range of interpretations and are therefore poor verb choices to use in formulating statements of performance objectives. On the other hand, the other verbs used in the previously stated performance objectives, such as *name, state, sketch, slice,* and *estimate* are clearer and certainly less ambiguous.

Since certain words are open to less interpretation than others, performance objectives should be formulated so there is some understanding and agreement concerning any observable student behavior associated with the verb used in the objective. As a matter of fact, the main criterion of a satisfactory performance objective is that it communicate clearly without any ambiguity the intent of its writer. One test of the clarity of a performance objective is whether another competent person can use that objective to write a question that will test a student on the achievement of that objective in such a way that the original writer will find that test question acceptable.

How To Write Performance Objectives

A unit plan on radicals was presented in Chapter 4. We now consider how a set of performance objectives may be developed using that unit as a model. But first, we suggest the following initial steps to be taken before actually writing the objectives in preparing a unit of work or a daily lesson plan:

1. Select the unit (or topic) to be taught.
2. Study relevant syllabi and texts, and speak to experienced colleagues.
3. List the major formulas, theorems, concepts, and the like.
4. Write a performance objective for each of the "skills" to be taught.
5. After the objective has been written, check it against the ability of your students. That is, are you requiring too much of them, or too little? Are your objectives realistic for the type of students you have? (We may indicate these as "high-" or "low-level" objectives.) Remember to write realistic objectives, but don't keep your expectations of pupil achievement too low just to be sure that the objectives will be met. Also

Sample 1. Performance Objectives for a Unit on Conic Sections

1. *Given eight equations of the form $Ax^2 + Bxy + Cy^2 + Dx + Ey + F = O$, the student will correctly name the described conic (or one of its special or degenerate cases) and state the coordinates of the center (if it exists) or the vertex (if it exists) for at least six of them within a forty-minute period.*

   a. Given Conditions: eight equations of the form $Ax^2 + Bxy + Cy^2 + Dx + Ey + F = O$
   b. Observable Student Behavior:
      Student will
      1. Name the conic
      2. State the coordinates of the center
   c. Minimum Level of Acceptable Performance: Students will correctly answer at least six questions within a forty-minute period.

2. *The student will use the coordinates of the center and the lengths of major and minor axes to sketch the graph represented by an equation of the form $Ax^2 + By^2 = C$.*

   a. Given Conditions: An equation of the form $Ax^2 + By^2 = C$
   b. Observable Student Behavior: Students will determine coordinates of the center, lengths of the major and minor axes. They will then sketch the curve using that information.
   c. Minimum Level of Acceptable Performance: the same as *b*.

3. *Given two second-degree equations, the student will estimate (correct to the nearest tenth) their intersection points, if any, graphically.*

   a. Given Conditions: Two second-degree equations
   b. Observable Student Behavior: Students will draw the graphs and estimate the coordinates at their intersection points
   c. Minimum Level of Acceptable Performance: Same as *b* and answer correct to the nearest tenth.
   d. Students will confirm their answers with a graphics calculator.

4. *The student will be able to state how a right circular cone ought to be "sliced" in order to obtain each of the regular conic sections. The special cases of these may be demonstrated for extra credit.*

   a. Given Conditions: A right circular cone.
   b. Observable Student Behavior: Students will describe how to "slice" the conic so that parabolic, elliptic, and hyperbolic sections will be formed; also they will show how to form two intersecting lines and one point.
   c. Minimum Level of Acceptable Performance: Students will be able to show the regular conics as described in *b*.

---

remember that the objectives should be written appropriately for students at various levels.

The following sample contains some possible performance objectives for the unit on radicals. These are written in a practical rather than an ideal form, for if a teacher were to prepare each objective in its ideal form, they would become too lengthy and cumbersome to write for each lesson plan.

USING PERFORMANCE OBJECTIVES

Now that you have seen examples of performance objectives, you can decide whether you would like to use them some of the time, all of the time, or none of the time. The objections to their use are mainly that the teacher will select those objectives that are relatively low-level, such as simple skills that lend themselves easily to direct observation and that more youngsters are likely to attain. Furthermore, higher-level skills that are not so easily observed and tested, but which may be even more important because they involve "power" thinking, may be neglected. Also, it may not be possible to state in advance all objectives of a lesson because of frequently unanticipated events that may occur during the lesson. These events may lead to the attainment of an objective that the teacher never even considered. There is also the danger that the teacher may use performance objectives as a "show" for a supervisor to indicate that mastery in a certain area had been attained as the teacher planned.

Sample 2.   Performance Objectives for a Unit on Radicals

---

1. *Powers and roots: square root table*

   Students will name the base, exponent, and power of any expression of the form A^b (low level).

   Students will evaluate four expressions such as 5^3; 16^2; $\sqrt{9}$; $\sqrt[3]{8}$.

   Students will determine the values of four expressions such as $\sqrt{12}$ using a square root table, correct to tenths.

   Students will use a standard secondary school square root table or a calculator to determine the values of four expressions such as $\sqrt{576}$ (high level).

2. *Pythagorean theorem and quadratic equations of the form $x^2 = 9$ and $x^2 = 3$*

   Students will recite the Pythagorean theorem (low level).

   Students will find the length of one side of a right triangle given the lengths of other two sides, correct to the nearest tenth. They will have the square root table or a calculator available.

   Students will find the positive integral root of three equations such as $x^2 = 9$.

   Students will find the positive root of three equations such as $x^2 = 12$, leaving answers either in radical form or expressing them to the nearest tenth. The square root table or a calculator may be used.

3. *Square root algorithm*

   Students will find values of four numbers such as $\sqrt{576}$, $\sqrt{27}$, $\sqrt{3}$ correct to the nearest tenth by using a square root algorithm.

4. *Simplifying radicals*

   Students will write three expressions such as $\sqrt{9x^2}$, $\sqrt{27a^4}$ $\sqrt{20y^5}$ in simplest radical form.

5. *Adding and subtracting radicals*

   Students will combine radicals in three expressions such as $2\sqrt{3} + \sqrt{27}$ and present the answer in simplest radical form.

   Students will combine radicals in three expressions such as $3\sqrt{18c^3} - 5c\sqrt{2c}$ and write answers in simplest radical form (high level).

6. *Multiplying radicals*

   Students will find the value of two expressions such as $\sqrt{3} \cdot \sqrt{12}$ without using the table or algorithm.

   Students will find the value, correct to the nearest tenth, of two expressions such as $\sqrt{5} \cdot \sqrt{6}$ by using the square root table or a calculator only once.

7. *Dividing radicals*

   Students will find the value of three expressions such as $\dfrac{\sqrt{12}}{\sqrt{3}}$ without using the square root table or the square root algorithm.

8. *Rationalizing denominators*

   Students will express each of two examples such as $\dfrac{2}{\sqrt{5}}$ as an equivalent fraction with a rational denominator.

   Students will express each of two examples such as $\dfrac{\sqrt{3} + \sqrt{2}}{\sqrt{3}}$ as an equivalent fraction with a rational denominator.

   Students will express each of two examples such as $\dfrac{2}{\sqrt{3} - 2}$ as an equivalent fraction with a rational denominator.

9. *Solving radical equations*

Students will solve two equations such as $\sqrt{x} = 3$ and $\sqrt{x-1} = 2$ and check answers by substitution.
Students will solve two equations such as $\sqrt{x-1} - 1 = 3$ and check answers by substitution.

10. *Review*

Students will correctly answer at least eleven of the following fourteen questions within forty minutes:

a. Evaluate 3^3; 14^2; $\sqrt{25}$; $3\sqrt{27}$.
b. Evaluate $\sqrt{13}$ and $\sqrt{27}$ correct to tenths.
c. Evaluate $\sqrt{121}$ and $\sqrt{324}$.
d. Find the positive root of $x^2 = 21$ correct to the nearest tenth.
e. Given a right triangle with a leg of length 8 and the hypotenuse of length 17, find the length of the other leg.
f. Use the square root table to find the positive root of $2x^2 = 10$ correct to the nearest hundredth.
g. Solve for x in terms of a: $x^2 = 9a^4$.
h. Solve for x and leave answer in simplest radical form: $x^2 = 24$.
i. Express in simplest radical form: $\sqrt{8y^4}$; $\sqrt{18a^5}$. Check by multiplication.
j. Combine and express in simplest radical form: $5\sqrt{2} + \sqrt{8}$.
k. Combine and express in simplest radical form: $3a\sqrt{2a} - \sqrt{8a^3}$.
l. Without any tables, find the value of $\dfrac{\sqrt{12}}{\sqrt{3}}$; $\sqrt{12} \cdot \sqrt{3}$.
m. Express $\dfrac{3}{\sqrt{2} + 1}$ as an equivalent fraction with a rational denominator.
n. Solve and check by substitution: $\sqrt{x-2} + 1 = 3$.

11. *Test*

This will reflect the review objectives stated above.

The performance objectives should appear in the lesson plan. They are often written immediately after the aim of the lesson, although some teachers have found it convenient to list these objectives at the end of the plan, as the culmination or summary of the lesson. This does not preclude their use at the beginning of the lesson as well.

It would appear advisable that if you choose to use performance objectives in your daily lessons and if in spite of the most careful planning on your part you find the lesson not progressing as planned, you should be prepared to adjust your lesson or your objectives on the spot! Remember, be flexible. If in fact the objectives are carefully thought out and well stated, they should be able to withstand most unexpected events. Your lesson should always be tailored to your audience, even if this "tailoring" must be done during the lesson.

SUMMARY

Whenever you prepare a unit of work, or a daily lesson plan, you are in effect writing a "script" to follow so that certain information, concepts, thought processes, and skills will be acquired by the pupils. Thus, the type of lesson selected, whether developmental, review, drill, or any other, is the one that is determined to be best suited for the particular purpose selected. Some professionals, however, feel that no unit or daily plan is complete until a set of performance objectives has been developed alongside it. Furthermore, students should be made well aware of these objectives so they will understand how the work being done is tied to the expected outcome. Some teachers believe that a student learns better knowing what the learning goal for a particular lesson is.

Those who disagree with this opinion feel that no set of objectives can ever be fully complete because they cannot all be anticipated in advance. Furthermore, the limitations imposed by predetermined objectives might tend to restrict the teacher's freedom to develop objectives that do not have clearly measurable outcomes, such as "the student will be inspired by the teacher," or "the student will learn to love the subject." Some teachers simply do not feel they need to use objectives. They may feel that a student's prior knowledge of the intent of the lesson diminishes the suspense the teacher would like to generate as a possible motivational device.

Once a teacher has decided to use performance objectives, she or he must formulate them well—using clear, unambiguous verbs. Well-formulated objectives contain three major parts:

1. Given conditions
2. Observable student behavior
3. Minimum level of acceptable performance

Finally, the teacher will know that the objectives have been attained by observing the written or oral behavior exhibited by the students at the conclusion of the lesson.

We note that although some teachers do not use performance objectives specifically, they still need to use the same *idea* in another form in such places, for example, as testing and drill work.

EXERCISES

1. Here is a poorly stated performance objective:
   The student must be able to understand the law of cosines.
   Indicate whether the following test questions are appropriate for testing whether the objective has been attained or not.
   a. Derive the formula for the law of cosines, for an acute or obtuse triangle.
   b. Given a triangle ABC and the measures of a, b, and $\angle C$, solve for c to the nearest tenth.

2. Suppose a supervisor came to your class and asked to see the performance objectives your students were expected to attain during the past week. She then randomly selected pupils to test them according to the objectives.
   a. Is this a fair way to measure your effectiveness?
   b. Would you choose low-level objectives from now on to ensure a better chance of demonstrating student success?
   c. Do you think that knowing that your supervisor will do this periodically will make you a more effective teacher? Justify your responses!

3. Write a list of twelve verbs that are too vague and unclear to be used in a performance objective statement. Write another twelve verbs that are unambiguous and that may be used to clearly state performance objectives.

4. Below are four performance objectives (not necessarily good ones). Write two questions that would test each objective to determine whether or not it had been attained. Also state whether the objective is well formulated.
   a. The pupils will state the domain and range of a function given the graph of the function.
   b. The pupils will understand how to solve a quadratic equation by "completing the square."
   c. The student will define parallelogram, rectangle, square, rhombus.
   d. The student will appreciate "indirect reasoning" in geometry.

5. Survey at least twelve high school or middle school mathematics teachers to determine how they use performance objectives in their teaching and in their lesson planning. If a respondent claims not to use performance objectives, try to elicit whether similar structures are used in teaching or in planning to teach their mathematics lessons. Write a report to summarize your findings.

REFERENCES

Bailey, G. D. *Teacher Self-Assessment: A Means for Improving Classroom Instruction.* Washington, DC: National Education Association, 1981.

Cooney, Thomas J. "Teachers' Decision Making." In *Mathematics Education Research: Implications for the Eighties.* Ed. E. Fennema. Reston, VA: NCTM, 1981, pp. 67–81.

Duke, D. L., and R. J. Stiggins. *Teacher Evaluation: Five Keys to Growth.* Washington, DC: National Education Association, 1986.

Emmer, Edmond T., et al. *Classroom Management For Secondary Teachers.* Englewood Cliffs, NJ: Prentice Hall, 1984, pp. 147–162.

Flanagan, John C., William M. Shanner, and Robert F. Mager. *Mathematics Behavioral Objectives. A Guide to Individualizing Learning.* Palo Alto, CA: Westinghouse Learning Press, 1971.

Howson, A. G., and J. P. Kahane. *The Popularization of Mathematics,* New York: Cambridge University Press, 1990.

Kenney, Robert. "Basic Competencies in Vermont." *Mathematics Teacher* 71 (1978): 702.

Leitzel, James R. C. *A Call for Change: Recommendations for the Mathematical Preparation of Teachers of Mathematics.* Washington, D.C.: Mathematical Association of America, 1991.

Mager, Robert F. *Preparing Instructional Objectives.* Palo Alto, CA: Fearon Publishers, 1962.

National Council of Teachers of Mathematics. *Guidelines for the Preparation of Teachers of Mathematics.* Washington, DC: NCTM, 1981.

This booklet provides the NCTM's position on what the preparation (both inservice and preservice) of mathematics teachers should entail.

New York City Board of Education, Division of Curriculum and Instruction. *Leadership Manual for High School Supervisors.* Vol. 1, 1984.

Otte, Michael. "The Education and Professional Life of Mathematics Teachers." *New Trends in Mathematics Teaching,* vol. 4. Paris, United Nations: UNESCO, 1979, pp. 107–132.

Ronshausen, Mena L., ed. *Facilitating Evaluation: The Role of a Mathematics Supervisor.* Reston, VA: NCTM, 1986.

Schult, Veryl. "A Giant Step for NCTM." *Mathematics Teacher* 66, no. 5 (1973): 391–92.

A brief history of the National Council of Teachers of Mathematics is given here.

Shuard, H., and D. Quadling. *Teachers of Mathematics, Some Aspects of Professional Life.* London: Harper & Row, 1980.

This book describes the professional life and responsibilities of the mathematics teacher in the United Kingdom. One can get an interesting perspective of one's professional position by viewing its analog in another country.

Swick, K. J., and P. E. Hanley. *Teacher Renewal: Revitalization of Classroom Teachers.* Washington, DC: National Education Association, 1983.

Taylor, Ross. *So You're A Mathematics Supervisor?* Washington, DC: NCTM, 1982.

Although this is addressed to the mathematics supervisor, the teacher of mathematics can benefit greatly from knowing what the supervisor expects and what the supervisor is trying to achieve within the profession.

Taylor, Ross, ed. *Professional Development for Teachers of Mathematics.* Reston, VA: NCTM, 1986.

Zumwalt, Karen K., ed. *Improving Teaching.* ASCD Yearbook. Alexandria, VA: Association for Supervision & Curriculum Development, 1986.

PART 3
PROFES-SIONAL STANDARDS FOR TEACHERS

The needs of mathematics teachers in preservice, in-service, and continuing education are addressed in Part 3. The first focus of preservice mathematics education is the acquisition of a body of mathematical knowledge that will serve the teacher well both in and out of the classroom. A second focus highlights the responsibility and autonomy that all classroom teachers, especially those attempting to implement the *Standards*, should attain.

Professional teachers know such aspects of the teaching process as how to question students properly, how to use calculators and computers effectively, and how to arrange for small group learning sessions and for class discussions. They pose challenging mathematical tasks and they know how to judge the effectiveness of a lesson. In short, they know how to teach mathematics to a wide range of learners, and they also know how students learn.

Continued professional development is generally the responsibility of each teacher. Participation in activities such as attending or speaking at local, national, and even international gatherings is valuable for professional growth and development, for it is at such meetings that new teaching strategies are presented and the latest in school mathematics thinking is often unfolded.

CHAPTER 16
TEACHING AS A PROFESSION

Every teacher ought to consider what factors constitute a *profession.* There is a knowledge base that every member of that profession must master. For the mathematics teacher that knowledge base includes, but is certainly not limited to, an appropriate knowledge of mathematics (both that which is being directly taught as well as that which forms the underlying basis for it), a knowledge of pedagogy appropriate for the level of teaching involved, and a knowledge of social and psychological factors that affect the teaching-learning process. It is this knowledge base that separates a professional mathematics teacher from the rest of the community.

A second factor that contributes to the establishment of a profession is the practitioner's power to make judgments. Teachers must be able to make professional judgments based on this knowledge base as well as other professional training they have received. A teacher must stay current not only in the knowledge base but also on current issues regarding the profession.

Functioning in a way that the public believes you will act in the best interest of the "client," in this case the student, is a third aspect in defining a profession. When the teacher has the ability and the "power" to exercise these three components of professionalism, he or she is well on the way toward strengthening the teaching profession. Professionalism is good for students because judgments are made immediately, in the best interest of the student and based on a foundation of knowledge.

THE PROFESSIONAL TEACHER

Teachers seeking to strengthen the profession must be aware of certain pitfalls. These relate to their functioning as professionals and their ability to interact with the community. One of the difficulties in our educational system is that within any grade level, for example the ninth or tenth grade, the ages of two students can vary by as much as a year because of the possible spread in birth date cutoff points for placement in school at the start of kindergarten as well as other factors. These possible one-year variations between students can affect the readiness level and ultimately a student's progressive achievement through the grades. A student's mathematical readiness may affect not only his or her academic performance but also social adjustments. The mathematics teacher must be able to recognize and deal with these possible problems.

A second concern is students' problem of relating to as many as six different teachers each day. They may have different personalities, teaching styles, and requirements. This problem takes on an even greater significance when one realizes how crucial it is for students to successfully cope with these oftentimes pronounced differences as they try to move through the educational system.

The teaching profession is further complicated by having to work with a student population that must master material in several different subject areas simultaneously, while each secondary school teacher is merely required to be a specialist in one subject. Although such demands on students are not uncommon, it is nevertheless important for mathematics teachers to be particularly aware of this as they meet students in their classes.

This is not an argument for laxity and reduced standards in the mathematics class but merely a call for sensitivity on the part of the mathematics teacher. A teacher's awareness of the students' perceptions of mathematics, of their

daily workload, and of the school in general is quite important for a professional to master. Securing these notions should further strengthen the teaching profession.

The *professional* mathematics teacher might do well to consider his or her responsibilities to extend beyond the mathematics classroom. Within the community there are numerous opportunities to provide some expertise either in mathematics or with pedagogical discussion. These might involve helping to resolve a problem with a mathematical solution, or to contribute to a local discussion on educational issues, in some cases extending to the greater community.

An example of this wider involvement might be to share some educational or mathematical ideas with a newspaper or periodical audience. Consider offering a regular column in a general-audience periodical on topics (such as recreational mathematics) designed to turn people on to the study of mathematics. Or if the opportunity presents itself, comment on a news report's mathematical significance as one of the authors did on a routine article in an issue of the *New York Times.*

More frequent comment of this sort would go far to serve mathematics education. It is imperative that people be constantly reminded of the importance of the mathematics around them.

Earliest Professional Encounters

Good mathematics teaching rests on pillars that are set in a firm foundation of undergraduate mathematics. These pillars extend toward graduate, preservice, in-service, and finally toward continuing mathematics education programs. Knowing mathematics, and particularly school mathematics, and how to teach it well and knowing the psychology of adolescent behavior and what motivates

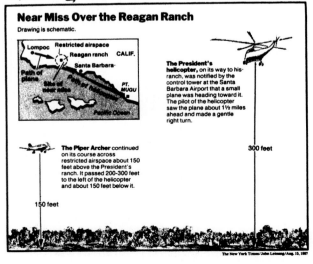

The New York Times

Near Miss Over the Reagan Ranch

Drawing is schematic.

Lompoc — Restricted airspace
Reagan ranch   CALIF.
Santa Barbara
Path of plane
PT. MUGU

The President's helicopter, on its way to his ranch, was notified by the control tower at the Santa Barbara Airport that a small plane was heading toward it. The pilot of the helicopter saw the plane about 1½ miles ahead and made a gentle right turn.

The Piper Archer continued on its course across restricted airspace about 150 feet above the President's ranch. It passed 200–300 feet to the left of the helicopter and about 150 feet below it.

300 feet

150 feet

The New York Times/John Leinung/Aug. 15, 1987

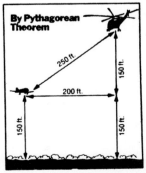

To the Editor:
Perhaps the most often asked questions of mathematics teachers are, "Why must we learn this stuff, and where are we ever to going to use it?" Although the answer is not "to correct The New York Times," it is still useful to enable students to read critically, and not just accept information because it is on a printed page.

On your front page Aug. 15, you report that the near miss of President Reagan's helicopter by a private plane over Santa Barbara, Calif., occurred "within 200 feet." Your diagram caption says the plane "passed 200-300 feet to the left of the helicopter," making the minimum horizontal distance 200 feet. With the vertical distance of 150 feet that you show, a right triangle may be formed, whose hypotenuse length is the actual distance the plane was from the helicopter. To apply the Pythagorean theorem $(a^2 + b^2 = c^2)$, the one thing most people remember from high school mathematics, this distance is 250 feet — more than "within 200 feet."

This is offered as the sort of thing

By Pythagorean Theorem

250 ft.   150 ft.

200 ft.

150 ft.   150 ft.

mathematics teachers (and even parents) ought to point out to students who question the value of mathematics.
    ALFRED S. POSAMENTIER
Professor of Mathematics Education
and Associate Dean
School of Education, City College
New York, Aug. 15, 1987

adolescents to learn mathematics are other pillars on which good mathematics teaching rests. These pillars are reinforced with further studies in the teacher's middle and later professional years, when college, government, and privately sponsored programs support these efforts.

Not all teachers encounter students who have the desire, background, capability, and interest to explore all topics that the teacher has studied, although over the course of a professional life every mathematics teacher will have an opportunity to serve as a resource and guide for many students. There is no such thing as a mathematics teacher being overprepared for a teaching assignment. Only the teacher with a broad mathematics background can have the confidence to create a classroom that empowers students to be members of a *miniature community* rather than merely a classroom filled with pupils. It will be a classroom where the teacher is not the sole authority for correct answers, where conjecturing, problem solving, and creating new ideas are nurtured, and where students freely discuss, explore, and invent mathematics.

The *Standards* proposes that mathematical content areas appropriate for investigation by secondary school *mathematics teachers* include topics in number systems, number theory, modern algebra, and linear algebra. Additionally, selected algebraic structures of isomorphic groups, vector spaces, rings, integral domains, and coding theory will be sure to serve every mathematics teacher well.

As for geometry, additional work in synthetic, coordinate, and transformational geometry should be supplemented with the non-Euclidean geometries and their historical development, such as the alternative approaches to the parallel postulate, the simplified wording of Playfair's postulate, and the seminal Saccheri quadrilateral. Foundations of modern geometry, as well as matrix representation of transformations, must not be overlooked.

Descriptive and inferential statistics and probability from experimental and theoretical viewpoints should include data analysis, the median-fit line for a scatter plot, confidence intervals, and hypothesis testing in addition to the traditional measures of dispersion.

It is expected that the mathematics training of secondary teachers will include modeling processes with real computer applications. Increased attention to discrete mathematics, symbolic logic, mathematical induction, recursive relationships, equivalence relations, sequences, and series will also be appropriate.

A firm grasp of the concepts of limit and continuity will provide a sound foundation for continued study of analysis in integral and differential calculus. Problems to be solved can now be expanded to include rate of change and optimization types.

An appreciation of the analytical power of the mind can be conveyed to students through the study of such seemingly diverse topics as non-Euclidean geometry and calculus. Historical anecdotes about the fascinating human frailties of mathematicians should be presented with wonder and excitement. A study of the history of mathematics may be one of the most valuable courses in which a prospective teacher can enroll, for it will open new vistas for his or her students and suggest alternative avenues for exploration and conjecture.

In-Service Professional Growth

NCTM endorses national, state, local, and regional conferences that offer teachers opportunities to learn the latest developments in school mathematics, conducted in informal, professional, and serious yet pleasant surroundings. Membership in the affiliated associations often includes literature such as locally prepared bulletins and guides that supplement the more sophisticated and professionally prepared *Mathematics Teacher, Mathematics Teaching in the Middle School,* and *Teaching Children Mathematics* (formerly called *Arithmetic Teacher*) of the National Council itself.

Additionally, the NCTM prepares yearbooks with such self-descriptive titles as

> Assessment in the Mathematics Classroom
> Calculators in Mathematics Education
> Discrete Mathematics Across the Curriculum
> The Secondary School Mathematics Curriculum
> Computers in Mathematics Education
> Teaching Statistics and Probability
> Applications in School Mathematics

A Research and Addenda Series are also available for additional instruction and guidance services for mathematics teachers. A number of additional books and videos are noted in their catalogs of educational materials.

Materials may be ordered from the National Council of Teachers of Mathematics, 1906 Association Drive, Reston, VA 22091-1593.

Summer Institutes

The National Science Foundation and the Woodrow Wilson Foundation are two examples of the scores of government and private summer institutes established and funded for the purpose of enhancing school mathematics programs. They often pay stipends to encourage attendance, and they are usually held in college and university facilities that become available during summer recess. These institutes often promote research and develop creative models that teachers are expected to implement when they return to classes. The courses are usually available without charge to mathematics teachers and are often credit bearing, so they may apply toward degrees higher than the baccalaureate.

They provide teachers with the opportunity to explore new mathematics, meet colleagues from different regions of the United States, and learn of other school systems, their problems, and their strengths. Appropriate new ideas may be applicable to a teacher's own situation.

Most schools and school systems receive enrollment information some time during the spring semester. Further information may be obtained from the NCTM and from the National Science Foundation, Department of Education, U.S. Government Printing Office, Washington, DC.

EXERCISES

1. Find the location and theme for local mathematics teacher conferences in the current academic year.

2. Prepare a fifteen-minute presentation for one of these conferences.

3. List three local institutions which offer in-service training for mathematics teachers.

REFERENCES

Cooney, Thomas J. "Teachers' Decision Making." In *Mathematics Education Research: Implications for the Eighties.* Ed. E. Fennema. Reston, VA: NCTM, 1981, pp. 67–81.

Leitzel, James R. C., *A Call for Change: Recommendations for the Mathematical Preparation of Teachers of Mathematics.* Washington, DC: Mathematical Association of America, 1991.

National Council of Teachers of Mathematics. *Guidelines for the Preparation of Teachers of Mathematics.* Washington, DC: NCTM, 1981.

Otte, Michael. "The Education and Professional Life of Mathematics Teachers." *New Trends in Mathematics Teaching,* vol. IV. Paris, United Nations: UNESCO, 1979, pp. 107–132.

Shuard, H., and D. Quadling. *Teachers of Mathematics: Some Aspects of Professional Life.* London: Harper & Row, 1980.

Taylor, Ross, ed. *Professional Development for Teachers of Mathematics.* Reston, VA: NCTM, 1986.

CHAPTER 17
TEACHER EVALUATION

Some teachers evoke strong, emotional reactions from pupils: "He's great" or "He stinks" sometimes describe the same teacher as seen by two different students sitting in the same room! More often than not, however, pupils' evaluations of a teacher are fairly consistent, whether favorable or not.

Although regular, formal evaluations and ratings by certified supervisors are usually mandated by school boards, informal assessments of teacher performance also may be made to guide the teacher toward improving his or her teaching skills. Pupils, parents, other teachers, as well as the teacher himself or herself can all participate in this type of evaluation process.

Is the classroom the only stage where the teacher's performance is judged? No, indeed! How the teacher affects student performance and attitude, both inside and outside the classroom, his or her skill in managing a classroom situation, as well as his or her professional and personal qualities also ought to play a role when judging his or her overall performance.

Professional growth demands an evaluation process based on an analysis of teaching that may be self-, colleague-, student-, or supervisor-generated. The purpose of each of the processes is the improvement of teaching. Evaluating a teacher's performance based on a single annual observation by a single observer is unreliable, though not uncommon. Ongoing involvement in a variety of professional activities is a good indicator of a teacher's commitment to helping all students to achieve mathematical power.

STUDENTS' TEACHER EVALUATIONS

The pupils' judgments of a teacher, especially when taken over a period of time and in different situations, are often very meaningful. That collective judgment determines the teacher's ''reputation'' and is arrived at ''informally,'' by word of mouth among students. Teachers may try to gain some insight into their reputations by asking students to express their opinions anonymously, in writing. A prepared form that includes a well-constructed checklist as well as some space for general comments might be a useful instrument for soliciting these feelings.

The following sample is an evaluation form similar to those distributed by some teachers to their students at the end of the term. These may be completed and returned anonymously. The results are seen only by the teacher who may then use them to adjust his or her teaching patterns. It is the kind of analysis that every young teacher should implement early in his or her career. Perhaps the adage about self-recognition being the first step toward improvement is what may motivate this exercise.

After analyzing the data in the form below, the teacher can determine the areas that might be in need of change. For example, if a teacher's tests are judged to be unfair, a supervisor or colleague might be asked to help write

Sample 1. Pupil's Evaluation Survey

TEACHER _____ DATE _____

Instructions:

Place a check (✔) in the appropriate space on the right.

The Teacher:	Usually	Usually Not	Comments (If Any)
Explains the work well			
Answers questions thoroughly			
Explains a second time if necessary			
Helps students outside class			
Knows the subject well			
Is always prepared			
Wastes time in class			
Gives unfair tests			
Prepares class for tests or quizzes			
Returns marked tests the next day			
Gives too much homework			
Arranges to have homework reviewed			
Is too strict in class			
Has a friendly personality			
Has a sense of humor			
Grades fairly			
Explains to class how grades are determined			
Meets pupils outside class to discuss problems			
Makes me like to go to math class			
I feel that I would like to have this teacher again			

OVERALL RATING: Satisfactory   Unsatisfactory

(circle one)

Comments or suggestions:

them for a while. (If students feel that she has a poor sense of humor, a Hollywood gag writer might help!) The only pressure to implement the findings of the survey is the teacher's own professional conscience. Very often this force promotes genuine concern, and ultimately real change follows.

Another type of informal evaluation technique is available in schools that have portable videotape equipment. This usually can be borrowed by the teacher for use in a class. Seeing oneself as others do affords the opportunity for self-analysis that is often more meaningful than the report or comments of others. With the assistance of a student (or teacher) "technician," it is possible to videotape an entire lesson as it unfolds before the class. The picture can be viewed at the teacher's leisure, and the tape can then be erased if so desired.

For some, the experience of being videotaped is so intimidating and frightening, even if no one but the teacher's own pupils are in the room, that they may reject this method of evaluation outright. For those who choose to participate in this type of self-analysis, a videotaped record of a teacher's performance will be most effective when viewed by the teacher together with several experienced colleagues who can point out what was done well, what was done poorly, and what corrections ought to be made. For a dramatic example, one teacher, after viewing himself on the video, remarked, "I didn't know I was so bald! (The next day he began parting his hair differently.) Another was astonished that she so frequently pushed her hair back during the lesson. Naturally the primary benefit of this immediate feedback is critical observation of the teacher's interaction with the class. This can be an extremely worthwhile activity.

Other informal evaluation techniques are available to those interested in using them. Take time out to answer the following questions honestly. Your answers should help guide you toward achieving the goal of excellence for which you ought to be striving.

1. Do I study more mathematics so that I will become a more competent and knowledgeable teacher?
2. Do I evaluate my classroom problems with fellow teachers at seminars, in-service courses, or even at the lunchroom table while offering opinions to and receiving advice from others?
3. Do I offer my services as an extracurricular advisor? Do mathematics teams, clubs, newspapers, speakers interest me?
4. Do I attend professional meetings of local and national mathematics teacher associations? Am I familiar with relevant professional literature as well as recent periodicals?
5. Do I observe other classes and ask other teachers to observe me for their reactions?
6. Do I inform parents or guidance counselors of students who have special problems?
7. What new and creative ideas have I offered lately to my colleagues, supervisor, or students?
8. Do I show an interest in the life of the school other than in the area of mathematics?

SUPERVISOR OBSERVATIONS

In many school systems, a teacher's overall performance is rated yearly. The rating, especially during the early nontenured (probationary) years, is taken very seriously, for it is often on that basis that tenure is granted or denied. While many aspects of the teacher's performance are considered when granting or denying tenure, the ability to teach a lesson well is of prime importance.

Whether a teacher is tenured or not, the formal observation is the technique used by supervisors to help formulate their opinions concerning a teacher's skill in the classroom. This observation may be an announced or unannounced visit to the classroom. It is sometimes preceded by a preobservation conference at which time the teacher and supervisor discuss the nature of the class to be observed, the topic to be taught, the type of lesson the teacher expects to teach, and the reason why the teacher selected that particular type of lesson. The supervisor may help the teacher plan the lesson by suggesting a challenging task, key questions, or types of practice exercises. It is then up to the teacher to implement that plan when the supervisor observes. The preobservation conference is usually held several days before the lesson is actually taught.

The observation is usually followed by a postobservation conference at which the lesson is discussed, suggestions are offered, criticisms are made, and alternatives are presented. A detailed written report on the observation follows this conference, and the report usually becomes part of the teacher's official record of performance in the school. While the tenured teacher may be formally observed once or twice a year, the nontenured teacher may be seen as many as six or even eight times annually, depending on the district's policy or the supervisor's determination of need.

Observation Reports

The sample observation report that follows, along with the one on page 260, will give you some general ideas of what supervisors look for in formal observations. Both are actual reports.

Although it is possible to incorporate more rating categories, such as "excellent" and "poor," into an observation form (see sample on page 262), such a refinement

Sample 2.   Observation Report of a First Year Algebra Class

Teacher _____ Class _____ Date _____

Description of the Lesson

As the pupils entered the room, they found a do-now exercise on the board, asking them to express algebraically four statements involving number relationships, using "*x*" to represent the number in question in each example. Thus, the attention of the class was directed to the work of the lesson immediately, and no time was wasted. After reminding the class that pupils needing extra help were urged to attend the after-school study sessions, the teacher circulated about the room to check on the quality of pupil work on the board exercises. A reasonable time was allowed for the class to do this work; then the teacher called on several pupils for their answers. These were given correctly in each instance: $x + 6$, $6x + 5$, $6x + 5 = 35$, and $7x - 4x = 24$.

Referring to the original statements, the teacher asked the class to distinguish between those that are sentences and those that are merely phrases. The pupils were able to do this, and the teacher emphasized that the last two were sentences, and therefore led to equations when translated into algebra, because of the presence of the verb "is" in their statements. The first two statements, both phrases, possessed no verbs in their statements. The teacher capitalized on a good opportunity here, both to link the study of mathematics with the work of his pupils in English and to introduce the concept of the mathematical sentence. The latter idea was carried further when the teacher elicited the solution of the equation $6x + 5 = 35$ from the pupils and then had a pupil point out that the number "5" makes the sentence "true." The use of the concept of the mathematical sentence is most valuable as a unifying device in the teaching of mathematics, especially in future work, where "sentences" include inequalities as well as equations.

After requiring the class to check the result of the solution of this equation in the original problem, a commendable procedure, the teacher paused to elicit a medial summary from the pupils, and he listed the steps for solving verbal problems on the board: 1. Read (the sentence). 2. State the unknown. 3. Set up equation. 4. Solve. and 5. Check. A pupil was then sent to the board to solve the equation $7x - 4x = 24$ while the rest of the class worked at their seats and the teacher circulated about the room to assist where help was needed. The work on the board was discussed and checked.

The remainder of the lesson was devoted to the solution of two additional problems of the same type as those already solved. These application exercises were considered carefully, the pupils working on them at their seats, the teacher checking their work, and then the class discussing and checking the solutions placed on the board. All checks were made orally in the original statements of the problems.

Commendations

The pupils were required to begin work immediately upon entering the room, since the do-now exercises were already on the board. Thus, no time was wasted in beginning the lesson.

The teacher repeatedly circulated about the room while the pupils were working on problems at their seats, thereby maintaining a continuous check on the quality of pupil work.

The work of the pupils in their English classes was brought into the lesson in connection with the recognition of phrases and sentences. The concept of the "mathematical sentence" also was introduced in the lesson and carefully illustrated.

Questioning was generally good. Nonvolunteers were frequently called on to answer questions. In addition to distributing questions widely, the teacher made an effort to increase pupil participation in the lesson by having pupils place their solutions to problems on the board.

The teacher elicited a medial summary from the pupils and wrote it on the board. This was the list of five steps to be taken in solving simple verbal problems. Applications of these steps were provided in subsequent problems. Of the five steps, the teacher especially stressed reading the problem (so important for all pupils, but especially for many of the slower ones in ninth year mathematics) and checking in the original statement of the problem.

Suggestions

Although the aim of the lesson became clear to this observer as the lesson unfolded, it would have been desirable to state it in concrete terms for the pupils, to enable them to take clearer and more meaningful notes. The aim could have been elicited from the class by asking for a title to the list of five steps presented as the medial summary. These pupils could have been expected to contribute a statement such as "Steps in solving problems," which the teacher could have refined, if he thought it necessary, before writing it on the board.

When teaching a lesson on problem solving, one must make a special effort to present at least some problems that will command considerable pupil interest and yet be simple enough for them to solve at their level. Most of the problems presented in this lesson were of the straight textbook type and lacked this special ''spark.'' The teacher could have had an effective challenge problem in the do-now set and more interesting problems throughout the lesson by relating them more closely with the pupils' experiences, such as their classroom test grades, their work experiences, their financial and earnings experiences, and so on.

Although the teacher attempted to elicit much of the material of the lesson from the pupils, he also gave them information in many instances that he could have obtained from them. Efforts should always be made to elicit the maximum amount of information from the class.

As with many new teachers, the teacher has a tendency to repeat most pupil answers. This practice should be avoided as much as possible, since it tends to foster pupil inattention to the original responses by fellow pupils. If it is necessary to have any pupil answers repeated, either because of inaudibility or because of a need for clarification, the pupil giving the answer or another pupil should be asked to repeat it.

Summary

Although new to the profession, Mr. X has been doing a very conscientious job with a program of generally weak classes. He has managed to maintain the interest of his pupils in their work, and he has made every effort to have them do their work faithfully. He has shown many signs of becoming a fine teacher, and I am certain that his techniques will improve as he becomes more experienced. It is a pleasure to welcome him to the department.

_____

Supervisor

Teacher's Signature: _____

---

could make an ''average'' rating appear to be worse because it would then be farther from the highest rating. The sample is merely one possible variation. Both items to be ranked as well as ranking intervals may be developed by supervisors and teachers to meet specific school needs.

COLLEGIAL OBSERVATIONS

After teachers have analyzed their own teaching through such means as videotaping their lessons, observing other teachers, and studying students' anonymous comments about their lessons, they are ready to consider and accept the opinions and recommendations of colleagues. The purpose of collegial analysis is not to issue a report on the teacher's competence but to provide a basis for self-improvement in such matters as the effectiveness and variety of the teacher's questions, of the proposed tasks, the organization of lessons, use of technology and manipulatives in the classroom, and all matters judged to be relevant by colleagues. Such analyses will usually be offered only on request by the teacher and may require one or more volunteers willing to give of their own time during one or more class sessions. It often requires coordination of teacher programs and other school schedules.

Enlightened administrators will create an atmosphere that encourages and assists teachers to solicit guidance in improving their instruction. Collegial observations are not to be viewed as a threat to the supervisor's authority but rather as an indicator of his or her professionalism. A teacher whose goal is professional growth will take advantage of every such opportunity.

EVALUATION TOWARD TENURE

The granting of tenure to a teacher is a serious matter to boards of education, for they and the state are thereby making a commitment to invest a large sum of money in a person over a span of many years. They would like to ''get their money's worth'' by acquiring the best ''product'' possible. The sums often include pensions, death benefits, health plans, and sick benefits, in addition to salaries.

In addition, a tenured teacher has certain legal and academic protections so that removal from the job for any reason must be well documented. In these matters, unions and professional associations such as the National Education Association and American Federation of Teachers are vigilant in protecting the rights of teachers against unscrupulous supervisors.

By granting tenure only after careful scrutiny, the state is thus protecting not only itself but also the children involved.

The probationary period for a teacher (often three years) is that time when a board of education, through its staff of administrators and supervisors, determines whether an individual merits tenured service. This determination is based on observations of classroom teaching techniques and classroom management, participation in school activities, and possibly in community activities. Professional and personal qualities are assessed. Willingness to accept and implement suggestions offered by supervisors and overall attendance patterns also are considered. Supervisors assess a teacher's overall cooperative effort as well as his suitability to the school district.

Sample 3. Observation Report of a High School Geometry Class

Teacher _____ Class _____ Date _____

Aim of Lesson: Introduction to parallel lines and corresponding angles formed by a transversal.

Procedure: The homework assignment for the following day was on the side board and the classroom exercise:

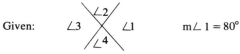

Given: $\angle 3 \quad \angle 1$ $m\angle 1 = 80°$

Find: $m\angle 2, m\angle 3, m\angle 4$

was at the front. After a few minutes, you told all students to stop writing and insisted that they put down their pens and pencils and listen to the discussion of the classwork exercise. You then stated that the topic to be discussed was "parallel lines." The definition and properties of parallel lines were stated, with emphasis on the importance of the two lines lying in the same plane. A transversal crossing two parallel lines was then drawn on the board, and the students were asked to guess which angles were equal in measure. After relating this diagram to the classwork exercise, you gave the pupils several appropriate exercises. The lesson ended with a review of the new work.

Commendations:

1. This was a well-prepared lesson.

2. Many students appeared to be eager to learn and followed instructions well.

3. The boardwork was generally clear and the use of colored chalk was effective.

4. Several excellent techniques were employed during the course of the lesson, especially when you had the students state the various properties of parallel lines that they knew from past experience; when you emphasized the possibility of two lines not meeting and yet not being parallel (skew lines); when you asked the students to "guess" which angles are congruent when a transversal is drawn; when you gave illustrations with two horizontal and two vertical parallel lines cut by a transversal; when you referred to the homework for the following day at appropriate times during the lesson; and when you summarized the lesson at the end of the period.

5. You praised students when their replies were correct, and when a particularly important answer was given such as, "We can't prove lines parallel because the angles (in a certain diagram in the textbook) are not corresponding angles," you asked another student to repeat it.

Shortcomings and Suggestions:

1. Avoid statements that are vague, unclear, and that may not be understood by the pupils. For example, after parallel lines were defined, you said, "The definition is not believed to be true by all people." You apparently had in mind one of the non-Euclidean geometries. Yet this statement, at this particular time, can serve only to confuse the students. In any event, the concept of truth or falsity does not apply to a definition. Also, after the class was able to conclude that "If two parallel lines are cut by a transversal, the corresponding angles are congruent," you should have told the pupils to simply postulate this, as they have done with other statements in the past. Instead, you said,"People have attempted to prove they are congruent and have succeeded. We won't prove it. It's an assumed proof." All this was unnecessary, for it was meaningless to the students.

2. You should not have attempted to illustrate skew lines with your drawing of two highways. You should only have referred to the diagram in the textbook instead of using a rather poor blackboard drawing.

3. At the beginning of the period when a boy walked in late, you said, "Oh my! Do you have a pass?" The boy answered, "No!" and you replied, "I'll have to mark you late. That's the second time—watch it!" While it was appropriate to ask for a pass, the "punishment" of marking him late, and the threat to "watch it!" were meaningless. You should simply have told him to explain his lateness at the end of the period, and if the explanation was not a satisfactory one, you would have to report it to the dean.

4. You should not wait to collect the homework until after the period has ended. This creates confusion. The collection should have been done earlier.

5. With more experience, you will realize that the lesson would have been more meaningful to the students if you had discussed not only the corresponding angles but also the alternate interior angles and interior angles on the same side of the transversal, all in a single period. You should also realize that these angles are formed if two *non*parallel lines are cut by a transversal.

General Estimate: Satisfactory

Teacher's Signature: _____   Supervisor _____

Rating Checklist

Sample 4. Rating Checklist

Name _____

School _____

Date _____

Lateness Record:

Attendance Record:

	Outstanding	Satisfactory	Unsatisfactory	Comments (If Any)
A. *Classroom Instruction and Management*				
1. Control of class				
2. Maintenance of a wholesome classroom atmosphere conducive to the learning process				
3. Planning and preparation of work				
4. Skill in adapting instruction to individual needs				
5. Effective use of appropriate methods				
6. Skill in making lessons attractive and interesting to pupils				
7. Evidence of pupil growth in knowledge, skills, appreciations, and attitudes				
8. Attention to pupil health, safety, and general welfare				
9. Attention to physical conditions of the classroom				
10. Housekeeping and appearance of room				
11. Care of equipment by teacher and students				
12. Attention to records and reports				
13. Attention to routine matters				
B. *Professional Qualities*				
1. Professional attitude				
2. Understanding of students				
3. Effect on character of students				
4. Resourcefulness and initiative				
5. Evidence of professional growth				
6. Willingness to accept special assignments in connection with the general school program				
7. Effort to establish and maintain good relationships with parents				
8. Maintenance of good relationships with other teachers and with supervisors				
C. *Personal Qualities*				
1. Appearance				
2. Voice, speech, English usage				

The sample on page 262 is a checklist that might be used by a school board (through its superintendent) when rating a probationer.

FORMAL EVALUATION AFTER TENURE

The process of evaluation and teacher growth is expected to continue throughout the teacher's professional career.

Yearly ratings of "satisfactory" or "unsatisfactory" are often given. As in the case of nontenured teachers, evaluations of tenured teachers are also based on formal observations of the type described earlier, though they are not nearly as frequent. The purpose, here, is to keep teachers on their professional "toes," through periodic evaluation of their performance. To make this a meaningful activity, recommendations are made and assistance is offered if it is determined that change is needed. Some supervisors prefer to use a simple form similar to this one to record their analysis of a lesson.

Sample 5.   Report with Ratings Categories

Teacher _____ Class _____ Date _____

A. *Brief Description of the Lesson:*

B. *Methods of Teaching:*	Good	Average	Needs Improvement	Comments
1. Challenge task				
2. Connection with pupils' previous knowledge				
3. Connections with other mathematics/real life illustrations				
4. Skill in questioning				
5. Effective use of small/large groups				
6. Discourse				
7. Stimulation of thought				
8. Summary or generalization				
9. Practice				
10. Effective use of technology				
11. Homework review				
C. *Responsiveness of Class*				
1. Attentiveness and interest				
2. Participation by students				
D. *Qualities of Teacher*				
1. Quality of voice				
2. Use of English				
3. Appearance				
E. *General*				
1. Talking too much?				
2. Repeating pupils' answers?				
3. Effective use of time				
4. Holding and reaching entire class				
5. Knowledge of subject				
6. Classroom management				

F. *Favorable Comments*

G. *Some Basic Suggestions*

Ultimately, the purpose of teacher evaluation programs is to improve student growth and learning. All the means used have that end in mind.

SUMMARY

Those teachers who are interested in growing professionally will find ways to do so. They become the "great" or "pretty good" teachers. They are usually teachers who actively participate in professional organizations, meetings, and programs, and regularly read professional journals. Those who pay mere lip service to their development (or who are honest enough to do not even that) become the teachers who are just passable or who, as described earlier in this chapter, "stink."

While continued self- and collegial analysis ought not become an obsession with a teacher, it ought to be a serious concern. Analyses result from informal evaluation that one's students can provide, videotape recording of a lesson, classroom observations by colleagues, critical questioning of one's role and effectiveness as an educator, and comments and suggestions made after formal observations by one's supervisor.

The postobservation conference consists of a serious and critical analysis of the lesson that was just presented. The written observation report is the written synthesis of this conference. This report becomes a permanent record of the description of the lesson, its strong and weak points, and suggestions and recommendations for future improvement.

The observation process continues throughout a teacher's career, for no one is immune to occasional slippage in technique, lesson presentation, or classroom management. A few reminders are often all that is needed to return the teacher to his or her previously high standards.

One experienced teacher, a former professional actor, always appreciated being observed, for he recalled its importance in his acting days when he would hire people to sit in the audience to observe his performance in the show. They would then report on every aspect of his performance, down to the most minute detail. It made him a better actor. He was an excellent teacher!

EXERCISES

1. Periodically, a teacher might send a student to the board to act as teacher for a portion of a lesson, while she sits in that pupil's seat. Comment on this as a type of teacher evaluation.

2. Some supervisors prefer to make *un*announced observations to see what a teacher's performance is "really" like. What are the merits of *announced* and *unannounced* visits?

3. "If a teacher gives the entire class high report card grades, all his students will like him, and this will be reflected in their evaluation of him." Comment on this.

4. Prepare a lesson from the unit plan on radicals for a first year algebra class (see p. 22, Chapter 4) and present it to your colleagues in this class. Have them evaluate your presentation.

5. Try to remember your own favorite high school mathematics teacher. What qualities impressed you most? Use the Pupil's Evaluation Survey in this chapter as a guide.

6. Suppose you are teaching in a high school and you find that one of your colleagues has aroused a strong negative feeling among his students. What would you do about this situation when one of his students comes to you for help (both in mathematics and in general regarding his classroom situation)?

7. After teaching for five years you find yourself teaching the same courses each year. You feel you are not being properly stimulated and are getting bored with your work. Explain how you might go about solving this dilemma.

8. The superintendent of your school district has come to observe you with an eye toward the granting of tenure. After the lesson, his comments to you are simply, "I see all this audio-visual equipment lying around the room, and you used none of it. If you don't use it from now on, we'll take it from you and pass it on to someone in another school." Comment on your probable feelings at that moment and your use of audio-visual equipment in the future.

9. A few days after a supervisor observes you, she sends you a report of the lesson that, in your judgment, is filled with inaccuracies and untruths. For example, she says you had no prepared lesson plan when indeed you did; she says you called on only a few students in class when, in fact, you involved virtually everyone. What is your reaction to this type of observation report, and what could you do?

10. Write to the National Council of Teachers of Mathematics (1906 Association Drive, Reston, Virginia, 22091) to request sample copies of *Mathematics Teacher, Mathematics Teaching in the Middle School,* and *Journal for*

Research in Mathematics Education journals along with membership application (half price for students). Read an article in each journal and write a brief review.

REFERENCES

Bailey, G. D. *Teacher Self-Assessment: A Means for Improving Classroom Instruction.* Washington, DC: National Education Association, 1981.

Cooney, Thomas J. ''Teachers' Decision Making.'' In *Mathematics Education Research: Implications for the Eighties.* Ed. E. Fennema. Reston, VA: NCTM, 1981, pp. 67–81.

Duke, D. L., and R. J. Stiggins. *Teacher Evaluation: Five Keys to Growth.* Washington, DC: National Education Association, 1986.

Emmer, Edmond T., et al. *Classroom Management For Secondary Teachers.* Englewood Cliffs, NJ: Prentice Hall, 1984, pp. 147–162.

Howson, A. G., and J. P. Kahane. *The Popularizaton of Mathematics.* New York: Cambridge University Press, 1990.

Kenney, Robert. ''Basic Competencies in Vermont.'' *Mathematics Teacher* 71 (1978): 702.

Leitzel, James R. C., *A Call for Change: Recommendations for the Mathematical Preparation of Teachers of Mathematics.* Washington, DC: Mathematical Association of America, 1991.

National Council of Teachers of Mathematics. *Guidelines for the Preparation of Teachers of Mathematics.* Washington, DC: NCTM, 1981.
This booklet provides the NCTM's position on what the preparation (both in-service and preservice) of mathematics teachers should entail.

New York City Board of Education, Division of Curriculum and Instruction. *Leadership Manual for High School Supervisors,* vol. 1. 1984.

Otte, Michael. ''The Education and Professional Life of Mathematics Teachers.'' *New Trends in Mathematics Teaching,* vol. IV. Paris, United Nations: UNESCO, 1979, pp. 107–132.

Ronshausen, Mena L., ed. *Facilitating Evaluation: The Role of a Mathematics Supervisor.* Reston, VA: NCTM, 1986.

Schult, Veryl. ''A Giant Step for NCTM.'' *Mathematics Teacher* 66, 5 (1973): 391–392.
A brief history of the National Council of Teachers of Mathematics is given here.

Shuard, H., and D. Quadling. *Teachers of Mathematics: Some Aspects of Professional Life.* London: Harper & Row, 1980.
This book describes the professional life and responsibilities of the mathematics teacher in the United Kingdom. One can get an interesting perspective of one's professional position by viewing its analog in another country.

Swick, K. J., and P. E. Hanley, *Teacher Renewal: Revitalization of Classroom Teachers.* Washington, DC: National Education Association, 1983.

Taylor, Ross. *So You're A Mathematics Supervisor?* Washington, DC: NCTM, 1982.
Although this is addressed to the mathematics supervisor, the teacher of mathematics can benefit greatly from knowing what the supervisor expects and what the supervisor is trying to achieve within the profession.

Taylor, Ross, ed. *Professional Development for Teachers of Mathematics.* Reston, VA: NCTM, 1986.

Zumwalt, Karen K, ed. *Improving Teaching.* ASCD Yearbook. Alexandria, VA: Association for Supervision & Curriculum Development, 1986.

PART 4
ENRICHMENT UNITS FOR THE SECONDARY SCHOOL CLASSROOM

A wide variety of mathematics topics are well suited as enrichment for secondary school mathematics courses. We can draw such topics from all branches of mathematics. Numerical curiosities, algebraic investigations of number relationships, geometric phenomena not usually available to this audience, as well as many other topics generally not found in the secondary school or college curricula are among the units found in this part of the book.

A very common topic viewed from a not-so-common viewpoint would certainly provide enrichment for the appropriate audience. The trick to providing students with enrichment activities is to present the material in a highly motivating and intelligible manner. This rather challenging objective will guide us through the many units presented here. It should be remembered from the outset that enrichment activities are *not* limited only to gifted students. As you will see throughout this part of the book, many enrichment activities can be successfully used with students of average mathematical ability as well as in remedial classes, provided proper adjustments are made. Naturally these modifications in the presentation (both in content and in method of presentation) can be made only by the classroom teacher using the material. With this in mind let us consider the format in which these enrichment units are presented.

Each enrichment unit treats a separate topic. With few exceptions, the topics can be considered in almost any order. Following a brief introduction, *Performance Objectives* for that unit are stated. Not only do these objectives succinctly foreshadow the content of the unit, but they provide you with a good indication of the scope of the material which follows. So that you can better determine the suitability of the unit for your particular class, a *Preassessment* section is offered. In addition to assisting you to ascertain your students' readiness for the unit, this section often also serves as a source for motivation which you may wish to use in presenting the topic to your class.

In the next section, *Teaching Strategies,* the enrichment topic is presented in a manner which you may use to introduce it to your class. Here the topic is carefully developed with an eye towards anticipating possible pitfalls and hurdles students may encounter along the way. The style is conversational throughout, making the reading more relaxed. Occasionally suggestions for extensions are offered so that the units do not appear to be terminal. Perhaps an underlying goal throughout these enrichment units is to allow them to serve as springboards for further investigation. Where appropriate, additional references are offered for further study.

One efficient way to ascertain whether the objectives for a particular unit have been met is to question the students on the topic presented. Sample questions are provided in the *Postassessment* section at the end of the unit. You are invited to augment these questions with some of your own where needed.

Since many of these enrichment units can be used in a variety of different mathematics classes and with students of different levels of mathematical ability, a cross-cataloguing chart is provided. This chart will enable you to select enrichment units according to subject, grade level, and student ability level. Naturally, you will need to make some modifications in the form to make the unit properly suited for the intended audience.

On the whole, you ought to make every effort to inject enrichment activities into all your mathematics instruction, regardless of the students' mathematical ability. Such activities can be just as rewarding in a remedial class as in one comprised of gifted students. The benefit, although manifested differently, should be about the same for all classes.

CROSS-CATALOGUE OF ENRICHMENT UNITS

To facilitate using the enrichment units found in this section, a cross-catalogue is provided. The units are listed in the order which they are presented in this section. In addition to providing page numbers for each unit, the grade level, the ability level and branch of mathematics to which each unit is related are also provided. These assessments are simply the opinion of the authors and some secondary school teachers. You may, however, try these units with audiences other than those specified.

You will notice that each ability level—Remedial, Average and Gifted—has been partitioned into four grade level divisions: 7–8, 9, 10, 11–12.

For the remedial student, grades 7–8 are usually the junior high school low level mathematics courses, while at grades 9 and 10 a general mathematics or introductory algebra is assumed. At grades 11–12 there is usually a continuation of the earlier courses, but with a greater degree of sophistication.

The average student partition refers to the junior high school pre-algebra program for grades 7–8, the elementary algebra course for grade 9, the high school geometry course for grade 10, and the second-year algebra (with trigonometry) course and beyond for grades 11–12.

Although very often the gifted student begins the study of elementary algebra in the eighth grade (or earlier), for the sake of simplicity we shall use the same course determination for the gifted students as for the average students (above). A greater ability in mathematics is assumed here, however.

The numbers 1 and 2 indicate the primary and secondary audiences for each unit. This implies that variations of these units can (and should) be used at all levels as you deem appropriate. Naturally, some modifications will have to be made. Some units may have to be "watered down" for weaker mathematics students, while for more gifted youngsters some units may serve as springboards for further investigation.

Ratings:
1—Primary use
   (specifically intended for that audience)
2—Secondary use
   (may be used for that audience with some modifications)

Another important consideration when selecting an enrichment unit is the branch of mathematics to which it is related. For many units this is difficult to isolate, since these units relate to many branches of mathematics. Using the code listed below, the *Subject* column indicates the related branches of mathematics. Although very often the order could easily be changed with no loss of accuracy, every attempt has been made to list the branches of mathematics in descending order of relevance to each unit, as judged by a group of mathematics teachers.

Subject Code:
1—Arithmetic
2—Number Theory
3—Probability
4—Logic
5—Algebra
6—Geometry
7—Analytic Geometry
8—Topology
9—Statistics
10—Problem Solving
11—Applications
12—Mathematical Curiosities

	Topic	Subject	Remedial Classes				Average Classes				Gifted Classes				Page Number
			7–8	9	10	11–12	7–8	9	10	11–12	7–8	9	10	11–12	
1	Constructing Odd Order Magic Squares	1,4,12	1	1	1	2	1	2							272
2	Constructing Even Order Magic Squares	1,12	1	1	1	2	1	2							274
3	Introduction to Alphametics	1,4	2	2	1	1	1	1			1	2			276
4	A Checkerboard Calculator	1,12	1	1	1	2	1	2			2	2			278
5	The Game of Nim	4,1,12	2	1	1	1	1	2			2	2			280
6	The Tower of Hanoi	4,1,12	2	1	1	1	1	2			2	2			282
7	What Day of the Week Was It?	4,1,12	2	2	1	1	1	1			1	2		2	284
8	Palindromic Numbers	2,1,12	1	1	2	2	1	1		2	1	1		2	289
9	The Fascinating Number Nine	1,2,12	2	1	1	1	1	2			1	2			290
10	Unusual Number Properties	1,2,12	2	1	1	1	1	2			1	2			292
11	Enrichment with a Hand-Held Calculator	1,2,12	1	1	1	1	1	2			1	2			294
12	Symmetric Multiplication	1,2,12	2	1	1	1	1	2		2	1	2			296
13	Variations on a Theme—Multiplication	1,2,12	2	1	1	1	1	2		2	1	2		2	298
14	Ancient Egyptian Arithmetic	2,1	1	2	2	1	1	2		2	1	1		2	300
15	Napier's Rods	1,2,11	1	1	1	1	1	2		2	2				302
16	Unit Pricing	1,11	1	1	1	1	1	2							303
17	Successive Discounts and Increases	1,11,12	2	2	1	1	1	1		2	1	2			304
18	Prime and Composite Factors of a Whole Number	1,2	1	1	1	2	2	2							306
19	Prime Numeration System	2,1,12		2		1	2	1		2	1				307
20	Repeating Decimal Expansions	2,1				2	2	1		2	2				309
21	Peculiarities of Perfect Repeating Decimals	2,1,12	1	1	2	2	1	1		2	1	2			311
22	Patterns in Mathematics	4,5	1	1	1	2	1	1			2	2			312
23	Googol and Googolplex	1,12	2	1	1	2	1	2			2		2		314
24	Mathematics of Life Insurance	3,9,5	2		2	2	2	2		1	2	1		2	316
25	Geometric Dissections	6,4,10			2	2	1	1	1		1	1			318

	Topic	Subject	Remedial Classes				Average Classes				Gifted Classes				Page Number
			7–8	9	10	11–12	7–8	9	10	11–12	7–8	9	10	11–12	
51	Introducing the Pythagorean Theorem	6,2,5						1	1	2		1	1	2	364
52	Trisection Revisited	6,5,12					2	1	1	1	2	1	1	2	366
53	Proving Lines Concurrent	6,10						2	2	2		2	1	2	368
54	Squares	6,10						1	1	2		1	1	2	370
55	Proving Points Collinear	6,10						2	2	2		2	1	1	371
56	Angle Measurement with a Circle	6						1	1	2		2	1		373
57	Trisecting a Circle	6 12						1	1	2		1	1	2	375
58	Ptolemy's Theorem	6,10						2	1	1		1	1	2	376
59	Constructing π	6,1						2	1	1		1	1	2	378
60	The Arbelos	6,5						2	1	1		1	1	1	380
61	The Nine Point Circle	6					2	2	1	2	2	1	1	2	382
62	The Euler Line	6					2	2	1	2	2	1	1	2	383
63	The Simson Line	6					2	2	1	2	2	1	1	2	385
64	The Butterfly Problem	6,10					2	2	1	2	2	1	1	1	386
65	Equicircles	6,5						2	1	2		2	1	1	388
66	The Inscribed Circle and the Right Triangle	6,5						2	2	2		2	1	1	390
67	The Golden Rectangle	6,5,2						2	1	1		1	1	2	392
68	The Golden Triangle	6,5,2						1	1	1		1	1	1	394
69	Geometric Fallacies	6,5						1	1	1		1	1	2	396
70	Regular Polyhedra	6,5				2	2	2	2	1	2	1	1	1	398
71	An Introduction to Topology	8,4		2	2	1	1	1	1	2		1	1	2	400
72	Angles on a Clock	1,5	1	1	1	1	1	1	1	2		1	2	2	401
73	Averaging Rates—The Harmonic Mean	5,1			2	2	1	1	2	1		1	2	2	403
74	Howlers	1,5	1	1	1	1	1	1	1	1	1	1	1	1	405
75	Digit Problems Revisited	5,1	1	1	1	1	1	1	1	1	1	1	1	1	407
76	Algebraic Identities	5,6						1	1	2		1	2		408
77	A Method for Factoring Trinomials of the Form: $ax^2 + bx + c$	5						1	2	1		1		2	410
78	Solving Quadratic Equations	5,10						1	2	1		1		1	411
79	The Euclidean Algorithm	2,5						1		1		1	1	1	413
80	Prime Numbers	2,5						2		2		1	1	1	415

	Topic	Subject	Remedial Classes				Average Classes				Gifted Classes				Page Number
			7–8	9	10	11–12	7–8	9	10	11–12	7–8	9	10	11–12	
105	A Parabolic Calculator	7,5				2		2	2	1		1	1	1	465
106	Constructing Ellipses	6,5,12,7						2	2	1		1	1	1	467
107	Constructing the Parabola	6,7,5			2	2	2	2	1	1			1	2	469
108	Using Higher Plane Curves to Trisect an Angle	7,5,6	2						2	1	1	1	1	1	471
109	Constructing Hypocycloid and Epicycloid Circular Envelopes	6,5,7						2	2	1		1	1	1	473
110	The Harmonic Sequence	5,6							1	1		1	1	1	475
111	Transformations and Matrices	5,7								2		2	2	1	476
112	The Method of Differences	1,5								1		2	2	1	479
113	Probability Applied to Baseball	3,5,4				2		1	1	1	2	1	1	1	480
114	Introduction to Geometric Transformations	6,5							1	1		2	1	1	482
115	The Circle and the Cardioid	6,5,11						2	1	1		1	1	1	484
116	Complex Number Applications	6,5,11							2	1		2	1	1	487
117	Hindu Arithmetic	2,1		2	2	1	1	2		2	1	1		2	489
118	Proving Numbers Irrational	5								1			2	1	491
119	How to Use a Computer Spreadsheet to Generate Solutions to Certain Mathematics Problems	1,2,10					1	2	1	1	1	1	2	2	492
120	The Three Worlds of Geometry	6										2	1	1	494
121	πie mix	5												1	497

1 Constructing Odd Order Magic Squares

This unit is intended for enrichment of students who have already mastered the fundamentals of elementary algebra. Carefully chosen parts of this unit may also prove effective in remedial classes, where students would appreciate some "recreational" mathematics.

Performance Objectives

1. *Students will construct magic squares of any odd order required.*

2. *Students will discover properties of given odd order magic squares.*

3. *Students will determine the sum of the elements of any row (or column, or diagonal) of any magic square, given only its order.*

Preassessment

Challenge students to form a 3×3 matrix with the numbers 1-9 so that the sum of the elements in each row, column or diagonal is the same. Indicate to them that such a matrix is called a *magic square* (of order 3).

Teaching Strategies

After students have had enough time to be either successful with, or thoroughly frustrated by, the challenge (usually less than 15 minutes), you may begin to attack the problem with them. Have them realize the advantage of knowing beforehand the sum of each row (or column, or diagonal).

In order to develop a formula for the sum of the elements in any row, column, or diagonal of a magic square*, students must be familiar with the formula for the sum of an arithmetic series, $S = \frac{n}{2} (a_1 + a_n)$. If they are not familiar with this formula it can be very easily related to them by telling the story of young Karl Friedrich Gauss (1777-1855) who, at the age of 10, successfully responded to his teacher's challenge.

His teacher had a habit of providing rather lengthy chores for the students to complete (while he knew of a shortcut formula). One day this teacher told the class to add a series of numbers of the sort: $1+2+3+4+\ldots+97+98+99+100$. As the teacher finished stating the problem, young Gauss submitted the answer. In amazement the teacher asked Gauss to explain his rapid solution. Gauss explained that rather than merely adding the 100 numbers in the order presented, he considered the following pairs $1+100=101$; $2+99=101$; $3+98=$

101; $4+97=101$; ...; $50+51=101$. Since there were 50 pairs of numbers whose sum was 101, his answer was $50×101=5,050$. In effect, he multiplied one-half the number of numbers to be added $(\frac{n}{2})$ by the sum of the first and last numbers in the series (a_1+a_n) in order to obtain the sum of the entire series.

From this formula, the sum of natural numbers from 1 to n^2 (the numbers used in an $n×n$ magic square) is $S = \frac{n^2}{2} (1+n^2)$. However, if it is required that each row must have the same sum, then the sum is $\frac{S}{n}$. (From here on the expression "the sum of a row" will actually refer to "the sum of the numbers in a row.") Therefore the sum of any row is $\frac{n}{2}(n^2+1)$. You might want to have students consider why the sum of a diagonal is also $\frac{n}{2}(n^2+1)$.

Students are now ready to begin to systematically consider the original problem. Have them consider the following matrix of letters representing the numbers 1-9.

	c_1	c_2	c_3
r_1	a	b	c
r_2	d	e	f
r_3	g	h	i

d_1 above left, d_2 above right.

Using the formula developed earlier, $S = \frac{n}{2} × (n^2+1)$, we find that the sum of a row of a third order (3×3) magic square is $\frac{3}{2} (3^2+1) = 15$. Therefore $r_2 + c_2 + d_1 + d_2 = 4 \cdot 15 = 60$. However $r_2 + c_2 + d_1 + d_2 = (d+e+f) + (b+e+h) + (a+e+i) + (c+e+g) = 3e + (a+b+c+d+e+f+g+h+i) = 3e + 45$ (since the sum of $1+2+3+\ldots+9 = \frac{9}{2}(1+9) = 45$). Therefore $3e + 45 = 60$ and $e = 5$.

Thus it is established that the center position of a third order magic square must be occupied by 5.

Since the sum of each row, column, and diagonal in this magic square is 15, $a + i = g + c = b + h = d + f = 15 - 5 = 10$. (Note: two numbers of an nth order magic square are said to be complementary if their sum is n^2+1; thus a and i are complementary.) Now lead your students through the following argument.

The number 1 cannot occupy a corner position. Suppose $a=1$; then $i=9$. However 2, 3, and 4 cannot be in the same row (or column) as 1, since there

---

*Unless stated otherwise this **unit** will be concerned with magic squares of consecutive natural numbers beginning with 1.

is no natural number less than 10 which would be large enough to occupy the third position of such a row (or column). This would leave only two positions (the non-shaded squares below) to accommodate these three numbers (2, 3, and 4). Since this cannot be the case, the numbers 1 and 9 may occupy only the middle positions of a row (or column).

1		
	5	
		9

The number 3 cannot be in the same row (or column) as 9, for the third number in such a row (or column) would then have to be 3, to obtain the required sum of 15. This is not possible because a number can be used only once in the magic square.

Now have students realize that neither 3 nor 7 may occupy corner positions. They should then use the above criteria to construct a magic square of order 3. Students should get any of the following magic squares.

2	7	6
9	5	1
4	3	8

4	3	8
9	5	1
2	7	6

8	1	6
3	5	7
4	9	2

6	1	8
7	5	3
2	9	4

2	9	4
7	5	3
6	1	8

4	9	2
3	5	7
8	1	6

8	3	4
1	5	9
6	7	2

6	7	2
1	5	9
8	3	4

Students might now want to extend this technique to constructing other odd order magic squares. However this scheme becomes somewhat tedious. Following is a rather mechanical method for constructing an odd order magic square.

Begin by placing a 1 in the first position of the middle column. Continue by placing the next consecutive numbers successively in the cells of the (positive slope) diagonal. This, of course, is impossible since there are no cells "above" the square.

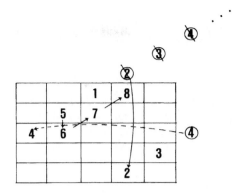

When a number must be placed in a position "above" the square, it should instead be placed in the last cell of the next column to the right. Then the next numbers are placed consecutively in this new (positive slope) diagonal. When (as in the figure above) a number falls outside the square to the right, it should be placed in the first (to the left) cell of the next row above the row whose last (to the right) cell was just filled (as illustrated). The process then continues by filling consecutively on the new cell until an already occupied cell is reached (as is the case with 6, above). Rather than placing a second number in the occupied cell, the number is placed below the previous number. The process continues until the last number is reached.

After enough practice students will begin to recognize certain patterns, e.g., the last number always occupies the middle position of the bottom row.

It should be noted that this is just one of many ways of constructing odd order magic squares. More adept students should be urged to justify this rather mechanical technique.

Postassessment
Have students do the following exercises:

1. Find the sum of a row of a magic square of order (a) 4; (b) 7; (c) 8.

2. Construct a magic square of order 11.

3. State some properties common to magic squares of odd order less than 13.

2 Constructing Even Order Magic Squares

This topic can be used with a remedial class in high school as well as with a more advanced class at any secondary school grade level. In the former case, only magic squares of doubly-even order should be considered, while in the latter case, singly-even order magic squares may be included. When used with a remedial class, the development of doubly-even order magic squares may serve as motivation for drill of arithmetic fundamentals.

Performance Objectives
1. *Students will construct magic squares of any even order required.*
2. *Students will discover properties of given even order magic squares.*

Preassessment
Begin your introduction with a historical note. Mention the German artist (and mathematician) Albrecht Dürer (1471-1528), who did considerable work with mathematics related to his art work. One of the more curious aspects of his work was the appearance of a magic square in an engraving of 1514 entitled "Melancholia" (Figure 1).

Figure 1

Figure 2

At the upper right hand corner of the engraving is the magic square (Figure 2). It is believed that this was one of the first appearances of magic squares in Western civilization. Of particular in-interest are the many unusual properties of this magic square. For example, the two center positions of the bottom row indicate the year the engraving was made, 1514. Offer your students some time to find other unusual properties (other than merely a constant sum of rows, columns, and diagonals).

Teaching Strategies
Students will probably enjoy discussing the many properties of this magic square, some of which are:

1. The four corner positions have a sum of 34.
2. The four corner 2×2 squares each has a sum of 34.
3. The center 2×2 square has a sum of 34.
4. The sum of the numbers in a diagonal equals the sum of those not in a diagonal.
5. The sum of the squares of the numbers in the diagonals (748) equals the sum of the squares of the numbers not in the diagonals.
6. The sum of the cubes of the numbers in the diagonals (9,248) equals the sum of the cubes of the numbers not in the diagonals.
7. The sum of the squares of the numbers in both diagonals equals the sum of the squares of the numbers in the first and third rows (or columns), which equals the sum of the squares of the numbers in the second and fourth rows (or columns.)
8. Note the following symmetries:
$$2+8+9+15 = 3+5+12+14 = 34$$
$$2^2+8^2+9^2+15^2 = 3^2+5^2+12^2+14^2 = 374$$
$$2^3+8^3+9^3+15^3 = 3^3+5^3+12^3+14^3 = 4,624$$
9. The sum of each adjacent upper and lower pair of numbers vertically or horizontally produces an interesting symmetry (see below).

vertically:	21	13	13	21
	13	21	21	13

horizontally:	19	15
	15	19
	15	19
	19	15

Consider first constructions of magic squares whose *order is a multiple of 4,* (sometimes referred to as *doubly-even order.*) Have students construct the square below with the diagonals as shown.

Figure 3

1	2	3	4
5	6	7	8
9	10	11	12
13	14	15	16

Then have them replace each number in a diagonal with its complement (i.e. that number which will give a sum of $n^2+1 = 16+1 = 17$.) This will yield a 4×4 magic square (Figure 4.) (Note: Durer simply interchanged columns 2 and 3 to obtain his magic square.)

A similar process is used to construct larger doubly-even order magic squares. To construct an 8×8 magic square, divide the square into 4×4 magic squares (Figure 5) and then replace the numbers in the diagonals of each of the 4×4 squares with their complements.

16	2	3	13
5	11	10	8
9	7	6	12
4	14	15	1

Figure 4

1	2	3	4	5	6	7	8
9	10	11	12	13	14	15	16
17	18	19	20	21	22	23	24
25	26	27	28	29	30	31	32
33	34	35	36	37	38	39	40
41	42	43	44	45	46	47	48
49	50	51	52	53	54	55	56
57	58	59	60	61	62	63	64

Figure 5

64	2	3	61	60	6	7	57
9	55	54	12	13	51	50	16
17	47	46	20	21	43	42	24
40	26	27	37	36	30	31	33
32	34	35	29	28	38	39	25
41	23	22	44	45	19	18	48
49	15	14	52	53	11	10	56
8	58	59	5	4	62	63	1

Figure 6

The resulting magic square is shown as Figure 6. Now have students construct a magic square of order 12.

A different scheme is used to construct magic squares of singly-even order, i.e., those whose order is even but *not* a multiple of 4. Any singly-even order (say, of order n) magic square may be separated into quadrants (Figure 7). For convenience label them A, B, C, and D.

Figure 7

A	C
D	B

Students should now be instructed to construct four *odd order* magic squares in the order A, B, C, and D (refer to the accompanying Model "Constructing Odd Order Magic Squares". That is, square A will be odd order magic square using the first $\frac{n^2}{4}$ natural numbers: square B will be an odd order magic square beginning with $\frac{n^2}{4}+1$; and ending with $\frac{n^2}{2}$; square C will be an odd order magic square beginning with $\frac{n^2}{2}+1$; and ending with $\frac{3n^2}{4}$; square D will be an odd order magic square beginning with $\frac{3n^2}{4}+1$ and ending with n^2. (Figure 8 illustrates the case where n=6.)

8	1	6	26	19	24
3	5	7	21	23	25
4	9	2	22	27	20
35	28	33	17	10	15
30	32	34	12	14	16
31	36	29	13	18	11

Figure 8

0 + 8	0 + 1	0 + 6	18 + 8	18 + 1	18 + 6
0 + 3	0 + 5	0 + 7	18 + 3	18 + 5	18 + 7
0 + 4	0 + 9	0 + 2	18 + 4	18 + 9	18 + 2
27 + 8	27 + 1	27 + 6	9 + 8	9 + 1	9 + 6
27 + 3	27 + 5	27 + 7	9 + 3	9 + 5	9 + 7
27 + 4	27 + 9	27 + 2	9 + 4	9 + 9	9 + 2

Figure 9

Have students notice the relation of the four magic squares of Figure 8 to the first magic square in the upper left position, A (Figure 9).

Now only some minor adjustments need be made to complete the construction of the magic squares. Let $n = 2(2m+1)$. Take the numbers in the first m positions in each row of A (except the middle row, where you skip the first position and take the next m positions) and interchange them with the numbers in the corresponding positions of square D. Then take the numbers in the last m-1 positions of square C and interchange them with the number in the corresponding posi-

35	1	6	26	19	24
3	32	7	21	23	25
31	9	2	22	27	20
8	28	33	17	10	15
30	5	34	12	14	16
4	36	29	13	18	11

Figure 10

tions of square B. Notice that for $n=6$ (Figure 10) $m\text{-}1=0$, hence squares B and C remain unaltered.

Have students apply this technique to the construction of a magic square of order 10 ($n=10$ and $m=2$; see Figures 11 and 12).

Figure 11

17	24	1	8	15	67	74	51	58	65
23	5	7	14	16	73	55	57	64	66
4	6	13	20	22	54	56	63	70	72
10	12	19	21	3	60	62	69	71	53
11	18	25	2	9	61	68	75	52	59
92	99	76	83	90	42	49	26	33	40
98	80	82	89	91	48	30	32	39	41
79	81	88	95	97	29	31	38	45	47
85	87	94	96	78	35	37	44	46	28
86	93	100	77	84	36	43	50	27	34

Figure 12

92	99	1	8	15	67	74	51	58	40
98	80	7	14	16	73	55	57	64	41
4	81	88	20	22	54	56	63	70	47
85	87	19	21	3	60	62	69	71	28
86	93	25	2	9	61	68	75	52	34
17	24	76	83	90	42	49	26	33	65
23	5	82	89	91	48	30	32	39	66
79	6	13	95	97	29	31	38	45	72
10	12	94	96	78	35	37	44	46	53
11	18	100	77	84	36	43	50	27	59

Postassessment

As a formal postassessment, have students

1. construct a magic square of order (a) 12; (b) 16;

2. construct a magic square of order (a) 14; (b) 18;

3. find additional properties of magic squares of order (a) 8; (b) 12.

3   Introduction to Alphametics

This unit can be used to reinforce the concept of addition.

Performance Objective

Given alphametic problems, students will solve them in a systematic fashion.

Preassessment

Have students solve the following addition problems, either by simple addition in (a) and by filling in the missing digits in (b).

```
a)    562          b)   5 6 7 __
     3943              __ 8 __ 9
     ____              _____
     8807              3 __ 3 3
```

Teaching Strategies

The preceding problems should serve as a motivation for this lesson. Alphametics are math-

ematical puzzles which appear in several disguises. Sometimes the problem is associated with the restoration of digits in a computational problem, while at other times, the problem is associated with decoding the complete arithmetical problem where letters of the alphabet represent all the digits. Basically, construction of this type of puzzle is not difficult, but the solution requires a thorough investigation of all elements. Every clue must be tested in all phases of the problem and carefully followed up. For example, suppose we were to eliminate certain digits in problem (a) above and supply the answer with some digits missing. Let us also assume that we do not know what these digits are. We may then be left with the following skeleton problem:

① ② ③ ④ ⑤

```
        _  6  2
     3  9  4  _
     _  8  _  7
  _  3  3  1  2
```

Have students analyze the problem. Lead them through the reconstruction as follows. From column five, 2 + __ + 7 = 12. Therefore the missing digit in the fifth column must be 3. In the fourth column, we have 1 + 6 + 4 + __ = 1, or 11 + __ = 1, therefore the digit must be zero. In the third column, we have 1 + __ + 9 + 8 = 23, and the missing digit must be 5. Now, from the second column, we have now 2 + 3 + __ = 13. This implies that the digit must be 8, and therefore, the digit to the left of 3 in the first column, botton row must be 1. Thus, we have reconstructed the problem. Students should now be able to find the missing digits in the second problem of the preassessment (if they haven't already solved it). The completed solution is

```
     5  6  7  ④
     ⑦  8  ⑤  9
  ①  3  ⑤  3  3
```

Have students make up their own problems and then interchange them with other students. We have considered problems that had exactly one solution. The following example will show a problem that has more than one solution.

① ② ③ ④

```
        _  8  7
     3  _  1
     5  6  _
  _  3  _  0
```

In 7 + 1 + __ = 10, the missing digit must be 2. In the third column, 1 + 8 + __ + 6 = _____, or 15 + __ = _____. An inspection must now be made of column two, so that all possible outcomes are considered. In the second column we have __ + 3 + 5 = 13. Thus, if we assigned the digits 5, 6, 7, 8, 9, for the value of the missing number in the third column, second row, we would have 15 + 5 = 20, 15 + 6 = 21, 15 + 7 = 22, 15 + 8 = 23, 15 + 9 = 24. This will then make the digit in column two equal to 3, since a 2 is being carried. Hence, we have as possible solutions:

387	387	387	387	387
351	361	371	381	391
562	562	562	562	562
1300	1310	1320	1330	1340

(or between each pair)

On the other hand, if we assigned values for the missing digit in the second row, third column, to be 0, 1, 2, 3, 4, then the digit in the first row, first column will be a 4, since a 1 was now carried. Therefore, there are ten different solutions which result from having two missing digits in the same column. Students should determine if this is true in all cases. Have students make up a similar problem where more than two digits are missing in the same column, and see what conclusion they can discover.

In the second type of problem, where all digits are represented by letters (hence the name alphametics), the problem is quite different from the preceding ones. Here, the clues from the "puzzle" must be analyzed for all different possible values to be assigned to the letters. No general rule can be given for the solution of alphametic problems. What is required is an understanding of basic arithmetic, logical reasoning, and plenty of patience.

One fine example of this type is the following addition problem:

① ② ③ ④ ⑤

```
  F  O  R  T  Y
        T  E  N
        T  E  N
  S  I  X  T  Y
```

Since the first line and the fourth line have **T Y** repeated, this would imply that the sum of both the **E**'s and the **N**'s in columns four and five must end in zero. If we let **N** = 0, then **E** must equal 5, and 1 is carried over to column three. We now have

```
  F  O  R  T  Y
     T  5  0
     T  5  0
  S  I  X  T  Y
```

Since there are two spaces before each **T E N,** the 0 in **F O R T Y** must be 9, and with 2 carried over from the hundred's place (column three), the **I** must be one. And a 1 is carried to column one, making **F** + 1 = **S**. Ask the students why 2 and not 1 was carried over to the second column. The reason 2 must be carried from column three is that if a 1 were carried, the digits **I** and **N** would both be zero. We are now left with the following numbers 2, 3, 4, 6, 7, 8 unassigned.

```
  F  9  R  T  Y
     T  5  0
     T  5  0
  S  1  X  T  Y
```

In the hundreds column, we have 2T + R + 1 (the 1 being carried over from column four), whose sum must be equal to or greater than 22; which implies **T** and **R** must be greater than 5. Therefore, **F** and **S** will be either 2, 3, or 4. Now **X** cannot be equal to 3, otherwise **F** and **S** would not be consecutive numbers. Then **X** equals 2 or 4, which is impossible if **T** is equal to or less than 7. Hence **T** must be 8, with **R** equal to 7 and **X** equal to 4. Then **F** = 2, **S** = 3, leaving **Y** = 6. Hence the solution to the problem is

```
        2 9, 7 8 6
             8  5  0
             8  5  0
        _____
        3 1, 4  8  6
```

Postassessment

Have students solve the following alphametic problems.

```
1)      4 __ __ 3
       __ __ 1 4 __
       _____
       __ __ 3 7 4 6
```

Answer
4603
99143
103746

```
2)    5 __ 4 __
       __ 4 5 __ 8
      6 __ 2 5 9
      _____
      9 4 1 9 6
```

Answer
5349
24588
64259
94196

```
3) T R I E D
   D R I V E
   _____
   R I V E T
```

Answer
17,465
57,496
74,961

```
4)   S E N D
     M O R E
     _____
   M O N E Y
```

Answer
9,567
1,085
10,652

```
5)   A L L S
     W E L L
     T H A T
     E N D S
     _____
   S W E L L
```

Answer
9,332
8,433
6,596
4,072
28,433

4 A Checkerboard Calculator

This enrichment unit will give students an easy, enjoyable method of operation with binary numerals.

Performance Objective
Students will be able to use a checkerboard calculator to do addition, subtraction, multiplication, and division with binary numerals.

Preassessment
Have students find:
a) $1100_2 + 110_2 = $ __   b) $12 + 6 = $ __
c) $111_2 \times 10_2 = $ __   d) $7 \times 2 = $ __

Teaching Strategies
John Napier, the 16th century mathematician who developed logarithms and Napier's Bones (the calculating rods), also described in his work *Rabdologia* a method for calculating by moving counters across a chessboard. Besides being the world's first binary computer, it is also a valuable teaching aid. Although use of checkered boards was common in the Middle Ages and Renaissance period, by adopting a binary system and basing algorithms on old methods of multiplying by

"doubling", Napier's Counting Board became much more efficient than any previous device.

Have students bring to school a standard chessboard or checkerboard. Begin by having students label rows and columns with the doubling series: 1, 2, 4, 8, 16, 32, 64, 128.

Now show how the board can be used for addition and subtraction. Every number is expressed by placing counters on a row. Each counter has the value of its column. For example, ask the students to add $89 + 41 + 52 + 14$. The fourth row (89) will show $64 + 16 + 8 + 1$ (Figure 1).

Figure 1

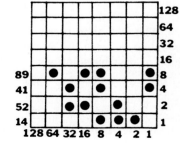

If the students think of each counter as a 1 and each empty space as a 0, 89 is represented in binary notation as 10110011_2.

The counters are positioned by starting at the left and putting a counter on the column of the largest number less than or equal to the number the student is representing. Place subsequent counters on the next largest number that when added to the previous number will not exceed the desired total, and so on.

To add, have students move all counters straight down (Figure 2).

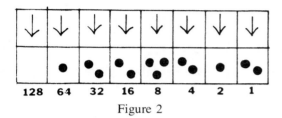

Figure 2

Adding the values of these counters will give the correct sum, but to use the board for binary notation, we must first "clear" the row of multiple counters on one cell. Have students start at the right, taking each cell in turn. Remove every PAIR of counters on a cell and replace them with a single counter on the next cell to the left. Assure students that this will not affect the sum as every two counters having value n, are replaced by one counter having value $2n$. In our example, the final result is the binary number 11000100_2 (Figure 3).

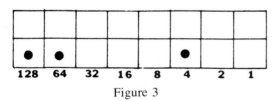

Figure 3

Subtraction is almost as simple. Suppose students want to take 83 from 108. Have them represent the larger number on the second row and the smaller number on the bottom row (Figure 4).

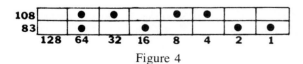

Figure 4

Students can now do subtraction in the usual manner, starting at the right and borrowing from cell to cell. Or instead, students can alter the entire second row until each counter on the bottom row has one or two counters above it, and no empty cell on the bottom row has more than one counter above it. This can be done by "doubling down" on

the second row; removing a counter and replacing it with two counters on the next cell to the right (Figure 5).

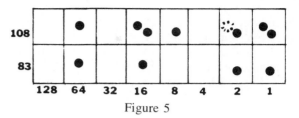

Figure 5

After this, "king" each counter in the bottom row by moving a counter on top of it from the cell directly above (Figure 6).

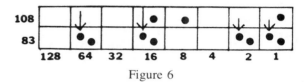

Figure 6

The top row now shows the difference of the two numbers in binary notation ($11001_2 = 25_{10}$).

Multiplication is also very simple. As an example use $19 \times 13 = 247$. Have students indicate one number, say 19, by marking below the board under the proper *columns* and the other number, 13, by marking the proper *rows*. Place a counter on every intersection of a marked column and marked row. (Figure 7A). Every counter not on the extreme right-hand column is next moved diagonally up and to the right as a bishop in chess (Figure 7B).

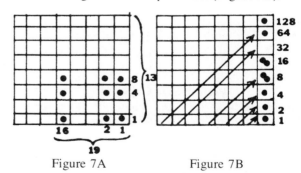

Figure 7A   Figure 7B

Clear the column by halving up as in addition, and the desired product is expressed in binary notation as 11110111_2 or 247_{10}, which students can quickly confirm.

Students will want to know how this works. Counters on the first row keep their values when moved to the right; counters on the second row double in value; counters on the third row quadruple in value; and so on. The procedure can be shown to be equivalent to multiplying with powers of the base 2. Nineteen is expressed in our example as $2^4 + 2^1 + 2^0$ and 13 as $2^3 + 2^2 + 2^0$. Multiplying the two trinomials gives us $2^7 +$

$2^6 + 2 \cdot 2^4 + 2 \cdot 2^3 + 2^2 + 2^1 + 2^0 = 247$. Moving the counters is equivalent to multiplying. We are, in effect, *multiplying* powers by *adding* exponents.

As an example of division, use $250 \div 13$. The procedure, as students may be expecting, is the reverse of multiplication. The divisor, in this case, 13, is marked at the bottom of the board and the dividend by counters on the column at the extreme right (Figure 8A). The dividend counters now move down and to the left, again like chess bishops, but in the opposite direction to multiplication. This procedure produces a pattern that has counters (one to a cell) only on marked columns, and each marked column must have its counters on the same rows. Only one such pattern can be formed. To do so it is necessary at times to double down on the right column; that is, remove single counters, replacing each with a pair of counters on the next lower cell. Have students start with the top counter and move it diagonally to the leftmost marked column. If the counter cannot proceed, have students return it to the original cell, double down, and try again. Have them continue in this way, gradually filling in the pattern until the unique solution is achieved (Figure 8B).

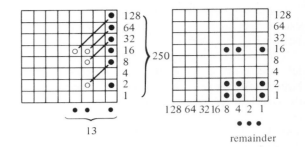

Figure 8A   Figure 8B

After the final counter is in place students should note that three counters are left over. This represents the remainder (3 or 11_2). The value of the right margin is now 10011_2 or 19_{10}, with $\frac{3}{13}$ left over.

Postassessment
Have students solve the following problems by using the checkerboard methods:

a) $27 \cdot 64 =$ b) $194 - 63 =$

c) $54 + 43 =$ d) $361 \div 57 =$

5   The Game of Nim

This unit will present an application of the binary system through the playing of a simple game called Nim.

Performance Objective
Students will play the game of Nim using binary notation system strategy to win.

Preassessment
Have students represent in binary notation:
(a) 14   (b) 7   (c) 13

Teaching Strategies
Nim, although sometimes played for money, can hardly be classified as a gambling game. This is because a player who knows the "secret" of the game can virtually always win.

The game of Nim may be played with sticks, pebbles, coins or any other small objects. Describe the game to students as played with toothpicks. Have students arrange the toothpicks in three piles (other numbers of piles may be used, also) with any number of toothpicks in each pile. Have two students be players. The two players take turns

making their moves. A move consists of taking away toothpicks according to certain rules. The rules are:

1. In each move a student may take away toothpicks from only one pile.

2. Each player may take any number of toothpicks, but must take at least one, and may take an entire pile at one time.

3. The player who takes away the last toothpick wins.

The "secret" of winning is quite simple, but practice is necessary to accurately perform mentally the arithmetic involved. Therefore, it is probably easier to start with a small number of toothpicks. The winning technique is based on choosing a move so that your opponent must draw from an *even set*.

First, it is necessary to learn how to identify an even set and an odd set. Suppose, for example, that the toothpicks are divided into three piles of (14), (7), and (13) toothpicks. Have students express each of these numbers in binary notation, and add the digits in each column in the same manner as when the decimal base is used. If at least one of the individual sums or digits is an odd number, the distribution is called an odd set. This example is an odd set because one sum is an odd number.

```
Fourteen  = 1 1 1 0
Seven     =   1 1 1
Thirteen  = 1 1 0 1
            2 3 2 2              (odd set)
```

If the toothpicks are divided into the piles (9), (13) and (4) toothpicks, each individual sum is even and so it is considered an even set.

```
Nine      = 1 0 0 1
Thirteen  = 1 1 0 1
Four      =   1 0 0
            2 2 0 2              (even set)
```

If a student draws from any even set, he necessarily must leave an odd set, for, considering the representation of the set in the binary scale, any draw will remove a one from at least one column, and the sum of the column will no longer be even.

On the other hand, if a player draws from an odd set, he can leave either an odd set or an even set. There are, however, usually only a few moves that can be made which will change an odd set into an even set. Therefore, a drawing at random from an odd set will very likely result in leaving an odd set.

Explain to the students that the object of the game is to try to force your opponent to draw from an even set, and his drawing will then leave an odd set. There are two winning end distributions that are even sets:

(a) Two piles of two toothpicks each, designated symbolically (2), (2).

(b) Four piles of one toothpick each, designated (1), (1), (1), (1).

If the student can leave an even set each time he plays, he is eventually able to force his opponent to draw from one of the above even sets, and the game is won. If at the start of the game the student has an even set before him, the best procedure is to draw a single toothpick from the largest pile leaving an odd set. If the opponent does not know the "secret" of the game, he or she will probably draw, leaving an odd set and you will then be able to force a win.

Have students follow moves in a sample game. Put toothpicks in piles of (7), (6) and (3) toothpicks each. /////// ////// ////

```
Seven    = 1 1 1
Six      = 1 1 0
Three    =   1 1
           2 3 2                (odd set)
```

To leave an even set, the first student must draw two toothpicks from any one pile. Drawing from the first pile would give:

///// ////// ///

```
Five     = 1 0 1
Six      = 1 1 0
Three    =   1 1
           2 2 2                (even set)
```

No matter how the second student moves, he is forced to leave an odd set. For instance, let him remove three toothpicks from the second pile.

///// /// ///

```
Five     = 1 0 1
Three    =   1 1
Three    =   1 1
           1 2 3                (odd set)
```

At this point the first student should draw all five toothpicks from the first pile.

/// ///

```
Three    = 1 1
Three    = 1 1
           2 2                  (even set)
```

Now, regardless of how the second student chooses the first will win. Students should now be permitted to play each other. This will provide reinforcement of the binary numeration system. After they have mastered the game as presented above, have them reverse the objective. (That is, let the loser be the player who must pick the last toothpick).

Postassessment

Have a student, who has been taught the strategy, play Nim against a student who only knows the rules. Use any (or all) of the following choices of piles of toothpicks:

(a) 17), (15), (4)   (b) (18), (15), (4)   (c) (18), (15), (3)

The student who has been taught the strategy of the game should always win.

6   The Tower of Hanoi

This unit provides students with an opportunity to construct and solve an ancient puzzle using the binary system of numeration. The puzzle, known as the Tower of Hanoi, was invented in 1883 by the French mathematician Edward Lucas.

Performance Objective

Each student will build and solve his own Tower of Hanoi puzzle using the binary system, and making use of knowledge required in this lesson.

Preassessment

Prior to this lesson students should be able to convert base 10 numerals to base 2 numerals. Administer the following quiz, instructing students to convert the given numerals (base 10) to base 2: a) 4 b) 8 c) 16 d) 60 e) 125.

Teaching Strategies

Begin the lesson by relating the "history" of the puzzle to the class:

W.W. Rouse Ball in his book *Mathematical Recreations and Essays*, relates an interesting legend of the origin of a puzzle called the Tower of Hanoi. In the great temple at Benares, beneath the dome that marks the center of the world, rests a brass plate in which are fixed three diamond needles, each a cubit high and as thick as the body of a bee. During creation, God placed 64 gold disks of diminishing size on one of these needles, the largest disk at the base resting on the brass plate. This is the tower of Bramah.

According to the legend the priests work day and night transferring the disks from one diamond needle to another according to the fixed laws of Bramah, which require that the priest on duty must *not* move *more than one disk at a time* and that he must place each disk on a needle so that *there is no smaller disk beneath it*. When the 64 disks have been transferred from the needle on which God placed them at creation to one of the other needles, tower, temple and Brahmins alike will crumble into dust, and with a thunderclap the world will vanish.

The puzzle, which is sold commercially, can easily be made by each member of the class. Instruct students to cut out eight cardboard circles, each of different size. Have them punch three holes into a piece of thick cardboard so that the distance between the holes is greater than the outside radius of the largest disk. Next have them glue a dowel or pencil upright into each hole. In each disk, they should cut a hole at the center, wide enough for the dowel to fit through. Now they can place each disk

on one of the dowels in order of size, with the largest one at the bottom. The arrangement of disks is called a *tower*.

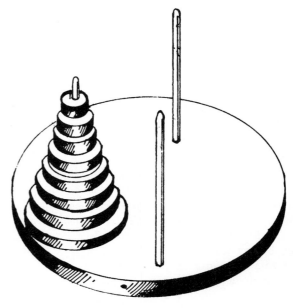

If you do not want to trouble yourself with cutting circles and gluing dowels into a board, you can make a simplified set by cutting eight squares of different sizes, and resting them on three plates instead of on dowels. In any case be sure to observe the rules:

At the start all the disks are placed on one post in order of size, the largest disk on the bottom. The puzzle involves shifting the disks, one at a time, from this post to another in such a way that a disk shall never rest on one smaller than itself. This should be done in the least possible number of moves. Remind students of the basic rules:

1) *Move only one disk at a time.*
2) *Never put a disk on top of a smaller disk.*

To familiarize students with the way the game works, demonstrate it first with only three disks. They should be able to transfer a tower of three disks in seven moves.

Now have them try it with four disks. To do this, seven moves are required to transfer the three top disks to one of the other two dowels. This frees the fourth disk which can then be moved to the vacant dowel. Seven more moves are now required to transfer the other three disks back on top the fourth. Thus, the total number of moves required is 15.

When students consider the game with five disks they must move the top four disks twice, once to free the bottom disk, and once to get them back on the bottom disk, after the bottom disk has been moved. Thus, moving five disks takes 31 moves: six disks, 63 moves. Ask the class how many moves are required to transfer seven disks. Eight disks?

As students begin to comprehend the challenge of the puzzle, an interesting mathematical problem will emerge: *What is the minimum number of moves required to shift a specific number of disks from one post to another?* To solve this problem, suggest that students denote the number of disks by n; the least number of moves required by 2^n-1. Therefore, if there are eight disks, the least number of moves is $2^8-1 = 256-1 = 255$.

Have students consider the Brahmins with their 64 disks of gold. How many moves will it take them? $2^{64}-1 = 18,446,744,073,709,551,615$.

If the priests were to make one transfer every second and work 24 hours a day, 365 days a year, they would need more than *580 billion years* to perform the feat, assuming that they never made a mistake. How long would it take the priests to transfer half (or 32) of the disks? $(4,294,967,296$ sec. $= 136$ years.)

Now have the class consider the problem of moving eight disks, the Tower of Hanoi. Suggest that students number the disks, one to eight according to size, from the smallest to the largest. Also, have them number the moves from 1 to 225 (2^8-1 $= 225$). As a class (or independent) project they should write the number of each move in the binary scale. To discover which disk to transfer at each move, and where to place it, they can refer to the binary scale numeral that corresponds to that move. Then have them count the digits from the right until the first unit digit is reached. The number of digits counted tells which disk to move. For example, if the first 1 from the right is the third digit, then the third disk is moved. Now its placement must be determined. If there are no other digits to the left of the first 1, then the disk is

placed on the dowel that has no disks on it. If there *are* other digits to the left of the first 1, students should count digits from the right again until they reach the second 1. The number of digits counted this time identifies a larger disk that was previously moved. Students must decide whether to place the disk they are moving on top of this larger disk or on the "empty" dowel. To decide which strategy to take, they should count the number of zeros between the first 1 from the right and the second 1 from the right. If there are no zeros between them, or if there is an even number of zeros between them, they should put the disk that they are moving onto the disk that the second 1 refers to. If the number of zeros between them is odd, they put the disk on the empty dowel.

The numbers 1 to 15, written in the binary scale are presented here, along with the instructions for the first fifteen moves.

1	Move disk 1.
10	Move disk 2.
11	Place disk 1 on disk 2.
100	Move disk 3.
101	Place disk 1 not on disk 3.
110	Place disk 2 on disk 3.
111	Place disk 1 on disk 2.
1000	Move disk 4.
1001	Place disk 1 on disk 4.
1010	Place disk 2 not on disk 4.
1011	Place disk 1 on disk 2.
1100	Place disk 3 on disk 4.
1101	Place disk 1 not on disk 3.
1110	Place disk 2 on disk 3.
1111	Place disk 1 on disk 2.

Postassessment

To assess student progress have them complete the above table. Then have them make the first 25 moves on their model of the Tower of Hanoi.

7 What Day of the Week Was It?

This topic may be used for enrichment in a recreational spirit, as well as an interesting application of mathematics. Students will also enjoy seeing the relationship between astronomy and mod 7. In addition, students will be surprised to see how many factors have to be considered in this seemingly simple problem.

Performance Objectives

1. Given any date, the student will determine the day of the week corresponding to this date.

2. Given any year, the student will determine the date of the Easter Sunday that year.

Preassessment

The students must be familiar with the construction of the calendar.

Give the students a date in this year and ask them to indicate the day corresponding to this date. After they try this, ask them to do this for a date in the past. The students will be anxious to develop a rapid and accurate method for doing this.

Teaching Strategy

Start with a brief history of the calendar. The students will be most interested in knowing the development of the present day Gregorian Calendar and fascinated by how it was changed.

Discuss the relationship of the calendar to astronomy. Time can be measured only by observing the motions of bodies that move in unchanging cycles. The only motions of this nature are those of the celestial bodies. Hence we owe to astronomy the establishment of a secure basis for the measurement of time by determining the lengths of the day, the month, and the year. A year is defined as the interval of time between two passages of the earth through the same point in its orbit in relation to the sun. This is the solar year. It is approximately 365.242216 mean solar days. The length of the year is not commensurable with the length of the day; the history of the calendar is the history of the attempts to adjust these incommensurable units in such a way as to obtain a simple and practical system.

The calendar story goes back to Romulus, the legendary founder of Rome, who introduced a year of 300 days divided into 10 months. His successor, Numa, added two months. This calendar was used for the following six and a half centuries until Julius Caesar introduced the Julian Calendar. If the year were indeed 365.25 days, the introduction of an additional day to 365 days once every four years, making the fourth year a leap year, would completely compensate for the discrepancy. The Julian Calendar spread abroad with other features of Roman culture, and was generally used until 1582.

The difficulty with this method of reckoning was that 365.25 was not 365.242216, and although it may seem an insignificant quantity, in hundreds of years it accumulates to a discrepancy of a considerable number of days. The Julian Year was somewhat too long and by 1582 the accumulated error amounted to ten days.

Pope Gregory XII tried to compensate for the error. Because the Vernal Equinox occurred on March 11 in 1582, he ordered that ten days be suppressed from the calendar dates in that year so that the Vernal Equinox would fall on March 21 as it should. When he proclaimed the calendar reform, he formulated the rules regarding the leap years. The Gregorian Calendar has years (based on approximately 365.2425 days) divisible by four as leap years, unless they are divisible by 100 and not 400. Thus 1700, 1800, 1900, 2100, . . . are not leap years, but 2000 is.

In Great Britain and its colonies the change of the Julian to the Gregorian Calendar was not made until 1752. In September of that year, eleven days were omitted. The day after September 2 was September 14. It is interesting to see a copy of the calendar for Sept. 1752 taken from the almanac of Richard Saunders, Gent., published in London (Figure A).

Mathematicians have pondered the question of the calendar and tried to develop ways of determining the days of any given date or holiday.

To develop a method for determining the day, the student should be aware that a calendar year (except for a leap year) is 52 weeks and one day long. If New Year's day in some year following a leap year occurs on a Sunday, the next New Year's will occur on Monday. The following New Year's day will occur on a Tuesday. The New Year's day of the leap year will occur on a Wednesday. Since there are 366 days in a leap year, the next New Year's day will occur on a Friday, and not on a Thursday. The regular sequence is interrupted every four years (except during years where numbers are evenly divisible by 100 but not evenly divisible by 400).

First develop a method to find the weekday for dates in the same year.

Suppose February 4 falls on Monday. On what day of the week will September 15 fall? Assuming that this calendar year is not a leap year, one need only: (1) Find the number of days between Feb. 4 and Sept. 15.

1752 September hath XIX Days this Year.

First Quarter, the 15th day at 2 afternoon.
Full Moon, the 23rd day at 1 afternoon.
Last Quarter, the 30th day at 2 afternoon.

M D	W D	Saints' Days Terms, &c.	Moon South	Moon Sets	Full Sea at Lond.	Aspects and Weather
1	f	Day br. 3.35	3 A 27	8 A 29	5 A 1	☐ ♃ ☿
2	g	London burn.	4 26	9 11	5 38	Lofty winds

According to an act of Parliament passed in the 24th year of his Majesty's reign and in the year of our Lord 1751, the Old Style ceases here and the New takes its place; and consequently the next Day, which in the old account would have been the 3d is now to be called the 14th; so that all the intermediate nominal days from the 2d to the 14th are omitted or rather annihilated this Year; and the Month contains no more than 19 days, as the title at the head expresses.

M D	W D	Saints' Days Terms, &c.	Moon South	Moon Sets	Full Sea at Lond.	Aspects and Weather
14	e	Clock slo. 5 m.	5 15	9 47	6 27	Holy Rood D.
15	f	Day 12 h. 30 m.	6 3	10 31	7 18	and hasty
16	g		6 57	11 23	8 16	showers
17	*A*	15 S. Aft. Trin.	7 37	12 19	9 7	
18	b		8 26	Morn.	10 22	More warm
19	c	Nat. V. Mary	9 12	1 22	11 21	and dry
20	d	Ember Week	9 59	2 24	Morn.	weather
21	e	St. Matthew	10 43	3 37	0 17	☌ ♀ ☿
22	f	Burchan	11 28	☾ rise	1 6	☐ ♃ ♀
23	g	Equal D. & N.	Morn.	6 A 13	1 52	☌ ☉ ♂
24	*A*	16 S. Aft. Trin.	0 16	6 37	2 39	☌ ☉ ☿
25	b		1 5	7 39	3 14	
26	c	Day 11 h. 52 m.	1 57	8 39	3 48	Rain or hail
27	d	Ember Week	2 56	8 18	4 23	☌ ♂ ☿
28	e	Lambert bp.	3 47	9 3	5 6	now abouts
29	f	St. Michael	4 44	9 59	5 55	✶ ♄ ♀
30	g		5 43	11 2	6 58	

Figure A

First find that Feb. 4 is the 35th day of the year and that Sept. 15 is the 258th day of the year. (The table Figure B expedites this). The difference of 258 and 35 is the number of days, namely, 223. (2) Since there are seven days in a week, divide 223 by 7. [223/7=31 + remainder 6.] (3) The 6 indicates that the day on which Sept. 15 falls is the sixth day after Monday, thus Sunday. In the case of a leap year, one day must be added after February 28 to account for February 29.

A similar method for finding the weekday of the dates in the same year can be discussed thusly.

Because January has 31 days, the same date in the subsequent month will be 3 days after that day in January; the same date in March will also be 3 days later than in January; in April, it will be 6 days later than in January. We can then construct a table of Index Numbers for the months which will adjust all dates to the corresponding dates in January:

Jan.	0	Apr.	6	July	6	Oct.	0
Feb.	3	May	1	Aug.	2	Nov.	3
Mar.	3	June	4	Sept.	5	Dec.	5

(The Index Numbers are actually giving you the days between the months divided by 7 to get the excess days as in the previous method.)

Now you need only add the date to the Index Number of the month, divide by 7 and the remainder will indicate the day of the week.

Example: Consider the year 1925. January 1 was on a Thursday. Find March 12.

To do this, add $12+3=15$; divide $15/7=2$ remainder 1. This indicates Thursday. In leap years an extra 1 has to be added for dates after February 29.

Students will now want to find the day for a date for any given year. Point out that first one need know what day January 1 of the Year 1 fell and also make adjustments for leap years.

The day of the week on which January 1 of Year 1 fell can be determined as follows. Using a known day and date, we find the number of days which have elapsed since January 1 of the Year 1. Thus, since January 1, 1952, was Wednesday, in terms of the value of the solar year, the number of days since January 1 is $1951 \times 365.2425 = 712588.1175$. Dividing by 7, we get 101,798 with a remainder of 2. The remainder indicates that 2 days should be counted from Wednesday. Since calculations refer to the past, the counting is done backwards, indicating that January 1 (in the Gregorian Calendar) fell on Monday.

One method for determining the day for any year suggests that dates in each century be treated separately. Knowing the weekday of the first day of that period, one could, in the same fashion as before, determine the excess days after that weekday (thus the day of the week that a given day would fall on for that century). For the years 1900–1999, the information needed is:

1. The Index Numbers of the months (see earlier discussion).
2. January 1 of 1900 was Monday.
3. The number of years (thus giving the number of

days over the 52 week cycles) that have elapsed since the 1st day of the year 1900.

4. The number of leap years (i.e., additional days) that have occurred since the beginning of the century. Knowing this, we can ascertain how many days in that Monday-week cycle we need count.

Examples:

1. *May 9, 1914.* Add 9 (days into the month), 1 (Index Number of the month), 14 (Number of years since the beginning of the century), and 3 (number of leap years in that century thus far). $9 + 1 + 14 + 3 = 27$. Divide by 7, leaves 6, which is Saturday.
2. *Aug. 16, 1937.* Add $16 + 2 + 37 + 9 = 64$. Divide by 7, leaves 1, which is Monday.

For the period, 1800–1899, the same procedure is followed except that January 1, 1800, was on Wednesday. For the period September 14, 1752, through 1799, the same procedure is followed except that the first day of that period would be Friday. For the period up to and including September 2, 1752, the same procedure is followed except that the whole year would be added and the number of the days would start with Friday.

Example: May 13, 1240. Add $13 + 1 + 1240 + 10 = 1264/7$, leaves 4, Monday.

There is another method for determining the day without having to consider separate periods.

Again we start by knowing the day of Jan. 1 of the Year 1. We will not count the actual number of days which have elapsed since Jan. 1 of Year 1, but count the number of excess days over weeks which have elapsed and to this number, add the number of days which have elapsed since January 1 of the given year. This total must be divided by 7, the remainder will indicate the number of days which must be counted for that week, thus the formula is, 1 (Monday) + the remainder of the division by 7 of (the number of years

DATE	1	2	3	4	5	6	7	8	9	10	11	12	13	14	15	16
JANUARY	1	2	3	4	5	6	7	8	9	10	11	12	13	14	15	16
FEBRUARY	32	33	34	35	36	37	38	39	40	41	42	43	44	45	46	47
MARCH	60	61	62	63	64	65	66	67	68	69	70	71	72	73	74	75
APRIL	91	92	93	94	95	96	97	98	99	100	101	102	103	104	105	106
MAY	121	122	123	124	125	126	127	128	129	130	131	132	133	134	135	136
JUNE	152	153	154	155	156	157	158	159	160	161	162	163	164	165	166	167
JULY	182	183	184	185	186	187	188	189	190	191	192	193	194	195	196	197
AUGUST	213	214	215	216	217	218	219	220	221	222	223	224	225	226	227	228
SEPTEMBER	244	245	246	247	248	249	250	251	252	253	254	255	256	257	258	259
OCTOBER	274	275	276	277	278	279	280	281	282	283	284	285	286	287	288	289
NOVEMBER	305	306	307	308	309	310	311	312	313	314	315	316	317	318	319	320
DECEMBER	335	336	337	338	339	340	341	342	343	344	345	346	347	348	349	350

Figure B

DATE	17	18	19	20	21	22	23	24	25	26	27	28	29	30	31
JANUARY	17	18	19	20	21	22	23	24	25	26	27	28	29	30	31
FEBRUARY	48	49	50	51	52	53	54	55	56	57	58	59			
MARCH	76	77	78	79	80	81	82	83	84	85	86	87	88	89	90
APRIL	107	108	109	110	111	112	113	114	115	116	117	118	119	120	
MAY	137	138	139	140	141	142	143	144	145	146	147	148	149	150	151
JUNE	168	169	170	171	172	173	174	175	176	177	178	179	180	181	
JULY	198	199	200	201	202	203	204	205	206	207	208	209	210	211	212
AUGUST	229	230	231	232	233	234	235	236	237	238	239	240	241	242	243
SEPTEMBER	260	261	262	263	264	265	266	267	268	269	270	271	272	273	
OCTOBER	290	291	292	293	294	295	296	297	298	299	300	301	302	303	304
NOVEMBER	321	322	323	324	325	326	327	328	329	330	331	332	333	334	
DECEMBER	351	352	353	354	355	356	357	358	359	360	361	362	363	364	365

Figure B (Continued)

which have elapsed thus far + the number of days which have elapsed since Jan. 1 of the given year + the number of leap years which have occurred since year 1) = the number of days of the week. The calculation of the number of leap years must take into account the fact that those years whose number ends with two zeros, which are not divisible by 400, are not leap years. Thus from the total number of leap years, a certain number of leap years must be subtracted.

Example: Dec. 25, 1954. $1 + 1953 + 488$ (leap years) -15 (century leap years $19 - 4$) $+ 358$ (number of days between Jan. 1, 1954, and Dec. 25, 1954) $= 2785$ Dividing by 7 gives remainder 6. Thus Dec. 25, 1954, fell on the sixth day of the week, Saturday.

Many other tables and mechanisms have been devised to solve the problem of determining days. The following are two nomograms devised for this.

The first (see Figure C) consists of four scales and is to be used as follows:

1. With a straightedge, join the point on the first scale indicating the date with the proper month on the third scale. Mark the point of intersection with the second scale.

2. Join this point on the second scale with the point on the fourth scale indicating the proper century. Mark the point of intersection with the third scale.

3. Join this point with the point indicating the appropriate year on the first scale. The point of intersection with the second scale gives the desired day of the week. (N.B. For the months of January and February use the year diminished by 1.)

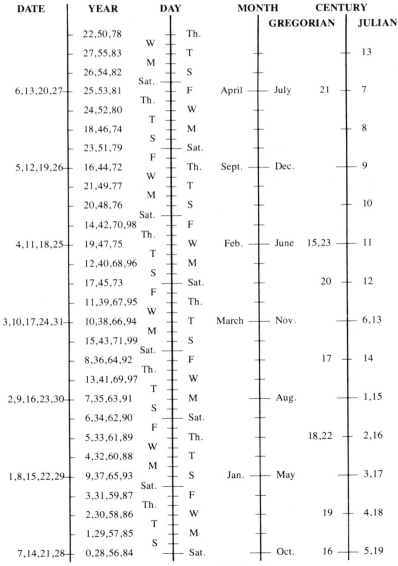

Figure C. *Perpetual Calendar.*

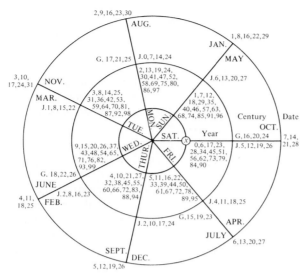

Figure D. *Perpetual Calendar, Radius-ring Type*.

The second arrangement (see Figure D) consists of three concentric rings intersected by seven radii. The procedure is: 1) Locate the date and the month on the outer ring; if they are two points, draw a line between them; if they coincide, draw a tangent. 2) Locate the century on the intermediate ring. Through this point draw a line parallel to the line drawn, until it intersects the intermediate ring at another point. The point found will be a ring-radius intersection. 3) From the point just found, follow the radius to the inner ring, then locate the year. (If the month is Jan. or Feb. use the preceding year.) Draw a line between these two points on the inner ring. (If they coincide on Saturday, then Saturday is the weekday sought.) 4) Now find the point where the Saturday radius cuts the inner ring, and through this Saturday point draw a line parallel to the line just drawn. The line will meet the inner ring at some radius-ring intersection. The weekday on this latter radius is the weekday of the date with which we began.

The problem of a perpetual calendar occupied the attention of many mathematicians and many of them devoted considerable attention to calculating the date of Easter Sunday. All church holidays fall on a definite date. The ecclesiastical rule regarding Easter is, however, rather complicated. Easter must fall on the Sunday after the first full moon which occurs after the Vernal (Spring) Equinox. Easter Sunday, therefore, is a movable Feast which may fall as early as March 22 or as late as April 25. The following procedure to find Easter Sunday in any year from 1900–1999 is based on a method developed by Gauss.

1. Find the remainder when the year is divided by 4. Call this remainder a.

2. Find the remainder when the year is divided by 7. Call this remainder b.

3. Find the remainder when the year is divided by 19. Multiply this remainder by 19, add 24, and again find the remainder when the total is divided by 30. Call this remainder c.

4. Now add $2a + 4b + 6c + 3$. Divide this total by 7 and call the remainder d.

The sum of c and d will give the number of days after March 22 on which Easter Sunday will fall.

Example: Easter 1921
(1) 21/4 leaves 1
(2) 21/7 leaves 0
(3) 21/19 leaves 2; [2(19) + 24]/30 leaves 2
(4) [2 + 0 + 12 + 3] /7 leaves 3
    2 + 3 = 5 days after March 22 = March 27

(The method above gives the date accurately except for the years 1954 and 1981. These years it gives a date exactly 1 week late, the correct Easters being April 18 and 19 respectively.)

Postassessment

1. Have the students determine the day of the week of their birth.

2. Have the students work out several given dates.

Oct. 12, 1492	May 30, 1920	Christmas 1978
April 1, 1945	Oct. 21, 1805	August 14, 1898
		July 4, 1776

3. Have the students find the dates of several Easter Sundays.

  1944, 1969, 1950, 1978, 1930, 1977, 1929

4. George Washington was born February 11, 1732. Why do we celebrate it February 22?

8   Palindromic Numbers

This unit will define palindromic numbers and introduce some of their properties. The study of palindromic numbers is suited for any class: while it provides all students an approach for analyzing numbers and their relationships, certain aspects of this topic can be selected for the slow students (e.g., the reverse addition property) while more advanced properties can be investigated by the more adept students (e.g., modular palindromes).

Performance Objectives

1. Students will state and analyze properties of palindromic numbers.

2. Students will construct new palindromes from any specified integer.

Preassessment

Have students analyze the expression "Madam I'm Adam" and the words "rotator" and "reviver" and point out their peculiarity (they spell the same backward and forward). Indicate to them that such an expression is called a palindrome and that in mathematics, numbers having the same property like 343 and 59695 are called palindromic numbers. Students can be asked to give their own examples of palindromic numbers and make a short list.

Teaching Strategies

After the students have compiled their lists, an analysis can be made of these numbers. Questions such as the following can be put to them to get a discussion going: Does a palindrome have an odd or even number of digits, or both? Are palindromic numbers prime, composite, or both? Is the square or cube of a palindromic number still a palindrome? Given a positive integer can a palindrome be constructed from some sort of operation on this integer? Students can attempt to answer these questions by testing their validity on the numbers from their lists or by seeking some new ones.

The students are ready at this point to study some of the following palindromic properties:

1. Palindromic numbers contain both prime and composite numbers (e.g., 181 is a palindromic prime while 575 is a composite palindrome); however, a palindromic prime, with the exception of 11, must have an odd number of digits.

Proof of the latter: (by contradiction)

Let p be a palindromic prime having an even number of digits. Let r be the sum of all digits in the even positions of the prime p and s be the sum of all the digits in the odd positions of the prime p. Since p is a palindrome with an even number of digits, the digits in odd positions duplicate the digits in even positions; therefore $s - r = 0$. But the test for divisibility by 11 states that a number is divisible by 11 if the difference between the sum of all digits in even positions and the sum of all digits in odd positions is 0 or a multiple of 11. Therefore, p has 11 as a factor and cannot be prime, a contradiction.

2. All integers N which yield palindromic squares are not necessarily palindromes. While there are infinitely many palindromes yielding palindromic squares (e.g., $22^2 = 484$ and $212^2 = 44944$), there exist some non-palindromic integers whose squares are palindromes (e.g., $26^2 = 676$ and $836^2 = 698896$) as well as some palindromic integers yielding non-palindromic squares (e.g., $131^2 = 17161$ and $232^2 = 53824$).

Repunits, numbers consisting entirely of 1's (by notation, R_k where k is the number of 1's) are palindromic numbers and produce palindromic squares when $1 \le k \le 9$: $R_2^2 = 121$: $R_3^2 = 12321$ and in general $R_k^2 = 12 \ldots k \ldots 21$, where $k = 9$. However, when $k > 9$ the carrying in addition would lose the palindromic product (e.g., $R_{10}^2 = 12 \ldots 6790098 \ldots 21$).

It has been found that square numbers are much richer in palindromes than randomly chosen integers.

3. In general, numbers which yield palindromic cubes (some of which are prime and some composite) are palindromic in themselves. The numbers N which yield palindromic cubes are as follows:

a) $N = 1, 7, 11$ ($1^3 = 1$, $7^3 = 343$, $11^3 = 1331$)

b) $N = 10^k + 1$ has a palindromic cube consisting of $k - 1$ zeros between each consecutive pair of 1,3,3,1: e.g., when $k = 1$, $N = 11$ and $N^3 = 1331$; when $k = 2$, $N = 101$ and $N^3 = 1030301$; when $k = 3$, $N = 1001$ and $N^3 = 1003003001$, etc. Notice that when $k = 2m + 1$, $m > 0$, then N is divisible by 11 and hence is composite.

c) N consisting of 3 1's and any desired number (which must be even) of zeros is divisible by 3 and has palindromic cubes: e.g., $(111)^3 = 1367631$, $(10101)^3 = 1030607060301$.

d) $N =$ any palindromic arrangement of zeros and four 1's is a non-prime and has a palindromic cube, except when the same number of zeros appears in the three spaces between the 1's: e.g., $(11011)^3 = 1334996994331$, $(10100101)^3 = 1003033091390931903303001$, whereas $(1010101)^3$ is not a palindrome.

The only $N < 2.8 \times 10^{14}$ which is not a palindrome yet yields a palindromic cube is $2201^3 = 10662526601$.

4. *Given any integer N we can often reach a palindrome by adding the number to its reversal (the number obtained by reversing the digits) and continuing the process until the palindrome is achieved.* For example, if $N = 798$, then $798 + 897 = 1695$, $1695 + 5961 = 7656$, $7656 + 6567 = 14223$, $14223 + 32241 = 46464$ (a palindrome). Whereas some numbers can reach a palindrome in only two steps (e.g., 75 and 48), there are others that reach it in 6 steps like 97, and still others like 89 and 98 that reach a palindrome in 24 steps. It has been found, however, that certain numbers like 196 when carried out to over 1000 steps still do not achieve palindromes so that this rule cannot be taken to hold for all integers but certainly for most since these cases are very rare. It has been proven that the rule does not hold in base two: the smallest counterexample is 10110 which after 4 steps reaches the sum 10*11*01*00*, after 8 steps it is 10*111*01*000*, after 12 steps it is 10*1111*01*0000*. Every fourth step increases by one digit each of the two sequences underlined and it is seen that each of these increasing sums is not a palindrome. There are some generalities found in this process of reverse addition:

(a) Different integers when subjected to this technique produce the same palindrome. For example, 554, 752, and 653 all produce the palindrome 11011 in 3 steps. In general, all integers in which the corresponding digit pairs symmetrical to the middle have the same sum will produce the same palindrome in the same number of steps. (In this case, all the digit pairs add up to 9.) There are however different integers

which produce the same palindrome in different numbers of steps. For example, 99 reaches 79497 in 6 steps whereas 7299 reaches it in 2 steps.

(b) Two digit numbers can be categorized according to the total sum of the two digits to ascertain the number of steps needed to produce a palindrome. It is obvious that if the sum of the digits is 9, only 1 step is needed; if their digit sum is 10 (e.g., 64 and 73), 2 steps are needed. Similar analyses will lead the students to conclude that if their digit sum is 11, 12, 13, 14, 15, 16, 17, or 18, a palindrome results after 1, 2, 2, 3, 4, 6, 24, and 1 respectively. The students can be asked to perform an analysis of this type and put their results in table form.

This topic of palindromes can be investigated further by more adept students. Further investigation lies in the areas of multigrades with palindromic numbers as elements, special palindromic prime numbers such as primes with prime digits as elements, modular palindromes, and triangular and pentagonal numbers that are also palindromes.

Postassessment

1. Do the following numbers yield palindromic cubes: (a) 1001001 (b) 1001001001 (c) 10100101 (d) 100101

2. Given the following 2 digit numbers, indicate the number of steps required in reversal addition to reach a palindrome: (a) 56 (b) 26 (c) 91 (d) 96

3. Perform the reverse addition technique on these integers and find other integers that will yield the same palindrome as these: (a) 174 (b) 8699

9   The Fascinating Number Nine

This unit is intended to offer a recreational presentation of the many interesting properties of the number 9. A long range goal of presenting these amusing number topics is to motivate further student investigation and insight into the properties of numbers.

Performance Objectives

1. Students will demonstrate at least three properties of the number nine.

2. Students will provide an example of a short-cut calculation involving the number nine.

Preassessment

Students should be familiar with the various field postulates and be reasonably adept with the operations

of addition, subtraction, multiplication, and division. A knowledge of algebra is helpful but not essential.

Teaching Strategies

In presenting new ideas to a class it is always best to build on what they already know. For example, ask students to multiply 53×99. Unsuspecting students will perform the calculation in the usual way. After their work has been completed, suggest the following:

$$\begin{aligned} \text{Since} \quad 99 &= 100 - 1 \\ 53 \times 99 &= 53\,(100 - 1) \\ &= 53\,(100) - 53(1) \\ &= 5300 - 53 \\ &= 5247 \end{aligned}$$

Now have them use this technique to multiply 42×999.

"Casting Out Nines" is a popular technique for checking calculations. For example, if students wish to check the addition $29+57+85+35+6 = 212$, they simply divide each number in the addition by 9 and retain only the remainder. Thus they have 2, 3, 4, 8, and 6, the sum of which is 23. (See below)

$$29 \rightarrow \quad 2$$
$$57 \rightarrow \quad 3$$
$$85 \rightarrow \quad 4$$
$$35 \rightarrow \quad 8$$
$$+ \; 6 \rightarrow + \; 6$$
$$\overline{212 \quad \quad 23}$$

The remainder of $212 \div 9$ is 5. If the remainder of $212 \div 9$ is the same as the remainder of $23 \div 9$, then 212 could be the correct answer. In this case, where 5 is the remainder of both divisions by 9; 212 *could* be the correct answer. Students cannot be sure from this checking method whether in fact this answer is correct since a rearrangement of the digits, to say 221, would also yield the same remainder when divided by 9.

It is interesting to note that division by 9 is not necessary to find the remainder. All one has to do is add the digits of the number (to be divided by 9) and, if the result is not a single digit number, repeatedly add the digits until a single digit remains. In the above example the remainders are:

for 29: $2 + 9 = 11; 1 + 1 = 2$
for 57: $5 + 7 = 12; 1 + 2 = 3$
for 85: $8 + 5 = 13; 1 + 1 = 4$
for 35: $3 + 5 = 8$
for   6: 6

for the sum of $2 + 3 + 4 + 8 + 6 = 23: 2 + 3 = 5$
for 212: $2 + 1 + 2 = 5$

Students can use a similar procedure for other operations. For example, to check a multiplication operation: $239 \times 872 = 208,408$, they will find the remainders (when divided by 9) of each of the above numbers.

for 239: $2 + 3 + 9 = 14; 1 + 4 = 5$
for 872: $8 + 7 + 2 = 17; 1 + 7 = 8$
for the product $5 \times 8 = 40; 4 + 0 = 4$
for 208,408: $2 + 0 + 8 + 4 + 0 + 8 = 22; 2 + 2 = 4$

Stress to your classes that this is not a fool-proof check of a calculation, but simply one indication of possible correctness. Present this topic in a way which will have them begin to marvel at the interesting properties of the number 9.

Another unusual property of 9 occurs in the multiplication of 9 and any other number of 2 or more digits. Consider the example $65,437 \times 9$. An alternative to the usual algorithm is as follows:

1. Subtract the units digit of the multiplicand from 10. $10 - 7 = \boxed{3}$
2. Subtract each of the remaining digits from 9 and add the rest to the preceding number of the multiplicand (at right). For any two-digit sums carry the tens digit to the next sum.

$9 - 3 = 6 + 7 = 1\boxed{3}$
$9 - 4 = 5 + 3 + 1 = \boxed{9}$
$9 - 5 = 4 + 4 = \boxed{8}$
$9 - 6 = 3 + 5 = \boxed{8}$

3. Subtract 1 from the left-most digit of the multiplicand. $6 - 1 = \boxed{5}$
4. Now list the results in reverse order to get the desired product. $\boxed{588,933}$

Although this method is somewhat cumbersome, it can set the groundwork for some rather interesting investigations into number theory.

To further intrigue your students with other fascinating properties of the number 9, have them multiply 12,345,679 by the first nine multiples of 9, and record their results:

12345679	×	9	=	111,111,111
12345679	×	18	=	222,222,222
12345679	×	27	=	333,333,333
12345679	×	36	=	444,444,444
12345679	×	45	=	555,555,555
12345679	×	54	=	666,666,666
12345679	×	63	=	777,777,777
12345679	×	72	=	888,888,888
12345679	×	81	=	999,999,999

Students should realize that in the sequence of natural numbers (making up the above multiplicands) the number 8 was omitted. In other words, the number that is two less than the base, 10, is missing. Ask students how to extend this scheme to bases other than 10.

Now have them reverse the sequence of natural numbers including the 8, and multiply each by the first nine multiples of 9. The results will be astonishing:

987654321	×	9	=	8 888 888 889
987654321	×	18	=	17 777 777 778
987654321	×	27	=	26 666 666 667
987654321	×	36	=	35 555 555 556
987654321	×	45	=	44 444 444 445
987654321	×	54	=	53 333 333 334
987654321	×	63	=	62 222 222 223
987654321	×	72	=	71 111 111 112
987654321	×	81	=	80 000 000 001

Some other interesting properties of the number 9 are exhibited below. Have students discover them by carefully guiding them to the desired result. Stronger students should be encouraged to investigate these relationships and discover *why* they "work."

1.
$$9 \times 9 = 81$$
$$99 \times 99 = 9801$$
$$999 \times 999 = 998001$$
$$9999 \times 9999 = 99980001$$
$$99999 \times 99999 = 9999800001$$
$$999999 \times 999999 = 999998000001$$
$$9999999 \times 9999999 = 99999980000001$$

2.
$$999999 \times 2 = 1999998$$
$$999999 \times 3 = 2999997$$
$$999999 \times 4 = 3999996$$
$$999999 \times 5 = 4999995$$
$$999999 \times 6 = 5999994$$
$$999999 \times 7 = 6999993$$
$$999999 \times 8 = 7999992$$
$$999999 \times 9 = 8999991$$

3.
$$1 \times 9 + 2 = 11$$
$$12 \times 9 + 3 = 111$$
$$123 \times 9 + 4 = 1111$$
$$1234 \times 9 + 5 = 11111$$
$$12345 \times 9 + 6 = 111111$$
$$123456 \times 9 + 7 = 1111111$$
$$1234567 \times 9 + 8 = 11111111$$
$$12345678 \times 9 + 9 = 111111111$$

4.
$$9 \times 9 + 7 = 88$$
$$98 \times 9 + 6 = 888$$
$$987 \times 9 + 5 = 8888$$
$$9876 \times 9 + 4 = 88888$$
$$98765 \times 9 + 3 = 888888$$
$$987654 \times 9 + 2 = 8888888$$
$$9876543 \times 9 + 1 = 88888888$$
$$98765432 \times 9 + 0 = 888888888$$

An interesting way to conclude this Model would be to offer your students a seemingly harmless challenge. That is, ask them to find an eight-digit number in which no digit appears more than once, and which, when multiplied by 9, yields a nine-digit number in which no digit appears more than once. Most of their attempts will fail. For example, $76541238 \times 9 = 688,871,142$, which has repeated 8's and 1's. Here are several correct numbers:

$$81274365 \times 9 = 731469285$$
$$72645831 \times 9 = 653812479$$
$$58132764 \times 9 = 523194876$$
$$76125483 \times 9 = 685129347$$

Postassessment

Ask students to:

1. Demonstrate three unusual properties of 9.

2. Show a short cut for multiplying 547×99.

3. Explain now to "check" a multiplication calculation by "casting out nines."

10   Unusual Number Properties

(Author's Note: This unit should be used after the unit entitled "Enrichment with a Hand-Held Calculator.")

The intention of this unit is to present a good supply of interesting number properties that can be best exhibited on a calculator.

Performance Objective

Students will investigate mathematical problems with the help of a hand calculator and then draw appropriate conclusions.

Preassessment

Students should be familiar with the basic functions of a calculator. The instrument required for this unit need only have the four basic operations.

Teaching Strategies

Perhaps one of the best ways to stimulate genuine excitement in mathematics is to demonstrate some short, simple and dramatic mathematical phenomena. The following are some examples that should provide you with ample material with which to motivate your students toward some independent investigations.

Example 1

When 37 is multiplied by each of the first nine multiples of 3 an interesting result occurs. Let students discover this using their calculators.

$$37 \times 3 = 111$$
$$37 \times 6 = 222$$
$$37 \times 9 = 333$$
$$37 \times 12 = 444$$
$$37 \times 15 = 555$$
$$37 \times 18 = 666$$
$$37 \times 21 = 777$$
$$37 \times 24 = 888$$
$$37 \times 27 = 999$$

Example 2

When 142,857 is multiplied by 2, 3, 4, 5, and 6, the products all use the same digits in the same order as in the original numbers, but each starting at a different point.

$$142,857 \times 2 = 285,714$$
$$142,857 \times 3 = 428,571$$
$$142,857 \times 4 = 571,428$$
$$142,857 \times 5 = 714,285$$
$$142,857 \times 6 = 857,142$$

When 142,857 is multiplied by 7, the product is 999,999. When 142,857 is multiplied by 8, the product is 1,142,856. If the millions digit is removed and added to the units digit (142,856 + 1) the original number is formed. Have students investigate the product $142,857 \times 9$. What other patterns can be found involving products of 142,857?

A similar pattern occurs with the following products of 76,923: 1, 10, 9, 12, 3, and 4; also 2, 5, 7, 11, 6, and 8. Ask students to inspect the sum of the digits of each of the products obtained. They should discover a truly fascinating result! Ask if they can find other such relationships.

Example 3

The number 1089 has many interesting properties. Have students consider the products of 1089 and each of the first nine natural numbers.

$$1089 \times 1 = 1089$$
$$1089 \times 2 = 2178$$
$$1089 \times 3 = 3267$$
$$1089 \times 4 = 4356$$
$$1089 \times 5 = 5445$$
$$1089 \times 6 = 6534$$
$$1089 \times 7 = 7623$$
$$1089 \times 8 = 8712$$
$$1089 \times 9 = 9801$$

Tell students to notice the symmetry of the first two and last two columns of the products. Each column lists consecutive integers. Encourage students not just to establish and explain this unusual occurrence, but also to build on it. What makes 1089 so unusual? What are the factors of 1089? Why does 1089×9 reverse the number 1089? Does a similar scheme work for other numbers? These questions and others should begin to set the tone for further investigation. Naturally students' calculators will be an indispensable tool in their work. The calculators will permit students to see patterns rapidly and without the side-tracking often caused by cumbersome calculations.

Example 4

Some other interesting number patterns for students to generate are given below. Be sure to encourage students to extend the patterns produced and to try to discover why they exist.

$$1 \times 8 + 1 = 9$$
$$12 \times 8 + 2 = 98$$
$$123 \times 8 + 3 = 987$$
$$1,234 \times 8 + 4 = 9,876$$
$$12,345 \times 8 + 5 = 98,765$$
$$123,456 \times 8 + 6 = 987,654$$
$$1,234,567 \times 8 + 7 = 9,876,543$$
$$12,345,678 \times 8 + 8 = 98,765,432$$
$$123,456,789 \times 8 + 9 = 987,654,321$$

$$11 \times 11 = 121$$
$$111 \times 111 = 12,321$$
$$1,111 \times 1,111 = 1,234,321$$
$$11,111 \times 11,111 = 123,454,321$$
$$111,111 \times 111,111 = 12,345,654,321$$
$$1,111,111 \times 1,111,111 = 1,234,567,654,321$$
$$11,111,111 \times 11,111,111 = 123,456,787,654,321$$
$$111,111,111 \times 111,111,111 = 12,345,678,987,654,321$$

Example 5

Have your students compute the divisions indicated by each of the following fractions. Tell them to record their results.

$$\frac{1}{7} = .\overline{142857} = \frac{142857}{999999}$$

$$\frac{2}{7} = .\overline{285714} = \frac{285714}{999999}$$

$$\frac{3}{7} = .\overline{428571} = \frac{428571}{999999}$$

$$\frac{4}{7} = .\overline{571428} = \frac{571428}{999999}$$

$$\frac{5}{7} = .\overline{714285} = \frac{714285}{999999}$$

$$\frac{6}{7} = .\overline{857142} = \frac{857142}{999999}$$

Students will notice the similar order of the repeating part along with the different starting points. Point out that the product of $7 \times .142857 = .999999$ (which is *close* to $7 \times \frac{1}{7} = 1$). Remind students that this is not the same as $7 \times .\overline{142857}$.

Some students may want to inspect this product in a nondecimal form:

$$7 \times 142,857 = 999,999$$
$$= 999,000 + 999$$
$$= 1,000(142 + 857) + (142 + 857)$$
$$= (142 + 857)(1000 + 1)$$
$$= 1001(142 + 857)$$
$$= 142,142 + 857,857$$

A better insight into an investigation of these fractions would come after students have already calculated the following quotients:

$$\frac{1}{13} = .\overline{076923} = \frac{076923}{999999}$$

$$\frac{3}{13} = .\overline{230769} = \frac{230769}{999999}$$

$$\frac{4}{13} = .\overline{307692} = \frac{307692}{999999}$$

$$\frac{9}{13} = .\overline{692307} = \frac{692307}{999999}$$

$$\frac{10}{13} = .\overline{769230} = \frac{769230}{999999}$$

$$\frac{12}{13} = .\overline{923076} = \frac{923076}{999999}$$

Once these have been fully discussed, students may wish to consider the remaining proper fractions with a denominator of 13. They should discover similar patterns and relationships.

The positive impact of the above *Examples* will be lost if students are not immediately guided to investigate and extend their discoveries. While the calculator is the guiding tool for discovering new relationships,

students' logical conjectures will come from a deeper investigation of the properties of numbers.

Postassessment

Have students complete the following exercises.

1. Multiply and add each of the following pairs of numbers:

$$\left.\begin{array}{c} 9,9 \\ 24,3 \\ 47,2 \\ 497,2 \end{array}\right\}.$$

How do their sums compare with their products? (reverses) ·

2. Perform the indicated operations and justify the resulting patterns. Then extend the pattern and see if it holds true.

$$12321 = \frac{333 \times 333}{1+2+3+2+1} = \frac{110889}{9}$$
$$= 12321$$

$$1234321 = \frac{4444 \times 4444}{1+2+3+4+3+2+1} = \frac{19749136}{16}$$
$$= 1234321$$

11   Enrichment With A Hand-Held Calculator

In recent years, with the increased accessibility of the hand-held calculator, mathematics teachers have had the responsibility of finding (or developing) a place for this useful tool in the current curriculum. One of the most frequently observed uses of the calculator is that of providing some excitement to remedial drill work. Here the calculator is merely used to check a student's drill calculation. Experience shows that this novelty seems to wear off soon and then loses its effectiveness as a motivational device.

A longer range and more effective use of the calculator is as a problem-solving facilitator. Students who have difficulty solving problems are often faced with a double dilemma. They are unable to interpret the given problem into a solvable form, and they are unable to do the calculations necessary to compute an answer. Normally they cannot concentrate on problem solving until they can do the necessary calculations. However, by using the calculator, they can temporarily avoid the calculations pitfall and thereby concentrate on the key to successful problem solving: interpretation. When this aspect has been

learned a student can concentrate on mastering calculations as an essential ingredient in problem solving.

The calculator also has a very definite place in mathematics enrichment. This unit presents some enrichment activities involving the calculator. In most cases the calculator will provide ideas which will serve as a springboard for further student investigation. In effect, the instrument will be a discovery and motivational device.

Performance Objective

Students will investigate mathematical problems with the help of a hand calculator and then draw appropriate conclusions.

Preassessment

Students should be familiar with the basic function of a calculator. The instrument required for this unit need have only the four basic operations.

For both practice and amusement, have students do the following on their calculators.

1. Compute:

   $2[60 - .243 + (12)(2400)] - 1$. To find what every man must pay read your answer upside down.

2. Compute:

   $4590.5864 + (568.3)(.007) - 1379.26$. Then turn your calculator upside down and after reading your answer, look inside your shoe.

These two exercises should give your students a relaxed feeling about working with calculators.

Teaching Strategies

Begin the lesson with a simple but intriguing oddity. Have students consider the calendar for the month of May 1977. Tell them to make a square around *any* nine dates; one way to do so is shown in the figure below.

Next, students should add 8 to the smallest number in the square and multiply it by 9. In the above example, we have $(11 + 8) \times 9 = 171$. Then students can use their calculators to multiply the sum of the numbers in the middle row (or column) by 3 and find the same result, 171. Have your students try this for other selections of 9 numbers. You should have them realize that the sum of the numbers in the middle row or column multiplied by 3 is in fact the sum of the 9 numbers. Students can verify this easily with their calculators.

From this point, you have an excellent opportunity to investigate properties of the arithmetic mean, as such study will shed more light on this cute "calendar trick." Students should realize that the *middle number* of the square of 9 numbers is in fact the arithmetic mean of the selected numbers. The use of the calculator will relieve them of burdensome computations and permit them to focus all their attention on the mathematical concepts being discovered.

For their next number investigation, have your students select any 3-digit number, say 538. Then have

them enter it twice into their calculators, without pressing any operation buttons. Their display should show 538538. Now have them divide by 7, then divide by 11, then divide by 13. Much to their surprise they will find their original number displayed. Immediately, student curiosity will arise. Ask them what single operation can be used to replace the 3 divisions. They should realize that a single division by $7 \times 11 \times 13 = 1001$ was actually performed. Since $538 \times 1001 = 538538$, the puzzle is essentially solved; yet students may wish to try this scheme on their calculators using other numbers. This should strengthen their knowledge about numbers, especially 1001, a rather significant number.

Students should now be motivated to try the following multiplications so that they can begin to appreciate (and predict) number patterns:

(a) $3 \times 11 = 33$ (b) $4 \times 101 = 404$
    $3 \times 111 = 333$ $4 \times 10101 = 40404$
    $3 \times 1111 = 3333$ $4 \times 1010101 = 4040404$
    $3 \times 11111 = 33333$ $4 \times 101010101 = 404040404$

(c) $5 \times 1001 = 5005$ (d) $65 \times 101 = 6565$
    $5 \times 110011 = 550055$ $65 \times 10101 = 656565$
    $5 \times 11100111 = 55500555$ $65 \times 1010101 = 65656565$

(e) $65 \times 1001 = 65065$ (f) $7 \times 11 = 77$
    $65 \times 10001 = 650065$ $7 \times 11 \times 101 = 7777$
    $65 \times 100001 = 6500065$ $7 \times 11 \times 10101 = 777777$
    $65 \times 1001001 = 65065065$ $7 \times 111 \times 1001 = 777777$

Now have students discover other ways of generating by multiplication: 777777, 7777777, and 77777777. At this point students ought to be interested enough to establish other number patterns from products.

Most of your students should now be ready to consider somewhat more sophisticated problems.

A *palindrome* is defined as "a word or verse reading the same backward or forward, e.g. *madam, I'm Adam.*" In mathematics a number which reads the same in either direction is a palindrome. For example, have your students select any 2-digit number and add to it the number whose digits are the reverse order of the original one. Now have them take the sum and add it to the number whose digits are in the reverse order. They should continue this process until a palindrome is formed. For example:

$75 + 57 = 132$
$132 + 231 = 363$, a *palindrome*

$79 + 97 = 176$
$176 + 671 = 847$
$847 + 748 = 1595$
$1595 + 5951 = 7546$
$7546 + 6457 = 14003$
$14003 + 30041 = 44044$, a *palindrome*

No matter which original 2-digit number is selected, a palindrome will eventually be formed. Using a calculator the students will see various patterns arising, which should lead them to discover why this actually "works."

Encourage your students to carefully conjecture about other possible number relationships and then verify them using a calculator.

Tell your students to use their calculators to verify

the following phenomenon for 6 different numbers. Then they should try to prove it.

Select any 3-digit number in which the hundreds digit and the units digit are unequal. Then write the number whose digits are in the reverse order from the selected number. Now subtract the smaller of these 2 numbers from the larger. Take the difference, reverse its digits, and add the "new" number to the original difference. What number do you always end up with? Why?

12 Symmetric Multiplication

This unit shows how some numbers, because of their symmetry, can be multiplied easily through the use of "form multiplication."

Performance Objective
Given a form multiplication example, students will perform the multiplication using the technique described in this unit.

Preassessment
Have students multiply each of the following by conventional means:
(a) 66666×66666 (b) 2222×2222 (c) 333×777

Teaching Strategies
After students have completed the above computations, they will probably welcome a more novel approach to these problems. Have them consider the following rhombic form approach.

$$
\begin{array}{r}
66666 \\
\times\ 66666 \\
\hline
36 \\
3636 \\
363636 \\
36363636 \\
3636363636 \\
36363636 \\
363636 \\
3636 \\
36 \\
\hline
44443555556
\end{array}
$$

Students might wonder if this scheme works for other numbers of this type. Have them square 88888 first by conventional method and then by rhombic form multiplication. To do the latter, students should replace the "36's" in the previous example with "64's." Soon students will wonder how to extend this multiplication technique to squaring a repeated-digit number where the square of a digit is a *one-digit* number.

In squaring a number such as 2222, students must write each partial product as 04.

$$
\begin{array}{r}
2222 \\
\times\ 2222 \\
\hline
04 \\
0404 \\
040404 \\
04040404 \\
040404 \\
0404 \\
04 \\
\hline
4937284
\end{array}
$$

At this juncture students may be convinced that this will be true for all numbers of this type. Have them consider squaring an n-digit number $uuu\ldots uuu$, where $u^2 = 10s + t$ (or written in base 10 as st). This multiplication would require an nth order rhombic form (i.e. one which increases the number of st's by one in each of the first n rows, and then decreases by one st in each of the remaining $n - 1$ rows). The case where $n = 5$ is shown below.

$$
\begin{array}{r}
uuuuu \\
\times\ uuuuu \\
\hline
st \\
stst \\
ststst \\
stststst \\
ststststst \\
stststst \\
ststst \\
stst \\
st \\
\hline
\end{array}
$$

Students will be interested to notice that this multiplication technique can be further extended to finding the product of two *different* repeated-digit numbers. That is, if the product of *uuu...u* and *vvvv...v* is sought, then the rhombic form of *st*'s is formed, where $uv = 10s + t$. For example, the product of $8888 \times 3333 = 29623704$ or:

```
        8888
      × 3333
          24
        2424
      242424
    24242424
      242424
        2424
          24
    29623704
```

When students have mastered the rhombic form of multiplying repeated-digit numbers, you might want to show them another form of repeated-digit multiplication. A *triangular* form of multiplication is shown below. Notice that after students sum the triangular array, they must multiply by 6.

```
         66666
       × 66666
             6
           666
         66666
       6666666
     666666666
     740725926
           × 6
    4444355556
```

In general, to square an *n* digit repeated-digit number, sum the columns of the triangular array of the repeated digit (where there are *n* rows beginning with a single digit and increasing succeeding rows by two digits), and then multiply this sum by the repeated digit.

This multiplication technique may be extended to finding the product of two different repeated digit numbers. Have students form their own rule after considering the following example.

```
        8888
      × 3333
           8
         888
       88888
     8888888
     9874568
         × 3
    29623704
```

```
        3333
      × 8888
           3
         333
       33333
     3333333
     3702963
         × 8
    29623704
```

Notice that the number of lines of the triangular form equals the number of digits in each number being multiplied. The rest of the rule can be easily elicited from the students.

The only other variation in the multiplication of repeated-digit numbers is when the number of digits of each number being multiplied is not the same. Suppose an *n* digit number is being multiplied by an *m* digit number. Set up the triangular form as if both numbers had *n* digits (as was done earlier). Then draw a diagonal to the right of the *m*th row and delete all the digits below the diagonal. The sum of the remaining digits is the desired product. The following example illustrates this procedure.

```
         44444
       × 666
            24
          2424
        242424
      24242424
    2424242424
      242.2424
        242424
          2424
            24
      29599704
```

Now have students multiply 66666×444. They should get the same array of numbers to be summed as above. This implies that $44444 \times 666 = 66666 \times 444$. After factoring, students should have no trouble justifying this equality.

Students should be encouraged to explain mathematically why the various form multiplications actually "work."

Postassessment

Have students compute each of the following using rhombic form multiplication:

a. 22222×77777 b. 9999×9999 c. 444×333

Have students compute each of the following using triangular form multiplication:

a. 555555×555555 b. 7777×4444

13 Variations on a Theme—Multiplication

This unit will present unconventional methods for determining the product of two integers.

Performance Objective
Given two integers and a method of multiplication, students will compute the product.

Preassessment
Have students compute the product of 43 and 92 by *more than one method.*

Teaching Strategies
The preceding problem should serve as excellent motivation for this unit. Most students will probably multiply the numbers correctly using the "conventional" method of multiplication shown below.

$$\begin{array}{r} 92 \\ \times\ 43 \\ \hline 276 \\ 368 \\ \hline 3956 \end{array}$$

Before discussing other methods of multiplication, the teacher should show why the "conventional" multiplication algorithm works. It may be easily seen that

$$\begin{aligned} 43 \times 92 &= (40+3) \times 92 \\ &= 40 \times 92 + 3 \times 92 \\ &= 3680 + 276 \\ &= 3956 \end{aligned}$$

which is exactly what is done, although mechanically.

The Doubling Method
To multiply 43 by 92 construct the following columns of numbers, starting with 1 and 92, and double each number.

•	1	92
•	2	184
	4	368
•	8	736
	16	1472
•	32	2944

We stop at 32 because twice 32 is 64 which is larger than 43. We start with the last number in the first column and add the appropriate numbers such that the sum is 43. Hence we choose (32, 8, 2, 1). Now we add the corresponding numbers in the second column.

$$\begin{array}{r} 92 \\ 184 \\ 736 \\ \underline{2944} \\ 3956 \end{array}$$

Therefore $43 \times 92 = 3956$. The reason this method works is illustrated below.

$$\begin{aligned} 43 \times 92 &= (32 + 8 + 2 + 1) \times 92 \\ &= (32 \times 92) + (8 \times 92) + (2 \times 92) + (1 \times 92) \\ &= 2944 + 736 + 184 + 92 \\ &= 3956 \end{aligned}$$

Russian Peasant Method
Again suppose we wish to multiply 43 and 92. Construct the following columns of numbers, starting with 43 and 92. In successive rows, halve the entries in the first column, rejecting the remainder of 1 when it occurs. In the second column, double each successive entry. This process continues until 1 appears in the first column.

*	43	92
*	21	184
	10	368
*	5	736
	2	1472
*	1	2944

Choose the numbers in the second column that corresponds to the "odd numbers" of the first column (those starred). Add those corresponding numbers of the second column and the result is the product of 43 and 92. That is, $92 + 184 + 736 + 2944 = 3956$. The proof that the Russian Peasant Method is always correct follows.

Assume "*a*" even: $a \cdot b = c$, where c is the desired result.

Assume "$\frac{1}{2}a$" odd: $\frac{1}{2}a - 2b = c$

The next step in the method is:

$$\left[\frac{1}{2}\left(\frac{1}{2}a \right) - \frac{1}{2} \right] \cdot 4b = y$$

Then using the distributive property:

$$\left[\frac{1}{4}a \cdot 4b \right] - \left[\frac{1}{2} \cdot 4b \right] = y$$

Since $\frac{1}{4}a \cdot 4b = c$, then $c - 2b = y$

Therefore the new product, y, will be short of the correct answer, c, by $2b$ (which is the first desired number to be added since it is paired with an odd number, $\frac{1}{2}a$).

As the process continues, the "new products" will remain the same if ka (an entry in the first column) is even. If ka is odd and $ka \cdot mb = w$, the next product will decrease by mb (the number matches with the odd number). For example, $\left(\dfrac{1}{2}ka - \dfrac{1}{2}\right) \cdot 2mb =$

$\left(\dfrac{1}{2}ka \cdot 2mb\right) - \left(\dfrac{1}{2} \cdot 2mb\right) = w - mb$

Finally when 1 appears in the first column:

$1 \cdot pb = Z$, with $pb = Z$

$Z = c -$ all deductions (numbers referred to above matched with odd ka's)

c (desired result) $= Z +$ all deductions

A further consideration of the Russian Peasant Method for multiplication can be seen from the following illustration:

$$
\begin{array}{llll}
*43 \cdot 92 & = (21 \cdot 2 + 1)(92) & = 21 \cdot 184 + 92 & = 3956 \\
*21 \cdot 184 & = (10 \cdot 2 + 1)(184) & = 10 \cdot 368 + 184 & = 3864 \\
10 \cdot 368 & = (5 \cdot 2 + 0)(368) & = 5 \cdot 736 + 0 & = 3680 \\
* \ 5 \cdot 736 & = (2 \cdot 2 + 1)(736) & = 2 \cdot 1472 + 736 & = 3680 \\
2 \cdot 1472 & = (1 \cdot 2 + 0)(1472) & = 1 \cdot 2944 + 0 & = 2944 \\
* \ 1 \cdot 2944 & = (0 \cdot 2 + 1)(2944) & = \quad\ \ 0 + 2944 & = 2944 \\
& & \hline & 3956
\end{array}
$$

Notice that summing only those numbers in the second column whose corresponding entries in the first column are odd, is justified by the above representation.

The teacher may wish to shed further light on this curiosity by presenting the binary nature of this multiplication.

$(43)(92)$

$= (1 \cdot 2^5 + 0 \cdot 2^4 + 1 \cdot 2^3 + 0 \cdot 2^2 + 1 \cdot 2^1 + 1 \cdot 2^0)(92)$

$= 2^0 \cdot 92 + 2^1 \cdot 92 + 2^3 \cdot 92 + 2^5 \cdot 92$

$= 92 + 184 + 736 + 2944$

$= 3956$

Other investigations should be encouraged by the students.

Lattice Multiplication

Once again consider the multiplication $43 \cdot 92$. To perform this method, a 2 by 2 array is constructed and diagonals are drawn as shown.

First multiply $3 \cdot 9 = 27$, the 2 is placed above the 7 as shown below.

The next step is to multiply $4 \cdot 9 = 36$. Again, the 3 is placed above the 6 in the appropriate box.

This process is continued, filling in the remainder of the square. Notice that $3 \cdot 2 = 6$ is recorded as $0/6$.

Now that there are entries in all cells, add the numbers in the diagonal directions indicated, beginning at the lower right. The sums are circled.

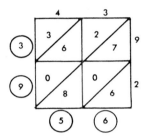

Notice that in the second addition, $8 + 0 + 7 = 15$, the 5 is recorded and the 1 is carried to the next diagonal addition. The correct answer (the product of $43 \cdot 92$) is then merely read from the circled numbers. That is, the answer is 3,956.

Trachtenberg System

The Trachtenberg System is a method for high-speed multiplication, division, addition, subtraction, and square root. There are numerous rules for these operations. Concern here will only be focused on the multiplication of two 2-digit numbers.

Again, suppose the product of 43 and 92 is desired.

Step 1. Multiply the two units digits

$$[3 \cdot 2 = 6]$$

$$
\begin{array}{r}
43 \\
\times 92 \\
\hline
6
\end{array}
$$

Step 2. Cross-multiply and add mentally

$$[(9 \cdot 3) + (2 \cdot 4) = 27 + 8 = 35]$$

Place the 5 as shown and carry the 3 (as an addend to the next step)

$$
\begin{array}{r}
43 \\
\times 92 \\
\hline
56
\end{array}
$$

Step 3. Multiply the two tens digits and then add any number carried over from the previous step.

$$[9 \cdot 4 = 36 \text{ and } 36 + 3 = 39]$$

$$
\begin{array}{r}
43 \\
\times \ 92 \\
\hline
3956
\end{array}
$$

The algebraic justification of this method is shown below:

Consider the two 2-digit numbers *ab* and *mn* (written in place-value form)

$$(10a + b) \cdot (10m + n)$$
$$= 10a \cdot 10m + 10a \cdot n + 10b \cdot m + bn$$
$$= \underbrace{100am}_{Step\ 3} + \underbrace{10an + bm}_{Step\ 2} + \underbrace{bn}_{Step\ 1}$$

Another Method

A multiple of ten "squared" is an easy mental computation. This method of multiplication incorporates this idea. Have students consider the product of $M \cdot N$. They then choose X such that $X = 10p$ and $M < X < N$ with $X - M = a$ and $N - X = b$. Then $M \cdot N = (X-a)(X+b) = X^2 - aX + bX - ab$.

Consider the multiplication of $43 \cdot 92$.

Let $X = 60$.

Then
$$43 \cdot 92 = (60-17)(60+32)$$
$$= 3600 + (-17 \cdot 60 + 60 \cdot 32) + (-17 \cdot 32)$$
$$= 3600 + (-1020 + 1920) + (-544)$$
$$= 3600 + 900 - 544$$
$$= 3956$$

However, if the numbers are the same distance from the multiple of ten, the method is much faster. The middle term will be eliminated!

Suppose students wish to multiply $57 \cdot 63$. Then $57 \cdot 63 = (60-3)(60+3) = 60^2 - 3^2 = 3600 - 9 = 3591$.

Part of the skill in working with different multiplication methods involves selection of the most efficient method for the particular problem. This should be stressed with the class.

Other Methods

Now that students have been exposed to several methods for multiplication, the teacher should suggest that students do research and explore other methods for multiplication. These could then be presented to the class.

Postassessment

1. Multiply 52 by 76 using any four different methods.

14 Ancient Egyptian Arithmetic

The study of a number system and its arithmetic is valuable to students on many levels. A student on a high level can delve into the mechanics of the system through an intricate comparison between that system and our own, and perhaps go off on a suitable tangent from there, such as an inspection of bases and still other number systems. For other students it can serve as a reinforcement of basic arithmetic (multiplication and division) both of integers and of fractions since the students will want to check if this system really works. This unit introduces students to the ancient Egyptian numerical notation and to their system of multiplying and dividing.

Performance Objectives

1) Given a multiplication problem, students will find the answer using an Egyptian method.

2) Given a division problem, students will find the answer using an Egyptian method.

3) Given a non-unit fraction, students will obtain its unit fraction decomposition.

Preassessment

Students should be familiar with addition and multiplication of fractions, as well as with the distributive property of real numbers. A knowledge of bases may also be useful.

Teaching Strategies

An example of a simple grouping system can be seen in the Egyptian hieroglyphics. This numeral system is based on the number 10. The symbols used when representing their numbers on stone, papyrus, wood and pottery were:

| for 1

∩ for 10

૭ for 10^2

ﻱ for 10^3

௴ for 10^4

Therefore, 13,521 would be represented as:

(Have students notice that the Egyptians wrote numbers from right to left.)

The Egyptians avoided a difficult multiplication or division method by using an easier (although at times longer) method. To multiply 14 by 27, they would have done the following:

	1	27
*	2	54
*	4	108
*	8	216
	16	432

To advance from any line to the next line, all the Egyptians had to do was double the number. Then, they picked out the numbers in the left-hand column that added up to 14 (the numbers with a *). By adding up the corresponding numbers in the right-hand column they arrived at the answer: $54 + 108 + 216 = 378$. This is an application of the distributive property of multiplication over addition, for what the Egyptians did is equivalent to:

$27(14) = 27(2 + 4 + 8) = 54 + 108 + 216 = 378$.

Further justification for the method lies in the fact that any number can be expressed as the sum of powers of two. Investigate this process with your students to the extent you feel necessary.

The Egyptians performed division in a similar way. They viewed the problem $114 \div 6$ as 6 times whatever number equals 114.

1	6 *
2	12 *
4	24
8	48
16	96 *

Now since $114 = 6 + 12 + 96$, the Egyptians would have found that $114 = 6(1 + 2 + 16)$ or $6 \times 19 = 114$. The answer is 19.

While no problems could arise in the Egyptian method of multiplication, a slight one occurs with respect to their method of division. To call attention to this problem, ask your class to use the above method to solve $83 \div 16$.

1	16 *
2	32
4	64 *
8	128

Using $16 + 64 = 80$, the Egyptians were still missing 3. Since $1 \times 16 = 16$, they found that they needed fractions to complete this problem.

In the Egyptian number system, every fraction except $\frac{2}{3}$ was represented as the sum of "unit fractions," fractions whose numerators are 1. In this way, the Egyptians avoided some of the computational problems one encounters when working with fractions. Since their arithmetic was based on doubling,

the only problem they had to deal with was how to change a fraction of the form $\frac{2}{n}$ to one of the form $\frac{1}{a} + \frac{1}{b} + \ldots$. They handled this problem with a table (found in the Rhind papyrus, dated approximately 1650 B.C.) which gives the decomposition of all fractions of the form $\frac{2}{n}$ for all odd n from 5 to 101. (Your class should be able to see why they considered only *odd n*.) A fraction such as $\frac{2}{37}$ was written as $\frac{1}{19} + \frac{1}{703}$ or, using the common notation for unit fractions, $\overline{19} + \overline{703}$. (This notation survives from the Egyptians who wrote a fraction such as $\frac{1}{4}$ as ⊓⊓⊓ and $\frac{1}{14}$ as ⊓⊓⊓ in hieroglyphics.) $\frac{2}{3}$ had its own symbol and sometimes $\frac{1}{2}$ appeared as .

The need now arises to consider a rule which can be used to decompose a fraction of the form $\frac{2}{pq}$ (where p or q may be 1). Have the class consider $\frac{2}{pq} = \frac{1}{\frac{p(p + q)}{2}} + \frac{1}{\frac{q(p + q)}{2}}$. They can add the fractions on the right side of the equation together to prove this is true. Also have them notice that since pq is odd (since we only need a rule to decompose $\frac{2}{n}$ where n is odd) p and q are odd, so $p + q$ will be even, and therefore $\frac{p + q}{2}$ will be an integer.

Students can decompose $\frac{2}{15}$ at least two ways. If they set $p = 3$ and $q = 5$ they will have $\frac{2}{15} = \frac{1}{\frac{3(8)}{2}} + \frac{1}{\frac{5(8)}{2}} = \frac{1}{12} + \frac{1}{20}$, or $\overline{12} + \overline{20}$. If they let $p = 1$ and $q = 15$ they will have $\frac{2}{15} = \frac{1}{\frac{1(16)}{2}} + \frac{1}{\frac{15(16)}{2}} = \frac{1}{8} + \frac{1}{120}$ or $\overline{8} + \overline{120}$.

It seems the Egyptians had other ways to decompose fractions so as to make the new denominator less complicated. For instance, we could also view $\frac{2}{15}$ as $\frac{4}{30}$.

Then we have $\frac{4}{30} = \frac{3}{30} + \frac{1}{30} = \overline{10} + \overline{30}$. Have students check these conversions.

Now, have students reconsider the earlier division problem $83 \div 16$.

1	16 *
2	32
4	64 *
8	128
$\overline{2}$	8
$\overline{4}$	4
$\overline{8}$	2 *
$\overline{16}$	1 *

By selecting a sum of 83 from the right column, they will arrive at the following answer: $1 + 4 + \overline{8} + \overline{16}$ $= 5 + \overline{8} + \overline{16} = 5\frac{3}{16}$. Students should now be able to solve their arithmetic problems using methods developed by the ancient Egyptians.

Postassessment

A. Have students write each of the following numbers in hieroglyphics.

1) 5,280   2) 23,057   3) $\frac{2}{25}$ 4) $\frac{2}{35}$

B. Have students change each of the following fractions into 2 different unit fraction decompositions.

1) $\frac{2}{27}$ 2) $\frac{2}{45}$ 3) $\frac{2}{99}$

C. Have students solve the following problems using Egyptian methods.

1) 30×41 2) 25×137 3) $132 \div 11$ 4) $101 \div 16$

15 Napier's Rods

Performance Objectives

1. Students will construct a cardboard set of Napier's Rods.

2. Students will successfully perform multiplication examples using Napier's Rods.

Preassessment

The only essential skill for this activity is the ability to do multiplication.

Teaching Strategies

Begin your presentation with a brief historical note about Napier's Rods. This multiplication "machine" was developed by John Napier (1550–1617), a Scotch mathematician, who was principally responsible for the development of logarithms. The device he developed consisted of flat wooden sticks with successive multiples of numbers 1–9. (See fig. 1)

Each student should be given an opportunity to construct his own set of Napier's Rods. Perhaps the best way to explain how to use Napier's Rods is to illustrate with an example using this device.

Consider the multiplication 523×467. Have students select the rods for 5, 2, and 3, and line them up adjacent to the Index Rod. (See fig. 2) Students must then select the appropriate rows from the index corresponding to the digits in the multiplier.

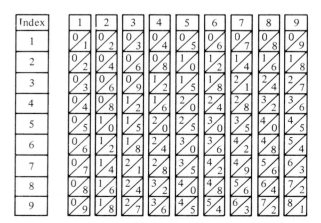

Figure 1

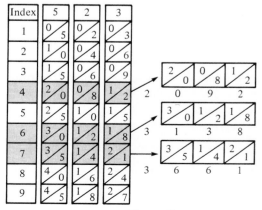

Figure 2

In a diagonal direction addition is done for each row (see fig. 2). The numbers thus obtained:

$$2092 = 4 \times 523$$
$$3138 = 6 \times 523$$
$$3661 = 7 \times 523$$

are added after considering the appropriate place values of the digits from which they were generated.

$$467 = 400 + 60 + 7$$
$$(467)(523) = (400)(523) + (60)(523) + (7)(523)$$
$$(467)(523) = 209200$$
$$31380$$
$$\underline{3661}$$
$$244241$$

A careful discussion of this last step will not only insure a working knowledge of the computing "machine" by your students, but also should give them a thorough understanding as to *why* this technique "works."

1. 561×49
2. 308×275
3. 4932×7655

Postassessment

Have students use a set of Napier's Rods (which they have constructed) to multiply each of the following:

16 Unit Pricing

Performance Objectives

1. Students will determine which of two given fractions is greater using the technique described on this card.

2. Students will determine which of two quantities of the same product has the more favorable price, given the quantity and the price for that quantity.

Preassessment

The only skill students need for this activity is multiplication of whole numbers.

Teaching Strategies

Ask your students if they would rather buy a 32 oz. jar of applesauce costing 30¢ or a 27 oz. jar costing 25¢. An organized thinker might translate the problem to one which asks which is larger, $\dfrac{30}{32}$ or $\dfrac{25}{27}$.

Students should realize that the fractions come from "price *per* ounce". The word "per" indicates division so a fraction $\dfrac{\text{price}}{\text{ounces}}$ can be attained.

There are many ways in which two fractions can be compared: dividing the numerator by the denominator and comparing the resulting decimal, changing both fractions to equivalent fractions with the same denominator, and so on.

We shall now consider another method, which could easily be the most efficient method. Draw two arrows as indicated below. Then multiply as the arrows show, writing the product under the arrowheads.

Simple inspection of these products indicates that 810 is the larger of the two; hence the fraction above the 810 (i.e., $\dfrac{30}{32}$) is the larger of the two fractions. Therefore, the unit price of the 27 ounce jar is lower and thus the better buy.

Before giving students problems involving comparison of unit prices, offer them some drill problems involving only comparison of fractions.

Postassessment

Select the larger of each for the following pairs of fractions.

1. $\dfrac{5}{6}, \dfrac{7}{8}$ 4. $\dfrac{13}{17}, \dfrac{19}{25}$

2. $\dfrac{8}{11}, \dfrac{17}{23}$ 5. $\dfrac{11}{19}, \dfrac{5}{9}$

3. $\dfrac{7}{9}, \dfrac{4}{5}$ 6. $\dfrac{7}{12}, \dfrac{18}{31}$

7. Which quantity has the lower unit price: a 7 oz. jar of mustard costing 11¢ or a 9 oz. jar of mustard costing 13¢?

17 Successive Discounts and Increases

This unit provides students with a simple technique for expressing various successive discounts and/or increases as one equivalent discount or increase. They may be rather fascinated by the ease of solution which this method brings to a usually complicated consumer situation.

Performance Objectives

1. Students will convert two or more successive discounts to one equivalent discount.

2. Students will convert two or more successive discounts and increases to one equivalent discount or increase.

Preassessment

Use the following problem for diagnostic purposes as well as to motivate discussion.

Ernie is deciding where to buy a shirt. Barry's Bargain Store offers the shirt at a 30% discount off the list price. Cheap Charlie's Store usually offers the same shirt at a 20% discount off the same list price. However, today Cheap Charlie's Store is offering the shirt at a 10% discount off the already discounted (20%) price. At which store will Ernie get a greater discount on the shirt today?

Teaching Strategies

Students may not immediately realize the difference in the discounts of the two stores mentioned in the problem above. Some students may feel that both stores offer the same discount. With your help they should begin to notice that, whereas Barry's Bargain Store offers a 30% discount off the original list price, Cheap Charlie's Store only offers a 20% discount off the original list price, while the 10% discount is taken off the lower, already discounted price. Hence, Ernie gets a greater discount with the 30% discount.

At this juncture your students may begin to wonder how large the actual difference is between the discounts offered by the two stores. You might then elicit from them that this quantitative comparison calls for finding a single discount equivalent to the two *successive discounts* of 20% and 10%.

Some students may suggest finding the required discounts by starting with a list price such as $10.00. This would work well as 100 is the basis of percents. That is, a discount of 20% off $10.00 yields a price of $8.00. Then a 10% discount off $8.00 yields a new price of $7.20. Since $7.20 may be obtained by a single discount of 28% off the original $10.00, *successive discounts* of 20% and 10% are equivalent to a single discount of 28%. It is simple to compare this with the 30% discount from the original problem.

Students should consider a general method of converting any number of successive discounts to a single discount. Illustrate with two successive discounts percents of d_1 and d_2 operating on a price p.

Use the same procedure as before:

$p - \dfrac{pd_1}{100} = p(1 - \dfrac{d_1}{100})$ represents the price after one discount has been computed; $[p(1 - \dfrac{d_1}{100})] - [p(1 - \dfrac{d_1}{100})] (\dfrac{d_2}{100}) = p(1 - \dfrac{d_1}{100})(1 - \dfrac{d_2}{100})$ represents the price after the second discount has been computed; $(1 - \dfrac{d_1}{100})(1 - \dfrac{d_2}{100})$ represents the percent that the new price is of the original price.

Therefore $1 - (1 - \dfrac{d_1}{100})(1 - \dfrac{d_2}{100})$ represents the discount taken off the original price in order to obtain the new price.

Hence, successive discounts of d_1% and d_2% are equivalent to a single discount percent of:

$1 - (1 - \dfrac{d_1}{100})(1 - \dfrac{d_2}{100})$. By translating this final algebraic expression into verbal form the students should be able to establish the following simple technique for converting two successive discounts to a single equivalent discount:

1) Change each of the successive discounts to decimal fractions.
2) Subtract each of these decimal fractions from the whole (i.e., 1.00).
3) Multiply the results of Step 2.
4) Subtract the results of Step 3 from the whole (i.e., 1.00).
5) Change the result of Step 4 to percent form.

Applying this to the successive discounts of 20% and 10% the students should show the following work:

1) 20% = .20 and 10% = .10
2) 1.00 − .20 = .80, and 1.00 − .10 = .90
3) (.80)(.90) = .72
4) 1.00 − .72 = .28
5) .28 = 28% (discount)

Students will notice that the rules above do not specify the number of successive discounts considered. This may prompt them to investigate the case where more than two successive discounts are to be converted to a single equivalent discount. Students should proceed in a manner similar to the one used above for two successive discounts. They should find that these same rules do in fact hold true in converting any number of successive discounts to a single equivalent discount.

A natural question to be expected at this juncture would probe the nature of *successive increases* or *successive decreases* and *increase*. Since an increase requires adding a percent of the price to the original price, while a discount requires subtracting a percent of the price from the original price, the students could be expected to guess that the technique for converting successive increases or combinations of successive increases and discounts to a single increase or discount will be similar to the conversion technique used for successive discounts. Suggest they work out this technique.

Broadening the scope of this conversion technique to include increases as well as discounts will allow students to consider problems such as the following:

When the entrance price to a basketball game was decreased by 25%, the attendance at the game increased by 35%. What was the effect of these changes on the daily receipts?

In solving this problem the student's work should resemble the following:

1) 25% = .25, and 35% = .35
2) 1.00 − .25 = .75 and 1.00 + .35 = 1.35
3) (.75)(1.35) = 1.0125
4) 1.0125 − 1.0000 = .0125
5) .0125 = 1.25% (increase)

You might wish to ask your students what they feel would be the net effect of a successive discount of 10% and increase of 10%. Students generally feel that these two changes counteract one another, leaving the original price unaltered. However they should be encouraged to apply the conversion technique. The net effect of these two changes is in fact a discount of 1%.

The following chart of successive discounts and increases of the same percent should lead students to making an intelligent conjecture about the "break even" point.

Successive Changes							
% Discount	20	15	10	5	1	.5	.1
% Increase	20	15	10	5	1	.5	.1
Equivalent % Discount Change	4	2.25	1	.25	.01	.0025	.0001

It might be satisfying for students to discover what combinations of successive discount and increase will leave the original price unaltered. One possible approach would be to use the conversion technique for a successive discount of d% and increase of i%:

$1 - (1 - d/100)(1 + i/100) = 0$; $1 - (1 - d/100 + i/100 - di/100^2) = 0$; $100d - 100i + di = 0$;

$$d = \frac{100i}{100 + i} \text{ or } i = \frac{100d}{100 - d}$$

The chart below lists possible values for d and i.

d	0	$9.09\overline{09}$	$16.66\overline{6}$	20	50	75	10	25
i	0	10	20	25	100	300	$11.11\overline{1}$	$33.33\overline{3}$

By now the students should have some insight into the topic of *successive percents*. The conversion technique introduced in this model is rather easy to remember as the basic steps merely call for: subtraction (and/or addition), multiplication, and subtraction (and/or addition).

Postassessment

Have students try to solve several problems such as the following.

1. Alice wants to buy a dress whose list price is $20. One store which generally discounts its dresses 12½% is offering an additional 20% on its already discounted price. A nearby store offers the same dress at a single 32% discount. Which store offers the lower price?

2. When the price of a magazine was decreased by 15% the sales increased by 20%. How were the receipts affected by these changes?

References

Posamentier, Alfred S. *A Study Guide for the Scho-*

lastic Aptitude Test, Mathematics Section. Boston Allyn and Bacon, 1983.

Posamentier, Alfred S., and Charles T. Salkind, *Challenging Problems in Algebra.* Palo Alto, CA: Dale Seymour Publications, 1988.

18 Prime and Composite Factors of a Whole Number

This unit presents a different approach to the process of factoring a number. It allows students to find the complete set of all different factors of a composite whole number. At the same time, this unit helps students better understand the factorization process.

Performance Objectives

1. Students will determine the total number of factors, prime and composite, of a given composite whole number.

2. Students will determine each of the elements of the set of prime and composite factors of this number.

3. Students will find the sum of all the elements of this set.

Preassessment

Students should be familiar with the basic rules of divisibility and able to find the prime factorization of a number.

Teaching Strategies

To find the set of prime and composite factors of the given number, you should first find the prime factorization of the number and then determine all possible products of these factors.

To find the prime factorization of the number, the "peeling" technique may be used. For example, to find the prime factorization of 3960, you should proceed as follows:

2)	3960		$3960 = 2 \times 1980$
2)	1980		$= 2 \times 2 \times 990$
2)	990		$= 2 \times 2 \times 2 \times 495$
3)	495		$= 2 \times 2 \times 2 \times 3 \times 165$
3)	165		$= 2 \times 2 \times 2 \times 3 \times 3 \times 55$
5)	55		$= 2 \times 2 \times 2 \times 3 \times 3 \times 5 \times 11$
	11		

The prime factorization of 3960 is:
$2 \times 2 \times 2 \times 3 \times 3 \times 5 \times 11 = 2^3 \times 3^2 \times 5 \times 11$

The total number of factors of a given number is determined by the product of the exponents (*each in-*

creased by one) of the different factors in the prime factorization of the number expressed in exponential form.

Therefore, the total number of factors of 3960 will be given by the product:
$(3 + 1)(2 + 1)(1 + 1)(1 + 1) = 4 \times 3 \times 2 \times 2 = 48$

To find each of the 48 factors, prepare the following self-explanatory table:

1	2	2^2	2^3
1	3	3^2	
1	5		
1	11		

Now have students multiply each number in the first row by each number in the second row:

1×1	1×2	1×2^2	1×2^3
1×3	2×3	$2^2 \times 3$	$2^3 \times 3$
1×3^2	2×3^2	$2^2 \times 3^2$	$2^3 \times 3^2$

Then each resulting product would be multiplied by each number in the third row:

$1 \times 1 \times 1$	$1 \times 1 \times 2$	$1 \times 1 \times 2^2$	$1 \times 1 \times 2^3$
$1 \times 1 \times 3$	$1 \times 2 \times 3$	$1 \times 2^2 \times 3$	$1 \times 2^3 \times 3$
$1 \times 1 \times 3^2$	$1 \times 2 \times 3^2$	$1 \times 2^2 \times 3^2$	$1 \times 2^3 \times 3^2$
$1 \times 1 \times 5$	$1 \times 2 \times 5$	$1 \times 2^2 \times 5$	$1 \times 2^3 \times 5$
$1 \times 3 \times 5$	$2 \times 3 \times 5$	$2^2 \times 3 \times 5$	$2^3 \times 3 \times 5$
$1 \times 3^2 \times 5$	$2 \times 3^2 \times 5$	$2^2 \times 3^2 \times 5$	$2^3 \times 3^2 \times 5$

You should continue this same process until all rows are exhausted. In the case of our example, 3960, we finally have:

$1\times1\times1\times1$	$1\times1\times1\times2$	$1\times1\times1\times2^2$	$1\times1\times1\times2^3$
$1\times1\times1\times3$	$1\times1\times2\times3$	$1\times1\times2^2\times3$	$1\times1\times2^3\times3$
$1\times1\times1\times3^2$	$1\times1\times2\times3^2$	$1\times1\times2^2\times3^2$	$1\times1\times2^3\times3^2$
$1\times1\times1\times5$	$1\times1\times2\times5$	$1\times1\times2^2\times5$	$1\times1\times2^3\times5$
$1\times1\times3\times5$	$1\times2\times3\times5$	$1\times2^2\times3\times5$	$1\times2^3\times3\times5$
$1\times1\times3^2\times5$	$1\times2\times3^2\times5$	$1\times2^2\times3^2\times5$	$1\times2^3\times3^2\times5$
$1\times1\times1\times11$	$1\times1\times2\times11$	$1\times1\times2^2\times11$	$1\times1\times2^3\times11$
$1\times1\times3\times11$	$1\times2\times3\times11$	$1\times2^2\times3\times11$	$1\times2^3\times3\times11$
$1\times1\times3^2\times11$	$1\times2\times3^2\times11$	$1\times2^2\times3^2\times11$	$1\times2^3\times3^2\times11$
$1\times1\times5\times11$	$1\times2\times5\times11$	$1\times2^2\times5\times11$	$1\times2^3\times5\times11$
$1\times3\times5\times11$	$2\times3\times5\times11$	$2^2\times3\times5\times11$	$2^3\times3\times5\times11$
$1\times3^2\times5\times11$	$2\times3^2\times5\times11$	$2^2\times3^2\times5\times11$	$2^3\times3^2\times5\times11$

However, students can obtain the same results in a

simpler and quicker way: Find the divisors of each of the factors in the number's prime factorization when written in exponential form. In our example:

$$2^3 \begin{cases} 2^1 = 2 \\ 2^2 = 4 \\ 2^3 = 8 \end{cases} \quad 3^2 \begin{cases} 3^1 = 3 \\ 3^2 = 9 \end{cases} \quad 5^1 \begin{cases} 5^1 = 5 \end{cases} \quad 11^1 \begin{cases} 11^1 = 11 \end{cases}$$
$$\quad\quad a \quad\quad\quad\quad b \quad\quad\quad\quad c \quad\quad\quad d$$

Have students prepare a table in which the first row is formed by number one and the numbers in *a* (see below). Have pupils draw a line and multiply each number in *b* by each number above this line. Students will draw a new line and multiply the element in *c* by all the numbers above the second line. The process will continue until all divisors of each of the factors in the number's prime factorization are multiplied.

1	2	4	8	I
3	6	12	24	
9	18	36	72	II
5	10	20	40	
15	30	60	120	III
45	90	180	360	
11	22	44	88	
33	66	132	264	
99	198	396	792	
55	110	220	440	IV
165	330	660	1320	
495	990	1980	3960	

The table which contains the 48 factors we are looking for starts with number 1 and ends with our given number 3960.

Part I is formed by number 1 and the factors in *a*. Part II is constituted by the products of each of the numbers in *b* and each of the numbers in I. Part III is made up by the products obtained when multiplying each of the numbers of *c* by each of the numbers in I and II. And finally, part IV is formed by multiplying each number of *d* by each of the numbers in I, II, and III. The table has 4 × 12 = 48 factors. All of the factors of 3960 appear in this table: The prime as well as the composite factors of 3960.

To find the sum of the factors of a number N, let us represent the prime factorization of N by $a^\alpha \cdot b^\beta \cdot c^\rho \cdot d^\theta$, such that, $N = a^\alpha \cdot b^\beta \cdot c^\rho \cdot d^\theta$. The sum of all the factors of N will be given by the formula:

$$s = \frac{a^{\alpha+1} - 1}{a - 1} \cdot \frac{b^{\beta+1} - 1}{b - 1} \cdot \frac{c^{\rho+1} - 1}{c - 1} \cdot \frac{d^{\theta+1} - 1}{d - 1}.$$

In our example: $N = 3960$, $a = 2$, $b = 3$, $c = 5$, $d = 11$, $\alpha = 3$, $\beta = 2$, $\rho = 1$, $\theta = 1$ as $3960 = 2^3 \times 3^2 \times 5 \times 11$ Therefore:

$$s = \frac{2^4 - 1}{2 - 1} \cdot \frac{3^3 - 1}{3 - 1} \cdot \frac{5^2 - 1}{5 - 1} \cdot \frac{11^2 - 1}{11 - 1}$$
$$= \frac{15}{1} \cdot \frac{26}{2} \cdot \frac{24}{4} \cdot \frac{120}{10}$$
$$= 15 \times 13 \times 6 \times 12$$
$$= 14{,}040$$

Postassessment

Have students calculate the total number of factors and then find each of them (either prime or composite), for each of the following:
a) 3600   b) 540   c) 1680   d) 25725

Find the sum of all the factors in each of the cases above.

19 Prime Numeration System

This unit will present an unusual way to express numbers. Consideration of this "strange" numeration system should strengthen student understanding of a place value system as well as appreciation of prime factorization.

Performance Objectives

1. *Students will convert numbers from the prime numeration system into base-ten numerals.*

2. *Students will convert numbers from base-ten into the prime numeration system.*

Preassessment

Students should know what a prime number is. Students should also be able to factor a base-ten numeral into its prime factors.

Teaching Strategies

To familiarize students with the prime numeration system, have students consider the following problems: a) 5·4 = 9, b) 12·24 = 36 c) 8÷2 = 6. Initially students will be quite puzzled. After further inspection those familiar with exponents will begin to conjecture along those lines. Yet, this system is probably quite different from any numeration system studied before.

In the prime numeration system, there is no base. The value of each place is a prime number. The first place (starting at the right) is the first prime, 2; the next place (to the left) is the next prime, 3. This continues with the consecutive prime numbers with each succeeding place (moving left) corresponding to the next consecutive prime. This can be shown by using a dash for each place and indicating its value below it.

$$\overline{29}\ \overline{23}\ \overline{19}\ \overline{17}\ \overline{13}\ \overline{11}\ \overline{7}\ \overline{5}\ \overline{3}\ \overline{2}$$

As with our base-ten system, this prime system continues indefinitely to the left.

In order to find the value of a number in base-ten, digits occupying each place are multiplied by their place value and then added. However, in this prime numeration system, the value of a number is obtained by taking each place value to the *power* of the number occupying that place and then *multiplying*. For example, the number 145_p (the subscript p will be used to indicate that the number is in the prime numeration system) equals $5^1 \cdot 3^4 \cdot 2^5 = 5 \cdot 81 \cdot 32 = 12960$. Notice the exponents of the prime numbers 5, 3, and 2 are 1, 4, and 5, respectively. Have students practice converting from the prime numeration system to base-ten numeration. When they begin to feel somewhat comfortable with this work, have them consider the representation of 0 and 1. Have students express 0_p and 10_p as a base-ten numeral. Indicate to the students that by definition $2^0 = 1$. Elicit from students that representation of zero will be impossible in the prime numeration system.

In order to convert a base-ten numeral into the prime numeration system, a review of prime factorization is necessary. Explain to students that any whole number greater than one can be expressed as the product of prime factors in precisely one way (The Fundamental Theorem of Arithmetic). For example, 420 can be factored as follows: $7^1 \cdot 5^1 \cdot 3^1 \cdot 2^2$. Therefore $420 = 1112_p$. Have students factor a) 144, b) 600, c) 1960, into their prime factors and represent their equivalents in the prime numeration system. Emphasize that exponents of the prime factors are the digits of the prime numeral.

When students have mastered this numeration system challenge them with multiplication; $5_p \cdot 4_p$

$5_p \cdot 4_p$ may be rewritten as $2^5 \cdot 2^4 = 2^9 = 512$. Therefore, $5_p \cdot 4_p = 9_p$. Now have them consider $25_p \cdot 4_p = 3^2 \cdot 2^5 \cdot 2^4 = 3^2 \cdot 2^9 = 29_p$ (or 4608). Other related exercises should be presented (e.g. $8_p \div 2_p$). It should be indicated that the operations of addition and subtraction would require conversion to base-ten numeration before actually adding or subtracting. These problems allow students to practice working with exponents in a new and unusual way.

The prime numeration system can be implemented to review the greatest common divisor and least common multiple of two numbers.

Suppose students were required to find the greatest common divisor of 18,720 and 3,150. They should change these two base-ten numerals to the prime numeration system to get: 100125_p and 1221_p. By listing the *smallest value of each place* to form a new number, they will obtain 121_p, which is the greatest common divisor of the two numbers.

Now suppose students were faced with the problem of finding the least common multiple of 18,720 and 3,150. Having changed these two base-ten numerals to the prime numeration system to get 100125_p and 1221_p, they must merely list the *largest value of each place* to get 101225_p, which is the least common multiple of the two numbers.

Students will enjoy applying the prime numeration system methods to other problems which require finding the greatest common divisor or the least common multiple of given numbers (more than two numbers may be considered at one time). The true value of these methods rests in the justification of these methods. Teachers should present these justifications as soon as students have mastered the techniques involved.

Now have students convert 0_p through 29_p into base-ten numerals and record their answers. Students will begin to see the base-ten numerals being generated in an unusual way.

Prime System	Base-Ten	
0_p	$2^0 =$	1
1_p	$2^1 =$	2
2_p	$2^2 =$	4
3_p	$2^3 =$	8
4_p	$2^4 =$	16
5_p	$2^5 =$	32
6_p	$2^6 =$	64
7_p	$2^7 =$	128
8_p	$2^8 =$	256
9_p	$2^9 =$	512
10_p	$3^1 \cdot 2^0 =$	3
11_p	$3^1 \cdot 2^1 =$	6
12_p	$3^1 \cdot 2^2 =$	12
13_p	$3^1 \cdot 2^3 =$	24
14_p	$3^1 \cdot 2^4 =$	48
15_p	$3^1 \cdot 2^5 =$	96
16_p	$3^1 \cdot 2^6 =$	192
17_p	$3^1 \cdot 2^7 =$	384
18_p	$3^1 \cdot 2^8 =$	768
19_p	$3^1 \cdot 2^9 =$	1536
20_p	$3^2 \cdot 2^0 =$	9
21_p	$3^2 \cdot 2^1 =$	18
22_p	$3^2 \cdot 2^2 =$	36
23_p	$3^2 \cdot 2^3 =$	72
24_p	$3^2 \cdot 2^4 =$	144
25_p	$3^2 \cdot 2^5 =$	288
26_p	$3^2 \cdot 2^6 =$	576
27_p	$3^2 \cdot 2^7 =$	1152
28_p	$3^2 \cdot 2^8 =$	2304
29_p	$3^2 \cdot 2^9 =$	4608

Elicit from students other possible applications of the prime numeration system.

Postassessment

Students should:

1. Express each of the following numbers in the base-ten numeration system.

a) 31_p b) 24_p c) 15_p d) 41_p e) 221_p f) 1234_p

2. Express each of the following base-ten numerals as a product of primes, and then in the prime numeration system.

a) 50 b) 100 c) 125 d) 400 e) 1000 f) 260 g) 350

3. Solve the following problems:

a) $3_p \cdot 6_p$ b) $12_p \cdot 13_p$ c) $6_p \div 3_p$

20 Repeating Decimal Expansions

The terms "never-ending" and "infinite" are often confusing to students. One of the first places they really come into contact with the concept is in the junior high school where they confront nonterminating decimal expansions. Students themselves realize the need for specific notation when they encounter the repeating decimals certain fractional forms produce. In this unit students discover the patterns and seemingly inconsistent arithmetic procedures that occur with repeating decimals.

Performance Objectives

1. *Students will be able to determine which rational numbers will yield repeating decimal expansions and which will terminate.*

2. *Students will determine minimum length of a repeating cycle.*

3. *Students will be able to use decimal equivalents to find other repeating decimals.*

4. *Students will examine an alternate method to determine decimal expansions.*

Preassessment

Students should know how to change from the fractional form ($\frac{a}{b}$) of a rational number to its decimal equivalent. They should be familiar with prime factorization.

Have students guess which of the following fractions would become repeating decimals: $\frac{1}{2}, \frac{1}{3}, \frac{1}{4}, \frac{1}{5}, \frac{1}{6}$. Have them work out these fraction-to-decimal conversions to check the accuracy of their guesses. Note also that a terminating decimal can be considered a repeating decimal with an infinite repetition of zeroes.

Teaching Strategies

Begin by having students work with fractions of the form $\frac{1}{n}$. This will force them to focus their attention (and guesswork) on the denominator. If they have difficulty figuring out how to determine repeating decimals without actually performing the expansion, suggest they factor into primes each of the denominators to see if any patterns become apparent. They will quickly see that the decimal terminates if, and only if, the prime factors of the denominator are 2's and/or 5's. They can easily justify that when the numerator takes on a decimal point and a series of zeroes, it becomes a multiple of 10 (for division purposes only); since the only prime factors of 10 are 5 and 2, it is only division by these factors that will terminate the division process.

Challenge students to determine to how many decimal places they must proceed before a pattern becomes evident. In some cases, as in $\frac{1}{3}$, it will take two decimal places before the pattern is clear. In others, it will not be so simple. Ask students to find the repeating pattern of $\frac{1}{17}$. This decimal expansion has 16 places before any pattern establishes itself $\frac{1}{17}$

$= .0588235294117647\overline{0588235294117647}.$

Some students may want to generalize and assume $\frac{1}{n}$ will have $(n-1)$ repeating digits. However, $\frac{1}{3} = .\overline{3}$, one repeating digit, which quickly disproves their theory. However, by examining each of the expansions of $\frac{1}{n}$, students will see that each expansion has at most $(n-1)$ repeating digits. They should realize that each of the expansion digits comes from the remainder after the division process of the previous step. For each of the remainders there are only $(n-1)$ choices. (The remainder cannot equal zero because then the process would terminate; it cannot equal n because then it would have been divisible once again.) If the remainder is the same as any previous remainder, students have found the repeating digits; if not they must continue until a remainder repeats. This will have to happen in, at most, $(n-1)$ steps. Therefore $\frac{1}{n}$, if repeating, will have at most $(n-1)$ repeating digits.

Students will also find it interesting to note that the repeating expansion for a number such as $\frac{1}{7}$ also yields the expansions for $\frac{2}{7}$, $\frac{3}{7}$, $\frac{4}{7}$, $\frac{5}{7}$, and $\frac{6}{7}$. The fraction $\frac{2}{7}$ can be rewritten in terms of $\frac{1}{7}$. Thus,

$$\frac{2}{7} = 2 \times \frac{1}{7} = 2 \times .\overline{142857} = .\overline{285714}.$$

By adding different repeating decimals, students will be able to find new repeating decimals. For example,

$$\begin{array}{r} \frac{1}{3} = \quad .\overline{333333} \\ + \quad \frac{1}{7} = + .\overline{142857} \\ \hline \frac{10}{21} = \quad .\overline{476190} \end{array}$$

To find the general repeating digits for $\frac{1}{n}$ when $n = 21$, have students divide $.\overline{476190}$ by the numerator, 10, to get $.\overline{047619}$.

In working with repeating decimals and in performing arithmetic operations, students may come upon the fact that $1 = .\overline{9}$. This is a difficult concept for a junior high school student to grasp. The following proof, which they can perform for themselves, should clarify the situation.

$$\begin{array}{r} \frac{1}{3} = .\overline{3} \\ + \quad \frac{2}{3} = .\overline{6} \\ \hline 1 = .\overline{9} \end{array}$$

Similarly, since

$$\frac{1}{9} \times 9 = .\overline{1} \times 9$$

$$\frac{9}{9} = .\overline{9}$$

$$1 = .\overline{9}$$

Students often concentrate and comprehend more thoroughly when they feel they are learning something new. The following method, which basically outlines the division process used to change from fractional to decimal form, gives students another means of finding the repeating decimal.

To find the decimal expansion of $\frac{3}{7}$, let $r_0 = \frac{3}{7}$, and multiply by 10 (comparable to bringing down the 0).

1. $\frac{3}{7} \times 10 = \frac{30}{7} = 4\frac{2}{7}$

Now let the 4 occupy the tenths place of the decimal and use $\frac{2}{7}$ as the new remainder, r_1. Repeat the process, using the fraction as the new remainder and retaining the whole as the decimal digit for the next place.

2. $\frac{2}{7} \times 10 = \frac{20}{7} = 2\frac{6}{7} \quad r_2 = \frac{6}{7}$

$\qquad$ hundredths place = 2

3. $\frac{6}{7} \times 10 = \frac{60}{7} = 8\frac{4}{7} \quad r_3 = \frac{4}{7}$

$\qquad$ thousandths place = 8

4. $\frac{4}{7} \times 10 = \frac{40}{7} = 5\frac{5}{7} \quad r_4 = \frac{5}{7}$

$\qquad$ ten thousandths place = 5

5. $\frac{5}{7} \times 10 = \frac{50}{7} = 7\frac{1}{7} \quad r_5 = \frac{1}{7}$

$\qquad$ hundred thousandths place = 7

6. $\frac{1}{7} \times 10 = \frac{10}{7} = 1\frac{3}{7} \quad r_6 = \frac{3}{7}$

$\qquad$ millionths place = 1

Tell students to repeat the process until the remainder is the same as the one with which they began. In this case $r_6 = r_0 = \frac{3}{7}$, and the decimal expansion is $\frac{3}{7} = .\overline{428571}$

A clear demonstration of this method is an excellent tool to help students better understand what is involved in the division process and why remainders are such a big factor in determining the length of the repetition.

Postassessment

Have students do the following:
1. Determine which of the following will terminate, without actually finding their decimal expansions: $\frac{2}{9}$, $\frac{1}{8}$, $\frac{3}{13}$, $\frac{19}{20}$
2. Determine the maximum number of digits in the repeating cycle of each: $\frac{1}{37}$, $\frac{4}{9}$, $\frac{3}{7}$
3. Knowing that $\frac{1}{14} = .0\overline{714285}$, find the decimal expansion for $\frac{3}{14}$ without dividing.
4. Show that $.5 = .4\overline{9}$. (Hint: think about the fractions $\frac{1}{3}$ and $\frac{1}{6}$).
5. Using the alternate method described, evaluate $\frac{2}{9}$ as a repeating decimal.

21   Peculiarities Of Perfect Repeating Decimals

This unit can be used as an interesting sidelight to the subject of decimals and fractions by showing "magical" properties of a certain class of numbers. These numbers are reciprocals of prime numbers whose decimal equivalents repeat after no less than P−1 places, where P is the prime number. Such numbers are said to have *perfect repetends*. In any repeating decimal, the sequence that repeats is called the repetend. It would be advisable to use this unit after the preceding one.

Performance Objectives
1. Students will test various examples of perfect repetends to verify specific principles.
2. Students will discover and reinforce important ideas about division, remainders, and decimal equivalents of fractions.

Preassessment
Students should know that the decimal equivalents of some fractions have 0 remainders, while others have repeating periods of various lengths. They should begin by converting $\frac{1}{7}$ to a decimal.

Teaching Strategies
It should be noted that in converting A/P to a decimal, the repetend can have no more than P−1 places, because in dividing A by P there can be at most P−1 different remainders, and as soon as a remainder appears for the second time, the same sequence will be repeated. Perfect repetends, as well as the sequence of P−1 remainders that accompanies each one, have several interesting properties. Only the simplest of these will be discussed here, but a more thorough listing of the principles of repeating decimals appears in *Philosophy of Arithmetic* by Edward Brooks, (Norwood Editions) pp. 460-485.

One of the simpler properties to explain is that multiples 1 to P−1 of 1/P are cyclic variations of the repetend of 1/P. After students find $\frac{1}{7}$ = $.\overline{142857}$, students can multiply the decimal by 2, 3, 4, 5, or 6, and get answers of $.\overline{285714}$, $.\overline{428571}$, $.\overline{571428}$, $.\overline{714285}$, $.\overline{857142}$, which are also decimal equivalents of $\frac{2}{7}$, $\frac{3}{7}$, $\frac{4}{7}$, $\frac{5}{7}$, $\frac{6}{7}$, respectively. Once this is understood, an easy way to find the multiples of $\frac{1}{7}$ is to find the last place first. For example, $4 \times .\overline{142857}$ ends in 8, so it must be $.\overline{571428}$. Where the period is longer, or where any digit appears more than once in the repetend, it may be necessary to find the last two or three digits

first. An explanation of this cyclic variation is that in dividing P into 1, at the point where the remainder is A, the same sequence will begin as occurs when dividing P into A. Remember also that every possible A (1<A<P) occurs as a remainder. Incidentally, when the repetend of 1/P is multiplied by P the result is .999999. Some other perfect repetends are:

$$\frac{1}{17} = .\overline{0588235294117647}$$

$$\frac{1}{19} = .\overline{052631578947368421}$$

$$\frac{1}{23} = .\overline{0434782608695652173913}$$

The only others for $P < 100$ are: $\frac{1}{29}$, $\frac{1}{47}$, $\frac{1}{59}$, $\frac{1}{61}$, $\frac{1}{97}$

Another curiosity of these numbers is that if the repetend is divided into two equal shorter sequences, their sum is $.\overline{99999}$. A graphic illustration of this is shown below. The inner circle is the repetend of $\frac{1}{29}$, and the outer circle is the sequence of remainders occurring after each number on the inner circle. The figure has the following properties (as do similar figures for all perfect repetends).

1) Any two diametrically opposite terms of the repetend add up to 9.
2) Any two opposite remainders add up to 29.
3) To multiply the repetend by a ($1<a<29$), find a in the circle of remainders and begin the new repetend with the decimal term following the one associated with a (clockwise).

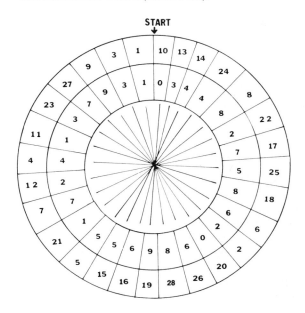

START

Some students may not have the patience to test out these generalizations on this figure, but of course a similar figure can be made for any of the perfect repetends. Students may construct their own figures, starting only with the information that $\frac{1}{17}$ is such a number.

Here is one alternative to plowing straight ahead with division when generating a repetend: after dividing 19 into 1 to five places, we get a remainder of 3. $\frac{1}{19} = .05263 \frac{3}{19}$.* But from this we know that $\frac{3}{19} = 3(.05263 \frac{3}{19}) = .15789 \frac{9}{19}$. So $\frac{1}{19} = .0526315789 \frac{9}{19}$.

But since we know that $\frac{1}{19}$ is a perfect repetend, 9 = first + tenth digit = second + eleventh = third + twelfth, etc., and we have generated all 18 digits.

This leads into a special property of the repetend of $\frac{1}{97}$. $\frac{1}{97} = .01 \frac{3}{97} = .0103 \frac{9}{97} = .010309 \frac{27}{97} =$

---

*$\frac{1}{19} = .05263 + \frac{3}{19} \times 10^{-5}$; i.e., $\frac{3}{19}$ represents the 6th decimal place.

$.01030927 \frac{81}{97}$. Unfortunately, 243 has 3 places, so this neat pattern changes, but we can still add powers of three in the following way to generate the repetend:
$.0103092781$
$\qquad 243$
$\qquad\quad 729$
$\qquad\quad 2187$
$\qquad\qquad 6561$ etc.
Students should be encouraged to discover other patterns of repetends.

Postassessment

Have students generate any of the perfect repetends by using the rules shown here, then find multiples of the repetend. Explore with the class for reasons why only primes have this peculiarity. For example, if $\frac{1}{14}$ had a perfect repetend, what happens to $\frac{2}{14}$ or $\frac{4}{14}$?

22 Patterns in Mathematics

This unit is designed for ninth year students of mathematics. Parts of this unit could be used for enrichment of remedial classes in finding the patterns by observation alone.

Performance Objectives

1. *Students will find patterns by observation.*
2. *Students will find formulas for the patterns by trial and error.*
3. *Students will find the formulas for the patterns by discovering the rules for finding the constant and the coefficients of* x *and* x^2.

Preassessment

Challenge students to find succeeding numbers in the following patterns and formulas for the patterns:

a)

x	y
0	1
1	3
2	5
3	7
4	?
5	?

b)

x	y
0	1
1	4
2	7
3	10
4	?
5	?

c)

x	y
0	1
1	5
2	9
3	13
4	?
5	?

d)

x	y
0	3
1	5
2	7
3	9
4	?
5	?

Most students will be able to find the patterns and the formulas by trial and error. Have students fill in

missing numbers, formulas, and note the differences between the successive *y*'s. The completed charts will look like this. D denotes difference between successive *y*'s:

a)

x	y	D
0	1	
1	3	2
2	5	2
3	7	2
4	9	2
5	11	2

$y = 2x + 1$

b)

x	y	D
0	1	
1	4	3
2	7	3
3	10	3
4	13	3
5	16	3

$y = 3x + 1$

c)

x	y	D
0	1	
1	5	4
2	9	4
3	13	4
4	17	4
5	21	4

$y = 4x + 1$

d)

x	y	D
0	3	
1	5	2
2	7	2
3	9	2
4	11	2
5	13	2

$y = 2x + 3$

Have students notice constants in each case. Do they observe any pattern? Perhaps they will notice that the constant is the value of *y* when *x* is zero. Draw their attention to the difference between the successive *y*'s. Do they observe anything? Yes, the difference between the *y*'s is the coefficient of *x*. Do several patterns of this type until students can quickly find the patterns and the formulas for the patterns.

Teaching Strategies

Give your students the following exercise and have them find the pattern and the formula if they can.

How many rectangles in all?   Complete the table

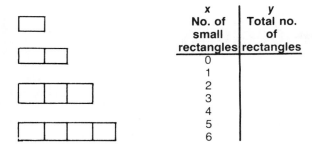

x No. of small rectangles	y Total no. of rectangles
0	
1	
2	
3	
4	
5	
6	

By observation of the rectangles, many will be able to find the pattern and fill in the table. Have them record the first difference. They will notice that it is not constant. Have them record the second difference. They will notice it is constant. Have them summarize their findings in a table. Perhaps some will find the formula also.

x No. of small rectangles	y Total no. of rectangles	D_1	D_2
0	0		
1	1	1	
2	3	2	1
3	6	3	1
4	10	4	1
5	15	5	1
6	21	6	1

$$y = \frac{x^2}{2} + \frac{x}{2}$$

Have them do the same with the following pattern: What is the largest number of pieces you can make with x cuts?

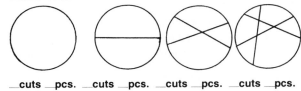

__cuts __pcs.   __cuts __pcs.   __cuts __pcs.   __cuts __pcs.

Have them fill out the following:

x No. of cuts	y No. of pcs.	D_1	D_2
0	1		
1	2	1	
2	4	2	1
3	7	3	1
4	11	4	1
5	16	5	

Notice the first difference. It is not constant. Notice the second difference. It is constant. Perhaps someone will be able to come up with the formula—

$$y = \frac{x^2}{2} + \frac{x}{2} + 1.$$

Are there any patterns one can see for the values of the constants or the coefficients in the two preceding problems? Yes, the constant is the value of y when x is zero.

Let us examine the formula $ax^2 + bx + c = y$ and find the values of y for various values of x.

x	y	D_1	D_2
0	c		
1	$a+b+c$	$a+b$	
2	$4a+2b+c$	$3a+b$	$2a$
3	$9a+3b+c$	$5a+b$	$2a$
4	$16a+3b+c$	$7a+b$	$2a$

Let us examine the pattern. As we found in the formulas, y is the constant when x is zero. The first difference is $a+b$, the sum of the coefficients of x^2 and x. The second difference is $2a$, twice the value of the coefficient of x^2. The value of the first difference when $x=1$ is $a+b$. Since we know the value of a (it is one-half of the second difference), we can find the value of b by subtracting a from the first difference $(a+b)$. So if we reexamine the earlier pattern, we can derive the formula.

The constant is the value of y when x is zero. Therefore the constant is 1. D_2 is $2a$. Since D_2 is 1, the value of a is ½. D_1 is $a+b$. Since D_1 is 1, and a is ½, the value of b is ½. The formula therefore is

$$y = \frac{1}{2}x^2 + \frac{1}{2}x + 1.$$

Postassessment

Finish the tables and find the formulas for the following patterns by finding the first and second differences:

x	y
0	3
1	6
2	13
3	24
4	
5	

x	y
0	0
1	5
2	14
3	27
4	
5	

x	y
0	0
1	13
2	34
3	63
4	
5	

x	y
0	2
1	3
2	6
3	11
4	
5	

23 Googol and Googolplex

This unit presents a discussion of large numbers. It introduces students to the finite world of large numbers and the ease of expressing large numbers using scientific notation.

Performance Objectives

1. *Students will give examples of scientific notation as used in science and mathematics.*
2. *Given any number, students will convert it into scientific notation.*

Preassessment

Students should be able to solve the following problems:

1. Compute the following products: Find the solution without using a pencil: *a*) 10 × 63 *b*) 100 × .05 *c*) 1000 × 951.
2. Compute the following quotients: *a*) 470 ÷ 10 *b*) 4,862 ÷ 1000 *c*) 46,000 ÷ 1000
3. What is the largest number you can think of?

Teaching Strategies

You might want to tell the old story of two children engaged in a violent argument in the street. The argument stems from the fact that each child is trying to state a larger number than the other. Finally, they realize each one can state a larger number than the other.

Numbers are fun to play with and many interesting things can be done with them. However, all too often we forget what a number really is. The students should be asked, how large is one million? Can we visualize the sum of the first billion natural numbers? Why should we care about numbers of great magnitude, we never use them— or do we?

At this point the teacher should state that scientists who use very large or very small numbers usually express these numbers in scientific notation. To learn how to use this system of numeration, we will recall some patterns in mathematics. It is up to the teacher at this point to introduce scientific notation. You may wish to refer to any standard textbook for an appropriate development.

1. When a number is expressed as the product of a power of 10 and a number that is less than ten but greater than or equal to one ($1 \leq n < 10$), the number is said to be written in scientific notation.
2. A science teacher may be able to suggest very large or very small numbers that students have used or read about in their science classes. These can then be converted into scientific notation.

A general discussion should ensue on when large numbers are used (for example, grains of sand on a beach, stars in the sky, or in economics, science, etc). Current newspaper and magazine articles abound with references to millions and billions, etc. How many people have seen a million of anything? Most people do not have a clear idea of the size of a million.

To earn a million dollars how long would you have to work at $100 a week? (almost 200 years). How many stars can you see with the naked eye on a clear night? No, not millions, but only about 3,500 (3.5×10^3 in scientific notation). A hundred sheets of paper make a stack about 5 millimetres thick or $\frac{1}{5}$ of an inch (25.4 millimetres equal an inch). A million sheets of paper would make a pile about 55 yards high, or roughly the height of a 12 story building. Suppose you are riding in a car at 65 mph. How long would it take you going constantly to travel one million miles? ($1\frac{3}{4}$ years).

Just how big is a billion? The 1981 federal budget calls for more tax dollars than there have been seconds since the birth of Christ. (Note: according to the ability of a particular class and allotted time all large numbers should be converted to scientific notation by the student.) Students should be led to the fact that it is virtually impossible for the human mind to comprehend the enormity of a billion. Remember how high a pile of a million sheets of paper would be—a hundred sheets of paper make a stack about 5 millimetres thick (about $\frac{1}{5}$ of an inch). A billion sheets of paper would make a pile 31 miles high.

A car traveling nonstop at 100 mph would take 1,140 years to travel a billion miles. If you earn $100 a week, you would have to work 192,307 years to earn a billion dollars. (Some of these illustrations may be calculated on an electronic calculator.)

You should pose the following problem. "John did me a favor the other day and I asked him what reward he would like. John, being very wise said, "Give me one penny for the first day, two pennies for the second day, four pennies for the third day, and likewise for sixty-four days, doubling the number of pennies for each successive day." How much money would I have to pay John?"

Making a table gives students an opportunity to see numbers growing and the magnitude they can reach.

Number of Days	Number of Pennies
1	1
2	2
3	4
4	8
5	16
etc.	etc.
64	9,223,372,036.854,775,808

Now the sum of all the numbers in the second column is the number of pennies needed to pay John:

$$18,446,744,073,709,551,615$$

It is read: Eighteen quintillion, four hundred forty-six quadrillion, seven hundred forty-four trillion, seventy-three billion, seven hundred nine million, five hundred fifty-one thousand, six hundred fifteen. Students should be able to see that even though it is an enormous number it is not infinite, but finite. Have them express it approximately in scientific notation.

The next question that may arise at this point concerns the largest number that can be expressed by three digits. In ordinary notation the answer is 999. What about 99^9? (review of exponents reveals the fact that this means 99 multiplied by itself 8 times.) But if exponents are permitted, the answer is 9^{9^9}, that is, 9 with the exponent 9^9, or simply 9 with the exponent 387,420,489. (the product of 387,420,489 nines). If printed with 16 figures to an inch, it has been estimated, this huge number would fill 33 volumes of 800 pages each, printing 14,000 figures on a page. It has been estimated that this number is more than four million times as large as the number of electrons in the universe, but a *finite* number. (Ask students to find the largest three digit number that can be written with fours.)

Say the number of grains of sand at Coney Island is about 10^{20}. Students could be asked to devise a method for establishing this estimate. The number of electrons which pass through the filament of an ordinary light-bulb in a minute equals the number of drops of water that flow over Niagara Falls in a hundred years. The reason for giving such examples of very large numbers to students is to emphasize that the elements of even very large sets can be counted.

Students may now ask what the largest number that has a name is. The term *googol* was coined to describe the figure 1 followed by a hundred zeros. Another term, *googolplex*, was invented for a still larger, but still finite, number consisting of a 1 followed by a googol of zeros. Thus, a googol times a googol would be a 1 with 200 zeros. Students who try to write a googolplex on the chalkboard or a sheet of paper will get some idea of the size of this very large but finite number (there would not be enough room to write it if you travelled to the farthest visible star, writing zeros all the way).

Astronomers find the light-year a very convenient unit of length in measuring great astromical distances. The North Star is 47 light years away. What does this mean? Light travels at the rate of 186,000 miles per-second. In one year light travels $6,000,000,000,000$ (6×10^{12}) miles. This tremendous distance is called a light year. The nearest star is 4.4 light-years away, and the farthest known star is 1.4×10^9 light years away. Have students consider this: It takes 47 light-years for light from Earth to reach the North Star. What would a person looking at the Earth from the North Star see today? (Events happening around 1934.)

Postassessment

Have students complete the following:

1. The distance of the planet Pluto from the earth is approximately 4,700,000,000,000 miles, Express this answer in scientific notation. (4.7×10^{12})

2. The circumference of the earth at the equator is approximately 25,000 miles. Express this in scientific notation. (2.5×10^4)

24 Mathematics of Life Insurance

This unit describes to students how insurance companies take into account probability and compound interest in calculating the net premium of life insurance.

Performance Objective

1. *Students will use a compound interest formula to compute the value of money left in a bank for a given period at a given rate.*

2. *Students will compute the present value of money that increases to a given amount when left in a bank for a given period at a given rate.*

3. *Students will use appropriate probabilities and interest rate to calculate the net premium a life insurance policy holder must pay.*

Preassessment

Use the following problem for diagnostic purposes as well as to motivate the lesson. Out of 200,000 men alive at age 40, 199,100 lived at age 41. What is the probability that an insured man of age 40 will live at least one year? What is the probability that he will die within one year?

Teaching Strategies

By posing the above problem, students become aware of the applicability of probability theory to life insurance. It is important for these companies to be able to measure the risks against which people are buying the life insurance. In order to decide on the premiums, a life insurance company must know how many people are expected to die in any group. They do this by collecting data about the number of people who died in the past from each age group. Since the data is collected from a large number of events, the law of large numbers applies. This law states that *with a large number of experiments, the ratio of the number of successes to the number of trials gets very close to the theoretical probability.*

Life insurance companies construct mortality tables based on past deaths in order to predict the number of people who will die in each age group. Below is a portion of the Commissioners 1958 Standard Ordinary Mortality Table. To construct this table a sample of ten million people was used. Their life span was recorded from birth till age 99. At each age level the table records the number of people alive at the start of the year and the number of deaths that occurred during the year. Then the following ratio is computed:

$$\frac{\text{Number of deaths during year}}{\text{Number of people alive at start of year}}$$

This ratio is then converted to deaths per 1000. The number of deaths per 1000 is called the *death rate*. This death rate, as students will see, is crucial in computing the premium that policyholders will pay.

Age	Number Living	Deaths Each Year	Deaths Per 1,000
0	10,000,000	70,800	7.08
1	9,929,200	17,475	1.76
2	9,911,725	15,066	1.52
3	9,896,659	14,449	1.46
4	9,882,210	13,835	1.40
10	9,805,870	11,865	1.21
11	9,794,005	12,047	1.23
12	9,781,958	12,325	1.26
13	9,769,633	12,896	1.32
18	9,698,230	16,390	1.69
25	9,575,636	18,481	1.93
30	9,480,358	20,193	2.13
42	9,173,375	38,253	4.17
43	9,135,122	41,382	4.53
44	9,093,740	44,741	4.92

Figure 1

After this introduction, the teacher should ask the class: What is the probability that an 18-year-old will die if out of 6,509 18-year-olds alive at the beginning of the year, 11 died? The probability is 11/6509. However, life insurance companies prefer to transform this ratio into death rate per 1000. The teacher should have the class change 11/6509 into $x/1000$ by setting up the following proportion:

$$\frac{x}{1000} = \frac{\text{Number of dying during the year}}{\text{Number alive at start of the year}}$$

x = death rate per 1000

The answer to the above problem is:

$$\frac{11}{6509} = \frac{x}{1000} \text{ or } x = 1.69$$

This means that 1.69 people out of the original 1000 will have died by the end of the eighteenth year. The insurance company uses this information to calculate the premium it will charge a group of 18-year-olds. Suppose there were 1000 people age 18 who insured themselves for $1000 each for one year. How much would the company have to pay out at the end of the year? If 1.69 people die, the company will pay out $1690 (1.69 × 1000 = 1690). Thus, how much must the company charge each of the 1000 policyholders? (This does not take into account profit or operating expenses). The $1690 divided evenly among 1000 people equals $1.69 per person.

In the previous discussion, students did not take into consideration the fact that money paid to the company earns interest during the year. So besides considering the death rate, the interest rate must also be taken into account when calculating the premium.

The teacher must now develop the concepts of compound interest. The teacher should ask the class how much money will be on deposit in a bank at the end of the year if one deposits $100 at 5 percent interest. The answer is $100 plus .05 (100) or 100×1.05 which is $105. If the $105 is kept in the bank another year, what will it amount to? $105 + .05(105)$ or $100 \times 1.05 \times 1.05$ or $100 \times (1.05)^2$ which amounts to $110.25. Have the students write the general formula using $P =$ original principal, $i =$ rate of interest per period, $A =$ the amount of money at the end of the specified time and $n =$ the number of years the principal is on deposit. The formula is $A = P (1 + i)^n$.

The teacher should now ask the students how much money they would have to deposit now in a bank whose rate of interest is 5 percent, if they wanted $100 accumulated in one year from now. In the previous example, the students saw that $100 grew to $105 in one year's time. This information is used to set up a proportion: $x/100 = 100/105 = .9524$. $x = 100(.9524) = 95.24.

How much would have to be deposited now in order to accumulate $100 at the end of two years from now? $x/100 = 100/110.25 = .9070$. $x = 90.70.

The students should now be able to derive a formula for calculating the present value from the formula for compound interest ($A = P(1 + i)^n$).

This formula is: $P = \dfrac{A}{(1 + i)^n}$.

Your students will now return to the original problem of the life insurance company that has to pay out $1690 at the end of the year to the deceased 18-year-olds. What is the present value of $1690? In other words, how much must the insurance company collect at the beginning of the year so that it can pay out $1690 at the end of the year? By using the present value formula, the students computed that for every $1 the company has to pay, it must collect $.9524 at the beginning of the year. If the company has to pay $1690, then it has to collect $1609.56 in total from its 1000 18-year-olds ($1690 \times .9524 = 1609.56). Thus each policyholder must contribute a premium of $1609.56/1000 = 1.60956$ or about $1.61.

You may now pose another problem. Suppose another group of 1000 people aged 25 bought policies for one year worth $1000 apiece (the death benefit is $1000). According to the mortality table their death rate is 1.93, or 1.93 out of 1000 25-year-olds die during their twenty-fifth year. What will the net premium be if the interest rate is 5 percent? Death rate per 1000 at age 25 = 1.93. Amount needed to pay claims = $(1.93 \times 1000) = $1930. Interest factor = $.9524. Present value of claims due in 1 year ($1930 \times .9524) = $1838.13. Number of persons paying premium = 1000. Net premium $1838.13/1000 = 1.83813$ of $1.84. This process may be continued for additional years of insurance.

Postassessment

Calculate the net premium for a two-year policy for a group of 1000 all age 30, with interest at 5 percent. Death rate at 30 is 2.13, death rate at 31 is 2.19.

25   Geometric Dissections

Unlike Humpty Dumpty, dissected geometric figures can be put back together again. In fact, the primary purpose of dissections is to cut a plane rectilinear figure with straight lines in such a way that the resulting pieces can be reassembled into a desired figure. This unit will introduce the wide range of geometric dissections by emphasizing their mathematical as well as recreational value.

Performance Objectives
1. Students will see familiar polygonal area formulas in a concrete and interrelated manner.

2. Students will transform certain polygonal figures into other polygonal figures of equal area through dissections.

Preassessment
Present your students with the following problem: Given an equilateral triangle, dissect the triangle into four pieces, which can be put together to form a rectangle. One possible solution: construct the perpendicular bisector from C to point D on side $\overline{AB}$; from D draw a line segment to the midpoint of $\overline{BC}$; bisect $\angle A$ extending the bisecting ray to point F on $\overline{CD}$. These four pieces will form a rectangle.;

Figure 1

Teaching Strategies
Begin discussion of dissections by demonstrating the area equality between a rectangle and a parallelogram with the same base. The dissection proceeds as follows. Using heavy paper or cardboard, construct a rectangle ABCD. Make a straight cut from vertex A to a point E on side $\overline{DC}$. Remove $\triangle$ ADE placing side $\overline{AD}$ along side $\overline{BC}$ to form parallelogram ABE'E.

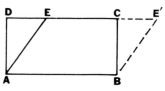

Figure 2

In a similar manner, you can also demonstrate that a parallelogram and a trapezoid with the same base have equal areas. Consider any trapezoid; find the midpoint E of side $\overline{BC}$, and through E draw a line parallel to $\overline{AD}$ which intersects $\overline{AB}$ at X and $\overrightarrow{DC}$ at Y. Since $\triangle$CEY and $\triangle$BEX are congruent, the areas of trapezoid ABCD and parallelogram AXYD are equal.

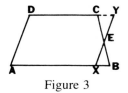

Figure 3

The range of possible transformations of polygons into other polygons by means of dissections is vast. Janos Bolyai, one of the founders of non-Euclidean geometry, was the first to suggest that given any two polygons with equal area, either figure could be dissected a finite number of times such that upon rearrangement it would be congruent to the other. However, we are concerned with specific transformations that require a minimum number of dissections.

For example, you could consider the problem of dissecting a given acute triangle to form a rectangle. In Figure 4, first find the midpoints of sides $\overline{AC}$ and $\overline{BC}$ and connect these points to form $\overline{DE}$. From C construct a perpendicular to $\overline{DE}$ at X. Take $\triangle$DXC and place it so that X is now at X' and $\angle$DCX is adjacent to $\angle$CAB. Similarly move $\triangle$EXC so that X is now at X" and $\angle$ECX is adjacent to $\angle$CBA.

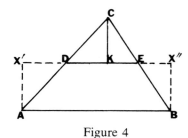

Figure 4

To encourage students to begin solving dissection problems on their own, suggest that they carefully construct a 10cm. by 10 cm. square as follows: Let $AL=BG=7$, $CT_1=3.1$, $AR_1=2.9$, $DN=4.2$; draw $\overline{AG}$ and $\overline{LN}$; on $\overline{LN}$ let $LS_1=1.6$; on $\overline{AG}$ locate points R,S,K, and T such that $AR=2.4$, $RS=3.3$, $SK=2.4$ and $KT=3.3$; draw $\overline{RR_1}$, $\overline{SS_1}$, $\overline{KB}$, and $\overline{TT_1}$.

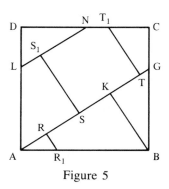

Figure 5

After cutting the student should have seven pieces. Using all of these pieces, students should attempt to form: (1) three squares of the same size, and (2) an isoceles trapezoid.

A beautiful dissection is possible with three regular hexagons. Leaving the first hexagon uncut, dissect the second and third as shown below in Figure 6. These 13 pieces can be combined to form a single hexagon.

Figure 6

It should be noted that this transformation can be considered in terms of rotations, and others in terms of reflections, translations, as well as rotations. You can then determine that a side of the larger hexagon is $\sqrt{3}$ times a side of the smaller hexagons. Since the area of the new hexagon is three times the area of each of the smaller hexagons, we have verified a significant relationship which holds between similar figures: that the ratio of their areas is the square of the ratio between any two corresponding sides.

Postassessment

Students should complete the following exercises.

1. Demonstrate by dissection that a rectangle can be divided into two congruent trapezoids which each have one-half the area of the rectangle.

2. With the pieces from the dissected 10cm by 10cm square, form: (1) a rectangle, and (2) a parallelogram.

3. Dissect the regular dodecagon which appears below into a square (cut along indicated lines).

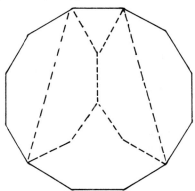

26   The Klein Bottle

This unit will provide students with an insight into one of the very fascinating topics of topology, the Klein bottle. They will be surprised to see a solid figure whose inside cannot be distinguished from its outside.

Performance Objectives

1. *Students will create a Klein bottle from a flat piece of paper.*

2. *Students will characterize a surface by certain topological properties.*

3. *Students will determine the Betti of topological surfaces.*

Teaching Strategies

Before demonstrating how the above situation can be created, briefly discuss the one-sided topological figure, the Klein bottle. The Klein bottle was invented by Felix Klein, a German mathematician, in 1882. If we were to compare the Klein bottle to something realistic, we would use a flexible object, such as a cylinder with a hole cut through the surface. We would then stretch one end to make a wide base and the other end narrowed like the neck of a bottle. But we would have to bring these two-end circles together with their arrows running in opposite directions (see diagram below). Imagine the narrow end of the cylinder bent up, and plunged through the hole on the cylinder and joined to the wide base as in the figure below.

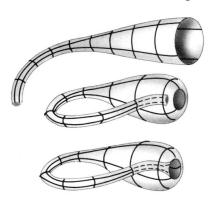

DIAGRAM 1

The hole on the surface of the cylinder should not be actually thought of as a hole but rather an intersection of surfaces covered by a continuation of the surface of the bottle.

Let us now return to the original problem. The situation can easily be visualized if we compare the sleeves of the jacket to the ends of the cylinder and one of the armholes to the hole in the cylinder. We have now created a figure that is topologically equivalent to the Klein bottle.

Once the students have a clear understanding as to what a Klein bottle appears to be, demonstrate how it can be created from a piece of paper. In order to construct a Klein bottle, what we are supposed to do with the flat piece of paper is to join the respective corners of the edges AB to A'B', but we are also to join the remaining edges AB' to A'B.

DIAGRAM 2

First create a cylinder by folding the sheet of paper in half and joining the open edges with a strip of tape. Cut a slot through the thickness of the paper nearest you about a quarter of the distance from the top. This will correspond to the "hole" in the surface of the cylinder. Fold the model in half and push the lower end through the slot. Join the edges as indicated by the arrows in the diagram. It is easily seen that this paper model is topologically identical to the Klein bottle created from the cylinder.

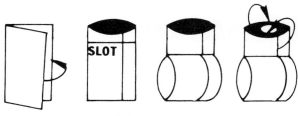

DIAGRAM 3

If we were now to examine the Klein bottle and try to distinguish the outside from the inside, and vice versa, we would find it impossible to do so. It would be evident that the surface is one-sided and edgeless, a notion very unusual to geometric figures.

Since it may be difficult to recognize a Klein bottle or any surface whose shape has been extremely distorted, it is necessary to be able to characterize each surface by simpler topological properties. Two of the properties have already been mentioned: number of edges and number of sides. A Klein bottle was found to be one-sided and have no edges. A third distinguishing feature of these surfaces is the *Betti number*. The Betti number is the maximum number of cross cuts (a simple cut with a pair of scissors which begins and ends on the edge) that can be made on a surface without dividing it into more than one piece. This means that a figure in the shape of a disk has a Betti number zero, since any cross cut will divide it into two pieces. On the other hand the lateral surface of a cylinder has a Betti number of one.

Ask students why it would be difficult to determine the Betti number of a doughnut shaped figure or a Klein bottle using the cross cut method. Most students should realize that the problem here is that both of these topological figures contain no edges. Therefore, an alternate method using a *loop-cut* (it starts at any point on the surface, and returns to it without crossing itself, avoiding the edge entirely) provides another way of determining the Betti number. When using the loop-cut to determine the Betti number, we count the number of edges and say that the Betti number equals the number of loop-cuts we can make in a surface without dividing it into more pieces than there were edges. A doughnut shaped figure requires two loop-cuts: one horizontally and the other vertically so the Betti number is two. The Klein bottle also requires two loop-cuts as shown in the diagram below.

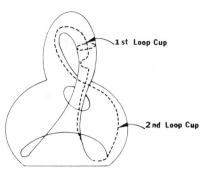

DIAGRAM 4

Postassessment

1. Have students determine the Betti number of the following surfaces:
   a. a tube
   b. a punctured tube
   c. a punctured sphere

2. Have students determine which figures would be created if you cut a Klein bottle in half.

27 The Four Color Map Problem

Topology is a branch of mathematics related to geometry. Figures discussed may appear on plane surfaces or on three-dimensional surfaces. The topologist studies those properties of a figure that remain *after* the figure has been distorted or stretched according to a set of rules. A piece of string with its ends connected may take on the shape of a circle, or a square. In going through this transformation, the order of the "points" along the string does not change. This retention of ordering has survived the distortion of shape, and is a property that attracts the interest of topologists.

Performance Objectives

1. Students will state the Four Color Map Problem.

2. Given a geographical map on a plane surface, the student will show, by example, that four colors are sufficient to successfully color the entire map.

Preassessment

Students should know the meaning of common boundaries and common vertices as applied to geographical maps on a plane surface.

Teaching Strategies

Begin by indicating that this problem was only recently solved with the extensive aid of computers. Previously it was considered one of the famous unsolved problems of mathematics.

Figure 1

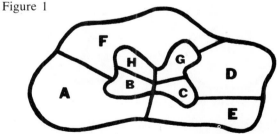

Have students analyze this fictional, geographic map of eight different countries, and list all countries that have a common boundary with country H and countries that share a common vertex with region H. A map will be considered correctly colored when each country is completely colored and two countries that share a common boundary have different colors. Two countries sharing a common vertex may also share the same color. Have students color in several maps according to the rules for coloring as stated above. (*b*/blue; *r*/red; *y*/yellow; *g*/green)

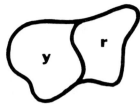

Figure 2

This map consists of two regions with one common boundary and therefore requires two colors to color correctly.

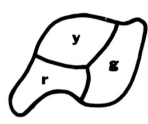

This map consists of three different regions and the students should conclude that three different colors are required to color it correctly. It seems as though a map with two regions requires two colors and a map with three regions requires three colors.

Ask the students if they can devise a map that has three different countries that will require less than three colors to color it. As an example see Figure 4.

Figure 4

Since the innermost country and the outermost country share no common boundary, they may share the color red and still retain their separate identity.

It seems reasonable to conclude that if a three-country map can be colored with less than three colors, a four-region map can be colored with less than four colors. Have the students create such a map.

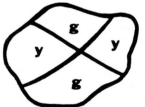 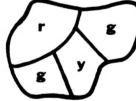

Figure 5   Figure 6

Figure 5 has four regions and requires only two colors for correct coloring. Figure 6 also consists of four regions and requires three colors for correct coloring.

Challenge students to devise a map that consists of four countries and requires exactly four colors for correct coloring. Before undertaking such a task students should now realize that this map calls for each of the four countries to share a common boundary with the other three. Figure 7 is an example of this map.

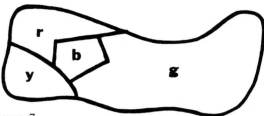

Figure 7

Ask students to take the next logical step in this series of map-coloring problems. They should come up with the idea of coloring maps involving five distinct regions. It will be possible to draw maps that have five regions and require two, three, or four colors to be colored correctly. The task of drawing a five-country map that *requires* five colors for correct coloring will be impossible. This curiosity can be generalized through further investigation and students should arrive at the idea that any map, on a plane surface, with any number of regions, can be successfully colored with four or fewer colors.

It is more satisfying to present the problem as a direct challenge in the following form: "Can you draw a geographic map, on a plane surface, with any number of regions, that requires five colors to be correctly colored?" This is the statement of the Four Color Problem. It should be noted that whereas the Three Famous Problems of antiquity have been proved to be impossible many years ago, this problem was only solved recently.

Postassessment

1. In a paragraph, using diagrams, describe what is meant by The Four Color Problem of Topology.

2. Using the colors *g*/green, *r*/red, *b*/blue, *y*/yellow, show that it is possible to correctly color each of the following maps with four or fewer colors.

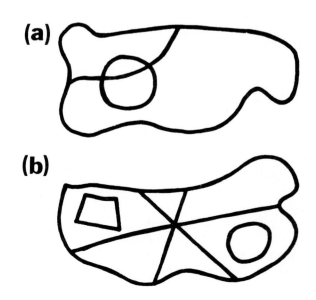

(a)

(b)

(c)

3. Draw a map that has an infinite number of regions but requires only two colors for correct coloring.

Reference

Appel, K. and Haken, W. "The Solution of the Four-Color-Map Problem." *Scientific American* 237, no. 4 (December 1977): 108–21.

28 Mathematics on a Bicycle

With the many variations of gears on the traditional ten speed bicycle, there are lots of applications of mathematics. These ought to help students better understand their bicycles while at the same time reinforce their mathematics.

Performance Objectives

1. Given the number of teeth (or sprockets) in the front and rear sprocket wheels, and diameter of the wheel, students will find gear ratios and distance traveled with each turn of the pedals. (New vocabulary will be developed.)

2. Students will be able to explain why pitch is important.

Preassessment

Students should have the basic skills of algebra, and be somewhat familiar with a bicycle.

Teaching Strategies

The adult bicycles which we shall consider have two wheels, front and rear cable brakes, gears—either three, five or ten, and are made of steel in its various alloys.

Let's examine first the differences in gearing between the three and ten speed bicycles, and in particular the mechanism of the ten speed bicycle.

In a three speed bicycle the gearing mechanism is located within the rear hub (or axle). It is a clutch type

Cross section

mechanism with pieces that interlock within the hub. It has constraints in that no ratio greater than the inside diameter of the rear hub can exist.

On a ten speed bicycle the back wheel has five sprocket wheels called a cluster, with the largest sprocket wheel closest to the spokes and then the rest gradually getting smaller. The gearing (i.e., the connection of sprocket wheels by a chain) is obtained by moving the chain from one sprocket to the other by means of a derailleur.

Let's examine closely the basic set-up.

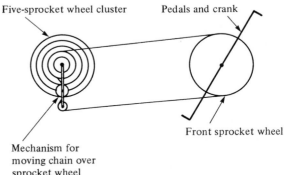

Five-sprocket wheel cluster   Pedals and crank

Front sprocket wheel

Mechanism for moving chain over sprocket wheel and changing gears

There exists a front and rear sprocket wheel with teeth set in gear by a connecting chain. The numbers of teeth on the front and rear sprocket wheels are important. Suppose the front sprocket wheel has 40 teeth and the rear sprocket wheel has 20 teeth; the ratio would then be 40/20 or 2. This means that the rear sprocket wheel turns twice every time the front sprocket wheel turns once. But the rear sprocket wheel is attached to the bicycle wheel and a translation of energy again occurs depending on the diameter of the wheel. On a ten speed bicycle the diameter of the wheel (including the tire) is 27 inches. This arrangement is shown in the diagram below.

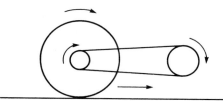

The relationship (when the bicycle wheel is included in the consideration is: gear ratio = ratio × diameter = $\frac{2}{1} = 27'' = 54$. The number generated here is usually between 36 and 108. It gives a comparison between gears and is useful for relating gear ratios to work performed.

For example, a rider using a sprocket wheel with 46 teeth in the front and a 16 tooth wheel in the rear along with a 27″ wheel gets a rear ratio of $77.625 \approx 78$. Another rider using a 50 tooth front sprocket wheel and 16 tooth sprocket wheel in the rear gets a gear ratio of $84.375 \approx 84$, which would be harder to pedal than a 78 gear ratio.

Where does this extra difficulty in pedaling benefit the rider? If one multiplies the gear ratio obtained in the formula above by π, one gets the distance traveled forward with each turn of the pedals. Students should recall that Circumference = π × Diameter.

For example, the rider with the 78 gear ratio goes approximately 245 inches forward for each turn of the pedals, while the rider with the 84 gear ratio goes approximately 264 inches forward for each complete turn of the pedals. Hence the increase in work (increased difficulty in pedaling) is returned in greater distance per pedal revolution.

Now let us examine applications of various gearing ratio to the average rider.

Suppose Mr. Carter was riding comfortably on level ground in a 78 gear ratio and then he came to a rather steep hill. Should he switch to a higher or lower gear ratio?

Your reasoning should be as follows: If Mr. Carter switches to an 84 gear ratio, he will go 264 inches forward for each turn of the pedals. This requires a certain amount of work. To overcome the effects of gravity to get up the hill requires additional energy. So Mr. Carter would probably end up walking his bicycle. If Mr. Carter had switched to a lower gear he would use less energy to turn the pedals and the additional energy required to climb the hill would make his gearing feel about the same as the 78 gear ratio. So the answer is to switch to a lower number gear ratio.

Mr. Carter will have to turn the pedal more revolutions to scale the hill; more than if he had chosen the 84 gear ratio and more than if he stayed in the 78 gear

ratio. Remember, his gearing only feels like 78 because of the hill. This is the "trade-off" Mr. Carter made: more revolutions at a constant torque (angular force) instead of the same number of revolutions per distance with varying force.

The benefit of this "trade-off" is understood by comparing the human body to the engine. An engine works most effectively at a constant torque than a varying torque and compensates by changing gear ratios with changing speed and revolutions per minute.

A more concise description is given below. A car uses gears to overcome static friction and accelerate to operating speed while providing constant torque or less torque than overload to the engine. This is not similar to the bicycle because the human machine can overcome an increase in torque for the short period of time to accelerate the bicycle. When a bicycle is in motion, the only force needed to keep it in motion at constant speed on level ground is that required to overcome internal friction and wind resistance. This is the same for a car. Should a rider wish to accelerate quickly, he would want to turn the pedals as fast as possible. All machines (including the human machine) have optimum torque capacity for this. There are two things that can happen to prevent the machine from reaching its maximum possible speed. First, if the torque is too high, it prevents rapid spin. This corresponds to a car in third gear trying to pass without a "downshift". The engine doesn't have the power for rapid acceleration and can only accelerate slowly. The same is true for a rider trying to accelerate quickly in the "harder gears"; he is without the necessary power. Second is "spin-out". This corresponds to when your car reaches 30 m.p.h. in first gear and cannot turn any faster even though there exists power for greater distance with each turn. An example is a manual shift car accelerating from a light in first without shifting. This compares on a bicycle to the rider turning the pedals as fast as possible but not at maximum force.

If the rider reaches maximum spin at maximum torque, he will reach maximum speed.

At this point you might want to have your students try some applications.

Model Problem: Mr. Bannister can turn a 68 gear ratio at 100 r.p.m. or a 72 gear ratio at 84 r.p.m. For maximum speed which should Mr. Bannister choose? (These are the very considerations bicycle racers use in determining which gear to use for the final sprint). Assume these speeds are constant for the duration of the sprint.

Solution: A 68 gear ratio times $\pi = 214$ inches per revolution (approximately). If Mr. Bannister spins 100 r.p.m., he is traveling at 21,400 inches/min. or 20.27 m.p.h.

A 72 gear ratio times $\pi = 226$ inches per revolution (approximately) at a rate of 84 r.p.m. would produce a speed of 18,984 inches/min. or 17.98 m.p.h. Therefore Mr. Bannister would be better off sprinting in the 68 gear ratio.

As mentioned earlier, these torque and spin performance items are given careful attention by racers. A racer will carefully select his back sprocket wheel cluster depending on the course. A relatively flat course would necessitate a 13–18 tooth range in the rear sprocket wheel cluster with a 47 tooth inner front sprocket wheel and 50 tooth outer front sprocket wheel.

This is where the ten speeds come from. When the chain is on the 47 tooth sprocket wheel, there are 5 different gear ratios as the rear derailleur moves the chain through the 5 rear sprocket wheels. When the chain is on the 50 tooth sprocket wheel, there are again 5 different gear ratios.

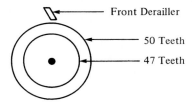

There is one other consideration a racer will make in selecting his gears and that is inertia. You will notice that a 54 front sprocket wheel and 18 tooth rear sprocket wheel gives the same gear ratio as would a 48 tooth front sprocket wheel and a 16 tooth rear sprocket wheel; that is, 48/16 = 3. The rider will choose the 48/16 because work is expended without return to accelerate through an angular acceleration a sprocket wheel of larger radius than a sprocket wheel of smaller radius due to inertia considerations. Since a 10″ radius sprocket wheel is the smallest to take the heavy shear forces, a 34 tooth sprocket wheel is the smallest available. We are currently using ½ pitch (distance between teeth), an improvement over 1″ pitch to increase the number of ratios without letting sprocket wheels get too large. A well-made sprocket wheel would look like the diagram below, where most of the unnecessary mass is cut out.

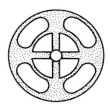

Inertia = M × distance from the axle of rotation squared. The smaller the distance, the smaller the inertia.

Thus in selecting a ten speed bicycle remember that with each difference in price goes a difference in thought toward design, performance, and work required for riding.

As a final example many inexpensive bicycles really only have 6–8 speeds because of duplication. Consider our previous example on inertia, where the choice was between a 48 tooth and 54 tooth front sprocket wheel. We saw duplication of the same gear ratio with a 16 and 18 rear sprocket wheel. This case occurs on many less expensive bicycles.

Postassessment

1. Lisa approaches a hill which raises whatever gear ratio she is in by 10. Lisa cannot pedal anything harder than a 62 gear ratio. If her 3 speed bicycle has 48, 58, and 78 gear ratio, which should she use?

2. How far forward with each revolution of the pedals will a 78 gear ratio move a bicycle whose wheel radius is 27″?

3. Josh can spin a 72 gear ratio 80 r.p.m. and a 96 gear ratio 48 r.p.m. Which gives a greater velocity?

29 Mathematics and Music

Students who are acquainted with operations on fractions but whose knowledge of music theory is limited will find a correlation between these fields.

Performance Objectives

1) *Students will demonstrate knowledge of certain formulas relating pitch of a note to properties of a string or an air column.*

2) *Students will know how to create Pythagoras' diatonic scale.*

3) *Students will show how Euclid proved that an octave is less than six whole tones.*

Preassessment

Obtain a stringed instrument such as a banjo, violin or a guitar. If these are unavailable the science department can probably lend you a sonometer, which is a scientific instrument with strings used in experimentation.

Perform the following three demonstrations. In each case, have students determine whether the pitch becomes higher or lower.

1) Pluck a string, tighten it, then pluck it again.

2) Pluck a string. Then by pressing down on the middle of the string (fretting) cause only half the string to vibrate.

3) Using two strings of different diameters (thickness), pluck each one.

Teaching Strategies

Elicit from the students the following three facts:

1) As tension increases, pitch becomes higher.

2) As length decreases, pitch becomes higher.

3) As diameter decreases, pitch becomes higher.

At this point explain that the above is grounded in mathematical formulas. However, these formulas use frequency, which is the number of vibrations of the string per second, rather than pitch. Since the pitch of a tone gets higher whenever the frequency increases, it will not really alter the formulas. They are:

$$\frac{F_1{}^2}{F_2{}^2} = \frac{T_1}{T_2}; \quad \frac{F_1}{F_2} = \frac{L_2}{L_1}; \quad \frac{F_1}{F_2} = \sqrt{\frac{D_2}{D_1}}$$

$$\left(\begin{array}{c}\text{strings are}\\\text{same type}\end{array}\right) \quad \left(\begin{array}{c}\text{tension}\\\text{constant}\end{array}\right) \quad \left(\begin{array}{c}\text{length and ten-}\\\text{sion constant}\end{array}\right)$$

where F = frequency
      T = tension
      D = diameter
         of string

Have students try numerical examples: A string which vibrates at a frequency of 400 vps (vibra-tions per second) is 20 inches long. A second string of the same type is plucked in a similar manner. (The tension being the same as in the first case.) If its frequency is 800 vps, how long is it? Have them solve $\frac{400}{800} = \frac{L_2}{20}$, concluding that the length of the second string is 10 inches. Another example could be the effect on the tension if the frequency of a string doubles. Elicit that the tension quad-ruples. $(\frac{1^2}{2^2} = \frac{1}{4})$

Music and mathematics are also related to the creation of a scale. Pythagoras, familiar to most students for his work with the right triangle, produced a scale that could make beautiful melodies, but limited the combination of tones possible and the use of harmony.

Pythagoras felt that those tones which were particularly pleasing, or *consonant,* were related to the numbers 1, 2, 3 and 4. He took several strings of the same length, letting the note C be the fundamental tone. If the sonometer is used, the teacher can demonstrate the basics of what Pythagoras did. This means that the string vibrates as a whole (See Diagram 1). To obtain the note C an octave higher, the string must vibrate in two parts, i.e., have twice the frequency (See Diagram 2). One can also accomplish the same thing by dividing a string into two parts of the ratio 1:2 (See Diagram 3).

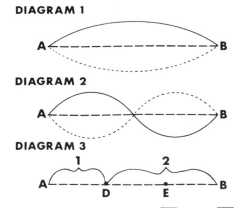

DIAGRAM 1

DIAGRAM 2

DIAGRAM 3

In Diagram 3, vibrating $\overline{AD}$ and $\overline{DB}$ sep-arately will have the same effect of producing 2 notes an octave apart. Thus, if C corresponds to the number 1, then C an octave higher would corre-spond to the number $\frac{2}{1}$ or 2. Pythagoras also added notes F and G corresponding to $\frac{4}{3}$ and $\frac{3}{2}$ respec-tively. Ask the students how the string can be divided into the ratio 3:2. Elicit that the string can be divided into five parts to obtain the result.

This is one reason why this note can be called a perfect fifth. To obtain a note corresponding to $\frac{4}{3}$ the string should be divided into seven parts as shown.

However, this note is called a fourth and not a seventh.

Pythagoras added to his scale $\frac{3}{2}$G or $\frac{3}{2} \cdot \frac{3}{2}$C $= \frac{9}{4}$C. Since C $= 1$ and the octave C $= 2$, $\frac{9}{4}$C $= 2\frac{1}{4}$C would not fit between these notes. Challenge the students to find a tone "basically" the same that would fit between C and its octave. Have them recall that doubling or halving a frequency only changes a tone by an octave. Thus, instead of $\frac{9}{4}$, Pythagoras used $\frac{1}{2}$ of $\frac{9}{4}$ or $\frac{9}{8}$. By adding the third harmonic of each successive tone (i.e. multiplying by $\frac{3}{2}$), students will be able to obtain tones whose relative frequencies are $1, \frac{3}{2}, \frac{9}{8}, \frac{27}{16}, \frac{81}{64}, \frac{243}{128}$. Of course, some additional "halving" was done when needed as in the case of $\frac{9}{8}$ Pythagoras' diatonic scale is thus obtained.

C	D	E	F	G	A	B	C	
1	$\frac{9}{8}$	$\frac{81}{64}$	$\frac{4}{3}$	$\frac{3}{2}$	$\frac{27}{16}$	$\frac{243}{128}$	2	$\left(\begin{smallmatrix}\text{Relative}\\\text{Frequencies}\end{smallmatrix}\right)$

G, which occupies the fifth position, is considered a perfect fifth. This occurs whenever the ratio of the fifth to the first is $\frac{3}{2}$. Throughout the discussion, the fact that frequencies are in the same ratio as their lengths should be stressed.

Have students study the scale in its new form. Elicit that there is a constant ratio of $\frac{9}{8}$ between notes (except between E and F and between B and C where the ratio is $\frac{256}{243}$). It should also be noted that $\frac{9}{8}$ corresponds to a whole tone (W) while the other is called a semitone (S). Thus, the pattern obtained is as follows:

C	D	E	F	G	A	B	C
1	$\frac{9}{8}$	$\frac{81}{64}$	$\frac{4}{3}$	$\frac{3}{2}$	$\frac{27}{16}$	$\frac{243}{128}$	2
	W	W	S	W	W	W	S

This is called a major scale.

However, there is some difficulty with harmony. When one sounds a tone on a musical instrument it not only vibrates in one piece making the fundamental tone, but also in parts creating tones called overtones. The overtones have 2, 3, 4 and 5 times the frequency of the fundamental. The fifth overtone corresponds to 5 or $\frac{5}{4}$ if it is to be placed between 1 and 2 (recall continuous halving like $\frac{1}{2} \cdot \frac{1}{2}$ creates a similar tone). The closest tone on the Pythagorean scale is E of frequency $\frac{81}{64}$. When a C is played and then followed by an E, the ear expects to hear the same E just heard as an overtone of C. However, to the individual the Pythagorean E can be quite disturbing. This disturbance is due to the fact that the two E's involved have only slightly different frequencies, one being $\frac{81}{64}$ and the other $\frac{5}{4}$ or $\frac{80}{64}$.

Postassessment

1) If the tension is constant and the length is increased, how is a string's pitch affected?

2) How does string tightening affect pitch?

3) Suppose C corresponds to $\frac{4}{5}$ instead of 1 in Pythagoras' scale. Find the relative frequencies of the next 8 notes of this major scale.

30   Mathematics In Nature

Performance Objective
Students will identify and explain where mathematics is found in nature in at least one situation.

Preassessment
A famous sequence of numbers (*The Fibonacci Numbers*) was the direct result of a problem posed by Leonardo of Pisa in his book *Liber Abaci* (1202) regarding the regeneration of rabbits. A brief review of this problem indicates that the total number of pairs of rabbits existing each month determined the sequence: 1,1,2,3,5,8,13,21,34,55, 89,. . . .

Fibonacci Numbers have many interesting properties and have been found to occur in nature.

Teaching Strategies
Have students divide each number in the Fibonacci sequence by its right hand partner to see what sequence develops. They will get a series of fractions:

$$\frac{1}{1}, \frac{1}{2}, \frac{2}{3}, \frac{3}{5}, \frac{5}{8}, \frac{8}{13}, \frac{13}{21}, \frac{21}{34}, \frac{34}{55}, \frac{55}{89}, \cdots$$

Ask students if they can determine a relationship between these numbers and the leaves of a plant (have a plant on hand). From the standpoint of Fibonacci Numbers, one may observe two items: (1) the number of leaves it takes to go (rotating about the stem) from any given leaf to the next one 'similarly placed' (i.e., above it and in the same direction) on the stem; and (2) the number of revolutions as one follows the leaves in going from one leaf to another one 'similarly placed'. In both cases, these numbers turn out to be the Fibonacci numbers.

In the case of leaf arrangement, the following notation is used: $\frac{3}{8}$ means that it takes three revolutions and eight leaves to arrive at the next leaf 'similarly placed'. In general, if we let r equal the number of revolutions, and s equal the number of leaves it takes to go from any given leaf to one 'similarly placed', then $\frac{r}{s}$ will be the *phyllotaxis* (the arrangement of leaves in plants). Have students look at Figure 1 and try to find the plant ratio. Draw a diagram on the board, and if possible, provide a live plant.

In this figure, the, plant ratio is $\frac{5}{8}$.

The pine cone, also presents a Fibonacci application. The bracts on the cone are considered to be modified leaves compressed into smaller space. Upon observation of the cone, one can notice two spirals, one to the left (clockwise) and the other to the right (counterclockwise). One spiral increases at a sharp angle, while the other spiral increases more gradually. Have students consider the steep spirals and count them as well as the spirals that increase gradually. Both numbers should be Fibonacci numbers. For example, a white pine cone has five clockwise spirals and eight counterclockwise spirals. Other pine cones may have different Fibonacci ratios. Later, have students examine the daisy to see where the Fibonacci ratios apply to it.

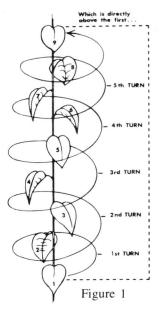

Figure 1

If we look closely at the ratios of consecutive Fibonacci numbers, we can approximate their decimal equivalents. Some are:

(1) $\frac{2}{3} = .666667$ (2) $\frac{3}{5} = .600000$

(3) $\frac{89}{144} = .618056$ (4) $\frac{144}{233} = .618026$

Continuing in this manner, we approach what is known as the *golden ratio*. Point B in Figure 2 divides line $\overleftrightarrow{AC}$ into the golden ratio, $\frac{AB}{BC} = \frac{BC}{AC} \approx .618034$.

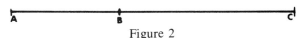

Figure 2

Now consider the series of golden rectangles (Fig. 3a and 3b), those whose dimensions are chosen so that the ratio of $\frac{width}{length}$ is the golden ratio (i.e., $\frac{w}{1} = \frac{1}{w + 1}$)

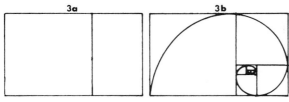

Figure 3

If the rectangle (Fig. 3a) is divided by a line into a square and a golden rectangle, and if we keep partitioning each new golden rectangle in the same way, we can construct a 'logarithmic spiral' in the successive squares (Fig. 3b). This type of curve is frequently found in the arrangements of seeds in flowers or in the shapes of sea-shells and snails. Bring in illustrations to show these spirals. (Fig. 4)

Figure 4

For another example of mathematics in nature, students should consider the pineapple. Here there are three distinct spirals of hexagons: a group of *five* spirals winding gradually in one direction, a second group of *13* spirals winding more steeply in the same direction, and a third group of *eight* spirals winding in the opposite direction. Each group of spirals consists of a Fibonacci number. Each pair of spirals interacts to give Fibonacci numbers. Figure 5 shows a representation of the pineapple with the scales numbered in order. This order is determined by the distance (relative) each hexagon is from the bottom. That is, the lowest is numbered 0, the next higher one is numbered 1. Note hexagon 42 is slightly higher than hexagon 37.

See if students can note three distinct sets of spirals in Figure 5 which cross each other, starting at the bottom. One spiral is the 0,5,10, etc., sequence, which increases at a slight angle. The second spiral is the 0,13,26, etc., sequence, which increases at a steeper angle. The third spiral has the 0,8,16, etc., sequence, which lies in the opposite direction from the other two. Have students figure out the common difference between the numbers in each sequence. In this case, the differences are 5,8,13, all of which are Fibonacci numbers. Different pineapples may have different sequences.

In concluding this topic, consider briefly the regeneration of male bees. Male bees hatch from unfertilized eggs; female bees from fertilized eggs. The teacher should guide students in tracing the regeneration of the male bees. The following pattern develops:

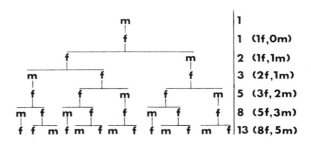

It should be obvious by now that this pattern is the Fibonacci sequence.

Postassessment

1) Ask students to explain two distinct ways mathematics manifests itself in nature.

2) Have students find examples of Fibonacci numbers in nature (other than those presented in this unit) and have them explain the manner in which the sequence is used.

References

Brother U. Alfred, *An Introduction to Fibonacci Discovery.* San Jose, Calif.: The Fibonacci Association, 1965.

Bicknell, M. and Verner E. Hoggatt, Jr., *A Primer for the Fibonacci Numbers.* San Jose, Calif.: The Fibonacci Association, 1972.

Hoggatt, Verner E., Jr. *Fibonacci and Lucas Numbers.* Boston: Houghton Mifflin, 1969.

Figure 5

31   The Birthday Problem

Students are fascinated by problems that involve surprise or unpredictable outcomes. The "birthday problem" will engage them in the study of mathematical probability.

Performance Objective

In problems involving sequences of successive events, such as indications of birthdays, tossing of coins, drawing of cards, throwing of dice, students will calculate the probability that a specified outcome (a) occurs at least once, (b) fails to occur at all.

Preassessment

Ask the class what they think the probability is of two students in the class sharing the same birthday. The students will respond that the chances of this being true are remote. Surprise them by telling them that, in a class of 30 students, the probability of at least two students having the same birthday is approximately 0.68 (a probability of 1.00 indicates an absolute certainty). In a class of 35 students, this probability rises to about 0.80. Restate these probabilities in the language of "odds." Point out that the odds in favor of the desired outcome in the first instance are better than two to one and in the second about four to one. Ditto and distribute a list of the 40 Presidents of the U.S.A. with the dates of their birth and death next to their names. Give students time to look for any dates the Presidents had in common. (Two, Polk and Harding, were born on November 2; two, Fillmore and Taft, died on March 8; and three, Adams, Jefferson, and Monroe, died on July 4.) Now take a class survey to determine if any students share the same birthday. If they do, this fact will reinforce the probability figures and will help convince them of the statistical plausibility. If they do not, indicate that no claim of absolute certainty was made.

Teaching Strategies

Review the following fundamental principles the students will need to know. Mathematical probabilities are stated as decimals between 0.00 and 1.00, and a probability of 0 (zero) means that a particular outcome is impossible while a probability of 1 (one) means that a particular outcome is a certainty.

Each of the principles enumerated here may be illustrated by simple examples in the tossing of coins, the throwing of dice, the drawing of cards, etc. For example, the probability of throwing a total of 13 with a pair of ordinary dice is equal to zero, while the probability of throwing some number between two and 12 inclusive is equal to one. The probability of a desired outcome occurring can be calculated by forming a fraction whose numerator represents the number of "acceptable" or "successful" outcomes and whose denominator represents the sum of the "successful" outcomes and the "unsuccessful" outcomes or "failures." Symbolically, $P = \dfrac{S}{S+F}$ or $P = \dfrac{S}{T}$. P represents the probability of a particular event occurring, S the number of successful outcomes, F the number of failures, and T the total number of outcomes possible. Either form of this fraction may be converted to a decimal between zero and one, since the numerator may never exceed the denominator.

The students should also note that the probability of a desired outcome <u>failing</u> to occur would be equal to $\dfrac{F}{S+F}$. Since $\dfrac{S}{S+F} + \dfrac{F}{S+F} = \dfrac{S+F}{S+F} = 1$, it follows that $\dfrac{S}{S+F} = 1 - \dfrac{F}{S+F}$.

The students should now state in words that the probability of a desired outcome <u>occurring</u> is equal numerically to 1.00 minus the probability of this outcome failing to occur. This statement enables them to complete the lesson.

Students should be familiar with a fundamental theorem of probability and it is presented here without proof: If the probability of an event is P_1, and if, after it has happened, the probability of a second event is P_2, then the probability that both events will happen is $P_1 P_2$. Point out that this principle may be generalized to calculate the probability that a sequence of n events will occur, given that each preceding event has occurred, and that the result would be $P_1 P_2 P_3 P_4 \ldots P_n$. For example, the students, by performing the following activities, will realize that the probability of drawing a spade from an ordinary deck of 52 cards is 13/52 or 0.25 and the probability of <u>not</u> drawing a spade is 39/52 or 0.75; where both probabilities refer to the drawing of a single card from the deck; they should note that 0.25 = 1.00 − 0.75. The probability of tossing a head, followed by a tail, followed by another tail, where a "true" coin is tossed three times in succession, is $1/2 \cdot 1/2 \cdot 1/2$ or 1/8, illustrating the use of the fundamental principle for dealing with successive events.

Back to the birthday problem. You might point

out that it will be simpler to calculate the probability that *no* students in the class share the same birthday and then to subtract this result from 1.00, than to directly calculate the probability that at least two students in the class have the same birthday. Help the students to formulate the following representation of the probability that *no* students in the class share the same birthday:

$$\frac{365}{365} \cdot \frac{364}{365} \cdot \frac{363}{365} \cdot \frac{362}{365} \cdot \frac{361}{365} \cdot \frac{360}{365} \cdot \frac{359}{365} \cdot \frac{358}{365} \cdot \frac{357}{365} \cdot \frac{356}{365} \cdot \ldots$$

There will be as many fractions in this product as there are students in the class. Note that this formulation is based on an ordinary year of 365 days. If any of your students has a February 29 birthday, use denominators of 366 and have the first fraction read 366/366.

Explain that these fractions represent the probabilities that students questioned in sequence as to their birthdays would *not* name a day already mentioned by a preceding student. Point out the fundamental principle for calculating the probability of successive events—sequential questioning. They will be interested in learning how they can best perform the sequence of multiplications and divisions—the simplest approach is through the use of calculators.

The students will discover that the value of their product has decreased to about 0.32 when the number of factors has reached 30, and to about 0.20 when the number of factors has reached 35. Since these figures represent the probabilities that no students in the class shared the same birthday, they represent "failures," in the terminology of this problem. Using the principle of subtraction from 1.00, already mentioned, to arrive at the probabilities of "successes"—the probabilities that at least two students in the class share the same birthday—we arrive at 0.68 or 0.80 or some other high decimal, depending on the size of the class. When the number of people in a group reaches just 55, the probability of finding at least two with the same birthday reaches the astonishing value of 0.99!

Evaluation

Students who have met the performance objective will be able to answer these or similar probabilities correctly:

1. Represent the probability that, given a group of 15 people, at least 2 share the same birthday.

2. If a coin is tossed into the air five times, what is the probability that (a) none of the tosses will turn up "heads" and (b) at least one of the tosses will turn up "heads"?

3. If a card is drawn from an ordinary deck of 52 cards, examined and replaced, and if this is repeated four times, what is the probability that (a) at least one of the cards drawn is a spade, and (b) none of the cards drawn is an ace?

32 The Structure of the Number System

Performance Objectives

Given any number, the student will identify it as belonging to the set of natural numbers, integers, rational numbers, real numbers, or complex numbers. The student will also convert any decimal representing a rational number to its equivalent fractional form and vice versa.

Preassessment

Assess students' ability with the following pretest, assuring them, of course, that this is a trial test and they will not be graded on it:

1. Identify the following numbers as belonging to the set of natural numbers, integers, rational numbers, real numbers, or complex numbers (name the "smallest" possible set in each case): -3, $5/3$, 17, $\sqrt{2}$, 3.14, $22/7$, $\sqrt{-9}$, $.\overline{4}$, $0.2133333\ldots$, $2.71828\ldots$, $0.121121112\ldots$, $.\overline{15}$, $.1\overline{5}$, $-1/4$, $-\sqrt{16}$, etc.

2. Convert each of the following fractions to decimals: $3/8$, $7/5$, $2/3$, $7/9$, $5/11$, $5/12$.

3. Convert each of the following decimals to fractions: 0.875, $.\overline{8}$, $.272727\ldots$, $0.8333333\ldots$.

Students who do well on the pretest have already attained the performance objective. Give them a different assignment while you present this lesson to the rest of the class.

Teaching Strategies

Ask your students to solve a simple linear equation such as $3x + 5 = 11$. When the correct solution, $x = 2$, is offered, ask what kind of number this is. Students may use such terms as "whole number" or "positive number" in their responses. Explain that 2 is a *counting* number and that the set of counting numbers is known mathematically as the set of natural numbers. Elicit other illustrations of natural numbers and have the students describe the set by roster: N =

{1, 2, 3, . . . }. They should note that the elements of this set are ordered and infinite in number, and that the set possesses a first or smallest element, the member 1.

Proceed in a similar fashion to develop the concept of the set of integers. Modify the equation just explored by reversing the two constants: $3x + 11 = 5$. When they obtain $x = -2$ as the solution, the students will volunteer that this is a negative whole number or some other similar description. Introduce the term ''integer'' if it is not mentioned by the class. They will readily understand that this term is synonymous with the term ''whole number'' and that the natural numbers just studied are a subset of the set of integers. This can be illustrated by a Venn diagram which, at this stage of the lesson, consists of an inner circle labeled ''N'' to represent the set of natural numbers and an outer circle labeled ''I'' to represent the set of integers. This diagram will be built up as the lesson develops by the addition of three more circles, each completely encircling all of the preceding circles. Elicit several illustrations of integers and help your students to describe this set by roster: I = { . . . , $-3, -2, -1, 0, 1, 2, 3$ . . . }. They will note that this set is also an infinite one and that it is ordered, but that it possesses *no* first element.

Now offer the equation $2x + 1 = 6$. When the answer, 5/2, is forthcoming, students will recognize that this number is *not* a member of the set of natural numbers or the set of integers since it is not a whole number but, rather, a fraction. Point out that such numbers are formed by setting up the ratio of two integers, *a/b,* where the denominator, *b,* is not equal to zero (ask your students why not!). The term ''rational number'' derives naturally from the word ''ratio.'' Add the third circle to your Venn diagram, completely enclosing the previous two circles. Label the new circle ''Q'' for quotient.

Elicit numerous illustrations of rational numbers, including proper and improper fractions, both positive and negative. Students should be aware that the set of rational numbers is infinite and ordered, but that no roster can be prepared for this set. You might explain that the rational numbers are ''everywhere dense'' and that an infinitude of rationals exists between any two rational numbers.

We are now ready to examine the decimals. Students will generally exhibit some uncertainty as to which of these represent rational numbers. We must consider terminating decimals, nonterminating but repeating decimals, and nonterminating and nonrepeating decimals. Your students can obtain some clues by converting a few fractions such as 1/8, 5/9, and 1/6 to decimals by dividing their numerators by their denominators. They will observe that the result

in every case is either a terminating decimal or a nonterminating but repeating decimal. Students can show easily that every terminating decimal represents a rational number by simply writing each one as a decimal fraction.

Next, introduce nonterminating decimals. Students who believe that $0.\overline{3}$ represents a rational number can be challenged to write it in fractional form. Some may recognize this decimal as being equal to 1/3. If so, challenge them with the decimal $0.\overline{5}$ which they obtained earlier themselves by converting 5/9 to a decimal, or with 0.16666 . . . which they also obtained themselves by converting 1/6 to a decimal. Ask them whether they could convert these decimals to fractions if they did *not* know the answers! Or, challenge them with the decimal $0.\overline{13}$, for which it is unlikely that they will know the result. If they need your help to convert such decimals to fractions, two illustrations will make the technique clear.

N = 0.131313 . . .
Multiply by 100:
100N = 13.131313 . . .
  N = 0.131313 . . .
 99N = 13 by subtraction
  $N = \dfrac{13}{99}$

N = .1666666 . . .
Multiply by 10:
10N = 1.666666 . . .
  N = 0.166666 . . .
 9N = 1.5 by subtraction
90N = 15
  $N = \dfrac{15}{90} = \dfrac{1}{6}$

Provide several illustrations for your students, including some with nonrepeating portions in the decimal before the repetand appears, as in the second example above. Help them to grasp the fact that such decimals represent rational numbers, even though their nonrepeating portions may be lengthy, as long as they are finite in length *and* they are followed by repetands of one or more digits.

Your students are now ready to consider the nonterminating, nonrepeating decimals. They are already familiar with some of these, notably $\pi = 3.14159$ . . . and perhaps the square roots of some of the nonperfect squares. (Be certain they understand that such numbers as 22/7 and 3.14 or 3.1416 are only *rational approximations* to the *irrational* number π.) Propose the equation $x^2 + 2 = 7$. Those who are familiar with the square root algorithm may be asked to work out $\sqrt{5}$ to a few decimal places to determine whether a pattern of repetition appears. They will discover, of course, that it does not, since $\sqrt{5}=2.236\ldots$ and is irrational.

Students unfamiliar with the algorithm may refer to a table of square roots. They will discover that the only square roots which contain a repetand in their decimal representations are those of perfect squares. All other square roots are irrational numbers, since they are nonterminating, nonrepeating decimals. You may also wish to generalize this result to the nth roots of nonperfect nth powers.

Explain to your students that the set of the rational numbers together with the set of irrational numbers form the set of real numbers. Add a fourth circle to your Venn diagram, labeling it ''R,'' and have it completely enclose the three circles previously drawn. The students should realize that the sets of natural numbers, integers, and rational numbers are each proper subsets of the set of real numbers.

This development of the structure of the number system may be concluded with a brief treatment of the complex numbers. Ask your students to try to solve the equation $x^2 + 4 = 0$. Help them to see why answers such as $+2$ and -2 are incorrect. They should soon realize that no real number squared can equal -4, or any other negative number, for that matter. Explain that numbers which are not real are called ''imaginary'' and that the imaginary numbers and the real numbers together form the set known as the ''complex numbers.'' You may wish to introduce the symbol $i = \sqrt{-1}$ so they can write a solution for their equation as $+2i$ and $-2i$. Complete the Venn diagram with the fifth and last circle, completely enclosing the other four circles, and showing the real numbers as a proper subset of the complex numbers, ''C.''

Evaluation

Give students a test similar to the pretest. Compare each student's pre- and posttest answers to measure progress.

33 Excursions in Number Bases

Students learn early in their school careers that the base used in our everyday number system (the ''decimal system'') is the number 10. Later, they discover that other numbers can serve as bases for number systems. For example, numbers written in base 2 (the ''binary system'') are used extensively in computer work. This lesson will explore a variety of problems involving numbers written in many different positive integral bases.

Performance Objective

Students will solve a variety of numerical and algebraic problems involving numbers expressed as numerals in any positive integral base b, $b \geq 2$.

Preassessment

How far you go in this lesson will depend somewhat on the algebraic background of the class. Question students or evaluate their previous work to determine how well they understand the idea of place value in writing numerals, the meaning of zero and negative exponents, and the techniques for solving quadratic and higher degree equations.

Teaching Strategies

Review briefly the fact that decimal numerals are written by using a system of place values. Point out, for example, that in the numeral 356 the digit *3* represents

300 rather than merely a *3*, the digit *5* represents *50* rather than merely a *5*, while the digit *6* is a units digit and really does represent a *6*. Briefly, $356 = 300 + 50 + 6 = 3(100) + 5(10) + 6 = 3(10)^2 + 5(10)^1 + 6(10)^0$. Likewise, $3,107 = 3(10)^3 + 1(10)^2 + 0(10)^1 + 7(10)^0$. Ask students for further illustrations. If necessary, review or teach at this point the meaning of the zero exponent and also of negative exponents, since these will be used later.

Explain that the use of the number 10 as a base is somewhat arbitrary, and students should note that other numbers can be used as bases. If the number 2 is used as a base, numbers are expressed as sums of powers of 2 rather than as sums of positive integral multiples of powers of 10, and the only digits used to represent numerals are 0 and 1. For example, the number 356 considered above is equal to $256 + 64 + 32 + 4 = 2^8 + 2^6 + 2^5 + 2^2 = 1(2)^8 + 0(2)^7 + 1(2)^6 + 1(2)^5 + 0(2)^4 + 0(2)^3 + 1(2)^2 + 0(2)^1 + 0(2)^0 = 101100100_{\text{two}}$, the subscript indicating the base. In base 3 (where the digits used to represent the numerals are 0, 1, and 2) $356 = 243 + 81 + 27 + 3 + 2(1) = 1(3)^5 + 1(3)^4 + 1(3)^3 + 0(3)^2 + 1(3)^1 + 2(3)^0 = 111012_{\text{three}}$. In base 5 (where the digits used are 0, 1, 2, 3, and 4) $356 = 2(125) + 4(25) + 1(5) + 1(1) = 2(5)^3 + 4(5)^2 + 1(5)^1 + 1(5)^0 = 2411_{\text{five}}$. Subscripts should be written in words rather than in numerals to avoid any possible confusion.

The class should note that when numerals are in base b, the only digits available for such representations are those from zero to $b - 1$, and that if the value of b is greater than 10, new digits must be created to represent the numerals 10, 11, 12, etc. Remind the class that numerals such as 2411_{five} should be read "two, four, one, one, base 5." Provide practice in writing and reading whole numbers in the numerals of bases other than base 10, according to class needs.

Next consider numbers other than integers. Help your students to see that 12.2_{ten} means $1(10)^1 + 2(10)^0 + 2(10)^{-1}$, since $10^0 = 1$ and $10^{-1} = 1/10$, and that this number can be represented in the numerals of other bases just as integers can. For example, in base 5 we have $12.2_{\text{ten}} = 2(5)^1 + 2(5)^0 + 1(5)^{-1}$, since $1/5 = 2/10$, so $12.2_{\text{ten}} = 22.1_{\text{five}}$. Illustrate further with such problems as the conversion of 7.5_{ten} to base 2: $7.5_{\text{ten}} = 1(2)^2 + 1(2)^1 + 1(2)^0 + 1(2)^{-1} = 111.1_{\text{two}}$. Decimal numerals whose decimal parts are .5 (1/2), .25 (1/4), .75 (3/4), .125 (1/8), etc., can be easily converted to base 2 numerals. For example, $8.75_{\text{ten}} = 1(2)^3 + 1(2)^{-1} + 1(2)^{-2}$, since $.75 = 3/4 = 1/2 + 1/4 = 1/2^1 + 1/2^2 = 2^{-1} + 2^{-2}$, so $8.75_{\text{ten}} = 1000.11_{\text{two}}$. Numbers can also be converted from numeral representations in one base to equivalent numeral representations in another base, where neither base is equal to 10. For example, 12.2_{four} can be represented in base 6 numerals as follows: $12.2_{\text{four}} = 1(4)^1 + 2(4)^0 + 2(4)^{-1} = 4 + 2 + 2/4 = 6 + 3/6 = 1(6)^1 + 0(6)^0 + 3(6)^{-1} = 10.3_{\text{six}}$. In base 10, this is the numeral 6.5. Provide practice with these types of numerical problems according to the interests and abilities of your students.

The class is ready to consider algebraic problems next. Offer the following challenge: "In a certain base b, the number 52 is double the number 25. Find the value of b." The students should note that 52 (read "five, two") really represents the expression $5b + 2$, since $52_b = 5(b)^1 + 2(b)^0$. Accordingly, the problem states that $5b + 2 = 2(2b + 5)$. Solve for b to get $b = 8$. Checking shows that $52_{\text{eight}} = 5(8) + 2 = 42_{\text{ten}}$ and $25_{\text{eight}} = 2(8) + 5 = 21_{\text{ten}}$ and $42 = 2(21)$. The above equation is only a linear one, but the following problem requires the use of a quadratic equation: "In what base b is the number represented by 132 twice the number represented by 33?" You have $132b = 1(b)^2 + 3(b)^1 + 2(b)^0$ and $33_b = 3(b)^1 + 3(b)^0$, so our equation becomes $b^2 + 3b + 2 = 2(3b + 3)$ or $b^2 - 3b - 4 = 0$. Solve for b in the usual fashion to obtain $b = -1$, (which must be rejected since the domain of b is positive), and $b = 4$, the only acceptable solution. Check: $132_{\text{four}} = 1(4)^2 + 3(4)^1 + 2(4)^0 = 1(16) + 3(4) + 2 = 30_{\text{ten}}$ and $33_{\text{four}} = 3(4)^1 + 3(4)^0 = 3(4) + 3 = 15_{\text{ten}}$; and 30 is twice 15. Offer students similar problems. If they have studied the solution of equations of degree higher than two, by synthetic division (since all results will be integral),

include numbers whose representations in the bases being used involve more than three digits. For example: "In what base b is the number represented by the numeral 1213 triple the number represented by the numeral 221?" You have $1(b)^3 + 2(b)^2 + 1(b)^1 + 3(b)^0 = 3[2(b)^2 + 2(b)^1 + 1(b)^0]$ or $b^3 + 2b^2 + b + 3 = 3(2b^2 + 2b + 1)$, which simplifies to $b^3 - 4b^2 - 5b = 0$. Since this equation can be factored without resorting to synthetic division, solve it as follows: $b(b - 5)(b + 1) = 0$ and $b = 0, 5, -1$. As before, the only acceptable solution is the positive one, $b = 5$. Ask the class to check this result.

A final interesting algebraic application of number base problems is suggested by the following: "In base 10, the numeral 121 represents a number that is a perfect square. Does the numeral represent a perfect square in any other positive integral base?" Help your students investigate this problem as follows: $121_b = 1(b)^2 + 2(b)^1 + 1(b)^0 = b^2 + 2b + 1 = (b + 1)^2$. Surprise! The numeral 121 represents a perfect square in *any* positive integral base $b \geq 3$, and is the square of one more than the base number! Are there any other such numerals? Students may discover others by squaring such expressions as $b + 2$ and $b + 3$ to obtain the numerals 144 and 169. These perfect squares in base 10 are also perfect squares in any positive integral base containing the digits used in them ($b \geq 5$ and $b \geq 10$, respectively). It's not necessary for the coefficient of b to equal 1. If you square $2b + 1$, for example, you obtain $4b^2 + 4b + 1 = 441_b$, which will be a perfect square in any positive integral base $b \geq 5$. Invite your students to try to square expressions such as $3b + 1, 2b + 2, 4b + 1$, etc., to obtain other perfect squares. Some may wish to continue this investigation into a search for perfect cubes, perfect fourth powers, etc. Help them to cube $b + 1$, for example, to obtain $b^3 + 3b^2 + 3b + 1$, indicating that the numeral 1331 is a perfect cube in any positive integral base $b \geq 4$ (in base 10, $1331 = 11^3$). As a matter of fact, 1331 is the cube of one more than the base number in each case! This study can be carried as far as the interest and ability of your class permits. Students familiar with the binomial theorem will find it convenient to use in expanding higher powers of such expressions as $b + 1, 2b + 1$, etc.

Evaluation

Students who have met the performance objective will be able to solve problems such as the following:

1. Represent the decimal numeral 78 as a numeral in base 5.

2. The number represented by the numeral 1000.1 in base 2 is represented by what numeral in base 8?

3. In a certain base b, the number represented by the numeral 54 is three times the number represented by the numeral 16. Find the value of b.

4. In a certain base b, the number represented by the numeral 231 is double the number represented by the numeral 113. Find the value of b.

5. In what bases would the numeral 100 represent a perfect square? In what bases would the numeral 1000 represent a perfect cube? Can you make a generalization of these results?

34 Raising Interest

Students are often confronted with advertisements by savings institutions offering attractive interest rates and frequent compounding of interest on deposits. Since most banks have a variety of programs, it's valuable for potential depositors to understand how interest is calculated under each of the available options.

Performance Objective

Students will use the formula for compound interest to calculate the return on investments at any rate of interest, for any period of time, and for any commonly used frequency of compounding, including instantaneous (continuous) compounding. They will also determine which of two or more alternatives gives the best return over the same time period.

Preassessment

Since this lesson requires the ability to apply the laws of logarithms, question students to be certain they're familiar with these laws. You should also determine the extent to which they are familiar with limits, since the class' background will help you determine how deeply you treat the concept of instantaneous compounding.

Teaching Strategies

Propose the following interesting problem: "In the year 1626, Peter Minuit bought Manhattan Island for the Dutch West India Company from the Indians for trinkets costing 60 Dutch guilders, or about $24. Suppose Indians had been able to invest this $24 at that time at an annual interest rate of 6%, and suppose further that this same interest rate had continued in effect all these years. How much money could the present-day descendants of these Indians collect if (1) only simple interest were calculated, and (2) interest were compounded (a) annually, (b) quarterly and (c) continuously?" The answers to a, b and c should surprise everyone!

Review briefly the formula for simple interest, studied in earlier lessons. The class will recall that simple interest is calculated by taking the product of the principle P, the annual interest rate r, and the time in years t. Accordingly, you have the formula $I = Prt$, and in the above problem $I = (24)(.06)(354) = \$509.76$ simple interest. Add this to the principle of 24.00 to obtain the amount A of 533.76 available at present. You have just used the formula for "amount," $A = P + Prt$.

With this relatively small sum in mind (for a return after 354 years!) turn to investigate the extent to which this return would have been improved if interest had been compounded annually instead of being calculated on only a simple basis. With a principle P, an annual rate of interest r, and a time $t = 1$, the amount A at the end of the first year is given by the formula $A_1 = P + Pr = P(1 + r)$. (The subscript indicates the year at the end of which interest is calculated.) Now $A_1 = P(1 + r)$ becomes the principle at the beginning of the second year, upon which interest will be credited during the second year. Therefore, $A_2 = P(1 + r) + P(1 + r)r = P(1 + r)(1 + r) = P(1 + r)^2$. Since the last expression represents the principle at the beginning of the third year, you have $A_3 = P(1 + r)^2 + P(1 + r)^2 r = P(1 + r)^2(1 + r) = P(1 + r)^3$. By now, your students will see the emerging pattern and should be able to suggest the generalization for the amount after t years, $A_t = P(1 + r)^t$.

Now try this formula on the $24 investment made in 1626! Assuming annual compounding at 6% per annum, you have $A_{354} = 24(1 + .06)^{354} = 21,801,558,740$. This means that the original $24 is now worth almost $22 billion! Most students are truly surprised by the huge difference between this figure and the figure $533.76 obtained by computing simple interest.

Most banks now compound not annually, but quarterly, monthly, daily, or continuously, so next generalize the formula $A = P(1 + r)^t$ to take into account compounding at more frequent intervals. Help your students observe that if interest is compounded semi-annually, the *periodic rate* would be only *one-half* the annual rate, but the number of periods would be *twice* the number of years: so

$$A = P\left(1 + \frac{r}{2}\right)^{2t}.$$ Likewise, if interest is com-

pounded quarterly $A = P\left(1 + \dfrac{r}{4}\right)^{2t}$. In general, if interest is compounded n times per year, you have $A = P\left(1 + \dfrac{r}{n}\right)^{nt}$. This formula may be used for any finite value of n. Letting $n = 4$ in the problem yields $A = 24\left(1 + \dfrac{.06}{4}\right)^{4(354)} = 24(1.015)^{1416} = 34{,}365{,}848{,}150$. The $24 has now risen to about $34 billion.

Students should note that changing the compounding from annually to quarterly increased the yield by about $12 billion.

Students may now ask whether the yield can be increased indefinitely by simply increasing the frequency of compounding. A complete treatment of this question requires a thorough development of the concept of limits, but an informal, intuitive approach will suffice here. Have students first explore the simpler problem of an investment of $1 at a nominal annual interest rate of 100% for a period of one year. This will give $A = 1\left(1 + \dfrac{1.00}{n}\right)^{n} = \left(1 + \dfrac{1.00}{n}\right)^{n}$ Ask the students to prepare a table of values for A for various common values of n, such as $n = 1$ (annual compounding), $n = 2$ (semiannual), $n = 4$ (quarterly), $n = 12$ (monthly). They should note that the amount A does *not* rise astronomically as n increases, but rather rises slowly from $2.00 ($n = 1$) to about $2.60 ($n = 12$). Explain that the amount A would approach, but not quite reach, the value $2.72. (The extent to which you may wish to discuss the fact that $\lim\limits_{n \to \infty} \left(1 + \dfrac{1}{n}\right)^{n} = e = 2.71828\ldots$ will depend on the backgrounds and abilities of your math students.)

Since investments generally don't draw 100% interest, you must next convert to a general interest rate or r. Setting $\dfrac{r}{n} = \dfrac{1}{k}$, you have $n = kr$, and $A = P\left(1 + \dfrac{r}{n}\right)^{nt}$ becomes $A = P\left(1 + \dfrac{1}{k}\right)^{krt} = P\left[\left(1 + \dfrac{1}{k}\right)^{k}\right]^{rt}$. Clearly, as n approaches infinity so does k, since r is finite, so the expression in brackets approaches the value e as a limit. You then have the formula $A = Pe^{rt}$ *for instantaneous compounding,*

where r is the nominal annual rate of interest and t is the time in years.

Students might be interested in knowing that this formula is a special representation of the general "Law of Growth," which is usually written in the $N = N_0 e^{rt}$ form, where N represents the final amount of a material whose initial amount was N_0. This law has applications in many other areas such as population growth (people, bacteria in a culture, etc.) and radioactive decay of elements (in which case it becomes the "Law of Decay," $N = N_0 e^{-rt}$).

Completing the investment problem, using 2.72 as an approximation to e, you have $A = 24(2.72)^{.06(354)} = 40{,}780{,}708{,}190$.

Students can see that the "ultimate" return on a $24 investment (at a nominal annual interest rate of 6% for 354 years) is about $41 billion.

Students may now apply the formulas developed. Banks currently offer interest rates ranging from 5% to as much as 12% (usually for time deposits of two years or more) and compounding is commonly done quarterly, monthly, daily or continuously. Students can work problems with varying principles, periodic rates, frequencies of compounding and time periods, and compare yields. They'll probably be surprised by what they learn!

Evaluation

Students who have met the performance objective will be able to answer questions such as these:

1. Banks offering 5% annual interest compounded quarterly claim that money doubles in 14 years. Is this claim accurate?

2. If you had $1,000 to invest for two years, would you get a greater return from a savings bank offering a 5% annual rate compounded quarterly or from a commercial bank offering a 4½% annual rate compounded continuously?

3. Banks offering a 6% nominal annual rate compounded continuously on term savings of two years or longer claim that this rate is equivalent to an "effective annual rate" (the rate under annual compounding) of 6.27%. Prove that this is true, assuming a deposit of $500 (the usual minimum) for a period of two years.

35 Reflexive, Symmetric, and Transitive Relations

In this lesson students will have the opportunity to explore some properties of mathematical relations between numbers, geometric figures, sets, propositions, persons, places and things.

Performance Objective
Students will identify a given relation as reflexive, symmetric, transitive, or as an equivalence relation.

Preassessment
Ask students to describe what the mathematical term "relation" refers to. If you are not satisfied they understand the term, present some examples before beginning the lesson. You may wish to vary the relations you present students, according to their grade level and background in such areas as algebra, geometry, set theory, number theory, and logic.

Teaching Strategies
Begin with a consideration of a very simple relation such as "is equal to" for real numbers. From their previous math experience, students will recognize that any quantity a is equal to itself; that if a quantity a is equal to another quantity b, then b is also equal to a; and that if a quantity a is equal to another quantity b, and b is in turn equal to a third quantity c, then a is equal to c. Symbolically, we have $a = a$, $a = b \rightarrow b = a$, and $a = b$ and $b = c \rightarrow a = c$. The arrow is read "implies" as in ordinary symbolic logic. (Replace the arrow with the word if the class is unfamiliar with this notation.) Explain that when a quantity a has a given relation to itself (as in $a = a$) that relation is called *reflexive*. Further, when a quantity a has a given relation to another quantity b and this results in b having the same relation to a (as in $a = b \rightarrow b = a$) that relation is called *symmetric*. Add that when a quantity a has a given relation to another quantity b and b has the *same* relation to a third quantity c, and this results in a having that *same* relation to c (as in $a = b$ and $b = c \rightarrow a = c$) that relation is called *transitive*. A relation possessing all three of these properties is an *equivalence relation*.

Now invite students to examine some of the relations with which they are familiar from earlier work in mathematics. You've just established that "is equal to" is an equivalence relation. Follow up by considering the relations "is greater than" and "is less than" for real numbers. Your class will quickly discover that these relations are neither reflexive nor symmetric, but that they *are* transi-

tive. An interesting variation is the relation "is not equal to" for real numbers. Although this relation is not reflexive, it *is* symmetric. Students may also think that this relation is transitive, but a simple counterexample will prove that it is not: $9 + 6 \neq 7 + 2$ and $7 + 2 \neq 11 + 4$, but $9 + 6 = 11 + 4$. So the relation "is not equal to" is not transitive.

Of course, none of the relations just considered is an equivalence relation. Have the class consider other relations, for example: "is a multiple of" (or "is divisible by") and "is a factor of" for integers. Both of these relations are reflexive and transitive, but neither is symmetric. Ask students to prove these facts algebraically. For the first relation, for example, they may write $a = kb$ and $b = mc$, where k and m are integers. Clearly, $a = 1a$ so a is divisible by a (reflexivity); $a/b = k$ since a is divisible by b but $b/a = 1/k$, which is *not* an integer, so b is not divisible by a (no symmetry); $a = kb$ and $b = mc \rightarrow a = k(mc)$ or $a/c = km$, which *is* an integer, since the product of two integers is an integer (the set of integers being closed under multiplication), so a is divisible by c (transitivity).

Consider next some relations in geometry. First explore the relations "is congruent to" and "is similar to" for geometric figures. Students will have little difficulty recognizing that both of these are equivalence relations. Ask the class to examine each of these relations when it is negated. Each will then possess only the symmetric property.

The relations "is parallel to" and "is perpendicular to" are very interesting when applied to lines in a plane and to planes themselves. For example, for lines in a plane, "is parallel to" is symmetric *and* transitive but "is perpendicular to" is *only* symmetric. Ask your students why! They should recall such ideas from geometry as "lines parallel to the same line are parallel to each other" and "lines perpendicular to the same line are parallel to each other." These relations may also be negated as exercises.

Students who have some familiarity with set theory may explore the relations "is equal to" and "is equivalent to" as applied to sets. Since *equal* sets are sets containing identical elements, it's obvious that "is equal to" is an equivalence relation. *Equivalent* sets have the same number of elements (their elements can be placed into one-to-one correspondence with each other), but not necessarily identical ones. A little reflection reveals that "is equivalent to" is also an equivalence relation. Another interesting relation is "is the complement of" as applied to sets. The class should discover that this relation is symmetric, but that it is neither reflexive nor transitive. (If a is the complement of b and b is the complement of c, then a is *not* the complement of c, but rather $a = c$.)

An interesting relation from number theory is "is congruent to, modulo m" for integers. Students familiar with this concept should be able to prove easily that this is an equivalence relation, using simple algebra: $a \equiv a \pmod{m}$ since $a - a = 0m$ (proving the reflexive property); $a \equiv b \pmod{m} \rightarrow b \equiv a \pmod{m}$ since $b - a = -(a - b) = -km$ (proving the symmetric property); $a \equiv b \pmod{m}$ and $b \equiv c \pmod{m} \rightarrow a \equiv c \pmod{m}$ since $a - c = (a - b) + (b - c) = km + pm = (k + p)m$ (proving the transitive property).

Students familiar with symbolic logic may be invited to consider the relation "implies" for propositions (e.g., as designated by p, q, r). The alert student will recognize that this relation is reflexive, $p \rightarrow p$ (since any proposition implies itself) and transitive, $(p \rightarrow q) \wedge (q \rightarrow r) \rightarrow (p \rightarrow r)$ (since this can be proved to be a tautology by using a truth table) but that it is *not* symmetric, $(p \rightarrow q) \rightarrow (q \rightarrow p)$ is *false*, (since the truth of a proposition does *not* guarantee the truth of its converse).

Now broaden the concept of relations from strictly mathematical settings to involve relations between persons, places and things. Your class should find this amusing as well as instructive. Suggest a relation such as "is the father of." A little reflection reveals that this relation is not reflexive, not symmetric and not transitive! It is obvious that a cannot be his own father (not reflexive); that if a is the father of b, then b is the son or daughter and not the father of a (not symmetric); and that if a is the father of b and b is the father of c, then a is the grandfather of c, not the father (not transitive)! Many similar relations may be considered, including "is the mother of," "is the brother of" (caution: *only* transitive, *not* symmetric, since b may be the sister of a), "is

the sister of," "is the sibling of" (this one *is* symmetric), "is the spouse of," "is the ancestor of," "is the descendent of," "is taller than" and "weighs more than." Any of these relations may be explored in the negative sense as well as in the positive one. With respect to places, students may consider relations such as: "is north of," "is west of" (caution: transitivity here is *not* necessarily true if places may be selected from anywhere on the globe rather than from merely a small area or only one country), "is at a higher altitude than," "is exactly one mile from" (symmetric only) and "is less than one mile from" (reflexive *and* symmetric). Relations among things may include "is above," "is older than," "costs as much as" and "costs more than," among others.

Evaluation

Students who have met the performance objective will be able to answer questions such as the following:

1. Identify each of the following relations as reflexive, symmetric, transitive or as an equivalence relation:
(a) "is supplementary to" for angles
(b) "is congruent to" for line segments
(c) "is a subset of" for sets
(d) "is a proper subset of" for sets
(e) "is equivalent to" for propositions
(f) "is wealthier than" for nations
(g) "is smaller than" for objects
(h) "is colder than" for places

2. Prove algebraically that the relation "is complementary to" for acute angles is symmetric but neither reflexive nor transitive.

3. Which of the following relations is reflexive and transitive but not symmetric?
(a) "is a positive integral power of" for real numbers
(b) "has the same area as" for triangles
(c) "is the converse of" for propositions
(d) "is younger than" for people

36 Bypassing An Inaccessible Region

This unit will present the problem of constructing a straight line through an inaccessible region using only straightedge and compasses, and without using the tools in or over this inaccessible region. This activity will provide an opportunity for students to exhibit creativity.

Performance Objectives

1. Given a straight line segment with an endpoint on the boundary of an inaccessible region, students, using straightedge and compasses, will construct another straight line segment collinear with the given one and on the other side of the inaccessible region (an endpoint will be on the boundary of this region).

2. Given one point on either side of an inaccessible region, students, using only straightedge and compasses, will construct two collinear straight line segments, each having one given point as an endpoint and neither intersecting the inaccessible region.

Preassessment

Students should be familiar with the basic geometric constructions using straightedge and compasses.

Teaching Strategies

To generate initial interest, begin this topic by developing a story about two countries which are separated by a mountain, and each of which wants to construct a straight road and tunnel through the mountain. Since neither country can decide how to dig the tunnel, they both decide to construct a road on one side of the mountain at the point where the anticipated tunnel (the continuation of a straight road on the other side of the mountain) will emerge from the mountain. Using only straightedge and compasses they seek to plot the path for this new road.

Once students understand the problem, have them draw a diagram (maps) of this situation.

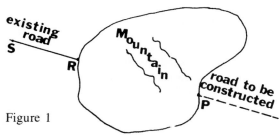

Figure 1

Students must construct the collinear "continuation of $\overline{SR}$" at point P (using straightedge and compasses) and never touch or go over the inaccessible region.

There are various ways to construct the collinear continuation of $\overline{SR}$ at P. One method is to erect a per-

pendicular (line ℓ) to $\overline{SR}$ at a convenient point N of $\overline{SR}$. Then at a convenient point M of line ℓ a perpendicular (line k) to ℓ is constructed (see Figure 2).

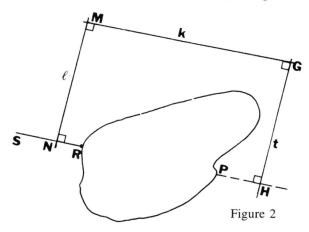

Figure 2

At a convenient point G of line k a perpendicular (line t) to line k is constructed. Point H is then obtained on line t, so that GH = MN. The line constructed perpendicular to line t at point H will be the required line through P and collinear with $\overline{SR}$. (It should be noted that although P was collinear with $\overline{SR}$ it was virtually not needed for the construction.) The justification for this method is that a rectangle (minus part of a side) was actually constructed.

Another method for solving this problem involves replacing the above rectangle with an equilateral triangle, since angles of measure 60° are rather simple to construct. Figure 3 presents this method and ought to be rather self-explanatory.

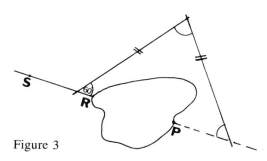

Figure 3

The problem of constructing a straight line "through" an inaccessible region, when only the two endpoints (at either side of the region) are given, is a much more challenging problem. Naturally an appropriate story can be built around this situation.

To construct two collinear straight line segments at each of two points (P and Q) situated at opposite sides of an inaccessible region, begin by drawing any convenient line segment from point P and construct a perpendicular line to it at a convenient point R. This perpendicular should not intersect the inaccessible region. See Figure 4.

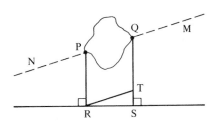

Figure 4

Now construct a perpendicular from Q, to this last line drawn, intersecting it at S. Locate T on $\overleftrightarrow{QS}$ so that PR = QS. Draw $\overline{RT}$. At P construct ∠RPN ≅ ∠PRT, and at Q construct ∠TQM ≅ ∠QTR. This completes the required construction, since $\overline{NP}$ and $\overline{QM}$ are extensions of side $\overline{PQ}$ of "parallelogram" PRTQ, and therefore are collinear.

There are many other methods of solving this problem. Many involve constructing similar triangles in order to then construct the two required lines. However students select to approach this problem, they are apt to be led to a creative activity.

Postassessment

1. Have students construct a "continuation" of $\overline{SP}$ on the other side of the inaccessible region (using only straightedge and compass and not touching or going over the inaccessible region).

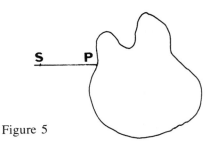

Figure 5

2. Have students construct two collinear segments at opposite ends (P and Q) of an inaccessible region (using only straightedge and compasses and not touching or going over the inaccessible region). These postassessment items become more challenging if original methods are sought.

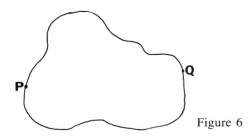

Figure 6

This decision depends upon the ability level of the class.

37 The Inaccessible Angle

Through a recreational application, this unit will provide the students the opportunity to use in novel ways various geometrical relationships they have learned. It also opens the door to a host of creative activities.

Performance Objective

Given an angle whose vertex is in an inaccessible region (hereafter referred to as an inaccessible angle), students will construct its angle bisector using straightedge and compasses.

Preassessment

Students should be familiar with the basic geometric constructions using straightedge and compasses.

See that students can properly bisect a given angle using only straightedge and compasses.

Teaching Strategies

After students have reviewed the basic geometric constructions present them with the following situation:

Problem: Given an angle whose vertex is inaccessible (i.e. tell students that the vertex of the angle is in a region in which, and over which, a straightedge and compasses cannot be used), construct the angle bisector using only straightedge and compasses.

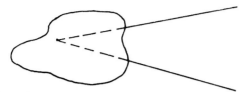

Figure 1

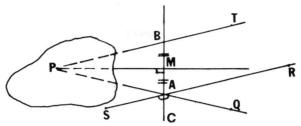

Figure 3

Most students' first attempts will probably be incorrect. However, careful consideration of students' responses should serve as a guide to a correct solution. Students will eventually present some rather strange (and creative) solutions. All should be given careful attention.

To best exhibit the true source of creativity that this problem provides, three different solutions are presented.

Solution I:

Draw any line ℓ intersecting the rays of the inaccessible angle at points A and B. Label the inaccessible vertex P.

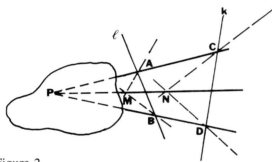

Figure 2

Construct the bisectors of ∠PAB and ∠PBA, which then intersect at M. Remind students that since the angle bisectors of a triangle (here ΔAPB) are concurrent, the bisector of ∠P, which we are trying to construct must contain point M.

In a similar way, draw any line *k*, intersecting the rays of the inaccessible angle at points C and D. Construct the bisectors of ∠PCD and ∠PDC, which intersect at N. Once again students should realize that, since the bisectors of a triangle (in this case ΔCPD) are concurrent, the bisector of ∠P must contain point N. Thus it has been established that the required line must contain points M and N, and therefore by drawing $\overleftrightarrow{MN}$ the construction is completed.

Solution II:

Begin this method by constructing a line parallel to one of the rays of the inaccessible angle. See Figure 3. This can be done in any one of various ways.

In Figure 3, $\overleftrightarrow{RS}$ is parallel to $\overrightarrow{PT}$ (a ray of the inaccessible ∠P), and intersects $\overrightarrow{PQ}$ at point A. Construct the bisector of ∠SAQ which will intersect $\overrightarrow{PT}$ at B. Since $\overleftrightarrow{SR}//\overrightarrow{PT}$, ∠SAC ≅ ∠PBA. However ∠SAC ≅ ∠CAQ ≅ ∠PAB. Therefore ∠PBA ≅ ∠PAB, thereby making ΔPAB isosceles. Since the perpendicular bisector of the base of an isosceles triangle also bisects the vertex angle, the perpendicular bisector of $\overline{AB}$ is the required angle bisector of the inaccessible angle (∠P).

Solution III:

Start by constructing a line ($\overline{MN}$) parallel to one of the rays ($\overrightarrow{PT}$) of the inaccessible angle (∠P), and intersecting the other ray at point A. See Figure 4.

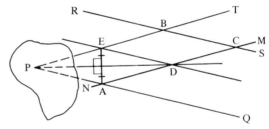

Figure 4

Then construct a line ($\overleftrightarrow{RS}$) parallel to the other ray ($\overrightarrow{PQ}$) of the inaccessible angle intersecting $\overrightarrow{PT}$ and $\overleftrightarrow{MN}$ at points B and C, respectively. With a pair of compasses, mark off a segment, $\overline{AD}$, on $\overline{AC}$ of the same length as $\overline{BC}$. Through D, construct $\overleftrightarrow{DE}//\overrightarrow{PQ}$, where E is on $\overrightarrow{PT}$. It can now be easily shown that ED = AD (since EBCD is a parallelogram and ED = BC. Since PEDA is a parallelogram with two adjacent sides congruent ($\overline{ED} \cong \overline{AD}$), it is a rhombus. Thus, the diagonal $\overline{PD}$ *is* the bisector of the inaccessible angle. $\overline{PD}$ can be constructed simply by bisecting ∠EDA or constructing the perpendicular bisector of $\overline{EA}$.

After presenting these solutions to your students, other solutions created by the students should follow directly. Free thinking should be encouraged to promote greater creativity.

Postassessment

Present students with an inaccessible angle and ask them to bisect it.

38   Triangle Constructions

Often teachers will justify the basic triangle congruence postulates by showing that unique triangles can be constructed with such given data as the lengths of three sides of a triangle or perhaps the lengths of two sides and the measure of the included angle. This unit will extend this usually elementary discussion of triangle constructions to some rather interesting problems.

Performance Objective
Given the measures of three parts of a triangle (which determine a triangle) students will analyze and construct the required triangle with straightedge and compasses.

Preassessment
Students should be familiar with the basic geometric constructions normally taught in the high school geometry course.

Teaching Strategies
To begin to familiarize students with this topic have them construct the triangle, where the measures of two angles and the length of the included side are given.

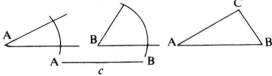

Figure 1

Students will draw a line and mark off the length of $\overline{AB}$ (sometimes referred to by c, the length of the side opposite $\angle C$). By constructing angles A and B at either end of $\overline{AB}$, they eventually find that they have constructed a *unique* $\triangle ABC$.

Surely, if the students were given the measures of the three angles of a triangle, each student would probably construct a triangle of different size (although all should be the same shape). Yet if the students were given the lengths of the three sides of a triangle they would all construct triangles congruent to one another. At this point students should realize that certain data will determine a *unique* triangle while other data will not. A student is thus limited in investigating such cases where the measures of only sides and angles are provided. Students will want to consider other parts of triangles as well. Present the following problem:

Construct a triangle given the lengths of two sides and the length of an altitude to one of these sides.

We shall write this problem as $[a,b,h_a]$, where h_a is the length of the altitude to side a.

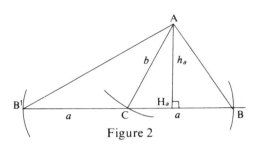

Figure 2

To do this construction, take the point H_a on any line and erect a perpendicular $H_a A$ (using the usual straightedge and compasses method) of length h_a. With arc (A,b) (Note: This ordered pair symbol is merely a short way of referring to the circle with center A and radius b) intersect the base line at C, then with arc (C,a), intersect this base line again at B and B'. The *two* solutions are $\triangle ABC$ and $\triangle AB'C$, each of which has the given $\{a,b,h_a\}$. Further inspection of this solution will indicate that $b > h_a$ was a necessary condition, and that if $b = h_a$ there would have only been *one* solution.

A much simpler problem is to construct a triangle given $\{a,b,h_c\}$. Here students begin in much the same way. On any line, erect at H_c a perpendicular length h_c. At C, the other extremity of h_c, draw (C,a) and (C,b). Their points of intersection with the original base line will determine points B and A, respectively. Once again a discussion of uniqueness should follow.

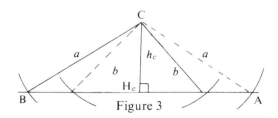

Figure 3

The figure above should help in this discussion.

Some triangle constructions require a good deal more analysis before actually beginning the construction. An example of such a problem is to construct the triangle given the lengths of its three medians $\{m_a, m_b, m_c\}$.

One approach for analyzing this problem is to consider the finished product, $\triangle ABC$.

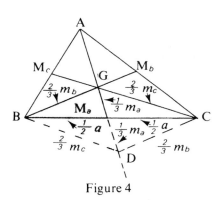

Figure 4

The objective here is to be able to construct one of the many triangles shown in the above figure by various elementary methods. By extending m_a (the median to side a), one third of its length to a point D and then drawing $\overline{BD}$ and $\overline{CD}$, we have created a triangle, $\triangle BGD$, which is easily constructible. Since the medians of a triangle trisect each other, we know that $BG = \frac{2}{3} m_b$. Since $GM_a = DM_a = \frac{1}{3} m_a$, (by construction) and $BM_? = CM_a$, we may conclude that BGCD is a parallelogram. Therefore $BD = GC = \frac{2}{3} m_c$. It is then rather simple to construct $\triangle BGD$, since its sides are each two thirds the length of one of the given medians (lengths easily obtained). After constructing $\triangle BGD$, the students should be able to complete the required construction by (1) extending BG one half its length to point M_b, (2) extending $\overline{DG}$ its own length to A, and (3) extending BM_a its own length to C (where M_a is the midpoint of $\overline{DG}$). The required triangle is then obtained by drawing $\overrightarrow{AM_b}$ to intersect $\overrightarrow{BM_a}$ at point C, and drawing $\overline{AB}$.

Not only does this problem review for the students many important concepts from elementary geometry, but it also provides an excellent opportunity for students to practice "reverse" reasoning in analyzing the problem.

For additional practice have students construct $\triangle ABC$ given $\{a, h_b, m_c\}$.

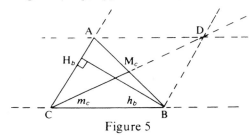

Figure 5

Once again have students first inspect the desired triangle. They should notice that $\triangle CBH_b$ can be easily constructed by erecting at H_c a perpendicular to $\overleftrightarrow{AC}$ of length h_b. At its extremity, B, draw (B, a) to intersect $\overleftrightarrow{AC}$ at C, to complete $\triangle CBH_b$. Further inspection of the above figure suggests that $\triangle CDB$ may also be constructed. Construct a line $\overleftrightarrow{(DB)}$ parallel to $\overleftrightarrow{AC}$ and intersecting arc $(C, 2m_c)$ at D. To find A, construct a line $\overleftrightarrow{(AD)}$ parallel to $\overleftrightarrow{CB}$ and intersecting $\overleftrightarrow{CH_b}$ at A. Since ADBC is a parallelogram, $\overleftrightarrow{CD}$ bisects $\overleftrightarrow{AB}$ at M_c, and $CM_c = \frac{1}{2} CD = m_c$. Thus the problem is analyzed in a rather reverse fashion, and then the required triangle is constructed.

When you consider the measures of other parts of a triangle such as angle bisectors, radius of the inscribed circle, radius of the circumscribed circle, and the semi-perimeter (as well as the measures of parts considered earlier in this Model), then there exist 179 possible triangle construction problems, where each consists of measures of three of these parts of a triangle. While some may be rather simple (e.g., $\{a, b, c\}$) others are somewhat more difficult (e.g., $\{h_a, h_b, h_c\}$).

This type of construction problem may very well serve as a springboard for a more careful study of this topic as well as various other geometric construction problems. A recently published book which contains much more on this topic (including the *complete* list of the 179 triangle constructions!) as well as a variety of other stimulating geometric construction topics (e.g., a review of the basic constructions, a variety of applications, circle constructions, restricted-tool constructions, etc.) is available from:

Dale Seymour Publications
P.O. Box 10888
Palo Alto, CA 94303
and is entitled:
Advanced Geometric Constructions
by: Alfred S. Posamentier and William Wernick

Postassessment

Have students construct triangles given:
1. $\{a, b, m_a\}$ 3. $\{a, h_b, h_c\}$ 5. $\{h_a, h_b, h_c\}$
2. $\{a, h_b, t_c\}$ 4. $\{h_a, m_a, t_a\}$

N.B. t_a is the length of the angle bisector of $\angle A$.

39 The Criterion of Constructibility

This unit will develop a criterion of construc-tibility for the Euclidean tools, straightedge and com-passes.

Performance Objectives

1. Students will state the criterion of construct-ibility.

2. Students will represent algebraic expressions geometrically (in terms of given lengths).

Preassessment

Ask students to represent geometrically AB + CD and AB − CD, given AB and CD.

Teaching Strategies

Most students should have been able to successfully do the above problem. Now let AB = a and CD = b.

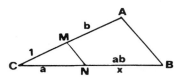

The next logical concern would be to represent the *product* of two given line segments. Here, however, a segment of unit length must be introduced.

To construct *ab,* two cases should be considered: (I) where $a > 1$ and $b > 1$, and (II) where $a < 1$ and $b < 1$.

In the first case (I), students would construct the figure below. Note $\overline{MN} \mathbin{/\!/} \overline{AB}$, and ∠C is any con-venient angle.

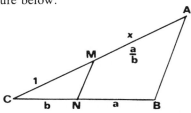

Since $\overline{MN} \mathbin{/\!/} \overline{AB}, \dfrac{x}{a} = \dfrac{b}{1}$, and $x = ab$; thus $\overline{NB}$ is the segment of desired length (i.e. ab). It should be noted that $ab > a$, and $ab > b$, which is expected if $a > 1$ and $b > 1$.

In the second case (II), students would proceed in the same way as in case I, however since $a < 1$ and $b < 1$, it should be made clear that geometrically $ab < a$, and $ab < b$.

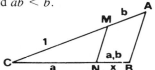

Students should now be challenged to discover a similar scheme for constructing a line segment which can represent the quotient of two given line segments, a and b. Again two cases should be considered:

Case I: $a < b < 1$. Once again have students con-struct the figure above, where $\overline{MN} \mathbin{/\!/} \overline{AB}$.

In this case either $a < \dfrac{a}{b} < b < 1$ or $a < b < \dfrac{a}{b} < 1$.

Students should be encouraged to verify this.

Case II: $b < a \leqslant 1$. Proceed as above to construct the figure below.

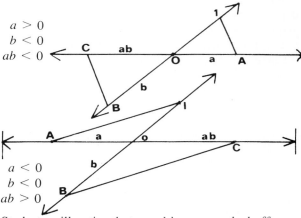

Here $b < a < \dfrac{a}{b}$

Until now all segments considered were of positive length. Students will now become curious about using segments of negative length to represent products and quotients.

In order to consider segments of negative length, we must introduce number line axes, horizontal and oblique. To find ab, locate A on the horizontal axis so that $OA = a$, and locate B on the oblique axis so that $OB = b$. Draw the line through the 1 on the oblique axis and A. Through B draw a line parallel to the first line, intersecting the horizontal axis in a point C. Thus $OC = ab$.

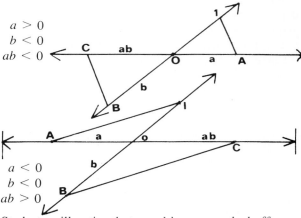

Students will notice that a and b were marked off on different axes and that in each case the product, ab, was appropriately less than or greater than zero.

As before, we shall find a quotient by considering division as the inverse of multiplication. To find

$\frac{a}{b}$, we find x such that $bx = a$. $a > 0$, and $b > 0$,

then $\frac{a}{b} > 0$.

$OB = b$
$OA = a$
$OC = 1$

$OD = \frac{a}{b}$

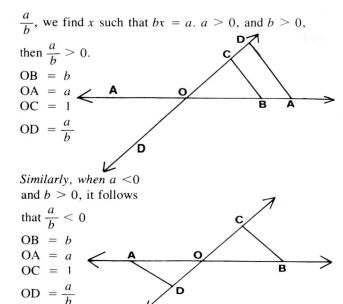

Similarly, when $a < 0$
and $b > 0$, it follows

that $\frac{a}{b} < 0$

$OB = b$
$OA = a$
$OC = 1$

$OD = \frac{a}{b}$

Have students consider division by zero. That is, where is B if $b = 0$? What happens to OD?

The only remaining operation for which a geometric representation is needed is square root extraction. Here students merely construct a semicircle on $1 + a$ (where $\sqrt{a}$ is sought). Then at the common endpoint, B, of segment 1 and a erect a perpendicular to intersect the semicircle at D. Thus $BD = \sqrt{a}$. Students should be able to apply mean proportional theorems to prove this.

The solution to a construction problem may be expressed as a root of an equation. For example, consider the problem of duplication of a cube. We must find the edge of a cube whose volume is twice that of a given cube. That is, we must find x, when $x^3 = 2$.

If we can obtain the solution by a finite number of applications of the operations $+$, $-$, $\times$, $\div$, and $\sqrt{}$, using given segments and a unit length, then the construction is possible.

Conversely, if the construction is possible, then we can obtain it by a finite number of applications of addition, subtraction, multiplication, division and extractions of square root, using the given segments and an arbitrary unit of length. We know that the straight lines and circles that we construct are deter-

mined either by given segments or those obtained from the intersections of two straight lines, a straight line and a circle, or two circles. To show the converse above, we must show that these intersections can be obtained from the coefficients of the equations by a finite number of applications of the operations of addition, subtraction, multiplication, division, and extraction of square root.

Two straight lines

$$y = mx + b$$
$$y = m'x + b' \qquad m \neq m'$$

have as their point of intersection the point (x, y) with

$$x = \frac{b - b'}{m - m'} \qquad\qquad y = \frac{mb' - m'b}{m - m'}$$

These relationships are obtained from the equations by applying the above operations. An equation for a circle with radius r and center (c, d) is $(x - c)^2 + (y - d)^2 = r^2$. To find the intersection of the circle with the line $y = mx + b$, we can substitute for y in the equation for the circle

$$(x - c)^2 + (mx + b - d)^2 = r^2$$

This forms a quadratic equation in x. Since the solution of the quadratic $ax^2 + bx + c = 0$ is

$$x = \frac{-b \pm \sqrt{b^2 - 4ac}}{2a}$$

we know that the quadratic $(x - c)^2 + (mx + b - d)^2 = r^2$ has a root that can be obtained from the known constants by applying the above five operations.

The intersection of two circles is the same as the intersection of one circle with the common chord. Thus, this case can be reduced to finding the intersection of a circle and a line.

Criterion of Constructibility   A proposed geometric construction is possible with straightedge and compass alone if and only if the numbers that define algebraically the required geometric elements can be derived from those defining the given elements by a finite number of rational operations and extractions of square root.

Postassessment

1. Restate and explain the Criterion of Constructibility.

2. Given lengths a, b, 1 construct a line segment of length $\sqrt{\dfrac{ab}{a + b}}$

Reference

Posamentier, Alfred S., and William Wernick, *Advanced Geometric Constructions*. Palo Alto, CA. Dale Seymour Publications, 1988.

40 Constructing Radical Lengths

Often students ask how a line of length $\sqrt{2}$ can be constructed. This activity will address itself to this question as well as find the length of other radical segments.

Performance Objective
Students will construct a segment of a given radical length after being given a unit length.

Preassessment
Students should be able to apply the Pythagorean Theorem and be familiar with the basics of geometric constructions with straightedge and compasses.

Teaching Strategies
Ask students to construct a triangle with one side of length $\sqrt{2}$ (be sure to tell them to select a convenient unit length). In all likelihood they will draw an isosceles right triangle with a leg of length 1. By the Pythagorean Theorem they will find that the hypotenuse has length $\sqrt{2}$.

Now have them construct a right triangle using this hypotenuse and have the other leg be of unit length. This newly formed right triangle has a hypotenuse of length $\sqrt{3}$. Students should easily discover that fact using the Pythagorean Theorem.

By repeating this process, students will generate, in sequence, radicals of integers, i.e., $\sqrt{2}, \sqrt{3}, \sqrt{4}, \sqrt{5}$, . . . The figure, frequently referred to as a "radical spiral", shows this process.

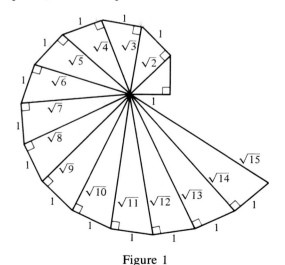

Figure 1

It could be expected that a student might ask if there is a more expedient method for constructing $\sqrt{15}$, rather than generating a radical spiral up to $\sqrt{15}$,

Lead students to recall one of the "mean proportional" theorems. In the figure below CD is the mean proportional between AD and BD.

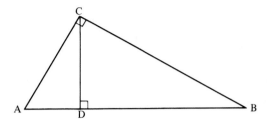

Figure 2

That is, $\dfrac{AD}{CD} = \dfrac{CD}{BD}$, or $(CD)^2 = (AD)(BD)$, which implies that $CD = \sqrt{(AD)(BD)}$

This relationship will help them construct a segment of length $\sqrt{15}$ in one construction. All they need do is to construct the above figure and let $AD = 1$ and $BD = 15$; then $CD = \sqrt{(1)(15)} = \sqrt{15}$.

What they should do is draw a segment of length 16 and partition it into two segments of lengths 1 and 15. At the partitioning point have them erect a perpendicular to this segment. The intersection of the perpendicular and the semicircle having the segment of length 16 as diameter determines the other endpoint of the perpendicular segment of length $\sqrt{15}$. See the figure below.

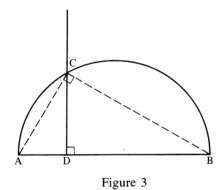

Figure 3

The dashed lines are merely needed to justify the construction.

Postassessment
1. Construct a radical spiral up to $\sqrt{18}$.
2. Construct a segment of length $\sqrt{18}$ using a given unit length. Do *not* construct a radical spiral here.

41 Constructing a Pentagon

Performance Objective
Students will construct a regular pentagon given the length of the radius of the circumscribed circle.

Preassessment
Students should be familiar with the properties of regular polygons.

Teaching Strategies
Begin your lesson by having the class consider a regular decagon whose radius is 1 (Figure 1).

Figure 1

With center O, draw $\overline{OA}$ and $\overline{OB}$ to form isosceles $\triangle AOB$. The class should easily see that $m\angle AOB = 36°$. (i.e. $\frac{360}{10} = 36$). Therefore $m\angle OAB = m\angle OBA = 72°$.

Isolate $\triangle AOB$ for clarity (Figure 2).

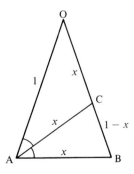

Figure 2

Draw angle bisector $\overline{AC}$. Therefore $m\angle OAC = 36°$, making $\triangle OCA$ isosceles. Similarly, $\triangle CAB$ is isosceles.

Moreover, $\triangle AOB \sim \triangle BAC$. If we let $x = OC$, then $CB = 1 - x$; also $CA = x = AB$. From the similarity students should obtain the proportion: $\frac{1}{x} = \frac{x}{1-x}$, which leads to the equation $x^2 + x - 1 = 0$.

This equation has two roots, one of which has geometric significance: $x = \frac{\sqrt{5} - 1}{2}$.

Now have students consider the construction of this value of x. At any point A of a line, erect a perpendicular of length $1 = OA$, and construct the unit circle (i.e. the circle with radius of length 1) tangent to that line at A. On the line make $AP = 2$ and then draw $\overline{OP}$. By using the Pythagorean Theorem, students should establish that $OP = \sqrt{5}$ and $PQ = OP - OQ = \sqrt{5} - 1$. Finally the perpendicular bisector of $\overline{PQ}$ gives us $QR = \frac{\sqrt{5} - 1}{2} = x$.

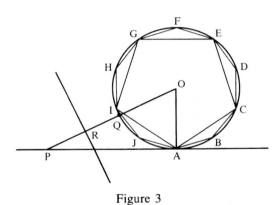

Figure 3

Students should now mark consecutive segments of x on the original unit circle. When done accurately, this value of x will give exactly 10 arcs on the circle. After students have constructed the decagon, they ought to realize that by joining the alternate vertices of the decagon, the desired pentagon is formed.

Postassessment
Have students construct a regular pentagon given a specific unit length.

42 Investigating the Isosceles Triangle Fallacy

This unit offers an opportunity to consider fully the Isosceles Triangle Fallacy. This fallacy can be used to reinforce the concept of betweeness.

Performance Objectives

1. *Students will exhibit the Isosceles Triangle Fallacy.*

2. *Students will indicate the "error" in the Isosceles Triangle Fallacy and prove their conjecture.*

Preassessment

Students should be familiar with the various methods for proving triangles congruent, as well as angle measurement in a circle.

Teaching Strategies

Begin the discussion by challenging your students to drawn any *scalene* triangle on the chalkboard which you will then prove isosceles.

To prove the scalene ΔABC isosceles, draw the bisector of ∠C and the perpendicular bisector of $\overline{AB}$. From their point of intersection, G, draw perpendiculars to $\overline{AC}$ and $\overline{CB}$, meeting them at points D and F, respectively.

It should be noted that there are four possibilities for the above description for various scalene triangles: figure 1, where $\overline{CG}$ and $\overline{GE}$ meet inside the triangle:

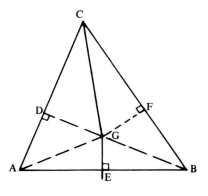

Fig. 1

figure 2, where $\overline{CG}$ and $\overline{GE}$ meet on $\overline{AB}$;

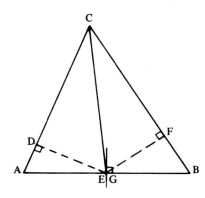

Fig. 2

figure 3, where $\overline{CG}$ and $\overline{GE}$ meet outside the triangle, but the perpendiculars $\overline{GD}$ and $\overline{GF}$ fall on $\overline{AC}$ and $\overline{CB}$;

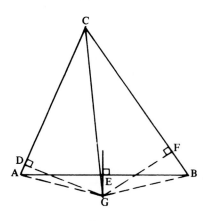

Fig. 3

figure 4, where $\overline{CG}$ and $\overline{GE}$ meet outside the triangle, but the perpendiculars $\overline{GD}$ and $\overline{GF}$ meet $\overrightarrow{CA}$ and $\overrightarrow{CG}$ outside the triangle.

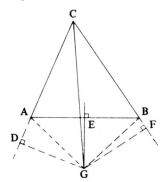

Fig. 4

The "proof" of the fallacy can be done with any of the above figures. Have students follow the "proof" on any (or all) of these figures.

Given:

ABC is scalene

Prove:

AC = BC (or △ABC is isosceles)

"Proof": Since ∠ ACG ≅ ∠ BCG and *rt* ∠ CDG ≅ *rt* ∠ CFG, △CDG ≅ △CFG (SAA). Therefore DG = FG and CD = CF. Since AG = BG (a point on the perpendicular bisector of a line segment is equidistant from the endpoints of the line segment) and ∠ADG and ∠ BFG are right angles, △DAG ≅ △FBG (H.L.). Therefore DA = FB. It then follows that AC = BC (by addition in figures 1, 2, and 3; and by substraction in figure 4).

At this point students will be quite disturbed. They will wonder where the error was committed which permitted this fallacy to occur. Some students will be clever enough to attack the figures. By rigorous construction students will find a subtle error in the figures:

a. The point G *must* be outside the triangle.

b. When perpendiculars meet the sides of the triangle, one will meet a side *between* the vertices, while the other will not.

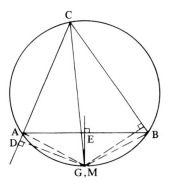

Fig. 5

Some discussion of Euclid's neglect of the concept of betweenness should follow. However, the beauty of this particular fallacy is the powerful proof of items *a* and *b* (above), which indicate the *error* of the fallacy.

Begin by considering the circumcircle of △ABC The bisector of ∠ ACB must contain the midpoint, M, of ⌢AB (since ∠ ACM and ∠ BCM are congruent inscribed angles). The perpendicular bisector of AB̄ must bisect ⌢AB, and therefore pass through M. Thus, the bisector of ∠ ACB and the perpendicular bisector of AB̄ intersect *outside* the triangle at M (or G). This eliminates the possibilities of figures 1 and 2.

Now have students consider inscribed quadrilateral ACBG. Since the opposite angles of an inscribed (or cyclic) quadrilateral are supplementary, *m∠*CAG + *m∠* CBG = 180. If ∠ CAG and ∠ CBG are right angles then CḠ would be a diameter and △ABC would be isosceles. Therefore since △ABC is scalene, ∠CAG and ∠CBG are not right angles. In this case one must be acute and the other obtuse. Suppose ∠CBG is acute and ∠CAG is obtuse. Then in △CGB the altitude on CB̄ must be *inside* the triangle, while in obtuse △CAG, the altitude on AC̄ must be *outside the triangle*. (This is *usually readily accepted by students but can be easily proved.*) The fact that one and *only one* of the perpendiculars intersects a side of the triangle *between* the vertices destroys the fallacious "proof." It is important that the teacher stress the importance of the concept of betweenness in geometry.

Postassessment

Have students:

1. "Prove" that any given scalene triangle is isosceles.

2. Indicate (and prove) where the "proof" in question 1 is fallacious.

3. Discuss the concept of betweenness in terms of its significance in geometry.

43 The Equiangular Point

This unit will develop interesting geometric relationships from an unusual geometric configuration. The topic is appropriate for any student who has mastered most of the high school geometry course.

Performance Objectives

1. Students will define the equiangular point of an acute triangle.

2. Students will locate the equiangular point of an acute triangle.

3. Students will state at least three properties of the figure used to locate the equiangular point of an acute triangle.

Preassessment

Before attempting to present this unit to your classes, review with them angle measurement of a circle and the basic properties of congruence and similarity.

Teaching Strategies

Begin your presentation by challenging students with the following problem:

Given: Acute △ABC.
△ACD and △ABF
are equilateral.

Prove: DB = CF

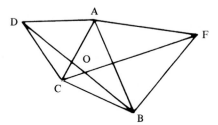

Figure 1

Although this problem uses only the most elementary concepts of the high school geometry course, students tend to find it somewhat challenging. What seems to be most perplexing is the selection of the proper pair of triangles to prove congruent. If, after a few minutes, students do not find these, tell them to name triangles that use the required segments $\overline{DB}$ and $\overline{CF}$ as sides. Soon they will realize that they must prove △CAF ≅ △DAB.

Next arises the problem of *how* to prove these triangles congruent. Lead students to realize that overlapping triangles usually share a common element. Here the common element is ∠CAB. Since △ACD and

△ABF are equilateral, m∠DAC = 60°, m∠FAB = 60°, and m∠DAB = m∠FAC (addition). Since △ACD is equilateral, AD = AC, and since △ABF is equilateral, AB = AF. Therefore △CAF ≅ △DAB (S.A.S.), and thus DB = CF.

Once students have fully understood this proof, have them consider a third equilateral triangle, △BCE, drawn on side $\overline{BC}$. Ask them to compare the length of $\overline{AE}$ to that of $\overline{DB}$ and $\overline{CF}$.

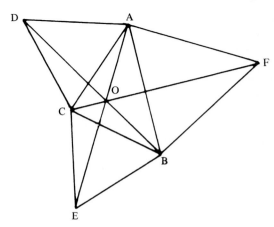

Figure 2

Most students will realize that all three segments have the same length. A proof of this is done in the same way as the previous one. That is, simply have them prove that △CAE ≅ △CDB to get AE = DB.

The fact that AE = DB = CF is quite astonishing when we bear in mind that △ABC was *any* acute triangle. A number of equally surprising results can now be established from this basis. Present each of these separately, but once each has been proved, carefully relate it to the previously established facts.

1. The line segments $\overline{AE}$, $\overline{DB}$, and $\overline{CF}$ are concurrent.

Proof: Consider the circumcircles of the three equilateral triangles, △ACD, △ABF, and △BCE.

Let K, L, and M be the centers of these circles (see Figure 3).

Circles K and L meet at points O and A. Since $m\overset{\frown}{ADC} = 240°$, and we know that $m\angle AOC = \frac{1}{2}(m\overset{\frown}{ADC})$, $m\angle AOC = 120°$. Similarly, $m\angle AOB = \frac{1}{2}(m\overset{\frown}{AFB}) = 120°$. Therefore $m\angle COB = 120°$, since a complete revolution = 360°.

Since $m\overset{\frown}{CEB} = 240°$, ∠COB is an inscribed angle and point O must lie on circle M. Therefore, we can see

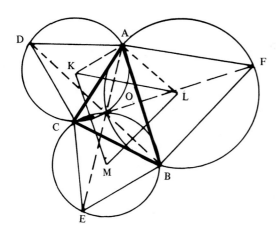

Figure 3

that the three circles are concurrent, intersecting at point O.

Now have students join point O with points A, B, C, D, E, and F. m∠ DOA = m∠ AOF = m∠ FOB = 60°, and therefore $\overleftrightarrow{DOB}$. Similarly $\overleftrightarrow{COF}$ and $\overleftrightarrow{AOE}$.

Thus it has been proved that $\overline{AE}$, $\overline{CF}$, and $\overline{DB}$ are concurrent, intersecting at point O (which is also the point of intersection of circles K, L, and M).

Now ask the class to determine the point in ΔABC at which the three sides subtend congruent angles. They should quickly recall that we just proved that m∠ AOB = m∠ AOC = m∠ BOC = 120°. Thus, the point—called the *equiangular point* of a triangle—at which the sides of ΔABC subtend congruent angles is point O.

2. *The circumcenters K, L, and M of the three equilateral triangles ΔACD, ΔABF, and ΔBCE, respectively, determine another equilateral triangle.*

Proof: Before beginning this proof, review briefly with students the relationship among the sides of a 30-60-90 triangle.

Have your students consider equilateral ΔDAC. Since AK is 2/3 of the altitude (or median), we obtain the proportion AC:AK = $\sqrt{3}$:1.
Similarly, in equilateral ΔAFB, AF:AL = $\sqrt{3}$:1.
Therefore, AC:AK = AF:AL.
m∠ KAC = m∠ LAF = 30°, m∠ CAL = m∠ CAL (reflexive) and m∠ KAL = m∠ CAF (addition).
Therefore, ΔKAL ~ ΔCAF.
Thus, CF:KL = CA:AK = $\sqrt{3}$:1.
Similarly, we may prove DB:KM = $\sqrt{3}$:1, and AE:ML = $\sqrt{3}$:1. Therefore, DB:KM = AE:ML = CF:KL. But since DB = AE = CF, as proved earlier, we obtain KM = ML = KL. Therefore, ΔKML is equilateral.

As a concluding challenge to your class, ask them to discover other relationships in Figure 3.

Postassessment

To test student comprehension of this lesson, give them the following exercises.
1. Define *the equiangular point* of an acute triangle.
2. Draw any acute triangle. Using straightedge and compasses, locate the equiangular point of the triangle.
3. State three properties found in Figure 3, above.

Reference

Posamentier, Alfred S., *Excursions in Advanced Euclidean Geometry*. Menlo Park, Ca.: Addison-Wesley, 1984.

44   The Minimum Distance Point of a Triangle

This unit will develop a search for the point in a triangle the sum of whose distances to the vertices is a minimum.

Performance Objectives

1. Students will prove that the sum of the distances to the sides of an equilateral triangle from an interior point is constant.

2. Students will locate the minimum distance point of a triangle with no angle of measure 120° or greater.

Preassessment

Students should be familiar with basic concepts of geometric inequalities.

Ask students to find the position of a point of a quadrilateral, the sum of whose distances to the vertices is a minimum.

Teaching Strategies

Begin the discussion by having students consider the location of the point in the interior of a given quadrilateral, the sum of whose distances from the vertices is the smallest possible (from here on we shall refer to such a point as the *minimum distance point*).

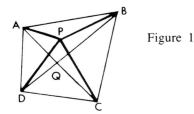

Figure 1

You can expect most students to guess that the point of intersection of the diagonals (point Q in Figure 1) would be this "minimum distance point." Although the conjecture is a clever one, try to elicit a justification (proof) for this point selection.

Let students select any point P (not at Q) in the interior of quadrilateral ABCD (Figure 1). PA + PC > QA + QC (since the sum of the lengths of two sides of a triangle is greater than the length of the third). Similarly, PB + PD > QB + QD. By addition, PA + PB + PC + PD > QA + QB + QC + QD, which shows that the sum of the distances from the point of intersection of the diagonals of a quadrilateral to the vertices is less than the sum of the distances from *any other* interior point of the quadrilateral to the vertices.

The next logical concern of students is usually, "What is the minimum distance point in a triangle?" Before tackling this question, it is useful to first consider another interesting theorem that will later help students develop the minimum distance point of a triangle.

Once again ask students to use their intuition and reason inductively. Have them construct a large equilateral triangle. Then have them select any interior point and carefully measure its distances from the three *sides* of the equilateral triangle. After students have recorded the sum of these three distances, ask them to repeat the procedure three times, each time with a different interior point. Accurate measurements should yield equal distance sums for each point selected. Consequently, students ought to be able to draw the following conclusion: *The sum of the distances from any point in the interior of an equilateral triangle to the sides of the triangle is constant.* Two proofs of this interesting finding are provided here:

Method I:

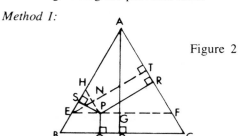

Figure 2

In equilateral $\triangle ABC$, $\overline{PR} \perp \overline{AC}$, $\overline{PQ} \perp \overline{BC}$, $\overline{PS} \perp \overline{AB}$, and $\overline{AD} \perp \overline{BC}$.
Draw a line through P parallel to $\overline{BC}$ meeting $\overline{AD}$, $\overline{AB}$, and $\overline{AC}$ at G, E, and F, respectively.
PQ = GD.
Draw $\overline{ET} \perp \overline{AC}$. Since $\triangle AEF$ is equilateral, $\overline{AG} \cong \overline{ET}$ (all the altitudes of an equilateral triangle are congruent).
Draw $\overline{PH}$ // $\overline{AC}$ meeting $\overline{ET}$ at N. $\overline{NT} \cong \overline{PR}$.
Since $\triangle EHP$ is equilateral, altitudes $\overline{PS}$ and $\overline{EN}$ are congruent.
Therefore, we have shown that PS + PR = ET = AG.
Since PQ = GD, PS + PR + PQ = AG + GD = AD, a constant for the given triangle.

Method II:

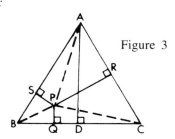

Figure 3

In equilateral $\triangle ABC$, $\overline{PR} \perp \overline{AC}$, $\overline{PQ} \perp \overline{BC}$, $\overline{PS} \perp \overline{AB}$, and $\overline{AD} \perp \overline{BC}$,
Draw $\overline{PA}$, $\overline{PB}$, and $\overline{PC}$.
The area of $\triangle ABC$
= area of $\triangle APB$ + area of $\triangle BPC$ + area of $\triangle CPA$
= $\frac{1}{2}$(AB)(PS) + $\frac{1}{2}$(BC)(PQ) + $\frac{1}{2}$(AC)(PR).

Since AB = BC = AC, the area of $\triangle ABC$ = $\frac{1}{2}$(BC) [PS + PQ + PR]. However, the area of $\triangle ABC$ = $\frac{1}{2}$(BC)(AD) therefore, PS + PQ + PR = AD, a constant for the given triangle.

Students are now ready to consider the original problem: to find the minimum distance point of a triangle. We shall consider a scalene triangle with no angle having a measure greater than 120°.

Students, realizing the apparent need for symmetry in this problem, may suggest selecting the point at which the sides subtend congruent angles. If they are to accept this conjecture, they must prove it.

We shall therefore prove that: *the point in the interior of a triangle (with no angle greater than 120°), at which the sides subtend congruent angles, is the minimum distance point of the triangle.*

Proof:

In Figure 4, let M be the point in the interior of $\triangle ABC$, where m$\angle$AMB = m$\angle$BMC = m$\angle$AMC = 120°.

Draw lines through A, B, and C which are perpendicular to $\overline{AM}$, $\overline{BM}$, and $\overline{CM}$, respectively.

These lines meet to form equilateral $\triangle PQR$. (To prove $\triangle PQR$ is equilateral, notice that each angle has measure 60°. This can be shown by considering, for example, quadrilateral AMBR. Since $m\angle RAM = m\angle RBM = 90°$, and $m\angle AMB = 120°$, it follows that $m\angle ARB = 60°$.)

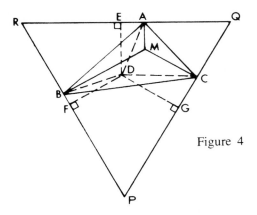

Figure 4

Let D be *any other* point in the interior of $\triangle ABC$. We must show that the sum of the distances from M to the vertices is less than the sum of the distances from D to the vertices.

From the theorem we proved above, MA + MB + MC = DE + DF + DG, (where $\overline{DE}$, $\overline{DF}$ and $\overline{DG}$

are the perpendiculars to $\overline{REQ}$, $\overline{RBP}$ and $\overline{QGP}$, respectively).

But DE + DF + DG < DA + DB + DC. (The shortest distance from an external point to a line is the length of the perpendicular segment from the point to the line.)

By substitution:

MA + MB + MC < DA + DB + DC.

Now having proved the theorem, students may wonder why we chose to restrict our discussion to triangles with angles of measure less than 120°. Let them try to construct the point M in an obtuse triangle with one angle of measure 150°. The reason for our restriction should become obvious.

Postassessment

To test student comprehension of the above exercises, ask them to:

1. Prove that the sum of the distances to the sides of an equilateral triangle from an interior point is constant.
2. Locate the minimum distance point of a triangle with no angle of measure greater than 120°.
3. Locate the minimum distance point of a quadrilateral.

Reference

Posamentier, Alfred S. *Excursions in Advanced Euclidean Geometry*. Menlo Park, Ca.: Addison-Wesley, 1984.

45 The Isosceles Triangle Revisited

Early in the high school geometry course, students perform many practice proofs using isosceles triangles. One such proof involves proving that the angle bisectors of the base angles of an isosceles triangle are congruent. Although this is a rather simple proof, its converse is exceedingly difficult; perhaps among the most difficult statements to prove in Euclidean geometry. This unit presents several methods by which students can prove the statement.

Performance Objectives

Students will prove that if two angle bisectors of a triangle are congruent, then the triangle is isosceles.

Preassessment

Students should have had practice with geometric proofs, including indirect proofs.

Teaching Strategies

Begin your presentation by asking students to prove: The angle bisectors of the base angles of an isosceles triangle are congruent.

You may wish to start them uniformly:

Given: Isosceles $\triangle ABC$, with AB = AC, $\overline{BF}$ and $\overline{CE}$ are angle bisectors

Prove: $\overline{BF} \cong \overline{CE}$

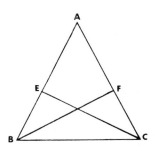

Proof: $m\angle FBC = \frac{1}{2}m\angle ABC$, and $m\angle ECB = \frac{1}{2}m\angle ACB$.

Since $m\angle ABC = m\angle ACB$ (base angles of an isosceles triangle), $m\angle FBC = m\angle ECB$. Since $\overline{BC} \cong \overline{BC}$, $\triangle FBC \cong \triangle ECB$ (ASA). Therefore $\overline{BF} \cong \overline{CE}$.

When students have completed this proof, ask them to state the converse of the statement just proved:

If two angle bisectors of a triangle are congruent, then the triangle is isosceles.

Challenge students to prove this new statement. Since it is highly unlikely that your students will be able to prove this statement in a short time, you may wish to show them some of the following proofs. They will be quite astonished that the converse of a rather simply proved statement is so difficult to prove. Each of the following proofs is quite instructional and merits special attention.

Given: $\overline{AE}$ and $\overline{BD}$ are angle bisectors of $\triangle ABC$.
$\overline{AE} \cong \overline{BD}$.

Prove: $\triangle ABC$ is isosceles.

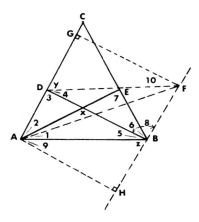

Proof: Draw $\angle DBF \cong \angle AEB$ so that $\overline{BF} \cong \overline{BE}$
Draw $\overline{DF}$.
Also draw $\overline{FG} \perp \overline{AC}$ and $\overline{AH} \perp \overline{FH}$.
By hypothesis, $\overline{AE} \cong \overline{DB}$, $\overline{FB} \cong \overline{EB}$.
And $\angle 8 \cong \angle 7$.
Therefore $\triangle AEB \cong \triangle DBF$ (SAS) $DF = AB$ and $m\angle 1 = m\angle 4$.

$m\angle x = m\angle 2 + m\angle 3$ (exterior angles) of a triangle)
$m\angle x = m\angle 1 + m\angle 3$ (substitution)
$m\angle x = m\angle 4 + m\angle 3$ (substitution)
$m\angle x = m\angle 7 + m\angle 6$ (exterior angles of a triangle)
$m\angle x = m\angle 7 + m\angle 5$ (substitution)
$m\angle x = m\angle 8 + m\angle 5$ (substitution)
Therefore, $m\angle 4 + m\angle 3 = m\angle 8 + m\angle 5$ (transitivity).

Thus $m\angle z = m\angle y$.
Right $\triangle FDG \cong$ right $\triangle ABH$(SAA), $DG = BH$, and $FG = AH$.
Right $\triangle AFG \cong$ right $\triangle FAH$ (HL) and $AG = FH$
Therefore, GFHA is a parallelogram.
Also, $m\angle 9 = m\angle 10$ (from $\triangle ABH$ and $\triangle FDG$)
$m\angle DAB = m\angle DFB$ (subtraction)
$m\angle DFB = m\angle EBA$ (from $\triangle DBF$ and $\triangle AEB$)
Therefore, $m\triangle DAB = m\triangle EBA$ (transitivity), and $\triangle ABC$ is isosceles.

The following proofs of this theorem are *indirect proofs* and may deserve special introduction.

Given: $\overline{BF}$ and $\overline{CE}$ are angle bisectors of $\triangle ABC$.
$\overline{BF} \cong \overline{CE}$

Prove: $\triangle ABC$ is isosceles

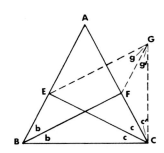

Indirect proof I:
Assume $\triangle ABC$ is *not* isosceles.
Let $m\angle ABC > m\angle ACB$
$\overline{BF} \cong \overline{CE}$ (hypothesis)
$\overline{BC} \cong \overline{BC}$
$m\angle ABC > m\angle ACB$ (assumption)
$\overline{CF} > \overline{BE}$.
Through F, construct $\overline{GF}$ parallel to $\overline{EB}$.
Through E, construct $\overline{GE}$ parallel to $\overline{BF}$.
BFGE is a parallelogram.
$\overline{BF} \cong \overline{EG}$, $\overline{EG} \cong \overline{CE}$, $\triangle GEC$ is isosceles.
$m\angle (g + g') = m\angle (c + c')$
but $m\angle g = m\angle b$
$m\angle (b + g') = m\angle (c + c')$
Therefore, $m\angle g' < m\angle c'$, since $m\angle b > m\angle c$.
In $\triangle GFC$, we have $CF < GF$
But $GF = BE$
Thus $CF < BE$.

The assumption of the inequality of $m\angle ABC$ and $m\angle ACB$ leads to two contradictory results, $CF < BE$ and $CF > BE$. Therefore $\triangle ABC$ is isosceles.

A second indirect proof follows:

Given: $\overline{BE}$ and $\overline{DC}$ are angle bisectors of $\triangle ABC$.
$\overline{BE} \cong \overline{DC}$

Prove: $\triangle ABC$ is isosceles.

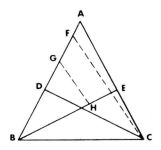

Indirect Proof II:

In ΔABC, the bisectors of angles ABC and ACB have equal measures (i.e., BE = DC). Assume that $m\angle ABC < m\angle ACB$; Then $m\angle ABE < m\angle ACD$.

We then draw $\angle FCD$ congruent to $\angle ABE$. Note that we may take F between B and A without loss of generality. In ΔFBC, FB > FC. (If the measures of two angles of a triangle are not equal, then the measures of the sides opposite these angles are also unequal, the side with the greater measure being opposite the angle with the greater measure.)

Choose a point G so that $\overline{BG} \cong \overline{FC}$.
Then draw $\overline{GH} \parallel \overline{FC}$
Therefore, $\angle BGH \cong \angle BFC$ (corresponding angles), and $\Delta BGH \cong \Delta CFD$ (ASA)
Then it follows that BH = DC.

Since BH < BE, this contradicts the hypothesis that the angle bisectors are equal. A similar argument will show that it is impossible to have $m\angle ACB < m\angle ABC$.

It then follows that $m\angle ACB = m\angle ABC$ and that ΔABC is isosceles.

Postassessment

Have students prove that if two angle bisectors of a triangle are congruent then the triangle is isosceles.

Reference

Posamentier, Alfred S., and Charles T. Salkind, *Challenging Problems in Geometry.* Palo Alto, CA: Dale Seymour Publications, 1988.

46   Reflective Properties of the Plane

Performance Objective

Given a line and two points on one side of a line, students will determine the shortest combined path from one point to the line and then to the second point.

Preassessment

Using the following illustration, ask students to locate the precise point on the cushion $\overline{PQ}$ of the "billiard table" which ball A must hit in order to then hit ball B (assume no "English" on the ball).

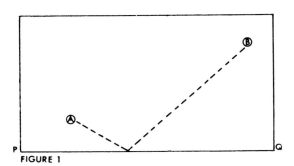

FIGURE 1

The disagreement as to where to hit the ball will develop enough interest to motivate the topic of the properties of reflection.

Teaching Strategies

Have the class try to prove the following property: "A ray of light will make equal angles with a mirror before and after reflecting off a mirror." (This theorem can be easily proved after considering the following proof.)

To find the *shortest path* from point A to line m then to point B in Figure 2, consider the perpendicular from A to line m (meeting line m at point C). Let D be the point on $\overrightarrow{AC}$ such that $\overline{AC} \cong \overline{CD}$. Point D is called the *reflected image* of point A in line m.

The point of intersection of $\overline{BD}$ and line m determines point P, the required point in the original problem. However, what must be shown now is

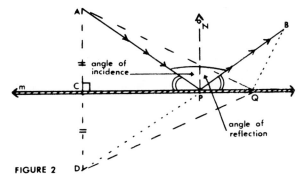

FIGURE 2

that AP + PB is less than *any other* path from A
to line m (say at point Q), and then to B.

Students might be more comfortable stating this
as a "formal proof":

Given: Points A and B are on the same side of line
    m $\overleftrightarrow{ACD}\perp\overleftrightarrow{CPQ}$, where Q is any point on $\overrightarrow{CP}$
    (other than P)
    $\overleftrightarrow{DPB}$
    $\overline{AC} \cong \overline{CD}$

Prove: AP + PB < AQ + QB

Outline of proof: Because line m is the perpendicu-
lar bisector of $\overline{ACD}$, $\overline{AP} \cong \overline{DP}$ and $\overline{AQ} \cong \overline{QD}$.
In $\triangle DQB$, BD < BQ + QD (triangle inequality).
Since BD = DP + PB, AP + PB < AQ + BQ.

You can now show the class that since $\angle$ BPQ
$\cong$ $\angle$ CPD, and $\angle$ APC $\cong$ $\angle$ CPD, that $\angle$ APC
$\cong$ $\angle$ BPQ. If $\overrightarrow{PN}\perp$ line m, then $\angle$ APN, the angle of
incidence, is congruent to $\angle$ BPN, the angle of
reflection.

Have students apply the properties of reflection
to the billiard table problem. A billiard ball will
rebound off a cushion as a ray of light "bounces"
off a mirror. Thus if a ball is at position A (Figure 3)
and the player desires to hit it off cushion $\overline{PQ}$ to position
B, he can aim his shot at the point on $\overline{PQ}$ where he would
see B (if a mirror were placed along $\overline{PQ}$).

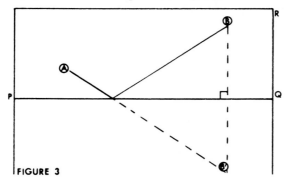

FIGURE 3

Now have students consider the problem of hit-
ting two cushions ($\overline{PQ}$ then $\overline{QR}$) before hitting B.

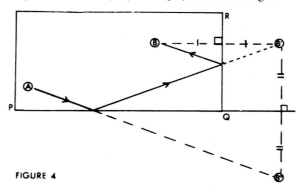

FIGURE 4

Consider the reflected image of B in $\overline{QR}$; call it
B′ (Figure 4). Now they merely have to consider

the problem of where to hit the ball from A off
cushion $\overline{PQ}$ so that it will roll toward B′. To do
this, have them take the reflected image of B′ in
$\overleftrightarrow{PQ}$, then the intersection of the line connecting A
and the reflected image of B′ (call it B″) and $\overrightarrow{PQ}$ is
the point to aim for to make this two-cushion shot.
Students may envision this point as the reflection
of the ball at B in the mirror placed along $\overrightarrow{PQ}$ that
they would see as the reflection in the mirror placed
along $\overline{QR}$.

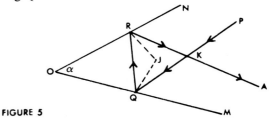

FIGURE 5

A motivated class may now wish to look beyond
the double reflection to where the angle between
the two planes is always fixed as a right angle.

Two mirrors with a fixed dihedral angle between
them are called *angle mirrors*. Have the class prove
that if an observer shines a light into the angle
mirrors so that the ray reflects off one mirror, then
the other, the final reflected ray will form an angle
with the original ray which is double the dihedral
angle between the two mirrors. In other words:

Given: Mirrors OM and ON, let $\angle$ NOM = α also
    a light ray originating at point P aimed at
    point Q reflecting off OM onto $\overrightarrow{ON}$ then
    to A

Prove: m $\angle$ PKR = 2 α (Figure 5)

Outline of proof: Draw the normals (the perpendiculars) to the planes (the mirrors) at the
points of incidence in each plane, i.e., $\overrightarrow{QJ}\perp\overrightarrow{OM}$,
at point Q, and draw $\overrightarrow{RJ}\perp\overrightarrow{ON}$, at point R (the
point of incidence in mirror $\overrightarrow{ON}$). Then, by the
property of reflection, $\overrightarrow{QJ}$ and $\overrightarrow{RJ}$ bisect $\angle$ PQR
and $\angle$ QRA, respectively. Then   m $\angle$ PKR
= m $\angle$ KQR + m $\angle$ KRQ, (exterior angle of a triangle theorem). Then m $\angle$ PKR = 2(m $\angle$ JQR
+ m $\angle$ QRJ) and m $\angle$ PKR = 2(180 − m $\angle$ RJQ).
But, since both $\angle$ JRO and $\angle$ JQO are right angles,
m $\angle$ ROQ = 180 − m $\angle$ RJQ (the sum of the measures of the interior angles of a quadrilateral is 360).
By substituting, m $\angle$ PKR = 2(m $\angle$ ROQ) = 2α.

One of the applications of angle mirrors is that
when the dihedral angle is 45° the ray will be
reflected 90°. Such a pair of mirrors is often
called an "optical square", because it is used to
determine perpendicular lines of sight.

To show how the optical square is used, station
one student at each of the three points O, A, and B,
so that the three points will define a triangle
(Figure 6). Using the optical square they will be

able to determine where the perpendicular from B to $\overrightarrow{AO}$ meets $\overrightarrow{AO}$. Have the student standing at O look at the student standing at A. Have another student, P, holding the optical square move along

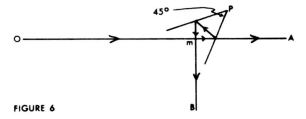

FIGURE 6

the line of sight from O to A until (at some point m) the student at O is able to see the student at B in the angle mirror. The point m is the foot of the altitude from B to $\overrightarrow{OA}$.

Postassessment
Using the property of reflection, have students prove that the height of a flagpole is

$$x = \frac{h \cdot BC}{AB}$$ where x is the height of the

flagpole and h is the height of an observer.

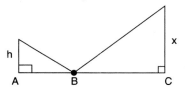

47 Finding The Length Of A Cevian Of A Triangle

This unit presents a method for finding the length of *any* line segment joining a vertex of a triangle with any point on the opposite side. Such a line segment is called a cevian, after Giovanni Ceva who developed a theorem about the concurrency of such line segments. This technique is particularly useful to students since it fills a void in many curricula. Students are usually taught methods for finding the lengths of special cevians such as altitudes and some medians. However, by using Stewart's Theorem (named after Matthew Stewart who published it in 1745), students will now be able to find the length of *any* cevian of a triangle.

Performance Objectives
1. Students will find the length of a specific cevian of a given triangle, all of whose side (and segment) lengths are known.

2. Students will use a special formula to find the length of an angle bisector of a triangle, given the lengths of its sides.

Preassessment
Students should have mastered most of the standard high school geometry course. For review purposes, have students work the following problem:

In a triangle whose sides have lengths 13, 14, and 15, what is the length of the altitude to the side of length 14?

Teaching Strategies
One of the major skills needed to develop Stewart's Theorem is a working knowledge of the Pythagorean

Theorem. The problem stated above requires this skill.

After students have drawn the diagram required by this problem, they will immediately see two right triangles.

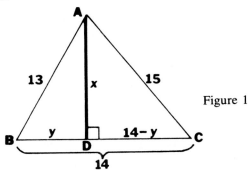

Figure 1

To this figure they will apply the Pythagorean Theorem twice, once to $\triangle ACD$ and a second time to $\triangle ABD$.

For $\triangle ACD$: $x^2 + (14 - y)^2 = 225$
For $\triangle ABD$: $x^2 + y^2 = 169$

By subtraction: $(14 - y)^2 - y^2 = 56$
                  $196 - 28y + y^2 - y^2 = 56$
                                    $y = 5$
          and then $x = 12$

Thus, students will see two right triangles with integral length sides: 5, 12, 13, and 9, 12, 15.

Now challenge your students to find the length of the angle bisector from vertex A of $\triangle ABC$. After a short time, their frustration will be evident. At this juncture, have the class stop working and discuss with them Stewart's Theorem:

Stewart's Theorem:

In Figure 2, the theorem states that:
$$a^2n + b^2m = c(d^2 + mn)$$

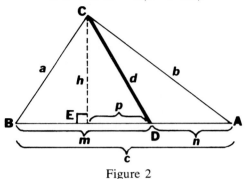

Figure 2

By this theorem, d may be found if a, b, m, and n are known. The proof of this most useful theorem follows.

Proof:

In $\triangle ABC$, let $\overline{BC} = a$, $AC = b$, $AB = c$, $CD = d$. Point D divides $\overline{AB}$ into two segments; $BD = m$ and $DA = n$. Draw the altitude $CE = h$ and let $ED = p$.

In order to proceed with the proof of Stewart's Theorem, we first derive two necessary formulas. The first one is applicable to $\triangle CBD$. We apply the Pythagorean Theorem to $\triangle CEB$ to obtain
$$(CB)^2 = (CE)^2 + (BE)^2.$$
Since $BE = m - p$, $a^2 = h^2 + (m - p)^2$.   (I)
However, by applying the Pythagorean Theorem to $\triangle CED$, we have $(CD)^2 = (CE)^2 + (ED)^2$, or $h^2 = d^2 - p^2$. Replacing h^2 in equation (I), we obtain
$$a^2 = d^2 - p^2 + (m - p)^2,$$
$$a^2 = d^2 - p^2 + m^2 - 2mp + p^2.$$
$$\text{Thus, } a^2 = d^2 + m^2 - 2mp.   \text{(II)}$$
A similar argument is applicable to $\triangle CDA$. Applying the Pythagorean Theorem to $\triangle CEA$, we find that
$$(CA)^2 = (CE)^2 + (EA)^2.$$
Since $EA = (n + p)$, $b^2 = h^2 + (n + p)^2$.   (III)
However, $h^2 = d^2 - p^2$, substitute for h^2 in (III) as follows:
$$b^2 = d^2 - p^2 + (n + p)^2,$$
$$b^2 = d^2 - p^2 + n^2 + 2np + p^2.$$
$$\text{Thus, } b^2 = d^2 + n^2 + 2np.   \text{(IV)}$$
Equations (II) and (IV) give us the formulas we need. Now multiply equation (II) by n to get
$$a^2n = d^2n + m^2n - 2mnp,   \text{(V)}$$
and multiply equation (IV) by m to get
$$b^2m = d^2m + n^2m + 2mnp.   \text{(VI)}$$
Adding (V) and (VI), we have
$$a^2n + b^2m = d^2n + d^2m + m^2n + n^2m + 2mnp - 2mnp.$$
Therefore, $a^2n + b^2m = d^2(n + m) + mn(m + n)$. Since $m + n = c$, we have $a^2n + b^2m = d^2c + mnc$, or
$$a^2n + b^2m = c(d^2 + mn).$$

Your students should now be ready to find the length of the median from vertex A of $\triangle ABC$, where $AB = 13$, $BC = 14$, and $AC = 15$. All they need do is apply Stewart's Theorem as follows:
$$c^2n + b^2m = a(d^2 + mn)$$
However, since $\overline{AD}$ is a median $m = n$.

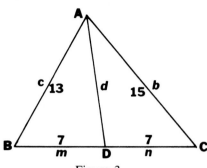

Figure 3

Substituting in the above formula:
$$13^2(7) + 15^2(7) = 14(d^2 + 49)$$
Therefore, $d = 2\sqrt{37}$.

To find the length of an angle bisector of a triangle, Stewart's Theorem leads to a very concise relationship, which students will find easy to use.

Have students consider $\triangle ABC$ with angle bisector $\overline{AD}$.

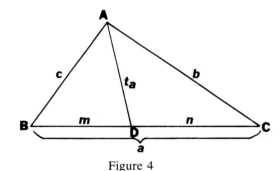

Figure 4

By Stewart's Theorem we obtain the following relationship: $c^2n + b^2m = a(t_a^2 + mn)$, or
$$t_a^2 + mn = \frac{c^2n + b^2m}{a}, \text{ or}$$
as illustrated by Figure 4.

But, $\frac{c}{b} = \frac{m}{n}$. (The bisector of an angle of a triangle divides the opposite side into segments whose measures are proportional to the measures of the other two sides of the triangle. The converse is also true.)
Therefore, $cn = bm$.
Substituting in the above equation,
$$t_a^2 + mn = \frac{cbm + cbn}{m + n} = \frac{cb(m + n)}{m + n} = cb.$$
Hence, $t_a^2 = cb - mn$.

At this juncture, your students should be able to find the length of *any* cevian of a triangle. For reinforcement, present problems involving angle bisectors and medians before going on to other types of cevians.

Postassessment

Have students complete the following exercises:

1. Find the length of an altitude drawn to the longest side of a triangle whose sides have lengths 10, 12, and 14.

2. Find the length of a median drawn to the longest side of a triangle whose sides have lengths 10, 12, and 14.

3. Find the length of an angle bisector drawn to the longest side of a triangle whose sides have lengths 10, 12, and 14.

4. In $\triangle PQR$, if $PR = 7$, $PQ = 8$, $RS = 4$, and $SQ = 5$, find PS when S is on $\overline{RQ}$.

48   A Surprising Challenge

This activity will alert geometry students to the fact that what may appear easy may actually be quite difficult.

Performance Objective
Given a geometric problem of the kind posed here, students will properly analyze it and solve it.

Preassessment
Students should be able to handle geometric proofs with relative ease before attempting this unit. The problem posed here is quite difficult to prove, yet easy to state. It ought to be within the reach of a slightly above average student of high school geometry.

Teaching Strategies
The geometric problem you are about to pose to your students appears to be quite simple and certainly innocent.

Problem: $\triangle ABC$ is isosceles ($CA = CB$). m $\angle ABD = 60°$, m $\angle BAE = 50°$, and m $\angle C = 20°$. Find the measure of $\angle EDB$.

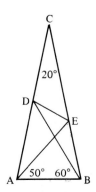

Figure 1

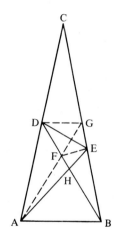

Figure 2

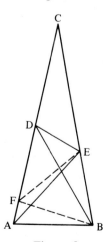

Figure 3

Students should be given a fair amount of time to grapple with this problem. Immediately, they will find the measures of most of the angles in the diagram. However, they will soon realize that this problem was not as simple as they first imagined, since they will be most likely unable to solve the problem. At this point you can begin your discussion of a solution of this problem.

Students will be quick to realize that auxiliary lines are necessary in order to solve this problem. Suggest that they draw $\overline{DG}$ // $\overline{AB}$, where G is on $\overline{CB}$. Then draw $\overline{AG}$ intersecting $\overline{BD}$ at F. The last segment to be drawn is $\overline{EF}$. (See Fig. 2.)

Students should be able to prove that $\angle ABD \cong \angle BAG$. Then m $< AGD = $ m $\angle BAG = 60°$ (alternate interior angles of parallel lines). Thus m $\angle AFB$ must be 60° and $\triangle AFB$ is equilateral, and $AB = FB$.

Since m $\angle EAB = 50°$, and m $\angle ABE = 80°$, m $\angle AEB = 50°$ making $\triangle ABE$ isosceles and $AB = EB$. Therefore $FB = EB$ (transitivity), and $\triangle EFB$ is isosceles.

Since m $\angle EBF = 20°$, m $\angle BEF = $ m $\angle BFE = 80°$. As m $\angle DFG = 60°$, m $\angle GFE = 40°$. $GE = EF$ (equal length sides of an isosceles triangle), and $DF = DG$ (sides of an equilateral triangle). Thus $DGEF$ is a kite, i.e., two isosceles triangles externally sharing a common base. $\overline{DE}$ bisects $\angle GDF$ (property of a kite), therefore m $\angle EDB = 30°$.

Another possible method of solution follows:
In isosceles $\triangle ABC$, m $\angle ACB = 20°$, m $\angle CAB = 80°$, m $\angle ABD = 60°$, and m $\angle EAB = 50°$.
Draw $\overline{BF}$ so that m $\angle ABF = 20°$; then draw $\overline{FE}$ (Fig. 3).
In $\triangle ABE$, m $AEB = 50°$ (sum of measures of the

angles of a triangle is 180°) therefore $\triangle ABE$ is isosceles and $AB = EB$.   (I)

Similarly, $\triangle FAB$ is isosceles, since m $\angle AFB = $ m $\angle FAB = 80°$.
Thus $AB = FB$.   (II)

From (I) and (II), $EB = FB$. Since m $\angle FBE = 60°$, $\triangle FBE$ is equilateral and $EB = FB = FE$.   (III)

Now, in $\triangle DFB$, m $\angle FDB = 40°$, and m $\angle FBD = $ m $\angle ABD - $ m $\angle ABF = 60° - 20° = 40°$.
Thus $\triangle DFB$ is isosceles and $FD = FB$.   (IV)

It then follows from (III) and (IV) that $FE = FD$, making $\triangle FDE$ isosceles, and m $\angle FDE = $ m $\angle FED$.
Since m $\angle AFB = 80°$ and m $\angle EFB = 60°$, then m $\angle AFE$, the exterior angle of isosceles $\triangle FDE$, equals 140°, by addition. It follows that m $\angle ADE = 70°$. Therefore, m $\angle EDB = $ m $\angle ADE - $ m $\angle FDB = 70° - 40° = 30°$.

There are various other methods for solving this problem. One source for seven solutions of this problem is *Challenging Problems in Geometry* by A. S. Posamentier, and C. T. Salkind, pp. 149–54 (Seymour, 1988).

Postassessment

Have students discover another solution for the above problem.

49 Making Discoveries in Mathematics

This activity is intended to permit the student to make discoveries based on observation, and then propose a conclusion.

Performance Objective
Faced with a mathematical pattern students will state their discoveries and propose a conclusion.

Teaching Strategies
This activity will be comprised of a series of mathematical mini-activities each of which will require the student to discover a pattern or relationship and then state his or her conclusion.

1. Select any two consecutive square numbers (e.g., 4 and 9). Give one prime between these two numbers. Repeat this for 10 other pairs of consecutive square numbers. Now try to find a pair of consecutive square numbers which do *not* have a prime number between them. What conclusion can you draw from this experiment?

2. Select any even integer greater than 2. Now express this even integer as the sum of exactly two prime numbers. For example, $8 = 3 + 5$, and $18 = 7 + 11$. Repeat this for at least 25 even integers before you draw any conclusions.

3. Draw *any* triangle. Using a protractor carefully trisect each of the angles of the triangle. Locate the points of intersection of the adjacent angle trisectors as illustrated below.

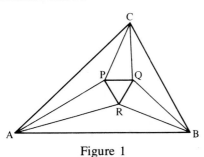

Figure 1

Join these three points and inspect the triangle formed. Repeat this construction for at least six different triangles before drawing any conclusion.

4. Draw *any* parallelogram. Construct an equilateral triangle externally on two adjacent sides as shown below. Then join the two remote vertices of the equilateral triangles to each other and to the farthest vertex of the parallelogram. What kind of triangle is formed? Before stating a conclusion repeat this experiment with at least six different parallelograms.

Students ought to be able to actually prove this last example. However, the other three examples should not be attempted; 1 and 2 have never been proved while 3 is extremely difficult to prove.*

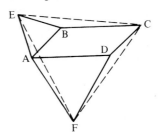

Figure 2

You might try to replicate these experiments with others similar to these. It is important for students to learn to trust their intuition in mathematics and be able to draw correct inductive conclusions.

Postassessment
Ask students to find the sum of the first 1,2,3,4,5,6, . . . 15 odd integers and list the 15 different sums. Then have the students state a logical conclusion.

---

*Two proofs of this theorem can be found in *Challenging Problems in Geometry* by A. S. Posamentier, and C. T. Salkind (Palo Alto, CA: Dale Seymour, 1988) pp. 158–61.

50

Tessellations

Performance Objectives

1. *Given a regular polygon, each student will determine whether it will tessellate a plane.*

2. *Given a combination of various regular polygons, each student will determine whether they will tessellate a plane.*

Preassessment

Before beginning this lesson explain to students that when polygons are fitted together to cover a plane with no spaces between them and no overlapping, the pattern is called a *tessellation*. (Mention the pattern of tiles on bathroom floors as one of the more common tessellations.) A tessellation which is made up entirely of congruent regular polygons that meet so that no vertex of one polygon lies on a side of another is referred to as a regular tessellation. Explain further that a network of equilateral triangles, a checkerboard pattern of squares and a hexagonal pattern are the *only* tessellations of regular polygons that exist.

Teaching Strategies

To mathematically show why the previous three patterns are the only tessellations which fit the description, ask the class to suppose m regular polygons are required to fill the space around one point (where the vertex of the angles of the polygon is situated). If they assume that each regular polygon has n sides, each interior angle of the polygon is equal to $\dfrac{(n-2)\ 180°}{n}$. Therefore $\dfrac{m(n-2)\ 180°}{n} =$ 360° and $(m-2)(n-2) = 4$.

Considering the nature of the problem, both integers m and n are greater than 2. If $m=3$, then $n=6$. If $m>3$, then $n<6$ and since $n>2$ only the values $n=3$, $n=4$ and $n=5$ need be considered. If $n=3$, then $m=6$; if $n=4$, then $m=4$. If $n=5$, m is non-integral; therefore, the only solutions are $m=3$, $n=6$; $m=4$, $n=4$; $m=6$, $n=3$. Have students suggest more convenient ways of symbolizing these tessellations (6^3, 4^4, 3^6). Use the following diagrams to show that no other regular polygon has an interior angle that will divide 360°. (Fig. 1 & 2)

Through further investigation the range of tessellations may be expanded. Tessellations can also be formed by fitting together two or more kinds of regular polygons, vertex to vertex, in such a way that the same polygons, in the same cyclic order, surround each vertex. These are called *semi-regular* tessellations in which there can be no fewer than three and no more than six polygons at any vertex.

Ask students to consider a ternary arrangement (three polygons share one point as vertex). Because the sum of the angles around any vertex must be 360°, a ternary arrangement of polygons of n_1, n_2 and n_3 sides respectively will be possible only if

$$\left(\frac{n_1-2}{n_1} + \frac{n_2-2}{n_2} + \frac{n_3-2}{n_3}\right) 180° = 360°.$$

From this we obtain

$$\left(\frac{n_1}{n_1} - \frac{2}{n_1} + \frac{n_2}{n_2} - \frac{2}{n_2} + \frac{n_3}{n_3} - \frac{2}{n_3}\right) 180° = 360°.$$

$$1 + 1 + 1 - 2\left(\frac{1}{n_1} + \frac{1}{n_2} + \frac{1}{n_3}\right) = 2.$$

Therefore, $\dfrac{1}{n_1} + \dfrac{1}{n_2} + \dfrac{1}{n_3} = \dfrac{1}{2}$.

In a similar way students can find the following conditions for other possible arrangements.

$$\frac{1}{n_1} + \frac{1}{n_2} + \frac{1}{n_3} + \frac{1}{n_4} = 1$$

$$\frac{1}{n_1} + \frac{1}{n_2} + \frac{1}{n_3} + \frac{1}{n_4} + \frac{1}{n_5} = \frac{3}{2}$$

$$\frac{1}{n_1} + \frac{1}{n_2} + \frac{1}{n_3} + \frac{1}{n_4} + \frac{1}{n_5} + \frac{1}{n_6} = 2$$

Following are the seventeen possible integer solutions that need be considered. (Table 1)

(Solutions 10, 14, and 17 have already been discussed. Solutions 1, 2, 3, 4, 6, and 9 each can be formed at a single vertex but they cannot be extended to cover the whole plane.) They are made up of different combinations of triangles, squares, hexagons, octagons, and dodecagons.

Any of the remaining solutions can be used as the only type of arrangement in a design covering a whole plane except #11, which must be used in conjunction with others, e.g. #5 or #15.

Have the class consider what happens in solution #5. Here two dodecagons and a triangle meet at a vertex. The extended figure can be formed by juxtaposing dodecagons as in figure 3. The remaining spaces form the triangles.

It may be noted that #7, composed of dodecagons, hexagons and squares, one at each vertex, gives a more complicated pattern (figure 4).

A juxtaposition of octagons (figure 5) forms #8. The empty spaces provide the areas needed for the squares.

Two different patterns can be obtained from #12 by the juxtaposition of hexagons. In one the hexagons have edges in common; in the other they have only vertices in common (figures 6 and 7). The empty spaces form triangles or diamond shapes composed of pairs of triangles.

Call on individual students to determine and draw the patterns for the remaining solutions.

Postassessment

1. Which of the following regular polygons will tessellate a plane: a) a square; b) a pentagon; c) an octagon; d) a hexagon.

2. Which of the following combinations of regular polygons will tessellate a plane: a) an octagon and a square; b) a pentagon and a decagon; c) a hexagon and triangle.

No.	n_1	n_2	n_3	n_4	n_5	n_6
1	3	7	42			
2	3	8	24			
3	3	9	18			
4	3	10	15			
5	3	12	12			
6	4	5	20			
7	4	6	12			
8	4	8	8			
9	5	5	10			
10	6	6	6			
11	3	3	4	12		
12	3	3	6	6		
13	3	4	4	6		
14	4	4	4	4		
15	3	3	3	4	4	
16	3	3	3	3	6	
17	3	3	3	3	3	3

Table 1

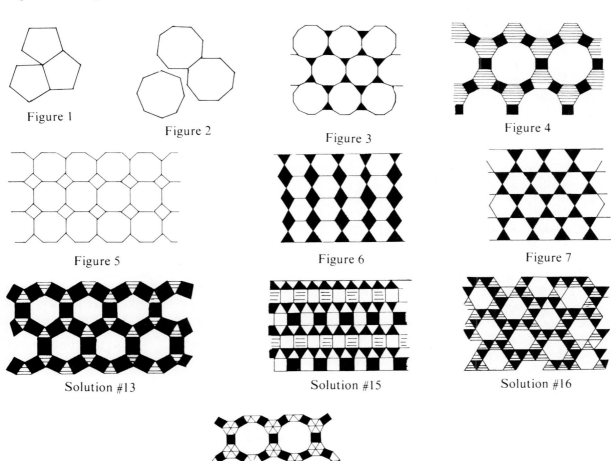

Figure 1

Figure 2

Figure 3

Figure 4

Figure 5

Figure 6

Figure 7

Solution #13

Solution #15

Solution #16

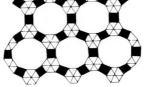

Solutions #11 & 17

51 Introducing the Pythagorean Theorem

This unit is intended for students taking the regular geometry course.

Performance Objective
Given appropriate measures, the student will use the Pythagorean Theorem to solve geometric problems.

In addition, it is expected that student appreciation for the Pythagorean Theorem will increase.

Preassessment
Have your students answer the following question:

Can a circular table top with a diameter of 9 feet fit through a rectangular door whose dimensions are 6 feet wide and 8 feet high?

Teaching Strategies
Students will immediately realize that the table top can possibly only fit through the door if it is tilted. Thereupon they will find a need for determining the length of the diagonal of this 6' by 8' rectangle. This is where you ought to introduce the Pythagorean Theorem. There are over 360 proofs of the Pythagorean Theorem available (see Elisha S. Loomis, *The Pythagorean Proposition,* National Council of Teachers of Mathematics, Washington, D.C., 1968.) A teacher may select the proof which he feels would be most interesting and intelligible for his particular class. Some proofs rely heavily on algebra while others are purely geometric.

Once the Pythagorean Theorem has been proved, the student is ready to apply his knowledge of the Theorem to some problems. Surely, he can now find that the length of the diagonal of the door (of the original problem) is 10 feet, and hence conclude that the table top would certainly fit through. There are many other "practical" problems which may be used to offer further application of the Pythagorean Theorem. For example, suppose your students wanted to find the diameter of a pipe. All they would have to do is place a carpenter's measuring square as shown in the figure. Then by measuring the length of x, the diameter would merely be $4.828\,x$. Students should of course be asked to analyze this. The broken lines in the diagram will help in the justification of this situation. Applying the Pythagorean Theorem to the right triangle shown:

$R^2 + R^2 = (R + x)^2$, or $R = x(1 + \sqrt{2})$.

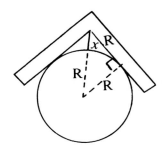

Another problem which you might have your students solve is that of finding the original diameter of broken plate where only a segment of the circle remains. Once again the diagram below depicts the situation: The lengths AB and CD

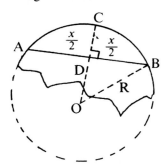

are measurable, and the broken lines are provided only for a discussion of the solution. Let $AB = x$, $CD = y$ and OB (the radius to be found) $= R$. Thus $OD = R - y$ and by the Pythagorean Theorem (in $\triangle ODB$) $(R - y)^2 + \dfrac{x^2}{4} = R^2$, and then $R = \dfrac{y}{2} + \dfrac{x^2}{8y}$ so that the diameter (in terms of the measurable lengths x and y) is $y + \dfrac{x^2}{4y}$.

From a strictly geometric point of view there are some rather interesting relationships which may be proved by applying the Pythagorean Theorem. You may wish to present some of these to your class as further application of this theorem.

1. If E is any point on altitude $\overline{AD}$, then $(AC)^2 - (CE)^2 = (AB)^2 - (EB)^2$.

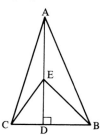

2. If medians $\overline{AD}$ and $\overline{BE}$ of $\triangle ABC$ are perpendicular then $AB = \sqrt{\dfrac{(AC)^2 + (BC)^2}{5}}$

3. If from any point inside a triangle, perpendiculars are drawn to the sides of the triangle, the sum of the squares of the measures of every other segment of the sides so formed equals the sum of the squares of the remaining three segments. That is in $\triangle ABC$ below:

$$(BD)^2 + (CE)^2 + (AF)^2$$
$$= (DC)^2 + (EA)^2 + (FB)^2.$$

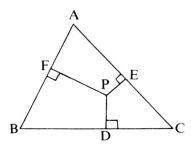

4. If $\overline{AD}$, $\overline{BE}$, and $\overline{CF}$ are medians of $\triangle ABC$,

(I) then $\dfrac{3}{4}[(AB)^2 + (BC)^2 + (CA)^2]$

$$= (AD)^2 + (BE)^2 + (CF)^2.$$

(II) then $5(AB)^2 = 4(AE)^2 + (BE)^2$, if $m \angle C = 90$.

The complete solutions of these problems and many other more challenging problems can be found in: Posamentier, Alfred S., and Charles T. Salkind. *Challenging Problems in Geometry* (Palo Alto, CA: Seymour, 1988).

Once students have a fair command of this celebrated theorem, they are ready to consider a generalization of it.

To this juncture the students have considered the Pythagorean Theorem as $a^2 + b^2 = c^2$, where a and b represented the *lengths* of the legs of a right triangle and c represented the *length* of its hypotenuse. However this statement could also be interpreted to mean the following: "The sum of the *areas* of the squares on the legs of a right triangle equals the *area* of the square on the hypotenuse." For the right triangle below $\mathcal{A} S_a + \mathcal{A} S_b = \mathcal{A} S_c$ ($\mathcal{A}$ represents "area of").

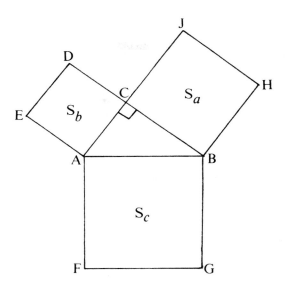

Now have students replace these squares with semicircles with diameters $\overline{BC}$, $\overline{AC}$, and $\overline{AB}$, or have them replace the squares with any similar polygons so that the corresponding sides are on the sides of $\triangle ABC$.

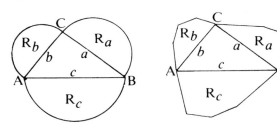

From a basic area relationship:

$$\frac{\mathcal{A} R_a}{\mathcal{A} R_c} = \frac{a^2}{c^2} \text{ and } \frac{R_b}{R_c} = \frac{b^2}{c^2}$$

Then $\dfrac{\mathcal{A} R_a + \mathcal{A} R_b}{\mathcal{A} R_c} = \dfrac{a^2 + b^2}{c^2}$

However, by the Pythagorean Theorem:

$a^2 + b^2 = c^2$ so that $\dfrac{\mathcal{A} R_a + \mathcal{A} R_b}{\mathcal{A} R_c} = 1$, and $\mathcal{A} R_a$ $+ \mathcal{A} R_b = \mathcal{A} R_c$. The interesting significance of this extension of the Pythagorean Theorem ought to be highlighted. Then have students pose other extensions.

Before leaving the geometric discussion of the Pythagorean Theorem, you might wish to show students how the converse of this theorem can be used to determine whether an angle of a triangle is acute, right or obtuse, given the lengths of the sides of the triangle.

That is,

if $a^2 + b^2 = c^2$, $\angle C$ is a right angle;

if $a^2 + b^2 > c^2$, $\angle C$ is acute;

if $a^2 + b^2 < c^2$, $\angle C$ is obtuse.

These relationships should prove to be quite fascinating and useful to the students.

Having considered the Pythagorean Theorem from a geometric standpoint, it should be interesting to consider this theorem from a number theoretic point of view. A *Pythagorean Triple,* written as (a, b, c), is a set of three positive integers a, b, and c, where $a^2 + b^2 = c^2$. For any Pythagorean Triple (a, b, c) and any positive integer k, (ka, kb, kc) is also a triple. Your students should be able to prove this.

A *Primitive Pythagorean Triple* is a Pythagorean Triple whose first two members are *relatively prime,* one even and the other odd. Introduce this: where $a^2 + b^2 = c^2$ (and m and n are natural numbers, and $m > n$), $a = m^2 - n^2$, $6 = 2mn$ and $c = m^2 + n^2$. (For a development of these relationships see: Sierpinski, W., *Pythagorean Triangles.* New York: Yeshiva University Press, 1962.) After setting up a table such as the following, students will begin to conjecture about properties of m and n which generate specific types of Pythagorean Triples. Students will also begin to group different types of Pythagorean Triples.

m	n	$m^2 - n^2$	$2mn$	$m^2 + n^2$
2	1	3	4	5
3	2	5	12	13
4	1	15	8	17
4	3	7	24	25
5	4	9	40	41
3	1	8	6	10
5	2	21	20	29

Some questions to anticipate are: What must be true about m and n in order for (a, b, c) to be a Primitive Pythagorean Triple? Can c of this triple ever be even? Why must the even member of a Primitive Pythagorean Triple be divisible by 4? What must be true about m and n in order that the third member of a Primitive Pythagorean Triple exceed one of the other members by 1? Why is one side of a Primitive Pythagorean Triple always divisible by 5? And why is the product of the three members of any Pythagorean Triple divisible by 60?

In a short while students will begin to probe the parity of numbers and the relationships of Pythagorean Triples. This genuine interest brought about by a rather elementary and superficial introduction to a topic in number theory may be the beginning of a student's investigation into a heretofore unfamiliar field.

Thus a study of the Pythagorean Theorem has a wide range of possibilities for interesting your students. *You* must take the initiative of introducing these variations on the theme. If this is properly done, your students will carry these endeavors further.

Reference
Posamentier, A.S., Banks, J.H., and Bannister, R.L. *Geometry, Its Elements and Structure*, 2d ed. New York: McGraw-Hill, 1977.

52   Trisection Revisited

Performance Objectives
1. Students will trisect a given angle using any of the four methods presented.

2. Students will prove the four methods of trisection.

Preassessment
Students should have a working knowledge of algebra. They should also have mastered constructions commonly taught in high school geometry and proofs of those constructions.

Teaching Strategies
After demonstrating and proving the following construction, discuss why it is not really a solution to the ancient problem of trisecting an angle using only Euclidean tools.

Given $\angle AOB_0$ with $m \angle AOB_0 = x$
Construct $\angle AOB_n$ such that $m \angle AOB_n = 2x/3$

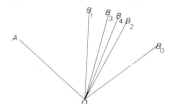

Figure 1

Construction and Proof
1. Construct $\overline{OB_1}$, the bisector of $\angle AOB_0$ then
$$m\angle AOB_1 = x - \frac{1}{2}x$$
    2. Construct $\overline{OB_2}$, the bisector of $\angle B_1OB_0$ then
$$m\angle AOB_2 = x - \frac{1}{2}x + \frac{1}{4}x$$

3. Construct $\overrightarrow{OB_3}$, the bisector of $\angle B_1OB_2$ then
$$m\angle AOB_3 = x - \frac{1}{2}x + \frac{1}{4}x - \frac{1}{8}x$$

4. Construct $\overrightarrow{OB_4}$, the bisector of $\angle B_3OB_2$ then
$$m\angle AOB_4 = x - \frac{1}{2}x + \frac{1}{4}x - \frac{1}{8}x + \frac{1}{16}x$$

5. Continuing in this fashion we will reach
$$m\angle AOB_n = x - \frac{1}{2}x + \frac{1}{4}x - \frac{1}{8}x + \ldots \pm (\frac{1}{2})^n x$$

then we multiply by $(\frac{1}{2})$ to obtain $(\frac{1}{2})m\angle AOB_n$
$$= \frac{1}{2}x - \frac{1}{4}x + \frac{1}{8}x - \frac{1}{16}x + \ldots \pm (\frac{1}{2})^{n+1}x.$$ Now
we add the second equation to the first to get
$$(\frac{3}{2})m\angle AOB_n = x \pm (\frac{1}{2})^{n+1}x$$
$$m\angle AOB_n = \frac{2x}{3}\left[1 \pm (\frac{1}{2})^{n+1}\right]$$

6. Now we observe that as n increases to infinity (which corresponds to carrying out an *infinite number* of construction operations) the term $(\frac{1}{2})^{n+1}$ approaches zero. Then $m\angle AOB_n$ approaches $\frac{2x}{3}$

The second construction adds to the Euclidean tools a strange looking device called a *tomahawk* (first published by Bergery in the third edition of *Geometrie Appliquee a l' Industrie*, Metz, 1835).

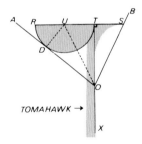

TOMAHAWK →

Figure 2

To construct a tomahawk, start with a line segment $\overline{RS}$ trisected at U and T. Draw a semicircle about U with radius $\overline{UT}$ and draw $\overline{TX}$ perpendicular to $\overline{RS}$. Complete the instrument as shown in the diagram.

To trisect any $\angle AOB$, simply place the implement on the angle so that S falls on $\overrightarrow{OB}$, TX passes through vertex O, and the semicircle is tangent to $\overline{AO}$ at some point, say D. Then, since we may easily show that $\triangle DOU \cong \triangle TOU \cong \triangle TOS$, we have $m\angle DOU = m\angle TOU = m\angle TOS = \frac{1}{3}m\angle AOB$

The third construction is implied by a theorem given by Archimedes. In it we use a straightedge upon which a line segment has been marked. This extension of Euclidean tools makes possible an *insertion principle trisection.*

To demonstrate the insertion principle to students, have them try the following problem using Euclidean tools.

Given $\overline{MN}$ with curves q and n (such that the smallest distance between q and n is $\leq MN$) and point O not on q or n

Construct a line through O which intersects q and n at M_1 and N_1 respectively so that $M_1N_1 = MN$.

Except for certain special cases, this problem is impossible using only Euclidean tools. Now have students mark a line segment on their straightedges whose measure is equal to MN. It is now a

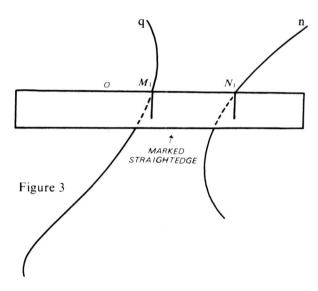

Figure 3

simple matter to adjust the marked straightedge until it describes a line through O with the distance between the two intersections equal to MN.

Now students are ready for the insertion principle trisection.

Given Circle O with central $\angle AOB$

Construct $\angle ADB$ so that $m\angle ADB = \frac{1}{3}m\angle AOB$

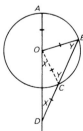

Figure 4

Construction
1. Draw $\overrightarrow{AO}$.
2. Mark AO on a straightedge.
3. Using the insertion principle draw $\overrightarrow{BD}$ such that D is on $\overrightarrow{AO}$ and $\overrightarrow{BD}$ intersects circle O at C with $\overline{AO} \cong \overline{CD}$. Then $m\angle ADB = \frac{1}{3}m\angle AOB$.

Proof
1. Draw $\overline{OC}$.
2. By construction $\overline{AO} \cong \overline{BO} \cong \overline{CO} \cong \overline{DC}$ (since the first three are radii of circle O and the last was constructed to be congruent to $\overline{AO}$).
3. $\triangle OCD$ and $\triangle BOC$ are isosceles.
4. Therefore $m\angle DOC = m\angle CDO = x$ and $m\angle OCB = m\angle OBC = y$
5. Since $\angle OCB$ is the exterior angle of $\triangle OCD$, $m\angle OCB = m\angle DOC + m\angle CDO = 2x$ or $y = 2x$.
6. Similarly since $\angle AOB$ is the exterior angle of $\triangle OBD$, $m\angle AOB = m\angle ADB + m\angle OBD = x + 2x = 3x$.
7. Thus, $m\angle ADB = \frac{1}{3}m\angle AOB$.

Ceva's method of trisection (the last of this unit) utilizes a device which consists of four hinged straightedges. In the diagram of Ceva's linkage, points C, D, E, and O are pivots such that the figure CDEO is a rhombus. To trisect a given angle A'O'B' one must first draw the circle about the vertex O' with radius equal to the length of a side of the rhombus CDEO. Ceva's instrument is then placed on the angle so that O and O' coincide. It is then adjusted until $\overrightarrow{DC}$ and $\overrightarrow{DE}$ go through the points where $\overrightarrow{OA'}$ and $\overrightarrow{OB'}$ intersect the circle,

points A and B respectively. Then $m\angle AOF = m\angle FOG = m\angle GOB = (\frac{1}{3})m\angle AOB$

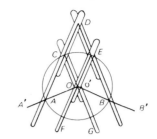

Figure 5

The proof uses the rhombus CDEO to obtain $m\angle ACG = m\angle COE = m\angle FEB = m\angle CDE = x$. Then $m\angle FOG = x$. Noting that points C and E are on the circle, we have $\angle ACG$ and $\angle FEB$ inscribed in the circle. Then $m\angle ACG = x = \frac{1}{2}m\angle AOG$ and $m\angle FEB = x = \frac{1}{2}m\angle FOB$ which gives us $2x = m\angle AOG$ and $2x = m\angle FOB$. Clearly then $m\angle AOF = m\angle FOG = m\angle GOB = \frac{1}{3}m\angle AOB$.

Postassessment
1. Prove the *tomahawk* trisection method valid.
2. Trisect any given arbitrary angle using any two of the methods presented in this unit.

53 Proving Lines Concurrent

This unit will present the student with a theorem which is quite useful in some cases when proving lines concurrent.

Performance Objective
Given appropriate problems, students will apply Ceva's Theorem to prove lines concurrent.

Preassessment
Have students try to prove any of the following:
1. Prove that the medians of a triangle are concurrent.
2. Prove that the angle bisectors of a triangle are concurrent.
3. Prove that the altitudes of a triangle are concurrent.

Teaching Strategies
An above average geometry student should, given enough time, be able to prove some of these theorems. It should be noted that the proofs they

would normally attempt (synthetically) are among the more difficult in the high school geometry course. Challenging students with these rather difficult problems sets the stage for the introduction of a theorem which will permit these problems to be done quite easily.

This theorem, first published in 1678 by the Italian mathematician Giovanni Ceva, is stated as follows:

Three lines drawn from the vertices A, B, and C of $\triangle ABC$ meeting the opposite sides in points L, M, and N, respectively, are concurrent if and only if
$$\frac{AN}{NB} \cdot \frac{BL}{LC} \cdot \frac{CM}{MA} = 1$$

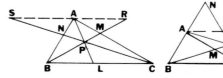

Note: There are two cases: The three lines meeting inside or outside the given triangle.

Before applying this theorem to the problems posed earlier, it might be wise to prove the theorem.

Given: $\triangle ABC$, with N on $\overleftrightarrow{AB}$, M on $\overleftrightarrow{AC}$ and L on $\overleftrightarrow{BC}$; also $\overleftrightarrow{AL}$, $\overleftrightarrow{BM}$, and $\overleftrightarrow{CN}$ are concurrent at P.

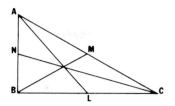

Prove: $\dfrac{AN}{NB} \cdot \dfrac{BL}{LC} \cdot \dfrac{CM}{MA} = 1$

Proof: Draw a line through A, parallel to $\overleftrightarrow{BC}$ meeting $\overleftrightarrow{CP}$ at S and $\overleftrightarrow{BP}$ at R.

$$\triangle AMR \sim \triangle CMB$$

Therefore $\dfrac{AM}{MC} = \dfrac{AR}{CB}$ (I)

$$\triangle BNC \sim \triangle ANS$$

Therefore $\dfrac{BN}{NA} = \dfrac{CB}{SA}$ (II)

$$\triangle CLP \sim \triangle SAP$$

Therefore $\dfrac{CL}{SA} = \dfrac{LP}{AP}$ (III)

$$\triangle BLP \sim \triangle RAP$$

Therefore $\dfrac{BL}{RA} = \dfrac{LP}{AP}$ (IV)

From (III) and (IV) we get $\dfrac{CL}{SA} = \dfrac{BL}{RA}$, or

$$\dfrac{CL}{BL} = \dfrac{SA}{RA} \qquad (V)$$

Now multiplying (I), (II), and (V) yields

$$\dfrac{AM}{MC} \cdot \dfrac{BN}{NA} \cdot \dfrac{CL}{BL} = \dfrac{AR}{CB} \cdot \dfrac{CB}{SA} \cdot \dfrac{SA}{RA} = 1$$

Since Ceva's Theorem is biconditional, it is necessary to prove the converse of the implication we have just proved.

Given: $\triangle ABC$ with N on $\overleftrightarrow{AB}$, M on $\overleftrightarrow{AC}$ and L on $\overleftrightarrow{BC}$; also $\dfrac{BL}{LC} \cdot \dfrac{CM}{MA} \cdot \dfrac{AN}{NB} = 1$.

Prove: $\overleftrightarrow{AL}$, $\overleftrightarrow{BM}$ and $\overleftrightarrow{CN}$ are concurrent.

Proof: Let $\overleftrightarrow{BM}$ and $\overleftrightarrow{AL}$ meet at P. Let $\overleftrightarrow{CP}$ meet AB at N'. Since $\overleftrightarrow{AL}$, $\overleftrightarrow{BM}$ and $\overleftrightarrow{CN}'$ are concurrent, by the part of Ceva's Theorem we have already proved we get:

$$\dfrac{BL}{LC} \cdot \dfrac{CM}{MA} \cdot \dfrac{AN'}{N'B} = 1.$$

However $\dfrac{BL}{LC} \cdot \dfrac{CM}{MA} \cdot \dfrac{AN}{NB} = 1$ (given)

Therefore $\dfrac{AN'}{N'B} = \dfrac{AN}{NB}$, so that N and N' must coincide. Thus the three lines are concurrent.

Students should now be ready to apply Ceva's Theorem to the three problems posed earlier.

1. Prove that the medians of a triangle are concurrent.

Proof: In $\triangle ABC$, $\overline{AL}$, $\overline{BM}$, and $\overline{CN}$ are medians (see figure below).

Therefore, AN = NB, BL = LC, and CM = MA. By multiplication $(AN)(BL)(MC) = (NB)(LC)(MA)$, or $\dfrac{AN}{NB} \cdot \dfrac{BL}{LC} \cdot \dfrac{CM}{MA} = 1$.

Thus by Ceva's Theorem $\overleftrightarrow{AL}$, $\overleftrightarrow{BM}$, and $\overleftrightarrow{CN}$ are concurrent.

2. Prove that the angle bisectors of a triangle are concurrent.

Proof: In $\triangle ABC$, $\overline{AL}$, $\overline{BM}$, and $\overline{CN}$ are interior angle bisectors (see figure below).

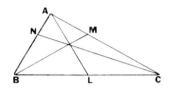

Since an angle bisector of a triangle partitions the opposite side into segments proportional to the two remaining sides of the triangle it follows that:

$$\dfrac{AN}{NB} = \dfrac{AC}{BC}, \quad \dfrac{BL}{LC} = \dfrac{AB}{AC} \text{ and } \dfrac{CM}{MA} = \dfrac{BC}{AB}.$$

Then by multiplying

$$\dfrac{AN}{NB} \cdot \dfrac{BL}{LC} \cdot \dfrac{CM}{MA} = \dfrac{AC}{BC} \cdot \dfrac{AB}{AC} \cdot \dfrac{BC}{AB} = 1$$

Thus by Ceva's Theorem the three angle bisectors are concurrent.

3. Prove that the altitudes of a triangle are concurrent.

Proof: In $\triangle ABC$, $\overline{AL}$, $\overline{BM}$, and $\overline{CN}$ are altitudes (see figures below).

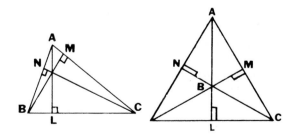

$\triangle ANC \sim \triangle AMB$, and $\dfrac{AN}{MA} = \dfrac{AC}{AB}$

$\triangle BLA \sim \triangle BNC$, and $\dfrac{BL}{NB} = \dfrac{AB}{BC}$

$\triangle CMB \sim \triangle CLA$, and $\dfrac{CM}{LC} = \dfrac{BC}{AC}$

By multiplying these three fractions we get:

$$\frac{AN}{MA} \cdot \frac{BL}{NB} \cdot \frac{CM}{LC} = \frac{AC}{AB} \cdot \frac{AB}{BC} \cdot \frac{BC}{AC} = 1$$

Thus by Ceva's Theorem the altitudes are concurrent.

These are some of the simpler applications of Ceva's Theorem. One source for finding more applications of Ceva's Theorem is *Challenging Problems in Geometry Vol. II*, by A.S. Posamentier and C.T. Salkind, Macmillan, 1970.

Postassessment

1. Have students use Ceva's Theorem to prove that when **Δ**ABC has points P, Q and R on sides $\overline{AB}$, $\overline{AC}$ and $\overline{BC}$, respectively, and when

$\dfrac{AQ}{QC} = \dfrac{BR}{RC} = 2$, and AP = PB, it follows that $\overline{AR}$, $\overline{BQ}$, and $\overline{CP}$ are concurrent.

2. **Δ**ABC cuts a circle at points E, E′, D, D′, F, F′ (see figure below). Prove that if $\overline{AD}$, $\overline{BF}$, and $\overline{CE}$ are concurrent, then $\overline{AD'}$, $\overline{BF'}$ and $\overline{CE'}$ are also concurrent.

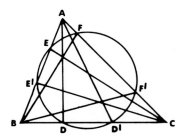

54   Squares

This unit will strengthen students' skills at proving quadrilaterals to be squares in addition to revisiting the topic of concurrency.

Performance Objective

Students will explain a method for proving concurrency.

Preassessment

Students should be familiar with the various properties of a square and should have had some experience in proving quadrilaterals to be squares.

Teaching Strategies

Have students construct a square externally on each side of a given parallelogram (see figure below). Have them locate the center of each square by drawing the diagonals. Ask the class what figure they believe will result by joining the centers of consecutive squares. Natural curiosity should motivate them to try to prove that PQRS is a square.

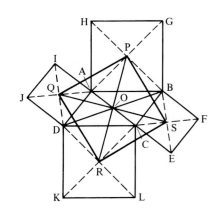

Proof:

ABCD is a parallelogram.

Points *P, Q, R,* and *S* are the centers of the four squares *ABGH, DAIJ, DCLK* and *CBFE*, respectively. *PA = DR* and *AQ = QD* (each is one-half a diagonal).

∠*ADC* is supplementary to ∠*DAB*, and ∠*IAH* is supplementary to ∠*DAB* (since ∠*IAD* and ∠*HAB* are right angles). Therefore ∠*ADC* ≅ ∠*IAH*.

Since m∠*RDC* = m∠*QDA* = m∠*HAP* = m∠*QAI* = 45°, ∠*RDQ* ≅ ∠*QAP*. Thus Δ*RDQ* ≅ Δ*PAQ* (SAS) and *QR = QP*.

In a similar fashion, it may be proved that *QP = PS* and *PS = RS*.

Therefore, *PQRS* is a rhombus.
Since △*RDQ* ≅ △*PAQ*, ∠ *DQR* ≅ ∠ *AQP*; therefore,
PQR ≅ ∠ *DQA* (by addition).
Since ∠ *DQA* ≅ right angle, ∠ *PQR* ≅ right angle, and
PQRS is a square.

Careful drawing of the figure above should indicate
that the diagonals of square *PQRS* and the diagonals
of parallelogram *ABCD* are concurrent. This proof
deserves special attention since it illustrates an all too
often neglected skill; proving concurrency.

To prove that the diagonals of square *PQRS* are
concurrent with the diagonals of parallelogram
ABCD, we must prove that a diagonal of the square
and a diagonal of the parallelogram bisect each other.
In other words, we prove that the diagonals of the
square and the diagonals of the parallelogram all-share

the same midpoint, (i.e., point *O*).

BAC ≅ ∠ *ACD*, and m∠ *PAB* = m∠ *RCD* = 45,
therefore ∠ *PAC* ≅ ∠ *RCA*.
Since ∠ *AOP* ≅ ∠ *COR* and *AP* = *CR*, △*AOP* ≅ △*COR*
(SAA)
Thus, *AO* = *CO*, and *PO* = *RO*.
Since $\overline{DB}$ passes through the midpoint of $\overline{AC}$,
(diagonals bisect each other) and similarly, $\overline{QS}$ passes
through the midpoint of $\overline{PR}$, and since $\overline{AC}$ and $\overline{PR}$
share the same midpoint (i.e., *O*) we have shown that
$\overline{AC}$, $\overline{PR}$, $\overline{DB}$, and $\overline{QS}$ are concurrent (i.e., all pass
through point *O*).

Postassessment

Ask students to explain a method for proving lines
concurrent. It is expected that they will explain the
method used in this lesson.

55   Proving Points Collinear

This unit will present the student with a
theorem which is quite useful in certain cases, when
proving points collinear.

Performance Objective
*Given appropriate problems students will apply
Menelaus' Theorem to prove points collinear.*

Preassessment
Have students try to prove that the interior angle
bisectors of two angles of a non-isosceles triangle
and the exterior angle bisector of the third angle
meet the opposite sides in three collinear points.

Teaching Strategies
The average student of high school geometry is
not properly trained or equipped to prove points
collinear. Thus, in most cases you will find the
preassessment problem beyond student ability.
However, this unit will provide you with sufficient student interest to introduce a theorem which
will provide a simple solution.

This theorem, originally credited to Menelaus
of Alexandria (about 100 A.D.) is particularly
useful in proving points collinear. It states that:
Points P, Q, and R on sides $\overline{AC}$, $\overline{AB}$, and $\overline{BC}$ of
△ABC are collinear if and only if

$$\frac{AQ}{QB} \cdot \frac{BR}{RC} \cdot \frac{CP}{PA} = 1$$

This is a two part (biconditional) proof.

Part I to prove $\dfrac{AQ}{QB} \cdot \dfrac{BR}{RC} \cdot \dfrac{CP}{PA} = 1$

Proof: Points P, Q, and R are collinear. Consider
the line through C, parallel to $\overline{AB}$, and meeting
$\overline{PQR}$ at D.

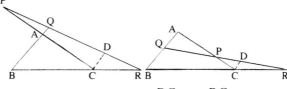

Since △DCR ~ △QBR, $\dfrac{DC}{QB} = \dfrac{RC}{BR}$ or

$DC = \dfrac{(QB)(RC)}{BR}$.   (a)

Similarly, since △PDC ~ △PQA, $\dfrac{DC}{AQ} = \dfrac{CP}{PA}$, or

$DC = \dfrac{(AQ)(CP)}{PA}$ (b)

From (a) and (b): $\dfrac{(QB)(RC)}{BR} = \dfrac{(AQ)(CP)}{PA}$.

Therefore (QB)(RC)(PA) = (AQ)(CP)(BR) which

indicates that $\dfrac{AQ}{QB} \cdot \dfrac{BR}{RC} \cdot \dfrac{CP}{PA} = 1$.

Part II involves proving the converse of the implication proved in Part I since this theorem is biconditional.

Proof: In the figures above let the line through R and Q meet $\overleftrightarrow{AC}$ at P'. Then by the theorem just proved $\dfrac{AQ}{QB} \cdot \dfrac{BR}{RC} \cdot \dfrac{CP'}{P'A} = 1$

However by hypothesis,

$\dfrac{AQ}{QB} \cdot \dfrac{BR}{RC} \cdot \dfrac{CP}{PA} = 1$

Therefore $\dfrac{CP'}{P'A} = \dfrac{CP}{PA}$ and P and P′ must coincide.

At this point students should be ready to apply Menelaus' Theorem to the problem presented in the preassessment.

Given: $\triangle ABC$, where $\overline{BM}$ and $\overline{CN}$ are interior angle bisectors and $\overline{AL}$ bisects the exterior angle at A

Prove: N, M and L are collinear.

Have students recall the important proportionality theorem about the angle bisector of a triangle.

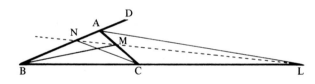

Proof: Since $\overline{BM}$ bisects $\angle ABC$, $\dfrac{AM}{MC} = \dfrac{AB}{BC}$

Since $\overline{CN}$ bisects $\angle ACB$, $\dfrac{BN}{NA} = \dfrac{BC}{AC}$.

Since $\overline{AL}$ bisects the exterior angle at A, $\dfrac{CL}{BL} = \dfrac{AC}{AB}$.

Therefore by multiplication:

$\dfrac{AM}{MC} \cdot \dfrac{BN}{NA} \cdot \dfrac{CL}{BL} = \dfrac{AB}{BC} \cdot \dfrac{BC}{AC} \cdot \dfrac{AC}{AB} = 1$

Thus, by Menelaus' Theorem N, M, and L must be collinear.

To provide further practice applying this useful theorem have students consider the following problem.

Prove that if tangents to the circumcircle of $\triangle ABC$, at A, B, and C, meet sides $\overleftrightarrow{BC}$, $\overleftrightarrow{AC}$ and $\overleftrightarrow{AB}$ at points P, Q, and R, respectively, then points P, Q, and R are collinear.

Proof: Since $m \angle BAC = \dfrac{1}{2} m \widehat{BC} = m \angle QBC$, $\triangle ABQ \sim \triangle BCQ$

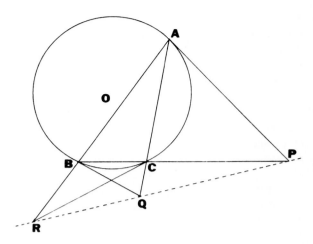

and $\dfrac{AQ}{BQ} = \dfrac{BA}{BC}$, or $\dfrac{(AQ)^2}{(BQ)^2} = \dfrac{(BA)^2}{(BC)^2}$.　　(I)

However $(BQ)^2 = (AQ)(CQ)$　　　　(II)

Substituting (II) into (I) yields $\dfrac{AQ}{CQ} = \dfrac{(BA)^2}{(BC)^2}$ (III)

Similarly, $m \angle BCR = \dfrac{1}{2} m \widehat{BC} = m \angle BAC$; therefore

$\triangle CRB \sim \triangle ARC$ and $\dfrac{CR}{AR} = \dfrac{BC}{AC}$, or

$\dfrac{(CR)^2}{(AR)^2} = \dfrac{(BC)^2}{(AC)^2}$.　　　　(IV)

However, $(CR)^2 = (AR)(RB)$.　　　　(V)

Substituting (V) into (IV) yields

$\dfrac{RB}{AR} = \dfrac{(BC)^2}{(AC)^2}$.　　　　(VI)

Students should now be asked to use the same scheme to prove $\triangle CAP \sim \triangle ABP$ and in a similar manner obtain $\dfrac{PC}{BP} = \dfrac{(AC)^2}{(BA)^2}$　　　(VII)

Now multiplying these proportions (i.e. (III), (VI), and (VII)) yields:

$\dfrac{AQ}{CQ} \cdot \dfrac{RB}{AR} \cdot \dfrac{PC}{BP} = \dfrac{(BA)^2}{(BC)^2} \cdot \dfrac{(BC)^2}{(AC)^2} \cdot \dfrac{(AC)^2}{(BA)^2} = 1$

Thus, by Menelaus' Theorem, P, Q and R are collinear.

Postassessment

Have students use Menelaus' Theorem to prove that the exterior angle bisectors of any non-isosceles triangle meet the opposite sides in three collinear points. The figure below should be useful.

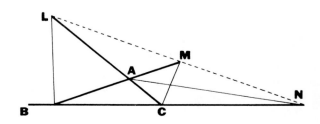

56 Angle Measurement with a Circle

This unit presents a rather unusual method for developing the theorems on angle measurement with a circle, normally considered in the tenth grade geometry course.

Performance Objectives

1. *Given appropriate materials, students will generate the various angle measurement theorems in the manner developed in this unit.*

2. *Given problems which require the use of the theorems discussed in this unit, students will be able to solve them successfully.*

Preassessment

Students should be familiar with an inscribed angle and the relationship of its measure to that of its intercepted arc.

Teaching Strategies

In addition to using the usual classroom materials, you should prepare the following:

a) A piece of cardboard with two dark colored pieces of string attached, forming an angle of convenient size.

b) A cardboard circle with an inscribed angle congruent to the "string angle."

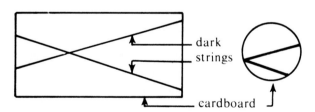

Naturally, it would be best if each student could prepare his own set of these materials in order to perform the following activities individually.

Refresh your students' memories about the relationship of an inscribed angle and its intercepted arc. Have them place the circle under the strings so that the two angles coincide:

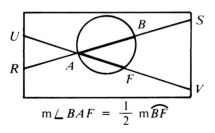

$$m\angle BAF = \frac{1}{2}\,m\widehat{BF}$$

Now have students slide the circle to the position illustrated below, where the rays of $\angle BAF$ are respectively parallel to the rays of the "string angle," $\angle NMQ$, and where the circle is tangent to $\overleftrightarrow{UQV}$ at M.

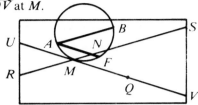

Students should realize that $m\widehat{FM} = m\widehat{AM}$, and $m\widehat{AM} = m\widehat{BN}$ (due to the parallel lines). Therefore $m\widehat{FM} = m\widehat{BN}$. Since $m\angle NMQ = m\angle BAF$, and

$$m\angle BAF = \frac{1}{2}\,m\widehat{BF} = \frac{1}{2}(m\widehat{BN} + m\widehat{NF}) =$$
$$\frac{1}{2}(m\widehat{FM} + m\widehat{NF}) = \frac{1}{2}m\widehat{MN}, \quad m\angle NMQ =$$
$$\frac{1}{2}m\widehat{MN}.$$ This proves the theorem that *the measure of an angle formed by a tangent and a chord of a circle is one half the measure of its intercepted arc.*

Now have your students slide the circle to a position where the vertex of the string angle is on a $\overline{AF}$ and where $\overline{AB}//\overline{RS}$.

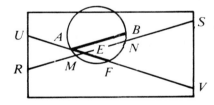

Once again because parallel lines exist here $(\overleftrightarrow{AB}//\overleftrightarrow{MN})$ $m\widehat{AM} = m\widehat{BN}$, and $m\angle BAF = m\angle NEF$. The students should now see that

$$m\angle BAF = \frac{1}{2}m\widehat{BF} = \frac{1}{2}(m\widehat{BN} + m\widehat{NF}) =$$
$$\frac{1}{2}(m\widehat{AM} + m\widehat{NF}).$$ They may then conclude that $m\angle NEF = \frac{1}{2}(m\widehat{AM} + m\widehat{NF})$. This proves the theorem that *the measure of an angle formed by two chords intersecting in a point in the interior of a circle is one half the sum of the measures of the arcs intercepted by the angle and its vertical angle.*

To consider the next type of angle, have your students slide the circle to the position illustrated below, where the string angle now appears as an angle formed by two secants.

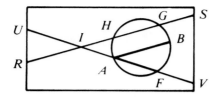

In this new position $\overrightarrow{AB} /\!/ \overrightarrow{GI}$ and $\overrightarrow{AF}$ is in $\overleftrightarrow{IF}$. Because $\overrightarrow{AB} /\!/ \overrightarrow{GI}$, $m\widehat{BG} = m\widehat{HA}$ and $m\angle BAF = m\angle GIF$. Have students once again follow the reasoning that $m\angle BAF = \frac{1}{2}m\widehat{BF} = \frac{1}{2}(m\widehat{BF} + m\widehat{BG} - m\widehat{BG}) = \frac{1}{2}(m\widehat{BF} + m\widehat{BG} - m\widehat{HA}) = \frac{1}{2}(m\widehat{GBF} - m\widehat{HA})$. They may then conclude that $m\angle GIF = \frac{1}{2}(m\widehat{GBF} - m\widehat{HA})$, which proves the theorem that *the measure of an angle formed by two secants intersecting in a point in the exterior of a circle is equal to one half the difference of the measures of the intercepted arcs.*

The next position of the circle will enable students to consider an angle formed by a tangent and a secant intersecting in the exterior of a circle. Have students slide the circle to the position as indicated in the following illustration.

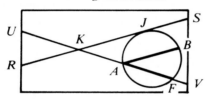

Here $\overrightarrow{AB} /\!/ \overleftrightarrow{KJS}$, $\overrightarrow{AF}$ is in $\overleftrightarrow{KV}$ and the circle is tangent to $\overleftrightarrow{KS}$ at J. Because $\overrightarrow{AB} /\!/ \overleftrightarrow{KJS}$, $m\widehat{JA} = m\widehat{JB}$ and $m\angle BAF = m\angle JKF$.

By now students should be able to produce the following without much difficulty:

$m\angle BAF = \frac{1}{2}m\widehat{BF} = \frac{1}{2}(m\widehat{BF} + m\widehat{JB} - m\widehat{JB})$
$= \frac{1}{2}(m\widehat{BF} + m\widehat{JB} - m\widehat{JA}) = \frac{1}{2}(m\widehat{JBF} - m\widehat{JA})$.
They should then conclude that $m\angle JKF = \frac{1}{2}(m\widehat{JBF} - m\widehat{JA})$, which proves the theorem that *the measure of an angle formed by a secant and a tangent to a circle intersecting in a point exterior to the circle is equal to one half the difference of the measures of the intercepted arcs.*

The last type of angle to be considered is an angle formed by two tangents. To form this angle the circle should be positioned tangent to each of the two strings so that each string is parallel to one of the rays of the angle in the circle.

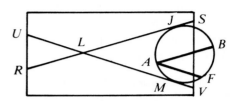

With the circle in the above position $\overrightarrow{AB} /\!/ \overleftrightarrow{LJS}$ and $\overrightarrow{AF} /\!/ \overleftrightarrow{LMV}$. Students should now be able to complete this proof independently. They should reason that $m\widehat{JB} = m\widehat{JA}$ and $m\widehat{MF} = m\widehat{MA}$; also $m\angle BAF = m\angle JLM$. Hence, $m\angle BAF = \frac{1}{2}m\widehat{BF}$
$= \frac{1}{2}(m\widehat{BF} + m\widehat{JB} + m\widehat{MF} - m\widehat{JB} - m\widehat{MF})$
$= \frac{1}{2}(m\widehat{BF} + m\widehat{JB} + m\widehat{MF} - m\widehat{JA} - m\widehat{MA}) = \frac{1}{2}(m\widehat{JBM} - m\widehat{JAM})$. Thus, $m\angle JLM = \frac{1}{2}(m\widehat{JBM} - m\widehat{JAM})$, which proves the theorem that *the measure of an angle formed by two tangents is equal to one half the difference of the measures of the intercepted arcs.*

To summarize this presentation have students realize that (1) the measure of an angle whose vertex is *on* the circle is one half the measure of the intercepted arc, (2) the measure of an angle whose vertex is *inside* the circle is one half the *sum* of the measures of the intercepted arcs, and (3) the measure of an angle whose vertex is *outside* the circle is one half *the difference* of the measures of the intercepted arcs.

As an alternative method for using this technique with your classes see *Geometry, Its Elements and Structure,* 2d ed., by A. S. Posamentier, J. H. Banks, and R. L. Bannister (McGraw-Hill, 1977), pp. 396–402.

Postassessment

Have students redevelop some of the above theorems using methods presented in this unit.

57 Trisecting a Circle

To partition a circle into two regions of equal area is a rather simple matter. However, to partition a circle into three regions of equal area is a more interesting problem. In this unit students will investigate various methods of accomplishing this.

Performance Objective
Students will be able to partition a circle into three regions of equal area.

Preassessment
Students should be able to perform some simple geometric constructions using a straightedge and compass. They should also be familiar with the Pythagorean Theorem and the formula for the area of a circle.

Teaching Strategies
Ask students to partition a circle into two regions of equal area. The obvious solution is for them merely to draw the diameter of the given circle. Now ask students to partition a circle into three regions of equal area (hereafter referred to as ''trisecting a circle''). This too, should cause no problem as students will realize that they must merely construct (using straightedge and compasses) three adjacent angles of measure 120°.

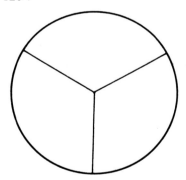

Figure 1

To construct this trisection they simply mark off six equal arcs along the circle with the compasses open to the radius of the circle. You may wish to justify this construction by referring to the inscribed hexagon, similarly constructed.

If you now ask students for another method of trisecting a circle, you will find them experimenting with another symmetry about the center. Ultimately this experimentation should lead to a consideration of two concentric circles, each concentric with the given circle. The problem then is to determine the lengths of the radii of the two circles.

Suppose students first find the radius, x, of a circle whose area is ⅓ that of a given circle of radius r. Then $\pi x^2 = \frac{1}{3}\pi r^2$, which yields $x = \frac{r}{\sqrt{3}} = \frac{r\sqrt{3}}{3}$. In a similar way they can find the radius, y, of a circle whose area is ⅔ that of a given circle of radius r. That is, $\pi y^2 = \frac{2}{3}\pi r^2$, which yields $y = \frac{r\sqrt{2}}{\sqrt{3}} = \frac{r\sqrt{6}}{3}$.

Now that the lengths have been established, the only problem remaining is to do the actual construction. Have students begin with a circle of radius r. To construct x, rewrite $x = \frac{r\sqrt{3}}{3}$ as $\frac{x}{\sqrt{3}} = \frac{r}{3}$. Then mark off the lengths r and 3 on a convenient line segment.

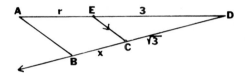

Figure 2

With any convenient angle, have students mark off a length $\sqrt{3}$ along this newly drawn ray. To construct a line segment of length $\sqrt{3}$ students may use any convenient method. For example, the radical spiral may be used (Figure 3).

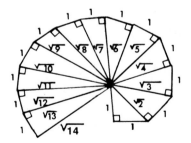

Figure 3

Another method for constructing a line segment of length $\sqrt{3}$ would involve setting up a diagram as shown in Figure 4.

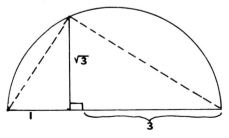

Figure 4

Once this length ($\sqrt{3}$) has been marked off along $\overline{DCB}$ (see Figure 2), students can construct a line through A parallel to $\overrightarrow{EC}$ to meet $\overrightarrow{DC}$ at B. Using proportions, they can establish that $x = BC = \dfrac{r\sqrt{3}}{3}$.

Thus, tell students to draw a circle of radius x concentric with the given circle. (Figure 5). The smaller circle has an area ⅓ that of the large circle. To complete the trisection students should construct a circle, radius y, concentric with the given circle.

The area of the circle of radius y must be ⅔ the area of the circle of radius r. Therefore, $\pi y^2 = \frac{2}{3}\pi r^2$, and $y = \dfrac{r\sqrt{2}}{\sqrt{3}} = \dfrac{r\sqrt{6}}{3}$. Have students construct y in a manner similar to the construction of x and then draw the circle concentric with the others (see the dotted-line circle in Figure 5).

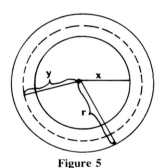

Figure 5

The resulting figure shows a trisected circle.

A more intriguing trisection of a circle involves a rather unusual partitioning.

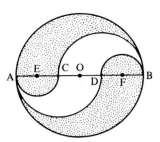

Figure 6

In Figure 6 the diameter of the given circle is trisected at points C and D. Four semicircles are then drawn as shown in the figure. Each of the two shaded regions is ⅓ the area of the given circle. Therefore the non-shaded region must also be ⅓ the area of the circle and thus the circle is trisected.

To prove this trisection valid, students need to show that one of the shaded regions has an area ⅓ that of the original circle. The area of the "upper" shaded region = area semicircle AB − area semicircle BC + area semicircle AC. If AE = r, AO = 3r, and BD = 2r. Therefore the area of the "upper" shaded region = $\frac{1}{2}\pi(3r)^2 - \frac{1}{2}\pi(2r)^2 + \frac{1}{2}\pi r^2 = \dfrac{9\pi r^2}{2}$ $- \dfrac{4\pi r^2}{2} + \dfrac{\pi r^2}{2} = 3\pi r^2$. However the area of the original circle to be trisected = $\pi(3r)^2 = 9\pi r^2$. Thus, the area of each shaded region is ⅓ the area of the original circle, which is then trisected.

Postassessment

Give students a circle and ask them to partition it into three regions of equal area.

58 Ptolemy's Theorem

This unit will offer the student a very powerful theorem about cyclic (inscribed) quadrilaterals.

Performance Objective

Given appropriate problems, students will apply Ptolemy's Theorem to successfully solve the problem.

Preassessment

Present students with an isosceles trapezoid with bases of length 6 and 8 and legs of length 5.

Ask them to find the length of a diagonal of the trapezoid.

Teaching Strategies

Students who are familiar with the Pythagorean Theorem should be able to solve this problem with two applications of this theorem. However, most students, after being shown this method, will certainly welcome a less tedious method of solution. This is when you introduce Ptolemy's Theorem.

Ptolemy's Theorem: In a cyclic (inscribed) quadrilateral, the product of the lengths of the diagonals is equal to the sum of the products of the lengths of the pairs of opposite sides.

Before proving this theorem be sure students understand the statement of the theorem and understand what a cyclic quadrilateral is. Some of the more popular theorems about cyclic quadrilaterals ought to be reviewed here. Examples of non-cyclic quadrilaterals should also be given, so that students better appreciate cyclic quadrilaterals.

Proof: Consider quadrilateral ABCD inscribed in circle *O*. Draw a line through A to meet $\overrightarrow{CD}$ at P, so that $m\angle BAC = m\angle DAP$.

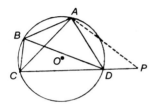

Since quadrilateral ABCD is cyclic, $\angle$ ABC is supplementary to $\angle$ ADC. However, $\angle$ ADP is supplementary to $\angle$ ADC. Therefore $m\angle$ ABC $= m\angle$ ADP. We can then prove $\triangle$ BAC $\sim \triangle$ DAP, and $\dfrac{AB}{AD} = \dfrac{BC}{DP}$, or $DP = \dfrac{(AD)(BC)}{AB}$.

Since $m\angle$ BAC $= m\angle$ DAP, $m\angle$ BAD $= m\angle$ CAP.

Since $\triangle$ BAC $\sim \triangle$ DAP, $\dfrac{AB}{AD} = \dfrac{AC}{AP}$. Therefore

$\triangle$ ABD $\sim \triangle$ ACP, then $\dfrac{BP}{CP} = \dfrac{AB}{AC}$, or $CP = \dfrac{(AC)(BD)}{AB}$.

But, $CP = CD + DP$.

By substitution $\dfrac{(AC)(BD)}{AB} = CD + \dfrac{(AD)(BC)}{AB}$

Now simplifying this expression gives us the desired result:

$$(AC)\ (BD) = (AB)\ (CD) + (AD)\ (BC)$$

which is Ptolemy's Theorem.

Show students how Ptolemy's Theorem may be used to solve the preassessment problem. Since an isosceles trapezoid is a cyclic quadrilateral, Ptolemy's Theorem may be used to get $d^2 = (6)(8) + (5)(5) = 73$.

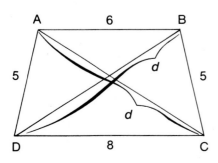

Therefore the length of a diagonal (*d*) is $\sqrt{73}$.

Students are often curious if a "new" theorem is consistent with theorems they learned earlier. Have students apply Ptolemy's Theorem to a rectangle (which is clearly a cyclic quadrilateral). For rectangle ABCD, Ptolemy's Theorem appears as: $(AC)(BD) = (AD)(BC + (AB)(DC)$.

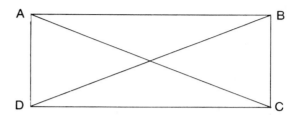

However, in the rectangle AB = DC, AD = BC, and AC = BD. Therefore by substitution $(AC)^2 = (AD)^2 + (DC)^2$, which is the Pythagorean Theorem.

Now have students consider a rather simple application of this celebrated theorem.

Problem: If point P is on arc AB of the circumscribed circle of equilateral $\triangle$ABC, and AP = 3 while BP = 4, find the length of $\overline{CP}$.

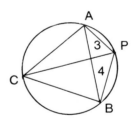

Solution: Let *t* represent the length of a side of equilateral $\triangle$ABC. Since quadrilateral APBC is cyclic, we may apply Ptolemy's Theorem, which yields:

$$(CP)\ (t) = (AP)\ (t) + (BP)\ (t).$$

Therefore CP = AP + BP = 3 + 4 = 7.

Students should be encouraged to investigate similar problems where the equilateral triangle is replaced with other regular polygons.

Often problems appear to be easier than they actually are. The next problem to be considered is one which seems to be easily solvable by simply using the Pythagorean Theorem. However, in solution it becomes useful to employ Ptolemy's Theorem.

Problem: On side $\overline{AB}$ of square ABCD, a right $\triangle$ABF, with hypotenuse $\overline{AB}$, is drawn externally to the square. If AF = 6 and BF = 8, find EF, where E is the point of intersection of the diagonals of the square.

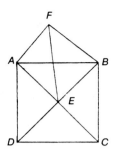

Solution: Applying the Pythagorean Theorem to right △AFB, we get AB = 10, and to right △AEB, we get AE = BE = 5√2. Since *m*∠AFB = *m*∠AEB = 90, quadrilateral AFBE is cyclic. Now we may apply Ptolemy's Theorem to quadrilateral AFBE, to get (AB)(EF) = (AF)(BE) + (AE)(BF)

Substituting the appropriate values gives us: (10)(EF) = (6)(5√2) + (5√2)(8), or EF = 7√2.

Students should be encouraged to reconsider this problem with right △ABF drawn internally to the square. In that case EF = √2.

Postassessment

Have students solve each of the following problems:

1. E is a point on side $\overline{AD}$ of rectangle ABCD, so that DE = 6, while DA = 8, and DC = 6. If $\overline{CE}$ extended meets the circumcircle of the rectangle at F, find the measure of chord $\overline{DF}$.

2. Point P on side $\overline{AB}$ of right △ABC is placed so that BP = PA = 2. Point Q is on hypotenuse AC so that $\overline{PQ}$ is perpendicular to $\overline{AC}$. If CB = 3, find the measure of $\overline{BQ}$, using Ptolemy's Theorem.

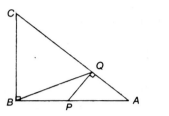
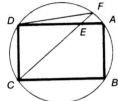

Reference

Posamentier, Alfred S., and Charles T. Salkind, *Challenging Problems in Geometry.* Palo Alto, CA: Seymour, 1988.

59   Constructing π

Performance Objectives

1) *Students will demonstrate a clear knowledge of the π ratio and its relationship to the circle.*

2) *Students will construct π in more than one way.*

Preassessment

Before beginning a discussion of π, review with students the meaning of diameter and circumference. Have students measure the diameter and circumference of a 25-cent piece. Also ask them to obtain similar measurements of other circular objects. Stress the importance of accurate measurement.

Teaching Strategies

Begin the lesson by writing the following chart on the chalkboard:

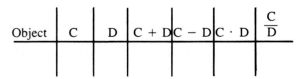

Object	C	D	C + D	C − D	C · D	$\dfrac{C}{D}$

Record some of the measurements that the students obtained. They should all have found that the diam-

eter of the quarter is *about* 2.4 mm long and that its circumference is *approximately* 7.8 mm. Have students then fill in the rest of the chart for the objects that they have measured. Ask them if any column seems to result in approximately the same value for each object measured and have them take the average of the numbers in that column. Their averages should be close to 3.14 (i.e. $\dfrac{C}{D} \approx 3.14$). It should be reemphasized that all the other columns produced varying results, whereas in the last column $\dfrac{C}{D}$ was the same regardless of the size of the object.

In 1737, this ratio was given the special name of "π" by Leonhard Euler, a famous Swiss mathematician. The exact value of π can never be determined; only approximations can be established. Here is the value of π correct to 50 decimal places:

π = 3.14159265358979323382462643
          38327950288841971693993751 . . .

Throughout the years, many attempts have been made to compute π, both algebraically and geometrically. This unit presents some of the geometric constructions involving π.

One of the first serious attempts to compute π to a certain degree of accuracy goes back to Archimedes, who tried to exactly determine π. His method was based on the fact that the perimeter of a regular polygon of n sides is smaller than the circumference of the circle circumscribed about it, while the perimeter of a similar polygon circumscribed about the circle is greater than the circle's circumference. By successively repeating this situation for larger values of n, the two perimeters will approach the circumference from both sides. Archimedes started with a regular hexagon and each time doubled the number of sides until he obtained a polygon of 96 sides. He was then able to determine that the ratio of the circumference of a circle to its diameter, or π, is less than $3\frac{10}{70}$ but greater than $3\frac{10}{71}$. We can write this in decimal notation as $3.14085 < \pi < 3.142857$. To aid in the students' understanding of this method, it might be beneficial if you illustrate with a few diagrams. The following chart might also aid in explaining this concept, as the students will see that as the number of sides increases, π is more accurately approximated.

Number of sides	Perimeter of circumscribed polygon	Perimeter of inscribed polygon
4	4.0000000	2.8284271
8	3.3137085	3.0614675
16	3.1825979	3.1214452
32	3.1517249	3.1365485
64	3.1441184	3.1403312
128	3.1422236	3.1412773
256	3.1417504	3.1415138
512	3.1416321	3.1415729
1024	3.1416025	3.1415877
2048	3.1415951	3.1415914

Figure A

Students will now see how they can actually construct a line segment whose length closely approximates π. This construction was developed in the mid 1800's and it involves the ratio $\frac{355}{113}$ (which had been previously discovered by a Chinese astronomer in the fifth century). $\frac{355}{113} = 3 + \frac{16}{113} = 3.1415929\ldots$ which is a correct approximation of π to six decimal places. The construction begins with a quadrant of unit radius. AO is $\frac{7}{8}$ of the radius, $\overline{AB}$ is drawn and a point C is marked off so that $CB = \frac{1}{2}$ of the radius. $\overline{CD}$ is drawn parallel to $\overline{AO}$ and $\overline{CE}$ is drawn parallel to $\overline{AD}$.

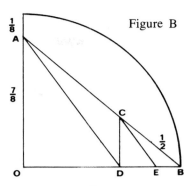

Figure B

Have students find AB: $(\frac{7}{8})^2 + 1^2 = (AB)^2$ $\therefore$ AB $= \frac{\sqrt{113}}{8}$.

Using similar triangles, the following relationships can easily be seen. (Have students explain why $\triangle CDB \sim \triangle AOB$ and $\triangle CEB \sim \triangle ADB$.)

$$\frac{DB}{OB} = \frac{CB}{AB} \text{ and } \frac{EB}{DB} = \frac{CB}{AB}$$

Multiplying these expressions we obtain

$$\frac{EB}{OB} = \frac{CB^2}{AB^2} = \frac{\frac{1}{4}}{\frac{113}{64}} = \frac{16}{113}$$

but since $OB = 1$, we get

$$\frac{EB}{1} = \frac{16}{113} \text{ or } EB = \frac{16}{113} \text{ or } \approx .1415929204\ldots$$

Since $\frac{355}{113} = 3 + \frac{16}{113}$, a line segment can now be drawn that is 3 times the radius extended by the distance EB. This will give us a line segment that differs from π by less than a millionth of a unit.

A slightly more difficult geometric approximation of π was developed in 1685 by Father Adam Kochansky, a librarian to King John III of Poland. A circle of unit radius is drawn. Then draw a tangent segment $\overline{QR}$, equal in length to 3 times the radius. Draw a diameter perpendicular to $\overline{QR}$ at Q, the point of tangency. Now draw a line, d, tangent at the other end of the diameter such that the measure of central angle $= 30°$. Connect points and extend line segments to form the figure pictured in the figure below. The students are now ready to calculate the value of π. (It will be shown that if the length of the radius is 1, line c approximates π.)

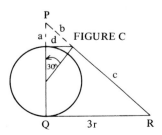

FIGURE C

If $r = 1$, in ΔPQR, $(a + 2)^2 + (3)^2 = (b + c)^2$ (1)

Also, using similar triangles, we have $\dfrac{a}{a + 2} = \dfrac{d}{3}$ (2)

and $\dfrac{b}{b + c} = \dfrac{d}{3}$ (3)

From equation (2) we obtain $3a = ad + 2d$ or

$a = \dfrac{2d}{3 - d}$. But $\tan 30° = \dfrac{d}{1} = d = \dfrac{\sqrt{3}}{3}$

Therefore $a = \dfrac{2\dfrac{\sqrt{3}}{3}}{3 - \dfrac{\sqrt{3}}{3}}$ or $a = \dfrac{2\sqrt{3}}{9 - \sqrt{3}}$ (4)

Similarly, from equation (3) we can obtain

$b = \dfrac{cd}{3 - d} = \dfrac{c\sqrt{3}}{9 - \sqrt{3}}$ (5)

Substituting equations (4) and (5) into equation (1) we

now have $\left(\dfrac{2\sqrt{3}}{9 - \sqrt{3}} + 2\right)^2 + 9 = \left(\dfrac{c\sqrt{3}}{9 - \sqrt{3}} + c\right)^2$

Students should be able to solve this equation for c

and obtain $c = \sqrt{\dfrac{40 - 2\sqrt{3}}{3}}$

Have students simplify this radical to obtain 3.141533 as an approximate value for c.

Throughout the lesson it should be emphasized that these are all *approximations* of the value π, since it is impossible to construct π with straightedge and compasses.

Posamentier, A. S. and Gordon, Noam. "An Astounding Revelation on the History of π." The Mathematics Teacher. Vol. 77, No. 1. Jan. 1984. NCTM.

Postassessment

1) Find the diameter of a circle whose circumference is 471 feet.

2) Construct a geometric approximation of π in more than one way.

60   The Arbelos

The region bounded by three semicircles in a manner resembling a shoemaker's knife has some rather interesting properties. This region, often called an arbelos, is the topic of this unit. Here the student will be introduced to this geometric figure with the intention of pursuing its properties further.

Performance Objectives

1. *Students will identify the arbelos.*
2. *Students will solve problems involving the arbelos.*

Preassessment

This unit should be presented to students who have studied geometry (or are currently enrolled in the last term of a geometry course). They should be able to compute lengths of arcs, areas of triangles and areas of circles.

Teaching Strategies

Have students draw a semicircle with center O and diameter $\overline{AB}$. Let $AB = 2R$. Have them then mark off a point C, between A and B. Then have them let $\overline{AC}$ and $\overline{CB}$ be diameters of semicircles D and E respectively. (see Figure 1) Let $AC = 2r_1$ and BC

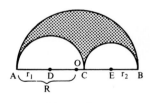

Figure 1

$= 2r_2$. The shaded portion of the figure is known as the *Arbelos* or *Shoemaker's Knife*. It has some very interesting properties which were considered by Archimedes, the famous Greek mathematician.

You should now direct student attention to the diagram. Try to elicit from your students the following property of the arbelos: that $\ell\widehat{AB} = \ell\widehat{AC} + \ell\widehat{CB}$. Once students understand this property, a proof should be established. In a circle, the length of an arc $= \dfrac{n}{360} \times 2\pi r$ (where n is the number of degrees of the arc and r is the length of the radius), we have

$$\ell\widehat{AB} = \dfrac{180}{360} \cdot 2\pi R = \pi R$$

$$\ell\widehat{AC} = \dfrac{1}{2} \cdot 2\pi r_1 = \pi r_1$$

$$\ell\widehat{CB} = \dfrac{1}{2} \cdot 2\pi r_2 = \pi r_2$$

Also $R = r_1 + r_2$, therefore multiplying by π we get $\pi R = \pi r_1 + \pi r_2$ or $\ell\widehat{AB} = \ell\widehat{AC} + \ell\widehat{CB}$. Have students consider the case where three semicircles (instead of two) are taken on $\overline{AB}$. Would a similar relationship hold true?

Students should now draw the perpendicular to $\overline{AB}$ at point C, which meets the circle at H. Also draw

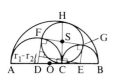

Figure 2

the common tangent to circles D and E and call the points of tangency F and G, respectively. Denote the point where these two segments intersect as S. (see Figure 2) Since a line segment drawn perpendicular to a diameter is the geometric mean between the segments of the diameter, we have that $(HC)^2 = 2r_1 \cdot 2r_2 = 4r_1r_2$. Also FG = JE (have students explain why from the diagram). Since JD = r_1 − r_2 and DE = $r_1 + r_2$, then $(JE)^2 = (r_1 + r_2)^2 - (r_1 - r_2)^2 = r_1^2 + 2r_1r_2 + r_2^2 - r_1^2 + 2r_1r_2 - r_2^2 = 4r_1r_2$. Therefore $(FG)^2 = 4r_1r_2$ or $(HC)^2 = (FG)^2 = 4r_1r_2$.

Ask your students if they can suggest another relationship that exists between $\overline{HC}$ and $\overline{FG}$. Once someone gives the response that $\overline{HC}$ and $\overline{FG}$ bisect each other at S, have the students try to prove it by themselves. SC is a common internal tangent to both circles, therefore, FS = SC and SC = SG, which gives us FS = SG. But since HC = FG (have students explain why), we also know that HS = SC. Also since FS = SG = HS = SC, the points F, H, G, C determine a circle with center S.

A very interesting property of the arbelos is one that involves this circle which has $\overline{HC}$ and $\overline{FG}$ as diameters. Have students try to express the area of the arbelos in terms of r_1 and r_2. Area of the arbelos = Area of semicircle AHB − (Area of semicircle AFC + Area of semicircle CGB)

Since Area of a semicircle = $\dfrac{\pi r^2}{2}$, we have

Area of the arbelos = $\dfrac{\pi R^2}{2} - (\dfrac{\pi r_1^2}{2} + \dfrac{\pi r_2^2}{2})$

$$= \frac{\pi}{2}(R^2 - r_1^2 - r_2^2)$$

We know that R = $r_1 + r_2$ and substituting we get

Area of the arbelos = $\dfrac{\pi}{2}((r_1+r_2)^2 - r_1^2 - r_2^2)$

$$= \frac{\pi}{2}(r_1^2 + 2r_1r_2 + r_2^2 - r_1^2 - r_2^2)$$

$$= \frac{\pi}{2}(2r_1r_2) = \pi r_1 r_2$$

Have the students now find the area of circle S. The diameter HC = $2\sqrt{r_1r_2}$, therefore the radius = $\sqrt{r_1r_2}$. The area of the circle then = $\pi(\sqrt{r_1r_2})^2 = \pi r_1r_2$. It is now apparent that they have must proved that the area of the arbelos is equal to the area of circle S.

You may wish to introduce another interesting arbelos.

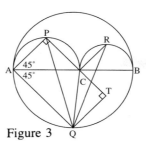

Figure 3

Let P and R be the midpoints of arcs $\overarc{AC}$ and $\overarc{CB}$ respectively. Let Q be the midpoint of the semicircle below $\overline{AB}$. Connect points P and R to C and to Q. A concave quadrilateral PQRC is formed (see Figure 3).

The area of this quadrilateral is equal to the sum of the squares of the radii, r_1 and r_2, of the two smaller semicircles.

A proof follows: The quadrilateral can be divided into two triangles by drawing $\overline{CQ}$. The area of $\triangle QCP$ can be shown to be equal to the area of right $\triangle APC$. The two triangles have a common base $\overline{CP}$, therefore their heights must be proved to be equal. To do this, draw $\overline{AP}$, $\overline{AQ}$ and draw $\overline{QT}$ perpendicular to $\overline{PC}$ extended. (see Figure 3) Since Q is the midpoint of semicircle AB, $m\overarc{QB} = 90°$. Therefore $m\angle QAB = 45°$. Also since $\triangle APC$ is an isosceles right triangle, $m\angle PAB = 45°$, which gives us that $m\angle PAQ = 90°$. But since $m\angle APC = 90°$ and $m\angle PTQ$ is also $= 90°$, quadrilateral APTQ is a rectangle and AP = QT.

Therefore, Area of $\triangle QCP = \dfrac{CP \cdot PA}{2}$

Since in isosceles right triangle APC, $(CP)^2 + (PA)^2 = (2r_1)^2$ or $2(CP)^2 = (2r_1)^2$

Therefore $(CP)^2 = 2r_1^2$ or $\dfrac{CP \cdot PA}{2} = r_1^2$

We therefore have that area of $\triangle QCP = r_1^2$ Similarly, it can be shown that area of $\triangle QCR = \dfrac{CR \cdot RB}{2} = r_2^2$. Therefore,

Area of the quadrilateral = $r_1^2 + r_2^2$.

Postassessment

1) If $r_1 = 16$ and $r_2 = 4$, show that $\overarc{AB} = \overarc{AC} + \overarc{CB}$; find the radius of circle S; find the area of the arbelos.

2) Describe semicircle D below $\overline{AB}$ (Figure 4). Let $\overline{AN}$ be tangent to circle E. Show that the area of the shaded region is equal to the area of the circle which has $\overline{AN}$ as its diameter.

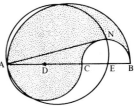

Figure 4

3) Find the area of quadrilateral PQRC (Figure 3), if $r_1 = 8$ and $r_2 = 5$.

4) What is the relationship between the arbelos in Figure 3 and Fibonacci numbers (see page 337).

Reference

Gardner, Martin. "The Diverse Pleasures of Circles that Are Tangent to One Another." *Scientific American*, 240 (1), January, 1979.

61 The Nine-Point Circle

An often neglected concept in the high school geometry curriculum is that of establishing points concyclic (on the same circle). This unit presents one of the more famous sets of concyclic points.

Performance Objectives
1. Students will define and construct the nine-point circle.

2. Students will locate the center of the nine-point circle.

Preassessment
Students should be aware of elementary methods of proving four points concyclic. For example, they should be aware of at least the following two theorems:

1. If one side of a quadrilateral subtends congruent angles at the two nonadjacent vertices, then the quadrilateral is cyclic (may be inscribed in a circle).

2. If a pair of opposite angles of a quadrilateral are supplementary, then the quadrilateral is cyclic.

Teaching Strategies
Present students with a $\triangle$ ABC, with midpoints of its sides A', B', C' (see Figure 1). Draw altitude $\overline{CF}$. Ask

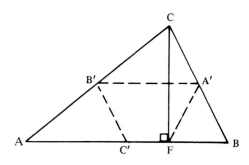

Figure 1

students to prove that quadrilateral A'B'C'F is an isosceles trapezoid. To do this they should realize that since $\overline{A'B'}$ is a segment joining the midpoints of two sides of a triangle, it is parallel to the third side of the triangle. Since $\overline{B'C'}$ joins the midpoints of $\overline{AC}$ and $\overline{AB}$, $B'C' = \frac{1}{2}(BC)$. Since the median to the hypotenuse of a right triangle is half the length of the hypotenuse, $A'F = \frac{1}{2}(BC)$. Therefore, $B'C' = A'F$, and trapezoid A'B'C'F is isosceles.

Now have students prove that an isosceles trapezoid is always cyclic (using Theorem 2, above).

To avoid confusion redraw $\triangle$ ABC with altitude $\overline{AD}$ as shown below.

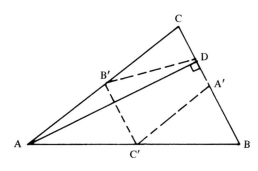

Figure 2

In the same way as for altitude $\overline{CF}$, have students independently prove that the points B', C', A' and D are concyclic. This should be done with the above proof as a guide.

Students should now be prepared to generalize a statement about the points B', C', A' and E, for altitude $\overline{BE}$. This will lead to the conclusion that the points D, F, and E each lie on the unique circle determined by points A', B', C'. Thus, students can summarize that the feet of the altitudes of a triangle are concyclic with the midpoints of the sides. So far they have established a "six-point circle."

By this time, students should have proved that the altitudes of a triangle are concurrent. This point is called the *orthocenter*. Have them consider the orthocenter, H, of $\triangle$ ABC, and the midpoint M of $\overline{CH}$.

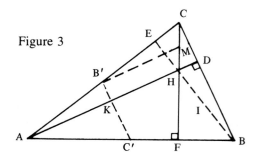

Figure 3

$\overline{B'M}$ is a segment joining the midpoints of two sides of $\angle$ ACH. Therefore $\overline{B'M}$ // $\overline{AH}$. Similarly in ∠ ABC, we have $\overline{B'C'}$ // $\overline{BC}$. Since altitude $\overline{AD} \perp \overline{BC}$, $\overline{B'M} \perp \overline{B'C'}$, or m ∠ MB'C' = 90°. Remember that m ∠ AFC = 90°. Therefore quadrilateral MB'C'F is cyclic, since its opposite angles are supplementary. This is the same circle established above, since three vertices (B', C', and F) are common with the six concyclic points, and three points determine a unique circle. Thus, a "seven-point circle" has been established.

To reinforce this proof, students should now prove that K and L (the midpoints of $\overline{AH}$ and $\overline{BH}$, respectively), also lie on this circle. To do this they merely need to repeat the above procedure for points K, C',

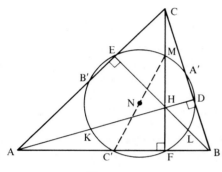

Figure 4

A', D and for points L, C', B', E. A brief review of the entire proof thus far will reveal a *nine-point circle*.

Have students consider $\overline{MC'}$ in Figure 4. Since it subtends right angles at points B' and F, it must be the diameter of the circle through B', C', F and M. To locate the center N, of this circle, simply tell students to find the midpoint of $\overline{MC'}$. This is the center of the nine-point circle.

Postassessment

To conclude the lesson ask students to do the following:

1. Define the nine-point circle.
2. Construct the nine-point circle using straightedge and compasses.
3. Locate the center of the nine-point circle.

Interesting relationships involving the nine-point circle can be found in the accompanying unit, The Euler Line.
Many other interesting relationships involving the nine point circle can be found in:
Posamentier, Alfred S. *Excursions in Advanced Euclidean Geometry.* Menlo Park, Ca.: Addison-Wesley, 1984.

62   The Euler Line

This unit should be presented to students *after* they have studied the unit on the nine-point circle. This unit uses some of the material developed in *The Nine-Point Circle* and relates it to other points of a triangle.

Performance Objectives
1. Students will locate the Euler line of a triangle.
2. Students will establish a relationship between the circumcenter, orthocenter, centroid and the center of the nine-point circle of a triangle.

Preassessment
Have students draw a scalene triangle and construct its nine-point circle as well as the circumcircle of the triangle.

Teaching Strategies
To facilitate the discussion, students should label their construction as in Figure 1 below.

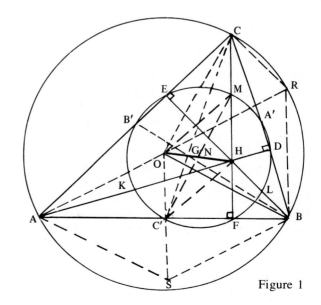

Figure 1

Students should now draw $\overline{OH}$, the segment joining the orthocenter (the point of intersection of the altitudes) and the circumcenter, (the point of intersection of the perpendicular bisectors of the sides of the triangle). This is the *Euler Line*.

Have students locate the center of the nine-point circle by finding the midpoint of $\overline{MC'}$, (this was proved in *The Nine-Point Circle*). An accurate construction should place this point on the midpoint of the Euler line $\overline{OH}$. Student curiosity should now request a proof of this astonishing occurrence.

1. Draw $\overleftrightarrow{OA}$ to intersect circle O at R.
2. $\overline{OC'} \perp \overline{AB}$ (since O is on the perpendicular bisector of $\overline{AB}$ and C' is the midpoint of $\overline{AB}$).
3. $m\angle ABR = 90°$ (an angle inscribed in a semicircle).
4. Therefore, $\overline{OC'} \,/\!/\, \overline{RB}$ (both are perpendicular to $\overline{AB}$).
5. Similarly, $\overline{RB} \,/\!/\, \overline{CF}$, and $\overline{RC} \,/\!/\, \overline{BE}$.
6. $\triangle AOC' \sim \triangle ARB$ (with a ratio of similitude of $\frac{1}{2}$).
7. Therefore $OC' = \frac{1}{2}(RB)$.
8. Quadrilateral RBHC is a parallelogram (both pairs of opposite sides are parallel).
9. Therefore, RB = HC, and $OC' = \frac{1}{2}(HC) = HM$.
10. Quadrilateral OC'HM is a parallelogram (one pair of sides is both congruent and parallel).
11. Therefore, since the diagonals of a parallelogram bisect each other, N, (the midpoint of $\overline{MC'}$), is the midpoint of $\overline{OH}$.

So far we proved that the center of the nine-point circle bisects the Euler Line. At this point we can easily prove that the radius of the nine-point circle is half the length of the radius of the circumcircle. Since $\overline{MN}$ is a line segment joining the midpoints of two sides of $\triangle COH$, it is half the length of the third side $\overline{OC}$. Thus the radius, $\overline{MN}$, of the nine-point circle is half the length of the radius, $\overline{OC}$, of the circumcircle.

In 1765, Leonhard Euler proved that the centroid of a triangle (the point of intersection of the medians) trisects the line segment joining the orthocenter and the circumcenter (the Euler line).

Since $\overline{OC'} \,/\!/\, \overline{CH}$, $\triangle OGC' \sim \triangle HGC$.

Earlier we proved that $OC' = \frac{1}{2}(HC)$,

Therefore, $OG = \frac{1}{2}(GH)$,

or $OG = (\frac{1}{3})(OH)$.

The only thing remaining is to show that G is the centroid of the triangle.

Since $\overline{CC'}$ is a median and $\overline{GC'} = \frac{1}{2}(GC)$,

G must be the centroid since it appropriately trisects the median.

Thus G trisects $\overline{OH}$.

Ask students why the median $\overline{BB'}$ also trisects $\overline{OH}$ (because it contains G, the centroid).

To this point we have bisected and trisected the Euler line with significant triangle points. Before ending the discussion of the Euler line, an interesting vector application should be considered. Review the concept of a vector and a parallelogram of forces. We shall show that $\overline{OH}$ is the resultant of $\overline{OA}$, $\overline{OB}$, and $\overline{OC}$. This was first published by James Joseph Sylvester (1814 - 1897).

Consider the point S on $\overline{OC'}$,
     where $\overline{OC'} = \overline{SC'}$.
Since $\overline{OC'S}$ is the perpendicular bisector of $\overline{AB}$, quadrilateral AOBS is a parallelogram (rhombus).
Therefore, $\overrightarrow{OS} = \overrightarrow{OA} + \overrightarrow{OB}$, or $\overrightarrow{OC'} = \frac{1}{2}(\overrightarrow{OA} + \overrightarrow{OB})$.
Since $\triangle OGC' \sim \triangle HGC$, $CH = 2(OC')$.
Thus $\overrightarrow{CH} = \overrightarrow{OA} + \overrightarrow{OB}$.
Since $\overrightarrow{HO}$ is the resultant of $\overrightarrow{OC}$ and $\overrightarrow{CH}$,
     $\overrightarrow{HO} = \overrightarrow{OC} + \overrightarrow{CH}$.
Therefore, $\overrightarrow{HO} = \overrightarrow{OC} + \overrightarrow{OA} + \overrightarrow{OB}$. (Substitution)

Postassessment

At the conclusion of this lesson ask students:
1. To construct the Euler line of a given scalene triangle, and
2. To state a relationship which exists between the circumcenter, orthocenter, centroid, and the center of the nine-point circle of a given scalene triangle.

63

The Simson Line

One of the more famous sets of collinear points is known as the *Simson Line*. Although this line was discovered by William Wallace in 1797, careless misquotes have, in time, attributed it to Robert Simson, (1687-1768). This unit will present, prove and apply the Simson Theorem.

Performance Objectives

1. Students will construct the Simson Line.

2. Students will prove that the three points which determine the Simson Line are, in fact, collinear.

3. Students will apply the properties of the Simson Line to given problems.

Preassessment

When students are presented with this unit, they should be well into the high school geometry course, having already studied angle measurement with a circle. Students should also review cyclic quadrilaterals (quadrilaterals which may be inscribed in a circle) before beginning this unit.

Teaching Strategies

Have each student construct a triangle inscribed in a circle. Then, from any convenient point on the circle (but not at a vertex of the triangle), have students construct perpendicular segments to each of the three sides of the triangle. Now, ask the class what relationship seems to be true about the three feet of the perpendiculars. If the constructions were done accurately, everyone should notice that these three points determine the *Simson Line*.

The obvious question should be quickly forthcoming: "Why are these three points collinear?" This is where you begin your proof.

Simson's Theorem: The feet of the perpendiculars drawn from any point on the circumcircle of a given triangle to the sides of the triangle are collinear.

Given: $\triangle ABC$ is inscribed in circle O.
  P is on circle O.
  $\overrightarrow{PY} \perp \overleftrightarrow{AC}$ at Y, $\overrightarrow{PZ} \perp \overleftrightarrow{AB}$ at Z, and $\overrightarrow{PX} \perp \overleftrightarrow{BC}$ at X.

Prove: Points X, Y, and Z are collinear.

Proof:

1. $\angle PYA$ is supplementary to $\angle PZA$ (both are right angles).

2. Quadrilateral PZAY is cyclic (opposite angles are supplementary).

3. Draw $\overline{PA}$, $\overline{PB}$, and $\overline{PC}$.

4. m $\angle PYZ$ = m $\angle PAZ$ (both are inscribed in the same arc).

5. $\angle PYC$ is supplementary to $\angle PXC$ (both are right angles).

6. Quadrilateral PXCY is cyclic (opposite angles are supplementary).

7. m $\angle PYX$ = m $\angle PCB$ (both are inscribed in the same arc).

8. m $\angle PAZ$ (m $\angle P\overline{A}B$) = m $\angle PCB$ (both are inscribed in the same arc of circle O).

9. m $\angle PYZ$ = m $\angle PYX$ (transitivity with steps 4, 7, and 8).

10. Since both angles, $\angle PYZ$ and $\angle PYX$, share the same ray $\overrightarrow{YP}$, and have the same measure, their other rays $\overrightarrow{YZ}$ and $\overrightarrow{YX}$ must coincide. Therefore, points X, Y, and Z are collinear.

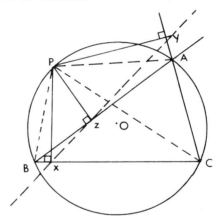

Figure 1

Present carefully to students this technique for proving collinearity. Although it is a somewhat unusual approach, it should prove quite useful to them in later work.

To strengthen the impact of the Simson Line, show students a proof of the converse of the above theorem.

Given: $\triangle ABC$ is inscribed in circle O.
  Points X, Y, and Z are collinear.
  $\overrightarrow{PY} \perp \overleftrightarrow{AC}$ at Y, $\overrightarrow{PZ} \perp \overleftrightarrow{AB}$ at Z, and $\overrightarrow{PX} \perp \overleftrightarrow{BC}$ at X.

Prove: P is on the circumcircle of $\triangle$ ABC.

Proof:

1. Draw PA, PB, and PC. (see Figure 1)

2. m $\angle PZB$ = 90° = m $\angle PXB$.

3. Quadrilateral PZXB is cyclic ($\overline{PB}$ subtends two congruent angles in the same half-plane).

4. $\angle PBX$ is supplementary to $\angle PZX$ (opposite angles of a cyclic quadrilateral).

5. ∠ PZX is supplementary to ∠ PZY (points X, Y, and Z are collinear).

6. Therefore, m ∠ PBX = m ∠ PZY (both are supplementary to ∠PZX).

7. Quadrilateral PZAY is cyclic (opposite angles, ∠ PYA and ∠ PZA, are supplementary).

8. m ∠ PZY = m ∠ PAY (both are inscribed in the same arc of the circumcircle of quadrilateral PZAY).

9. Therefore, m∠ PBX = m ∠ PAY (transitivity of steps 6 and 8).

10. Thus, ∠ PBC is supplementary to ∠ PAC (since $\overrightarrow{YAC}$ is a line).

11. Quadrilateral PACB is cyclic (opposite angles are supplementary), and, therefore, P is on the circumcircle of ΔABC.

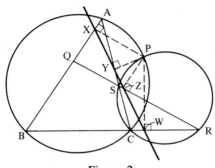

Figure 2

Students should now be ready to apply the Simson Line to a geometric problem.

Sides $\overleftrightarrow{AB}$, $\overleftrightarrow{BC}$, and $\overleftrightarrow{CA}$ of ΔABC are cut by a transversal at points Q, R, and S, respectively. The circumcircles of ΔABC and ΔSCR intersect at P. Prove that quadrilateral APSQ is cyclic.

Draw perpendiculars $\overline{PX}$, $\overline{PY}$, $\overline{PZ}$ and $\overline{PW}$ to $\overleftrightarrow{AB}$, $\overleftrightarrow{AC}$, $\overleftrightarrow{QR}$, and $\overleftrightarrow{BC}$, respectively, as in Figure 2. Since point P is on the circumcircle of ΔABC, points X, Y, and W are collinear (Simson's Theorem). Similarly, since point P is on the circumcircle of ΔSCR, points Y, Z, and W are collinear. It then follows that points X, Y, and Z are collinear. Thus, P must lie on the circumcircle of ΔAQS (converse of Simson's Theorem), or quadrilateral APSQ is cyclic.

Postassessment
Have students complete the following exercises.
1. Construct a Simson Line of a given triangle.
2. How many Simson Lines does a triangle have?
3. Prove Simson's Theorem.
4. From a point P on the circumference of circle O, three chords are drawn meeting the circle in points A, B, and C. Prove that the three points of intersection of the three circles with $\overline{PA}$, $\overline{PB}$, and $\overline{PC}$ as diameters, are collinear.

64 The Butterfly Problem

One of the most intriguing geometric relationships involves a figure which resembles a butterfly. Most students will easily understand the problem and think it just as simple to prove. But this is where the problem begins to generate further interest since the proof is somewhat elusive. This unit will suggest ways of presenting the problem to your class and provide a number of different proofs of this celebrated theorem.

Performance Objective
1. Students will state the Butterfly Problem.
2. Students will prove the Butterfly Problem valid.

Preassessment
Students should have mastered most of the high school geometry course (especially the study of circles and similarity).

Teaching Strategies
Use a duplicating machine to prepare a sheet of paper for each student with a large circle containing a chord, $\overline{AB}$, (not the diameter), and its midpoint, M, clearly marked. Tell students to draw *any* two chords, $\overline{EF}$, and $\overline{CD}$, containing M. Now have them draw the chords $\overline{CE}$ and $\overline{FD}$ which intersect $\overline{AB}$ at points Q and P, respectively. Their diagrams should resemble the Figure below.

Figure 1

Ask your class to measure any segments that appear congruent in their diagrams, and to list the pairs. You should find that most students will have included on their lists the segments $\overline{AP} \cong \overline{BQ}$ and $\overline{MP} \cong \overline{MQ}$ Remind students that they all started their diagrams with *different* segments $\overline{CE}$ and $\overline{FD}$, and, although their diagrams resemble a butterfly in a circle, their art may differ substantially from their classmates'. This should dramatize the most astonishing result of this situation, that *everyone's* $\overline{MP} \cong \overline{MQ}$!

Students will now want to prove this remarkable result. Toward this end, a number of proofs of this celebrated theorem are presented here.

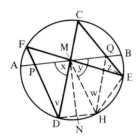

Figure 2

Proof I With M the midpoint of $\overline{AB}$ and chords $\overline{FME}$ and $\overline{CMD}$ drawn, we now draw $\overline{DH} \,//\, \overline{AB}$, $\overline{MN} \perp \overline{DH}$, and line segments $\overline{MH}$, $\overline{QH}$, and $\overline{EH}$. Since $\overline{MN} \perp \overline{DH}$ and $\overline{DH} \,//\, \overline{AB}$, MN $\perp$ AB.

$\overline{MN}$, the perpendicular bisector of $\overline{AB}$, must pass through the center of the circle. Therefore $\overline{MN}$ is the perpendicular bisector of $\overline{DH}$, since a line through the center of the circle and perpendicular to a chord, bisects it.

Thus MD = MH, and $\Delta MND \cong \Delta MNH$, (H.L.). m∠ DMN = m∠HMN, so m∠x = m∠y (they are the complements of congruent angles). Since $\overline{AB} \,//\, \overline{DH}$, m$\widehat{AD}$ = m$\widehat{BH}$, m ∠x = ½(m$\widehat{AD}$ + m$\widehat{CB}$) (angle formed by two chords) m ∠x = ½(m$\widehat{BH}$ + m$\widehat{CB}$) (substitution). Therefore, m ∠y = ½(m$\widehat{BH}$ + m$\widehat{CB}$). But m∠CEH = ½(m$\widehat{CAH}$) (inscribed angle). Thus, by addition, m∠y + m∠CEH = ½(m$\widehat{BH}$ + m$\widehat{CB}$ + m$\widehat{CAH}$). Since m$\widehat{BH}$ + m$\widehat{CB}$ + m$\widehat{CAH}$ = 360°, m∠y + m∠CEH = 180°. It then follows that quadrilateral MQEH is inscriptable, that is, a circle may be circumscribed about it. Imagine a drawing of this circle. ∠ w and ∠ z are measured by the same arc, $\widehat{MQ}$ (inscribed angle), and thus m∠w = m∠z.

Now consider our original circle m∠v = m∠z, since they are measured by the same arc, $\widehat{FC}$ (inscribed angle.) Therefore, by transitivity, m∠v = m∠w, and $\Delta MPD \cong \Delta MQH$ (A.S.A.). Thus, MP = MQ.

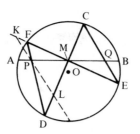

Figure 3

Proof II Extend $\overline{EF}$ through F. Draw $\overline{KPL} \,//\, \overline{CE}$.

m∠ PLC = m∠ ECL (alternate interior angles),

therefore, $\Delta PML \sim \Delta QMC$ (A.A.), and $\dfrac{PL}{CQ} = \dfrac{MP}{MQ}$

m∠ K = m∠ E (alternate interior angles),

therefore, $\Delta KMP \sim \Delta EMQ$ (A.A.), and $\dfrac{KP}{QE} = \dfrac{MP}{MQ}$

By multiplication,
$$\frac{(PL)\,(KP)}{(CQ \cdot (QE)} = \frac{(MP)^2}{(MQ)^2}. \qquad (I)$$

Since m∠ D = m∠ E (inscribed angle), and m∠ K = m∠ E (alternate interior angles), m ∠D = m∠K. Also, m∠ KPF = m ∠ DPL (vertical angles). Therefore, $\Delta KFP \sim \Delta DLP$ (A.A.), and $\dfrac{PL}{DP} = \dfrac{FP}{KP}$; and so
$$(PL)\,(KP) = (DP)\,(FP). \qquad (II)$$

In equation (I), $\dfrac{(MP)^2}{(MQ)^2} = \dfrac{(PL)\,(KP)}{(CQ)\,(QE)}$; we substitute from equation (II) to get
$$\frac{(MP)^2}{(MQ)^2} = \frac{(DP)\,(FP)}{(CQ)\,(QE)}$$

Since (DP) (FP) = (AP) (PB), and (CQ) (QE) = (BQ) (QA), (product of segments lengths of intersecting chords), $\dfrac{(MP)^2}{(MQ)^2} = \dfrac{(AP)\,(PB)}{(BQ)\,(QA)} =$

$$\frac{(MA - MP)\,(MA + MP)}{(MB - MQ)\,(MB + MQ)} = \frac{(MA)^2 - (MP)^2}{(MB)^2 - (MQ)^2}$$

Then $(MP)^2 (MB)^2 = (MQ)^2 (MA)^2$.
But MB = MA. Therefore, $(MP)^2 = (MQ)^2$, or MP = MQ.

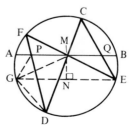

Figure 4

Proof III Draw a line through E parallel to $\overline{AB}$ meeting the circle at G, and draw $\overline{MN} \perp \overline{GE}$. Then draw $\overline{PG}$, $\overline{MG}$ and $\overline{DG}$.

m∠ GDP (∠ GDF) = m∠ GEF (inscribed angles). (I)
m∠ PMG = m∠ MGE (alternate interior angles). (II)
Since the perpendicular bisector of $\overline{AB}$ is also the perpendicular bisector of $\overline{GE}$,
then GM = ME, and m∠ GEF = m∠ MGE (base angles).   (III)
From (I), (II), and (III), m∠ GDP = m∠ PMG. (IV)

Therefore, points P,M,D, and G are concyclic (A quadrilateral is cyclic if one side subtends congruent angles at the two opposite vertices). Hence, m∠PGM = m∠ PDM (inscribed angles, in a new circle).   (V)
However, m∠ CEF = m∠ PDM (∠ FDM) (inscribed angles).   (VI)
From (V) and (VI), M∠ PGM = m∠ QEM (∠ CEF).
From (II), we know that m∠ PMG = m∠ MGE.
Thus, m∠ QME = m∠ MEG (alternate interior angles), and m∠ MGE = m∠ MEG (base angles).

Therefore, m∠ PMG = m∠ QME and ΔPMG ≅ ΔQME   (A.S.A.). It follows that PM = QM.

Although these proofs of the Butterfly Problem are not of the sort the average student is likely to discover independently, they do provide a very rich learning experience in a well motivated setting.

Postassessment
Ask students to:
1. State the Butterfly Problem.
2. Explain why the Butterfly Problem is true. (Students should either present one of the above proofs or one of their own.)

Additional solutions can be found in:
Posamentier, Alfred S., and Charles T. Salkind, *Challenging Problems in Geometry.* Palo Alto, CA: Seymour, 1988.

65   Equicircles

Equicircles is a term used to refer to both the inscribed and escribed circles of a triangle. This unit will develop a number of fascinating relationships between these circles.

Performance Objectives
1. Students will define equicircles.
2. Students will state at least four properties involving equicircles.
3. Students will state and prove one property of equicircles.

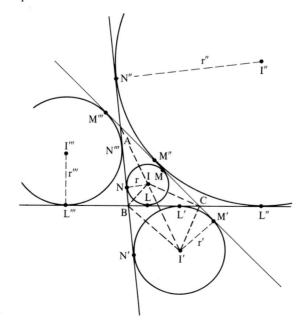

Preassessment
Students should have mastered the topic of circles in their high school geometry course.

Present the following figure to your students and ask them to find the length of $\overline{AN'}$, if the perimeter of ΔABC = 16. (Points M', N' and L' are points of tangency.)

Teaching Strategies
Although the problem posed above is quite simple, its approach is rather unusual and therefore could cause your students some difficulty. The only theorem they need to recall is that two tangent segments from an external point to a circle are congruent. Applying this theorem to the above problem we get:
$$BN' = BL' \text{ and } CM' = CL'$$
The perimeter of ΔABC = AB + BC + AC
$$= AB + (BL' + CL') + AC$$
which by substitution yields:
$$AB + BN' + CM' + `AC$$
or
$$AN' + AM'$$
However, AN' = AM' (they too are tangent segments from the same external point to the same circle).

Therefore AN' = $\frac{1}{2}$ (perimeter of ΔABC) = 8. By summarizing this rather fascinating fact, students will be motivated towards pursuing further relationships in this figure.

Next, let s = semiperimeter of ΔABC
$$a = BC; b = AC; c = AB$$

With your guidance, students should now be able to establish the following relationship:

$$BN' = BL' = AN' - AB = s - c$$
$$CM' = CL' = AM' - AC = s - b$$

At this point you ought to indicate to students that these are just a few of the segments that will be expressed in terms of the lengths of the sides of $\triangle ABC$. Here the relationship of the two circles to the triangle should be defined. Students will recognize circle I as the *inscribed* circle of $\triangle ABC$. Most likely they are not familiar with circle I'. This circle, which is also tangent to the lines of the three sides of $\triangle ABC$, yet contains no interior points of the triangle, is called an *escribed* circle. A triangle has four equicircles, one inscribed, and three escribed. The center of an escribed circle, called an *excenter*, is the point of intersection of two exterior angle bisectors and one interior angle bisector.

Students should gain further familiarity with these circles by expressing other segments in terms of the lengths of the sides of $\triangle ABC$. Once again provide guidance where necessary.

$$\begin{aligned} AN + AM &= (AB - NB) + (AC - MC) \\ &= (AB - LB) + (AC - LC) \\ &= (AB + AC) - (LB + LC) \\ &= c + b - a \end{aligned}$$

Challenge your students to show that

$$c + b - a = 2(s - a).$$

Therefore $AN + AM = 2(s - a)$.
However $AN = AM$, thus $AN = s - a$.
Have your students conjecture how BN and CL can be expressed in terms of the lengths of the sides of $\triangle ABC$.

$$BN = s - b$$
$$CL = s - c$$

We are now ready to apply some of these expressions to establish two interesting relationships. These are: $BL = CL'$, and $LL' = b - c$, the difference between the lengths of the other two sides of $\triangle ABC$.

Since both BL and CL' were shown to be equal to $s - b$, $BL = CL'$.
Consider LL' which equals $BC - BL - CL'$
By substitution $LL' = a - 2(s - b) = b - c$.

We can now prove rather easily that the length of the common external tangent segment of an inscribed and escribed circle of a triangle equals the length of the side contained in the line which intersects the tangent segment.

The proof proceeds as follows: $NN' = AN' - AN$
Earlier we showed that $AN' = s$, and $AN = s - a$.
By substitution, $NN' = s - (s - a) = a$
The same argument holds true for MM'.

Another interesting theorem states that the length of the common external tangent segment of two escribed circles of a triangle equals the sum of the lengths of the two sides which intersect it.

To prove this theorem, have students recall that $BL'' = s$ and $CL''' = s$. This was proved when the *Preassessment* problem was solved. Therefore

$$\begin{aligned} L''L''' &= BL'' + CL''' - BC \\ &= s + s - a \\ &= b + c \end{aligned}$$

We can also show that the length of each of the common internal tangent segments of two escribed circles of a triangle equals the length of the side opposite the vertex they determine. The proof is rather simple:

$$L'L'' = BL'' - BL' = BL'' - BN' = s - (s - c) = c$$

Encourage students to investigate the above figure and discover other relationships. A consideration of the radii of the equicircles will produce some interesting results. These radii are called *equiradii*.

A theorem states that the radius of the inscribed circle of a triangle equals the ratio of the area to the semiperimeter. That is:

$$\cancel{A}\triangle ABC = \cancel{A}\triangle BCI + \cancel{A}\triangle CAI + \cancel{A}\triangle ABI \text{(note: } \cancel{A} \text{ reads "area of")}$$

$$\begin{aligned} \cancel{A}\triangle ABC &= \frac{1}{2}ra + \frac{1}{2}rb + \frac{1}{2}rc \\ &= \frac{1}{2}r(a + b + c) = sr. \end{aligned}$$

Therefore $r = \dfrac{\cancel{A}\triangle ABC}{s}$

A natural extension of this theorem states that the radius of an escribed circle of a triangle equals the ratio of the area of the triangle to the difference between the semiperimeter and the length of the side to which the escribed circle is tangent.

To prove this have students consider:

$$\begin{aligned} \cancel{A}\triangle ABC &= \cancel{A}\triangle ABI' + \cancel{A}\triangle ACI' - \cancel{A}\triangle BCI' \\ &= \frac{1}{2}r'c + \frac{1}{2}r'b - \frac{1}{2}r'a \\ &= \frac{1}{2}r'(c + b - a) \\ &= r'(s - a) \end{aligned}$$

Therefore $r' = \dfrac{\cancel{A}\triangle ABC}{s - a}$

In a similar manner students should show that

$$r'' = \frac{\cancel{A}\triangle ABC}{s - b}$$

and

$$r''' = \frac{\cancel{A}\triangle ABC}{s - c}$$

To conclude this discussion, have students find the product of all the equiradii of a circle. All they need do is multiply the last few expressions:

$$rr'r''r''' = \frac{(\cancel{A}\triangle ABC)^4}{s(s - a)(s - b)(s - c)}$$

However by Heron's formula:

$$\angle\triangle ABC = \sqrt{s(s-a)(s-b)(s-c)}$$

Therefore: $rr'r''r''' = (\angle\triangle ABC)^2$.

At this point ask students to summarize the various theorems and relationships developed in this Model.

Postassessment

To conclude the lesson, have students complete the following exercises.

1. Define equicircles and equiradii.
2. State four properties of equicircles.
3. State and prove one property of equicircles.

Reference

Posamentier, Alfred S., *Excursions in Advanced Euclidean Geometry.* Menlo Park, Ca.: Addison-Wesley, 1984.

66   The Inscribed Circle and the Right Triangle

After having completed a unit on circles and a separate unit dealing with right triangles, students may enjoy seeing some relationships that integrate these units. This unit will deal with some interesting properties of the radius of an inscribed circle of a right triangle.

Performance Objectives

1. *Given a right triangle with integral length sides, students will be able to show that the inradius is an integer.*

2. *Students will be able to explain how the altitude drawn to the hypotenuse of a right triangle is related to the inradii of the triangles formed.*

3. *Students will know and be able to derive a formula relating the inradius to the area and perimeter of a right triangle.*

4. *Given a particular integral inradius, students will be able to determine the number of right triangles with integral relatively prime sides having this given inradius.*

5. *Students will be able to give one possible triple of the lengths of sides of a right triangle when given a positive integral value of the inradius.*

Preassessment

Have students try the following problems:

1. Find the radius of a circle inscribed in a right triangle whose sides have lengths 3, 4, 5.

2. Repeat this problem for a triangle whose sides have lengths 5, 12, 13.

Teaching Strategies

After having completed the above problems either individually or as a class, students will want to con-

sider the following question. "Given a right triangle of integral sides, will this guarantee that the radius of the inscribed circle is also an integer?" In order to prove that the answer is affirmative, consider the diagram below. Here, r is the inradius, (i.e., the radius of the inscribed circle) and $\triangle ABC$ has a right angle at

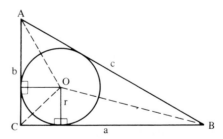

C and sides of lengths a, b, c. The proof involves finding a relationship between r, a, b and c. If the center of the circle is joined to each of the three vertices, three triangles are formed. The area of one triangle is $\frac{1}{2}ra$, the second triangle's area is $\frac{1}{2}rb$ and the third's is $\frac{1}{2}rc$. The area of $\triangle ABC$ is $\frac{1}{2}ab$. Challenge the students to set up a relationship between r and a, b, c. By adding areas one gets $\frac{1}{2}ra + \frac{1}{2}rb + \frac{1}{2}rc = \frac{1}{2}ab$ which is the area of $\triangle ABC$. Thus, $r = \frac{ab}{a+b+c}$. But this only seems to make r rational for integral a, b and c. At this point, remind students (or show them for the first time) how integral values of a, b and c are obtained from a formula. That is, show them this generating formula for sides of right triangles.

$$a = (m^2 - n^2)$$
$$b = 2mn$$
$$c = (m^2 + n^2),$$ where $m > n$ and m and n are relatively prime positive integers of different parity.

Using $r(a+b+c) = ab$, substitute a, b and c. Thus, $2r(m^2 + mn) = 2mn(m^2 - n^2)$ or $r = n(m-n)$.

Since m and n are integers, $m > n$, then r is also an integer. Therefore, *whenever a right triangle has integral sides it also has an integral inradius.*

As a result of the above, a concise formula can be established relating the inradius to the area and perimeter of a right triangle. Since $r = \dfrac{ab}{a+b+c}$, substitute p (perimeter) for $a+b+c$. Also note that the area of $\triangle ABC = \mathscr{A} \dfrac{ab}{2}$ or $2 \mathscr{A} \triangle ABC = ab$ (where $\mathscr{A}$ represents "area of"). Thus $r = \dfrac{2 \mathscr{A} \Delta}{p}$. For practice, have students find the inradius, given various values of $\mathscr{A} \Delta$ and p.

Students have probably worked for some time with right triangles whose altitude to the hypotenuse is drawn (see figure below). Now they can relate the inradius to this familiar diagram.

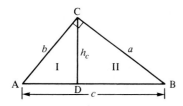

Let $\triangle ADC$ be called $\triangle I$ with inradius r_I. Similarly, $\triangle DCB$ ($\triangle II$) has inradius r_{II} and $\triangle ABC$ ($\triangle III$) has inradius r_{III}. It can be shown that the sum of the inradii of $\triangle I$, $\triangle II$ and $\triangle III$ equals the length of the altitude from C, which will be called h_c. Note that $\triangle ADC \sim \triangle DCB \sim \triangle ABC$. Since the corresponding inradii of the similar triangles are in the same ratio as any pair of corresponding sides, $\dfrac{r_I}{r_{III}} = \dfrac{b}{c}$ or $r_I = \dfrac{b}{c} r_{III}$. In the same manner, $r_{II} = \dfrac{a}{c} r_{III}$. Therefore, $r_I + r_{II} + r_{III} = \dfrac{a+b+c}{c} r_{III}$.

Recalling that $r = \dfrac{2 \mathscr{A} \Delta III}{p}$, $\dfrac{a+b+c}{c} r_{III} =$

$\left(\dfrac{a+b+c}{c} \right) \left(\dfrac{2 \mathscr{A} \Delta III}{p} \right) = \dfrac{2 \mathscr{A} \Delta III}{c}$. But

$\mathscr{A} \Delta III = \dfrac{1}{2} h_c c$. Thus $\dfrac{2 \mathscr{A} \Delta III}{c} = h_c$ making $r_I + r_{II} + r_{III} = h_c$ which is what was to be proved.

One can also use the above to prove that the area of the inscribed circle in $\triangle I$ plus the area of the inscribed circle in $\triangle II$ equals the area of the inscribed circle in $\triangle III$. This can be seen by recalling

that it has been shown that $r_I = \dfrac{b}{c} r_{III}$ and $r_{II} = \dfrac{a}{c} r_{III}$. Thus $r_I{}^2 + r_{II}{}^2 = \dfrac{b^2}{c^2} r_{III}{}^2 + \dfrac{a^2}{c^2} r_{III}{}^2 = \dfrac{a^2 + b^2}{c^2} r_{III}{}^2 = r_{III}{}^2$ (since $a^2 + b^2 = c^2$). Multiplying by π one gets $\pi r_I{}^2 + \pi r_{II}{}^2 = \pi r_{III}{}^2$ which is the theorem to be proved.

Another interesting relationship concerning the inradius is: "The number of primitive Pythagorean Triples is 2^{ℓ}, where ℓ is the number of odd prime divisions of r ($\ell \geq 0$), and r is the length of the corresponding inradius." The full meaning of this theorem should be clear to students before embarking on the proof. Show students that for every natural number r there exists at least one right triangle of sides $2r+1$, $2r^2 + 2r$ and $2r^2 + 2r + 1$ where r is the inradius. Students should be able to check that this satisfies the Pythagorean Theorem. As an example, have them try various values for r. For $r = 1$, one gets a triangle of side lengths 3, 4 and 5.

Getting back to proving the above theorem, let a, b and c be sides of a right triangle with sides of integral length, where b is even, a, b and c are relatively prime. The inradius of this triangle is the positive integer r. Recall that $r = \dfrac{ab}{a+b+c}$ r can also be written as $\dfrac{1}{2}(a+b-c)$ by noting that $\dfrac{ab}{a+b+c} = \dfrac{a+b-c}{2}$ is an identity. Students should be urged to verify this identity remembering that $a^2 + b^2 = c^2$. From the original generating formula substitute for a, b and c. Students should obtain $r = (m-n)n$. Since m and n are relatively prime, then $(m-n)$ and n are also relatively prime. (Note: $(m-n)$ is odd since m and n are relatively prime and of opposite parity.) Thus, the inradius can be decomposed into a product of two positive integers which are relatively prime and where the factor $(m-n)$ is odd.

Now consider r as any positive integer where $r = xy$ is any decomposition of r into a product of two relatively prime positive integers where one is odd. Let $m = x+y$, $n = y$. Then m and n are also relatively prime. Also, since x is odd, if $n = y$ is odd, then $m = x+y$ is even. Similarly, if m is odd, n must be even. Thus, one of the numbers m and n is even.

Recall $m > n$. Letting $a = m^2 - n^2$, $b = 2mn$, $c = m^2 + c^2$ one obtains the type of triangle desired with inradius $r = (m - n) \cdot nab$. Therefore, every decomposition of the number r into a product of two relatively prime numbers where one is odd will determine the type of triangle desired of inradius r. It can be shown that if $\ell \geq 0$ where $r = 2 p_1{}^{x_1} p_2{}^{x_2} p_3{}^{x_3} \ldots p_{\ell}{}^{x_{\ell}}$ with p_i being an odd prime integer (i a positive integer), **then the number of decompositions of r is 2^{ℓ}. Thus**

2_ℓ must be the number of decompositions or r into two relatively prime factors where one is odd.

Thus, for every positive integer r, there exists as many distinct right triangles whose sides have lengths which are relatively prime integers with inradius r as there are distinct decompositions of r into a product of two relatively prime factors of which one is odd. The numbers of such triangles are 2_ℓ. This completes the proof.

Students desiring to look into the matter further might try to prove that if r is a positive even integer, then the total number of right triangles with intregal length sides which are not necessarily relatively prime, having r as an inradius, is given by $(x + 1)(2x_1 + 1)(2x_2 + 1) \cdots (2x_\ell + 1)$ where x and ℓ are the numbers found by decomposing r into $2^x p_1^{x_1} p_2^{x_2} \ldots p_\ell^{x_\ell}, x \geq 0, \ell \geq 0$ and p_ℓ = odd prime, $x_1 \geq 1$ and $2 < p_1 < p_2 < \ldots < p_\ell$. Any positive integer can be so decomposed.

Other interesting relationships concerning the inradius might be researched by the students. For example, they might try to prove the formula (for any triangle) that the inradius r of ΔXYZ (sides x,y,z and

$s = \dfrac{x + y + z}{2}$) is r $= \sqrt{\dfrac{(s - x)(s - y)(s - z)}{5}}$. Other investigations should prove to be challenging to the class.

Postassessment

1. If a right triangle has sides of 5, 12 and 13 does this guarantee r will also be an integer? If so, which integer is it? If not, explain why.

2. If an altitude drawn to the hypotenuse of a right triangle creates three similar triangles of inradii 2, 3 and 4 find the length of this altitude.

3. Find the number of distinct right triangles whose sides have lengths which are relatively prime integers having 70 as its inradii.

4. If the inradius equals 3, find the lengths of the sides of one right triangle with this inradius.

5. ΔXYZ has an area of 6 and a perimeter of 12. Find the length of its inradius.

67   The Golden Rectangle

In this unit, the concept of the Golden Ratio will be introduced together with some of its elementary algebraic and geometric ramifications.

Performance Objectives

1. Students will construct a golden rectangle.
2. Students will state the golden ratio.
3. Students will demonstrate certain properties of the golden rectangle and the golden ratio.

Preassessment

Some knowledge of geometry and intermediate algebra is necessary.

Teaching Strategies

Have your students draw a golden rectangle using the following construction. Given square ABCD, with each side one unit long, locate the midpoint, M, of $\overline{AD}$. Draw $\overline{MC}$. By the Pythagorean theorem, MC $= \dfrac{\sqrt{5}}{2}$. With center of compasses at M and radius $\overline{MC}$, have students describe an arc cutting $\overrightarrow{AD}$ at E. Then,

DE = ME − MD $= \dfrac{\sqrt{5}}{2} - \dfrac{1}{2}, = \dfrac{\sqrt{5} - 1}{2}$. (1)

From this result, it follows that AE = AD + DE

$= 1 + \dfrac{\sqrt{5} - 1}{2}$, or $= \dfrac{\sqrt{5} + 1}{2} = 1.61803\cdots$.

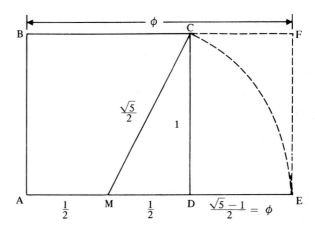

Figure 1

By erecting a perpendicular at E to meet $\overrightarrow{BC}$ at F, rectangle ABFE is constructed, where the ratio of length to width is

$$\frac{AE}{AB} = \frac{\frac{\sqrt{5}+1}{2}}{1} = \frac{\sqrt{5}+1}{2}. \tag{2}$$

The ratio (2) is called the *golden ratio* or *golden section,* denoted by the Greek letter phi (ϕ), and a rectangle having such a ratio of length to width is called a *Golden Rectangle.* Note that the value of (2), $\phi = 1.61803\cdots$, is an irrational number approximately equal to $\frac{8}{5}$. A rectangle with such a ratio of length to width was thought by the ancient Greeks, and corroborated experimentally by the psychologist Fechner in 1876, to be the most pleasing and harmoniously balanced rectangle to the eye.

Have your students solve the equation $x^2 - x - 1 = 0$, solutions for which are

$$r_1 = \frac{\sqrt{5}+1}{2} \text{ and } r_2 = \frac{-\sqrt{5}+1}{2}. \tag{3}$$

From (2), $r_1 = \phi$, and r_2, when evaluated, is equal to $-0.61803\cdots$.

A relation between ϕ and r_2 will become apparent if we first evaluate the reciprocal of ϕ, i.e., determine $\frac{1}{\phi}$. From (2),

$$\frac{1}{\phi} = \frac{1}{\frac{\sqrt{5}+1}{2}} = \frac{\sqrt{5}-1}{2} = 0.61803\cdots.$$

The ratio $\frac{\sqrt{5}-1}{2}$ is denoted by ϕ'. Thus, from (3), $r_2 = \frac{-\sqrt{5}+1}{2}$ is the additive inverse of ϕ' and is denoted by $-\phi'$. In summary, then,

$$\phi = \frac{\sqrt{5}+1}{2} = 1.61803\cdots, \tag{4}$$

$$-\phi = \frac{-\sqrt{5}-1}{2} = -1.61803\cdots, \tag{5}$$

$$\frac{1}{\phi} = \phi' = \frac{\sqrt{5}-1}{2} = 0.61803\cdots, \tag{6}$$

$$-\phi' = \frac{-\sqrt{5}+1}{2} = -0.61803\cdots. \tag{7}$$

In passing, it should be kept in mind that the ratio of width to length for a Golden Rectangle is ϕ', whereas the ratio of length to width is ϕ. Thus, in Figure 1, $\frac{DE}{DC} = \phi'$, so that CDEF is a golden rectangle.

Some rather unique relationships can be derived from (4) − (7). For example, using (4) and (6),

$$\phi \cdot \phi' = 1, \tag{8}$$

and $\phi - \phi' = 1$. $\tag{9}$

ϕ and ϕ' are the only two numbers in mathematics which bear the distinction of having both their products and differences equal to one!

$$\phi^2 = \left(\frac{\sqrt{5}+1}{2}\right)^2 = \frac{5+2\sqrt{5}+1}{4} = \frac{3+\sqrt{5}}{2}. \tag{10}$$

But, $\quad \phi + 1 = \frac{\sqrt{5}+1}{2} + 1 = \frac{3+\sqrt{5}}{2}. \tag{11}$

Thus, from (10) and (11),

$$\phi^2 = \phi + 1. \tag{12}$$

Furthermore, by using (6) and (12),

$$(\phi')^2 + \phi = \frac{1}{\phi^2} + \phi = \frac{1}{\phi+1} + \phi = \frac{1+\phi^2+\phi}{\phi+1}$$

$$= \frac{\phi^2+\phi^2}{\phi^2} = \frac{2\phi^2}{\phi^2} = 2. \tag{13}$$

Again, using (6) and (12),

$$\phi^2 - \phi' = \phi + 1 - \frac{1}{\phi} = \frac{\phi^2+\phi-1}{\phi} = \frac{\phi+1+\phi-1}{\phi} = 2. \tag{14}$$

Hence, from (13) and (14)

$$(\phi')^2 + \phi = \phi^2 - \phi' \tag{15}$$

Powers of ϕ: A fascinating occurrence of the Fibonacci series can be obtained if we derive powers of ϕ in terms of ϕ and take note of the coefficients and constants that arise.

For example, using (12),

$$\phi^3 = \phi^2 \cdot \phi = (\phi + 1)\phi = \phi^2 + \phi = \phi + 1 + \phi = 2\phi + 1, \tag{16}$$

$$\phi^4 = \phi^3 \cdot \phi = (2\phi + 1)\phi = 2\phi^2 + \phi = 2(\phi + 1) + \phi = 2\phi + 2 + \phi = 3\phi + 2, \tag{17}$$

and $\phi^5 = \phi^4 \cdot \phi = (3\phi + 2)\phi = 3\phi^2 + 2\phi = 3(\phi + 1) + 2\phi = 3\phi + 3 + 2\phi = 5\phi + 3. \tag{18}$

Have students generate further powers of ϕ.

$$\begin{aligned}
\phi^1 &= 1\phi + 0 \\
\phi^2 &= 1\phi + 1 \\
\phi^3 &= 2\phi + 1 \\
\phi^4 &= 3\phi + 2 \\
\phi^5 &= 5\phi + 3 \\
\phi^6 &= 8\phi + 5 \\
\phi^7 &= 13\phi + 8 \\
\phi^8 &= 21\phi + 13 \\
\vdots \quad & \quad \vdots \quad\ \vdots
\end{aligned} \tag{19}$$

Let us return to figure 1. If, along $\overline{CD}$, the length $DE = \phi'$ is marked off, we obtain square DEGH, each side equal in length to ϕ'.

Thus, $CH = 1 - \phi'$ (remember that originally CD = one unit). But $1 - \phi' = 1 - \frac{1}{\phi} = \frac{\phi-1}{\phi} = \frac{\frac{1}{\phi}}{\phi} =$

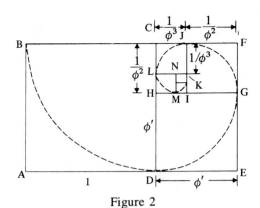

Figure 2

$\frac{1}{\phi^2} = (\phi')^2 = \frac{1}{\phi^2}$. With CF (or GH) $= \phi' = \frac{1}{\phi}$,

$\frac{CH''}{CF} = \frac{(\phi')^2}{\phi'} = \phi'$.

Thus, CFGH is also a golden rectangle.

In like fashion, a square, each of whose sides is $(\phi')^2$ units in length, can be partitioned along side CF of CFGH, whereby we obtain another golden rectangle CJIH. CJIH can similarly be partitioned to obtain square GJKL, leaving golden rectangle IKLH. This process of partitioning squares from golden rectangles to obtain another golden rectangle can be indefinitely continued in the manner suggested in figure 2.

If points B,D,G,J,L,M are connected by a smooth curve (see figure 2), a spiral-shaped curve will result. This is part of an equiangular spiral, a detailed discussion of which is not possible at this time.

Postassessment

1. A line segment $\overline{AE}$ is said to be divided into *extreme and mean ratio* if a point D can be located on $\overline{AE}$ such that $\dfrac{\overline{AE}}{\overline{AD}} = \dfrac{\overline{AD}}{\overline{DE}}$ (20)

In figure 1, let AE $= x$ and AD $= 1$. Then, from (20), derive the quadratic equation which was used to determine the value of ϕ in (3).

Reference

Posamentier, Alfred S., *Excursions in Advanced Euclidean Geometry*. Menlo Park, Ca.: Addison-Wesley, 1984.

68   The Golden Triangle

This unit will help to develop student understanding in areas of mathematics not usually dealt with.

Performance Objectives

1. Students will demonstrate understanding of various relationships between the pentagon, the pentagram and the golden ratio.

2. Students will construct a Golden Triangle.

3. Students will demonstrate certain properties of the Golden Triangle with trigonometric functions.

Preassessment

Some knowledge of geometry and intermediate algebra is necessary.

Teaching Strategies

Have your students construct a regular pentagon ABCDE by any method, after which they should draw pentagram ACEBD (see Figure 1.) Let each side of the pentagon be ϕ units in length. Review with your students the various angle measures and isosceles triangles formed by the pentagram and pentagon. Particular note should be made of similar isosceles triangles BED and DEF since they

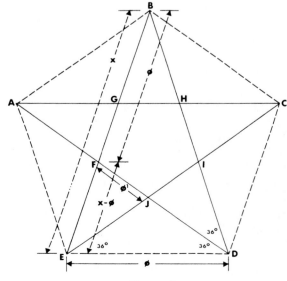

Figure 1

will be chosen, quite arbitrarily, from the many similar triangles in Figure 1, for the discussion that follows.

With $\overline{DF}$ the bisector of $\angle BDE$, triangles DEF and BDF are isosceles, so that

$$ED = DF = FB = \phi. \tag{1}$$

Let $BE = BD = x$. Then $FE = x - \phi$, and

$$\frac{BF}{FE} = \frac{BD}{ED}, \frac{\phi}{x - \phi} = \frac{x}{\phi}, \tag{2}$$

so that $x^2 - \phi x - \phi^2 = 0.$ (3)

The positive root of (3), from the quadratic formula, is

$$x = \phi\left(\frac{1 + \sqrt{5}}{2}\right). \tag{4}$$

But by definition, $\dfrac{1 + \sqrt{5}}{2} = \phi.$

Hence, from (4),

$$x = \phi \cdot \phi = \phi^2 = BE, \tag{5}$$

and $EF = x - \phi = \phi^2 - \phi = \phi + 1 - \phi = 1.$ (6)

Thus, in $\triangle BED$, the ratio of leg to base, using

(5), is $\dfrac{BE}{ED} = \dfrac{\phi^2}{\phi} = \phi,$

and in $\triangle DEF$, the ratio of leg to base is again ϕ,

since $\dfrac{DE}{EF} = \dfrac{\phi}{1} = \phi,$

so that in any 72°-72°-36° isosceles triangle

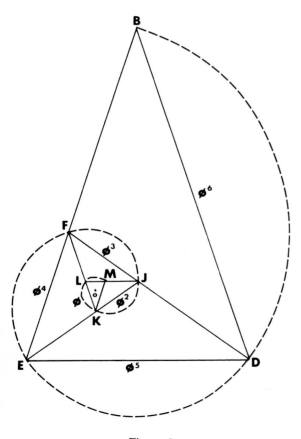

Figure 2

(hereafter referred to as *The Golden Triangle*), the ratio of

$$\frac{\text{leg}}{\text{base}} = \phi \tag{7}$$

This is the same ratio of length to width defined for the Golden Rectangle.

In isosceles $\triangle EFJ$, $FJ = \phi'$, since, using (6) and

(7), $\dfrac{EF}{FJ} = \dfrac{1}{FJ} = \phi,$ implying that $FJ = \dfrac{1}{\phi} = \phi'.$ (8)

Thus, regular pentagon FGHIJ has side length of ϕ'.

Returning to isosceles $\triangle DEF$, it is apparent that $\overline{EJ}$ is the bisector of $\angle DEF$. In figure 2, let $\overline{FK}$ be the bisector of $\angle EFJ$. Then $FJ = FK = \dfrac{1}{\phi}$ and

base $JK = \dfrac{1}{\phi^2}.$ Moreover, $\overline{FK} \parallel \overline{BD}$, since $m\angle KFJ = m\angle JDB.$

In like fashion, the bisector of $\angle FJK$ is parallel to $\overline{ED}$ and meets $\overline{FK}$ at L, forming another golden triangle, $\triangle JKL$. This process of bisecting a base angle of a golden triangle can be continued indefinitely to produce a series of smaller and smaller golden triangles which converge to a limiting point, 0. This point, comparable to that obtained in the golden rectangle, is the pole of an equiangular spiral which passes through the vertices B,D,E,F,J,K,L, . . . of each of the golden triangles.

A number of additional properties of the golden triangle are worth mentioning:

1. In figure 2, let ML be of unit length. Then, from (7),

$$\begin{aligned}
LK &= \phi &&= 1\phi + 0 \\
KJ &= \phi^2 &&= 1\phi + 1 \\
JF &= \phi^3 &&= 2\phi + 1 \\
FE &= \phi^4 &&= 3\phi + 2 \\
ED &= \phi^5 &&= 5\phi + 3 \\
DB &= \phi^6 &&= 8\phi + 5
\end{aligned} \tag{9}$$

forming a Fibonacci Series.

2. The bisector of the vertex angle of a golden triangle divides the bisectors of the base angles in the golden ratio (see Figure 1.) Since the angle bisectors of a triangle are concurrent, the bisector of $\angle EBD$ must pass through J. However, from

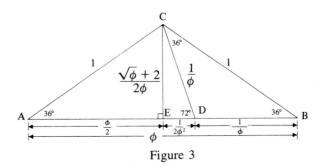

Figure 3

(6), EF = 1 = EJ = JD, and from (8), FJ = ϕ'.

Hence, $\dfrac{JD}{FJ} = \dfrac{1}{\phi'} = \phi$.

3. The golden triangle can be used to represent certain trigonometric functions in terms of ϕ (see Figure 3.) Let $\triangle ABC$ be a 36°-36°-108° isosceles triangle, with AC = CB = 1. Let one of the trisectors of angle C meet $\overline{AB}$ at D. Then $\triangle ACD$ is a golden triangle with $m\angle CDA = m\angle DCA = 72°$. Since AC = 1, then AD = 1, and from (7), CD = $\dfrac{1}{\phi}$. Furthermore, $\triangle BCD$ is isosceles with

$m\angle BCD = m\angle DBC = 36°$. Thus CD = DB = $\dfrac{1}{\phi}$, and AB = AD + DB = $1 + \dfrac{1}{\phi} = \phi$.

From C, drop a perpendicular to meet $\overline{AB}$ at E. This makes AE = EB = $\dfrac{\phi}{2}$. Immediately, in

right $\triangle ACE$ cos 36° = $\dfrac{\phi}{2}$, implying that (10)

$$\sin 54° = \frac{\phi}{2}. \tag{11}$$

Furthermore,

$$ED = AD - AE = 1 - \frac{\phi}{2} = \frac{2-\phi}{2} = \frac{1}{2\phi^2}. \tag{12}$$

Now in right $\triangle CED$,

$$\cos 72° = \frac{ED}{CD} = \frac{\dfrac{1}{2\phi^2}}{\dfrac{1}{\phi}} = \frac{1}{2\phi} = \sin 18°. \tag{13}$$

Postassessment

1. Using the reciprocal trigonometric identities, determine values in terms of ϕ for tan, cot, sec and csc for the angle measures indicated in (10), (11) and (13) above.

2. Using the half-angle formulas, determine trigonometric function values for 18° and 27° in terms of ϕ.

This unit should be used in conjunction with "The Golden Rectangle."

Reference

Huntley, H.E., *The Divine Proportion*. New York: Dover, 1970.

69 Geometric Fallacies

Geometry students studying proofs using auxiliary sets often question the need for a rigorous reason for that set's existence. Often they don't appreciate the need for proving the existence and uniqueness of these sets. Students also develop a dependence upon a diagram without analyzing its correctness. This unit introduces fallacious proofs to students in the hope that they can better grasp the need for such rigor.

Performance Objective

Given a geometric fallacy, students will determine where the fallacy occurs.

Preassessment

Students should be well acquainted with geometric proofs of both congruent and similar triangles.

Present your students with the following proof. They will recognize that it contains a fallacy. Ask them to try to determine where the error occurs.

Given: ABCD is a rectangle
$\overline{FA} \cong \overline{BA}$
R is the midpoint of $\overline{BC}$
N is the midpoint of $\overline{CF}$

To Prove: A right angle is equal in measure to an obtuse angle ($\angle CDA \cong \angle FAD$)
Draw $\overrightarrow{RL}$ perpendicular to $\overline{CB}$.
Draw $\overrightarrow{NM}$ perpendicular to $\overline{CF}$.
$\overrightarrow{RL}$ and $\overrightarrow{NM}$ intersect at point O. If they didn't intersect, $\overrightarrow{RL}$ and $\overrightarrow{NM}$ would be parallel and this would mean $\overline{CB}$ is parallel to $\overline{CF}$ which is impossible.
Draw $\overline{DO}$, $\overline{CO}$, $\overline{FO}$ and $\overline{AO}$.
Since $\overline{RO}$ is the perpendicular bisector of $\overline{CB}$ and $\overline{DA}$, $\overline{DO} \cong \overline{AO}$.
Since $\overline{NO}$ is the perpendicular bisector of $\overline{CF}$, $\overline{CO} \cong \overline{FO}$.
And, since $\overline{FA} \cong \overline{BA}$ and $\overline{BA} \cong \overline{CD}$, we have $\overline{FA} \cong \overline{CD}$.
$\therefore \triangle CDO \cong \triangle FAO$ (SSS $\cong$ SSS), so $\angle ODC \cong \angle OAF$.
Since $\overline{OD} \cong \overline{OA}$ we have $\angle ODA \cong \angle OAD$.

Now, $m \angle ODC - m \angle ODA = m \angle OAF - m \angle OAD$ or $m \angle CDA = m \angle FAD$.

Teaching Strategies

When students have inspected the proof and have found nothing wrong with it, ask them to use rulers and compasses to reconstruct the diagram. The correct diagram looks like this:

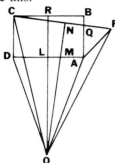

Although the triangles are congruent, our ability to subtract the specific angles no longer exists. Thus, the difficulty with this proof lies in its dependence upon an incorrectly drawn diagram.

In order to show that $\angle OAF$ cannot be obtuse, we must show that when $\overline{OF}$ intersects $\overline{AB}$ and $\overline{AD}$, and point O is on the perpendicular bisector of $\overline{CF}$, then point O cannot be on the perpendicular bisector of $\overline{AD}$.

Suppose point O is the intersection of the two perpendicular bisectors. (As in the original diagram.) Since $\overline{CD} /\!/ \overline{AQ}$, $\angle DCF \cong \angle AQF$. In isosceles $\triangle ABF$, $\angle ABF \cong \angle AFB$. But $m \angle AFB > m \angle AFC$; by substitution $m \angle ABF > m \angle AFC$. Since $\angle AQF$ is an exterior angle of $\triangle BQF$, $m \angle AQF > m \angle ABF$. Therefore $m \angle AQF > m \angle ABF > m \angle AFC$, or $m \angle AQF > m \angle AFC$. By substitution $m \angle DCF > m \angle AFC$. Since $\angle OCF \cong \angle OFC$ by subtraction we have $m \angle DCO > m \angle OFA$. Thus, $DO > OA$. This is a contradiction since $DO = AO$ if O is bisector of $\overline{DA}$ on the perpendicular. Therefore point O cannot be on the perpendicular bisector of $\overline{DA}$ for any point O such that $\angle OAF$ is obtuse.

The above proof also holds true for the following diagram which shows that $\angle OAF$ cannot be acute.

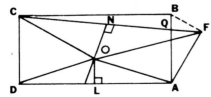

Now present your students with the following proof that any point in the interior of a circle is also on the circle.

Given: Circle O, with radius r
      Let A be any point in the interior of the circle distinct from O.
Prove: A is on the circle

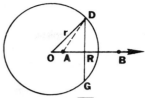

Let B be on the extension of $\overline{OA}$ through A such that $OA \cdot OB = r^2$. (Clearly OB is greater than r since OA is less than r.) Let the perpendicular bisector of $\overline{AB}$ meet the circle in Points D and G, where R is the midpoint of $\overline{AB}$.

We now have $OA = OR - RA$ and $OB = OR + RB = OR + RA$.

$\therefore r^2 = (OR - RA)(OR + RA)$
$\quad r^2 = OR^2 - RA^2$
$\quad r^2 = (r^2 - DR^2) - (AD^2 - DR^2)$ by the Pythagorean Theorem
$\quad r^2 = r^2 - AD^2$
$\therefore AD^2 = 0$
$\therefore$ A coincides with D, and lies on the circle.

The fallacy in this proof lies in the fact that we drew an auxiliary line ($\overleftrightarrow{DRG}$) with *two* conditions—that $\overline{DRG}$ is the perpendicular bisector of $\overline{AB}$ and that it intersects the circle. Actually, all points on the perpendicular bisector of $\overline{AB}$ lie in the exterior of the circle and therefore cannot intersect the circle.

$r^2 = OA (OB)$
$r^2 = OA (OA + AB)$
$r^2 = OA^2 + (OA)(AB)$

now, the proof assumes $OA + \dfrac{AB}{2} < r$

$\qquad\qquad 2(OA) + AB < 2r$
$\qquad 4(OA)^2 + 4(OA)(AB) + AB^2 < 4r^2$
$\qquad$ Since $r^2 = OA^2 + (OA)(AB)$
$\qquad$ we have $4r^2 + AB^2 < 4r^2$
$\qquad AB^2 < 0$
$\qquad$ which is impossible.

This proof points to the care we must take when drawing auxiliary sets in using *one* condition only.

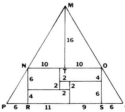

Here is a "triangle" consisting of four right triangles, four rectangles and a "hole."

1. Have your students calculate the area of the eight regions (not the hole) [416]
2. Now have them calculate the area of the entire figure. [Since PQ = 32 and height = 26, $\frac{1}{2}$PQ$\cdot h$ = 416] We are now faced with this problem: how did we arrive at the same area with and without the hole?

The fallacy occurs because of an error in 2. The figure is *not* a triangle, since points M, N and P are not collinear.

If points M, N and P were collinear,
since ∠RNO is a right angle, ∠PNR is the complement of ∠MNT
since ∠NRP is a right angle, ∠PNR is the complement of ∠RPN
∴ ∠MNT ≅ ∠RPN
∴ △MNT ∼ △NPR

But, this is not the case.
The same argument holds for points M, O and Q. Therefore the figure is a pentagon; thus the formula we used in 2 is incorrect.

Postassessment

Have students select a geometric fallacy from any of the following books and explain the "error" in the proof

References

Maxwell, E. A., *Fallacies in Mathematics*, Cambridge University Press, 1963.

Northrop, E. P., *Riddles in Mathematics*, D. Van Nostrand Co., 1944.

Posamentier, A. S., J. H. Banks, and R. L. Bannister, *Geometry, Its Elements and Structure*, 2d ed., McGraw-Hill, 1977. pp 240–44, 270–71.

70 Regular Polyhedra

This unit will present a method which can be used to prove that there are not more than five regular polyhedra.

Performance Objective

Students will define a regular polyhedron, identify all regular polyhedra, and explain why no more than five regular polyhedra exist.

Preassessment

Display physical models of various polyhedra and have students count the number of vertices (V), the number of edges (E), and the number of faces (F) of each polyhedron. After tabulating their results they should notice the relationship:
$$V + F = E + 2$$

Teaching Strategies

Having empirically established Euler's Theorem, $(V + F = E + 2)$, students may wish to apply it to reach other conclusions about polyhedra. Depending upon class interest, proof of this theorem may be in order. One source for the proof is *Geometry, Its Elements and Structure* by A.S. Posamentier, J.H. Banks, and R.L. Bannister, pp. 574–576 (McGraw-Hill, 1977).

One interesting application of this theorem is the proof that more than five *regular* polyhedra cannot exist. You should begin by defining a regular polyhedron as *a solid figure bounded by portions of planes called faces, each of which is a regular polygon* (congruent sides and angles). The cube is a common example of a regular polyhedron.

To begin the proof that *there are only five regular polyhedra*, let s represent the number of sides of each face and let t represent the number of faces at each vertex.

Since there are t faces at each vertex students should realize that there are also t edges at each vertex. Suppose in counting the number of edges (E) of a given polyhedron, the number of edges at each vertex were counted and then multiplied by the number of vertices (V). This would produce *twice* the number of edges (2E) of the polyhedron, as each edge was counted twice, once at each of the two vertices it joins. Hence:

$$tV = 2E, \text{ or } \frac{V}{\frac{1}{t}} = \frac{E}{\frac{1}{2}}$$

Similarly, in counting the number of edges of the polyhedron, the number of sides (s) of each face were counted and then multiplied by the number of faces (F) of the polyhedron. This would also produce *twice* the number of edges of the polyhedron, as each side (edge) counted belongs to two faces. Hence, $sF = 2E$, or $\frac{F}{\frac{1}{s}} = \frac{E}{\frac{1}{2}}$

$$\text{Therefore } \frac{V}{\frac{1}{t}} = \frac{E}{\frac{1}{2}} = \frac{F}{\frac{1}{s}}$$

Students should recall the following theorem on proportions: $\frac{a}{b} = \frac{c}{d} = \frac{e}{f} = \frac{a+c+e}{b+d+f}$
Then have them apply it to the following:

$$\frac{V}{\frac{1}{t}} = \frac{-E}{-\frac{1}{2}} = \frac{F}{\frac{1}{s}} = \frac{V - E + F}{\frac{1}{t} - \frac{1}{2} + \frac{1}{s}}$$

However, by Euler's Theorem (V − E + F = 2),

$$\frac{V}{\frac{1}{t}} = \frac{E}{\frac{1}{2}} = \frac{F}{\frac{1}{s}} = \frac{2}{\frac{1}{t} - \frac{1}{2} + \frac{1}{s}}$$

Students may now solve for V, E, and F:

$$V = \frac{4s}{2s + 2t - st}$$

$$E = \frac{2st}{2s + 2t - st}$$

$$F = \frac{4t}{2s + 2t - st}$$

Students should be asked to inspect the nature of V, E, and F. Realizing that these numbers must be positive, elicit from students that the denominators must be positive (since *s* and *t* are positive, as well as the numerators). Thus,

$$2s + 2t - st > 0$$

To enable factoring add −4 to both members of the inequality to get:

$$2s + 2t - st - 4 > -4$$

Then multiply both sides by −1:

$$-2s - 2t + st + 4 < 4, \text{ or } (s-2)(t-2) < 4.$$

At this point have students place restrictions on *s* and *t*. They should be quick to state that no polygon may have less than three sides; hence $s \geq 3$. Also, they should realize that at each vertex of the polyhedron there must at least be three faces; hence $t \geq 3$.

These facts will indicate that $(s-2)$ and $(t-2)$ must be positive. Since their product must be less than four, students should be able to generate the following table:

(s−2)(t−2)	(s−2)	(t−2)	s	t	V	E	F	Name of Polyhedron
1	1	1	3	3	4	6	4	Tetrahedron
2	2	1	4	3	8	12	6	Hexahedron (cube)
2	1	2	3	4	6	12	8	Octahedron
3	3	1	5	3	20	30	12	Dodecahedron
3	1	3	3	5	12	30	20	Icosahedron

Since there are no other possible values for *s* and *t* the above table is complete, and hence there are only five regular polyhedra. More able students should be encouraged to investigate the existence of these five regular polyhedra. One source is Euclid's *Elements*, Book XIII.

Further inspection of the above table reveals an interesting symmetry between the hexahedron and the octahedron as well as the dodecahedron and the icosahedron. That is, if *s* and *t* are interchanged these symmetries will be highlighted. Furthermore, this table indicates that the faces of these regular polyhedra are either equilateral triangles, squares, or regular pentagons (see column *s*). Students should also be encouraged to

further verify Euler's Theorem (V + F = E + 2) with the data in the above table.

The figure shows the five regular polyhedra as well as "patterns" which can be used to construct (by cutting them out and appropriately folding them) these polyhedra.

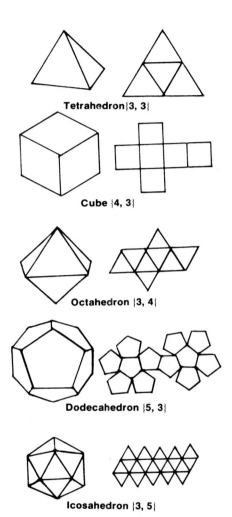

Tetrahedron {3, 3}

Cube {4, 3}

Octahedron {3, 4}

Dodecahedron {5, 3}

Icosahedron {3, 5}

Although often referred to as the five Platonic Solids, it is believed that three (tetrahedron, hexahedron, and dodecahedron) of the five solids were due to Pythagoreans, while the remaining two solids (octahedron, and icosahedron) were due to the efforts of Theaetetus (414 − 369 B.C.). There is enough history about these solids to merit a brief report by one of the students.

Postassessment

1. Have students define and identify regular polyhedra.

2. Have students explain why more than five regular polyhydra cannot exist.

71   An Introduction to Topology

A lesson on topology can be taught immediately after teaching geometry. This unit will present some basic concepts of topology and their applications.

Performance Objectives

1. *Given two geometric drawings students will determine whether they are topologically equivalent.*

2. *Given a polyhedron or a plane figure students can show that $V + F - E = 2$ (space), and $V + F - E = 1$ (plane).*

Preassessment

A basic knowledge of seventh grade geometry is desirable preceding this unit.

Teaching Strategies

Have students draw several closed curves. Then have them distinguish between those that are simple closed curves and those that are not. Some possible student responses may be the following.

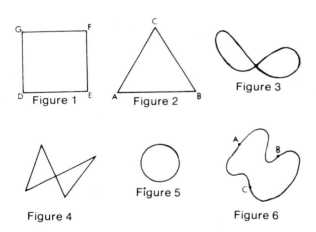

Figure 1   Figure 2   Figure 3

Figure 4   Figure 5   Figure 6

Ask students to redraw each of the figures without lifting their pencils off their paper. Students should realize that if Figure 1 were drawn on a rubber sheet they could twist and bend it into figures 2, 5, and 6.

Suppose they now consider some geometric figures in space. Have them draw a cube.

Figure 7

Ask students if this cube can be transformed into any of figures 8, 9, or 10 by twisting or bending it.

Figure 8   Figure 9   Figure 10

They should find that the only figure of these that the cube can be transformed into is a sphere.

It may therefore be said that a cube is topologically equivalent to a sphere. Tell students that studying figures in this way leads to a branch of mathematics called *topology* or "rubber sheet geometry."

One of the more fascinating relationships in geometry is directly taken from topology. This relationship involves the vertices (V), edges (E) and faces (F) of a polyhedron or polygon. It reads: $V + F - E = 2$ (in three-dimensional space) or $V + F - E = 1$ (in a plane). Have students consider a pentagon. A pentagon has five vertices, five edges and one face; hence $V + F - E = 5 + 1 - 5 = 1$. Students may now wish to consider a three-space figure. The cube (figure 7) has eight vertices, six faces and twelve edges. Therefore, $V + F - E = 8 - 12 + 6 = 2$. These relationships can be demonstrated to the class by using overhead projector transparencies or with physical models.

Suppose a plane were to cut all edges of one of the trihedral angles of a cube (a piece of clay in the form of a cube would be useful here). This plane would then separate one of the vertices from the cube. However, in the process, there would be added to the original polyhedron: 1 face, 3 vertices and 3 edges. Thus, for this new polyhedron, V is increased by 2, F is increased by 1 and E is increased by 3; yet, $V + F - E$ remains unchanged. More such experiments should be encouraged.

Figures are topologically equivalent if one can be made to coincide with the other by distortion, shrinking, stretching, or bending. If one face of a polyhedron is removed the remaining figure is topologically equivalent to a region of a plane. This new figure (see figure 11) will not have the same shape or size, but its *boundaries* are preserved. The edges will become sides of polygonal regions, and there will be the same number of edges and vertices in the plane figure as in the polyhedron. Each polygon that is not a triangle can be cut into triangles, or triangular regions, by drawing diagonals. Each time a diagonal is drawn, we increase the number of edges by one but we also increase the number of faces by one. The value of $V - E + F$ is preserved. Triangles on the outer edge of the region will have either one edge on the boundary of the region, as △ABC in the accompanying figure, or have two edges on the boundary, as △DEF. Triangles such as △ABC can be removed by removing the one boundary side (i.e., $\overline{AC}$). By doing this we decrease the number of faces by one and the number of edges by one. Still V − E + F is unchanged. Triangles such as DEF can be removed by removing two edges (i.e., $\overline{DF}$ and $\overline{EF}$). By doing this we decrease the number of edges by two, the number of faces by one, and the number of vertices by one. V − E + F is still preserved. We continue in this manner until we are left with one triangle. This triangle has three vertices, three edges, and one face. Hence, V − E + F = 1 in the plane. We conclude that when we replace the face we removed we have V − E + F = 2 for a polyhedron in space.

After students have had a chance to familiarize themselves with this theorem, they should be encouraged to test it empirically with student constructed polyhedra. Clay is a good medium for this activity. Students may want to record their results on a chart.

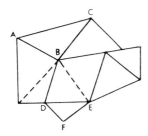

Figure 11

Figure 12a

Figure 12b

Figure 13a

Figure 13b

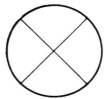

Figure 14a

Figure 14b

Postassessment

1. Have students decide if any of Figures 12, 13, or 14 can be bent into the other figures.
2. Show that V + F − E = 2 holds for a tetrahedron and an octahedron.
3. Show that V + F − E = 1 holds for a hexagon and a dodecagon.

72   Angles On A Clock

This unit can be used in earlier junior high school grades as a recreational activity where some interesting relationships can be discovered, or it can be used as an enrichment application for beginning algebra students studying the topic of uniform motion.

Performance Objectives

1. Students will determine the precise time that the hands of a clock form a given angle.

2. Students will solve problems related to the positions of the hands on a clock.

Preassessment

Ask students at what time (exactly) will the hands of a clock overlap after 4 o'clock.

Teaching Strategies

Your students' first reaction to the solution to this problem will be that the answer is simply 4:20. When you remind them that the hour hand moves uniformly, they will begin to estimate the answer to be between 4:21 and 4:22. They will realize that the hour hand moves through an interval between minute markers every 12 minutes. Therefore it will leave the interval 4:21-4:22 at 4:24. This however doesn't answer the original question about the exact time of this overlap.

In a beginning algebra class studying uniform motion problems, have students consider this problem in that light. The best way to have a student begin to understand the movement of the hands of a clock is by having him or her consider the hands traveling independently around the clock at uniform speeds. The minute markings on the clock (from now on referred to as "markers") will serve to denote distance as well as time. An analogy should be drawn here to the uniform motion of automobiles (a popular and overused topic for verbal problems in an elementary algebra course). A problem involving a fast automobile overtaking a slower one would be appropriate.

Experience has shown that the analogy should be drawn between specific cases rather than mere generalizations. It might be helpful to have the class find the distance necessary for a car traveling at 60 m.p.h. to overtake a car with a head start of 20 miles and traveling at 5 m.p.h.

Now have the class consider 4 o'clock as the initial time on the clock. Our problem will be to determine exactly when the minute hand will overtake the hour hand after 4 o'clock. Consider the speed of the hour hand to be r, then the speed of the minute hand must be $12r$. We seek the distance, measured by the number of markers traveled, that the minute hand must travel to overtake the hour hand.

Let us refer to this distance as d markers. Hence the distance that the hour hand travels is $d-20$ markers, since it has a $20-$marker head start over the minute hand. For this to take place, the times required for the minute hand, $\dfrac{d}{12r}$, and for the hour hand, $\dfrac{d-20}{r}$, are the same. Therefore, $\dfrac{d}{12r} = \dfrac{d-20}{r}$, and $d = \dfrac{12}{11} \cdot 20 = 21\dfrac{9}{11}$. Thus the minute hand will overtake the hour hand at exactly $4:21\dfrac{9}{11}$.

Consider the expression $d = \dfrac{12}{11} \cdot 20$. The quantity 20 is the number of markers that the minute hand had to travel to get to the desired position, assuming the hour hand remained stationary. However, quite obviously, the hour hand does not remain stationary. Hence, we must multiply this quantity by $\dfrac{12}{11}$ as the minute hand must travel $\dfrac{12}{11}$ as far. Let us refer to this fraction$(\dfrac{12}{11})$ as the correction factor. Have the class verify this correction factor both logically and algebraically.

To begin to familiarize the students with use of the correction factor, choose some short and simple problems. For example, you may ask them to find the exact time when the hands of a clock overlap between 7 and 8 o'clock. Here the students would first determine how far the minute hand would have to travel from the "12" position to the position of the hour hand, assuming again that the hour hand remains stationary. Then by multiplying the number of markers, 35, by the

correction factor, $\dfrac{12}{11}$, they will obtain the exact time $(7:38\dfrac{2}{11})$ that the hands will overlap.

To enhance students' understanding of this new procedure ask them to consider a person checking a wristwatch against an electric clock and noticing that the hands on the wristwatch overlap every 65 minutes (as measured by the electric clock). Ask the class if the wristwatch is fast, slow, or accurate.

You may wish to have them consider the problem in the following way. At 12 o'clock the hands of a clock overlap exactly. Using the previously described method we find that the hands will again overlap at exactly $1:05\dfrac{5}{11}$, and then again at exactly $2:10\dfrac{10}{11}$, and again at exactly $3:16\dfrac{4}{11}$ and so on. Each time there is an interval of $65\dfrac{5}{11}$ minutes between overlapping positions. Hence, the person's watch is inaccurate by $\dfrac{5}{11}$ of a minute. Have students now determine if the wristwatch is fast or slow.

There are many other interesting, and sometimes rather difficult, problems made simple by this correction factor. You may very easily pose your own problems. For example, you may ask your students to find the exact times when the hands of a clock will be perpendicular (or form a straight angle) between, say, 8 and 9 o'clock.

Again, you would have the students determine the number of markers that the minute hand would have to travel from the "12" position until it forms the desired angle with the stationary hour hand. Then have them multiply this number by the correction factor $(\dfrac{12}{11})$ to obtain the exact actual time. That is, to find the exact time that the hands of a clock are *first* perpendicular between 8 and 9 o'clock, determine the desired position of the minute hand when the hour hand remains stationary (here, on the 25 minute marker). Then, multiply 25 by $\dfrac{12}{11}$ to get $8:27\dfrac{3}{11}$, the exact time when the hands are *first* perpendicular after 8 o'clock.

For students who have not yet studied algebra, you might justify the $\dfrac{12}{11}$ correction factor for the interval between overlaps in the following way:

Think of the hands of a clock at noon. During the next 12 hours (i.e. until the hands reach the same position at midnight) the hour hand makes one revolution, the minute hand makes 12 revolutions, and the minute hand coincides with the hour hand 11 times (including midnight, but not noon, starting just after the hands separate at noon).

Since each hand rotates at a uniform rate, the hands overlap each $\frac{12}{11}$ of an hour, or $65\frac{5}{11}$ minutes.

This can be extended to other situations.

Your students should derive a great sense of achievement and enjoyment as a result of employing this simple procedure to solve what usually appears to be a very difficult clock problem.

Postassessment

1. At what time will the hands of a clock overlap after 2 o'clock?

2. At what time will the hands of a clock be perpendicular after 3 o'clock?

3. How would the "correction factor" change if our clock were a 24-hour cycle clock?

4. What would the "correction factor" be if we sought the exact time when the second hand and the minute hand were perpendicular after: *(fill in a specified time)*?

5. What angle is determined by the hands of a clock at: *(fill in a specified time)*?

6. What is the first time (exactly) when the second hand bisects the angle formed by the minute and hour hands of a clock after: *(fill in a specified time)*?

73 Averaging Rates—The Harmonic Mean

This unit will present a shortcut method for determining the average of two or more rates, (rates of speed, cost, production, etc.).

Performance Objectives

1. Given various rates for a common base, students will find the average of these rates.
2. Given a problem calling for the average of given rates, students will correctly apply the concept of a harmonic mean when applicable.

Preassessment

Have students solve the following problem:

Noreen drives from her home to work at the rate of 30 mph. Later she returns home from work over the same route at the rate of 60 mph. What is her average rate of speed for both trips?

Teaching Strategies

The preceding problem should serve as excellent motivation for this unit. Most students will probably incorrectly offer 45 mph as their answer to this problem. Their explanation will be that 45 is the average of 30 and 60. True! You must convince them that since the numbers 30 and 60 represent rates, they cannot be treated as simple quantities. Students will wonder what difference this should make.

The first task is to convince your students that their original answer, 45 mph, is incorrect. Have them realize that when Noreen drove from home to work she had to drive twice as much time than she did on her return trip. Hence, it would be incorrect to give both rates the same "weight." If this still

does not convince your students, ask them that if their test scores throughout the semester were 90, 90, 90, 90 and 40, which of the following methods would they use to find their average:

90 (average of first four tests)
+40 (their last test score)
130 ÷ 2 = 65

Or: 90 + 90 + 90 + 90 + 40 = 400; 400 ÷ 5 = 80.

It would be expected that students would now suggest that the answer to the original problem could be obtained by: $\frac{30 + 30 + 60}{3} = 40$. This is perfectly correct; however, a simple solution as this would hardly be expected if one rate were not a multiple of the other. Most students would now welcome a more general method of solution. One such solution is based on the relationship: *Rate × Time = Distance*. Consider the following:

T_1 (time going to work) $= \dfrac{D}{30}$

T_2 (time returning home) $= \dfrac{D}{60}$

T (total time for both trips) $= T_1 + T_2 = \dfrac{D}{20}$

R (rate for the entire trip) $= \dfrac{2D}{T} = \dfrac{2D}{\dfrac{D}{20}} = 40$

R is actually the *average rate* for the entire trip, since problems of this nature deal with uniform motion.

Of particular interest are those problems where the rates to be averaged are for a common base (e.g., the same distance for various rates of speed). Have students consider the original problem in general terms, where the given rates of speed are R_1 and R_2 (instead of 30 and 60), each for a distance D. Therefore, $T_1 = \dfrac{D}{R_1}$ and $T_2 = \dfrac{D}{R_2}$, so that

$$T = T_1 + T_2 = D(\frac{1}{R_1} + \frac{1}{R_2}) = \frac{D(R_1 + R_2)}{R_1 R_2}.$$

However, have students consider:

$$R = \frac{2D}{T} = \frac{2D}{D\ (\frac{1}{R_1} + \frac{1}{R_2})} = \frac{2}{\frac{1}{R_1} + \frac{1}{R_2}} = \frac{2R_1 R_2}{R_1 + R_2} \quad (1)$$

They should notice that $\dfrac{2R_1 R_2}{R_1 + R_2}$ is actually the reciprocal of the average of the reciprocals of R_1 and R_2. Such an average is called the *harmonic mean*.

Perhaps a word about the harmonic mean would be in order. A progression of numbers is said to be harmonic if any three consecutive members of the progression, a, b and c have the property that:

$$\frac{a}{c} = \frac{a - b}{b - c} \quad (2)$$

This relationship may also be written as:

$$a(b-c) = c(a-b) \quad (3)$$

Dividing by abc we get:

$$\frac{1}{c} - \frac{1}{b} = \frac{1}{b} - \frac{1}{a} \quad (4)$$

This relationship shows that the reciprocals of a harmonic progression are in an arithmetic progression, as with $\dfrac{1}{a}$, $\dfrac{1}{b}$ and $\dfrac{1}{c}$. When three terms are in an arithmetic progression the middle term is their mean. Thus $\dfrac{1}{b}$ is the arithmetic mean between $\dfrac{1}{a}$ and $\dfrac{1}{c}$; b is the harmonic mean between a and c.

Expressing b in terms of a and c in equation (4):

$$\frac{2}{b} = \frac{1}{a} + \frac{1}{c}, \text{ and } b = \frac{2ac}{a + c} \quad (5)$$

Have students compare (1) with (5)!

In a similar manner you may wish to have the class consider the harmonic mean of three numbers, r, s and t:

$$\frac{3}{\frac{1}{r} + \frac{1}{s} + \frac{1}{t}} = \frac{3rst}{st + rt + rs}$$

Students may even wish to extend this to determine a "formula" for the harmonic mean of four numbers, k, m, n and p:

$$\frac{4}{\frac{1}{k} + \frac{1}{m} + \frac{1}{n} + \frac{1}{p}} = \frac{4kmnp}{mnp + knp + kmp + kmn}.$$

Have students consider the following problem: Lisa bought 2 dollars worth of each of three different kinds of pencils, priced at 2¢, 4¢ and 5¢ each respectively. What is the average price paid per pencil?

The answer to this question is $3\dfrac{3}{19}$, the harmonic mean of 2, 4 and 5. Stress the point that this was possible since each rate acted on the same base, 2 dollars. Similar problems (see the Posttest) may be posed and solved by the students at this time.

You may wish to consider a geometric illustration of the concept. Although the harmonic mean enjoys the most prominence geometrically in projective geometry, it might be more appropriate to give an illustration of the harmonic mean in synthetic geometry.

Have the students consider the length of the segment containing the point of intersection of the diagonals of a trapezoid and parallel to the bases, with its endpoints in the legs. (see $\overline{EGF}$ below.) The length of this segment, $\overline{EGF}$, is the harmonic mean between the lengths of the bases, $\overline{AD}$ and $\overline{BC}$. In the figure below, ABCD is a trapezoid, with $\overline{AD}$ // $\overline{BC}$ and diagonals intersecting at G. Also $\overline{EGF}$ // $\overline{BC}$, and $\overline{DEC}$ and $\overline{AFB}$.

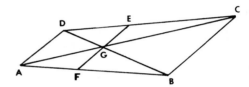

Since $\overline{GF}$ // $\overline{BC}$, $\triangle AFG \sim \triangle ABC$, and $\dfrac{AF}{FG} = \dfrac{AB}{BC}$. Similarly, since $\overline{GF}$ // $\overline{AD}$, $\triangle GBF \sim \triangle DBA$, and $\dfrac{BF}{FG} = \dfrac{AB}{AD}$. Therefore, $\dfrac{AF}{FG} + \dfrac{BF}{FG} = \dfrac{AB}{BC} + \dfrac{AB}{AD}$. Since $AF + BF = AB$, $\dfrac{AB}{FG} = \dfrac{AB}{BC} + \dfrac{AB}{AD}$, or $FG = \dfrac{(BC)\ (AD)}{BC + AD}$. In a similar manner it can be shown that $EG = \dfrac{(BC)\ (AD)}{BC + AD}$. Therefore, $EF = FG + EG = \dfrac{2(BC)\ (AD)}{BC + AD}$; hence, EF is the harmonic mean between BC and AD.

Postassessment

1) If a jet flies from New York to Rome at 600 mph and back along the same route at 500 mph, what is the average rate of speed for the entire trip?

2) Alice buys 2 dollars worth of each of three kinds of nuts, priced at 40¢, 50¢ and 60¢ per pound, respectively. What is the average price Alice paid per pound of nuts?

3) In June, Willie got 30 hits for a batting average of .300; however, in May he got 30 hits for a batting average of .400. What is Willie's batting average for May and June?

4) Find the harmonic mean of 2, 3, 5, 6, 2 and 9.

References:

Posamentier, Alfred S. *A Study Guide for the Mathematics Section of the Scholastic Aptitude Test,* Boston, Mass.: Allyn & Bacon, 1983.

Posamentier, Alfred S., and Charles T. Salkind, *Challenging Problems in Algebra.* Palo Alto, CA: Dale Seymour, 1988.

Posamentier, Alfred S., and Charles T. Salkind, *Challenging Problems in Geometry.* Palo Alto, CA: Dale Seymour, 1988.

Posamentier, A. S. "The Harmonic Mean and Its Place Among Means." in *Readings for Enrichment in Secondary School Mathematics.* Edited by Max A. Sobel. Reston, VA: NCTM.

74 Howlers

In *Fallacies in Mathematics*, E.A. Maxwell refers to the following cancellations as *howlers:*

$$\frac{1\cancel{6}}{\cancel{6}4} = \frac{1}{4}$$

$$\frac{2\cancel{6}}{\cancel{6}5} = \frac{2}{5}$$

This unit will offer a method of presenting these howlers to elementary algebra students so students better understand number concepts.

Performance Objectives
1. *Students will develop a howler not already presented in class.*
2. *Students will explain why there are only four howlers composed of two-digit fractions.*

Preassessment
Students should be able to reduce fractions to lowest terms. They should also be familiar with such concepts as factor, prime number, and be able to perform all operations on fractions.

Teaching Strategies
Begin your presentation by asking students to reduce to lowest terms the following fractions: $\frac{16}{64}, \frac{19}{95}, \frac{26}{65}, \frac{49}{98}$. After they have reduced to lowest terms each of the fractions in the usual manner, tell them that they did a lot of unnecessary work. Show them the following cancellations:

$$\frac{1\cancel{6}}{\cancel{6}4} = \frac{1}{4}$$

$$\frac{1\cancel{9}}{\cancel{9}5} = \frac{1}{5}$$

$$\frac{2\cancel{6}}{\cancel{6}5} = \frac{2}{5}$$

$$\frac{4\cancel{9}}{\cancel{9}8} = \frac{4}{8} = \frac{1}{2}$$

At this point your students will be somewhat amazed. Their first reaction is to ask if this can be done to any

fraction composed of two-digit numbers. Challenge your students to find another fraction (comprised of two-digit numbers) where this type of cancellation will work. Students might cite $\frac{5\cancel{5}}{\cancel{5}5} = \frac{5}{5} = 1$ as an illustration of this type of cancellation. Indicate to them that although this will hold true for all multiples of eleven, it is trivial, and our concern will be only with proper fractions (i.e. whose value is less than one).

After they are thoroughly frustrated you may begin a discussion on why the four fractions above are the only ones (composed of two-digit numbers) where this type of cancellation will hold true.

Have students consider the fraction $\frac{10x + a}{10a + y}$. The nature of the above four cancellations was such that when cancelling the a's the fraction was equal to $\frac{x}{y}$. Therefore $\frac{10x + a}{10a + y} = \frac{x}{y}$.

This yields: $y(10x + a) = x(10a + y)$

$$\text{or } 10xy + ay = 10ax + xy$$
$$9xy + ay = 10ax$$
$$\text{and } y = \frac{10ax}{9x + a}$$

At this point have students inspect this relationship. They should realize that it is necessary that x, y, and a be integers since they were digits in the numerator and denominator of a fraction. It is now their task to find the values of a and x for which y will also be integral.

To avoid a lot of algebraic manipulation you might have students set up a chart which will generate values of y from $y = \frac{10ax}{9x + a}$. Remind them that x, y and a must be *single digit* integers. Below is a portion of the table they will construct. Notice that the cases where $x = a$ are excluded since $\frac{x}{a} = 1$.

		$\dfrac{x\quad}{\quad}\!\!\diagdown\!\!^{a}$	1	2	3	4	5	6	...	9
		1	▨	$\dfrac{20}{11}$	$\dfrac{30}{12}$	$\dfrac{40}{13}$	$\dfrac{50}{14}$	$\dfrac{60}{15}=4$		
		2	$\dfrac{20}{19}$	▨	$\dfrac{60}{21}$	$\dfrac{80}{22}$	$\dfrac{100}{23}$	$\dfrac{120}{24}=5$		
		3	$\dfrac{30}{28}$	$\dfrac{60}{29}$	▨	$\dfrac{120}{31}$	$\dfrac{150}{32}$	$\dfrac{180}{33}$		
		⋮								
		9								

The portion of the chart pictured above already generated two of the four integral values of y; that is, when $x = 1$, $a = 6$, then $y = 4$, and when $x = 2$, $a = 6$ and $y = 5$. These values yield the fractions $\dfrac{16}{64}$, and $\dfrac{26}{65}$, respectively. The remaining two integral values of y will be obtained when $x = 1$, $a = 9$, then $y = 5$; and when $x = 4$, $a = 9$, then $y = 8$. These yield the fractions $\dfrac{19}{95}$ and $\dfrac{49}{98}$, respectively. This should convince students that there are only four such fractions composed of two-digit numbers.

Students may now wonder if there are fractions composed of numerators and denominators of more than two digits, where this strange type of cancellation holds true. Have students try this type of cancellation with $\dfrac{49\not{9}}{9\not{9}8}$. They should find that, in fact,

$$\frac{499}{998} = \frac{4}{8} = \frac{1}{2}.$$

Soon they will realize that

$$\frac{49}{98} = \frac{499}{998} = \frac{4999}{9998} = \frac{49999}{99998} = \dots$$

$$\frac{16}{64} = \frac{166}{664} = \frac{1666}{6664} = \frac{16666}{66664} = \frac{166666}{666664} = \dots$$

$$\frac{19}{95} = \frac{199}{995} = \frac{1999}{9995} = \frac{19999}{99995} = \frac{199999}{999995} = \dots$$

$$\frac{26}{65} = \frac{266}{665} = \frac{2666}{6665} = \frac{26666}{66665} = \frac{266666}{666665} = \dots$$

Students with higher ability may wish to justify these extensions of the original howlers.

Students who at this point have a further desire to seek out additional fractions which permit this strange cancellation should be shown the following fractions. They should verify the legitimacy of this strange cancellation and then set out to discover more such fractions.

$$\frac{3\not{2}2}{8\not{2}0} = \frac{32}{80} = \frac{2}{5}$$

$$\frac{3\not{8}5}{8\not{8}0} = \frac{35}{80} = \frac{7}{16}$$

$$\frac{1\not{7}8}{\not{7}45} = \frac{18}{45} = \frac{2}{5}$$

$$\frac{27\not{5}}{7\not{7}0} = \frac{25}{70} = \frac{5}{14}$$

$$\frac{16\not{3}}{\not{3}2\not{6}} = \frac{1}{2}$$

$$\frac{2\not{0}3}{6\not{0}9} = \frac{1}{3}$$

Postassessment

Have students:

a. Generate a "howler" not already presented in this discussion.

b. Explain why there are only four howlers, each composed of two-digit numbers.

75   Digit Problems Revisited

Problems involving the digits of a number as presented in the elementary algebra course are usually very straightforward and somewhat dull. Often they serve merely as a source of drill for a previously taught skill. This unit shows how digit problems (perhaps somewhat "off the beaten path" in nature) can be used to improve a student's concept of numbers.

Performance Objectives
1. Students will solve problems involving the digits of a number.
2. Students will analyze a mathematical fact about the nature of certain numbers.

Preassessment
Students should be able to solve simple linear equations as well as simple simultaneous equations.

Teaching Strategies
Begin your presentation by asking your students to select any three-digit number in which the hundreds digit and units digit are unequal. Then have them write the number whose digits are in the reverse order from the selected number. Now tell them to subtract these two numbers (the smaller number from the greater one). Once again tell them to take this difference, reverse its digits and add the "new" number to the *original difference*. They *all* should end up with 1,089.

For example, suppose a student selected the number 934. The number with the digits reversed is 439. The computation would appear as:

$$\begin{array}{rl} 934 & \\ 439 & \\ \hline 495 & \text{(difference)} \\ 594 & \text{(reversed digits)} \\ \hline 1089 & \text{(sum)} \end{array}$$

When students compare results they will be amazed to discover uniformity in their answers. At this point they should be quite eager to find out why they all came up with the same result.

Begin by letting them represent the original number by $100h + 10t + u$, where h, t and u represent the hundreds, tens and units digits, respectively. Let $h > u$, which would have to be true in one of the original numbers. In subtracting, $u - h < 0$; therefore take 1 from the tens place to make the units place $10 + u$ (of the minuend).

Since the tens digits of the two numbers to be subtracted are equal, and 1 was taken from the tens digit of the minuend, then the value of this digit is $10(t - 1)$. The hundreds digit of the minuend is $h - 1$, since 1 was taken away to enable subtraction in the tens place, making the

value of the tens digit $10(t - 1) + 100 = 10(t + 9)$. Pictorially this appears as:

$$\begin{array}{lll} 100(h-1) & +10(t+9) & +(u+10) \\ 100u & +10t & +h \\ \hline 100(h-u-1) & +10(9) & +u-h+10 \end{array}$$

reversing the digits of this difference yields
$$100(u-h+10) + 10(9) + h-u-1$$
Adding the last two lines yields:
$$100(9) + 10(18) + (10-1) = 1089$$

Another problem involving the digits of a number and presenting a somewhat unusual twist follows:

Seven times a certain two-digit number equals a three-digit number. When the digit 6 is written after the last digit of the three-digit number, the three-digit number is increased by 1,833. Find the two-digit number.

The major obstacle students encounter in the solution of this problem is how to indicate placing a 6 after a number. Let students represent the two-digit number by a. Therefore the three-digit number is $7a$. Now to place a 6 after a number is to multiply the number by 10 and add the 6. The required equation is then $70a + 6 = 7a + 1833$, and $a = 29$.

To further exhibit the usefulness of working algebraically with a digital expression of a number, you may find it exciting to show students why a number is divisible by 9 (or 3) if the sum of its digits is divisible by 9 (or 3). Have them consider any five digit number, say, ab,cde, that is $10,000a + 1,000b + 100c + 10d + e$. Since this number may be rewritten as $(9,999+1)a + (999+1)b + (99+1)c + (9+1)d + e$, or $9,999a + 999b + 99c + 9d + a + b + c + d + e$, and the sum of the first four terms is divisible by 9 (or 3), the sum of the remaining terms must also be divisible by 9 (or 3). That is, in order for the number to be divisible by 9 (or 3), $a + b + c + d + e$ must be divisible by 9 (or 3).

Another digit problem with a rather nonroutine solution should now be presented. Students will find the following analysis a bit unusual.

Find the two-digit number N such that when it is divided by 4 the remainder is zero, and such that all of its positive integral powers end in the same two digits as the original number, N.

Students will naturally want to begin solving this problem by letting $N = 10t + u$. Since $10t + u = 4m$ (i.e. a multiple of 4), u is even. Ask students which even digits have squares terminating with the same digit as the original digit. Once students establish that only 0 and 6 satisfy this property, therefore $u = 0$ or 6.

The case $u = 0$ implies that $t = 0$ so that N $= 00$, a trivial case, for if $t = 0$, N will terminate in 0 while its square will terminate in 00.

Now have students consider $u = 6$. Then N $= 10t + 6 = 4m$, or $5t + 3 = 2m$. This indicates that $t = 1,3, 5,7$, or 9. But N² $= (10t + 6)^2 = 100t^2 + 120t + 36 = 100t^2 + 100d + 10e + 36$, where $120t = 100d + 10e$. Since the last two digits of N² are the same as those of N, $10e + 36 = 10t + 6$, and $t = e + 3$, so that $t \geq 3$. Also, $120t = 100d + 10(t-3)$, whereby $11t = 10d - 3$, and $11t \leq 87$, or $t \leq 7$.

Have students try $t = 3$, $36^2 = 1296$ (reject) then try $t = 5$, $56^2 = 3136$ (reject). Finally try $t = 7$, then $76^2 = 5776$ (accept since N $= 76$).

There are many other problems involving the digits of numbers which you may wish to present to your class to advance the number theory introduction which this model provided.

Postassessment

1. Show, using a digital representation of a number, that a given number is divisible by 8, if the last three digits (considered as a new number) are divisible by 8.

2. There are two numbers formed of the same two digits—one in reverse of the other. The difference between the squares of the two numbers is 7,128 and the sum of the number is 22 times the difference between the two digits. What are the two numbers?

3. By shifting the initial digit 6 of the positive integer N to the end, we obtain a number equal to ¼N. Find the smallest possible value of N that satisfies the conditions.

76   Algebraic Identities

This unit will present a geometric process for carrying out algebraic identities. With only the representation of a number by a length, and lacking sufficient algebraic notation, early Greeks devised the method of application of areas to prove these identities.

Performance Objective
Students will geometrically establish algebraic identities using the method of application of areas.

Preassessment
1. Have students expand $(a+b)^2$.
2. Have students expand $a(b+c)$.
3. Have students expand $(a-b)^2$.
4. Elicit for what values of a and b each of the above generated equalities are true.

Teaching Strategies
After students have considered questions above, they should be reacquainted with the properties of an identity. Once students understand the concept of an identity, introduce the method of application of areas by illustrating geometrically the identity $(a+b)^2 = a^2 + 2ab + b^2$. To begin, have students draw a square of side length $(a+b)$. The square should then be partitioned into various squares and rectangles. (See Figure 1) The lengths of the various sides are appropriately labeled.

Figure 1

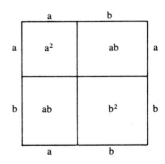

Students can easily determine the area of each region. Since the area of the large square equals the areas of the four quadrilaterals into which it was partitioned, students should get,
$(a+b)^2 = a^2 + ab + ab + b^2 = a^2 + 2ab + b^2$.
A more rigorous proof can be found in Euclid's *Elements*, Proposition 4, Book II.

Next illustrate geometrically the identity $a(b+c) = ab + ac$. To begin, have students draw a rectangle whose adjacent sides are of lengths a and $(b+c)$. The rectangle should then be partitioned into various rectangles. (See *Figure 2*) The lengths of these sides are also labeled.

Students can easily determine the area of each partition. Elicit from students that since the area of the large rectangle equals the areas of the two quadrilaterals into which it was partitioned, the diagram illustrates $a(b+c) = ab + ac$.

Figure 2

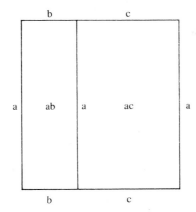

Have students consider the following identity $(a+b) \times (c+d) = ac + ad + bc + bd$. Guide students to draw the appropriate rectangle with side lengths $(a+b)$ and $(c+d)$. The rectangle should be partitioned into various rectangles. (See Figure 3) The lengths of sides and areas of regions have been labeled. As in the other cases, the area of the large rectangle equals the areas of the four quadrilaterals into which it was partitioned.

The diagram (Fig. 3) illustrates the identity $(a+b) \times (c+d) = ac + ad + bc + bd$. Explain to students that the method of application of areas can be used to prove most algebraic identities. The difficulty will lie in their choice of dimensions for the quadrilateral and the partitions made.

Figure 3

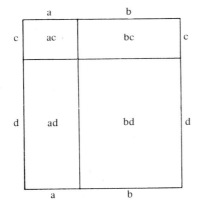

After students feel comfortable using areas to represent algebraic identities, have them consider the Pythagorean relationship, $a^2 + b^2 = c^2$. Although this is not an identity, the application of areas is still appropriate. Have students draw a square of side length $(a+b)$. Show students how to partition this square into four congruent triangles and a square. (See *Figure 4*) The lengths of the sides have been labeled.

Figure 4

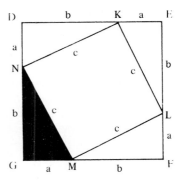

The diagram (Fig. 4) illustrates:

1. Area DEFG = 4 × (Area of $\triangle$GNM) + Area KLMN.

2. Therefore, $(a+b)^2 = 4(\frac{1}{2}ab) + c^2$

3. If we now substitute the identity for $(a+b)^2$, which was proven before, we obtain, $a^2 + 2ab + b^2 = 2ab + c^2$.

Elicit from students the remainder of the proof to conclude that $a^2 + b^2 = c^2$. Students should now be able to pose and solve geometrically their own identities.

Postassessment

1. Have students indicate how to establish the following algebraic identities geometrically.

a). $(a-b)^2 = a^2 - 2ab + b^2$

b). $a^2-b^2 = (a+b) \times (a-b)$

2. Have students determine other identities that can be proved using the method of application of areas.

77 A Method For Factoring Trinomials of the Form $ax^2 + bx + c$

This unit presents a rather unusual method for factoring, when possible, trinomials of the form $ax^2 + bx + c$, where $a, b,$ and c are integers. This technique is especially helpful when the coefficient a of $ax^2 + bx + c$ is different from 1, because in this case the usual method based on trial and error is rather tedious for most of the trinomials.

Performance Objectives
1. *Given various trinomials of the form* $ax^2 + bx + c$, *students will analyze and factor them.*
2. *Students will be able to apply this technique to the solution of quadratic equations.*

Preassessment
Students should be familiar with multiplications and factorizations of binomials and with factorizations of perfect square trinomials.

Teaching Strategies
Begin this lesson by giving several examples of multiplications of binomials: $(x + 5)(x + 2)$, $(2x - 3)(x + 1)$, $(5x - 2)(3x - 7)$, etc. Have students notice the following properties of these multiplications:

(a) They always yield trinomials of the form $ax^2 + bx + c$, where $a, b,$ and c are integers.

(b) The product of the first terms of the binomials is the first term of the trinomial.

(c) It is impossible for a to obtain the value of zero from the product of any two binomials. Thus a is always different from zero in the trinomial of the form $ax^2 + bx + c$.

Once students have practiced these multiplications, have them consider the inverse operation. That is, given trinomials of the form $ax^2 + bx + c$, have students factor them as the product of two binomials. Ask for suggestions on how to factor different trinomials; for example: $x^2 + 5x + 6$, $2x^2 - 7x - 4$, and so on. Then have students consider the factorization of the general trinomial $ax^2 + bx + c$ in the following fashion:

$$ax^2 + bx + c = \frac{a(ax^2 + bx + c)}{a} = \frac{a^2x^2 + abx + ac}{a},$$

this being possible because a is always different from zero.

If $a^2x^2 + abx + ac$ can be factored, one factorization could be: $(ax + y)(ax + z)$ where y and z are to be determined. Thus, we have:

$$ax^2 + bx + c = \frac{a^2x^2 + abx + ac}{a} = \frac{(ax + y)(ax + z)}{a}$$
$$= \frac{a^2x^2 + a(y + z)x + yz}{a}$$

If the second and fourth equalities are now compared, we notice that: $y + z = b$ and $yz = ac$. Thus, to factor a trinomial of the form $ax^2 + bx + c$, it is only necessary to express it as the product $\frac{(ax + y)(ax + z)}{a}$ where y and z can be determined by noticing that their sum must be b and their product must be ac. Also have students notice that because $\frac{(ax + y)(ax + z)}{a} = \frac{a^2x^2 + abx + ac}{a}$, it follows that the numerator is a multiple of a, and therefore, it will always be possible to cancel the constant a.

EXAMPLE 1.
Factor $5x^2 + 8x + 3$

We have $5x^2 + 8x + 3 = \frac{(5x + y)(5x + z)}{5}$ where $y + z = 8$ and $yz = (5)(3) = 15$. An analysis of the constant term 15 reveals that the possible pairs of numbers y and z whose product is 15 are: 15 and 1, -15 and -1, 5 and 3, and -5 and -3; but because their sum must be 8, the only possible combination of y and z is 5 and 3. Therefore,

$$5x^2 + 8x + 3 = \frac{(5x + 5)(5x + 3)}{5} = \frac{5(x + 1)(5x + 3)}{5}$$
$$= (x + 1)(5x + 3)$$

EXAMPLE 2.
Factor $6x^2 + 5x - 6$

We have: $(6x^2 + 5x - 6) = \frac{(6x + y)(6x + z)}{6}$, where $y + z = 5$ and $yz = (6)(-6) = -36$. An analysis of the product yz, that is, of -36 reveals that the possible pairs of numbers whose product is -36 are: 36 and -1, -36 and 1, 18 and -2, -18 and 2, 12 and -3, -12 and 3, 9 and -4, -9 and 4, and 6 and -6. But, because the algebraic sum of y and z must be $+5$, we have that the only possible combination is 9 and -4. Therefore,

$$6x^2 + 5x - 6 = \frac{(6x + 9)(6x - 4)}{6} = \frac{3(2x + 3)\,2(3x - 2)}{6}$$
$$= (2x + 3)(3x - 2)$$

If $a = 1$, we have the simpler form $x^2 + bx + c$. Thus,
$$x^2 + bx + c = \frac{(1x + y)(1x + z)}{1} = (x + y)(x + z)$$
where $y + z = b$ and $yz = c$.

EXAMPLE 3.

Factor $x^2 - 4x - 5$

We have: $x^2 - 4x - 5 = (x + y)(x + z)$ where $y + z$ is -4 and yz is -5. Thus, the possible pairs of numbers are: 5 and -1, and -5 and 1, but because the algebraic sum is -4 the only possible combination is -5 and $+1$. Therefore, $x^2 - 4x - 5 = (x - 5)(x + 1)$. This technique is also applicable to the solution of quadratic equations, that is, equations of the form $ax^2 + bx + c = 0$.

EXAMPLE 4.

Solve $2x^2 - 7x - 4 = 0$

We first factor $2x^2 - 7x - 4$. Thus, $2x^2 - 7x - 4 = \dfrac{(2x + y)(2x + z)}{2}$ where $y + z$ is -7 and yz is -8.

Because the product is -8, we find that the possible pairs are: 8 and -1, -8 and 1, 4 and -2, and -4 and 2. But because the algebraic sum is -7, the only pos-

sible combination is -8 and 1. Thus, $2x^2 - 7x - 4 = \dfrac{(2x - 8)(2x + 1)}{2} = (x - 4)(2x + 1)$. Therefore we have: $2x^2 - 7x - 4 = (x - 4)(2x + 1) = 0$ and the roots of this quadratic equation will be 4 and $-\frac{1}{2}$. It is important for students to understand that there is no guarantee that "any" given trinomials can be factored; $x^2 - 5x - 7$ and $x^3 - 5x - 6$ *cannot* be factored.

Postassessment

Students who have met the *Performance Objectives* should be able to do the following exercises:

1. Factor the following trinomials
   (a) $x^2 - 8x + 12$ (b) $4x^2 + 4x - 3$
   (c) $x^2 + 10x + 25$ (d) $3x^2 - 5x$
   (e) $2r^2 + 13r - 7$ (f) $9m^2 - 1$
2. Solve the following quadratic equations:
   (a) $x^2 - 3x - 4 = 0$
   (b) $6x^2 + x = 2$

78 Solving Quadratic Equations

This unit presents four new methods for solving quadratic equations.

Performance Objective

Students will solve a given quadratic equation in at least four different ways.

Preassessment

Students should be able to solve the equation:
$$x^2 - 7x + 12 = 0$$

Teaching Strategies

In all likelihood most of your students solved the above equation by the *Factoring* method. That is, to solve they performed the following operations:

$$x^2 - 7x + 12 = 0$$
$$(x - 3)(x - 4) = 0$$
$$x - 3 = 0 \ | \ x - 4 = 0$$
$$x = 3 \ | \ x = 4$$

This method cannot be used to solve all types of quadratic equations. If the trinomial $ax^2 + bx + c$ from the equation $ax^2 + bx + c = 0$ is not factorable, then this method cannot be used to solve the equation.

The rest of this lesson develops four new methods for solving quadratic equations.

Completing the Square

Consider the equation $ax^2 + bx + c = 0$, where a, b and c are integers and $a \neq 0$.

$$ax^2 + bx + c = x^2 + \frac{b}{a}x + \frac{c}{a} = 0$$

Add the square of one-half the coefficient of x to both sides:

$$x^2 + \frac{b}{a}x + \left(\frac{b}{2a}\right)^2 = -\frac{c}{a} + \left(\frac{b}{2a}\right)^2$$

$$\left(x + \frac{b}{2a}\right)^2 = -\frac{c}{a} + \frac{b^2}{4a^2}$$

Take the square root of both sides:

$$x + \frac{b}{2a} = \pm\sqrt{\frac{b^2 - 4ac}{4a^2}}$$

$$x = \frac{-b \pm \sqrt{b^2 - 4ac}}{2a}$$

This is the quadratic formula:

Example: Solve $x^2 - 7x + 12 = 0$

$$x^2 - 7x + \left(\frac{-7}{2}\right)^2 = -12 + \left(\frac{-7}{2}\right)^2$$

$$\left(x - \frac{7}{2}\right)^2 = -12 + \frac{49}{4} = \frac{-48 + 49}{4} = \frac{1}{4}$$

$$x - \frac{7}{2} = \pm\sqrt{\frac{1}{4}} = \pm\frac{1}{2}$$

$$x = \frac{7}{2} \pm \frac{1}{2} \qquad x = 3, 4$$

Splitting the Difference

Let x_1 and x_2 be the roots of the given equation $ax^2 + bx + c = 0$. Then $x^2 + \frac{b}{a}x + \frac{c}{a} = 0$ or

$$(x - x_1)(x - x_2) = 0$$

We know that the sum of the roots $x_1 + x_2 = \dfrac{-b}{a}$ and

that the product of the roots $x_1 x_2 = \dfrac{c}{a}$

Let $x_1 = \dfrac{-b}{2a} + N$, where N is some rational number

and $x_2 = \dfrac{-b}{2a} - N$

Then the product of the roots, $\dfrac{c}{a} = x_1 x_2 =$

$(-\dfrac{b}{2a} + N)(-\dfrac{b}{2a} - N)$

In solving for N, we get:

$$N = \pm \dfrac{\sqrt{b^2 - 4ac}}{2a}$$

Therefore the roots are $x = \dfrac{-b}{2a} \pm \dfrac{\sqrt{b^2 - 4ac}}{2a}$

Example: Solve $x^2 - 7x + 12 = 0$

Students will establish that the sum of the roots $x_1 + x_2$

$= 7$. Therefore one root must be $\dfrac{7}{2} + N$ and the other

must be $\dfrac{7}{2} - N$, where N is some rational number.

Since the produce of the roots is 12, $x_1 x_2 =$

$(\dfrac{7}{2} + N)(\dfrac{7}{2} - N) = \dfrac{49}{4} - N^2 = 12.$

Therefore $N^2 = \dfrac{1}{4}$. and $N = \pm \dfrac{1}{2}$

Thus the roots are: $x_1 = \dfrac{7}{2} + N = \dfrac{7}{2} + \dfrac{1}{2} = 4$

$x_2 = \dfrac{7}{2} - N = \dfrac{7}{2} - \dfrac{1}{2} = 3$

Method of Simultaneous Equations:

Rather than developing the general case first, we shall first solve the given equation $x^2 - 7x + 12 = 0$. This order should be easier to follow for this method.

Example: Solve $x^2 - 7x + 12 = 0$

Consider the sum and product of the roots: $x_1 + x_2 = 7$ and $x_1 x_2 = 12$

Square the sum: $(x_1 + x_2)^2 = 49$

Multiply the product by -4: $-4x_1 x_2 = -48$

By addition $(x_1 + x_2)^2 - 4x_1 x_2 = 49 - 48 = 1$

However, the left side simplifies to $(x_1 - x_2)^2$

Therefore $x_1 - x_2 = \pm \sqrt{1} = \pm 1$

Remember that $x_1 + x_2 = 7$

Now solving these equations simultaneously:

$2x_1 = 8 \quad x_1 = 4 \quad x_2 = 3$

The general case for $ax^2 + bx + c = 0$ follows:

The square of the sum of the roots,

$$(x_1 + x_2)^2 = x_1^2 + 2x_1 x_2 + x_2^2 = \dfrac{b^2}{a^2}$$

The product of the roots and -4 is:

$$-4x_1 x_2 = \dfrac{-4c}{a}$$

As above, we add these last two equations:

$$x_1^2 - 2x_1 x_2 + x_2^2 = \dfrac{b^2}{a^2} - \dfrac{4c}{a}$$

$$(x_1 - x_2)^2 = \dfrac{b^2 - 4ac}{a^2}$$

Therefore:

$$x_1 - x_2 = \pm \dfrac{\sqrt{b^2 - 4ac}}{a}$$

Since $x_1 + x_2 = \dfrac{-b}{a}$

$$x_1 \text{ or } x_2 = \dfrac{1}{2}\left(\dfrac{-b}{a} \pm \dfrac{\sqrt{b^2 - 4ac}}{a} \right)$$

$$= \dfrac{-b \pm \sqrt{b^2 - 4ac}}{2a}$$

Method of Root Reduction:

Again we start the discussion with the solution for a specific equation before considering the general form.

Example: Solve $x^2 - 7x + 12 = 0$

Let $r = x - n$, then $x = r + n$, and $x^2 = (r + n)^2 = r^2 + 2rn + n^2$

We now substitute the appropriate values in the original equation.

$(r^2 + 2rn + n^2) - 7(r + n) + 12 = 0$

$r^2 + r(2n - 7) + (n^2 - 7n + 12) = 0$

If $2n - 7 = 0$ then the r term is annihilated.

This will happen when $n = \dfrac{7}{2}$.

We then have $r^2 + (n^2 - 7n + 12) = 0$ or by substituting

$n = \dfrac{7}{2}: \quad r^2 + \left(\dfrac{49}{4} - 7(\dfrac{7}{2}) + 12 \right) = 0$

$r^2 = \dfrac{49}{4} - 12 = \dfrac{1}{4};$ and $r = \pm \dfrac{1}{2}$

Thus the roots $(x = r + n)$ are:

$x_1 = +\dfrac{1}{2} + \dfrac{7}{2} = 4 \qquad x_2 = -\dfrac{1}{2} + \dfrac{7}{2} = 3$

The general case proceeds in a similar manner. Consider the equation $ax^2 + bx + c = 0$. Let $r = x - n$, then $x = r + n$ and

$x^2 = (r + n)^2 = r^2 + 2rn + n^2$

Now substitute these values into the original equation:

$x^2 + \dfrac{bx}{a} + \dfrac{c}{a} = 0$

$(r^2 + 2rn + n^2) + \dfrac{b}{a}(r + n) + \dfrac{c}{a} = 0$

or $\quad r^2 + r(2n + \dfrac{b}{a}) + (n^2 + \dfrac{bn}{a} + \dfrac{c}{a}) = 0$

In order to annihilate the r term we let

$2n + \dfrac{b}{a} = 0$, or $n = \dfrac{-b}{2a}$

This then gives us:

$r^2 + (n^2 + \dfrac{b}{a}n + \dfrac{c}{a}) = 0$

or $\qquad r^2 = -(n^2 + \dfrac{b}{a}n + \dfrac{c}{a})$

However, since $n = \dfrac{-b}{2a}$

$$r^2 = -\left(\dfrac{b^2}{4a^2} - \dfrac{b^2}{2a^2} + \dfrac{c}{a}\right)$$

$$r^2 = \dfrac{b^2 - 4ac}{4a^2} \quad \text{and} \quad r = \pm \dfrac{\sqrt{b^2 - 4ac}}{2a}$$

Therefore, since $x = r + n$, $x = \dfrac{-b}{2a} \pm \dfrac{\sqrt{b^2 - 4ac}}{2a}$

or $\qquad x = \dfrac{-b \pm \sqrt{b^2 - 4ac}}{2a}$

Although some of these methods for solving quadratic equations are not too practical, they do offer students a better understanding of many of the underlying concepts.

Postassessment

Ask students to use at least four of the methods presented in this lesson to solve the following equations.

1. $x^2 - 11x + 30 = 0$
2. $x^2 + 3x - 28 = 0$
3. $6x^2 - x - 2 = 0$

79 The Euclidean Algorithm

This unit presents a method of introducing students to the Euclidean Algorithm for finding the greatest common divisor of two given integers.

Performance Objectives

1. Given any two integers, students will determine the greatest common divisor of the two integers, regardless of the magnitude of the two integers.

2. Having determined the greatest common divisor, the students will then be able to express the greatest common divisor in terms of the two integers.

Preassessment

Ask students how they would weigh 12 ounces, 2 ounces, 3 ounces, 4 ounces, 1 ounce and 11 ounces using only a set of two pan balance scales and some 5 and 7 ounce weights.

Teaching Strategies

Students should be able to suggest weighing the weights in the following manner:

a. **12 ounces:** Place one 5 oz. and one 7 oz. weight on the same pan, and the 12 ounces can be weighed on the other pan.

b. **2 ounces:** Place one 7 oz. weight on one pan and a 5 oz. weight on the other pan. Then the desired 2 oz. weight is that which must be placed on the pan containing the 5 oz. weight in order to balance the scales.

c. **3 ounces:** Place two 5 oz. weights on one pan and a 7 oz. weight on the other pan. The desired 3 oz. weight is that which must be added to the 7 oz. weight in order to balance the scales.

d. **4 ounces:** Place two 5 oz. weights on one pan and two 7 oz. weights on the other. The desired weight is that which must be added to the two 5 oz. weights in order to balance the scales.

e. **1 ounce:** Place three 5 oz. weights on one pan and two 7 oz. weights on the other. The desired weight is that which must be added to the two 7 oz. weights in order to balance the scales.

f. **11 ounces:** Place five 5 oz. weights on one pan and two 7 oz. weights on the other pan. The desired weight is that which must be added to the two 7 oz. weights in order to balance the scales.

Students should then be asked to weigh one ounce, two ounces, three ounces and four ounces using other combinations of given weights. They should soon be able to discover that the smallest weight which can be weighed using any combination of given weights is equal to the *greatest common divisor* of the two weights:

Given Weights	G.C.D.	Minimum Weighable
2 and 3	1	1
2 and 4	2	2
3 and 9	3	3
8 and 20	4	4
15 and 25	5	5

The greatest common divisor of A and B will be referred to as either G.C.D. of A and B or (A,B).

In order to find (945, 219) we can use the *Euclidean Algorithm*. The Euclidean Algorithm is based on a lemma which states: A and B are integers where A does not equal zero. If B is divided by A a quotient Q and remainder R is obtained $(B = QA + R)$, then $(B,A) = (A,R)$. Using the following procedure the G.C.D. of 945 and 219 can be found:

Divide 945 by 219: $945 = (4)(219) + 69$ (1)

Divide 219 by 69: $219 = (3)(69) + 12$ now   (2)
continue this process

$$69 = (5)(12) + 9 \qquad (3)$$
$$12 = (1)(9) + 3 \qquad (4)$$
$$9 = (3)(3) + 0 \dots \text{ until R}$$
equals 0.

Therefore, the G.C.D. of 945 and 219 is 3, which was the last non-zero remainder in the successive divisions. This method may be used to find (A,B) where A and B are any two integers. Have students practice this algorithm with some exercises before continuing the lesson.

For stronger students in the class (or just for your interest) a proof of this algorithm is provided. The following is a statement and proof of the *Euclidean Algorithm:*

For given non-zero integers a and b, divide a by b to get remainder r_1; divide b by r_1 to get remainder r_2. This is continued so that when remainder r_k is divided by r_{k+1} the remainder r_{k+2} is obtained. Eventually there will be an r_n such that $r_{n+1} = 0$. It follows that $|r_n|$ is the greatest common divisor of a and b.

Proof: The division algorithm will determine integers $q_1, r_1, q_2, r_2, q_3, r_3, \dots$ where

$$a = q_1 b + r_1$$
$$b = q_2 r_1 + r_2$$
$$r_1 = q_3 r_2 + r_3$$
$$\cdot$$
$$\cdot$$
$$\cdot$$

and where $0 \le \dots < r_3 < r_2 < r_1 < |b|$. There are only $|b|$ non-negative integers less than $|b|$. Therefore there must be an $r_{n+1} = 0$ for $n+1 \le |b|$. If $r_1 = 0$ then $(a, b) = b$. If $r_1 \ne 0$ then:

$$a = q_1 b + r_1$$
$$b = q_2 r_1 + r_2$$
$$r_1 = q_3 r_2 + r_3$$
$$\cdot$$
$$\cdot$$
$$\cdot$$
$$r_{n-2} = q_n r_{n-1} + r_n$$
$$r_{n-1} = q_{n+1} r_n$$

Let $d = (a,b)$. Since $d|a$, and $d|b$, then $d|r_1$. Similarly, since $d|b$ and $d|r_1$, then $d|r_2$. Again, since $d|r_1$ and $d|r_2$, then $d|r_3$. Continuing this reasoning eventually yields $d|r_{n-2}$, and $d|r_{n-1}$, then $d|r_n$.

Since $r_n \ne 0$, $r_n \mid r_{n-1}$. Also $r_n \mid r_n$; therefore $r_n|r_{n-2}$. Similarly, $r_n|r_{n-3}, r_n|r_{n-4}, \dots r_n|r_2, r_n|r_1, r_n|b$, and $r_n|a$. Since $r_n|a$ and $r_n|b$, therefore $r_n|d$. Thus, $r_n \mid d$ and $d \mid r_n$, it follows that $r_n = d$, or $r_n = (a,b)$.

At this juncture it would be nice to be able to express the G.C.D. of two integers in terms of the two integers, that is, $MA + NB = (A,B)$, where M and N are integers. In the earlier case of (945, 219), $3 = M(219) + N(945)$. By working backwards, ("up" the Euclidean Algorithm), we can accomplish the following:

From line (4) above: $3 = 12 - 9$

Substituting for 9 from line (3) above:
$$3 = 12 - (69 - 5 \cdot 12), \ 3 = 6 \cdot 12 - 69$$

Substituting for 12 from line (2):
$$3 = 6(219 - 3 \cdot 69) - 69$$

Substituting for 69 from line (1):
$$3 = 6 \cdot 219 - 19(945 - 4 \cdot 219), \text{ or}$$
$$3 = 82(219) - 19(945).$$

Earlier students have determined the minimum which can be weighed by a 945 oz. and a 219 oz. weight by finding (945, 219). Now they can also determine how many 945 oz. weights to place on one pan and how many 219 oz. to place on the other pan, by expressing (945, 219) in terms of 945 and 219. That is, they must place 82 219 oz. weights on one pan and 19 945 oz. weights on the other pan. The desired weight is that which must be added to the 19 945 oz. weights in order to balance the weights. This scheme may be used to develop an understanding of Diophantine Equations.

Postassessment

Students should be able to compute the G.C.D. of the following pairs of integers and express the G.C.D. in terms of the two integers:

1) 12 and 18   2) 52 and 86
3) 865 and 312   4) 120 and 380

80   Prime Numbers

This unit will introduce students to fascinating facts concerning prime numbers.

Performance Objectives
1. Given a number, students will use Euler's ϕ function to find the number of positive integers less than the given number that are relatively prime to it.

2. Students will explain why it is not possible for a polynomial with integral coefficients to exist that will generate only primes.

Preassessment
Ask students to identify which of the following are prime numbers:

a) 11	b) 27	c) 51
d) 47	e) 91	f) 1

Teaching Strategies
Mathematicians have spent years trying to find a general formula that would generate primes. There have been many attempts, but none have succeeded.

Have students test the expression $n^2 - n + 41$ by substituting various positive values for n. Make a chart on the chalkboard recording their findings. As they proceed they should begin to notice that as n ranges in value from 1 through 40, only prime numbers are being produced. (If they have not substituted $n = 40$, have them do so.) Then ask them to try $n = 41$. The value of $n^2 - n + 41$ is $(41)^2 - 41 + 41 = (41)^2$ which is not prime. A similar expression, $n^2 - 79n + 1601$, produces primes for all values of n up to 80. But for $n = 81$, we have $(81)^2 - 79 \cdot 81 + 1601 = 1763 = 41 \cdot 43$ which is not a prime. Students might now wonder if it is possible to have a polynomial in n with integral coefficients whose values would be primes for every positive integer n. Advise them not to try to find such an expression; Leonhard Euler (1707-1783) proved that none can exist. Euler showed that any proposed expression will produce at least one non-prime.

Euler's proof follows. First, assume that such an expression exists, being in the general form: $a + bx + cx^2 + dx^3 + \ldots$ (understanding that some of the coefficients may be zero.) Let the value of this expression be s when $x = m$. Therefore: $s = a + bm + cm^2 + dm^3 + \ldots$. Similarly, let t be the value of the expression when $x = m + ns$: $t = a + b(m + ns) + c(m + ns)^2 + d(m + ns)^3 \ldots$ This may be transformed to:
$$t = (a + bm + cm^2 + dm^3 + \ldots) + A$$
where A represents the remaining terms all of which are multiples of s. But the expression within the parentheses is, by hypothesis, equal to s. This makes the whole expression a multiple of s, and the number produced is not a prime. Every such expression will produce at least one prime, but not necessarily more than one. Consequently, no expression can generate primes exclusively.

Although this last statement was recognized early in mathematical history, mathematicians continued to conjecture about forms of numbers that generated only primes.

Pierre de Fermat (1601-1665), who made many significant contributions to the study of number theory, conjectured that all numbers of the form $F_n = 2^{2^n} + 1$, where $n = 0, 1, 2, 3, 4, \ldots$ were prime numbers. Have students find F_n for $n = 0, 1, 2$. They will see that the first three numbers derived from this expression are 3, 5, and 17. For $n = 3$, students will find that $F_n = 257$; by telling them $F_4 = 65,537$, they should notice these numbers are increasing at a very rapid rate. For $n = 5$, $F_n = 4,294,967,297$, and Fermat could not find any factor of this number. Encouraged by his results, he expressed the opinion that all numbers of this form are probably also prime. Unfortunately he stopped too soon, for in 1732, Euler showed that $F_5 = 4,294,967,297 = 641 \times 6,700,417$ (not a prime!). It was not until 150 years later that the factors of F_6 were found: $18,446,744,073,709,551,617 = 247,177 \times 67,280,421,310,721$. As far as is now known, many more numbers of this form have been found but *none* of them have been prime. It seems that Fermat's conjecture has been completely turned around, and one now wonders if any primes beyond F_4 exist.

Euler also continued further into his study of primes. He began examining those integers that are *relatively prime* (two integers are relatively prime if they have no common positive factor except 1). Have students write down the number 12 and the positive integers less than 12. Tell them to cross out 12 itself and then all the integers that have a factor greater than 1 in common with 12.

$$1\ \cancel{2}\ \cancel{3}\ \cancel{4}\ 5\ \cancel{6}\ 7\ \cancel{8}\ \cancel{9}\ \cancel{10}\ 11\ \cancel{12}$$

They will see that 1, 5, 7, 11 are the only integers remaining. Therefore, there are four positive integers less than 12 which are relatively prime to it. The number of such integers is denoted by $\phi(n)$ and is known as Euler's ϕ function. For $n = 1$, we have $\phi(n) = 1$. For $n > 1$, $\phi(n) =$ the number of positive integers less than n and relatively prime to it. Thus, as we just saw, $\phi(12) = 4$.

Let students now find values of $\phi(n)$ for n = 1, 2, 3, 4, 5. A chart, such as Figure 1 below is convenient for this.

n	integers relatively prime to and less than n	$\phi(n)$
1		1
2	1 2	1
3	1 2 3	2
4	1 2 3 4	2
5	1 2 3 4 5	4
6	1 2 3 4 5 6	2
7	prime	6
8	1 2 3 4 5 6 7 8	4
9	1 2 3 4 5 6 7 8 9	6
10	1 2 3 4 5 6 7 8 9 10	4
11	prime	10
12	1 2 3 4 5 6 7 8 9 10 11 12	4

Students should notice that when n is prime, it is not necessary to list all the numbers. Since a prime is relatively prime to all positive integers less than it, we therefore have $\phi(n) = n - 1$, for n a prime.

Have students continue to find $\phi(n)$ for $n = 6$ through 12. Looking down the $\phi(n)$ column, it does not seem that any particular pattern is emerging. We would like to, though, obtain an expression for the general term, so that $\phi(n)$ can be calculated for any number. We have already stated that if n is prime, then $\phi(n) = n - 1$. In order to discover an expression for $\phi(n)$ if n is not prime, we will look at a particular case. Let $n = 15$. Decomposing 15 into primes, we obtain $15 = 3 \cdot 5$. We can write this as $n = p \cdot q$, where $n = 15$, $p = 3$, and $q = 5$. Next, have students write down 15 and all positive integers less than 15. Have them cross out all integers having 3 (which is p) as a factor:

1 2 3̸ 4 5 6̸ 7 8 9̸ 10 11 1̸2̸ 13 14 1̸5̸

They will see that there are 5 or $5 = \frac{15}{3} = \frac{n}{p}$ of these. There are 10 numbers remaining or $10 = 15$

$- \frac{15}{3} = n - \frac{n}{p} = n \left(1 - \frac{1}{p}\right)$.

From these 10 integers, have students cross out those having 5 (which is q) as a factor:

1 2 4 5̸ 7 8 1̸0̸ 11 13 14

There are only 2 of these or $2 = \frac{1}{5}(10) = \frac{1}{q}[n(1 - \frac{1}{p})]$. There are now 8 numbers left: $8 = 10 - \frac{1}{5}(10) = n(1 - \frac{1}{p}) - \frac{1}{q}[n(1 - \frac{1}{p})]$. $n(1 - \frac{1}{p})$ is a factor of both terms of the expression. We have therefore established a formula for the number of positive integers less than n and relatively prime to it:

$$\phi(n) = n(1 - \frac{1}{p})(1 - \frac{1}{q})$$

The number n, though, might have more than 2 factors in its prime decomposition, so let us now state a more general formula (given without proof). Let the number n be decomposed into its prime factors $p, q, r, \ldots, w$. Then $n = p^a \cdot q^b \cdot r^c \cdot \ldots \cdot w^h$, where $a, b, c, \ldots, h$ are positive integers (which may or may not be all 1's). Then $\phi(n) = n(1 - \frac{1}{p})(1 - \frac{1}{q})(1 - \frac{1}{r}) \ldots (1 - \frac{1}{w})$. The teacher should also show the students that if n is a prime, the formula still holds since $\phi(n) = n - 1 = n(\frac{n-1}{n}) = n(1 - \frac{1}{n})$. To see how the formula works, work together with students in finding the following: $\phi(21), \phi(43), \phi(78)$.

Solutions: $\phi(21) = \phi(7 \cdot 3) = 21(1 - \frac{1}{7})(1 - \frac{1}{3}) = 21$

$(\frac{6}{7})(\frac{2}{3}) = 12$

$\phi(43) = 43 - 1$ (since 43 is a prime) $= 42$

$\phi(78) = \phi(2 \cdot 3 \cdot 13) = 78(1 - \frac{1}{2})(1 - \frac{1}{3})$

$(1 - \frac{1}{13}) = 78(\frac{1}{2})(\frac{2}{3})(\frac{12}{13}) = 24$

At this point, some students might have noticed that every value of $\phi(n)$ is even. Justification of this may serve as a springboard for further investigation.

Postassessment

1. Find each of the following:
a. $\phi(13)$ b. $\phi(14)$ c. $\phi(48)$ d. $\phi(73)$ e. $\phi(100)$

2. Have students explain why there is no polynomial with integral coefficients that will generate only primes.

81　　　Algebraic Fallacies

All too often students make errors in their mathematics work which are more subtle than an errors in computation or some other careless act. To prevent errors which are the results of violations of mathematical definitions of concepts, it would be wise to exhibit such flaws beforehand. This is the main mission of this unit.

Performance Objective
Given an algebraic fallacy, students will analyze and determine where the fallacy occurs in the algebraic "proof".

Preassessment
Students should be familiar with the basic algebraic operations normally taught in the high school elementary algebra course.

Teaching Strategy
When the theory behind mathematical operations is poorly understood, there exists the possibility that the operations will be applied in a formal and perhaps illogical way. Students, not aware of certain limitations on these operations, are likely to use them where they do not necessarily apply. Such improper reasoning leads to an absurd result called a fallacy. The following paradoxes will illustrate how such fallacies can arise in algebra when certain algebraic operations are performed without realizing the limitations upon those operations.

Almost everyone who has been exposed to elementary algebra will come across, at one time or another, a proof that $2 = 1$ or $1 = 3$, etc. Such a "proof" is an example of a fallacy.

"Proof":

1) Let　　　　　　　　　　　　　　　$a = b$
2) Multiply both sides by a:　　　　$a^2 = ab$
3) Subtract b^2 from both sides:　$a^2 - b^2 = ab - b^2$
4) Factoring:　　　　　　　$(a + b)(a - b) = b(a - b)$
5) Dividing both sides by $(a - b)$: $(a + b) = b$
6) Since $a = b$, then　　　　　　　$2b = b$
7) Dividing both sides by b:　　　　$2 = 1$

Ask the students to analyze the "proof" and find out where the reasoning breaks down. Of course, the trouble is in the fifth step. Since $a = b$, then $a - b = 0$. Therefore, division by zero was performed, which is *not permissible*. It would be appropriate at this time to discuss what division means in terms of multiplication. To divide a by b implies that there exists a number y such that $b \cdot y = a$, or $y = \dfrac{a}{b}$. If $b = 0$, there are two

possibilities, either $a \neq 0$ or $a = 0$. If $a \neq 0$, then $y = \dfrac{a}{0}$ or $0 \cdot y = a$. Ask your students if they can find a number which when multiplied by zero will equal a. Your students should conclude that there is no such number y. In the second case, where $a = 0$, $y = \dfrac{0}{0}$ or $0 \cdot y = 0$. Here any number for y will satisfy the equation, hence any number multiplied by zero is zero. Therefore we have the "rule" that division by zero is not permissible. There are other fallacies based on division by zero. Have your students discover for themselves where and how the difficulty occurs in each of the following examples.

1) To "prove" that any two unequal numbers are equal. Assume that $x = y + z$, and x, y, z are positive numbers. This implies $x > y$. Multiply both sides by $x - y$. Then $x^2 - xy = xy + xz - y^2 - yz$. Subtract xz from both sides:

$$x^2 - xy - xz = xy - y^2 - yz$$

Factoring, we get $x(x - y - z) = y(x - y - z)$. Dividing both sides by $(x - y - z)$ yields $x = y$. Thus x, which was assumed to be greater than y, has been shown to equal y. The fallacy occurs in the division by $(x - y - z)$, which is equal to zero.

2) To "prove" that all positive whole numbers are equal. By doing long division, we have, for any value of x

$$\frac{x - 1}{x - 1} = 1$$

$$\frac{x^2 - 1}{x - 1} = x + 1$$

$$\frac{x^3 - 1}{x - 1} = x^2 + x + 1$$

$$\frac{x^4 - 1}{x - 1} = x^3 + x^2 + x + 1$$

$$\vdots$$

$$\frac{x^n - 1}{x - 1} = x^{n-1} + x^{n-2} + \ldots + x^2 + x + 1$$

Letting $x = 1$ in all of these identities, the right side then assumes the values $1, 2, 3, 4, \ldots, n$. The left side members are all the same. Consequently, $1 = 2 = 3 = 4 = \ldots = n$. In this example, the left-hand side of each of the identities assumes the value $\dfrac{0}{0}$ when $x = 1$. This problem serves as evidence that $\dfrac{0}{0}$ can be any number.

Consider the following, and ask your students if they would agree with the following statement, "If two fractions are equal and have equal numerators, then they also have equal denominators." Let the students give illustrations using any fractions they choose. Then have them solve the following equation.

$$6 + \frac{8x - 40}{4 - x} = \frac{2x - 16}{12 - x} \qquad (1)$$

Add terms on the left-hand side, to get

$$\frac{6(4 - x) + 8x - 40}{4 - x} = \frac{2x - 16}{12 - x} \qquad (2)$$

Simplifying: $\dfrac{2x - 16}{4 - x} = \dfrac{2x - 16}{12 - x}$

Since the numerators are equal, this implies $4 - x = 12 - x$. Adding x to both sides, $4 = 12$. Again, as in some of the previous examples, the division by zero is disguised. Have students find the error. It should be pointed out that the axioms cannot be blindly applied to equations without considering the values of the variables for which the equations are true. Thus, equation (1) is not an identity true for all values of x, but it is satisfied only by $x = 8$. Have students solve $(12 - x)(2x - 16) = (4 - x) \times (2x - 16)$ to verify this. Thus $x = 8$, implies that the numerators are zero. You may also have the students prove the general case for $\dfrac{a}{b} = \dfrac{a}{c}$, to show that a cannot be zero.

Another class of fallacies includes those which neglect to consider that a quantity has two square roots of equal absolute value; however one is positive and the other is negative. As an example, take the equation $16 - 48 = 64 - 96$. Adding 36 to both sides gives $16 - 48 + 36 = 64 - 96 + 36$. Each member of the equation is now a perfect square, so that $(4 - 6)^2 = (8 - 6)^2$. Taking the square root of both sides, we get $4 - 6 = 8 - 6$, which implies $4 = 8$. Ask the students where the fallacy occurs. The fallacy in this example lies in taking the improper square root. The correct answer should be $(4 - 6) = -(8 - 6)$.

The following fallacies are based upon the failure to consider all the roots of a given example.

Have students solve the equation $x + 2\sqrt{x} = 3$ in the usual manner. The solutions are $x = 1$ and $x = 9$. The first solution satisfies the equation, while the second solution does not. Have students explain where the difficulty lies.

A similar equation is $x - a = \sqrt{x^2 + a^2}$. By squaring both sides and simplifying we get $-2ax = 0$, or $x = 0$. Substituting $x = 0$ in the original equation, we find that this value of x does not satisfy the equation. Have the students find the correct root of the given equation.

So far we have dealt with square roots of positive numbers. Ask the students what happens when we apply our usual rules to radicals containing imaginary numbers, in light of the following problem. The students have learned that $\sqrt{a} \cdot \sqrt{b} = \sqrt{ab}$, for example, $\sqrt{2} \cdot \sqrt{5} = \sqrt{2 \cdot 5} = \sqrt{10}$. But this gives then, $\sqrt{-1} \cdot \sqrt{-1} = \sqrt{(-1)(-1)} = \sqrt{1} = 1$. However $\sqrt{-1} \cdot \sqrt{-1} = (\sqrt{-1})^2 = -1$. It therefore may

be concluded that $1 = -1$, since both equal $\sqrt{-1} \times \sqrt{-1}$. Students should try to explain the error. They should realize that we cannot apply the ordinary rules for multiplication of radicals to imaginary numbers.

Another proof that can be used to show $-1 = +1$ is the following:

$$\sqrt{-1} = \sqrt{-1}$$
$$\sqrt{\frac{1}{-1}} = \sqrt{\frac{-1}{1}}$$
$$\frac{\sqrt{1}}{\sqrt{-1}} = \frac{\sqrt{-1}}{\sqrt{1}}$$
$$\sqrt{1} \cdot \sqrt{1} = \sqrt{-1} \cdot \sqrt{-1}$$
$$1 = -1$$

Have students replace i for $\sqrt{-1}$, and -1 for i^2 to see where the flaw occurs.

Before concluding the topic on algebraic fallacies, it would be appropriate to consider a fallacy involving simultaneous equations. The students, by now, should realize that in doing the preceding proofs a certain law or operation was violated. Consider an example where hidden flaws in equations can bring about ludicrous results. Have students solve the following pairs of equations by substituting for x in the first equation:

$2x + y = 8$ and $x = 2 - \dfrac{y}{2}$. The result will be $4 = 8$.

Have students find the error. When students graph these two equations, they will find the two lines to be parallel and therefore have *no* points in common.

Further exhibition of such fallacies will prove a worthwhile activity due to the intrinsically dramatic message they carry.

Postassessment

Have students determine where and how the fallacy occurs in the following examples.

1) a. $x = 4$
   b. $x^2 = 16$
   c. $x^2 - 4x = 16 - 4x$
   d. $x(x - 4) = 4(4 - x)$
   e. $x(x - 4) = -4(x - 4)$
   f. $x = -4$

2) a. $(y + 1)^2 = y^2 + 2y + 1$
   b. $(y + 1)^2 - (2y + 1) = y^2$
   c. $(y + 1)^2 - (2y + 1) - y(2y + 1) = y^2 - y(2y + 1)$
   d. $(y + 1)^2 - (y + 1)(2y + 1) + \dfrac{1}{4}(2y + 1)^2 =$
      $y^2 - y(2y + 1) + \dfrac{1}{4}(2y + 1)^2$
   e. $\left[(y + 1) - \dfrac{1}{2}(2y + 1) \right]^2 = \left[y - \dfrac{1}{2}(2y + 1) \right]^2$
   f. $y + 1 - \dfrac{1}{2}(2y + 1) = y - \dfrac{1}{2}(2y + 1)$
   g. $y + 1 = y$

82 Sum Derivations with Arrays

Performance Objectives

(1) *Students will derive the formula for the sum of the first* n *natural numbers, triangular numbers, square numbers, or pentagonal numbers.*

(2) *Given any integral value of* n, *students will apply the proper formula to find the sum of the first* n *figurate numbers.*

Preassessment

Before beginning this lesson, be sure students are familiar with the meanings of *figurate numbers* and *formation of sequences of figurate numbers.* They should also have some knowledge of elementary algebra.

Teaching Strategies

To begin to familiarize students with this topic, have them construct dot arrays on graph paper to illustrate the first few terms in the sequences of various figurate numbers.

Natural numbers

1   2   3   4   5

Triangular numbers

1   3   6   10   15

Square numbers

1   4   9   16   25

Pentagonal numbers

1   5   12   22   35

Discuss with the class the visual relationships. Most students will clearly see that we can represent the sum of the first n natural numbers as follows:

N_n = Sum of the first n natural numbers

= $1 + 2 + 3 + \ldots + n$

= $1 + (1+1) + (1+1+1) + \ldots + (1+1+ \ldots +1)$

n

N_n can also be represented as the sum of the numbers in an array:

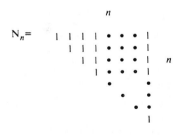

By switching the rows with the columns, N_n can be made to look slightly different:

N_n =

n

n

These two representations of N_n in array form can now be combined to produce an array for $2N_n$ as shown below:

$2N_n$ =

$(n+1)$

n

Students can distinctly see that $2N_n = n(n+1)$ from an inspection of the array for $2N_n$. We therefore have:

$$N_n = \frac{n(n+1)}{2}$$

This resulting formula for N_n can be applied whenever it is required to find the sum of the first n natural numbers.

Have students consider trying to derive a formula for the first n triangular numbers. Clearly, from the dot arrays presented earlier, the following can be established:

T_n = Sum of the first n triangular numbers

= $1 + 3 + 6 + \ldots + N_n$

= $1 + (1+2) + (1+2+3) + \ldots + (1+2+3+ \ldots +n)$

T_n can now be represented as the sum of the numbers in an array:

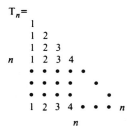

By applying the previously determined formula for **N** to each row of this array we obtain:

$$T_n = \frac{1(1+1)}{2}$$
$$+ \frac{2(1+2)}{2}$$
$$+ \frac{3(1+3)}{2}$$
$$+ \frac{4(1+4)}{2}$$
$$+ \ldots$$
$$+ \frac{n(1+n)}{2}$$

Students should now see that:

$2T_n = 1(2) + 2(3) + 3(4) + 4(5) + \ldots + n(n+1)$

which can be represented in a very convenient form as the sum of the numbers in an array:

$$2T_n = \begin{array}{cccccccc} & 2 & 3 & 4 & 5 & \bullet & \bullet & \bullet & (n+1) \\ & & 3 & 4 & 5 & \bullet & \bullet & \bullet & (n+1) \\ & & & 4 & 5 & \bullet & \bullet & \bullet & (n+1) \\ & & & & 5 & \bullet & \bullet & \bullet & (n+1) \quad n \\ & & & & & \bullet & & & \bullet \\ & & & & & & \bullet & & \bullet \\ & & & & & & & \bullet & \bullet \\ & & & & & & & & (n+1) \end{array}$$

The combination of the array for T_n and the array for $2T_n$ produces an array for $3T_n$ which is easy to sum up:

$$3T_n = \begin{array}{c} \qquad\qquad (n+1) \\ \begin{array}{ccccccccc} 1 & 2 & 3 & 4 & 5 & \bullet & \bullet & \bullet & (n+1) \\ 1 & 2 & 3 & 4 & 5 & \bullet & \bullet & \bullet & (n+1) \\ 1 & 2 & 3 & 4 & 5 & \bullet & \bullet & \bullet & (n+1) \\ 1 & 2 & 3 & 4 & 5 & \bullet & \bullet & \bullet & (n+1) \quad n \\ \bullet & \bullet & \bullet & \bullet & \bullet & & & & \bullet \\ \bullet & \bullet & \bullet & \bullet & & & & \bullet & \\ \bullet & \bullet & \bullet & & & & \bullet & & \bullet \\ 1 & 2 & 3 & 4 & \bullet & \bullet & \bullet & n & (n+1) \end{array} \end{array}$$

Our formula for N_n directly yields

$$3T_n = n \frac{(n+1)\ (1+[n+1])}{2}$$

$$\boxed{T_n = \frac{n(n+1)\ (n+2)}{6}}$$

Students are now ready to consider the sum of the first n square numbers.

$S_n =$ Sum of the first n square numbers
$= 1^2 + 2^2 + 3^2 + 4^2 + \ldots + n^2$

In array form this appears as:

$$S_n = \begin{array}{c} \qquad\qquad n \\ \begin{array}{cccccccc} 1 & 2 & 3 & 4 & \bullet & \bullet & \bullet & n \\ & 2 & 3 & 4 & \bullet & \bullet & \bullet & n \\ & & 3 & 4 & \bullet & \bullet & \bullet & n \\ & & & 4 & \bullet & \bullet & \bullet & n \quad n \\ & & & & \bullet & & \bullet & \\ & & & & & \bullet & \bullet & \\ & & & & & & \bullet & \\ & & & & & & & n \end{array} \end{array}$$

Combining the array for T_n with this array for S_n, we obtain an array for $S_n + T_n$:

$$S_n + T_n = \begin{array}{c} \qquad\qquad n \\ \begin{array}{ccccccccc} 1 & 2 & 3 & 4 & \bullet & \bullet & \bullet & n \\ 1 & 2 & 3 & 4 & \bullet & \bullet & \bullet & n \\ 1 & 2 & 3 & 4 & \bullet & \bullet & \bullet & n \\ 1 & 2 & 3 & 4 & \bullet & \bullet & \bullet & n \quad (n+1) \\ 1 & 2 & 3 & 4 & & & \bullet & \\ \bullet & \bullet & \bullet & \bullet & & & & \bullet \\ \bullet & \bullet & \bullet & & & & \bullet & n \\ 1 & 2 & 3 & 4 & \bullet & \bullet & \bullet & n \end{array} \end{array}$$

Students should observe that each row of the array for $S_n + T_n$ is the sum of the first n natural numbers. In the present notation, this is N_n. Since the array has $(n+1)$ rows, we clearly obtain

$$S_n + T_n = (n+1)N_n.$$

Substituting the formulas previously derived for T_n and N_n is an exercise in elementary algebra which quickly yields

$$\boxed{S_n = \frac{n(n+1)\ (2n+1)}{6}}$$

Postassessment

To measure students' attainment of the performance objective, have each student:

(1) Derive a formula for the sum of the first n pentagonal numbers using arrays.

(2) Apply the various formulas the class has derived to find the sum of the first n figurate numbers for several integral values of n.

83 Pythagorean Triples

While teaching the Pythagorean Theorem at the secondary school level, teachers often suggest that students recognize (and memorize) certain common ordered sets of three numbers which can represent the lengths of the sides of a right triangle. Some of these ordered sets of three numbers, known as Pythagorean triples, are: (3, 4, 5), (5, 12, 13), (8, 15, 17), (7, 24, 25). The student is asked to discover these Pythagorean triples as they come up in selected exercises. How can one generate more triples without a trial and error method? This question, often asked by students, will be answered in this unit.

Performance Objectives

1. *Students will generate six primitive Pythagorean triples using the formulas developed in this unit.*
2. *Students will state properties of various members of a primitive Pythagorean triple.*

Preassessment

Students should be familiar with the Pythagorean Theorem. They should be able to recognize Pythagorean triples and distinguish between primitive Pythagorean triples and others.

Teaching Strategies

Ask your students to find the missing member of the following Pythagorean triples:

1. (3, 4, ____)
2. (7, ____, 25)
3. (11, ____, ____)

The first two triples can be easily determined using the Pythagorean Theorem. However, this method will not work with the third triple. At this point you can offer your students a method for solving this problem. This is the topic of this unit.

Before beginning the development of the desired formulas, we must consider a few simple lemmas.

Lemma 1: When 8 divides the square of an odd number, the remainder is 1.

Proof: We can represent an odd number by $2k + 1$, where k is an integer.
$$(2k + 1)^2 = 4k^2 + 4k + 1 = 4k(k + 1) + 1$$
Since k and $k+1$ are consecutive, one of them must be even. Therefore $4k(k+1)$ must be divisible by 8.
Thus $(2k + 1)^2$, when divided by 8, leaves a remainder of 1.

The following lemmas follow directly.

Lemma 2: When 8 divides the sum of two odd square numbers, the remainder is 2.

Lemma 3: The sum of two odd square numbers cannot be a square number.

Proof: Since the sum of two odd square numbers, when divided by 8, leaves a remainder of 2, the sum is even but not divisible by 4. It therefore cannot be a square number.

We are now ready to begin our development of formulas for Pythagorean triples. Let us assume that (a, b, c) is a primitive Pythagorean triple. This implies that a and b are relatively prime. Therefore they cannot both be even. Can they both be odd?

If a and b are both odd, then by Lemma 3: $a^2 + b^2 \neq c^2$. This contradicts our assumption that (a, b, c) is a Pythagorean triple; therefore a and b cannot both be odd. Therefore one must be odd and one even.

Let us suppose that a is odd and b is even. This implies that c is also odd.

We can rewrite $a^2 + b^2 = c^2$ as
$$b^2 = c^2 - a^2$$
$$b^2 = (c + a) \cdot (c - a)$$

Since the sum and difference of two odd numbers is even,

$c + a = 2p$, and $c - a = 2q$ (p and q are natural numbers).

By solving for a and c we get:
$$c = p + q, \quad \text{and} \quad a = p - q$$

We can now show that p and q must be relatively prime. Suppose p and q were not relatively prime; say $g > 1$ was a common factor. Then g would also be a common factor of a and c. Similarly g would also be a common factor of $c + a$ and $c - a$. This would make g^2 a factor of b^2, since $b^2 = (c + a) \cdot (c - a)$. It follows that g would then have to be a factor of b. Now if g is a factor of b and also a common factor of a and c, then $a, b,$ and c are not relatively prime. This contradicts our assumption that (a, b, c) is a *primitive* Pythagorean triple. Thus p and q must be relatively prime.

Since b is even, we may represent b as
$$b = 2r$$
But $b^2 = (c + a)(c - a)$.

Therefore $b^2 = (2p) \cdot (2q) = 4r^2$, or $pq = r^2$

If the product of two relatively prime natural numbers (p and q) is the square of a natural number (r), then each of them must be the square of a natural number. Therefore we let

$$p = m^2 \quad \text{and} \quad q = n^2$$

where m and n are natural numbers. Since they are factors of relatively prime numbers (p and q), they (m and n) are also relatively prime.

Since $a = p - q$ and $c = p + q$
$\quad\quad a = m^2 - n^2$ and $c = m^2 + n^2$

Also, since $b = 2r$ and $b^2 = 4r^2 = 4pq = 4m^2n^2$
$\quad\quad b = 2mn$

To summarize we now have formulas for generating Pythagorean triples:

$$a = m^2 - n^2 \quad\quad b = 2mn \quad\quad c = m^2 + n^2$$

The numbers m and n cannot both be even, since they are relatively prime. They cannot both be odd, for this would make $c = m^2 + n^2$ an even number, which we established earlier as impossible. Since this indicates that one must be even and the other odd, $b = 2mn$ must be divisible by 4. Therefore no Pythagorean triple can be composed of three prime numbers. This does *not* mean that the other members of the Pythagorean triple may not be prime.

Let us reverse the process for a moment. Consider relatively prime numbers m and n (where $m > n$) and where is even and the other odd. We will now show that (a, b, c) is a primitive Pythagorean triple where $a = m^2 - n^2$, $b = 2mn$ and $c = m^2 + n^2$.

It is simple to verify algebraically that

$$(m^2 - n^2)^2 + (2mn)^2 = (m^2 + n^2)^2$$

thereby making it a Pythagorean triple. What remains is to prove that (a, b, c) is a *primitive* Pythagorean triple.

Suppose a and b have a common factor $h > 1$. Since a is odd, h must also be odd. Because $a^2 + b^2 = c^2$, h would also be a factor of c. We also have h a factor of $m^2 - n^2$ and $m^2 + n^2$ as well as of their sum, $2m^2$, and their difference $2n^2$.

Since h is odd, it is a common factor of m^2 and n^2. However m and n (and as a result m^2 and n^2) are relatively prime. Therefore h cannot be a common factor of m and n. This contradiction establishes that a and b are relatively prime.

Having finally established a method for generating primitive Pythagorean triples, students should be eager to put it to use. The table below gives some of the smaller primitive Pythagorean triples

Pythagorean Triples

m	n	a	b	c
2	1	3	4	5
3	2	5	12	13
4	1	15	8	17
4	3	7	24	25
5	2	21	20	29
5	4	9	40	41
6	1	35	12	37
6	5	11	60	61
7	2	45	28	53
7	4	33	56	65
7	6	13	84	85

A fast inspection of the above table indicates that certain primitive Pythagorean triples (a, b, c) have $c = b + 1$. Have students discover the relationship between m and n for these triples.

They should notice that for these triples $m = n + 1$. To prove this will be true for other primitive Pythagorean triples (not in the table), let $m = n + 1$ and generate the Pythagorean triples.

$$a = m^2 - n^2 = (n + 1)^2 - n^2 = 2n + 1$$
$$b = 2mn = 2n(n + 1) = 2n^2 + 2n$$
$$c = m^2 + n^2 = (n + 1)^2 + n^2 = 2n^2 + 2n + 1$$

Clearly $c = b + 1$, which was to be shown!

A natural question to ask your students is to find all primitive Pythagorean triples which are consecutive natural numbers. In a method similar to that used above, they ought to find that the only triple satisfying that condition is (3, 4, 5).

Other investigations can be proposed for student consideration. In any case students should have a far better appreciation for Pythagorean triples and elementary number theory after completing this unit.

Postassessment

1. Find six primitive Pythagorean triples which are not included in the above table.

2. Find a way to generate primitive Pythagorean triples of the form (a, b, c) where $b = a + 1$.

3. Prove that every primitive Pythagorean triple has one member which is divisible by 3.

4. Prove that every primitive Pythagorean triple has one member which is divisible by 5.

5. Prove that for every primitive Pythagorean triple the product of its members is a multiple of 60.

6. Find a Pythagorean triple (a, b, c) where $a^2 = b + 2$.

84 Divisibility

The unit will present methods for finding divisors without doing division.

Performance Objectives
1. Given any integer, students will determine its prime factors, without doing any division.

2. Students will produce rules for testing divisibility by all natural numbers less than 49, and some greater than 49.

Preassessment
Have students indicate without doing any division which of the following numbers are divisible by 2, by 3, and by 5.

a) 792   b) 835   c) 356   d) 3890   e) 693   f) 743

Teaching Strategies
Students are probably aware that any even number is divisible by 2; hence of the above numbers, a, c, and d are divisible by 2. Many will also recognize that a number whose terminal digit (units digit) is either 5 or 0, is divisible by 5; hence, b and d are divisible by 5. At this point students will be eager to extend this rule to hold true for testing divisibility by 3. Of the above numbers, c, e, and f are the only numbers whose terminal digit is a multiple of 3; yet only one of these numbers, 693, is in fact divisible by 3. This should stir up sufficient curiosity so as to create a desire among the students to develop rules to test divisibility by numbers other than 2 and 5.

There are various ways to develop rules for testing divisibility by various numbers. They may be developed in order of magnitude of the numbers. This method may be appealing to some; however it detracts from the various patterns which students so often appreciate in the development of mathematics. In this unit we shall consider the rules in groups of related methods.

Divisibility by powers of 2: *A given number is divisible by 2^1 (or 2^2, 2^3, . . . 2^n, respectively) if the last 1 (or 2, 3, . . . n, respectively) digit(s) is (are) divisible by 2^1 (or 2^2, 2^3, . . . 2^n, respectively).*

Proof: Consider the following *n*-digit number:
$$a_{n-1}a_{n-2}a_{n-3} \ldots a_2 a_1 a_0$$
which can be written as:
$$10^{n-1}a_{n-1} + 10^{n-2}a_{n-2} + \ldots + 10^2 a_2 + 10^1 a_1 + 10^0 a_0$$
Since all terms except the last are always divisible by 2, we must be assured of the divisibility of the last term when testing divisibility by 2. Similarly, since all the terms except the last two are always divisible by 2^2, we must merely determine if the last two digits (considered as a number) is divisible by 2^2. This scheme may easily be extended to the nth case.

Divisibility by powers of 5: *A given number is divisible by 5^1 (or 5^2, 5^3, . . . 5^n, respectively) if the last 1 (or 2, 3, . . . n, respectively) digit(s) is (are) divisible by 5^1 (or 5^2, 5^3, . . . 5^n, respectively).*

Proof: The proof of these rules follows the same scheme as the proof for testing divisibility by powers of two, except the 2 is replaced by a 5.

Divisibility by 3 and 9: *A given number is divisible by 3 (or 9) if the sum of the digits is divisible by 3 (or 9).*

Proof: Consider the number $a_8 a_7 a_6 a_5 a_4 a_3 a_2 a_1 a_0$ (the general case $a_n a_{n-1} \ldots a_3 a_2 a_1 a_0$ is similar). This expression may be written as $a_8(9 + 1)^8 + a_7(9 + 1)^7 + \ldots + a_1(9 + 1) + a_0$. Using the expression $M_i(9)$ to mean a multiple of 9, for $i = 1, 2, 3, \ldots, 7, 8$, we can rewrite the number as:
$$a_8[M_8(9) + 1] + a_7[M_7(9) + 1] + \ldots + a_1[M_1(9) + 1] + a_0$$
(A mention of the binomial theorem may be helpful here.) The number equals $M(9) + a_8 + a_7 + a_6 + a_5 + a_4 + a_3 + a_2 + a_1 + a_0$, where $M(9)$ is a multiple of 9. Thus the number is divisible by 9 (or 3) if the sum of the digits is divisible by 9 (or 3).

A rule for testing divisibility by 11 is proved in a manner similar to the proof for divisibility by 3 and 9.

Divisibility by 11: *A given number is divisible by 11 if the difference of the two sums of alternate digits is divisible by 11.*

Proof: Consider the number $a_8 a_7 a_6 a_5 a_4 a_3 a_2 a_1 a_0$ (using the general case is similar). This expression may be written as:
$$a_8(11-1)^8 + a_7(11-1)^7 + \ldots + a_1(11-1) + a_0$$
$$= a_8[M_8(11) + 1] + a_7[M_7(11) - 1] + \ldots + a_1[M_1(11) - 1] + a_0$$
This expression then equals $M(11) + a_8 - a_7 + a_6 - a_5 + a_4 - a_3 + a_2 - a_1 + a_0$. Thus the number is divisible by 11 if $a_8 + a_6 + a_4 + a_2 + a_0 - (a_7 + a_5 + a_3 + a_1)$ is divisible by 11.

You would be wise to indicate the extensions in bases other than ten of each of the previously mentioned divisibility rules. Often students are able to make these generalizations on their own (especially with appropriate coaxing). The remainder of this Model will deal with rules for testing divisibility of primes ≥ 7 and composites.

Divisibility by 7: *Delete the last digit from the given number, then subtract* twice *this deleted digit from the remaining number. If the result is divisible by 7, the original number is divisible by 7. This process may be repeated if the result is too large for simple inspection of divisibility by 7.*

Proof: To justify the technique, consider the various possible terminal digits and the corresponding subtraction:

Terminal digit	Number subtracted from original	Terminal digit	Number subtracted from original
1	$20 + 1 = 21 = 3 \cdot 7$	5	$100 + 5 = 105 = 15 \cdot 7$
2	$40 + 2 = 42 = 6 \cdot 7$	6	$120 + 6 = 126 = 18 \cdot 7$
3	$60 + 3 = 63 = 9 \cdot 7$	7	$140 + 7 = 147 = 21 \cdot 7$
4	$80 + 4 = 84 = 12 \cdot 7$	8	$160 + 8 = 168 = 24 \cdot 7$
		9	$180 + 9 = 189 = 27 \cdot 7$

In each case a multiple of 7 is being subtracted one or more times from the original number. Hence, if the remaining number is divisible by 7, then so is the original number.

Divisibility by 13: *This is the same as the rule for testing divisibility by 7, except that the 7 is replaced by 13 and instead of subtracting* twice *the deleted digit, we subtract* nine times *the deleted digit each time.*

Proof: Once again consider the various possible terminal digits and the corresponding subtraction:

Terminal digit	Number subtracted from original	Terminal digit	Number subtracted from original
1	$90 + 1 = 91 = 7 \cdot 13$	5	$450 + 5 = 455 = 35 \cdot 13$
2	$180 + 2 = 182 = 14 \cdot 13$	6	$540 + 6 = 546 = 42 \cdot 13$
3	$270 + 3 = 273 = 21 \cdot 13$	7	$630 + 7 = 637 = 49 \cdot 13$
4	$360 + 4 = 364 = 28 \cdot 13$	8	$720 + 8 = 728 = 56 \cdot 13$
		9	$810 + 9 = 819 = 63 \cdot 13$

In each case a multiple of 13 is being subtracted one or more times from the original number. Hence, if the remaining number is divisible by 13, then the original number is divisible by 13.

Divisibility by 17: *This is the same as the rule for testing divisibility by 7 except that the 7 is replaced by 17 and instead of subtracting* twice *the deleted digit, we subtract* five times *the deleted digit each time.*

Proof: The proof for the rule for divisibility by 17 follows a similar pattern to those for 7 and 13.

The patterns developed in the preceding three divisibility rules (for 7, 13, and 17) should lead students to develop similar rules for testing divisibility by larger primes. The following chart presents the "multipliers" of the deleted digits for various primes.

To test divisibility by	7	11	13	17	19	23	29	31	37	41	43	47
Multiplier	2	1	9	5	17	16	26	3	11	4	30	14

To fill in the gaps in the set of integers, a consideration of divisibility of composites is necessary.

Divisibility by composites: *A given number is divisible by a composite number if it is divisible by each of its relatively prime factors.* The chart below offers illustrations of this rule. You or your students should complete the chart to 48.

To be divisible by	6	10	12	15	18	21	24	26	28
The number must be divisible by	2,3	2,5	3,4	3,5	2,9	3,7	3,8	2,13	4,7

At this juncture the student has not only a rather comprehensive list of rules for testing divisibility, but also an interesting insight into elementary number theory. Have students practice using these rules (to instill greater familiarity) and try to develop rules to test divisibility by other numbers in base ten and to generalize these rules to other bases. Unfortunately lack of space prevents a more detailed development here.

Postassessment

Students who have met the performance objectives should be able to do these exercises.

1. State a rule for testing divisibility by
   a) 8   b) 18   c) 13   d) 23   e) 24   f) 42
2. Determine the prime factors of
   a) 280   b) 1001   c) 495   d) 315   e) 924

Further references on this topic may be found in:

Posamentier, Alfred S. *A Study Guide for the Mathematics Section of the Scholastic Aptitude Test,* Boston, Mass.: Allyn & Bacon, 1983.

Posamentier, Alfred S., and Charles T. Salkind. *Challenging Problems in Algebra.* Palo Alto, CA: Dale Seymour, 1988.

Posamentier, Alfred S., and Charles T. Salkind. *Challenging Problems in Geometry.* Palo Alto, CA: Dale Seymour, 1988.

85   Fibonacci Sequence

Performance Objectives
Students will:
1. *define the Fibonacci Sequence.*
2. *find sums of various Fibonacci numbers.*
3. *find the sum of squares of the first Fibonacci numbers.*
4. *discover properties of Fibonacci numbers.*

Preassessment
Have students try to solve the following problem:
How many pairs of rabbits will be produced in a year, beginning with a single pair, if in one month each pair bears a new pair which becomes productive from the second month on?

Teaching Strategies
Italian mathematician Leonardo of Pisa (he was the son, figlio, of Bonaccio, hence the name Fibonacci) presented the above problem in his book *LIBER ABACI* published in 1202. Consider its solution with students. Begin by drawing a chart as pictured below.

Figure 1

let A = Adult pairs, B = Baby pairs

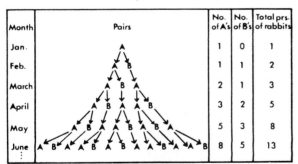

Month	Pairs	No. of A's	No. of B's	Total prs. of rabbits
Jan.		1	0	1
Feb.		1	1	2
March		2	1	3
April		3	2	5
May		5	3	8
June		8	5	13

Start with first month and proceed to the next months explaining the procedure as you go along. Remind students that a baby pair must mature one month before becoming productive.

Continue the chart until the twelfth month where it will be discovered that 377 pairs of rabbits are produced in a year. Now focus students' attention on the third column (Number of A), the Fibonacci Sequence. Have them try to discover a rule for continuing this sequence. Tell students to notice that each term is the sum of the two preceding terms. This can be written as a general expression: $f_n = f_{n-1} + f_{n-2}$, where f_n stands for the nth Fibonacci number. For example, $f_3 = f_1 + f_2$; $f_4 = f_2 + f_3$; $f_7 = f_5 + f_6$. Also $f_1 = f_2 = 1$.

The Fibonacci Sequence has many interesting properties that students can observe by studying the relationships between the terms. It can be proved that the sum of the first n Fibonacci numbers, $f_1 + f_2 + \ldots + f_n = f_{n+2} - 1$ (A)

It has already been noted that the following relations hold: $f_1 = f_3 - f_2$ (since $f_3 = f_1 + f_2$)
$$f_2 = f_4 - f_3$$
$$f_3 = f_5 - f_4$$
.
.
$$f_{n-1} = f_{n+1} - f_n$$
$$f_n = f_{n+2} - f_{n+1}$$

By *termwise* addition of all these equations it follows that $f_1 + f_2 + f_3 + \ldots + f_n = f_{n+2} - f_2$, but we know that $f_2 = 1$. Therefore $f_1 + f_2 + f_3 + \ldots + f_n = f_{n+2} - 1$.

In a similar manner we can find an expression for the sum of the first n Fibonacci numbers with odd indices: $f_1 + f_3 + f_5 + \ldots + f_{2n-1} = f_{2n}$ (B)
To do this we write:
$$f_1 = f_2$$
$$f_3 = f_4 - f_2 \text{ (since } f_4 = f_2 + f_3)$$
$$f_5 = f_6 - f_4$$
$$f_7 = f_8 - f_6$$
$$f_{2n-3} = f_{2n-2} - f_{2n-4}$$
$$f_{2n-1} = f_{2n} - f_{2n-2}$$
Again by termwise addition, we obtain:
$$f_1 + f_3 + f_5 + \ldots + f_{2n-1} = f_{2n}$$
The sum of the first n Fibonacci numbers with even indices is $f_2 + f_4 + f_6 + \ldots + f_{2n} = f_{2n+1} - 1$ (C)
To prove this we subtract equation (B) from twice equation (A), that is, $f_1 + f_2 + f_3 + \ldots + f_{2n} = f_{2n+2} - 1$, to obtain $f_2 + f_4 + \ldots + f_{2n} = f_{2n+2} - 1 - f_{2n} = f_{2n+2} - f_{2n} - 1 = f_{2n+1} - 1$ (since $f_{2n+2} = f_{2n} + f_{2n+1}$ and $f_{2n+1} = f_{2n+2} - f_{2n}$) which is what we wanted to prove.

By yet another application of the process of termwise addition of equations we can derive a formula for the sum of the squares of the first n Fibonacci numbers. We must first note that for $k > 1$:
$$f_k f_{k+1} - f_{k-1} f_k = f_k (f_{k+1} - f_{k-1}) = f_k \cdot f_k = f_k{}^2$$
This gives us the following relations:
$$f_1{}^2 = f_1 f_2 - f_0 f_1 \text{ (where } f_0 = 0)$$
$$f_2{}^2 = f_2 f_3 - f_1 f_2$$
$$f_3{}^2 = f_3 f_4 - f_2 f_3$$
.
.
$$f_{n-1}{}^2 = f_{n-1} f_n - f_{n-2} f_{n-1}$$
$$f_n{}^2 = f_n f_{n+1} - f_{n-1} f_n$$
By adding termwise we obtain:
$$f_1{}^2 + f_2{}^2 + f_3{}^2 + \ldots + f_n{}^2 = f_n \cdot f_{n+1}$$

The Fibonacci Sequence is also connected to a famous, ancient topic in mathematics. Examining the ratios of the first successive pairs of numbers in the sequence we obtain the following:

$$\frac{1}{1} = 1.0000 \qquad \frac{2}{1} = 2.0000$$

$$\frac{3}{2} = 1.5000 \qquad \frac{5}{3} = 1.6667$$

$$\frac{8}{5} = 1.6000 \qquad \frac{13}{8} = 1.6250$$

$$\frac{21}{13} = 1.6154 \qquad \frac{34}{21} = 1.6190$$

$$\frac{55}{34} = 1.6176 \qquad \frac{89}{55} = 1.6182$$

$$\frac{144}{89} = 1.6180 \qquad \frac{233}{144} = 1.6181$$

The ratios f_n/f_{n-1} ($n > 0$) form a decreasing sequence for the odd values of n and an increasing sequence for the even values of n. Each ratio on the right hand side is larger than each corresponding ratio on the left hand side. The ratio approaches a limiting value between 1.6180 and 1.6181. It can be shown that this limit is $\frac{1 + \sqrt{5}}{2}$ or approximately 1.61803 to five decimal places.

The ratio was so important to the Greeks that they gave it a special name, the "Golden Ratio" or the "Golden Section." They did not express the relationship in decimal form but with a geometric construction in which two line segments are in the exact golden ratio, 1.61803 . . . to 1.

The golden ratio yields the basic connection between the Fibonacci Sequence and geometry. Consider again the ratios of consecutive Fibonacci numbers. As we said earlier, the table of fractions above seems to be approaching the golden ratio. Let us investigate this notion further by considering the line segment $\overline{APB}$, with P partitioning $\overline{AB}$ so that $\frac{AB}{AP} = \frac{AP}{PB}$.

A————•————B
        P

Let $x = \frac{AB}{AP}$. Therefore $x = \frac{AB}{AP} = \frac{AP + PB}{AP} = 1 + \frac{PB}{AP} = 1 + \frac{AP}{AB} = 1 + \frac{1}{x}$. Thus $x = 1 + \frac{1}{x}$ or $x^2 - x - 1 = 0$.

The roots of this equation are:

$$a = \frac{1 + \sqrt{5}}{2} \approx 1.6180339887, \text{ and}$$

$$b = \frac{1 - \sqrt{5}}{2} \approx -.6180339887$$

Since we are concerned with lengths of line segments, we shall use only the positive root, a. As a and b are roots of the equation $x^2 - x - 1 = 0$, $a^2 = a + 1$ (1) and $b^2 = b + 1$ (2).

Multiplying (1) by a^n (where n is an integer) $a^{n+2} = a^{n+1} + a^n$. Multiplying (2) by b^n (where n is an integer) $b^{n+2} = b^{n+1} + b^n$. Subtracting equation (2) from equation (1):

$$a^{n+2} - b^{n+2} = (a^{n+1} - b^{n+1}) + (a^n - b^n)$$

Now dividing by $a - b = \sqrt{5}$ (non-zero!):

$$\frac{a^{n+2} - b^{n+2}}{a - b} = \frac{a^{n+1} - b^{n+1}}{a - b} + \frac{a^n - b^n}{a - b}$$

If we now let $t_n = \frac{a^n - b^n}{a - b}$, then $t_{n+2} = t_{n+1} + t_n$ (same as the Fibonacci Sequence definition). All that remains to be shown in order to be able to establish t_n as the nth Fibonacci number, f_n, is that $t_1 = 1$ and $t_2 = 1$:

$$t_1 = \frac{a^1 - b^1}{a - b} = 1$$

$$t_2 = \frac{a^2 - b^2}{a - b} = \frac{(a - b)(a + b)}{a - b} = \frac{(\sqrt{5})(1)}{(\sqrt{5})} = 1$$

Therefore $f_n = \frac{a^n - b^n}{a - b}$, where $a = \frac{1 + \sqrt{5}}{2}$, $b = \frac{1 - \sqrt{5}}{2}$ and $n = 1, 2, 3, \ldots$

Postassessment

1. Find the sum of the first 9 Fibonacci numbers.
2. Find the sum of the first 5 Fibonacci numbers with odd indices.

References

Brother, U. Alfred, *An Introduction to Fibonacci Discovery.* San Jose, Calif.: The Fabonacci Association, 1965.

Bicknell, M. and Verner E. Hoggatt, Jr., *A Primer for the Fibonacci Numbers.* San Jose, California: The Fibonacci Association, 1972.

Hoggatt, Verner E., Jr., *Fibonacci and Lucas Numbers.* Boston: Houghton Mifflin, 1969.

Posamentier, Alfred S. *Excursions in Advanced Euclidean Geometry.* Menlo Park, Ca.: Addison-Wesley, 1984.

86   Diophantine Equations

This unit may be presented to any class having mastered the fundamentals of elementary algebra.

Performance Objectives
1. Given an equation with two variables, students will find integral solutions (if they exist.)
2. Given a verbal problem which calls for a solution of a Diophantine equation, students will determine (where applicable) the number of possible solutions.

Preassessment
Have students solve the following problem: Suppose you are asked by your employer to go to the post office and buy 6-cent and 8-cent stamps. He gives you 5 dollars to spend. How many combinations of 6-cent and 8-cent stamps could you select from to make your purchase?

Teaching Strategies
Most students will promptly realize that there are two variables which must be determined, say x and y. Letting x represent the number of 8-cent stamps and y represent the number of 6-cent stamps, the equation: $8x + 6y = 500$ should follow. This should then be converted to: $4x + 3y = 250$. At this juncture the student should realize that although this equation has an infinite number of solutions, it may or may not have an infinite number of *integral* solutions; moreover, it may or may not have an infinite number of *positive integral* solutions (as called for by the original problem). The first problem to consider is whether integral solutions, in fact, exist.

For this a useful theorem may be employed. It states that if the greatest common factor of a and b is also a factor of k, where a, b, and k are integers, then there exist an infinite number of integral solutions for x and y in $ax + by = k$. Equations of this type whose solutions must be integers are known as *Diophantine equations* in honor of the Greek mathematician Diophantus, who wrote about them.

Since the greatest common factor of 3 and 4 is 1, which is a factor of 250, there exist an infinite number of integral solutions to the equation $4x + 3y = 250$. The question now facing your students is how many (if any) *positive* integral solutions exist?

One possible method of solution is often referred to as Euler's method (Leonhard Euler, 1707-1783). To begin, students should solve for the variable with the coefficient of least absolute value; in this case, y. Thus $y = \dfrac{250 - 4x}{3}$. This is to be rewritten to separate the integral parts as:

$$y = 83 + \frac{1}{3} - x - \frac{x}{3} = 83 - x + \frac{1 - x}{3}.$$

Now introduce another variable, say t; and let $t = \dfrac{1 - x}{3}$. Solving for x yields $x = 1 - 3t$. Since there is no fractional coefficient in this equation, the process does *not* have to be repeated as it otherwise would have to be (i.e., each time introducing new variables, as with t above). Now substituting for x in the above equation yields: $y = \dfrac{250 - 4(1 - 3t)}{3} = 82 + 4t$. For various integral values of t, corresponding values for x and y will be generated. A table of values such as that below might prove useful.

t	...	-2	-1	0	1	2	...
x	...	7	4	1	-2	-5	...
y	...	74	78	82	86	90	...

Perhaps by generating a more extensive table, students will notice for what values of t positive integral values for x and y may be obtained. However, this procedure for determining the number of positive integral values of x and y is not very elegant. The students should be guided to the following inequalities to be solved simultaneously:

$$1 - 3t > 0 \qquad \text{and} \qquad 82 + 4t > 0.$$

Thus $\quad t < \dfrac{1}{3} \qquad$ and $\qquad t > -20\dfrac{1}{2}$,

or $-20\dfrac{1}{2} < t < \dfrac{1}{3}$. This indicates that there are 21 possible combinations of 6-cent and 8-cent stamps which can be purchased for 5 dollars.

Students might find it helpful to observe the solution to a more difficult Diophantine equation. The following is such an example:

Solve the Diophantine equation $5x - 8y = 39$.
1. Solve for x, since its coefficient has the lower absolute value of the two coefficients

$$x = \frac{8y + 39}{5} = y + 7 + \frac{3y + 4}{5}.$$

2. Let $t = \dfrac{3y + 4}{5}$, then solve for y:

$$y = \frac{5t - 4}{3} = t - 1 + \frac{2t - 1}{3}.$$

3. Let $u = \dfrac{2t - 1}{3}$, then solve for t:

$t = \dfrac{3u + 1}{2} = u + \dfrac{u + 1}{2}$.

4. Let $v = \dfrac{u + 1}{2}$, then solve for u:

$u = 2v - 1$.

We may now reverse the process since the coefficient of v is an integer.

5. Now substituting in the reverse order:

$t = \dfrac{3u + 1}{2}$

therefore: $t = \dfrac{3(2v - 1) + 1}{2} = 3v - 1$.

also: $y = \dfrac{5t - 4}{3}$

therefore: $y = \dfrac{5(3v - 1) - 4}{3} = \boxed{5v - 3 = y}$

Similarly: $x = \dfrac{8y + 39}{5}$

therefore: $x = \dfrac{8(5v - 3) + 39}{5} = \boxed{8v + 3 = x}$

v	...	-2	-1	0	1	2	...
x	...	-13	-5	3	11	19	...
y	...	-13	-8	-3	2	7	...

The above table indicates how the various solutions of this Diophantine equation may be generated. Students should be urged to inspect the nature of the members of the solution set.

Another method of solving Diophantine Equations is presented in Unit 87.

Postassessment

Have students solve each of the following Diophantine equations and then determine the number of positive integral solutions (if any.)

1. $2x + 11y = 35$ 3. $3x - 18y = 40$
2. $7x - 3y = 23$ 4. $4x - 17y = 53$

Reference: Related works by the author include: Posamentier, Alfred S., and Charles T. Salkind, *Challenging Problems in Algebra.* Palo Alto, CA: Seymour, 1988.

87   Continued Fractions And Diophantine Equations

This lesson should be considered after the accompanying unit, "Diophantine Equations" is presented. This unit describes another method of solving Diophantine equations.

Performance Objectives

1. Given an equation with two variables, students will find integral solutions (if they exist).

2. Given a verbal problem which calls for a solution of a Diophantine equation, students will determine (where applicable) the number of possible solutions.

3. Given an improper fraction, students will write an equivalent continued fraction.

Preassessment

Students should have successfully mastered the concepts of the unit "Diophantine Equations."

Teaching Strategies

Before discussing this method of solution of Diophantine equations, an excursion into continued fractions would be appropriate. Every improper fraction (reduced to lowest terms) has an equivalent continued fraction. For example:

$$\frac{11}{7} = 1 + \frac{4}{7} = 1 + \frac{1}{\frac{7}{4}} = 1 + \frac{1}{1 + \frac{3}{4}}$$

$$= 1 + \frac{1}{1 + \frac{1}{\frac{4}{3}}} = 1 + \frac{1}{1 + \frac{1}{1 + \frac{1}{3}}}$$

The last expression is called a *simple continued fraction*, since all the numerators after the first term are 1. These are the only types of continued fractions we shall consider here.

Consider a general improper fraction (reduced to lowest terms) and its equivalent simple continued fraction:

$$\frac{r}{s} = a_1 + \cfrac{1}{a_2 + \cfrac{1}{a_3 + \cfrac{1}{a_4 + \cfrac{1}{a_5}}}}$$

We shall call $c_1 = a_1$ the first convergent;

$c_2 = a_1 + \cfrac{1}{a_2}$ the second convergent;

$c_3 = a_1 + \cfrac{1}{a_2 + \cfrac{1}{a_3}}$ the third convergent;

$c_4 = a_1 + \cfrac{1}{a_2 + \cfrac{1}{a_3 + \cfrac{1}{a_4}}}$ the fourth convergent;

$c_5 = a_1 + \cfrac{1}{a_2 + \cfrac{1}{a_3 + \cfrac{1}{a_4 + \cfrac{1}{a_5}}}}$ the last convergent.

For example, for the above continued fraction equivalent to: $\frac{11}{7}$,

$$c_1 = 1; c_2 = 2; c_3 = \frac{3}{2}; c_4 = \frac{11}{7}$$

It would be appropriate at this juncture to derive a method for finding the nth convergent of a general continued fraction.

Let $c_n = \frac{r_n}{s_n}$ (the nth convergent)

$c_1 = a_1$, therefore $r_1 = a_1$ and $s_1 = 1$.

$c_2 = a_1 + \cfrac{1}{a_2} = \cfrac{a_1 a_2 + 1}{a_2}$

therefore $r_2 = a_1 a_2 + 1$, and $s_2 = a_2$.

$c_3 = a_1 + \cfrac{1}{a_2 + \cfrac{1}{a_3}} = a_1 + \cfrac{1}{\cfrac{a_2 a_3 + 1}{a_3}}$

$= a_1 + \cfrac{a_3}{a_2 a_3 + 1} = \cfrac{a_1 a_2 a_3 + a_1 + a_3}{a_2 a_3 + 1}$

$= \cfrac{a_3(a_1 a_2 + 1) + a_1}{a_3 a_2 + 1}$, since

$a_1 a_2 + 1 = r_2; a_1 = r_1; a_2 = s_2; 1 = s_1$; we get

$c_3 = \cfrac{a_3 r_2 + r_1}{a_3 s_2 + s_1}$. Therefore, $r_3 = a_3 r_2 + r_1$,

and $s_3 = a_3 s_2 + s_1$.

Similarly $c_4 = \cfrac{a_4 r_3 + r_2}{a_4 s_3 + s_2}$. Following this pattern

$$\boxed{c_n = \frac{a_n r_{n-1} + r_{n-2}}{a_n s_{n-1} + s_{n-2}} = \frac{r_n}{s_n}}$$

(This can be proved by mathematical induction.)
Now consider the general case for $n = 2$:

$c_2 = \cfrac{a_2 r_1 + r_0}{a_2 s_1 + s_0}$. Earlier c_2 was found to

equal $\cfrac{a_1 a_2 + 1}{a_2}$.

Equating corresponding parts yields:
$a_2 r_1 + r_0 = a_1 a_2 + 1$
Therefore, $r_1 = a_1$ and $r_0 = 1$
also, $a_2 s_1 + s_0 = a_2$
Therefore, $s_1 = 1$ and $s_0 = 0$.
In a similar way consider the general case for $n = 1$:

$c_1 = \cfrac{a_1 r_0 + r_{-1}}{a_1 s_0 + s_{-1}}$ Earlier this was found

equal to $\frac{a_1}{1}$.

Equating corresponding parts yields:
$a_1 r_0 + r_{-1} = a_1$
Therefore, $r_0 = 1$ and $r_{-1} = 0$
also, $a_1 s_0 + s_{-1} = 1$
Therefore, $s_0 = 0$ and $s_{-1} = 1$

Have students convert $\frac{117}{41}$ to the equivalent

continued fraction, $2 + \cfrac{1}{1 + \cfrac{1}{5 + \cfrac{1}{1 + \cfrac{1}{5}}}}$

Now set up a table:

Convergents

n	-1	0	1	2	3	4	5
a_n			2	1	5	1	5
$c_n = \dfrac{r_n}{s_n}$	$\dfrac{0}{1}$	$\dfrac{1}{0}$	$\dfrac{2}{1}$	$\dfrac{3}{1}$	$\dfrac{17}{6}$	$\dfrac{20}{7}$	$\dfrac{117}{41}$

The first two columns for r_n and s_n are constant. However, the other values vary with the particular fraction. The values of a_n are taken directly from the continued fractions. Each value of r_n and s_n is obtained from the general formula derived earlier. To check if this chart was constructed properly students should notice that the last convergent is in fact the original improper fraction.

An inspection of the various cross-products suggests: $r_n \cdot s_{n-1} - r_{n-1} \cdot s_n = (-1)^n$
With this background material learned, the students are now ready to apply their knowledge of continued fractions to solving Diophantine equations of the form $ax + by = k$, where the greatest common factor of a and b is a factor of k. First they should form an *improper* fraction using the two coefficients, say $\frac{a}{b}$. Then convert this fraction to a continued fraction: $\dfrac{a}{b} = \dfrac{r_n}{s_n}$

Using the previously discovered formula:

$$r_n \cdot s_{n-1} - r_{n-1} \cdot s_n = (-1)^n$$

and substituting: $a \cdot s_{n-1} - b \cdot r_{n-1} = 1$
(or multiply by -1.)   Now multiplying by k:
$a(k \cdot s_{n-1}) - b(k \cdot r_{n-1}) = k$.
Thus, $x = k \cdot s_{n-1}$, and $y = -k \cdot r_{n-1}$ is a solution
of the Diophantine equation.
For example, consider the Diophantine equation:
$$41x - 117y = 3.$$
After setting up the above table, the $n-1$ convergent is used. That is, $r_{n-1} = 20$ and $s_{n-1} = 7$. The
above relationship:
$a(k \cdot s_{n-1}) - b(k \cdot r_{n-1}) = k$
yields with appropriate substitution:
$41(3 \cdot 20) - 117(3 \cdot 7) = 3$
Thus one solution of $41x - 117y = 3$ is $x = 60$ and
$y = 21$.

In order to find the remaining solutions the
following scheme is used.
Subtract $41(60) - 117(21) = 3$ from $41x - 117y = 3$
to obtain $41(x-60) - 117(y-21) = 0$
Therefore, $41(x-60) = 117(y-21)$;

$$\text{or} \quad \frac{x-60}{117} = \frac{y-21}{41} = t$$

Thus, $t = \dfrac{x-60}{117}$ and $\boxed{x = 117t + 60}$

Also $t = \dfrac{y-21}{41}$ and $\boxed{y = 41t + 21}$

A table of solutions may then be constructed.

t	$\cdots$		-2	-1	0	1	2		$\cdots$
x	$\cdots$		-174	-57	60	177	294		$\cdots$
y	$\cdots$		-61	-20	21	62	103		$\cdots$

Postassessment

Have students change each of the following improper fractions to equivalent continued fractions.

1. $\dfrac{37}{13}$ 2. $\dfrac{47}{23}$ 3. $\dfrac{173}{61}$

Have students solve each of the following Diophantine equations and then determine how many
(if any) positive solutions exist.

4. $7x - 31y = 2$ 6. $5x - 2y = 4$
5. $18x - 53y = 3$ 7. $123x - 71y = 2$

88   Simplifying Expressions Involving Infinity

This unit presents simple algebraic methods
(appropriate for elementary algebra students) to solve
seemingly difficult problems involving infinity.

Performance Objective

*Given an algebraic problem involving infinity, students will use a simple algebraic method to solve the
problem.*

Preassessment

Students should be able to work with radical equations and quadratic equations.

Teaching Strategies

Offer the following problem to your students for
solution:
Find the value of x if

$$x^{x^{x^{x^{\cdot^{\cdot^{\cdot}}}}}} = 2.$$

Most students' first reaction will be one of bewilderment. Since they have probably never worked with an
infinite expression they are somewhat overwhelmed.
Students may try to substitute into the expression
values for x, in order to estimate an answer to the
problem. Before they are entirely frustrated, begin by

explaining the infinite nature of the expression. Explain also that

$$3^{3^3} \neq 27^3 = 19{,}683 \text{ but rather } 3^{3^3} = 3^{27} = 7{,}625{,}597{,}484{,}989.$$

Now have your students inspect
the original expression in the following way: if

$x^{x^{x^{x^{\cdot^{\cdot}}}}} = 2$, then, since there are an infinite number
of x's, one x less would not affect the expression.
Therefore the exponent of the first x (lowest base) is 2.

Thus, this expression simplifies to $x^2 = 2$, and
$x = \sqrt{2}$. Students should be asked to consider the
possibility of $x < 0$.

It would be natural for students to wonder if they could compose a similar problem by replacing 2 with, say, 5 or 7. Without elaborating, indicate to them that values to replace 2 may not be chosen at random, and that in fact these replacement values may not exceed e (i.e. the base of the natural system of logarithms, approximately 2.7182818284 . . .).

To reinforce the scheme used in the solution of the above problem, have students consider the value of the nest of radicals

$$\sqrt{5 + \sqrt{5 + \sqrt{5 + \sqrt{5 + \sqrt{5 + \ldots}}}}}.$$

In order to find x, where

$x = \sqrt{5 + \sqrt{5 + \sqrt{5 + \sqrt{5 + \sqrt{5 + \ldots}}}}}$, have students realize that nothing is lost by deleting the first 5 of this nest of radicals, since there are an infinite number of them. Thus

$x = \sqrt{5 + \underbrace{\sqrt{5 + \sqrt{5 + \sqrt{5 + \sqrt{5 + \ldots}}}}}_{= x}}$

or $x = \sqrt{5 + x}$, which is a simple radical equation. Students merely square both sides of the equation and solve the resulting quadratic equation:

$$x^2 = 5 + x$$
$$x^2 - x - 5 = 0$$
$$x = \frac{1 \pm \sqrt{21}}{2}$$

Since x is positive, $x = \dfrac{1 + \sqrt{21}}{2} \approx 2.79$.

An alternative approach to evaluating a nest of radicals is to first square both sides of the original equation to get

$x^2 = 5 + \sqrt{5 + \sqrt{5 + \sqrt{5 + \sqrt{5 + \ldots}}}}$ and then substitute x, so that $x^2 = 5 + x$. The rest is as in the previous method.

It is important that you stress inspecting the reasonability of the value of the nest of radicals. That is, should the value be positive or negative, real or imaginary, etc.

Another application of this method of evaluating expressions involving infinity is with continued fractions. Before introducing infinite continued fractions, you ought to refresh your students' memories about continued fractions. You may wish to have them write $\dfrac{13}{5}$ as a continued fraction:

$$\frac{13}{5} = 2 + \frac{3}{5} = 2 + \frac{1}{\frac{5}{3}} = 2 + \frac{1}{1 + \frac{2}{3}}$$

$$= 2 + \frac{1}{1 + \frac{1}{\frac{3}{2}}} = 2 + \frac{1}{1 + \frac{1}{1 + \frac{1}{2}}}$$

Further, you may also want to have them simplify the continued fraction $1 + \dfrac{1}{2 + \dfrac{1}{3 + \dfrac{1}{4}}}$

$$1 + \frac{1}{2 + \frac{1}{3 + \frac{1}{4}}} = 1 + \frac{1}{2 + \frac{1}{\frac{13}{4}}} = 1 + \frac{1}{2 + \frac{4}{13}}$$

$$= 1 + \frac{1}{\frac{30}{13}} = 1 + \frac{13}{30} = \frac{43}{13}$$

Now have students consider the infinite continued fraction: $1 + \dfrac{1}{1 + \dfrac{1}{1 + \dfrac{1}{1 + \dfrac{1}{1 + \ldots}}}}$

They will soon realize that the previous method of simplification will no longer work. At this point you would show them the following method:

Let $x = 1 + \dfrac{1}{1 + \dfrac{1}{1 + \dfrac{1}{1 + \ldots}}}$

Once again deleting the first "part" of the infinite continued fraction will not affect its value (because of the nature of infinity).

Therefore $x = 1 + \dfrac{1}{\underbrace{1 + \dfrac{1}{1 + \dfrac{1}{1 + \ldots}}}_{= x}}$

or $x = 1 + \dfrac{1}{x}$, which yields $x^2 = x + 1$

$$x^2 - x - 1 = 0$$

and $x = \dfrac{1 \pm \sqrt{5}}{2}$, however since $x > 0$, $x = \dfrac{1 + \sqrt{5}}{2}$. Some of your students may recognize this value as that of the golden ratio.

More advanced students might wonder how a non-repeating infinite expression is evaluated. For these students you may wish to present the following:

Evaluate $\sqrt{1 + 2\sqrt{1 + 3\sqrt{1 + 4\sqrt{1 + 5\sqrt{1 + \ldots}}}}}$.

To evaluate this expression some preliminary work must first be done. Since

$(n+2)^2 = n^2 + 4n + 4 = 1 + (n+1)(n+3)$,

$n+2 = \sqrt{1 + (n+1)(n+3)}$.

$n(n+2) = n\sqrt{1 + (n+1)(n+3)}$

Let $f(n) = n(n+2)$

then $f(n+1) = (n + 1)(n+3)$

Thus $f(n) = n\sqrt{1 + (n+1)(n+3)}$

$\qquad f(n) = n\sqrt{1 + f(n+1)}$

$\qquad f(n) = n\sqrt{1 + (n+1)\sqrt{1 + f(n+2)}}$

$\qquad f(n) = n\sqrt{1 + (n+1)\sqrt{1 + (n+2)\sqrt{1 + f(n+3)}}},$
and so on.

Now if $n = 1$, then $f(n) = 1(1+2) = 3$ and $3 =$

$1\sqrt{1 + (1+1)\sqrt{1 + (1+2)\sqrt{1 + (1+3)\sqrt{1 +}}}} \ldots$

$= 1\sqrt{1 + 2\sqrt{1 + 3\sqrt{1 + 4\sqrt{1 +}}}} \ldots$

As a result of presenting the methods considered in this model, your students should have a more solid concept of infinite expressions.

1. Simplify: $\sqrt{7 + \sqrt{7 + \sqrt{7 + \sqrt{7 + }}}} \ldots$

2. Simplify: $2 + \cfrac{1}{3 + \cfrac{1}{3 + \cfrac{1}{3 + \cfrac{1}{3 + \ldots}}}}$

3. Simplify: $1 + \cfrac{1}{2 + \cfrac{1}{1 + \cfrac{1}{2 + \cfrac{1}{1 + \cfrac{1}{2 + \ldots}}}}}$

89 Continued Fraction Expansion of Irrational Numbers

Performance Objectives

1. Given an irrational number, students will write an equivalent continued fraction.

2. Given an infinite expansion, students will get back to the irrational number.

Preassessment

Students should be familiar with continued fractions.

Teaching Strategies

The procedure for expanding an irrational number is essentially the same as that used for rational numbers. Let x be the given irrational number. Find a_1, the greatest integer less than x, and express x in the form

$$x = a_1 + \frac{1}{x_2}, \; 0 < \frac{1}{x_2} < 1$$

where the number

$$x_2 = \frac{1}{x - a_1} > 1 \text{ is irrational; for, if an integer}$$

is subtracted from an irrational number, the difference and the reciprocal of the difference are irrational.

Find a_2, the largest integer less than x_2 and express x_2 in the form

$$x_2 = a_2 + \frac{1}{x_3}, \; 0 < \frac{1}{x_3} < 1, \; a_2 \geq 1$$

where again the number

$$x_3 = \frac{1}{x_2 - a_2} > 1$$

This calculation may be repeated indefinitely, producing in succession the equations

$$x = a_1 + \frac{1}{x_2}, \; x_2 > 1$$

$$x_2 = a_2 + \frac{1}{x_3}, \; x_3 > 1, \; a_2 \geq 1$$

$$x_3 = a_3 + \frac{1}{x_4}, \; x_4 > 1, \; a_3 \geq 1$$

$$\vdots \qquad \vdots \qquad \vdots$$

$$x_n = a_n + \frac{1}{x_{n+1}}, \; x_{n+1} > 1, \; a_n \geq 1$$

$$\vdots \qquad \vdots \qquad \vdots$$

where $a_1, a_2, a_3, \ldots, a_n, \ldots$ are all integers and the numbers $x, x_2, x_3, \ldots$ are all irrational. This process cannot end because the only way this could happen would be for some integer a_n to be equal to x_n. This is impossible since each successive x_i is irrational.

Substituting x_2 from the second equation above into the first equation, then x_3 from the third into this result, and so on, produces the required infinite simple continued fraction

$$x = a_1 + \frac{1}{x_2} = a_1 + \cfrac{1}{a_2 + \cfrac{1}{x_3}} = a_1 + \cfrac{1}{a_2 + \cfrac{1}{a_3 + \cfrac{1}{x_4}}}$$

or sometimes written as $x = [a_1, a_2, a_3, a_4, \ldots]$, where the three dots indicate that the process is continued indefinitely.

Example 1. Expand $\sqrt{3}$ into an infinite simple continued fraction.

Solution: The largest integer less than $\sqrt{3}$ is 1. Therefore, $a_1 = 1$ and

$$\sqrt{3} = 1 + \frac{1}{x_2}$$

Solving this equation for x_2, we get

$$x_2 = \frac{1}{\sqrt{3} - 1} \cdot \frac{\sqrt{3} + 1}{\sqrt{3} + 1} = \frac{\sqrt{3} + 1}{2}$$

Therefore: $\sqrt{3} = a_1 + \dfrac{1}{x_2} = 1 + \dfrac{1}{\dfrac{\sqrt{3} + 1}{2}}$

$x_2 = a_2 + \dfrac{1}{x_3}$ where $a_2 = 1$, since it is the largest integer less than $\dfrac{\sqrt{3} + 1}{2}$

Therefore:

$$x_3 = \frac{1}{\dfrac{\sqrt{3} + 1}{2} - 1} = \frac{2}{\sqrt{3} - 1} \cdot \frac{\sqrt{3} + 1}{\sqrt{3} + 1}$$

$$= \sqrt{3} + 1$$

$$\sqrt{3} = 1 + \frac{1}{1 + \dfrac{1}{\sqrt{3} + 1}}$$

Continuing this process:

$x_3 = 2 + \dfrac{1}{x_4}, a_3 = 2$ since 2 is the largest integer less than $\sqrt{3} + 1$.

$$x_4 = \frac{1}{\sqrt{3} - 1} \cdot \frac{\sqrt{3} + 1}{\sqrt{3} + 1} = \frac{\sqrt{3} + 1}{2}$$

$$\sqrt{3} = 1 + \frac{1}{1 + \dfrac{1}{2 + \dfrac{1}{\dfrac{\sqrt{3} + 1}{2}}}}$$

Since $x_4 = \dfrac{\sqrt{3} + 1}{2}$ is the same as $x_2 = \dfrac{\sqrt{3} + 1}{2}$, x_5 will produce the same result as x_3, namely $\sqrt{3} + 1$. All the following partial quotients will be 1,2,1,2 and the infinite expansion of $\sqrt{3}$ will be

$$\sqrt{3} = 1 + \frac{1}{1 + \dfrac{1}{2 + \dfrac{1}{1 + \dfrac{1}{2 + \cdots}}}} = [1, 1, 2, 1, 2, \ldots] = [1, \overline{1, 2}].$$

The bar over the 1 and 2 indicates that the numbers 1 and 2 are repeated indefinitely.

Example 2. Find the infinite continued fraction expansion for

$$x = \frac{\sqrt{30} - 2}{13}$$

Solution: Since $\sqrt{30}$ is between 5 and 6, the largest integer less than x is $a_1 = 0$. Then

$$x = \frac{\sqrt{30} - 2}{13} = 0 + \frac{1}{x_2}$$

where $x_2 = \dfrac{1}{x} = \dfrac{13}{\sqrt{30} - 2} \cdot \dfrac{\sqrt{30} + 2}{\sqrt{30} + 2}$

$$= \frac{\sqrt{30} + 2}{2} > 1$$

The largest integer less than x_2 is $a_2 = 3$, therefore,

$$x_2 = a_2 + \frac{1}{x_3} = 3 + \frac{1}{x_3}$$

Therefore $x_3 = \dfrac{1}{x_2 - 3} = \dfrac{1}{\dfrac{\sqrt{30} + 2}{2} - 3}$

$$= \frac{2}{\sqrt{30} - 4} \cdot \frac{\sqrt{30} + 4}{\sqrt{30} + 4}$$

$$= \frac{2(\sqrt{30} + 4)}{14} = \frac{\sqrt{30} + 4}{7}$$

The largest integer less than x_3 is $a_3 = 1$.

Therefore $x_4 = \dfrac{1}{x_3 - 1} = \dfrac{1}{\dfrac{\sqrt{30} + 4}{7} - 1}$

$$= \frac{7}{\sqrt{30} - 3} \cdot \frac{\sqrt{30} + 3}{\sqrt{30} + 3} = \frac{\sqrt{30} + 3}{3}$$

In a similar way we get $x_5 = \dfrac{\sqrt{30} + 3}{7}$, $x_6 = \dfrac{\sqrt{30} + 4}{2}$, and $x_7 = \dfrac{\sqrt{30} + 4}{7} = x_3$

Further investigation will show that the sequence 1,2,1,4 repeats. The required expansion is

$$x = 0 + \frac{1}{x_2} = 0 + \frac{1}{3 + \dfrac{1}{x_3}} = 0 + \frac{1}{3 + \dfrac{1}{1 + \dfrac{1}{x_4}}}$$

$$= 0 + \frac{1}{3 + \dfrac{1}{1 + \dfrac{1}{2 + \dfrac{1}{x_5}}}} = 0 + \frac{1}{3 + \dfrac{1}{1 + \dfrac{1}{2 + \dfrac{1}{1 + \dfrac{1}{x_6}}}}}$$

$$= 0 + \frac{1}{3 + \dfrac{1}{1 + \dfrac{1}{2 + \dfrac{1}{1 + \dfrac{1}{4 + \dfrac{1}{x_7}}}}}}$$

so finally we obtain

$$x = \frac{\sqrt{30} - 2}{13} = [0, 3, \overline{1, 2, 1, 4}].$$

Students may prove that a given infinite continued fraction actually represents an irrational number. Consider showing that $[2, \overline{2, 4}]$ represents $\sqrt{6}$. Begin by writing:

Let $x = 2 + \dfrac{1}{2 + \dfrac{1}{4 + \dfrac{1}{2 + \dfrac{1}{4 + \cdots}}}}$.

where $y = 2 + \cfrac{1}{4 + \cfrac{1}{2 + \cfrac{1}{4 + \cdots}}}$

Therefore $y = 2 + \cfrac{1}{4 + \cfrac{1}{y}} = 2 + \cfrac{y}{4y + 1}$

Solving for y yields: $\dfrac{2 + \sqrt{6}}{2}$

However $x = 2 + \dfrac{1}{y} = 2 + \dfrac{2}{2 + \sqrt{6}}$

Hence, $x = 2 + \sqrt{6} - 2 = \sqrt{6}$

Postassessment

Have students change each of the following into an infinite simple continued fraction.

1. $\sqrt{2}$ 2. $\sqrt{43}$ 3. $\dfrac{25 + \sqrt{53}}{22}$

Have students show that the infinite continued fraction $[\overline{3,6}] = \sqrt{10}$.

90   The Farey Sequence

This unit presents a discussion of a rather unusual sequence of numbers. This topic can be presented to students at various levels. However, the emphasis will change with the various ability and maturity levels of the students.

Performance Objectives

(1) Students will show that the fraction immediately before $\dfrac{1}{2}$ and its immediate successor of the Farey Sequence are complementary.

(2) Students will establish the relationship between π and the number of terms in the Farey Sequence.

Preassessment

Using the sequence of fractions below, have students find the sum of the two fractions:

a. fifth term to the left and fifth term to the right of $\dfrac{1}{2}$;

b. third term to the left and third term to the right of $\dfrac{1}{2}$;

c. second term to the left and second term to the right of $\dfrac{1}{2}$;

$\dfrac{1}{7}, \dfrac{1}{6}, \dfrac{1}{5}, \dfrac{1}{4}, \dfrac{2}{7}, \dfrac{1}{3}, \dfrac{2}{5}, \dfrac{3}{7}, \dfrac{1}{2}, \dfrac{4}{7}, \dfrac{3}{5}, \dfrac{2}{3},$
$\dfrac{5}{7}, \dfrac{3}{4}.$

Ask students to generalize their results.

Teaching Strategies

A review of the preassessment activity will indicate that the three sums students were asked to find all resulted in 1. That is,

$\dfrac{1}{4} + \dfrac{3}{4} = 1; \dfrac{1}{3} + \dfrac{2}{3} = 1$ and $\dfrac{2}{5} + \dfrac{3}{5} = 1.$

We shall refer to a pair of fractions whose sum is 1 as *complementary*. Let us now inspect the given sequence.

If we list all proper common fractions in their lowest terms in order of magnitude up to some arbitrarily assigned limit—such as with denominators not exceeding 7—we have the 17 fractions

$\dfrac{1}{7}, \dfrac{1}{6}, \dfrac{1}{5}, \dfrac{1}{4}, \dfrac{2}{7}, \dfrac{1}{3}, \dfrac{2}{5}, \dfrac{3}{7}, \dfrac{1}{2}, \dfrac{4}{7}, \dfrac{3}{5}, \dfrac{2}{3},$
$\dfrac{5}{7}, \dfrac{3}{4}, \dfrac{4}{5}, \dfrac{5}{6}, \dfrac{6}{7}.$

This is called the Farey Sequence. The Farey Sequence F_n, of order n, is defined as the *ordered set consisting of $\dfrac{0}{1}$, the irreducible proper fractions with denominators from 2 to* n, *arranged in order of increasing magnitude, and $\dfrac{1}{1}$.* There are many characteristic properties of the Farey Sequence. One is the relationship students discovered earlier: fractions equidistant from $\dfrac{1}{2}$ are complementary; that is, their sum equals one. Another interesting relationship involves the number of terms in the Farey Sequence of order n and π.

Before beginning a development of this sequence, students should be given some background on the Farey Sequence. They should be told that Farey, in 1816, discovered the sequence while perusing lengthy tables of decimal quotients. Apparently the numerator of any fraction in the Farey Sequence is obtained by adding the numerators of the fractions on each side of it, and similarly for the denominators. Since the result must be in lowest terms, this holds true for triplet:

$\dfrac{1}{3}, \dfrac{2}{5}, \dfrac{3}{7}$ where $\dfrac{3+1}{3+7} = \dfrac{4}{10} = \dfrac{2}{5}$.

Students will see that the sum of fractions equidistant from $\dfrac{1}{2}$ equals 1. This can be proved many ways.

Suppose that $\dfrac{\ell}{n}$ is a number of the series which is less than $\dfrac{1}{2}$ and such that ℓ and n are relatively prime. Comparing the corresponding number of the other side of $\dfrac{1}{2}$, we find $\dfrac{(n-\ell)}{n}$. Since this belongs to the Farey Sequence it is necessary that g.c.d. $(n-\ell, n) = 1$. Supposing that $(n-\ell)$ and n are not relatively prime, then $n-\ell = qd$ and $n = qd+\ell$. Also $n = rd$ and thus $rd = qd + \ell$. Therefore d divides ℓ and consequently d divides $(n-\ell)$ for d divides n. This however contradicts the fact that $(n - \ell)/n$ was in its lowest terms (which is the definition of terms in the Farey Sequence) and therefore g.c.d. $(n-\ell, n) = 1$.

Now to prove that $\dfrac{\ell}{n} + \dfrac{a}{b} = 1$. Let $\dfrac{\ell}{n}$ be the immediate predecessor of $\dfrac{1}{2}$. If there was another term immediately succeeding $\dfrac{1}{2}$ and belonging to F_n, then the fractions are arranged as follows:

$$\dfrac{\ell}{n}, \dfrac{1}{2}, \dfrac{a}{b} \text{ where } \dfrac{1}{2} = \dfrac{\ell+a}{n+b}$$

(one of the properties of the sequence). To prove that $\dfrac{\ell}{n} + \dfrac{a}{b} = 1, \dfrac{a}{b}$ must be in lowest terms if it belongs to F_n. If two fractions whose sum is 1 are in lowest terms, then their denominators are equal. Thus if $\dfrac{\ell}{n} + \dfrac{a}{b} = 1$, b must equal n. Therefore $\dfrac{\ell+a}{n} = 1$ and $\ell + a = n$, or $a = n - \ell$. But $\dfrac{\ell}{n}$ was the immediate predecessor of $\dfrac{1}{2}$ and $\dfrac{a}{b} = \dfrac{n-\ell}{n}$. Thus the immediate predecessor of $\dfrac{1}{2}$ and its immediate successor are complementary since their sum equals 1.

Another very interesting property results between π and the sum of the terms in the Farey Sequence. The number of fractions of order n is obtained as follows. Since the fractions are all in lowest terms, it follows that for a given denominator b, the number of numerators is the number of integers less than, and prime to, b. Students should then see the number of fractions N, in the Farey Sequence is equal to $\phi(2) + \phi(3) + \phi(4) + \ldots + \phi(n)$, where $\phi(n)$ is the number of positive integers less than or equal to n that are relatively prime to n. If $n = 7$, we have N = $\phi(2) + \phi(3) + \phi(4) + \phi(5) + \phi(6) + \phi(7) = 1 + 2 + 2 + 4 + 2 + 6$. The value of N increases rapidly as n increases and when $n = 100$, N = 3043. Thus there are many irreducible common fractions with numerators and denominators not exceeding 100.

There is a remarkable formula involving the ϕ function and π (the ratio of the circumference to the diameter of the circle).

The ϕ function refers to Euler's function. The sum of the Farey Sequence can be written by using a formula in terms of Euler's function ϕ. If $\dfrac{h}{k}$ is a term in the Farey Sequence then g.c.d. $(h,k) = 1$. For any fixed number $k>1$ the number of terms of the form $\dfrac{h}{k}$ is $\phi(k)$. It can be demonstrated that the sum $\phi(1) + \phi(2) + \ldots + \phi(n)$ is approximated by the expression $3n^2/\pi^2$, the approximation becoming more and more accurate as n increases. Except for the first term this sum represents the number of terms, N in a Farey Sequence of order n. Since we know the value of π to any desired degree of accuracy, this means we can find approximately the number of terms in a Farey Sequence without evaluating separately $\phi(1)$, $\phi(2)$, $\phi(3)$ .... $\phi(n)$. Thus for $n = 100$ we would have N = $3 \cdot 100^2/\pi^2 = 3039.6355 \ldots$ whereas the true value is 3043.

Thus the number of terms of the Farey series approaches $\dfrac{3n^2}{\pi^2}$.

Postassessment

1. Given $n = 200$, $n = 8$, find the number of terms in the Farey Sequence using the expression $\dfrac{3n^2}{\pi^2}$.

2. Have students find other properties of the Farey Sequence.

91   The Parabolic Envelope

This unit describes briefly the mechanical construction of the parabolic envelope and shows how students can use the envelope to derive a host of related curves.

Performance Objectives

Using the envelope as a foundation, students will draw a variety of curves by different techniques without point by point plotting from an equation. In the process, they will be introduced to the visual concepts of an envelope, evolute and pedal to a given curve.

Preassessment

Students should have completed a basic geometry course and be familiar with the conic sections.

Teaching Strategies

Have your students construct tangents to a parabola in the following manner:
Draw an angle of any measure, and divide each side of the angle into the same number of equally-spaced intervals. In Figure 1, we have an angle, A, of measure 50°, divided on each side into 17 equally-spaced, numbered intervals. Starting, as we did, at the lower left of the angle, lines were drawn connecting points 1

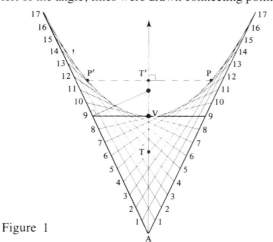

Figure 1

to 17, 2 to 16, 3 to 15, and so on, terminating with 17-1, (where the notation ''17-1'' means the segment connecting point 17 to point 1, or conversely). The resulting array of lines are tangents which *envelope* a parabola.

The midpoint, V, of the line 9-9, is the *vertex* of the parabola, and 9-9 is the tangent to the parabola at V. A line from A to V, extended beyond V, is the parabola's *axis of symmetry,* and is also included in Figure 1. Ask students why 9-9 is the tangent perpendicular to AV.

Erect a perpendicular to either side of the angle at point 9. We state without proof that the intersection of this perpendicular with the axis of symmetry determines the *focus,* F, of the parabola. More ambitious students may wish to prove this. At any rate, it would be meaningful to mention the reflective and locus properties of the focus.

Specific points of tangency on the parabola can be visually approximated directly from Figure 1. They can be more exactly located from the fact that a tangent to the parabola intersects the axis at a distance from the vertex equal to the ordinate of the point of tangency. As an example in Figure 1, tangent 14-4 intersects the axis at T. Locate a point T′ on the axis above V such that TV = VT′. Draw a line through T′ parallel to 9-9 so as to intersect the envelope at P and P′, then P and P′ are the points on the parabola where 14-4 and 4-14 are tangent. Other points on the parabola can be determined in the same manner.

Evolute to the Parabola

Having located all such points of tangency P and P′ on the parabola, use a right-angled triangle or carpenter's square to erect perpendiculars at each of these points. These perpendiculars to a curve at the point of tangency are called *normals*. The envelope of all such normals defines the *evolute* to the curve; that is, the normals are then tangents to the evolute of the given curve. Thus, the evolute to the parabola can be shown to be a one-cusped curve called a *semi-cubic parabola*. This is shown in Figure 2.

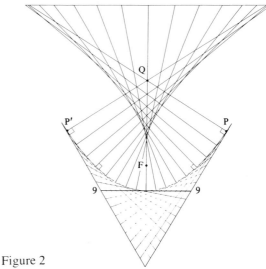

Figure 2

To realize an accurately drawn evolute, utilize the symmetry of the parabola about the axis. Hence, normals to P and P intersect at Q on the axis of symmetry.

Pedal Curves to the Parabola

Figure 3 shows a given curve, C, and a fixed point, F, on or in the neighborhood of C. Dropping perpendiculars from F to each of the tangents to the curve, we find that the locus of the feet of the perpendiculars, P, defines the *pedal curve* to the given curve with respect to F. For a given curve, different choices of F will result in different pedal curves.

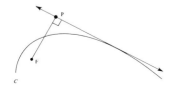

Figure 3

Now let the focus, F, of the parabola in Figure 1 be the fixed point for consideration. If perpendiculars are dropped to each of the tangents, students will note that the locus of the feet of these perpendiculars is the line 9-9. That is, the tangent to the vertex is the pedal curve to a parabola with respect to its focus. Conversely, it can be shown that a perpendicular erected to a tangent with 9-9 will pass through F. This latter fact justifies the technique used earlier to locate the parabola's focus. (Students should recall that to prove a locus, a biconditional statement must be proved.)

Next let V be the fixed point. From V, we drop perpendiculars to each of the tangents obtained in Figure 1. The locus of the feet is shown in Figure 4 as a curve having a cusp at V, and symmetric to the axis. We state without proof that the locus is the *cissoid of Diocles*. Locate F′ on the axis, below V, such that FV = VF′. Through F′ draw a line parallel to 9-9. This line is the parabola's *directrix*, and can be shown to be the asymptotic line which the cissoid approaches.

At this point you may wish to discuss the various properties of a parabola, such as its reflective properties. You may also define the parabola in terms of a locus, now that the focus and direction have been determined. Thus, a parabola is the locus of points equidistant from a point (the focus), and a line (the directrix), not containing the point. Folding waxed paper clearly demonstrates this locus. Draw a line and an external point on a piece of wax paper. Fold the wax paper repeatedly in such a manner that the point is superimposed on the line. The creases produced form a parabolic envelope.

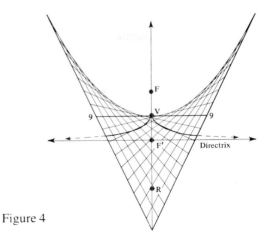

Figure 4

Postassessment

Have students draw two additional pedal curves to the parabola. Tell them to use the following as a guide:

a.) Let F′ be the fixed point. The pedal curve will be seen to the *Right Strophoid*.

b.) Locate R (Figure 4), the reflection of F through the directrix such that FF′ = F′R. Have R be the fixed point. The pedal curve is the *trisectrix of MacLaurin*.

c.) The *contrapedal* to a given curve is the locus of the feet of the perpendiculars from a given fixed point to the normals to a given curve. In Figure 2, with F as fixed point, determine the locus of the contrapedal. From F, drop perpendiculars to each of the normals you drew to obtain the evolute. The locus of the contrapedal is a parabola whose turning point concurs with F.

d.) Confirm by measurement that the contrapedal locus in c.) is identical to the locus of the midpoints of the segment of a normal from the point of tangency on the parabola to the point of intersection of the normal and the parabola's axis of symmetry.

References

Lockwood, E. H., *A Book of Curves*, Cambridge University Press, 1961.

Zwikker, C., *The Advanced Geometry of Plane Curves and their Applications*, Dover Publications, 1963.

92 Application of Congruence to Divisibility

Performance Objectives

1. *Given any integer, students will determine its prime factors without doing any division.*

2. *Students will produce rules for testing divisibility by natural numbers other than those presented in this unit.*

Preassessment

1. Have students find the prime factors of each of the following: (a) 144   (b) 840   (c) 360
2. Have students indicate, without doing any division, which of the following numbers are divisible by 2, 3, and 5: (1) 234   (b) 315

Teaching Strategies

Begin the lesson by introducing the concept of number congruences. Two numbers which have the same remainder when divided by 7 are said to be *congruent modulo 7.*

For example, 23 and 303 give the same remainder when divided by 7. Therefore, we say that 23 and 303 are congruent modula 7. This statement can be represented by symbols as follows: $23 \equiv 303 \pmod 7$.

In general, two integers a and b are congruent modulo m (written as $a \equiv b \pmod{m}$, if they give the same non-negative remainder when divided by the integer $m \neq 0$.

Because of this definition, we have the following double implication:

$$a \equiv b \pmod m \iff \begin{cases} a = mk + r \\ b = mk' + r \end{cases} \quad 0 \le r < |m|$$

The symbol "$\equiv$" was first used in 1801 by Karl Friedrich Gauss (1777—1855), the famous German mathematician. It is suggested by its similarity with the ordinary equality. It has nothing to do with geometric congruence. The sign $\not\equiv$ means "is not congruent to."

Example 1: $17 \equiv -4 \pmod 7$

Because:
$$17 = 7\cdot2 + 3$$
$$-4 = 7\cdot(-1) + 3$$

In this example, we must use -1 as a quotient. If we use 0, the remainder would be negative against the definition of congruence.

Example 2: $a \equiv 0 \pmod a$ This is true because they both give the same remainder 0.

Another Definition of Congruences:

Two numbers are congruent modulo m, *if and only if their difference is divisible by* m. We want to prove that: $a \equiv b \pmod m \iff a - b = \overline{m}$ ($\overline{m}$ reads "a multiple of m.")

Proof

If $a \equiv b \pmod m \iff \begin{array}{l} a = mk_1 + r \\ b = mk_2 + r \end{array}$

Subtracting: $a - b = m(k_1 - k_2)$ or $a - b = \overline{m}$

Therefore: $a \equiv b \pmod m \Rightarrow a - b = \overline{m}$

Conversely: if $a - b = \overline{m} \Rightarrow a = b + \overline{m}$
$$\Rightarrow a = b + km \quad (1)$$

But $b = mk' + r$ (2). Thus, from (1) and (2) we have:
$$a = b + km = (mk' + r) + km$$
$$= m(k' + k) + r$$
$$= mk'' + r \ (3)$$

From (2) and (3) we then have:
$$\begin{array}{l} a = mk'' + r \\ b = mk' + r \end{array} \text{therefore: } a \equiv b \pmod m$$

Thus, $a - b = \overline{m} \Rightarrow a \equiv b \pmod m$

Therefore, $a \equiv b \pmod m \Rightarrow a - b = \overline{m}$, *Q.E.D.*

Students should now be ready to consider the following:

Some Elementary Properties of Congruences

If $a \equiv b \pmod m$ and $c \equiv d \pmod m$, then:

I) $a + c \equiv b + d \pmod m$

II) $ac \equiv bd \pmod m$

III) $ka \equiv kb \pmod m$ for every integer k.

These properties follow from the definition of congruences. We shall prove II); the others can be proved by following the same method:

Since $a \equiv b \pmod m \iff a = b + \overline{m}$ (1)
and $c \equiv d \pmod m \iff c = d + \overline{m}$ (2)

Then, multiplying (1) and (2):
$$ac = bd + b\overline{m} + d\overline{m}$$
$$= bd + (b + d)\overline{m}$$
$$= bd + \overline{m}$$

Therefore, $ac \equiv bd \pmod m$.

Another interesting aspect of modular system are *power residues*. The *power residues* of a number a with respect to another number m are *the remainders obtained when the successive powers* a^0, a^1, $a^2, \ldots,$ *of a are divided by* m.

Example 3: Find the power residues of **5** with respect to 3. Since:

$5^0: 3 = \quad 1 : 3 = \quad 0\cdot3 + 1$ therefore $r_0 = 1$.
$5^1: 3 = \quad 5 : 3 = \quad 1\cdot3 + 2$ therefore $r_1 = 2$.
$5^2: 3 = \quad 25 : 3 = \quad 8\cdot3 + 1$ therefore $r_2 = 1$.
$5^3: 3 = 125 : 3 = 41\cdot3 + 2$ therefore $r_3 = 2$.

and so on.

Therefore, the power residues of 5 with respect to 3 will be: 1, 2, 1, 2, ... Have students consider why no number other than 1 or 2 appears in this sequence.

Example 4: Find the power residues of 10 modulo 2. Also indicate the different congruences. We have:

$10^0 : 2 = 1 : 2 = 0 \cdot 2 + 1$ therefore $r_0 = 1$.
$10^1 : 2 = 10 : 2 = 5 \cdot 2 + 0$ therefore $r_1 = 0$.
$10^2 : 2 = 100 : 2 = 50 \cdot 2 + 0$ therefore $r_2 = 0$.
Therefore, the power residues are 1, 0, 0, ...
Thus, the congruences will be:

$$10^0 \equiv 1, 10^1 \equiv 0, 10^2 \equiv 0, \ldots, (\text{mod } 2)$$

Students should be able to justify the appearance of this sequence.

Once students have mastered the concept of power residues, they should be ready to consider various *properties of power residues*.

I) The power residue of a^0, when divided by m, is always 1.

Proof: We have that: $a^0 : m = 1 : m = 0 \cdot 1 + 1$. i.e., a remainder of 1. Hence, $a^0 \equiv 1 \pmod{m}$.

II) If a power residue is zero, then the following power residues are also zero.

Proof: Let a^h give a zero power residue when divided by m. Then, $a^h \equiv 0 \pmod{m}$ If both sides are multiplied by a, we have: $a \cdot a^h \equiv a \cdot 0 \pmod{m}$ or $a^{h+1} \equiv 0 \pmod{m}$ Therefore, $a^{h+1}, a^{h+2}, \ldots$ will give zero power residues also. This was evident in example 4 above.

Criteria for Divisibility

Have students consider any number $N = a_n a_{n-1} \ldots a_2 a_1 a_0$ written in base 10. Therefore: $N = a_0 10^0 + a_1 10^1 + a_2 10^2 + \ldots + a_n 10^n$. Let $r_0, r_1, \ldots, r_n$ be the power residues of 10 $(\text{mod } m)$ Therefore, $10^0 \equiv 1, 10^1 \equiv r_1, \ldots, 10^n \equiv r_n \pmod{m}$ Have students multiply each congruence by $a_0, a_1, \ldots, a_n$, respectively, to get:

$a_0 10^0 \equiv a_0, a_1 10^1 \equiv a_1 r_1, \ldots, a_n 10^n \equiv a_n r_n \pmod{m}$ If they are added in order, we will get: $a_0 10^0 + \ldots + a_n 10^n \equiv a_0 + a_1 r_1 + a_2 r_2 + \ldots + a_n r_n \pmod{m}$ Thus, $N \equiv a_0 + a_1 r_1 + a_2 r_2 + \ldots + a_n r_n$

From this last congruence, N will be divisible by m if and only if $a_0 + a_1 r_1 + \ldots + a_n r_n$ is divisble by m. This statement can be used to find the different criteria for divisibility the following way:

Divisibility by 2 and 5
We have for any number N that:
$N \equiv a_0 + a_1 r_1 + \ldots + a_n r_n \pmod{m}$. If students consider $m = 2$ (or $m = 5$), they will have that $r_1 = 0$ because $10^1 \equiv 0 \pmod{2}$ (or mod 5) therefore, $r_2 = 0, r_3 = 0, \ldots$ Hence they will have $N \equiv a_0 \pmod{2 \text{ or } 5}$. This means that: *A number is divisible by 2 or 5, if and only if its last digit is divisible by 2 or 5.*

Divisibility by 3 and 9
We have that: $10^0 \equiv 1, 10^1 \equiv 1, \ldots \pmod{3 \text{ or } 9}$. Since $N \equiv a_0 + a_1 r_1 + a_2 r_2 + \ldots + a_n r_n \pmod{m}$. Thus, $N \equiv a_0 + a_1 + a_2 + \ldots + a_n \pmod{3 \text{ or } 9}$. Therefore, a given number is divisible by 3 or 9, if and only if the sum of its digits is divisible by 3 or 9.

Divisibility by 11
Since $10^0 \equiv 1, 10^1 \equiv -1, 10^2 \equiv 1, \ldots, \pmod{11}$ Hence, $N \equiv a_0 - a_1 + a_2 - \ldots + (-1)^n a_n \pmod{11}$ Therefore, a given number is divisible by 11 if and only if the difference of the two sums of the alternate digits is divisible by 11.

The previous method will lead students to develop similar rules for testing divisibility by other primes. It should be emphasized and justified that a number is divisible by a composite number if it is divisible by each of its *relative prime* factors.

Therefore, if we want to determine if a number is divisible by 6, we only have to test its divisibility by 2 and 3.

With sufficient discussion students should be able to establish a comprehensive list of rules for testing divisibility as well as develop insight into some elementary theory of congruences.

Postassessment
Have students perform these exercises:
1) State a rule for testing divisibility by:
   (a) 4 and 25   (b) 7 (c) 13 (d) 101
2) Determine the prime factors of:
   (a) 1220 (b) 315 (c) 1001
3) Find the criteria for divisiblity by 6 and 11 in base 7.

93 Problem Solving—A Reverse Strategy

Geometry teachers are frequently asked, "How did you know which approach to take in order to prove these two line segments parallel?" Generally, the teacher would like to think that experience prompted the proper conclusion. This would, of course, be of no value to the questioning student. He or she would like to learn a definite procedure to follow. The teacher would be wise to describe to the student a reverse strategy which would have the student begin with the desired conclusion and discover each preceding step in order.

Performance Objective

Given a problem situation which lends itself to a reverse strategy of solution, students will employ this strategy to successfully solve the problem.

Preassessment

Have students solve the following problem:

If the sum of two numbers is 2, and the product of the same two numbers is 3, find the sum of the reciprocals of these numbers.

Teaching Strategies

A reverse strategy is certainly not new. It was considered by Pappus of Alexandria about 320 A.D. In Book VII of Pappus' *Collection* there is a rather complete description of the methods of "analysis" and "synthesis". T.L. Heath in his book, *A Manual of Greek Mathematics* (Oxford University Press, 1931, p. 452-3) provides a translation of Pappus' definitions of these terms:

Analysis takes that which is sought as if it were admitted and passes from it through its successive consequences to something which is admitted as the result of synthesis; for in analysis we assume that which is sought as if it were already done, and we inquire what it is from which this results, and again what is the antecedent cause of the latter, and so on, until, by so retracing our steps, we come upon something already known or belonging to the class of first principles, and such a method we call analysis as being solution backwards.

But in *synthesis*, reversing the process, we take as already done that which was last arrived at in the analysis and, by arranging in their natural order as consequences what before were antecedents, and successively connecting them one with another, we arrive finally at the construction of that which was sought; and this we call *synthesis*.

Unfortunately, this method has not received its due emphasis in the mathematics classroom. This discussion will reinforce the value of reverse strategy in problem solving.

To better understand this technique for problem solving, a number of appropriate problems will be presented. Discussion of their solutions should help students attain a better grasp of this method.

Let us first consider the following simple problem from basic geometry.

Problem 1:

Given: $\overline{AB} \cong \overline{DC}$

$\overline{AB} \; // \; \overline{DC}$

$\angle BAH \cong \angle DCG$

$\overline{BEGHFD}$

$\overline{GE} \cong \overline{HF}$

Prove: $\overline{AE} \; // \; \overline{CF}$

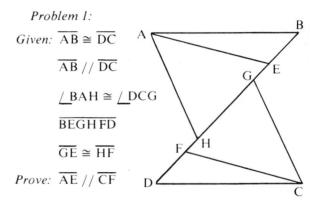

Solution: The first thoughts of a student trying to do this proof is to consider what information is given, and then what is to be proved. Having considered the given information, the poorly trained student will usually proceed blindly, proving segments, angles and triangles congruent until (if ever) he or she reaches the desired conclusion.

On the other hand, a well-trained student, after considering the given information, will immediately look at the desired conclusion and begin working in reverse from that conclusion ("analysis"). First this student will ask what methods there are for proving lines parallel. This will for the most part lead to proving angles congruent. In this proof clever students will realize that if they were able to prove $\angle AED \cong \angle CFB$, they would then be able to prove $\overline{AE}$ parallel to $\overline{CF}$. But how can they prove $\angle AED \cong \angle CFB$? Because of the type of training they receive, most students will generally react to this question by trying to find a pair of congruent triangles, which have $\angle AED$ and $\angle CFB$ as a pair of corresponding angles. Continuing this reverse approach, students must now locate such a pair of congruent triangles. It would be helpful if students could prove $\triangle AEH \cong \triangle CFG$, as these triangles have $\angle AED$ and $\angle CFB$ as a pair of corresponding angles. Can these triangles be proven congruent? Evidently not. All that students know about these triangles at this point is that $\overline{HE} \cong \overline{GF}$. Using this type of reasoning she or he soon will prove that $\triangle ABH \cong \triangle CDG$, which will help to prove $\triangle AEH$

$\cong \triangle$CFG. Then, by retracing steps of reverse reasoning in the opposite order ("synthesis") students will easily attain the desired conclusion. It is clear that reverse strategy was instrumental in formulating a path to the desired conclusion.

The reverse approach to solving a problem becomes dramatically stronger, when the resulting solution becomes significantly more elegant. As an example, let us consider the following problem offered in the preassessment.

Problem 2:

> If the sum of two numbers is 2 and the product of these same two numbers is 3, find the sum of the reciprocals of these two numbers.

Solution: A first reaction after reading this problem would be to set up the equation: $x + y = 2$, and $xy = 3$. A well-trained student of algebra would promptly set out to solve these equations simultaneously. She or he may solve the first equation for y to get $y = 2 - x$, and then substitute appropriately in the second equation so that $x(2-x) = 3$ or $x^2 - 2x + 3 = 0$. As $x = 1 \pm \sqrt{-2}$ the two numbers are $1 + i\sqrt{2}$ and $1 - i\sqrt{2}$. Now the sum of their reciprocals is

$$\frac{1}{1+i\sqrt{2}} + \frac{1}{1-i\sqrt{2}} = \frac{(1-i\sqrt{2}) + (1+i\sqrt{2})}{(1+i\sqrt{2}) \cdot (1-i\sqrt{2})} = \frac{2}{3}$$

This solution is by no means elegant.

Had students used a reverse strategy ("analysis"), they would have first inspected the desired conclusion; that is, $\dfrac{1}{x} + \dfrac{1}{y}$.

The sum of these fractions is $\dfrac{x + y}{xy}$. The two original equations immediately reveal the numerator and the denominator of this fraction. This produces the answer, $\dfrac{2}{3}$, immediately. It is quite obvious that for this particular problem, a reverse strategy was superior to more common, straightforward approach.

Problem 3: If the sum of two numbers is 2, and the product of the same two numbers is 3, find the sum of the squares of the reciprocals of these numbers.

Solution: To find the sum of the squares of the reciprocals (of the numbers described in the above problem) by a reverse approach, the student must first consider the conclusion, that is: $\left(\dfrac{1}{x}\right)^2 + \left(\dfrac{1}{y}\right)^2$ or $\dfrac{1}{x^2} + \dfrac{1}{y^2}$ Once again students would be required to add the fractions to get: $\dfrac{x^2 + y^2}{x^2y^2}$. Therefore the denominator of the answer is $(xy)^2 = 9$. However, the numerator is not as simple to evaluate as it was earlier. Students must now

find the value of $x^2 + y^2$. Once again students must look backward. How can they somehow generate $x^2 + y^2$? Students will be quick to suggest that $(x + y)^2$ will yield $x^2 + y^2 + 2xy$, which in part produces $x^2 + y^2$. Besides, $(x + y)^2 = (2)^2 = 4$ and $2xy = 2 \cdot 3 = 6$. Hence $x^2 + y^2 = -2$. The problem is therefore solved, as $\dfrac{1}{x^2} + \dfrac{1}{y^2} = \dfrac{x^2 + y^2}{x^2y^2} = \dfrac{-2}{9}$.

A similar procedure can be employed to find the value of $(\dfrac{1}{x})^3 + (\dfrac{1}{y})^3$ from the original two equations $x + y = 2$ and $xy = 3$. Once again beginning with the conclusion and working in reverse, $\dfrac{1}{x^3} + \dfrac{1}{y^3} = \dfrac{x^3 + y^3}{(xy)^3}$. Since students already know that $(xy)^3 = (3)^3 = 27$, they need only to find the value of $x^3 + y^3$. How can they generate $x^3 + y^3$?

From: $(x + y)^3 = x^3 + y^3 + 3x^2y + 3xy^2$
We get: $x^3 + y^3 = (x + y)^3 - 3xy(x + y)$
$$x^3 + y^3 = (2)^3 - 3(3)(2)$$
$$x^3 + y^3 = -10$$

Therefore: $\dfrac{1}{x^3} + \dfrac{1}{y^3} = \dfrac{x^3 + y^3}{(xy)^3} = \dfrac{-10}{27}$

This procedure may also be used to find the sum of higher powers of these reciprocals.

Another problem whose solution lends itself nicely to a reverse strategy ("analysis") involves geometric constructions.

Problem 4: Construct a triangle given the lengths m_a and m_b, of two medians of a triangle and the length, c, of the side whose endpoints are each an endpoint of one of the medians.

Solution: Rather than immediately trying to perform the required construction, students would be wise to use a reverse strategy. They may assume construction and inspect the results.

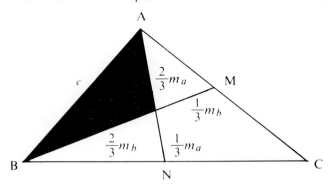

Students will soon realize that they would be able to construct the shaded triangle above as they can easily obtain the lengths of its sides (c, $\dfrac{2m_a}{3}$, $\dfrac{2m_b}{3}$). Points M and N can then be located using the property of the centroid. Then point C will be determined by the intersection of $\overrightarrow{AM}$ and $\overrightarrow{BN}$.

Having started from the conclusion and working in reverse, students have formulated a plan for constructing the required triangle, by merely retracing steps in the reverse direction ("synthesis").

Although there are many problems whose solutions can be significantly simplified by using a reverse strategy, there are also a great number of problems where a straightforward approach is best. It is natural for a student to approach a problem in a straightforward manner. Yet we as teachers must encourage our students to abandon the straightforward approach when a solution is not easily forthcoming, and attempt a reverse solution.

Some problems require only a partial reverse strategy. In such problems it is useful to begin with the conclusion and work backwards until a path to the conclusion is established. Let us consider the following problems.

Problem 5: Find the solution of the following: $(x - y^2)^2 + (x - y - 2)^2 = 0$, where x and y are real numbers.

Solution: Students of algebra might naturally use a straightforward approach to solve this equation. After squaring each of the polynomials as indicated, confusion would mount. Students previously exposed to a reverse strategy would then try to analyze the solution set of the equation. The values of x and y must be such that the sum of the squares of the polynomials equals zero. How can the sum of two positive numbers equal zero? Students can answer this question by saying that $x - y^2 = 0$ and $x - y - 2 = 0$. Up to this point students used a reverse strategy ("analysis"). However, now they must proceed in a straightforward manner ("synthesis") solving the equations $x - y^2 = 0$ and $x - y - 2 = 0$ simultaneously.

In his book *How to Solve It*, George Polya discusses a backward method of problem solving which is similar to a reverse strategy discussed in this article. Polya emphasizes the importance of the role of a teacher in presenting such methods to students when he states that "there is some sort of psychological repugnance to this reverse order which may prevent a quite able student from understanding the method if it is not presented carefully."

It is the responsibility of the mathematics teacher to make a conscious effort to stress the importance, benefits and possible limitations of a reverse strategy in problem solving.

Postassessment

1. If $x + y = 2$ and $xy = 3$, find $\dfrac{1}{x^4} + \dfrac{1}{y^4}$.

2. Construct a triangle given the lengths of two sides and the length of an altitude to one of these sides.

3. Have students use analysis and synthesis to prove the following:

"In right $\triangle ABC$, $\overline{CF}$ is the median drawn to hypotenuse $\overline{AB}$, $\overline{CE}$ is the bisector of $\angle ACB$, and $\overline{CD}$ is the altitude to $\overline{AB}$.
Prove that $\angle DCE \cong \angle ECF$.

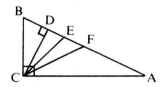

4. Evaluate $x^5 + \dfrac{1}{x^5}$, if $x^2 + \dfrac{1}{x^2} = 7$.

(Answer: $\pm\ 123$)

94 Decimals and Fractions in Other Bases

Performance Objectives

(2) Students will rationalize repeating decimals or repeating fractions in other bases.

Preassessment

Ask students to find the decimal number equivalent to $\frac{87}{99}$ $\left(=\frac{87}{10^2-1}\right)$. Challenge students to represent a repeating decimal by a simple rational number.

Teaching Strategies

Decimal numbers are usually classified as repeating and non-repeating. Repeating decimals are further partitioned into terminating and non-terminating decimals. Students are usually readily aware that a terminating decimal represents a particular rational number. But the nature of a non-terminating decimal is more intriguing. We begin this exploration by confining ourselves to non-terminating repeating decimals. Consider the repeating decimal: $.1212\overline{12}$. (The bar over the last two digits indicates the repeating digits.) What we want to do is to represent this decimal by an equivalent rational simple fraction. If we let $x = .12\overline{12}$. . . and then $100x = 12.12\overline{12}$ . . . subtracting the former from the latter yields the equation: $100x - x = 12$, or $x = \frac{12}{100-1} = \frac{12}{99}$. We have now found a ratio representation for $.1212$ . . . .

Some further exploration is in order now. Notice that $\frac{12}{99}$ $+ \frac{88}{99} = 1$. However, if we add the equivalent decimal representations $\begin{array}{r} .1212\overline{12} \\ +.8787\overline{87} \\ \hline .999999 \end{array}$ one would think that $.999999\overline{99} = 1$. Indeed, applying the above technique yields: $x = .9999\overline{9}$ and $10x = 9.9999\overline{9}$; therefore $10x - x = 9$, and $x = \frac{9}{10-1}$, $x = 1$.

This illustration leads us to an important theorem: any repeating decimal can be represented as a rational number (i.e., the *ratio* of two integers, the denominator not zero).

Proof:

Let the repeating decimal be represented by $.a_1a_2$ . . . a_n . . . where a_i is a digit and n is an integer that represents the length of the repetition. As before, let

$$x = .a_1a_2 \ldots a_n \ldots$$

and

$$10^n x = a_1a_2 \ldots a_n.a_1a_2 \ldots a_n \ldots .$$

Now

$$10^n x - x = a_1a_2 \ldots a_n$$
$$x(10^n - 1) = a_1a_2 \ldots a_n$$
$$x = \frac{a_1a_2 \ldots a_n}{10^n - 1}$$

The repeating decimal is now represented by a rational number.

Students will now want to consider repeating fractions in bases other than 10 (no longer called decimals!). Suppose we have in base 3 the repeating fraction: $.12\overline{12}$. Students should be guided to asking the following:

(1) Can this repeating fraction be represented by a rational number in base 3?

(2) In general can *any* repeating fraction in *any* given base be represented by a rational number?

Begin by using the approach applied earlier to repeating decimals. Let $x = .12\overline{12}$. Ask students how the ternary point may be shifted two places to the right (note the ternary point in base 3 is analogous to the decimal point in base 10). How $3^2 x = 12.12\overline{12}$. By subtracting x we get: $3^2 x - x = 12$, $x(3^2 - 1) = 12$, $x = \frac{12}{3^2 - 1} = \frac{12}{22}$. Thus the repeating fraction in base 3 can be represented by a rational number. Have students notice the analogous form in base 10.

Using these illustrations as models we shall prove that a repeating fraction in any base can be represented by a rational number in that base.

Proof:

Consider any base B and any repeating fraction in that base: $.a_1a_2 \ldots a_n \ldots$ where a_i is a digit of the number and n is an integer that represents the length of the repetition $x = .a_1a_2 \ldots a_n \ldots$

$$B^n x = a_1a_2 \ldots a_n.a_1a_2 \ldots a_n \ldots$$
$$B^n x - x = a_1a_2 \ldots a_n$$
$$x = \frac{a_1a_2 \ldots a_n}{B^n - 1}$$

This proves that any repeating fraction can be represented by a rational number.

Postassessment

Have students do the following exercises:

1. If $x = \frac{123}{10^3 - 1}$, what is its decimal representation?

2. If $x = \frac{11256}{7^4 - 1}$, represent x as a rational fraction.

3. Rationalize the repeating fraction $x = .23\overline{23}$ when x is in base 10, 8 and 5.

95 Polygonal Numbers

This unit can be taught to a class that has a reasonably good command of the basic algebraic skills. Since most of the unit employs intuitive thinking, a good degree of this training should result. It would be helpful if the students were familiar with arithmetic sequences and the formula for the sum of its series. However, if students are not familiar with this topic, essentials can be developed in a reasonably short time.

Performance Objectives
1. *Given the rank of any regular polygon, the student will find a number that corresponds to it.*
2. *The student will discover relations between two or more different polygonal numbers of given ranks.*

Preassessment
The ancient Babylonians discovered that some whole numbers can be broken down into patterns of units. This link between arithmetic and geometry was also of concern to the ancient Greeks. For example, the number 3 can be represented as three dots forming a triangle, as can the number 6.

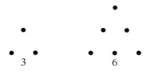

Which regular polygon do you think the number 4 represents? The number 9? After the students have had some time to find such polygons, ask them to provide the answers.

Numbers that can be related to geometric figures are called *figurate* or *polygonal* numbers.

Teaching Strategies
Tell the students that it would be very easy to find the number which corresponds to a given regular polygon if we could find a formula such that given any regular polygon and its rank we could obtain that number from it.

Begin by telling the students what the rank of a regular polygon indicates. For any regular polygon, the rank indicates, in order, the corresponding polygonal number. For example, for a triangle, rank $1 = 3$ (the first triangular number), rank $2 = 6$ (the second triangular number), rank $3 = 10$, etc.

Now draw five figures that will show how to get the first five ranks of the first five figurate numbers (triangular, square, pentagonal, hexagonal, heptagonal). To save time you may use an overhead projector instead, or you may distribute mimeographed sheets with the drawings. Make a corresponding table. Both the drawings and the table which follow indicate what might be shown to your students.

Table 1

Rank *r*

| Triangle | Square | Pentagon | Hexagon | Heptagon |

It should be clear to the student that making a figure to obtain every possible triangular, square, etc. number is a very tedious task. Instead we will study how consecutive polygonal numbers of a given polygon follow each other and, by looking at the sequence formed, try to obtain a formula for the rth rank of each given polygon.

If we look at the first row of figurate numbers corresponding to triangular numbers, and if we also look at their corresponding ranks (table 1) we will notice that they can be written as:

Table 2

Figure	No. sides		Rank *r*			
	N	1	2	3	4	5
Triangular	3	1	3	6	10	15
Square	4	1	4	9	16	25
Pentagonal	5	1	5	12	22	35
Hexagonal	6	1	6	15	28	45
Heptagonal	7	1	7	18	34	55

$$1 = r$$
$$3 = (r - 1) + r$$
$$6 = (r - 2) + (r - 1) + r$$
$$10 = (r - 3) + (r - 2) + (r - 1) + r$$
$$15 = (r - 4) + (r - 3) + (r - 2) + (r - 1) + r$$

If we look at the ranks we will also notice that their sequence forms an arithmetic sequence and that each triangular number of rank r is the sum of that arithmetic sequence $1, 2, 3, \ldots, r$ from 1 to r. Thus we can conclude that the rth triangular number is given by:

$T_r = r(r + 1)/2$

Next, let's look at the square numbers:

$$1 = r^2 = 1^2$$
$$4 = r^2 = 2^2$$
$$9 = r^2 = 3^2$$
$$16 = r^2 = 4^2$$
$$25 = r^2 = 5^2$$

It is clear that each square number is the square of its corresponding rank. So the r square number is r^2.

The formula for the rth pentagonal number can be obtained if we write each number in the following way:

$$1 = r^2 + 0 = 1 + 0$$
$$5 = r^2 + 1 = 2^2 + 1$$
$$12 = r^2 + 3 = 3^2 + 3$$
$$22 = r^2 + 6 = 4^2 + 6$$
$$35 = r^2 + 10 = 5^2 + 10$$

If we study the second part of the sums $0, 1, 3, 6, 10$, we will see that each of the numbers correspond to the sum of the arithmetic sequence $0, 1, 2, \ldots, (r - 1)$ which is $(r - 1)r/2$. So the rth pentagonal number is

$$r^2 + \frac{(r - 1)r}{2} = \frac{2r^2 + (r - 1)r}{2} = \frac{(2r^2 + r^2 - r)}{2}$$
$$= \frac{(3r^2 - r)}{2} = \frac{r(3r - 1)}{2}$$

To find a formula for the rth hexagonal number, consider the first five as follows:

$$1 = 1r$$
$$6 = 3r = 3(2)$$
$$15 = 5r = 5(3)$$
$$28 = 7r = 7(4)$$
$$45 = 9r = 9(5)$$

An inspection of the coefficients of r: $1, 3, 5, 7, 9$, would reveal that each corresponds to the sum of the corresponding rank and the rank immediately before it. That is, each coefficient is equal to $r + (r - 1)$. Therefore the rth hexagonal number is $[r + (r - 1)]r = (2r - 1)r$.

The rth heptagonal number is found as follows. Write the first seven heptagonal numbers in the following way:

$$1 = 2r^2 - 1 = 2(1)^2 - 1$$
$$7 = 2r^2 - 1 = 2(2)^2 - 1$$
$$18 = 2r^2 + 0 = 2(3)^2 + 0$$
$$34 = 2r^2 + 2 = 2(4)^2 + 2$$
$$55 = 2r^2 + 5 = 2(5)^2 + 5$$

It probably will be very difficult for the students to arrive at a formula for the second part X of each number $2r^2 + X$. Therefore after the students have looked at the numbers for a short time the teacher should immediately point out that each X is equal to the sum of the arithmetic sequence $-1, 0, 1, 2, 3, \ldots, (r - 2)$ minus one, which is $\frac{(r - 2)(r - 1)}{2} - 1$.

Students should test the formula on each of the given numbers above. So the rth heptagonal number is

$$2r^2 + \frac{(r - 2)(r - 1)}{2} - 1 = 2r^2 + \frac{(r - 2)(r - 1) - 2}{2} =$$
$$2r^2 + \frac{r^2 - 3r + 2 - 2}{2} = \frac{r(5r - 3)}{2}$$

Call attention to the fact that we now have a formula for the rth rank of each of the first 5 polygonal numbers. So we are now able to find any triangular, square, pentagonal, hexagonal and heptagonal number. But, there are regular polygons of $8, 9, \ldots 20, 100$, etc. sides and we would also like to have a formula for the rth rank of each of them. It is our next task to find such formulas.

To do this let's write the formulas we have already found as follows:

No. sides	Rank $= r$		
3	$\dfrac{r(r + 1)}{2}$	$= \dfrac{r^2 + r}{2}$	$= \dfrac{1r^2}{2} + \dfrac{r}{2}$
4	r^2	$= \dfrac{2r^2}{2}$	$= \dfrac{2r^2}{2} + \dfrac{0}{2}$
5	$\dfrac{r(3r - 1)}{2}$	$= \dfrac{3r^2 - r}{-2}$	$= \dfrac{3r^2}{2} - \dfrac{r}{2}$
6	$r(2r - 1)$	$= \dfrac{4r^2 - 2r}{2}$	$= \dfrac{4r^2}{2} - \dfrac{2r}{2}$
7	$\dfrac{r(5r - 3)}{2}$	$= \dfrac{5r^2 - 3r}{2}$	$= \dfrac{5r^2}{2} - \dfrac{3r}{2}$
.			
.			
.			
.			
.			
.			
.			
N			

Let's now look at the last column. We will notice that the coefficients of the $\frac{r^2}{2}$ terms can be written as $(N-2)$. Also the coefficients of the $\frac{r}{2}$ terms can be written as $-(N-4)$. Therefore, the rth rank of a N-gonal number is

$$\frac{(N-2)r^2}{2} - \frac{(N-4)r}{2} = \frac{(N-2)r^2 - (N-4)r}{2} =$$
$$\left(\frac{r}{2}\right)\left[(N-2)r - (N-4)\right] = \left(\frac{r}{2}\right)\left[(r-1)N - 2(r-2)\right]$$

The completed table (including the first 5 ranks of the N-gonal number looks like this:

No. sides	\multicolumn{6}{c}{Rank}
	1	2	3	4	5	r
3	1	3	6	10	15	$\frac{r(r+1)}{2}$
4	1	4	9	16	25	r^2
5	1	5	12	22	35	$\frac{r(3r-1)}{2}$
6	1	6	15	28	15	$\frac{r(2r-1)}{}$
7	1	7	18	34	55	$\frac{r(5r-3)}{}$
.						
.						
.						
N	1		.....		$\left(\frac{r}{2}\right)\left[(r-1)N - 2(r-2)\right]$	

At this point it would be instructive for the students to work out some simple examples using the formula for the rth N-gonal number.

Example 1

Find the third octagonal number.

Solution: Let $N=8$ and $r=3$. Substitute these numbers in the formula $\frac{r}{2}\left[(r-1)N - 2(r-2)\right]$

$= \frac{3}{2}\left[(3-1)8 - 2(3-2)\right] = \frac{3}{2}(2)8 - 2(1)$

$= \frac{3}{2}\left[16-2\right] = \frac{3 \times 14}{2} = 21$

Example 2

To what regular polygon does the number 40 correspond if $r=4$?

Solution: In this case we know the rank and the number, but we must find N. We substitute into and solve the following equation:

$$\left(\frac{r}{2}\right)\left[(r-1)N - 2(r-2)\right] = 40$$
$$\left(\frac{4}{2}\right)\left[(4-1)N - 2(4-2)\right] = 40$$
$$2\left[3N - 2(2)\right] = 40, \quad \text{and} \quad N=8.$$

So the figure is a regular octagon.

The following examples are a little more difficult for they call for applications of the formulas to find relationships between different types of polygonal numbers.

Example 3

Show that the rth pentagonal number is equal to r plus three times the $(r-1)$th triangular number.

Solution: In order to do this problem we must first write the formula for the rth pentagonal number:

$$P_r = \frac{r(3r-1)}{2} = \frac{3r^2}{2} - \frac{r}{2}$$

Rewrite $\frac{-r}{3}$ as $\frac{-3r}{2} + r$.

Now we have $\frac{3r^2}{2} - \frac{3r}{2} + r = \frac{3(r^2-r)}{2} + r$

$\frac{3r(r-1)}{2} + r = 3T_{r-1} + r$, where

T_{r-1} is the $(r-1)^{\text{st}}$ triangular number.

Example 4

Show that any hexagonal number is equal to the sum of a pentagonal number of the same rank and a triangular number of the preceding rank.

Solution: $(\text{Hex})_r = r(2r-1) = 2r^2 - r$

$= \frac{3r^2 - r}{2} + \frac{r^2 - r}{2}$

$= \frac{r(3r-1)}{2} + \frac{r(r-1)}{2} = P_r + T_{r-1}$

Postassessment

After students have studied the previous examples they should be able to do the following problems:

1. Draw a regular octagon corresponding to the third octagonal number of example 1 (study the drawings of the first 5 figurate numbers before doing this problem).

2. Find the first 3 dacagonal (10 sides) numbers.

3. Show that any heptagonal number is equal to the sum of a hexagonal number of the same rank and a triangular number of the previous rank (i.e., show: $(\text{Hep})_r = (\text{Hex})_r + T_{r-1}$).

4. Show that any N-gonal number ($N \geqslant 5$) is equal to the sum of the $(N-1)$-gonal number of the same rank and a triangular number of the previous rank. (Hint: Begin with the $(N-1)$-gonal number of rank

r and T_{r-1}. Carry out the addition).

5. Show that the sum of any number of consecutive odd integers, starting with 1 is a perfect square (i.e., a square number).

96 Networks

This unit will serve as an introductory lesson in topology.

Performance Objective

Given a closed curve, students will determine if it is traversible or nontraversible.

Preassessment

Have students try to trace with a pencil each of the following configurations without missing any part and without going over any part twice.

Ask students to determine the number of arcs or line segments which have an endpoint at each of A, B, C, D, E.

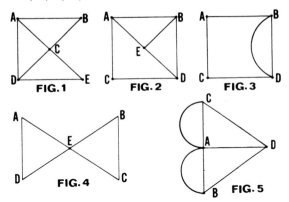

FIG.1   FIG.2   FIG.3   FIG.4   FIG.5

Teaching Strategies

Configurations such as Figures 1-5, which are made up of line segments and/or continuous arcs are called *networks*. The number of arcs or line segments which have an endpoint at a particular vertex, is called the *degree* of the vertex.

After trying to trace these networks without taking their pencils off the paper and without going over any line more than once, students should notice two direct outcomes. The networks can be traced (or *traversed*) if they have (1) all even degree vertices or (2) exactly two odd degree vertices. The proof of these two outcomes follows.

There are an even number of odd degree vertices in a connected network.

Proof: Let V_1 be the number of vertices of degree 1, let V_3 be the number of vertices of degree 3, and

V_n the number of vertices of degree n. Also let $N = V_1 + V_3 + V_5 + \ldots + V_{2n-1}$. N is the number of odd degree vertices in a given connected network ("connected" meaning without loose ends). Since there are 3 arc endpoints at V_3, 5 at V_5 and n at V_n, the total number of arc endpoints in a connected network is $M = V_1 + 2V_2 + 3V_3 + 4V_4 + \ldots + 2nV_{2n}$.

$$M - N = 2V_2 + 2V_3 + 4V_4 + 4V_5 + \ldots + (2n-2)V_{2n-1} + 2nV_{2n}$$
$$= 2(V_2 + V_3 + 2V_4 + 2V_5 + \ldots + (n-1)V_{2n-1} + nV_{2n})$$

Since the difference of two even numbers is an even number, $M - (M - N) = N$ is an even number.

A connected network can be traversed, only if it has at most two odd degree vertices.

Proof: On a continuous path the inside vertices must be passed through. That is, if a line "enters" the point another must "leave" the point. This accounts for the endpoints. The only vertices which do not conform to this rule are the beginning and endpoints in the traversing. These *two* points may be of odd order. By the previous theorem, it was established that there must be an even number of odd vertices; therefore there can only be *two* or *zero* vertices of odd order in order to traverse a network.

Have students now draw both traversible and nontraversible networks (using these two theorems). Network 1 in the Preassessment has five vertices. Vertices B,C,E are of even degree and vertices A and D are of odd degree. Since Figure 1 has exactly two odd degree vertices as well as three even degree vertices it is traversible. If we start at A then go down to D, across to E, back up to A, across to B, and down to D we have chosen a desired route.

Network 2 has five vertices. Vertex C is the only even degree vertex. Vertices A,B,E, and D, are all of odd degree. Consequently, since the network has more than two odd vertices, it is not traversible.

Network 3 is traversible because it has two even vertices and exactly two odd degree vertices.

Network 4 has five even degree vertices and can be traversed.

Network 5 has four odd degree vertices and *cannot* be traversed.

To generate interest among your students present them with the famous Königsberg Bridge Problem. In the eighteenth century the small Prussian city of Königsberg, located where the Pregel River formed two branches, was faced with a recreational dilemma: Could a person walk over each of the seven bridges exactly once in a continuous walk through the city? In 1735 the famous mathematician Leonhard Euler (1707-1783) proved that this walk could not be performed. Indicate to students that the ensuing discussion will tie in their earlier work with networks to the solution of the Königsberg Bridge Problem.

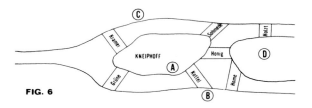

FIG. 6

Tell pupils to indicate the island by A, the left bank of the river by B, the right one by C, and the area between the two arms of the upper course by D. If we start at Holzt and walk to Sohmede and then through Honig, through Hohe, through Kottel, through Grüne we will never cross Kramer. On the other hand if we start at Kramer and walk to Honig, through Hohe, through Kottel, through Sohmede, through Holzt we will never travel through Grüne.

The Königsberg Bridge Problem is the same problem as the one posed in Figure 5. Let's take a look at Figures 5 and 6 and note the similarity. There are seven bridges in Figure 6 and there are seven lines in Figure 5. In Figure 5 each vertex is of odd degree. In Figure 6 if we start at D we have three choices, we could go to Hohe, Honig, or Holzt. If in Figure 5 we start at D we have three line paths to choose from. In both figures if we are at C we have either three bridges we could go on or three lines. A similar situation exists for locations A and B in Figure 6 and vertices A and B in Figure 5. Emphasize that this network *cannot* be traversed.

Another example of a problem where the consideration of the traversibility of a network is important is the Five Room House Problem. Have

students consider the diagram of a five-room house.

Each room has a doorway to each adjacent room and a doorway leading outside the house. The problem is to have a person start either inside or outside the house and walk through each doorway *exactly once*.

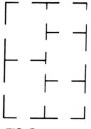

FIG. 7a

Students should be encouraged to try various paths. They will realize that although the number of attempts is finite, there are far too many to make a trial-and-error solution practical. They should be guided to a network diagram analogous to this problem.

Figure 7b shows various possible paths joining the five rooms A, B, C, D, and E, and the outside F. The problem now reduces to merely determining if this network is traversible. There are *four vertices* of odd degree and two vertices of even degree. Since there are not *exactly* two or zero vertices of odd order, this network *cannot* be traversed; hence the Five-Room House Problem does not have a solution path.

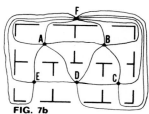

FIG. 7b

Other problems of a similar nature may now be presented to the students.

Postassessment

1. Have students find out if the following figures can be traced without removing their pencils from the paper and without going over any line twice. (i.e., traversed)

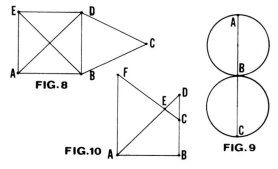

FIG. 8

FIG.10

FIG. 9

2. Have students draw a house floor plan and then determine if one can walk through each doorway exactly once.

97   Angle Trisection—Possible or Impossible?

Of the Three Famous Problems of Antiquity, the one most instructive to a high school student is the angle trisection. This unit will present a discussion and proof that any angle cannot be trisected with only straightedge and compasses.

Performance Objective
Students will outline a proof that an angle of measure 120° cannot be trisected. '

Preassessment
Students should be familiar with the basic geometric constructions.

Teaching Strategies
Ask students to trisect an angle of measure 90° using only straightedge and compasses. With little difficulty they ought to be able to construct an angle of measure 60° at the vertex of the given angle. This virtually completes the trisection. However, now ask students to trisect an angle of measure 120°. This will cause difficulty because it is impossible with straightedge and compasses. At this point, begin discussion of the impossibility of angle trisection using only straightedge and compasses.

With the aid of a unit length and an angle of measure A, it is possible to construct a line segment of length cos A. (see figure below)

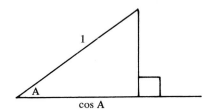

If we can trisect ∠A, then we can also construct the $\cos \frac{A}{3}$. If we can show that $\cos \frac{A}{3}$ cannot be constructed, then we have shown that ∠A cannot be trisected. Here we shall let $m\angle A = 120°$, and show ∠A cannot be trisected.

We shall first obtain an expression for cos A in terms of $\cos \frac{A}{3}$.

$\cos 3y = \cos (2y+y) = \cos 2y \cos y - \sin 2y \sin y$
But, $\cos 2y = 2 \cos^2 y - 1$.
Substituting:
$\cos 3y = \cos y (2 \cos^2 y - 1) - \sin 2y \sin y$
$= \left[2 \cos^3 y - \cos y \right] - \sin 2y \sin y.$

But, $\sin 2y = 2 \sin y \cos y$
Therefore:

$\cos 3y = \left[2 \cos^3 y - \cos y \right] - \sin y (2 \sin y \cos y)$
$\cos 3y = \left[2 \cos^3 y - \cos y \right] - 2 \sin^2 y \cos y$
$\cos 3y = \left[2 \cos^3 y - \cos y \right] - 2 \cos y(1 - \cos^2 y)$
$\cos 3y = \left[2 \cos^3 y - \cos y \right] - 2 \cos y + 2 \cos^3 y$
$\cos 3y = 4 \cos^3 y - 3 \cos y$

Let $3y = A$ to obtain:

$\cos A = 4 \cos^3 \dfrac{A}{3} - 3 \cos \dfrac{A}{3}$

Multiply by 2 and replace $2 \cos \dfrac{A}{3}$ with x to get:

$2 \cos A = x^3 - 3x.$

Since $\cos 120° = -\dfrac{1}{2}$, $x^3 - 3x + 1 = 0.$

Students should now recall that one of the criteria of constructibility (see p. 256) indicates that constructible roots must be of the form $a + b\sqrt{c}$, where a and b are rational and c is constructible.

First, then, we must show that $x^3 - 3x + 1 = 0$ has no rational roots. To do this, we assume that there is a rational root, $\dfrac{p}{q}$, where p and q have no common factor greater than 1. Substituting for $\dfrac{p}{q}$, we have

$(\dfrac{p}{q})^3 - 3(\dfrac{p}{q}) + 1 = 0$
$p^3 - 3pq^2 + q^3 = 0$
$q^3 = 3pq^2 - p^3$
$q^3 = p(3q^2 - p^2)$

This means that q^3, and hence q, has the factor p. Therefore p must equal ± 1. Also, solving for p^3
$\quad p^3 = 3pq^2 - q^3$
$\quad p^3 = q^2(3p - q)$
This means p and q must have a common factor, and hence $q = \pm 1$. We can conclude from this that the only rational root of $x^3 - 3x + 1 = 0$ is $r = \pm 1$. By substitution, we can show that neither $+1$ nor -1 is root.

Next, assume $x^3 - 3x + 1 = 0$ has a constructible root $a + b\sqrt{c}$. By substitution in the equation $x^3 - 3x + 1 = 0$, we can show that if $a + b\sqrt{c}$ is a root, then its conjugate, $a - b\sqrt{c}$, is also a root. The sum of the roots of the polynomial equation $x^n + a_1 x^{n-1} + a_2 x^{n-2} + \ldots + a_n = 0$ is $r_1 + r_2 + r_3 + \ldots + r_n = -a_1.$

It follows from this that the sum of the roots $x^3 - 3x + 1 = 0$ is zero. If two roots are $a + b\sqrt{c}$ and $a - b\sqrt{c}$, with the third root r, we have
$$a + b\sqrt{c} + a - b\sqrt{c} + r = 0$$
$$r = -2a$$
But a is rational and hence r is rational, and we have a contradiction. Hence the angle whose measure is 120° cannot be trisected. This essentially proves that any angle cannot be trisected with only straightedge and compasses.

Postassessment
Have students write an outline of the proof presented in this unit as well as a discussion of its significance.

98 Comparing Means

This unit can be used as a major part of a lesson on statistics.

Performance Objectives
1. Students will compare magnitudes of three means for any two or more numbers.

2. Students will prove comparison relationships between means.

Preassessment
After students have reviewed the arithmetic and geometric means, have students express h in terms of a and b, where a,h,b is a harmonic sequence.

Teaching Strategies
Begin by defining the three means (arithmetic, harmonic and geometric) in the following way.

Suppose a,m,b are an arithmetic sequence. The middle term (m) is said to be the *arithmetic mean*. Since a,m,b have a common difference $m - a = b - m$,

and $\boxed{m = \dfrac{a+b}{2} = \text{arithmetic mean (A.M.)}}$

Now suppose a,h,b are a harmonic sequence. The middle term (h) is said to be the *harmonic mean*. Since a,h,b have reciprocals with a common difference, $\dfrac{1}{h} - \dfrac{1}{a} = \dfrac{1}{b} - \dfrac{1}{h}$ and

$\boxed{h = \dfrac{2ab}{a+b} = \text{harmonic mean (H.M.)}}$

Finally suppose a,g,b are a *geometric sequence*.

Since a,g,b have a common ratio, $\dfrac{g}{a} = \dfrac{b}{g}$ and

$\boxed{g = \sqrt{ab} = \text{geometric mean (G.M.)}}$

Since often a pictorial model crystalizes understanding, a geometric interpretation is appropriate here. Consider the semicircle with diameter $\overline{AOPB}$ with $\overline{AO} \cong \overline{OB}$ and $\overline{PR} \perp \overline{APB}$. (R is on the semicircle). Also $\overline{PS} \perp \overline{RSO}$. Let $AP = a$ and $PB = b$.

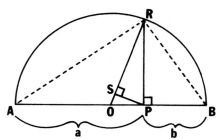

Since $RO = \frac{1}{2}AB = \frac{1}{2}(AP + PB) = \frac{1}{2}(a+b)$, RO is the *arithmetic mean* (A.M.) between a and b.

Consider right $\triangle ARB$. Since $\triangle BPR \sim \triangle RPA$, $\dfrac{PB}{PR} = \dfrac{PR}{AP}$ or $(PR)^2 = (AP) \cdot (PB) = ab$. Therefore $PR = \sqrt{ab}$. Thus PR is the *geometric mean* (G.M.) between a and b.

Since $\triangle RPO \sim \triangle RSP$, $\dfrac{RO}{PR} = \dfrac{PR}{RS}$. Therefore $RS = \dfrac{(PR)^2}{RO}$. But $(PR)^2 = ab$ and $RO = \frac{1}{2}AB = \frac{1}{2}(a+b)$. Thus $RS = \dfrac{ab}{\frac{1}{2}(a+b)} = \dfrac{2ab}{a+b}$ which is the *harmonic mean* (H.M.) between a and b.

This geometric interpretation lends itself quite well to a comparison of the magnitudes of these three means. Since the hypotenuse of a right triangle is its longest side, in $\triangle ROP$, $RO > PR$ and in $\triangle RSP$, $PR > RS$. Therefore, $RO > PR > RS$. However, since it is possible for these triangles to degenerate, $RO \geqq PR \geqq RS$ which implies that A.M. $\geqq$ G.M. $\geqq$ H.M.

Since the student is familiar with both arithmetic mean and geometric mean (sometimes called the mean proportional), a brief introduction to the harmonic mean would be in order.

The *harmonic mean* between two numbers is the *reciprocal of the arithmetic mean between the reciprocals* of these two numbers. This is because a harmonic sequence is a sequence of reciprocals of members of an arithmetic sequence. For a and b,

$$\text{H.M.} = \cfrac{1}{\cfrac{\cfrac{1}{a}+\cfrac{1}{b}}{2}} = \frac{2ab}{a+b}$$

Example 1: Find the harmonic mean of $a, b,$ and c.
Solution: by the definition

$$\text{H.M.} = \cfrac{1}{\cfrac{\cfrac{1}{a}+\cfrac{1}{b}+\cfrac{1}{c}}{3}} = \frac{3abc}{ab+ac+bc}$$

Both the arithmetic mean and the geometric mean have popular applications in secondary school curriculum. The harmonic mean also has a very useful and often neglected application in elementary mathematics. The harmonic mean is the "average of rates." For example, suppose the average rate of speed for the trip to and from work is desired, when the rate of speed to work is 30 m.p.h. and returning (over the same route) is 60 m.p.h. The average speed is the harmonic mean between 30 and 60; that is, $\frac{(2)(30)(60)}{30+60} = 40$.

To show that the average rate of speed of two (or more) speeds is in fact the harmonic mean of these speeds, consider rates of speed $r_1, r_2, r_3, \ldots, r_n$, each traveled for a time $t_1, t_2, t_3, \ldots, t_n$, respectively and *each* over a distance d.

$$t_1 = \frac{d}{r_1}, \ t_2 = \frac{d}{r_2}, \ t_3 = \frac{d}{r_3}, \ \ldots \ t_n = \frac{d}{r_n}$$

The average speed (for the entire trip) is

$$\frac{\text{total distance}}{\text{total time}} = \frac{nd}{t_1+t_2+t_3+\ldots+t_n}$$

$$= \frac{nd}{\dfrac{d}{r_1}+\dfrac{d}{r_2}+\ldots+\dfrac{d}{r_n}} = \frac{n}{\dfrac{1}{r_1}+\dfrac{1}{r_2}+\dfrac{1}{r_3}+\ldots+\dfrac{1}{r_n}},$$

which is the harmonic mean.

Example 2: If Lisa bought $1.00 worth of each of three kinds of candy, 15¢, 25¢ and 40¢ per pound, what was her average price paid per pound?
Solution: Since the harmonic mean is the average of rates (taken over the same base), the average price per pound was

$$\frac{(3)(15)(25)(40)}{(15)(25)+(15)(40)+(25)(40)} = 22\frac{62}{79}¢$$

To complete the discussion of a comparison of the magnitude of the three means, consider with the class a more general (algebraic) discussion.

In general terms,

$$\text{A.M.} = \frac{a_1+a_2+a_3+\ldots+a_n}{n}$$

$$\text{G.M.} = \sqrt[n]{a_1 \cdot a_2 \cdot a_3 \cdot \ldots \cdot a_n}$$

$$\text{H.M.} = \frac{n}{\dfrac{1}{a_1}+\dfrac{1}{a_2}+\dfrac{1}{a_3}+\ldots+\dfrac{1}{a_n}}$$

Theorem 1: A.M. $\geq$ G.M.

Proof: Let $g = \sqrt[n]{a_1 \cdot a_2 \cdot a_3 \cdot \ldots \cdot a_n}$;

then $1 = \sqrt[n]{\dfrac{a_1}{g} \cdot \dfrac{a_2}{g} \cdot \dfrac{a_3}{g} \cdot \ldots \cdot \dfrac{a_n}{g}}$

Therefore $1 = \dfrac{a_1}{g} \cdot \dfrac{a_2}{g} \cdot \dfrac{a_3}{g} \cdot \ldots \cdot \dfrac{a_n}{g}$

However $\dfrac{a_1}{g} + \dfrac{a_2}{g} + \dfrac{a_3}{g} + \ldots + \dfrac{a_n}{g} \geq n$ since if the product of n positive numbers equals 1, their sum is *not* less than n. Therefore

$$\frac{a_1+a_2+a_3+\ldots+a_n}{n} \geq g$$

Hence $\dfrac{a_1+a_2+a_3+\ldots+a_n}{n} \geq \sqrt[n]{a_1 \cdot a_2 \cdot a_3 \cdot \ldots \cdot a_n}$,

or A.M. $\geq$ G.M.

This proof for two numbers a and b $(a > b)$ is rather cute:
Since $a - b > 0$, $(a-b)^2 > 0$, or $a^2 - 2ab + b^2 > 0$. By adding $4ab$ to both sides of the inequality:
$$a^2 + 2ab + b^2 > 4ab$$
Taking the positive square root yields:
$$\frac{a+b}{2} > \sqrt{ab}$$
Hence A.M. $>$ G.M. (Note: if $a = b$ then A.M. = G.M.)

Theorem 2: G.M. $\geq$ H.M.

Proof: Since A.M. $\geq$ G.M. for $a_1^b, a_2^b, a_3^b \ldots, a_n^b$

$$\frac{a_1^b + a_2^b + a_3^b + \ldots + a_n^b}{n} \geq \sqrt[n]{a_1^b \cdot a_2^b \cdot a_3^b \ldots a_n^b}.$$

when $\dfrac{1}{b} < 0$, $\left[\sqrt[n]{a_1^b \cdot a_2^b \cdot a_3^b \cdot \ldots \cdot a_n^b}\right]^{\frac{1}{b}} \geq$

$$\left[\frac{a_1^b + a_2^b + a_3^b + \ldots + a_n^b}{n}\right]^{\frac{1}{b}}$$

Take $b = -1$, then $\sqrt[n]{a_1 \cdot a_2 \cdot a_3 \ldots \cdot a_n} \geq$

$$\left[\frac{a_1^{-1} + a_2^{-1} + a_3^{-1} + \ldots + a_n^{-1}}{n}\right]^{-1}$$

Hence; $\sqrt[n]{a_1 \cdot a_2 \cdot a_3 \ldots \cdot a_n} \geq$

$$\frac{n}{\dfrac{1}{a_1}+\dfrac{1}{a_2}+\dfrac{1}{a_3}+\ldots+\dfrac{1}{a_n}} \text{, or G.M.} \geq \text{H.M.}$$

Once again for two numbers a and b $(a > b)$ the proof becomes much simpler:

Since (from above) $a^2 + 2ab + b^2 > 4ab$,
$ab(a+b)^2 > (4ab)(ab)$

Therefore $ab > \dfrac{4a^2b^2}{(a+b)^2}$, or $\sqrt{ab} > \dfrac{2ab}{a+b}$

Hence, G.M. > H.M. (Note if $a = b$ then G.M. = H.M.)

Postassessment

1. Find the A.M., G.M., and H.M. for each of the following:

    a) 20 and 60;   b) 25 and 45   c) 3, 15 and 45.

2. Arrange the G.M., H.M., and A.M. in ascending order of magnitude.

3. Show that for two given numbers the G.M. is the geometric mean between the A.M. and H.M.

4. Prove that the G.M. > H.M. for a, b, and c.

99   Pascal's Pyramid

The ability to expand and generalize is one of the most important facilities a teacher can help a student develop. In this unit, the familiar application of Pascal's triangle to determine the coefficients of a binomial expansion $(a + b)^n$ is expanded by the use of "Pascal's pyramid" to consider the coefficients of $(a + b + c)^n$.

Performance Objectives

1) *Students will evaluate trinomial expansions* $(a + b + c)^n$ *of lower powers.*

2) *Students will discover important relationships between Pascal's triangle and Pascal's pyramid.*

Preassessment

If your students are familiar with Pascal's triangle, have them perform the following expansions:

    a) $(a + b)^3$; b) $(a - b)^4$; c) $(x + 2y)^5$.

Ask your students to test their algebraic multiplication (and patience) by evaluating:

a) $(a + b + c)^3$; b) $(a + b + c)^4$.

Teaching Strategies

Begin by reviewing Pascal's triangle. You might mention that this triangle is not Pascal's alone. In fact, the triangle was well known in China before 1300 and was also known to Omar Khayyam, author of the *Rubiyat,* almost 600 years before Pascal. Historical accuracy aside, each row of Pascal's (or Khayyam's or Ying Hui's) triangle yields the coefficients of $(a + b)^n$.

1	$(a + b)^0$
1 1	$(a + b)^1$
1 2 1	$(a + b)^2$
1 3 3 1	$(a + b)^3$
1 4 6 4 1	$(a + b)^4$
1 5 10 10 5 1	$(a + b)^5$

For example, to find $(a + b)^4$ use the coefficients in row 5 of the triangle: $a^4 + 4a^3b + 6a^2b^2 + 4ab^3 + b^4$:

Whereas a binomial expansion can be represented by a readily visible triangle, the trinomial expansion is represented by the more complex pyramid. The first expansion $(a + b + c)^0$ has the single coefficient 1. We can visualize this as the vertex of the pyramid. Each succeeding expansion is then represented by a triangular cross section of the pyramid with the coefficient 1 at each of the vertices.

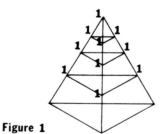

Figure 1

Therefore each of the lateral edges of the pyramid consists of a sequence of 1's. The second expansion $(a + b + c)^1$ has coefficients: $1a + 1b + 1c$, which are represented by the first layer triangle with entries only at the vertices,   1
        1 1.

There are two methods of generating the coefficients of higher powers by means of the pyramid. In the first, again consider each expansion as a triangular cross-section of a pyramid. The numbers on the outer edge of each layer (the numbers between the vertices) are found by adding the two numbers that lie directly above. For example, $(a + b + c)^2$ has 1's at each vertex, and 2's between   1
         2   2
      1   2   1

To determine the terms in the interior of the triangle, add the three terms that lie above; for example, $(a + b + c)^3$ has the following coefficients:

```
          1
        3   3
      3   6   3
    1   3   3   1
```

or referring to the pyramid:

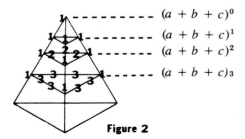

Figure 2

To assign these coefficients to the correct variables:

1) let the coefficient in the first row of the pyramid be "a" to the highest power of that expansion;

2) let the elements of the second row be the coefficients of the product of "a" to the second highest power and the other variables to the first power;

3) in the third row again decrease the power of "a" and arrange the other variables such that the sum of the exponents of each term equals the power the original expansion was raised to;

4) within each row the powers of "a" remain the same while ths power of "b" decreases left to right and the power of "c" increases.

Specifically, consider $(a + b + c)^3$ which has a coefficient configuration:

```
          1
        3   3
      3   6   3
    1   3   3   1
```

The full expansion would then be: $a^3 + 3a^2b + 3a^2c + 3ab^2 + 6abc + 3ac^2 + b^3 + 3b^2c + 3bc^2 + c^3$.

In working with these pyramids students may notice that the edge of each triangle corresponds exactly to a row of the Pascal triangle i.e., the edge of $(a + b + c)^3$,

1 3 3 1, is the same as the fourth row in Pascal's triangle. This observation leads to the second method of deriving the pyramid.

Let the left edge of the trinomial expansion be represented by the corresponding row of Pascal's triangle. Then multiply each row of Pascal's triangle by the number on the left edge to generate the coefficients for the trinomial expansion. For example, the left edge of $(a + b + c)^4$ will be 1 4 6 4 1, corresponding to the fifth row of Pascal's triangle.

```
        1                    (1×1)
      1   1              (4×1) (4×1)
    1   2   1        (6×1) (6×2) (6×1)
  1   3   3   1    (4×1) (4×3) (4×3) (4×1)
1   4   6   4   1  (1×1) (1×4) (1×6) (1×4) (1×1)
```

Multiplying these elements along the edge by the consecutive rows of the triangle yields $(a + b + c)^4$.

```
          1
        4   4
      6   12   6
    4   12   12   4
  1   4   6   4   1
```

This may at first appear to be a complicated procedure, but practice in its use will clear up intitial confusion and introduce an intriguing and useful technique.

Postassessment

Students should perform the following exercises:

1) Have the students compare the time required to expand $(a + b + c)^4$ algebraically versus the pyramid expansion.

2) Expand $(a + b + c)^5$, $(a + b + c)^6$.

3) Expand $(a + 2b + 3c)^3$, $(a + 4b + c)^4$.

4) Some students may be interested in constructing a working model of the pyramid, composed of detachable triangular sections with the appropriate coefficients noted on each surface.

100 The Multinomial Theorem

This unit should be used with a class which has already studied the Binomial Theorem.

Performance Objectives

1. *Students will find the coefficient of any given term of a given multinomial expansion without actually expanding it.*

2. *Students will justify the existence of the coefficients of the multinomial expansion.*

3. *Students will successfully apply Multinomial Theorem to a given trinomial.*

Preassessment

Have students expand $(a + b)^4$ by using the Binomial Theorem. Ask students to determine the number of different arrangements which can be formed from the letters AAABBBCC.

Teaching Strategies

Begin by reviewing student responses concerning the number of arrangements of AAABBBCC. They should realize that this problem differs from asking them to determine the number of arrangements of ABCDEFGH (where each symbol to be arranged is different from the rest). In the latter case the first place (of the eight places) can be filled in any one of eight ways, the second place can be filled in any one of seven ways, the third in six ways, the fourth in five ways, . . ., the eighth in only one way. Using the counting principle, the total number of ways is $8 \cdot 7 \cdot 6 \cdot 5 \cdot 4 \cdot 3 \cdot 2 \cdot 1 = 8!$ (read "8 factorial").

Having already studied Binomial Theorem, students should be familiar with the basic concepts of *combinations*. That is, $_nC_r = \binom{n}{r} = \frac{_nP_r}{r!}$

$= \frac{n!}{r!\,(n-r)!}$

Students should now be ready to consider the original problem, finding the number of arrangements of AAABBBCC. They should be carefully led through the following development.

Let #(A) represent the "number of ways of selecting positions for the A's." Since there are three A's, from the 8 positions 3 must be selected.

This can be done $_8C_3$ or $\binom{8}{3}$ ways. Hence #(A)

$= \binom{8}{3} = \frac{8!}{3! \cdot 5!}$

Similarly $\#(B) = \binom{5}{3} = \frac{5!}{3! \cdot 2!}$, since 3 posi-

tions for the three B's must be selected from the remaining 5 positions. This leaves 2 positions to be selected for the two C's. Since only 2 positions remain, there is only one way of selecting these 2 positions, that is $\binom{2}{2} = \frac{2!}{2! \cdot 0!} = 1$. Indicate that $0! = 1$ by definition. By using the counting principle, #(A and B and C) = #(A)·#(B)·#(C) =

$$\frac{8!}{3! \cdot 5!} \cdot \frac{5!}{3! \cdot 2!} \cdot \frac{2!}{2! \cdot 0!} = \frac{8!}{3! \cdot 3! \cdot 2!}$$

This last expression is usually symbolized as $\binom{8}{3,3,2}$

which represents the number of ways of arranging eight items consisting of repetitions of 3 items, 3 items and 2 items.

To reinforce this technique, ask your students to determine the number of ways in which the letters of *Mississippi* can be arranged. Taking into consideration the repetitions (i.e. 1-M, 4-I's, 4-S's, 2-P's) students should obtain

$$\frac{11\ 10\ 9\ \cancel{8}\ 7\ \cancel{6}\ 5\ \cancel{4}\ \cancel{3}\ \cancel{2}\ \cancel{1}}{1\ \cancel{4}\ \cancel{3}\ \cancel{2}\ 1\ \cancel{4}\ \cancel{3}\ \cancel{2}\ 1\ \cancel{2}\ \cancel{1}} = 34,650.$$

Students should now be guided to generalizing this scheme for counting to n items which include n_1 items of one kind, n_2 items of another, n_3 items of a third kind, . . . , n_r items of a last kind. Clearly $n_1 + n_2 + n_3 + \ldots + n_r = n$. Applying the scheme from before, $\#(N_1)$ shall represent "the number of ways in which n_1 positions may be selected from the n positions available." Hence $\#(N_1) = \frac{n!}{n_1!\,(n-n_1)!}$ Similarly, $\#(N_2) = \frac{(n-n_1)!}{n_2!(n-n_1-n_2)!}$, since only $n-n_1$ places remained from which to select n_2 positions. Similarly, $\#(N_r) =$

$\frac{(n-n_1-n_2-\ldots-n_{r-1})!}{n_r!(n-n_1-n_2-\ldots-n_r)!}$. Since $n_1 + n_2 + n_3 + \ldots + n_r = n$, $\#(N_r) \ldots 1, \frac{n_r!}{n_r! \cdot 0!} = 1$

Using the counting principle for these r cases the numbers of ways of arranging these n items (with r items being repeated) is obtained:

$$\frac{n!}{n_1!(n-n_1)!} \cdot \frac{(n-n_1)!}{n_2!(n-n_1-n_2)!} \cdot \frac{(n-n_1-n_2)!}{n_3!(n-n_1-n_2-n_3)!}$$

$$\ldots \cdot 1 = \frac{n!}{n_1! \cdot n_2! \cdot n_3! \ldots n_r!} = \binom{n}{n_1,n_2,n_3,\ldots,n_r}$$

which is a convenient symbol to use here.

Students should apply this general formula to the case where $r = 2$. They will get:

$\binom{n}{n_1 n_2} = \dfrac{n!}{n_1! \cdot n_2!} = \dfrac{n!}{n_1!(n-n_1)!}$, which is the famil-

iar $_nC_{n_1}$ or $\binom{n}{n_1}$.

The students should now be ready to tackle Multinomial Theorem. In the preassessment they were asked to expand $(a+b)^4$. They should note that certain terms appear more than once. For example, the term *aaab*, commonly written a^3b, appears $\binom{4}{3}$ times. This corresponds to the number of arrangements of aaab. For each such term the same argument holds.

Students should now consider the expansion of $(a+b+c)^4$. To actually compute this expansion, students may multiply a different combination of the members of each of the factors to obtain each term. For example, some of the 81 terms will appear as *aaaa, aaab, aabb, abac, abab, cbcb, . . .* These are commonly written as a^4, a^3b, a^2b^2, a^2bc, a^2b^2, b^2c^2. In the above list a^2b^2 appeared twice; however, in the complete expansion (of 81 terms) it would appear $\binom{4}{2,2,0} = \dfrac{4!}{2!\ 2!\ 0!}$

$= 6$ times. Thus if a student were asked to find the coefficient of the term a^3bc^2 in the expansion $(a+b+c)^6$, he would merely evaluate $\binom{6}{3,1,2} = \dfrac{6!}{3! \cdot 1! \cdot 2!} = 60$. Hence the entire expansion may be written as: $(a+b+c)^4 =$

$$\sum_{n_1 + n_2 + n_3 = 4} \frac{4!}{n_1! \cdot n_2! \cdot n_3!} \cdot a^{n_1} \cdot b^{n_2} \cdot c^{n_3}.$$

From here the general Multinomial Theorem follows easily: $(a_1 + a_2 + a_3 + \ldots + a_r)^n =$

$$\sum_{n_1 + n_2 + \ldots + n_r = n} \frac{n!}{n_1! \cdot n_2! \cdot \ldots \cdot n_r!} \cdot a_1^{n_1} \cdot a_2^{n_2}$$
$$\cdot a_3^{n_3} \cdot \ldots \cdot a_r^{n_r}$$

Although rather cumbersome, some students might wish to prove this theorem by mathematical induction.

Following are two applications of the Multinomial Theorem.

1) Expand and simplify: $(2x + y - z)^3$

$= \binom{3}{3,0,0}(2x)^3(y)^0(-z)^0 + \binom{3}{0,3,0}(2x)^0(y)^3(-z)^0$

$+ \binom{3}{0,0,3}(2x)^0(y)^0(-z)^3 + \binom{3}{2,1,0}(2x)^2(y)^1(-z)^0$

$+ \binom{3}{2,0,1}(2x)^2(y)^0(-z)^1 + \binom{3}{1,1,1}(2x)^1(y)^1(-z)^1$

$+ \binom{3}{0,2,1}(2x)^0(y)^2(-z)^1 + \binom{3}{0,1,2}(2x)^0(y)^1(-z)^2$

$+ \binom{3}{1,2,0}(2x)^1(y)^2(-z)^0 + \binom{3}{1,0,2}(2x)^1(y)^0(-z)^2$

$(2x + y - z)^3 = 8x^3 + y^3 - z^3 + 12x^2y - 12x^2z + 6xy^2 + 6xz^2 - 12xyz - 3y^2z + 3yz^2$.

2) Find the term in the expansion of $(2x^2 - y^3 + \frac{1}{2}z)^7$ which contains x^4 and z^4. The general

term of the expansion is: $\binom{7}{a, b, c}(2x^2)^a (-y^3)^b \left(\dfrac{1}{2}z\right)^c$,

where $a + b + c = 7$. Thus the terms containing x^4 and z^4 have $a = 2$ and $c = 4, \therefore b = 1$. Substituting in the above gives:

$\binom{7}{2,1,4}(2x^2)^2(-y^3)^1 (\frac{1}{2}z)^4 = \dfrac{7!}{2!1!4!}(4x^4)(-y^3) \times$

$(\frac{1}{16}z^4) = \dfrac{-105}{4} x^4y^3z^4$.

Postassessment

1. Have students find the coefficient of a^2b^5d in the expansion of $(a+b-c-d)^8$.

2. Ask students to explain how the coefficients for any term of a multinomial expansion are derived.

3. Have students expand $(2x + y^2 - 3)^5$

101 Algebraic Solution of Cubic Equations

Man's interest in cubic equations can be traced back to the times of the early Babylonians about 1800–1600 B.C. However, the algebraic solution of third degree equations is a product of the Italian Renaissance.

The algebraic solution of cubic equations is thus associated with the names of the Italian mathematicians: Scipione del Ferro, Nicolo de Brescia (called Tartaglia), Girolamo Cardan, and Rafael Bombelli.

Performance Objectives
1. *Given some cubic equations, students will find their solutions.*
2. *Given a verbal problem which calls for a solution of a cubic equation, students will determine (where applicable) the real solutions to the problem.*

Preassessment
Students should have mastered operations with quadratic equations. They should also have a solid background in complex numbers and trigonometry.

Teaching Strategies
Review roots of complex numbers in the following fashion:

The nth root of a complex number z is obtained by taking the nth root of the absolute value r, and dividing the amplitude ϕ by n. This will give you the principal value of that root. The general formula to get all the roots of z is:

$$\sqrt[n]{z} = \sqrt[n]{r}\left[\text{Cos}\,\frac{\phi + 2k\pi}{n} + i\,\text{Sin}\,\frac{\phi + 2k\pi}{n}\right]$$

For $k = 0$, this yields the principal value, and for $k = 1, 2, 3, \ldots, n-1$, we get the rest of the roots.

Example 1: Find the cube roots of unity. We have that $1 = \text{Cos}\,0° + i\,\text{Sin}\,0°$, therefore, $\phi = 0°$ and $r = 1$.

The general formula is then, $z = \text{Cos}\,\frac{2k\pi}{3} + i\,\text{Sin}\,\frac{2k\pi}{3}$ where $k = 0, 1,$ and 2.

If $k = 0, z_1 = \text{Cos}\,0 + i\,\text{Sin}\,0 = 1$ (Principal value)

If $k = 1, z_2 = \text{Cos}\,\frac{2\pi}{3} + i\,\text{Sin}\,\frac{2\pi}{3} = \text{Cos}\,120°$
$+ i\,\text{Sin}\,120°$
$= -\text{Cos}\,60° + i\,\text{Sin}\,60° = -\frac{1}{2} + \frac{\sqrt{3}}{2}i$

If $k = 2, z_3 = \text{Cos}\,\frac{4\pi}{3} + i\,\text{Sin}\,\frac{4\pi}{3} = \text{Cos}\,240° +$
$i\,\text{Sin}\,240°$
$= -\text{Cos}\,60° - i\,\text{Sin}\,60° = -\frac{1}{2} - \frac{\sqrt{3}}{2}i$

Notice that each one of the complex roots of unity generates the other roots. To do so, we only have to take the second and third powers of those roots. For example, if we take $\alpha = z_2 = -\frac{1}{2} + \frac{\sqrt{3}}{2}i$, we get:

$$\alpha^2 = (-\frac{1}{2} + \frac{\sqrt{3}}{2}i)^2 = (-\frac{1}{2})^2 + 2(-\frac{1}{2})(\frac{\sqrt{3}}{2}i)$$
$$+ (\frac{\sqrt{3}}{2}i)^2$$

$\alpha^2 = \frac{1}{4} - \frac{\sqrt{3}}{2}i + \frac{3}{4}i^2$, but $i^2 = -1$, thus,

$\alpha^2 = \frac{1}{4} - \frac{3}{4} - \frac{\sqrt{3}}{2}i = -\frac{1}{2} - \frac{\sqrt{3}}{2}i = z_3$

Similarly,

$\alpha^3 = \alpha^2 \cdot \alpha = (-\frac{1}{2} - \frac{\sqrt{3}}{2}i)(-\frac{1}{2} + \frac{\sqrt{3}}{2}i)$

$\alpha^3 = (-\frac{1}{2})^2 - (\frac{\sqrt{3}}{2}i)^2 = \frac{1}{4} - \frac{3}{4}i^2$

$ = \frac{1}{4} + \frac{3}{4} = 1 = z_1$

Therefore, the three roots of unity are: 1, α, and α^2 where α can be either $z_2 = -\frac{1}{2} + \frac{\sqrt{3}}{2}i$ or $z_3 = -\frac{1}{2} - \frac{\sqrt{3}}{2}i$.

Example 2: Find the cubic roots of the real number a. We have that $a = a\,(\text{Cos}\,0° + i\,\text{Sin}\,0°)$, therefore, $\sqrt[3]{a} = \sqrt[3]{r}\,(\text{Cos}\,\frac{2k\pi}{3} - i\,\text{Sin}\,\frac{2k\pi}{3})$, where $k = 0, 1,$ or 2. But, $\text{Cos}\,\frac{2k\pi}{3} - i\,\text{Sin}\,\frac{2k\pi}{3}$ where $k = 0, 1$ or 2, will give the three roots of unity (see Example 1). Thus, if the real root of a is a', the three roots of a will be: a', $a'\alpha$, and $a'\alpha^2$, where α can be either $-\frac{1}{2} + \frac{\sqrt{3}}{2}i$, or $-\frac{1}{2} - \frac{\sqrt{3}}{2}i$.

Let us now consider the general cubic equation:
$$ax^3 + bx^2 + cx + d = 0,$$
where $a, b, c,$ and d are arbitrary complex numbers. This equation can be reduced to a simpler form without the second degree term, by making the transformation $x = y - \frac{b}{3a}$. Thus, we have:

$$a\left(y - \frac{b}{3a}\right)^3 + b\left(y - \frac{b}{3a}\right)^2 + c\left(y - \frac{b}{3a}\right) + d = 0$$

$$a\left(y^3 - \frac{b}{a}y^2 + \frac{b^2}{3a^2}y - \frac{b}{27a^3}\right) + b\left(y^2 - \frac{2b}{3a}y + \right.$$

$$\left.\frac{b^2}{9a^2}\right) + c\,(y - \frac{b}{3a}) + d = 0, \text{ and we have,}$$

$$ay^3 + \left(\frac{b^2}{3a} - \frac{2b^2}{3a} + c\right)y + \left(-\frac{b^3}{27a^2} + \frac{b^3}{9a^2} - \frac{bc}{3a} + d\right) = 0$$

Now, if we make:

$$\frac{b^2}{3a} - \frac{2b^2}{3a} + c = c' \quad \text{and} \quad \frac{-b^3}{27a^2} + \frac{b^3}{9a^2} - \frac{bc}{3a} + d = d',$$

the general equation will become:

$$ay^3 + c'y + d' = 0$$

To avoid fractions in the solution of this equation, we divide it by a, and write it in the following fashion:

$$y^3 + 3py + 2q = 0$$

This last equation is called the reduced cubic equation and, as we have shown, any cubic equation can be reduced to that form.

To solve the reduced equation, the following identity is considered:

$$(a+b)^3 - 3ab\,(a+b) - (a^3+b^3) = 0$$

If this identity is compared with the reduced equation, we have that:

$$a+b = y, \quad ab = -p, \quad \text{and} \quad a^3+b^3 = -2q$$

From these equations, we see that we only have to find the values of a and b to find y. This can be done by solving the system:

$$\begin{matrix} ab = -p \\ a^3+b^3 = -2q \end{matrix} \quad \text{or} \quad \begin{matrix} a^3b^3 = -p^3 \\ a^3+b^3 = -2q \end{matrix}$$

From the second equation we have that: $b^3 = -2q - a^3$, and substituting this value in the first equation, we have: $-a^3(2q + a^3) = -p^3$, therefore, $a^6 + 2a^3q - p^3 = 0$

If we make $a^3 = v$, we obtain the following quadratic equation: $v^2 + 2qv - p^3 = 0$.

The roots of this quadratic equation are:

$$v_1 = -q + \sqrt{q^2 + p^3} \quad \text{and}$$

$$v_2 = -q - \sqrt{q^2 + p^3}.$$

Because of the symmetry of a and b in the system, we can take v_1 or v_2 to be a^3 or b^3 randomly.

So, $a^3 = -q + \sqrt{q^2 + p^3}$ and

$$b^3 = -q - \sqrt{q^2 + p^3}$$

Therefore, $a = \sqrt[3]{-q + \sqrt{q^2 + p^3}}$ and

$$b = \sqrt[3]{-q - \sqrt{q^2 + p^3}},$$

But $y = a + b$, thus,

$$y = \sqrt[3]{-q + \sqrt{q^2 + p^3}} + \sqrt[3]{-q - \sqrt{q^2 + p^3}},$$

which is called Cardan's formula for the cubic.

Since a^3 and b^3 have three roots each, it seems that the equation has nine roots. This is not the case, for since $ab = -p$, the cubic roots of a^3 and b^3 are

to be taken in pairs so that their product (which is ab) is a rational number $-p$.

Now, we know that the cubic roots of a^3 are: a (the principal value), $a\alpha$, and $a\alpha^2$, where α is one of the complex roots of unity. Similarly, the cubic roots of b^3 are: b, $b\alpha$, and $b\alpha^2$.

However, if the product of a and b must be rational, we have that the only admissible solutions are: (a,b), $(a\alpha,b\alpha^2)$, and $(a\alpha^2,b\alpha)$, because:

$$ab = -p$$
$$a\alpha \cdot b\alpha^2 = ab\alpha^3 = ab = -p \text{ (because } \alpha^3 = 1)$$
$$a\alpha^2 \cdot b\alpha = ab\alpha^3 = ab = -p$$

Therefore, the values of y are:

$$a + b, \quad a\alpha + b\alpha^2, \quad \text{and} \quad a\alpha^2 + b\alpha.$$

But $x = y - \dfrac{b}{3a}$ and so, the roots of the general cubic equation will be found once we know y.

Example 3: Solve the equation $x^3 + 3x^2 + 9x - 13 = 0$. First, we must reduce this equation to eliminate the second degree term. The transformation is: $x = y - \dfrac{b}{3a}$. In this example, $a = 1$, $b = 3$, $c = 9$, and $d = -13$. Therefore, $x = y - \dfrac{3}{3(1)} = y - 1$.

Thus, substituting $y-1$ for x in the equation, $(y-1)^3 + 3(y-1)^2 + 9(y-1) - 13 = 0$, or $(y^3 - 3y^2 + 3y - 1) + 3(y^2 - 2y + 1) + 9(y-1) - 13 = 0$
So, $y^3 - 6y - 20 = 0$ is the reduced equation.

Therefore,
$3p = 6$, $p = 2$, and $p^3 = 8$
$2q = -20$, $q = -10$, and $q^2 = 100$.

Thus, $\sqrt{q^2 + p^3} = \sqrt{108} = 6\sqrt{3}$, and,

$$a = \sqrt[3]{10 + 6\sqrt{3}} = \sqrt[3]{1 + 3\sqrt{3} + 9 + 3\sqrt{3}}$$
$$= \sqrt[3]{(1+\sqrt{3})^3} = 1 + \sqrt{3}$$
$$b = \sqrt[3]{10 - 6\sqrt{3}} = \sqrt[3]{1 - 3\sqrt{3} + 9 - 3\sqrt{3}}$$
$$= \sqrt[3]{(1-\sqrt{3})^3} = 1 - \sqrt{3}$$

The solutions for the reduced equation are then,

$$y_1 = a + b = (1 + \sqrt{3}) + (1 - \sqrt{3}) = 2$$
$$y_2 = a\alpha + b\alpha^2 = (1 + \sqrt{3})\left(-\frac{1}{2} + \frac{\sqrt{3}}{2}i\right)$$
$$\quad + (1 - \sqrt{3})\left(-\frac{1}{2} - \frac{\sqrt{3}}{2}i\right) = -1 + 3i$$
$$y_3 = a\alpha^2 + b\alpha = (1 + \sqrt{3})\left(-\frac{1}{2} - \frac{\sqrt{3}}{2}i\right)$$
$$\quad + (1 - \sqrt{3})\left(-\frac{1}{2} + \frac{\sqrt{3}}{2}i\right)$$
$$\quad = -1 - 3i.$$

But, $x = y - 1$. Therefore:

$$x_1 = y_1 - 1 = 2 - 1 = 1$$
$$x_2 = y_2 - 1 = -1 + 3i - 1 = -2 + 3i$$
$$x_3 = y_3 - 1 = -1 - 3i - 1 = -2 - 3i$$

Thus, in this example, we have for solutions one real and two conjugate complex roots. In this first of two units, we have studied the general solution of the cubic. In a second, we will study the different cases, reducible and irreducible, in the solution of cubic equations using Cardan's formula.

Postassessment

Students who have met the performance objectives should be able to do the following exercises:

1) Find the roots of $x^3 + 6x^2 + 17x + 18 = 0$
2) Solve: $x^3 - 11x^2 + 35x - 25 = 0$
3) Find the solution of $x^3 - 3x^2 + 3x - 1 = 0$

102 Solving Cubic Equations

In the first of two units on cubic equations, we have studied the general solution of the cubic. In this second, we will study the different cases, reducible and irreducible, in the solution of cubic equations using Cardan's formula.

Performance Objectives

1. *Given some cubic equations, students will analyze them to see the kind of solutions they are going to obtain when the equation is solved.*

2. *Students will solve given cubic equations.*

Preassessment

Students should have mastered operations with complex numbers and quadratic equations. They should also have a solid background in trigonometry.

Teaching Strategies

Review the content of the previous unit on cubic equations in the following fashion: Given a general cubic equation $Ax^3 + Bx^2 + Cx + D = 0$, it is always possible to eliminate the second degree term by making the change of variables $x = y - \dfrac{B}{3A}$. This transformation will lead to an equation of the form $y^3 + 3py + 2q = 0$, which is called the reduced or normal cubic equation.

The solution of the reduced equation is given by the Cardan's formula $y = \sqrt[3]{-q + \sqrt{q^2 + p^3}} + \sqrt[3]{-q - \sqrt{q^2 + p^3}}$. If $a = \sqrt[3]{-q + \sqrt{q^2 + p^3}}$ and $b = \sqrt[3]{-q - \sqrt{q^2 + p^3}}$, the roots of the reduced equations are: $y_1 = a + b$, $y_2 = a\alpha + b\alpha^2$, and $y_3 = a\alpha^2 + b\alpha$ where $\alpha = -\dfrac{1}{2} + \dfrac{\sqrt{3}}{2} i$ and $\alpha^2 = \dfrac{1}{2} - \dfrac{\sqrt{3}}{2} i$ are cube roots of unity.

Once the values y_1, y_2, and y_3 are found, the solutions of the general cubic equation will be obtained by using the transformation $x = y - \dfrac{B}{3A}$.

From the Cardan's formula, it is obvious that the nature of the solutions will depend on the value of $q^2 + p^3$ which for this reason is called the discriminant of the cubic. This is so, because $q^2 + p^3$, being under a square root will yield real or imaginary values according to the sign of the sum $q^2 + p^3$.

Before discussing the discriminant, it is useful to rewrite solutions of the reduced equation in the following fashion:

$$y_1 = a + b; \; y_2 = a\alpha + b\alpha^2 = a(-\frac{1}{2} + \frac{\sqrt{3}}{2}i)$$
$$+ b(-\frac{1}{2} - \frac{\sqrt{3}}{2}i); \; y_3 = a\alpha^2 + b\alpha = a(-\frac{1}{2} - \frac{\sqrt{3}}{2}i)$$
$$+ b(-\frac{1}{2} + \frac{\sqrt{3}}{2}i)$$

and simplifying:

$$y_1 = a + b; \; y_2 = -\frac{a + b}{2} + \frac{a - b}{2} \sqrt{3}\, i;$$
$$y_3 = -\frac{a + b}{2} - \frac{a - b}{2} \sqrt{3}\, i.$$

Let us now consider the discriminant $q^2 + p^3$.

I) If $q^2 + p^3 > 0$, a and b have each one real value, then we can suppose a and b will be real also. Consequently, $a + b$ and $a - b$ will be real also. Therefore, we have that if $a + b = m$ and $a - b = n$, the solutions of the reduced equation are:

$$y_1 = a + b = m; \; y_2 = -\frac{m}{2} + \frac{n}{2}\sqrt{3}\, i; \; y_3 = -\frac{m}{2} - \frac{n}{2}\sqrt{3}\, i.$$

Thus, if $q^2 + p^3 > 0$, we have one real root and two conjugate imaginary.

Example 1: Solve $x^3 - 6x^2 + 10x - 8 = 0$
First, we must eliminate the square term. The transformation for this example is:

$$x = y - \frac{B}{3A} = y - \frac{-6}{3} = y + 2$$

Thus, substituting $y + 2$ for x in the equation:

$(y + 2)^3 - 6(y + 2)^2 + 10(y + 2) - 8 = 0$

$y^3 + 6y^2 + 12y + 8 - 6y^2 - 24y - 24 + 10y$
$\quad + 20 - 8 = 0$

$y^3 - 2y - 4 = 0$ (Reduced equation)

Therefore:

$$3p = -2 \quad p = -\frac{2}{3} \quad \text{and} \quad p^3 = -\frac{8}{27}$$

$$2q = -4 \quad q = -2 \quad \text{and} \quad q^2 = 4$$

Thus, $q^2 + p^3 = 4 - \dfrac{8}{27} = \dfrac{100}{27} > 0.$

Therefore, we know that in the solution one root must be real and two conjugate imaginary.

The values for a and b are:

$$a = \sqrt[3]{-q + \sqrt{q^2 + p^3}} = \sqrt[3]{2 + \sqrt{\frac{100}{27}}} = \sqrt[3]{2 + \frac{10}{3\sqrt{3}}}$$

$$b = \sqrt[3]{-q - \sqrt{q^2 + p^3}} = \sqrt[3]{2 - \sqrt{\frac{100}{27}}} = \sqrt[3]{2 - \frac{10}{3\sqrt{3}}}$$

and simplifying:

$$a = \sqrt[3]{\frac{6\sqrt{3} + 10}{3\sqrt{3}}} = \sqrt[3]{\frac{3\sqrt{3} + 9 + 3\sqrt{3} + 1}{\sqrt{27}}} = \sqrt[3]{\frac{(3 - 1)^3}{\sqrt{27}}}$$

$$b = \sqrt[3]{\frac{6\sqrt{3} - 10}{3\sqrt{3}}} = \sqrt[3]{\frac{3\sqrt{3} - 9 + 3\sqrt{3} - 1}{\sqrt{27}}} = \sqrt[3]{\frac{(\sqrt{3} - 1)^3}{\sqrt{27}}}$$

$$a = \frac{\sqrt{3} + 1}{\sqrt{3}} \quad \text{and} \quad b = \frac{\sqrt{3} - 1}{\sqrt{3}}$$

The solutions for the reduced equation are then:

$$y_1 = a + b = \frac{\sqrt{3} + 1}{\sqrt{3}} + \frac{\sqrt{3} - 1}{\sqrt{3}} = 2$$

$$y_2 = a\alpha + b\alpha^2 = \left(\frac{\sqrt{3} + 1}{\sqrt{3}}\right)\left(-\frac{1}{2} + \frac{\sqrt{3}}{2} i\right)$$
$$+ \left(\frac{\sqrt{3} - 1}{\sqrt{3}}\right)\left(-\frac{1}{2} - \frac{\sqrt{3}}{2} i\right)$$

$$y_3 = a\alpha^2 + b\alpha = \left(\frac{\sqrt{3} + 1}{\sqrt{3}}\right)\left(-\frac{1}{2} - \frac{\sqrt{3}}{2} i\right)$$
$$+ \left(\frac{\sqrt{3} - 1}{3}\right)\left(-\frac{1}{2} + \frac{\sqrt{3}}{2} i\right)$$

and simplifying

$y_1 = 2; \quad y_2 = -1 + i; \quad y_3 = -1 - i.$

Therefore the solutions of the general equation are:

$x_1 = y_1 + 2 = 2 + 2 = 4$
$x_2 = y_2 + 2 = -1 + i + 2 = 1 + i$
$x_3 = y_3 + 2 = -1 - i + 2 = 1 - i$

II) If $q^2 + p^3 = 0$, a and b are equal; therefore if m represents the common real value of a and b, we have:

$y_1 = m + m = 2m$

$$y_2 = -\frac{m + m}{2} + \frac{m - m}{2} \sqrt{3}\, i = -m$$

$$y_3 = -\frac{m + m}{2} - \frac{m - m}{2} \sqrt{3}\, i = -m$$

Thus, in this case we have that all the roots are real and two are equal.

Example 2: Find the roots of $x^3 - 12x + 16 = 0$

In this example we already have the reduced equation, therefore:

$3p = -12 \quad p = -4 \quad \text{and} \quad p^3 = -64$
$2q = \quad 16 \quad q = \quad 8 \quad \text{and} \quad q^2 = \quad 64$

thus, $q^2 + p^3 = 64 - 64 = 0$. This means that the solution will have three real roots, two of them equal. The values of a and b are:

$$a = \sqrt[3]{-q + \sqrt{q^2 + p^3}} = \sqrt[3]{-8} = -2$$

$$b = \sqrt[3]{-q - \sqrt{q^2 + p^3}} = \sqrt[3]{-8} = -2$$

Therefore the roots are:

$y_1 = a + b = -4$

$$y_2 = a\alpha + b\alpha^2 = -2(\alpha + \alpha^2)$$
$$= -2\left(-\frac{1}{2} + \frac{\sqrt{3}}{2} i - \frac{1}{2} - \frac{\sqrt{3}}{2} i\right) = 2$$

$$y_3 = a\alpha^2 + b\alpha = -2(\alpha^2 + \alpha)$$
$$= -2\left(-\frac{1}{2} - \frac{\sqrt{3}}{2} i - \frac{1}{2} + \frac{\sqrt{3}}{2} i\right) = 2$$

III) If $q^2 + p^3 < 0$, a and b will be complex numbers because of the square root of the discriminant which is negative in this case. Therefore, if the values a and b are $a = M + Ni$ and $b = M - Ni$, the solutions of the reduced equation will be:

$y_1 = a + b = 2M$

$$y_2 = -\frac{2M}{2} + \frac{2Ni}{2} \sqrt{3} i = -M - \sqrt{3}\, N$$

$$y_3 = -\frac{2M}{2} - \frac{2Ni}{2} \sqrt{3} i = -M + \sqrt{3}\, N$$

which are all real roots and unequal.

However, there is no general arithmetic or algebraic method of finding the exact value of the cubic root of complex numbers. Therefore, Cardan's formula is of little use in this case, which for this reason is called the irreducible case.

The solution of this case can be obtained with the use of trigonometry. Thus, when the Cardan's formula has the form $y = \sqrt[3]{u + vi} + \sqrt[3]{u - vi}$ we call $r = \sqrt{u^2 + v^2}$ and $\tan \Theta = \dfrac{v}{u}$; therefore, the cubic root of them will be:

$$y = \sqrt[3]{r} \left[\text{Cos} \frac{\Theta + 2k\pi}{3} + i\, \text{Sin} \frac{\Theta + 2k\pi}{3}\right]$$
$$+ \sqrt[3]{r} \left[\text{Cos} \frac{\Theta + 2k\pi}{3} - i\, \text{Sin} \frac{\Theta + 2k\pi}{3}\right]$$

where $k = 0, 1,$ and 2.

If we simplify this expression we obtain:

$$y = 2\sqrt[3]{r}\, \text{Cos} \frac{\Theta + 2k\pi}{3} \quad \text{where } k = 0, 1, \text{ and } 2.$$

Therefore the three roots are:

$$y_1 = 2\sqrt[3]{r}\, \text{Cos} \frac{\Theta}{3}; \quad y_2 = 2\sqrt[3]{r}\, \text{Cos} \frac{\Theta + 2\pi}{3};$$

$$y_3 = 2\sqrt[3]{r}\, \text{Cos} \frac{\Theta + 4\pi}{3}$$

Example 3: Solve $x^3 - 6x - 4 = 0$

From this equation we have: $3p = -6$ and $2q = -4$; therefore, $p^3 = -8$, $q^2 = 4$, $p^3 + q^2 = -4$ and $\sqrt{p^3 + q^2} = 2i$

The solution then would be: $y = \sqrt{2 + 2i} + \sqrt{2 - 2i}$, thus, $r = \sqrt{4 + 4} = \sqrt{8}$, $\tan \Theta = \frac{2}{2}$ or $\tan \Theta = 1$ and $\Theta = \frac{\pi}{4}$. Therefore, the roots of the equation are:

$$x_1 = 2\sqrt[3]{r} \, \text{Cos} \, \frac{\Theta}{3} = 2\sqrt[3]{\sqrt{8}} \, \text{Cos} \, \frac{\pi}{12} = 2\sqrt{2} \, \text{Cos} \, 15°$$

$$x_2 = 2\sqrt[3]{r} \, \text{Cos} \, \frac{\Theta + 2\pi}{3} = 2\sqrt{2} \, \text{Cos} \, \frac{\pi/4 + 2\pi}{3} = 2\sqrt{2} \, \text{Cos} \, 135°$$

$$x_3 = 2\sqrt[3]{r} \, \text{Cos} \, \frac{\Theta + 14\pi}{3} = 2\sqrt{2} \, \text{Cos} \, \frac{\pi/4 + 4\pi}{3} = 2\sqrt{2} \, \text{Cos} \, 255°$$

But,

$$\text{Sin} \, \frac{y}{2} = \sqrt{\frac{1 - \text{Cos} \, x}{2}} \quad \text{and} \quad \text{Cos} \, \frac{x}{2} = \sqrt{\frac{1 + \text{Cos} \, x}{2}}$$

Therefore,

$$\text{Sin} \, 15° = \sqrt{\frac{1 - \text{Cos} \, 30°}{2}} = \sqrt{\frac{1 - \sqrt{3}/2}{2}} = \frac{\sqrt{2 - \sqrt{3}}}{2}$$

and

$$\text{Cos} \, 15° = \sqrt{\frac{1 + \text{Cos} \, 30°}{2}} = \sqrt{\frac{1 + \sqrt{3}/2}{2}} = \frac{\sqrt{2 + \sqrt{3}}}{2}$$

Thus, the roots are:

$$x_1 = 2\sqrt{2} \frac{\sqrt{2 + \sqrt{3}}}{2} = \sqrt{4 + 2\sqrt{3}}$$
$$= \sqrt{1 + 2\sqrt{3} + 3} = 1 + \sqrt{3}$$

$$x_2 = 2\sqrt{2} \cos 135° = 2\sqrt{2}(-\cos 45°)$$
$$= 2\sqrt{2} \left(-\frac{\sqrt{2}}{3} \right) = -2$$

$$x_3 = 2\sqrt{2}(\sin 15°) = 2\sqrt{2} \left(\frac{\sqrt{2 - \sqrt{3}}}{2} \right)$$
$$= \sqrt{1 + 2\sqrt{3} + 3} = 1 - \sqrt{3}$$

The reducible cases may also employ the aid of trigonometry.

Postassessment

Students who have met the performance objectives should be able to do the following exercises: Analyze and then solve the following cubics:

1) $x^3 - 6x^2 + 11x - 6 = 0$
2) $x^3 - 5x^2 + 9x - 9 = 0$
3) $x^3 - 75x + 250 = 0$
4) $x^3 - 6x^2 + 3x + 10 = 0$

103 Calculating Sums of Finite Series

Mathematical induction has become thoroughly entrenched in secondary school curricula. Many textbooks provide a variety of applications of this technique of proof. Most popular among these applications is proving that specific series have given formulas as sums. Although most students merely work the proof as required, some may question how the sum of a particular series was actually generated.

This unit will provide you with a response to students' requests for deriving formulas for certain series summations.

Performance Objectives

1. Given some finite series, students will find their sum.

2. Students will develop formulas for determining the sum of various finite series.

Preassessment

Students should have mastered operations with algebraic expressions, functions, and concepts of finite sequence and series.

Teaching Strategies

Review concepts of sequences and series in the following fashion.

A *finite sequence* is a finite set of ordered elements or terms, each related to one or more of the preceding elements in some specifiable way.
Examples: 1) $1, 3, 5, 7, \ldots, 19$
2) $\sin x, \sin 2x, \sin 3x, \ldots, \sin 20x$
3) $2, 4, 6, 8, \ldots, 2n$

Let us now consider any finite sequence of elements $u_1, u_2, \ldots, u_n$. We can obtain the following partial sums:

$$s_1 = u_1$$
$$s_2 = u_1 + u_2$$
$$s_3 = u_1 + u_2 + u_3$$
$$\cdots\cdots\cdots\cdots\cdots$$
$$s_n = u_1 + u_2 + \ldots + u_n$$

We call this sum $u_1 + u_2 + \ldots + u_n$ a *finite series* of the elements of the sequence $u_1, u_2, \ldots, u_n$. S_n represents the total sum of these elements. For example, if we have the sequence $1, 2, 3, 4$, the series is $1 + 2 + 3 + 4$, and the sum S_4 is 10.

This example is a simple one. However, if instead of considering four terms 1, 2, 3, and 4, we consider "n" terms 1, 2, 3, . . . , n, it will not be that simple to calculate their sum $S_n = 1 + 2 + 3 + \ldots + n$. Sometimes, there are easy ways to calculate the sum of a specific series, but we cannot apply that particular method to all the series.

For example, the previous series $1 + 2 + 3 + \ldots + n$, could be calculated by using the following artifice:

$$1 = 1 = \frac{1 \cdot 2}{2}$$

$$1 + 2 = 3 = \frac{2 \cdot 3}{2}$$

$$1 + 2 + 3 = 6 = \frac{3 \cdot 4}{2}$$

$$\cdots\cdots\cdots\cdots\cdots\cdots\cdots$$

$$1 + 2 + \ldots + n = \frac{n(n + 1)}{2}$$

which is the total sum of the series.

This means that if we want to calculate the sum of the series $1 + 2 + 3 + \ldots + 10$, we will have:

$$S_{10} = \frac{10(10 + 1)}{2} = \frac{10 \cdot 11}{2} = 55.$$

We cannot apply this artifice to every series, therefore, we must find a more general method which permits us to calculate the sum of several series. This method is given by the following theorem:

Theorem: Let us consider a finite series $u_1 + u_2 + u_3 + \ldots + u_n$ If we can find a function $F(n)$ such that $u_n = F(n + 1) - F(n)$ then, $u_1 + u_2 + \ldots + u_n = F(n + 1) - F(1)$.

Proof: We have by hypothesis that: $u_n = F(n + 1) - F(n)$; therefore, if we apply it for $n - 1, n - 2, \ldots, 3, 2, 1$, we will get the following relations:

$$u_n = F(n + 1) - F(n)$$
$$u_{n-1} = F(n) - F(n - 1)$$
$$u_{n-2} = F(n - 1) - F(n - 2)$$
$$\cdot \qquad \cdot \qquad \cdot$$
$$\cdot \qquad \cdot \qquad \cdot$$
$$\cdot \qquad \cdot \qquad \cdot$$
$$u_2 = F(3) - F(2)$$
$$u_1 = F(2) - F(1)$$

If we now add these relations, we will get: $u_1 + u_2 + u_3 + \ldots + u_n = F(n + 1) - F(1)$ which proves the theorem

Before having students embark on applications, have them consider the following examples:

1. Find the sum of the series $1 + 2 + 3 + \ldots + n$. Because $u_n = n$, we consider $F(n) = An^2 + Bn + C$.

(A polynomial one degree higher than u_n should be used.) Therefore, $F(n + 1) = A(n + 1)^2 + B(n + 1) + C$. According to the theorem above, we must have:

$$u_n = F(n + 1) - F(n)$$
$$n = [A(n + 1)^2 + B(n + 1) + C] - [An^2 + Bn + C]$$
$$n = 2An + (A + B)$$

Therefore, by equating coefficients of powers of n we get: $2A = 1$, and $A + B = 0$. By solving these simultaneously we get: $A = \frac{1}{2}$ and $B = -\frac{1}{2}$

Therefore, $F(n) = \frac{1}{2}n^2 - \frac{1}{2}n + C$,
$$F(n + 1) = \frac{1}{2}(n + 1)^2 - \frac{1}{2}(n + 1) + C,$$
and $F(1) = C$

Thus, $1 + 2 + 3 + \ldots + n = F(n + 1) - F(1)$
$$= \frac{1}{2}(n + 1)^2 - \frac{1}{2}(n + 1)$$
$$= \frac{1}{2}n(n + 1).$$

2. Find the sum of the series $1^2 + 2^2 + 3^2 + \ldots + n^2$. Since $u_n = n^2$, we consider $F(n) = An^3 + Bn^2 + Cn + D$ (One degree higher than u_n, since the highest power of $F(n)$ will be annihilated in $F(n + 1) - F(n)$. Thus $F(n + 1) = A(n + 1)^3 + B(n + 1)^2 + C(n + 1) + D$.

Now, $u_n = n^2 = F(n + 1) - F(n)$
$$n^2 = [A(n + 1)^3 + B(n + 1)^2 + C(n + 1) + D] - [An^3 + Bn^2 + Cn + D]$$
$$n^2 = 3An^2 + (3A + 2B)n + (A + B + C)$$

By equating coefficients of powers of n, we get $3A = 1$; $3A + 2B = 0$; and $A + B + C = 0$ and solving simultaneously:

$$A = 1/3; B = -1/2; C = 1/6$$

Thus, $F(n) = \frac{1}{3} n^3 - \frac{1}{2} n^2 + \frac{1}{6} n + D$

$$F(n + 1) = \frac{1}{3} (n + 1)^3 - \frac{1}{2}(n + 1)^2 + \frac{1}{6}(n + 1) + D$$

$$F(1) = \frac{1}{3} - \frac{1}{2} + \frac{1}{6} + D = D$$

Hence, $1^2 + 2^2 + 3^2 + \ldots + n^2$
$$= F(n + 1) - F(1)$$
$$= \frac{1}{3}(n + 1)^3 - \frac{1}{2}(n + 1)^2 + \frac{1}{6}(n + 1)$$
$$= \frac{n(n + 1)(2n + 1)}{6}$$

3. Find the sum of the series $1^3 + 3^3 + 5^3 + \ldots + (2n - 1)^3$. Since u_n is of third degree, $F(n) = An^4 + Bn^3 + Cn^2 + Dn + E$ and $F(n + 1) = A(n + 1)^4 + B(n + 1)^3 + C(n + 1)^2 + D(n + 1) + E$.

Thus, $u_n = (2n - 1)^3 = F(n + 1) - F(n)$; or $8n^3 - 12n^2 + 6n - 1 = 4An^3 + (6A + 3B)n^2 + (4A + 3B + 2C)n + (A + B + C + D)$.

Equating coefficients:
$4A = 8$, and $A = 2$; $6A + 3B = -12$, and $B = -8$;
$4A + 3B + 2C = 6$; and $C = 11$; $A + B + C + D = -1$, and $D = -6$

Therefore, $F(n) = 2n^4 - 8n^3 + 11n^2 - 6n + E$;
$$F(n + 1) = 2(n + 1)^4 - 8(n + 1)^3$$
$$+ 11(n + 1)^2 - 6(n + 1) + E;$$
and $F(1) = -1 + E$.
Thus,
$1^3 + 3^3 + 5^3 + \ldots + (2n - 1)^3 = F(n + 1) - F(1)$
$= 2(n + 1)^4 - 8(n + 1)^3 + 11(n + 1)^2 - 6(n + 1)$
$+ E - (-1 + E) = 2n^4 - n^2 = n^2(2n^2 - 1)$.

4. Find the sum of the series $\frac{1}{2} + \frac{1}{4} + \ldots + \frac{1}{2^n}$.

Let us consider $F(n) = \dfrac{A}{2^n}$ and therefore, $F(n + 1)$

$= \dfrac{A}{2^{n+1}}$ Hence, $u_n = F(n + 1) - F(n)$. Thus,

$\dfrac{1}{2^n} = \dfrac{A}{2^{n+1}} - \dfrac{A}{2^n}$, therefore $A = -2$. Hence,

$F(n + 1) = -\dfrac{1}{2^n}$; and $F(1) = -1$. Therefore,

$$\frac{1}{2} + \frac{1}{4} + \ldots + \frac{1}{2^n} = F(n + 1) - F(1)$$
$$= -\frac{1}{2^n} + 1$$
$$= 1 - \frac{1}{2^n}$$

After sufficient practice students should be able to find $F(n)$ more easily.

Postassessment

Students who have met the performance objectives should be able to do the following exercises:

1) Find the sum of the series $1 + 8 + 27 + \ldots + n^3$.

2) Find the sum of the series $1/5 + 1/25 + 1/125 + \ldots + 1/5^n$.

3. Find the formula for the sum of a finite arithmetic progression.

104 A General Formula For The Sum Of Series Of The Form $\sum\limits_{t=1}^{n} t^r$

The calculation of the sum of convergent series is an important topic. There is not, however, a general formula to calculate the sum of any given convergent series.

This unit will provide you with a general formula to calculate the sum of series of the specific type $\sum\limits_{t=1}^{n} t^r$.

Performance Objectives

1. Given some finite series of the form $\sum\limits_{t=1}^{n} t^r$, students will find their sum.
2. Students will demonstrate an understanding of the technique used to find general formulas for certain specific series.

Preassessment

Students should know the Binomial Theorem and have a fair knowledge of series and elementary linear algebra.

Teaching Strategies

Review the concept of series and the Binomial Theorem in the following fashion.

A series is a sum of the elements of a given sequence. For example, if we have the sequence of elements $u_1, u_2, \ldots, u_n$, the series is $u_1 + u_2 + \ldots + u_n$. This series can also be represented by the symbol $\sum\limits_{r=1}^{n} u_r$. Thus, the symbol $\sum\limits_{n=1}^{n} k^2$ means $1^2 + 2^2 + \ldots + n^2$.

Another example of series is the one represented by $\sum\limits_{m=0}^{k} \binom{k}{m} a^{k-m} b^m$, where a and b are arbitrary real numbers, k is any positive integer, and $\binom{k}{m} = \dfrac{k!}{m!(k-m)!}$. This series can be proved to be equal to $(a + b)^k$, and this fact is known as the *Binomial Theorem*.

There is also a less known but important theorem from the theory of series whose proof we are going to give in this unit. We are going to use this theorem and the Binomial Theorem in the development of our discussion.

Lemma: Let us consider a finite series $\sum\limits_{r=1}^{n} u_r$. If we can find a function $f(n)$ such that $u_n = f(n+1) - f(n)$, then $\sum\limits_{r=1}^{n} u_r = f(n+1) - f(1)$

Proof: We have by hypothesis that: $u_n = f(n+1) - f(n)$; therefore, if we apply it for $n-1, n-2, \ldots, 3, 2, 1$, we will get the following relations:

$$u_n = f(n+1) - f(n)$$
$$u_{n-1} = f(n) - f(n-1)$$
$$u_{n-2} = f(n-1) - f(n-2)$$
$$\cdots\cdots\cdots\cdots\cdots\cdots\cdots$$
$$u_2 = f(3) - f(2)$$
$$u_1 = f(2) - f(1)$$

If we now add these relations, we will get $\sum\limits_{r=1}^{n} u_r$ equal to $f(n+1) - f(1)$ which proves the theorem.

Let $\sum\limits_{t=1}^{n} t^r$ be the series whose sum we want. In order to apply the previous Lemma to this series, we may consider the arbitrary function $f(n) = \sum\limits_{k=0}^{r+1} b_k n^k$ where b is any real number and n is any positive integer. Thus, $f(n+1) = \sum\limits_{k=0}^{r+1} b_k (n+1)^k$. If we now impose the condition of the hypothesis of the Lemma to this function for the series $\sum\limits_{t=1}^{n} t^r$, we have:

$$u_n = f(n+1) - f(n)$$

or

$$n^r = \sum_{k=0}^{r+1} b_k (n+1)^k - \sum_{k=0}^{r+1} b_k n^k$$

$$n^r = \sum_{k=0}^{r+1} b_k \, [(n+1)^k - n^k] \qquad \text{(I)}$$

But according to the Binomial Theorem,

$$(n+1)^k = \sum_{m=0}^{k} \binom{k}{m} n^{k-m} \text{ and thus,}$$

$$(n+1)^k - n^k = \sum_{m=1}^{k} \binom{k}{m} n^{k-m}.$$

Therefore in (I) we have:

$$n^r = \sum_{k=0}^{r+1} b_k \, [\sum_{m=1}^{k} \binom{k}{m} n^{k-m}]$$

This equation leads to the following system of equations:

$$\binom{r+1}{1} b_{r+1} = 0$$

$$\binom{r+1}{2} b_{r+1} + \binom{r}{1} b_r = 0$$

$$\binom{r+1}{3} b_{r+1} + \binom{r}{2} b_r + \binom{r-1}{1} b_{r-1} \ldots \ldots = 0$$

$$\ldots \ldots \ldots \ldots \ldots \ldots \ldots \ldots \ldots \ldots = 0$$

$$\binom{r+1}{m} b_{r+1} + \binom{r}{m-1} b_r + \binom{r-1}{m-2} b_{r-1} + \ldots = 0$$

$$\ldots \ldots \ldots \ldots \ldots \ldots \ldots \ldots \ldots \ldots = 0$$

$$\binom{r+1}{r+1} b_{r+1} + \binom{r}{r} b_r + \ldots \ldots + \binom{1}{1} b_1 \ldots = 0$$

This system of equations can be expressed in matrix form as follows:

$$
\begin{bmatrix}
\binom{r+1}{1} & 0 & 0 & 0 & \ldots & 0 \\
\binom{r+1}{2} & \binom{r}{1} & 0 & 0 & \ldots & 0 \\
\binom{r+1}{3} & \binom{r}{2} & \binom{r-1}{1} & 0 & \ldots & 0 \\
\cdot & \cdot & \cdot & & & \cdot \\
\cdot & \cdot & \cdot & & & \cdot \\
\binom{r+1}{m} & \binom{r}{m-1} & \binom{r-1}{m-2} & 0 & \ldots & 0 \\
\cdot & \cdot & \cdot & & & \cdot \\
\binom{r+1}{r+1} & \binom{r}{r} & \binom{r-1}{r-1} & \binom{r-2}{r-2} & \ldots & 1
\end{bmatrix}
\begin{bmatrix}
b_{r+1} \\ b_r \\ b_{r-1} \\ \cdot \\ \cdot \\ b_m \\ \cdot \\ b_1
\end{bmatrix}
=
\begin{bmatrix}
1 \\ 0 \\ 0 \\ \cdot \\ \cdot \\ 0 \\ \cdot \\ 0
\end{bmatrix}
$$

If we call these three matrices A, X, and B respectively, we have that AX = B. But A is a diagonal matrix, thus, det $A = \prod\limits_{s=1}^{r+1} \binom{s}{1} = 0$ and therefore A^{-1} exists. (Det A is the determinant of A, which for a simple case is $\begin{vmatrix} a_1 & b_1 \\ a_2 & b_2 \end{vmatrix} = a_1 b_2 - a_2 b_1$. The Π represents "product," in the way the Σ represents "sum.") Thus we have $X = A^{-1}B$. If a_{ij} represents any element of A^{-1}, that implies that $X = A^{-1}B = \begin{pmatrix} a_{11} \\ a_{21} \\ \vdots \\ a_{r+1,1} \end{pmatrix}$ because

B is a column vector. Thus,

$$
\begin{pmatrix} b_{r+1} \\ b_r \\ \vdots \\ b_1 \end{pmatrix}
=
\begin{pmatrix} a_{11} \\ a_{21} \\ \vdots \\ a_{r+1,1} \end{pmatrix}
$$

But this means that: $b_{r+2-i} = a_{i,1}$ for all $i \in \{1,2,3, \ldots , r+1\}$.

Therefore for the function $f(n) = \sum\limits_{k=0}^{r+1} b_k n^k$ we have:

$$f(n+1) = \sum_{k=0}^{r+1} b_k \, (n+1)^k \text{ and } f(1) = \sum_{k=0}^{r+1} b_k \text{ where } b_{r+2-i}$$

$$= a_{i,1} \text{ for all } i \in \{1,2,3, \ldots , r+1\}$$

Thus, by the previous Lemma,

$$\sum_{t=1}^{n} t^r = \sum_{k=0}^{r+1} b_k \, (n+1)^k - \sum_{k=0}^{r+1} b_k \text{ or}$$

$$\sum_{t=1}^{n} t^r = \sum_{k=0}^{r+1} b_k \, [(n+1)^k - 1] \qquad \text{(II)}$$

But by the Binomial Theorem we have that:

$$(n+1)^k - 1 = \binom{k}{0} n^k + \binom{k}{1} n^{k-1} + \ldots + \binom{k}{k-1} n$$

Thus, in (II)

$$\sum_{t=1}^{n} t^r = \sum_{k=0}^{r+1} b_k \, [\binom{k}{0} n^k + \binom{k}{1} n^{k-1} + \ldots + \binom{k}{k-1} n]$$

or

$$\sum_{t=1}^{n} t^r = n \sum_{k=0}^{r+1} [b_k \binom{k}{0} n^{k-1} + b_k \binom{k}{1} n^{k-2} + \ldots + b_k \binom{k}{k-1}]$$

And if we call $b_k \binom{k}{j} = c_j$, we have $\sum\limits_{t=1}^{n} t^r = n \sum\limits_{j=0}^{r} c_j n^j$ because when $k = 0$, $b_0 \binom{0}{j} = c_j = c_0$

which implies that $j = 0$ and when $k = r+1$, $b_{r+1} \binom{r+1}{j} = c_j$, which implies that $j = r$. Thus:

Theorem: The general formula for series of the form $\sum_{t=1}^{n} t^r$ is $n \sum_{j=0}^{r} c_j n^j$ where $c_j = b_k \binom{k}{j}$ for all $j \in \{0,1,3, \ldots , r\}$ and $b_{r+2-i} = a_{i,1}$ for all $i \in \{1,2,3, \ldots , r+1\}$

Example 1. Find $\sum_{t=1}^{n} t^2$.

In this example $r = 2$, therefore we have

$$\begin{pmatrix} \binom{3}{1} & 0 & 0 \\ \binom{3}{2} & \binom{2}{1} & 0 \\ \binom{3}{3} & \binom{2}{2} & \binom{1}{1} \end{pmatrix} \begin{pmatrix} b_3 \\ b_2 \\ b_1 \end{pmatrix} = \begin{pmatrix} 1 \\ 0 \\ 0 \end{pmatrix}$$

Thus, $A = \begin{pmatrix} 3 & 0 & 0 \\ 3 & 2 & 0 \\ 1 & 1 & 1 \end{pmatrix}$ and A^{-1} is

$$A^{-1} = \frac{(\text{Adj. } A)'}{\text{Det. } A} = \frac{\begin{pmatrix} 2 & -3 & 1 \\ 0 & 3 & -3 \\ 0 & 0 & 6 \end{pmatrix}'}{\begin{vmatrix} 3 & 0 & 0 \\ 3 & 2 & 0 \\ 1 & 1 & 1 \end{vmatrix}} \quad \text{or}$$

$$A^{-1} = \frac{\begin{pmatrix} 2 & 0 & 0 \\ -3 & 3 & 0 \\ 1 & -3 & 6 \end{pmatrix}}{6}$$

Therefore,

$$X = \frac{1}{6} \begin{pmatrix} 2 & 0 & 0 \\ -3 & 3 & 0 \\ 1 & -3 & 6 \end{pmatrix} \begin{pmatrix} 1 \\ 0 \\ 0 \end{pmatrix} = \frac{1}{6} \begin{pmatrix} 2 \\ -3 \\ 1 \end{pmatrix}$$

and $\begin{pmatrix} b_3 \\ b_2 \\ b_1 \end{pmatrix} = \frac{1}{6} \begin{pmatrix} 2 \\ -3 \\ 1 \end{pmatrix}$ implies that $\begin{cases} b_3 = \frac{1}{6} \ (2) \\ b_2 = \frac{1}{6} \ (-3) \\ b_1 = \frac{1}{6} \ (1) \end{cases}$

Thus, $f(n) = \frac{1}{6}[2n^3 - 3n^2 + n + b_0]$

$f(n + 1) = \frac{1}{6}[2(n + 1)^3 - 3(n + 1)^2 + (n + 1) + b_0]$

and, $f(1) = \frac{1}{6}(b_0)$

Hence, the sum of the series will be:

$k^2 = f(n+1) - f(1)$

$\quad = \frac{1}{6}[2(n+1)^3 - 3(n+1)^2 + (n+1)]$

$\quad = \frac{1}{6} n(n+1)(2n+1)$

Example 2. Find the sum of $1 + 2 + 3 + \ldots + n$

In this example the series is $\sum_{k-1}^{n} k$ and $r = 1$. Thus, the equation will be:

$$\begin{pmatrix} \binom{2}{1} & 0 \\ \binom{2}{2} & \binom{1}{1} \end{pmatrix} \cdot \begin{pmatrix} b_0 \\ b_1 \end{pmatrix} = \begin{pmatrix} 1 \\ 0 \end{pmatrix} \quad \text{Then, } A = \begin{pmatrix} 2 & 0 \\ 1 & 1 \end{pmatrix}$$

The inverse of A will then be, $A^{-1} = \begin{pmatrix} 1 & 0 \\ -1 & 2 \end{pmatrix} \frac{}{2}$ and

$$X = \frac{1}{2} \begin{pmatrix} 1 & 0 \\ -1 & 2 \end{pmatrix} \begin{pmatrix} 1 \\ 0 \end{pmatrix} = \frac{1}{2} \begin{pmatrix} 1 \\ -1 \end{pmatrix}$$

This implies that $b_0 = \frac{1}{2}(1)$ and $b_1 = \frac{1}{2}(-1)$

Then, $f(n) = \frac{1}{2}(n^2 - n + a_2)$

$f(n + 1) = \frac{1}{2}[(n + 1) - (n + 1) + a_2]$

and $f(1) = \frac{1}{2}(a_2)$

Then, $\sum_{k=1}^{n} k = f(n + 1) - f(1) = \frac{1}{2}[(n + 1)^2 - (n + 1)]$

$\quad = \frac{1}{2} n (n + 1)$

After sufficient practice students should be able to do the following exercises.

Postassessment

Have students complete the following exercises:

1) Find the sum of $1^3 + 2^3 + \ldots + n^3$

2) Find the sum of $\sum_{k=1}^{n} k^5$

3) What are the changes in the general theorem if in $\sum_{t=1}^{n} t^r$, t is an even number?

105 A Parabolic Calculator

After having taught the properties of the parabola to an eleventh grade mathematics class, the teacher might want to discuss some applications of the parabola. The teacher may discuss the reflective properties of a parabolic surface such as a searchlight or the mirror in a telescope. The light source at the focus of a parabolic reflecting surface (fig. 1) reflects its rays off the surface in *parallel paths*. It may be noted that the angle of incidence, $\angle FTP$, equals the angle of reflection, $\angle FTQ$.

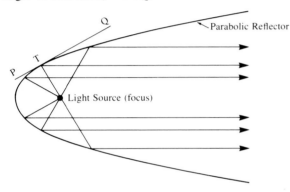

Figure 1

The same principal is used in a telescope (fig. 2) (or radar unit). However here the rays are generated from external sources and reflected off the mirror (or radar screen) to the focus, which may consist of a camera or other sensing device.

Other applications such as the parabolic path of a thrown object may be considered. However a rather unusual application of the parabola involves its properties on the Cartesian plane. This model will present a method of using a parabola on the Cartesian plane as a calculating device for performing multiplication and division. The only supplies students will need are graph paper and a straightedge.

Performance Objectives

• *Students will draw an appropriate parabola, and perform a given multiplication with it.*
• *Students will draw an appropriate parabola and perform a given division with it.*
• *Students will justify (analytically) why the multiplication method presented in this unit "works."*

Preassessment

Before presenting this unit to the class the teacher should be sure that students are able to graph a

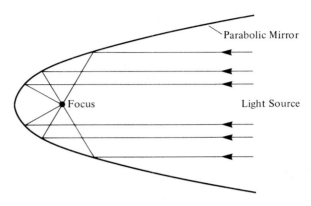

Figure 2

parabola and are able to find the equation of a line, given two points on the line.

Teaching Strategies

On a large sheet of graph paper (preferably one with small squares) have students draw coordinate axes and graph the parabola $y = x^2$. This must be done very accurately. Once this has been completed students are ready to perform some calculations. For example, suppose they wish to multiply 3×5. They would simply draw the line joining the point on the parabola whose abscissa is 3 with the point whose abscissa is -5. The point product of 3 and 5 is the ordinate of the point where this line intersects the y-axis. (Figure 3, AB)

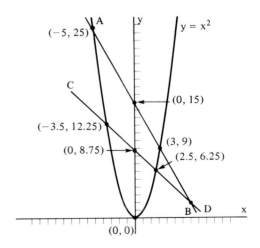

Figure 3

For further practice have students multiply 2.5 $\times$ 3.5. Here they must draw the line containing the points (2.5, 6.25) and (−3.5, 12.25). (These are the points on parabola $y = x^2$, whose abscissas are 2.5 and −3.5) The ordinate of the point where this line (Figure 3, $\overset{\leftrightarrow}{CD}$) intersects the y-axis is the product of 2.5 and 3.5, that is, 8.75. Naturally the size of the graph will determine the degree of accuracy which can be obtained. Students should realize that the points on the parabola whose abscissas were −2.5 and 3.5 could just as well have been used in place of the points whose abscissas were 2.5 and −3.5 in the past example.

At this point the teacher may ask students how this same scheme can be used to do division. Students, noting that division is the inverse operation of multiplication, should suggest that $\overset{\leftrightarrow}{CD}$ could have been used to divide the following: 8.75 ÷ 3.5. The other point of intersection which $\overset{\leftrightarrow}{CD}$ makes with the parabola, point (2.5, 6.25) yields the answer 2.5.

The teacher would be wise to offer students a variety of drill exercises to better familiarize them with this technique. Students can use a straightedge (without drawing a line) to read the answers from the graph.

After sufficient drill, students may become curious about the reason why this technique of calculation actually "works." To prove that it does work, have the class consider the following general case (Figure 4).

Let $\overset{\leftrightarrow}{PQ}$ intersect the parabola $y = x^2$ at points (x_1, y_1) and (x_2, y_2), and intersect the y-axis at $(0, y_3)$. This proof must conclude that $y_3 = |x_1 x_2|$.

Proof:

The slope of $\overset{\leftrightarrow}{PQ} = \dfrac{y_2 - y_1}{x_2 - x_1} = \dfrac{x_2^2 - x_1^2}{x_2 - x_1} =$

$x_1 + x_2$ (since $y_2 = x_2^2$, and $y_1 = x_1^2$).

The slope of $\overset{\leftrightarrow}{PQ}$ expressed with any point (x, y)

is $\dfrac{y - y_1}{x - x_1}$.

Therefore $\dfrac{y - y_1}{x - x_1} = x_1 + x_2$ is the equation of $\overset{\leftrightarrow}{PQ}$.

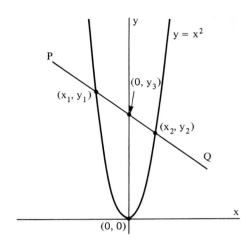

Figure 4

At the point $(0, y_3)$ $\dfrac{y_3 - y_1}{0 - x_1} = x_1 + x_2$ and

$y_3 = -x_1^2 - x_1 x_2 + y_1$.

But $y_1 = x_1^2$, thus $y_3 = -x_1 x_2$, but this is positive, so $y_3 = |x_1 x_2|$.

With a knowledge of this proof students may wish to experiment with other parabolas in an attempt to replace $y = x^2$ with a more "convenient" parabola.

This scheme also provides the student with a host of further investigations. For example, it may be used to "construct" a line of length $\sqrt{a}$. The student need only construct a line parallel to the x-axis and intersecting the y-axis at $(0, a)$. The segment of that line which is between the y-axis and the parabola has length $\sqrt{a}$. Further student investigations should be encouraged.

Postassessment

1. Have students draw the parabola $y = x^2$ and then use it to do the following exercises:
   a) 4 × 5   b) 4.5 × 5.5   c) 4 ÷ 2.5   d) 1.5 ÷ .5
2. Have students show how $y = \frac{1}{2}x^2$ may be used to perform multiplication and division operations.

106 Constructing Ellipses

This unit provides a means of constructing ellipses using a straightedge and a compass.

Performance Objectives

1. Students will plot points on an ellipse without the use of an equation.

2. The relation of the circle to the ellipse will be used by students in the constructions of ellipses.

Preassessment

Students should have completed tenth year mathematics and be familiar with fundamental trigonometric identities. Knowledge of analytic geometry is helpful, but not necessary. Ask students to construct an ellipse using any method (i.e., analytically or with special tools).

Teaching Strategies

After inspecting student attempts to construct an ellipse, have them consider the accuracy of their work. Some students may have attempted a "freehand" drawing, while others may have plotted an appropriate curve on a piece of graph paper. This should lead comfortably to Method I.

Method I: Point-by-point construction. One of the definitions of an ellipse is: *the locus of a point, P, which moves such that the sum of its distances from two given fixed points, F and F', is a constant.* From Figure 1, the definitions just given implies that PF + PF' = a constant. (1)

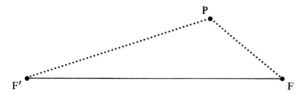

Figure 1

Customarily, this constant is given the value 2a, and it is not too difficult to derive from this definition the equation of the ellipse:

$$\frac{x^2}{a^2} + \frac{y^2}{b^2} = 1 \qquad (2)$$

Indeed, the popular thumbtack and string-loop construction is directly based on this definition (where a string-loop is held taut between two thumbtacks and a pencil which changes position).

Procedure: Place an 8½″ × 11″ sheet in the horizontal position and center on it a 4″ horizontal line whose endpoints F and F' are the ellipse's foci (see

Figure 2). Let the constant in (1) equal 6″. Thus, PF + PF' = 6″. (3)

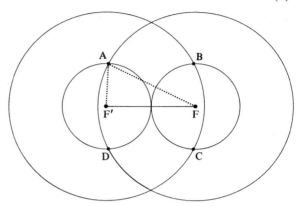

Figure 2

With F as center, draw a circle of 4″ radius. Do likewise with F' as center. Next, again use F and F' as centers for circles of 2″ radius. Note that these four circles intersect in four points A, B, C and D which lie on the ellipse. For, if point A is arbitrarily chosen, by construction FA = 2″ and F'A = 4″; hence FA + F'A = 6″, satisfying (3).

A rather accurate construction can be made by using increments of ½″ for the radii of each circle centered on F and F', starting with $9\frac{1}{2}$″ and $2\frac{1}{2}$″ radii. The next set of four points on the ellipse would be obtained by drawing two circles of 5″ and 1″ radius, both on F and F'. These two pairs of circles would be followed by another two pairs of radii 9″ and 3″, and so on, as indicated in Figure 3. Indeed, additional ellipses can then be sketched from Figure 3.

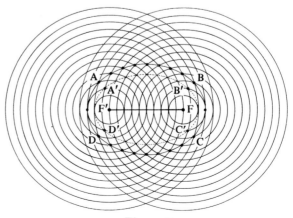

Figure 3

Assume that PF + PF′ = 5″.   (4)

Then, one need only mark the intersections of those circles centered on F and F′, the sum of whose radii is 5. For example, in constructing (3) by using the suggested ¼″ increment, it was necessary at some point to use a radius of 3½″ centered on F and F′ and another radius of 1½″ again centered on F and F′. The intersection of these four circles, A′, B′, C′ and D′, provide four points on *another* ellipse such that, using A′ arbitrarily, FA′ + F′A′ = 5″.

Figure 3 thus shows the two ellipses sketched, both of which have F and F′ as their foci. Other ellipses can be sketched in a similar manner from the same figure.

Method II: Tangent construction. Centered on an 8½″ by 11″ sheet of paper, have students draw a circle of radius 3″. Locate a point F in the interior of the circle 2¼″ from the center (see Figure 4).

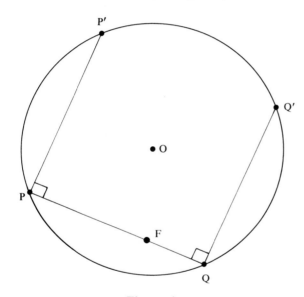

Figure 4

Through F draw a chord to intersect the circle at P and Q. Using a right triangle template or carpenter's T-square, erect perpendiculars at P and Q to meet the circle at P′ and Q′, respectively. Then $\overleftrightarrow{PP'}$ and $\overleftrightarrow{QQ'}$ are each tangents to an ellipse having F as one of its foci. Continue this procedure for many such chords $\overline{PQ}$, obtaining a diagram similar to that shown in Figure 5.

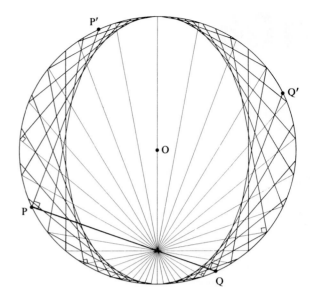

Figure 5

The proof of this construction is based on the converse of the following theorem: *The locus of the intersection of the tangent to an ellipse with the perpendicular on it from either focus is a circle.* A proof of this theorem can be found in Bowser's *An Elementary Treatise on Analytic Geometry,* pages 139-140.

Varying the position of F will change the size and shape of the ellipse. Furthermore, the second focus, F′ is located on $\overrightarrow{FO}$ extended through O its own distance.

Postassessment

1. Have students draw Figure 3 on a larger scale, such as FF′ = 6″. Coloring in the numerous regions formed by the intersections of the circles may prove quite satisfying.

2. Have students draw a circle of radius *r*, with O as center. They then locate a fixed point, F, inside the circle, and draw $\overline{OF}$. Clearly, *r* > OF. Then have them draw an arbitrary radius OQ. Connect FQ, and construct its midpoint, M. At M, they should erect a perpendicular to intersect $\overline{OQ}$ at P. Then P lies on an ellipse with F as one of its foci. Moreover, $\overrightarrow{MP}$ extended through P is a tangent to the same ellipse. Have students complete this construction and justify it.

107 Constructing the Parabola

Performance Objective
With straightedge and compasses, students will construct a parabola without using an equation.

Preassessment
Ask students to construct the parabola $y = x^2$ on a sheet of graph paper. When this has been done, have them draw any other parabola on a sheet of "blank" paper.

Teaching Strategies
In all likelihood students will be unable to draw a parabola without use of graph paper. At this point the teacher may define the parabola in terms of locus. That is, it is the locus of points equidistant from a fixed point and a fixed line. Perhaps students will find this a useful hint in deriving a method of construction of a parabola. After considering students' suggestions, have them consider the following methods.

Method I. Point-by-point Construction. Towards the left of an 8½-by-11-inch sheet of paper held horizontally, lightly draw about 15 vertical parallel lines each spaced ½ inch apart (see Figure 1). Each line segment should be eight inches long. Draw the

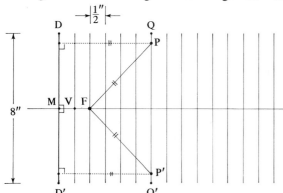

Figure 1

common perpendicular bisector of these lines. Label your drawing as shown in Figure 1, being sure to place F at the intersection of the third parallel line and the perpendicular bisector. Let $\overleftrightarrow{QQ'}$ be any arbitrary parallel line, say the sixth one from $\overleftrightarrow{DD'}$. By construction, $\overleftrightarrow{QQ'}$ is $(6 \cdot \frac{1}{2}) = 3''$ from $\overleftrightarrow{DD'}$. Maintaining this distance, using F as center, swing an arc with your compasses cutting $\overleftrightarrow{QQ'}$ above and below the perpendicular bisector at P and P'. Then P and P' are on the parabola with F as the *focus* of the parabola. Repeat this procedure for the other parallel lines, joining all the points so determined (see Figure 2).

Discussion: By construction, the perpendicular distance of either P or P' from $\overleftrightarrow{DD'}$ is equal to FP

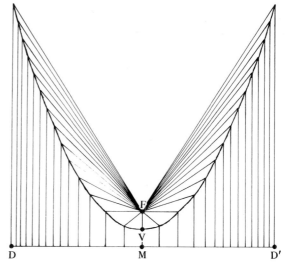

Figure 2

or FP'. The definition of a parabola is based on such an equivalence of distance of a varying point from a fixed line and a fixed point. A parabola is the locus of points each of whose distances from a fixed point equals its distance from a fixed line. The line $\overleftrightarrow{DD'}$ is referred to as the *directrix* and its perpendicular bisector is the *axis* of the parabola. If M is the intersection of the axis and the directrix $\overleftrightarrow{DD'}$, by letting FM = 2p, it is not difficult, using the distance formula and the above definition, to show that the parabola's equation is $y^2 = 4px$. (1) The midpoint, V, of $\overline{MF}$ is the parabola's *vertex*, and is often referred to as the parabola's turning point.

Method II. Point-by-point Construction. Draw a rectangle ABCD (see Figure 3), letting V and G be the midpoints of $\overline{AD}$ and $\overline{BC}$, respectively.

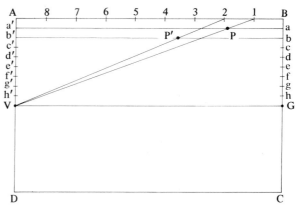

Figure 3

Divide $\overline{AB}$ and $\overline{BG}$ into the same *number* of equal parts. Starting from B, let the successive points of equal division be 1, 2, 3, . . . on $\overline{AB}$ and *a, b, c* . . . on $\overline{BG}$. Draw $\overline{aa'}$ perpendicular to $\overline{BG}$. Note that *a'*, *b'*, *c'* . . . . are points on $\overline{AV}$). Draw $\overline{V1}$, meeting $\overline{aa'}$ at P. Similarly, draw $\overline{bb'}$ perpendicular to $\overline{BG}$ and draw $\overline{V2}$, meeting $\overline{bb'}$ at P'. Continue this for the other points. Then P and P', and other points so obtained are on a parabola with V as its vertex and $\overline{VG}$ as its axis.

Proof: From Figure 3, let $\overleftrightarrow{AD}$ be the *y*-axis and $\overleftrightarrow{VG}$ the *x*-axis (see Figure 4). Let *b* on $\overline{BG}$ now be called

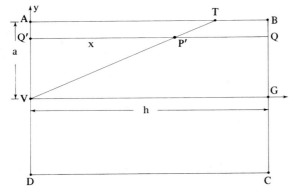

Figure 4

Q, *b'* on $\overline{AV}$ to be labelled Q'. Similarly, let point 2 in Figure 3 be called T. Draw $\overline{VT}$ and $\overline{QQ'}$, meeting at P'. Let VQ' = GQ = *y*, Q'P' = *x*, VG = *h*, AV = *a*.

By construction (i.e., points T and Q were selected with this property),

$$\frac{AT}{AB} = \frac{GQ}{GB}, \text{ or } \frac{AT}{h} = \frac{y}{a}. \quad (2)$$

From similar triangles VQ'P' and VAT, $\dfrac{x}{y} = \dfrac{AT}{AV}$

$$= \frac{AT}{a}, \text{ or } AT = \frac{ax}{y}. \quad (3)$$

Substituting this value of AT in (2), $\dfrac{\frac{ax}{y}}{h} = \dfrac{y}{a}$, or

$$\frac{a^2 x}{y} = hy. \quad (4)$$

Solving (4) for y^2 yields $y^2 = \dfrac{a^2 x}{h}$, *(5)*

which is of the same form as (1) in which

$$4p = \frac{a^2}{h}. \quad (6)$$

Since *p* is the distance from the vertex to the focus, solving (6) for *p* will locate the focus in terms of *a* and *h* of the original rectangle.

Method III. Envelope construction. Near the bottom edge of a vertically-held 8½x11-inch sheet of paper, draw a horizontal line the full width of the paper (see Figure 5). Label this line $\overleftrightarrow{AA'}$. Draw the perpendicular bisector of $\overline{AA'}$, with midpoint V. Locate F on the perpendicular bisector, one inch above V. On $\overline{AA'}$, on either side of V, mark off points Q, Q', Q'', . . . , gradually increasing, by a very small increment, the successive distances from V to Q, Q to Q', Q' to Q'', ... Place a right triangle template or carpenter's T-square such that a leg passes through F and the vertex of the right angle is concurrent with

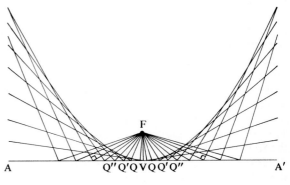

Figure 5

any of the points Q, Q', Q'', ... Construct a right angle with one ray $\overline{FQ}$ and drawing an extended line to the edge of the paper with the other ray of the right angle. Repeat this procedure for other points Q', Q'', ... The resulting diagram should be similar to Figure 5, and the shape "enveloped" by all these lines is a parabola.

Postassessment

Have your students draw an angle of any measure, making both sides equal in length. Starting from the vertex, have them measure off equally spaced intervals along each side, labeling the intervals on each side 1, 2, 3, 4, . . . , 10, with the vertex labelled 0. Then ask them to connect point 10 on one side with point 1 on the other side. See that they do likewise for points 9 and 2, 8 and 3, and so forth, always being sure that the sum of the numbers joined is 11. The resulting appearance will be somewhat similar to Figure 5. Students will have drawn an envelope to a parabola. Have students attempt to justify this construction, as well as that for Figure 5.

108 Using Higher Plane Curves to Trisect an Angle

This unit will introduce two higher plane algebraic curves, showing analytically and visually (experimentally) how the trisection is done.

Performance Objective

1. Given a certain locus condition, students will learn how to sketch a curve directly from the locus without using an equation.

2. Given a polar equation, students will plot the curve on polar coordinate paper.

3. Given one of the curves discussed in this unit, students will trisect any angle.

Preassessment

Students should have done some work with polar coordinates.

Teaching Strategies

The trisection of an angle can be considered a consequence of the following locus problem: Given $\triangle OAP$ with fixed base $\overline{OA}$ and variable vertex P, find the locus of points P such that $m\angle OPA = 2\,m\angle POA$. (See figure 1.) Let O be the pole of a polar coordinate system and $\overrightarrow{OA}$ the initial line, with A having coordinate $(2a,0)$.

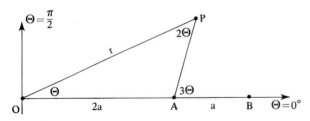

Figure 1

Let $m\angle AOP = \theta$ and $OP = r$. Then by hypothesis, $m\angle APO = 2\theta$, from which it follows $m\angle OAP = \pi - 3\theta$, ($\pi$ radians $= 180°$). Extend $\overline{OA}$ through A a distance of a units, thereby locating point B. Then $m\angle BAP = 3\theta$. By the law of sines,

$$\frac{r}{\sin(\pi - 3\theta)} = \frac{2a}{\sin 2\theta} \qquad (1)$$

from which it follows $r = \dfrac{2a \cdot \sin(\pi - 3\theta)}{\sin 2\theta}$ (2)

Since $\sin(\pi - 3\theta) = \sin 3\theta$ and $\sin 2\theta = 2\sin\theta\cos\theta$, the appropriate substitutions for equation (2) yield

$$r = \frac{a \cdot \sin 3\theta}{\sin\theta\cos\theta}. \qquad (3)$$

With $\sin 3\theta = 3\sin\theta - 4\sin^3\theta = \sin\theta(3 - 4\sin^2\theta)$,

(3) yields $r = \dfrac{3a - 4a \cdot \sin^2\theta}{\cos\theta}$. (4)

Letting $\sin^2\theta = 1 - \cos^2\theta$ in (4),

$r = \dfrac{-a + 4a \cdot \cos^2\theta}{\cos\theta}$, which can easily be simplified, by letting $\dfrac{1}{\cos\theta} = \sec\theta$, to $r = a(4\cos\theta - \sec\theta)$ (5)

the required polar equation for the *Trisectrix of Maclaurin*.

By placing P on the other side of $\overleftrightarrow{OA}$ (Fig. 1) a similar derivation will yield

$r = a(4\cos\theta - \sec\theta)$ (6)

Since $\cos(-\theta) = \cos\theta$ and $\sec(-\theta) = \sec\theta$, it follows that (5) is symmetric with respect to $\overleftrightarrow{OA}$. Thus, as confirmed by (6), for all points of the locus above $\overleftrightarrow{OA}$, there are corresponding points below it as well. (These corresponding points are reflections in $\overleftrightarrow{OA}$.)

To sketch the locus, assigning values to θ in (5) and (6) will, of course, furnish points of the Trisectrix. Have students make an exact copy of $\triangle AOP$ on polar coordinate graph paper, so that O is at the origin and $\overrightarrow{OA}$ is on the horizontal axis (at $\theta = 0$ radians.) Then students should plot various points of the curve and draw the curve.

Students may now use the original diagram (on regular paper.) A novel approach to curve sketching would be to plot points and draw lines directly from the given locus condition. One need only assign various values to θ and a corresponding 3θ value to $\angle$ BAP. With $\overrightarrow{OB}$ a fixed base for each of these angles, the intersection of the second side of each angle will yield point P. Figure 2 shows such a construction for values of $0° \leq \theta \leq 55°$ in $5°$ intervals.

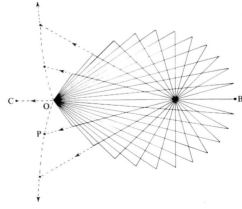

Figure 2

For $\theta = 0°$ and $60°$, there is no triangle, merely $\overline{OB}$. For $\theta > 60°$, consider some arbitrary point C such that $\overleftrightarrow{COA}$. Let the measure of reflex

$m\angle$BAP $= 195°$, thus placing P below $\overleftrightarrow{COA}$. Then $m\angle$COP $= 65°$, preserving the trisection property. Note that for $|\Theta| \angle 60°$, there will be two asymptotic branches above and below $\overrightarrow{OB}$.

Conversely, given (5), it is a bit more difficult to show that for any point P on the Trisectrix, $m\angle$BOP $= \frac{1}{3}$. $m\angle$BAP. The proof rests on showing that $m\angle$OPA $= 2\Theta$, from which it follows that $m\angle$BAP $= 3\Theta$.

Equation (5) for the Trisectrix of Maclaurin can also be obtained from the following locus problem (see Figure 3):

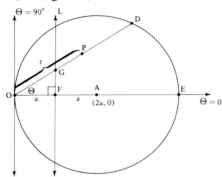

Figure 3

Given O, the pole of a polar coordinate system and E $(4a,0)$. At A $(2a,0)$ as center, draw a circle of radius $2a$. Through F $(a,0)$ draw a line L perpendicular to $\overleftrightarrow{OE}$. Locate an arbitrary point D on the "upper" semicircle's circumference and draw $\overleftrightarrow{OD}$, intersecting L at G. Arbitrarily locate P on $\overleftrightarrow{OD}$. As D varies along the semicircle, find the locus of P on $\overleftrightarrow{OD}$ such that OP $=$ GD. The resulting polar equation will be identical to (5). (*Hints for solution:* Let $m\angle$AOD $= \Theta$, OP $= r =$ GD. Draw $\overline{DE}$, forming right triangle ODE. Express OD in terms of a and $\cos\Theta$, and express OG in terms of a and $\sec\Theta$).

The student now has a method for trisecting an angle (using an additional tool, a curve.) Once students have grasped the above, they may consider another curve, the Limacon of Pascal, which also

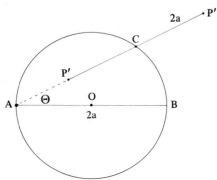

Figure 4

can be used to trisect an angle. However, the following construction for the Limacon should be attempted first.

Draw a circle of diameter AB $= 2a$, center O. Locate an arbitrary point C, distinct from A or B, on the circle's circumference. Place the edge of a ruler at C in such a way that the ruler's midpoint rests on C and that the same edge passes through A. Locate two points P and P' at a distance of a units on either side of C. Repeat this for different positions of C. P and P' are then points on the Limacon.

For a visual effect analogous to Figure 2, divide the circle's circumference into 18 evenly spaced arcs. Repeat the procedure in the preceding paragraph for each of these 18 points, thereby yielding 36 points on the Limacon's circumference. Be sure to draw a line to connect all corresponding points P and P', taking note of the loop that occurs *inside* the Limacon. A suggested diameter for the base circle O is 3″, making P'C $=$ CP $= 1\frac{1}{2}″$.

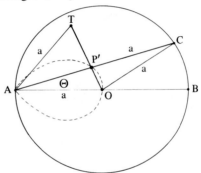

Figure 5

Figure 5 shows the base circle O, the Limacon's inner loop, as well as a few other points and lines used for the following trisection: Let $\angle$BAT be congruent to the angle to be trisected, making AT$=a$. Draw $\overline{TO}$, intersecting the loop at P', and then draw $\overline{AP'}$. We now show that $m\angle$BAT $= 3$ times $m\angle$BAP'.

Extend $\overline{AP'}$ to intersect the circle at C. Since P' is a point on the Limacon, CP' $=a$, from the above construction. Draw $\overline{OC}$ and let $m\angle$OAP' $= \Theta$. Immediately, OA $=$ OC, $m\angle$C $= \Theta$, therefore $m\angle$AOC $=\pi - 2\Theta$. Since $\triangle$OCP' is isosceles, each of its base angles has measure $\frac{\pi}{2} - \frac{1}{2}\Theta$. $m\angle$AP'O $= \frac{\pi}{2} + \frac{1}{2}\Theta$, and it follows that $m\angle$AOP' $= \frac{\pi}{2} - \frac{3}{2}\Theta$.

However, $\triangle$ATO is also isosceles, hence $m\angle$T $= \frac{\pi}{2} - \frac{3}{2}\Theta$, from which it follows that $m\angle$BAT $= 3\Theta$, which was to be proved.

Postassessment

Construct the Limacon of Figure 4 by locating P and P' a distance of $2a$ units on either side of c.

109 Constructing Hypocycloid and Epicycloid Circular Envelopes

In this unit, two elementary cycloidal curves will be related to each other. Students will then create a circular envelope which will simultaneously encompass both curves.

Performance Objectives

1. Students will define: hypocycloid and epicycloid.

2. Students will construct a hypocycloid and an epicycloid.

3. Students will generalize these constructions to other hypocycloids and epicycloids.

Preassessment

Tenth year mathematics is necessary. A minimal knowledge of polar coordinates is helpful.

Teaching Strategies

Initiate the introduction of hypocycloid and epicycloid curves by rolling varying sized circular discs about the interior and exterior circumference, respectively, of a fixed circular disc of constant radius. If possible, let the radius of the fixed circle be some integral multiple of the radius of the rolling circle. Have your students speculate on the loci obtained by a fixed point on the circumference of the varying sized rolling circles. For the interior rotations, it will be necessary for the fixed circle to be hollowed out. A Spirograph Kit, if available, is an excellent motivational source.

This unit analyzes the case when the interior and exterior rolling circles each have radius $b = \dfrac{a}{3}$, as shown in Figure 1 (next column). O is the center of the fixed circle, radius a, and is also the pole of a polar coordinate system. C and C' are the centers, respectively, of the interior and exterior rolling circles. We will assume that both rotating circles are continuously in tangential contact with each other at T. Therefore, $\overrightarrow{OT}$, making an angle of measure Θ with the initial line, intersects circles C and C' at I, T, and I', and contains the centers, C and C'. It is understood that initially each circle was tangent to the fixed circle at B; furthermore, P and P' are respectively fixed points on the circumference of circles C and C'. At the instant both circles began their circuits, P and P' were coincident with B. The partial loci from B to P and P' are shown in Figure 1.

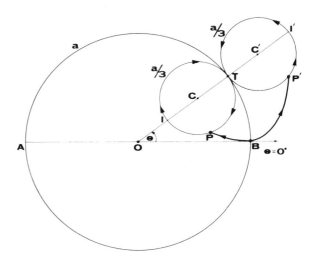

Figure 1

In Figure 2, we show the complete loci swept out by each fixed point. The locus of P is a *hypocycloid of three cusps*, often called the *deltoid;* whereas the locus of P' is an *epicycloid of three cusps*. Each circle requires three complete rotations before returning to point B. The fixed circle is then a circumcircle for the deltoid and an incircle for the three-cusped epicycloid.

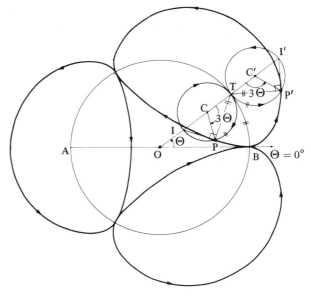

Figure 2

The following lines are drawn in each circle: $\overline{IP}$, $\overline{CP}$ and $\overline{TP}$ for circle C; $\overline{TP'}$, $\overline{C'P'}$ and $\overline{I'P'}$ for circle C'. Have your students explain why

length $\overset{\frown}{TP}$ = length $\overset{\frown}{TB}$ = length $\overset{\frown}{TP'}$.   (1)
Then show that

m $\angle$TCP = 3Θ = m $\angle$TC'P'.   (2)

Since the radii of circles C and C' are equal, ΔTPC $\cong$ ΔTP'C' (SAS); and corresponding sides,

TP = TP'.   (3)

Observe that m$\angle$TPI = 90 = m$\angle$TP'I'. Furthermore, we state without proof that $\overline{PI}$ and $\overline{P'I'}$ are respectively tangents to the deltoid at P and the epicycloid at P'. Further details can be found in reference (2).

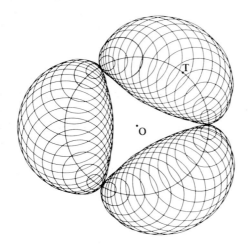

Figure 3

The above equation (3) implies that a circle centered at T, with radius TP = TP' will be tangent to each curve at P and P'. Certainly, as T varies, there is a corresponding change in the length of $\overline{TP'}$ (or $\overline{TP}$). We show in Figure 3 the final result obtained when circles are drawn for 60 equally spaced positions of T along the fixed circle. We utilize symmetry properties of each curve to minimize the work required to determine the varying lengths of $\overline{TP}$: since each curve repeats itself every 120°, and $\overline{OI'}$ divides the curve symmetrically at m$\angle\Theta$ = 60, it is only necessary to obtain those lengths of $\overline{TP}$ between 0°$\leqslant\Theta\leqslant$60°, in intervals of measure 6. These lengths were obtained by making an

accurate drawing of the required ten positions of either rolling circle.

Postassessment

To test student comprehension of hypocycloids and epicycloids, have them complete the following exercises.

1. Figure 4 (below) shows the results obtained when $b = \dfrac{a}{4}$. Justify the occurrence of a four cusped hypocycloid and a four cusped epicycloid.

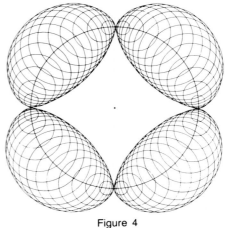

Figure 4

2. Generalize for $b = \dfrac{a}{n}$, $n = 5, 6, \ldots$

3. Make a drawing for the case $b = \dfrac{a}{2}$ (the *nephroid*). Visually show that the locus of a fixed point on the interior rolling circle is a diameter of the fixed circle.

4. Repeat for $b = a$, the *cardioid*. Show that all the circles centered on T pass through a fixed point; i.e., one of the loci degenerates to a point.

References

Beard, Robert S., *Patterns in Space,* Creative Publications, 1973.

Lockwood, E. H., *A Book of Curves,* Cambridge University Press, 1961.

110   The Harmonic Sequence

This unit is best presented to a class after arithmetic and geometric sequences have been mastered.

Performance Objectives

1. *Students will define harmonic sequence.*

2. *Students will illustrate a harmonic sequence geometrically.*

3. *Students will solve simple problems with harmonic sequences.*

Preassessment

Ask students to find the fourth term of the sequence:
$1\frac{1}{3}, 1\frac{11}{17}, 2\frac{2}{13}$.

Teaching Strategies

A natural response on the part of your students is to try to find the fourth term of the above sequence by trying to find a common difference, and when that fails, a common ratio. In a short time your students will feel frustrated. This will offer you a good opportunity to motivate your students towards a "new" type of sequence. Ask students to write each term in improper fraction form and then write its reciprocal. This will yield: $\frac{3}{4}, \frac{17}{28}, \frac{13}{28}$ or $\frac{21}{28}, \frac{17}{28}, \frac{13}{28}$. Further inspection of this new sequence will indicate it to be an arithmetic sequence with a common difference of $\frac{-4}{28}$. Students will now easily obtain the required fourth term, $\frac{1}{\frac{9}{28}} = \frac{28}{9} = 3\frac{1}{9}$.

Students should now be motivated to learn more about the harmonic sequence.

Consider three or more terms in an arithmetic sequence: for example, $a_1, a_2, a_3 \ldots, a_n$. The sequence of reciprocals of these terms, $\frac{1}{a_1}, \frac{1}{a_2}, \frac{1}{a_3}, \ldots, \frac{1}{a_n}$ is called a harmonic sequence. The term "harmonic" comes from a property of musical sounds. If a set of strings of uniform tension whose lengths are proportional to $1, \frac{1}{2}, \frac{1}{3}, \frac{1}{4}, \frac{1}{5}, \frac{1}{6}$ are sounded together, the effect is said to be "harmonious" to the ear. This sequence is harmonic, as the reciprocals of the terms from an arithmetic sequence, 1, 2, 3, 4, 5, 6.

There is no general formula for the sum of the terms in a harmonic series. Problems dealing with a harmonic sequence are generally considered in terms of the related arithmetic sequence.

Two theorems would be useful to consider:

Theorem 1: If a constant is added to (or subtracted from) each term in an arithmetic sequence, then the new sequence is also arithmetic (with the same common difference.)

Theorem 2: If each term in an arithmetic sequence is multiplied (or divided) by a constant, the resulting sequence is also arithmetic (but with a different common difference).

The proofs of these theorems are left as exercises.

The proofs of these theorems are simple and straightforward and do not merit special consideration here. However, the following example will help students gain facility in work with harmonic sequences.

Example: If a, b, c forms a harmonic sequence, prove that $\frac{a}{b+c}, \frac{b}{c+a}, \frac{c}{a+b}$ also forms a harmonic sequence.

Solution: Since $\frac{1}{a}, \frac{1}{b}, \frac{1}{c}$ forms an arithmetic sequence, $\frac{a+b+c}{a}, \frac{a+b+c}{b}, \frac{a+b+c}{c}$ also forms an arithmetic sequence. This may be written as $1 + \frac{b+c}{a}$, $1 + \frac{a+c}{b}$, $1 + \frac{a+b}{c}$. Therefore $\frac{b+c}{a}, \frac{a+c}{b}, \frac{a+b}{c}$. forms an arithmetic sequence. Thus $\frac{a}{b+c}, \frac{b}{a+c}, \frac{c}{a+b}$ forms a harmonic sequence.

Perhaps one of the more interesting aspects of any sequence is to establish a geometric model of the sequence.

One geometric interpretation of a harmonic sequence can be taken from the intersection points of the interior and exterior angle bisectors of a triangle with the side of the triangle.

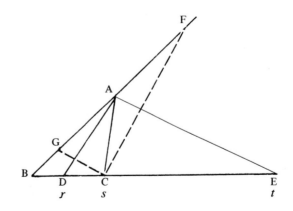

Consider $\triangle ABC$, where $\overline{AD}$ bisects $\angle BAC$ and $\overline{AE}$ bisects $\angle CAF$, and B, D, C, and E are collinear. (see fig. a) It can easily be proved that for exterior angle bisector $\overline{AE}$, $\dfrac{BE}{CE} = \dfrac{AB}{AC}$ (i.e. draw $\overline{GC}\!/\!/\overline{AE}$;

$AG = AC$; also $\dfrac{BE}{CE} = \dfrac{AB}{AG} = \dfrac{AB}{AC}$)

Similarly for interior angle bisector $\overline{AD}$,

$$\frac{BD}{CD} = \frac{AB}{AC}.$$

(The proof is done by drawing $\overline{CF}\!/\!/\overline{AD}$; $AF = AC$;

$\dfrac{BD}{CD} = \dfrac{AB}{AF} = \dfrac{AB}{AC}$.)

Therefore $\dfrac{BE}{CE} = \dfrac{BD}{CD}$ or $\dfrac{CD}{CE} = \dfrac{BD}{BE}$. It is then said that the points B and C separate the points D and E harmonically.

Now suppose $\overleftarrow{BDCE}$ is a number line with B as the zero point, point D at coordinate r, point C at coordinate s, and point E at coordinate t. Therefore $BD = r$, $BC = s$, and $BE = t$. We shall show that r, s, t forms a harmonic sequence. Since $\dfrac{CD}{CE} = \dfrac{BD}{BE}$,

$\dfrac{BC-BD}{BE-BC} = \dfrac{BD}{BE}$, or $\dfrac{s-r}{t-s} = \dfrac{r}{t}$. Therefore $t(s-r) = r(t-s)$ and $ts-tr = rt-rs$. Dividing each term by rst, we get $\dfrac{1}{r} - \dfrac{1}{s} = \dfrac{1}{s} - \dfrac{1}{t}$, which indicates that $\dfrac{1}{t}, \dfrac{1}{s}, \dfrac{1}{r}$ forms an arithmetic sequence. Thus, r, s, t forms a harmonic sequence.

Students should now have reasonably good insight into a harmonic sequence.

Postassessment

1. Set up an equation with the terms of the harmonic sequence a, b, c. (Use the definition.)
2. Find the 26th term of the sequence:

$$2\frac{1}{2}, \ 1\frac{12}{13}, \ 1\frac{9}{16}, \ 1\frac{6}{19} \ \cdots$$

3. Prove that if a^2, b^2, c^2 forms an arithmetic sequence, then $(b + c)$, $(c + a)$, $(a + b)$ forms a harmonic sequence.

111 Transformations and Matrices

This unit will algebraically formalize a discussion of geometric transformations by use of matrices.

Performance Objectives

1. *Given a particular geometric transformation, students will name the 2 × 2 matrix that effects this transformation.*

2. *Given certain 2 × 2 matrices, students will, at a glance, name the transformation each matrix effects.*

Preassessment

1. On a cartesian plane, graph $\triangle ABC$ with vertices at A(2,2), B(4,2), C(2,6). Write the coordinates of A', B', C' which result when $\triangle ABC$ undergoes each of the following transformations:

   a. Translation by −5 units in the x direction tion and 2 units in the y direction.
   b. Reflection across the x-axis.
   c. Rotation of 90° about the origin.
   d. Enlargement scale factor 2 with center at (2,2).

2. Given an equilateral triangle as shown with each vertex the same distance from the origin, list geometric transformations which leave the position of the triangle unchanged, assuming the vertices are indistinguishable.

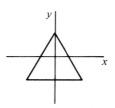

Figure 1

Teaching Strategies

The teacher should first make students aware of a matrix array of numbers. Tell the students that a matrix of size $a \times b$ has a rows and b columns enclosed in brackets. When $a = b$ the matrix is said to be *square*. The class should see that adding matrices involves adding the numbers in corresponding positions in each matrix, for example

$$\begin{bmatrix} a \\ b \end{bmatrix} + \begin{bmatrix} c \\ d \end{bmatrix} = \begin{bmatrix} a + c \\ b + d \end{bmatrix} \quad \text{and the students must}$$

see that matrices must be of the same size (dimension) to be added.

When showing students how to multiply matrices you should use the following general form. Note carefully the column-row relationship between the two matrix factors in the product.

$$\begin{bmatrix} a & b \\ c & d \end{bmatrix} \cdot \begin{bmatrix} x \\ y \end{bmatrix} = \begin{bmatrix} ax + by \\ cx + dy \end{bmatrix}$$

Students may now describe the position of a point either by its coordinates (x,y) or by a 2×1 matrix, called a *position vector*, $\begin{bmatrix} x \\ y \end{bmatrix}$, which represents the vector from the origin to the point.

You may find it effective to use the phrase "is mapped onto" when describing the effect of a transformation. The symbol for this phrase using matrices is "$\longrightarrow$."

Translations provide a simple introduction into the use of matrices.

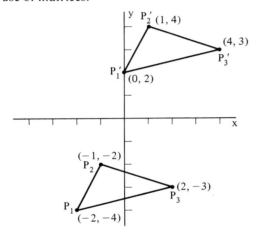

A translation of the triangle $P_1P_2P_3$ to $P'_1P'_2P'_3$ can be generalized in matrix form

$$\begin{bmatrix} x \\ y \end{bmatrix} \longrightarrow \begin{bmatrix} x \\ y \end{bmatrix} + \begin{bmatrix} 2 \\ 6 \end{bmatrix}$$

$\begin{bmatrix} 2 \\ 6 \end{bmatrix}$ represents here a "translation vector," meaning it translates (x,y) 2 units in the x direction and 6 units in the y direction. Students should readily see that by matrix addition each point P_1, P_2, P_3 is mapped onto P'_1, P'_2, P'_3 respectively. That is,

$$P_1 \begin{bmatrix} -2 \\ -4 \end{bmatrix} + \begin{bmatrix} 2 \\ 6 \end{bmatrix} = P'_1 \begin{bmatrix} 0 \\ 2 \end{bmatrix}, P_2 \begin{bmatrix} -1 \\ -2 \end{bmatrix} + \begin{bmatrix} 2 \\ 6 \end{bmatrix} =$$

$$P'_2 \begin{bmatrix} 1 \\ 4 \end{bmatrix}, P_3 \begin{bmatrix} 2 \\ -3 \end{bmatrix} + \begin{bmatrix} 2 \\ 6 \end{bmatrix} = P'_3 \begin{bmatrix} 4 \\ 3 \end{bmatrix}$$ Matrix ad-

dition of 2×1 position vectors can therefore describe any translation in the two-dimensional plane. Students should be given several examples and exercises where a particular point (x_1, y_1) is translated into any other point (x_2, y_2) by a suitable

choice of 2×1 matrix $\begin{bmatrix} x \\ y \end{bmatrix}$ such that

$$\begin{bmatrix} x_1 \\ y_1 \end{bmatrix} + \begin{bmatrix} x \\ y \end{bmatrix} = \begin{bmatrix} x_2 \\ y_2 \end{bmatrix}$$

Rotations, reflections and *enlargements* are more interesting, and to describe them algebraically requires 2×2 matrices. Students should first be given two or three examples of the type

$$\begin{bmatrix} 2 & 3 \\ -1 & 2 \end{bmatrix} \cdot \begin{bmatrix} 3 \\ 2 \end{bmatrix} = \begin{bmatrix} 12 \\ 1 \end{bmatrix}$$ for two reasons. For

one, they may need practice in matrix multiplication, a skill they must master before embarking on the rest of this topic, and second, and most important in this strategy, is that students begin to think of

the matrix $\begin{bmatrix} 2 & 3 \\ -1 & 2 \end{bmatrix}$ (or any 2×2 matrix) as a

transformation of the point $P(3,2)$ onto the point $P'(12,1)$. Each example of this type should be accompanied by an illustration, as in Figure 2.

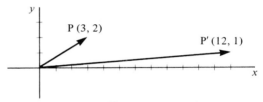

Figure 2

When the students are familiar with the notion that any 2×2 matrix represents a transformation, the teacher should be ready to show them that some 2×2 matrices represent special transformations with which they are familiar. For example, the teacher may give them the matrix and point, respectively (which follow):

1. $\begin{bmatrix} -1 & 0 \\ 0 & 1 \end{bmatrix} \cdot \overset{P_1}{\begin{bmatrix} 2 \\ 3 \end{bmatrix}} = \overset{P'_1}{\begin{bmatrix} -2 \\ 3 \end{bmatrix}}$

and

2. $\begin{bmatrix} 0 & -1 \\ 1 & 0 \end{bmatrix} \cdot \overset{P_2}{\begin{bmatrix} 3 \\ 1 \end{bmatrix}} = \overset{P'_2}{\begin{bmatrix} -1 \\ 3 \end{bmatrix}}$

and

3. $\begin{bmatrix} 3 & 0 \\ 0 & 3 \end{bmatrix} \cdot \overset{P_3}{\begin{bmatrix} 2 \\ -1 \end{bmatrix}} = \overset{P'_3}{\begin{bmatrix} 6 \\ -3 \end{bmatrix}}$

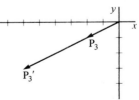

Students may have recognized the transformations in these examples as (1) a reflection (across the y axis), (2) a positive rotation of 90°, and (3) an enlargement, scale factor 3. To emphasize the point that it was not merely by chance that the matrices accomplished these transformations, ask the students to take the general point $\begin{bmatrix} x \\ y \end{bmatrix}$ and multiply it by each of the matrices. The students' answers will be, respectively, $\begin{bmatrix} -x \\ y \end{bmatrix}$, $\begin{bmatrix} -y \\ x \end{bmatrix}$, $\begin{bmatrix} 3x \\ 3y \end{bmatrix}$. Students will therefore see (the second case may require some insight) that the matrices $\begin{bmatrix} -1 & 0 \\ 0 & 1 \end{bmatrix}$, $\begin{bmatrix} 0 & -1 \\ 1 & 0 \end{bmatrix}$, and $\begin{bmatrix} 3 & 0 \\ 0 & 3 \end{bmatrix}$ do indeed accomplish, in the general case, the transformations they recognized in the particular examples.

To achieve performance objectives, whereby matrices provide a handy tool in transformational work, show what 2×2 matrices do to the unit vectors i $\begin{bmatrix} 1 \\ 0 \end{bmatrix}$ and j $\begin{bmatrix} 0 \\ 1 \end{bmatrix}$.

Choose any 2×2 matrix, as in the previous example, $\begin{bmatrix} 2 & 3 \\ -1 & 2 \end{bmatrix}$, and ask your students to multiply the unit vectors i and j by this matrix.

$$\begin{bmatrix} 2 & 3 \\ -1 & 2 \end{bmatrix} \cdot \begin{bmatrix} 1 \\ 0 \end{bmatrix} = \begin{bmatrix} 2 \\ -1 \end{bmatrix},$$

$$\begin{bmatrix} 2 & 3 \\ -1 & 2 \end{bmatrix} \cdot \begin{bmatrix} 0 \\ 1 \end{bmatrix} = \begin{bmatrix} 3 \\ 2 \end{bmatrix}$$

Use another example:

$$\begin{bmatrix} -1 & 0 \\ 0 & -1 \end{bmatrix} \cdot \begin{bmatrix} 1 \\ 0 \end{bmatrix} = \begin{bmatrix} -1 \\ 0 \end{bmatrix},$$

$$\begin{bmatrix} -1 & 0 \\ 0 & -1 \end{bmatrix} \cdot \begin{bmatrix} 0 \\ 1 \end{bmatrix} = \begin{bmatrix} 0 \\ -1 \end{bmatrix}$$

Continue with more examples until it is obvious to the students that

In any 2×2 matrix $\begin{bmatrix} a & b \\ c & d \end{bmatrix}$, multiplying by $\begin{bmatrix} 1 \\ 0 \end{bmatrix}$ gives the first column $\begin{bmatrix} a \\ c \end{bmatrix}$ and multiplying by $\begin{bmatrix} 0 \\ 1 \end{bmatrix}$ gives the second column $\begin{bmatrix} b \\ d \end{bmatrix}$. In other words, the matrix maps the base vectors $\begin{bmatrix} 1 \\ 0 \end{bmatrix}$ and $\begin{bmatrix} 0 \\ 1 \end{bmatrix}$ onto $\begin{bmatrix} a \\ c \end{bmatrix}$ and $\begin{bmatrix} b \\ d \end{bmatrix}$ respectively.

When this conclusion is reached and appreciated by each student, the class then holds the key to reaching the performance objectives. Check whether the class can answer each of the following two types of problems:

1. Which transformation is performed by applying the matrix $\begin{bmatrix} 2 & 0 \\ 0 & 2 \end{bmatrix}$ to the unit vectors?

Show them that $\begin{bmatrix} 2 & 0 \\ 0 & 2 \end{bmatrix} \cdot \begin{bmatrix} 1 \\ 0 \end{bmatrix} = \begin{bmatrix} 2 \\ 0 \end{bmatrix}$

and so $\begin{bmatrix} 1 \\ 0 \end{bmatrix}$ has been mapped onto $\begin{bmatrix} 2 \\ 0 \end{bmatrix}$

and $\begin{bmatrix} 2 & 0 \\ 0 & 2 \end{bmatrix} \cdot \begin{bmatrix} 0 \\ 1 \end{bmatrix} = \begin{bmatrix} 0 \\ 2 \end{bmatrix}$.

and so $\begin{bmatrix} 0 \\ 1 \end{bmatrix}$ has been mapped onto $\begin{bmatrix} 0 \\ 2 \end{bmatrix}$.

Conclude that $\begin{bmatrix} 2 & 0 \\ 0 & 2 \end{bmatrix}$ is therefore an enlargement, scale factor 2.

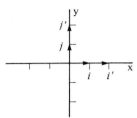

2. Which matrix effects the transformation: rotation by 180°, centered at the origin? Ask the students to draw the effect of 180 rotation on the base vectors.

Check with them that $\begin{bmatrix} 1 \\ 0 \end{bmatrix} \rightarrow \begin{bmatrix} -1 \\ 0 \end{bmatrix}$ and $\begin{bmatrix} 0 \\ 1 \end{bmatrix} \rightarrow \begin{bmatrix} 0 \\ -1 \end{bmatrix}$. Ask them what 2×2 matrix will give the results $\begin{bmatrix} a & d \\ c & d \end{bmatrix} \cdot \begin{bmatrix} 1 \\ 0 \end{bmatrix} = \begin{bmatrix} -1 \\ 0 \end{bmatrix}$ and $\begin{bmatrix} a & b \\ c & d \end{bmatrix} \cdot \begin{bmatrix} 0 \\ 1 \end{bmatrix} = \begin{bmatrix} 0 \\ -1 \end{bmatrix}$. They should by now know that $\begin{bmatrix} -1 \\ d \end{bmatrix}$ gives the first column of the 2×2 matrix and $\begin{bmatrix} 0 \\ -1 \end{bmatrix}$ gives the second column.

Therefore the desired matrix is $\begin{bmatrix} -1 & 0 \\ 0 & -1 \end{bmatrix}$.

Numerous examples and exercises should follow, such as those found in the posttest.

Depending on his aims, the teacher may want to go on at this point to discuss inverse transformations (i.e., ones that reverse the effect of the original transformation) and transformations followed in the same problem by other transformations. The teacher should be aware here too of the value of using matrices, for the inverse of a matrix represents the inverse of a transformation, and multiplying two 2×2 matrices represents the effect of one transformation followed by another.

Postassessment

1. What transformation does the matrix
a.) $\begin{bmatrix} 0 & 1 \\ -1 & 0 \end{bmatrix}$ b.) $\begin{bmatrix} 2 & 0 \\ 0 & -2 \end{bmatrix}$ c.) $\begin{bmatrix} 0 & -1 \\ -1 & 0 \end{bmatrix}$ represent?
2. Find the matrix of each of the following transformations:
  a.) Reflection across the line y = x.
  b.) Enlargement with center at the origin, scale factor ½.
  c.) Rotation by −90°.

112 The Method of Differences

Many students familiar with arithmetic and geometric progressions will welcome the opportunity to extend their knowledge of sequences and series to a much broader class of simple functions.

Performance Objectives

(1) Given sufficient terms of a sequence whose *nth* term is a rational, *integral function of* n, *students will form an array consisting of the successive orders of differences.*

(2) *Given such an array, students will then use the method of differences to find expressions for the nth term and the sum of the first* n *terms.*

Preassessment

Students should be acquainted with the Binomial Theorem for positive, integral exponents as it is ordinarily taught in high schools.

Teaching Strategies

Begin the lesson by challenging the class to find the general term of the sequence 2, 12, 36, 80, 150, 252 . . . After initial efforts of most students to find the familiar arithmetic and geometric progressions have proved unsuccessful hint that sequences of this sort might be generated by single polynomials e.g. n^2 (1, 4, 9, . . .) or n^3 (1, 8, 27, . . .). One student or another may shortly recognize that the *n*th term is given by $n^3 + n^2$.

Elicit that an infinite number of such sequences could be produced by using familiar polynomial functions. Then explain that a simple method exists for finding both the general term and the sum of these sequences. It is called the "Method of Differences" and although it is not generally taught to high school students, it is nonetheless well within their grasp.

Have the class form the "difference between successive terms" of the above sequence, and then continue the process as shown below.

$$
\begin{array}{ccccccc}
2 & 12 & 36 & 80 & 150 & 252 & \ldots \\
 & 10 & 24 & 44 & 70 & 102 & \ldots \\
 & & 14 & 20 & 26 & 32 & \ldots \\
 & & & 6 & 6 & 6 & \ldots
\end{array} \quad (1)
$$

Observe that we reach a line of differences in which all terms are equal. To test whether this occurrence is merely accidental, have the students form sequences from polynomials such as $n^3 + 5n$, $2n^3 + 3$, and so forth, and then repeat the process of taking successive differences. A consensus will soon emerge that an eventual line of equal terms is indeed characteristic of such sequences. The formal proof of this proposition (although simple) is not necessary at this time. Suffi-

cient motivation will have been produced to examine the general case shown below.

Given sequence:	$U_1, U_2, U_3, U_4, U_5, U_6, \ldots$
1st order of difference:	$\Delta U_1, \Delta U_2, \Delta U_3, \Delta U_4, \Delta U_5, \ldots$ (2)
2nd order of difference:	$\Delta_2 U_1, \Delta_2 U_2, \Delta_2 U_3, \Delta_2 U_4, \ldots$
3rd order of difference:	$\Delta_3 U_1, \Delta_3 U_2, \Delta_3 U_3, \ldots$

The notation will be self-evident to all who have written out several previous arrays. Thus: $\Delta U_3 = U_4 - U_3$, $\Delta_2 U_3 = \Delta U_4 - \Delta U_3$, etc. If the delta symbol, Δ, appears too forbidding for some, it can simply be replaced by the letter D.

From the method of forming each entry in (2) it can be seen that: any term is equal to the sum of the term immediately preceding it added to the term below it on the left.

Using nothing more than this simple observation, we will now express each term of the given sequence as a function of the descending terms making up the left-hand boundary. Thus: $\boxed{U_2 = U_1 + \Delta U_1}$ (3)

Also, $U_3 = U_2 + \Delta U_2$ with $\Delta U_2 = \Delta U_1 + \Delta_2 U_1$.
$U_3 = (U_1 + \Delta U_1) + (\Delta U_1 + \Delta_2 U_1)$
$$\boxed{U_3 = U_1 + 2\Delta U_1 + \Delta_2 U_1} \quad (4)$$

By referring to (2) students should be able to follow the reasoning that leads to an expression for U_4 in terms of U_1.
$U_4 = U_3 + \Delta U_3$; however, $\Delta U_3 = \Delta U_2 + \Delta_2 U_2$.
But, $\Delta U_2 = \Delta U_1 + \Delta_2 U_1$, and $\Delta_2 U_2 = \Delta_2 U_1 + \Delta_3 U_1$.
Therefore, $\Delta U_3 = \Delta U_1 + 2\Delta_2 U_1 + \Delta_3 U_1$
Now, using (3) and (4):
$U_4 = (U_1 + 2\Delta U_1 + \Delta_2 U_1) + (\Delta U_1 + 2\Delta_2 U_1 + \Delta_3 U_1$
$$\boxed{U_4 = U_1 + 3\Delta U_1 + 3\Delta_2 U_1 + \Delta_3 U_1} \quad (5)$$

Calling attention to the boxed expressions for U_2, U_3, U_4 the teacher can elicit the fact that the numerical coefficients involved are those of the Binomial Theorem. Note, however, that the coefficients used for the *fourth* term (1, 3, 3, 1) are those found in a binomial expansion for the exponent *three*. If this remains true generally, we shall be able to write:

$$\boxed{\begin{aligned} U_n = {} & U_1 + (n-1)\Delta U_1 + \frac{(n-1)(n-2)}{1\cdot 2}\Delta_2 U_1 + \\ & \ldots + {}_{n-1}C_r\Delta_r U_1 + \ldots + \Delta_{n-1}U_1 \end{aligned}} \quad (6)$$

If desired, the formal proof of (6) can be easily obtained by mathematical induction once the identity $_nC_r + {_nC_{r-1}} = {_{n+1}C_r}$ is established.

Some teachers may wish to rewrite (6) so as to resemble the notation typically used in treating arithmetic progressions. To do this, let the first term of the sequence be "*a*", while the first terms of each successive order of difference are $d_1, d_2, d_3 \ldots$. Then the *nth* term will be:

$$\ell = a + (n-1)d_1 + \frac{(n-1)(n-2)}{1 \cdot 2} d_2 + \ldots \quad (7)$$

Finding the Sum of the First n-*Terms*

Examine the following array, in which $U_1, U_2 \ldots$ are again the terms of the given sequence we wish to sum.

$$0_1 \quad S_2 \quad S_3 \quad S_4 \quad S_5 \quad \ldots$$
$$U_1 \quad U_2 \quad U_3 \quad U_4 \quad \ldots \qquad (8)$$
$$\Delta U_1 \quad \Delta U_2 \quad \Delta U_3 \quad \ldots$$

Observe that the S-terms are formed by relations such as
$$S_2 = 0 + U_1 = U_1$$
$$S_3 = S_2 + U_2 = U_1 + U_2$$
$$S_4 = S_3 + U_3 = U_1 + U_2 + U_3$$
$$S_5 = S_4 + U_4 = U_1 + U_2 + U_3 + U_4$$

Thus, if we can find an expression for S_{n+1} we will have also found the sum of the first *n*-terms. To find S_{n+1} one simply applies the previously determined equation (6) to the above array (8). Before doing so, students should carefully compare (8) with (2). Then

it should become evident that the proper application of equation (6) yields:

$$S_{n+1} = 0 + nU_1 + \frac{n(n-1)}{1 \cdot 2}\Delta U_1 + \ldots + \Delta_n U_n \text{ or}$$

$$\boxed{U_1 + U_2 + \ldots + U_n = nU_1 + \frac{n(n-1)}{1 \cdot 2}\Delta U_1 + \ldots + \Delta_n U_n} \quad (9)$$

As an illustration, let us sum the first *n* squares of the integers.
$$1, \quad 4, \quad 9, \quad 16, \quad 25 \quad \ldots$$
$$3, \quad 5, \quad 7, \quad 9 \quad \ldots$$
$$2, \quad 2, \quad 2 \quad \ldots$$

$$\text{Sum of } n^2 = n \cdot 1 + \frac{n(n-1)}{1 \cdot 2} \cdot 3 + \frac{n(n-1)(n-2)}{1 \cdot 2 \cdot 3} \cdot 2$$
$$= \frac{6n + 9n(n-1) + 2n(n-1)(n-2)}{6} = \frac{n}{6}(n+1)(2n+1)$$

Students may readily confirm the validity of this expression. Again, as before, the teacher may elect to rewrite (9) in terms of $a, d_1, d_2, \ldots$ and so forth.

Postassessment

Have students find the *nth* term and the sum of *n* terms for
1) 2, 5, 10, 17, 26 . . .
2) 1, 8, 27, 64, 125 . . .
3) 12, 40, 90, 168, 280, 432 . . .

Have students create sequences of their own from simple polynomials, and then challenge their classmates to discover the general term.

113 Probability Applied To Baseball

Each year the first months of school coincide with the last months of major league baseball. The playing of the World Series in October normally provides a source of distraction. For mathematics teachers, however, this event can be harnessed to provide useful motivation for a host of probability applications that have high intrinsic academic value.

Performance Objectives

1) *Given odds for opposing World Series teams, students will calculate the expected number of games to be played.*

2) *Given the batting average of any hitter, students will estimate the probability of his attaining any given number of hits during a game.*

Preassessment

Previous study of permutations and probability is not necessary if some introductory discussion is provided. The topic is thus suitable for younger senior high school students (who have not yet learned the binomial theorem). Older students need even less preparation.

Teaching Strategies

The lesson should begin with an informal, spirited discussion of which team is likely to win the World Series. Newspaper clippings of the "odds" should be brought in. This leads directly to the question of how many games will be required for a decision.

Length of Series

If the outcome of a World Series is designated by a sequence of letters representing the winning team (NAANAA means National League won the first and fourth games while losing the rest), challenge the class to find the total number of possible outcomes.

Discuss the solution in terms of "permutations of objects that are not all different." Observe that separate cases of four, five, six, or seven objects must be considered. Elicit that a constraint in the problem is that the winning team must always win the last game. The results can be tabulated as:

No. of Games Played	4	5	6	7
No. of Sequences	2	8	20	40

Table 1

As to the probabilities that the series will actually last four, five, six or seven games, these clearly depend on the relative strengths of the teams. Most students will recognize intuitively that the prospects for a long series increase when the teams are closely matched, and vice versa.

If newspaper "odds" are available these should be translated into the probability of A's winning (p) and N's winning ($q = 1 - p$). If the odds are $m{:}n$ then $p = m/(m + n)$.

After a brief discussion reviewing the principle that governs the probability of independent events (perhaps illustrated by coin throws), it should become clear that the probability of an American League sweep is $P(A \text{ in } 4) = p \cdot p \cdot p \cdot p = p^4$. Similarly $P(N \text{ in } 4) = q^4$ and the overall probability of a four-game series is simply $p^4 + q^4$.

It is rewarding for students to find their intuitions confirmed, so it will be illuminating to substitute the various values for p and q that result from different odds, as shown by Table 2 below.

If odds favoring A are	1:1	2:1	3:1
P (4-game series)	.13	.21	.32

Table 2

Students should be encouraged to extend this table of values.

Before calculating the likelihood of a five-game series, recall work done at the outset to determine the number of possible five-game sequences. There were eight such sequences (NAAAA, ANAAA, AANAA, AAANA, ANNNN and so forth) and the probability associated with *each* of the first four is given by $q \cdot p \cdot p \cdot p \cdot p = p \cdot q \cdot p \cdot p \cdot p = p \cdot p \cdot q \cdot p \cdot p = p \cdot p \cdot p \cdot q \cdot p = p^4 q$
Since these outcomes are mutually exclusive, the probability of $P(A \text{ in } 5) = 4p^4q$. In identical fashion $P(N \text{ in } 5) = 4pq^4$ and the overall chance for a five-game series is: $4p^4q + 4pq^4 = 4pq (p^3 + q^3)$.

Similarly, by falling back on the work done on permutations at the start of the lesson, it is simple to show that $P(\text{six-game series}) = 10p^2q^2 (p^2 + q^2)$ and $P(\text{seven-game series}) = 20p^3q^3 (p + q) = 20 p^3q^3 [p + q = 1]$

As more complete information is derived, Table 2 can be extended to five, six, and seven games for various initial odds.

At this point, students may be introduced to (or reminded of) the important concept of Mathematical Expectation, E(X). With probabilities available for each outcome, E(X) for the length of the series can be calculated

Odds 1:1

X — no. of Games	4	5	6	7
P(X)	.13	.24	.31	.31

$$E(X) = \Sigma X_i P(X_i) = 5.75$$
[Σ notation can be avoided]

Table 3

Batting Probabilities

Most students who follow baseball believe they have a clear understanding of the meaning of "batting average", and its implications for a hitter going into a game. Challenge the class to estimate the chances of a player getting at least one hit in four times at bat if his season-long batting average has been .250. Some may feel there is a virtual certainty of a hit since $.250 = \frac{1}{4}$.

Begin the analysis, as before, by using a sequence of letters to denote the hitter's performance (NHNN means a hit the second time up). Again, calculate the total number of possible sequences, which will be seen to be 16. Weaker students would be advised to write out each of these permutations.

Select the simplest case of NNNN. From previous work, the probability of this outcome should be evident to the class as $P(\text{hitless}) = \frac{3}{4} \cdot \frac{3}{4} \cdot \frac{3}{4} \cdot \frac{3}{4} = \frac{(3)^4}{(4)} = \frac{81}{256} = 0.32$ (Recall: $P(H) = \frac{1}{4}$ and $P(N) = \frac{3}{4}$.) Since all other sequences involve at least one hit, their combined probability is $1 - .32 = 0.68$. Thus there is only a 68 percent chance that the batter will achieve at least one hit in four times. While this result is not startling, it may definitely entail some readjustment in the thinking of some students.

In a similar manner, probabilities can be calculated for the cases of one hit (four possible sequences), two hits (six possible sequences), and so on.

The above topics represent examples of Binomial Experiments and Bernouilli Trials. Discuss with the class the definition of a Bernouilli Trial and the criteria for a Binomial Experiment, using illustrations from dice tossing, coin throwing and so forth. Elicit their estimation of whether these concepts might be usefully applied to other real life events such as gamete unions in genetics; the success of medical procedures such as surgery, and finally, the success of a batsman in baseball.

There are inherent limitations in attempting to treat baseball performances as Bernouilli Trials, especially in a unique situation like a World Series. Nonetheless, there is value in having students acquire a sense of "first-order approximations".

At the same time, their insight into the applications of mathematics can be deepened by confronting a topic with which they feel familiar and are competent to evaluate.

Postassessment

Have students:
(1) Extend Table 2 for P(five-game series), P(6), P(7) for the odds shown, as well as other realistic odds.

(2) Reconstruct Table 3 for odds of 2:1, 3:1 and then calculate E(X) for these cases.

114 Introduction to Geometric Transformations

Beginning with an introduction to the three basic rigid motion transformations, this unit will show how a group can be developed, where the elements are transformations.

Performance Objectives

1. Students will define translation, rotation, and reflection.
2. Students will identify the appropriate transformation from a diagram showing a change of position.
3. Students will test the group postulates for a given set of transformations under composition.

Preassessment

This unit should be presented when students have mastered the basics of geometry. They should be familiar with the concept of group, but do not need to have had any exposure to transformations prior to this unit. A knowledge of functions is also helpful for this unit.

Teaching Strategies

The first part of this unit will concern itself with a brief introduction to the three basic rigid motion transformations: translations, rotations, and reflections.

Students should recall that a one-to-one and onto function is a congruence. That is, $\overline{AB} \xrightarrow[\text{onto}]{1=1} \overline{CD}$ implies that $\overline{AB} \cong \overline{CD}$.

Translations

Consider   T: $\alpha \xrightarrow[\text{onto}]{1=1} \alpha$, that is, a mapping of the entire plane onto itself in the direction of a given vector **v**.

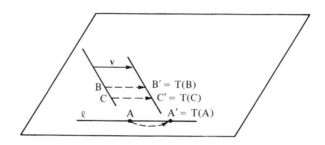

In the figure above each point in the plane is taken to a new point in the plane in the direction and distance of the translation vector **v**. Here T(B)=B′, B′ is the image of B under the translation. Points along line ℓ, which is parallel to **v**, are mapped onto other points of ℓ. To insure a good understanding of this type of transformation ask your students the following questions:

1. Which lines are mapped onto themselves? (those parallel to the translation vector)
2. Which points are mapped onto themselves? (none)
3. Which vector determines the inverse of T? (the negative of **v**)

Rotations

Consider R: $\alpha \xrightarrow[\text{onto}]{1-1} \alpha$, that is a mapping of the entire plane onto itself as determined by a rotation of any angle about a point. We shall agree to consider only counterclockwise rotations unless specified otherwise.

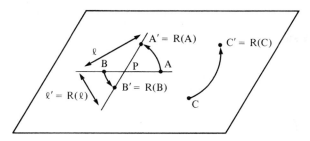

In the figure above R represents a rotation of 90° about P. The following questions should help your students understand this transformation:

1. Are any points mapped upon themselves by a rotation R? (yes, P)
2. Are any lines mapped upon themselves by a rotation R? (No, unless the rotation is 180°, written R_{180}, then any line through the center of rotation (P) is mapped upon itself.)
3. If ℓ is in the plane, how are ℓ and $\ell' = R_{90}(\ell)$ related? (perpendicular)
4. What is the inverse of R_{90}? (either R_{270}, or R_{630}, etc., or R_{-90}.)
5. What is the inverse of R_{180}? (R_{180})
6. If $R_a\,R_b$ means a rotation of $b°$ followed by a rotation of $a°$, describe R_a^2, R_b^3, R_a^4 (R_{2a}, R_{3b}, R_{4a}).
7. Simplify $R_{200} \cdot R_{180}$. ($R_{380} = R_{380-360} = R_{20}$)
8. Simplify $R_{90} \cdot R_{270}$. ($R_{360} = R_0$)
9. Simplify R_{120}^4. ($R_{480} = R_{480-360} = R_{120}$)

Reflections

Consider M_ℓ: $\alpha \xrightarrow[\text{onto}]{1=1} \alpha$, a mapping of the entire plane onto itself as determined by a reflection in a point or a line.

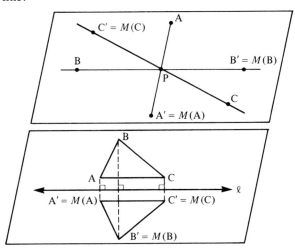

To find the reflection of a point A in a given point P, simply locate the point A′ on ray $\overrightarrow{AP}$ (on the opposite side of P as is A) so that A′P = AP. In the top figure above, A′ is the image (or reflection) of A.

To find the reflection of a point A in a given line ℓ, locate the point A′ on the line perpendicular to ℓ and

containing A, at the same distance from ℓ as A, but on the opposite side. In the bottom figure above, the points of a triangle (and hence the triangle itself) are reflected in ℓ.

Once again some questions for your students:

1. What is the inverse of M_ℓ? (M_ℓ)
2. How does an image differ from its pre-image? (different orientation, or "mirror image")
3. How does the reflection of a line in a given point change the line's orientation? (changes the order of points on the line from given to the reverse of that)
4. Describe each of the following:
    a) $M_\ell(m)$, where $\ell \,//\, m$.
       ($m'\,//\,\ell$ on the opposite side of ℓ as is m)
    b) $M_\ell(n)$, where $\ell \perp n$.
       (n' is the same line as n)
    c) $M_\ell(k)$, where ℓ is oblique to k.
       (k' forms the same angle with ℓ as does k at the same point as k but on the opposite side of ℓ)

Groups

In order to discuss a group of transformations it would be helpful to review the definition of a group.

1. A set with one operation.
2. Associative property must hold true.
3. An identity element must exist.
4. Every element must have an inverse.

To consider the elements as the three types of transformations would be confusing. We shall therefore show that (I) any translation is the product of two reflections, and (II) any rotation is the product of two reflections. This will enable us to work exclusively with reflections. The word "product" as it was used above refers to the "composition" of transformations; that is, one transformation performed after the other.

I. To show that any translation $T_\mathbf{v}$ is equivalent to the composition of two reflections consider the figure below.

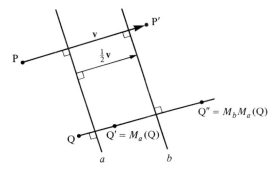

At either end of any vector $\frac{1}{2}\,\mathbf{v}$ consider the lines perpendicular to $\mathbf{v}$. By reflecting any point Q in line a

and then in line *b*, Q″ is obtained, which is T$_v$(Q). That is, $M_a(Q) = Q'$ and $M_b(M_a(Q)) = Q'' = M_bM_a(Q)$.

II. To show that any rotation R$_\Theta$ is equivalent to the composition of two reflections consider the figure below.

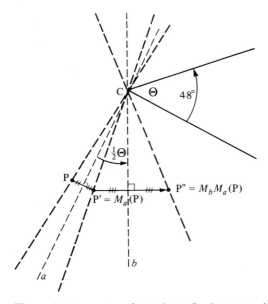

Through the center of rotation, C, draw two lines forming an angle of measure $\frac{1}{2}\Theta$. Select any point P and reflect it through line *a* and then reflect that image through line *b*.

For convenience we shall use line *a* before line *b*. Using the two pairs of congruent triangles in the figure above, we can easily prove that $M_bM_a(P) = P''$ is in fact equal to R$_\Theta$ (P).

Now that we can replace translations and rotations with combinations of reflections, ask your students to verify that a group of transformations is at hand. They must demonstrate *all* four properties listed above.

Postassessment

1. Define translation, rotation, and reflection.
2. Describe each of the following as a single transformation.
3. Show that reflections form a group under the operation of composition.

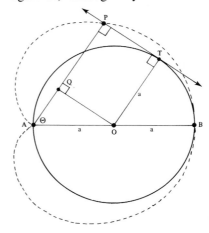

---

115   The Circle and the Cardioid

Performance Objectives

1. Given a circle, students will be able to draw a cardioid without using an equation.

2. Students will be able, by experimentation, to generate curves other than the cardioid.

Preassessment

Introduce students to the cardioid by having them set up a table of values for $r = 2a(1 + \cos\theta)$ Then have students locate the corresponding points on a polar coordinate graph. After they have constructed this curve, which was first referred to as a *cardioid* (heart-shaped) by de Castillon in 1741, students should be enticed to consider some rather unusual methods for constructing this curve.

Teaching Strategies

Method I. Ask the students to draw a base circle, O, of diameter 3 inches, centered evenly on an

8½″ × 11″ sheet. With a protractor, divide the circumference into 36 equally spaced points (see figure 1.) Through any of these 36 points, T, con-

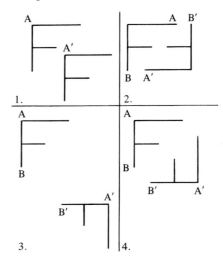

Figure 1

struct a tangent, t, to the circle. This need not necessarily be constructed in the classical way using straightedge and compasses, but rather with a right triangle template, or a carpenter's T-square, in which one leg of the triangle passes through the center of the circle. Drawing a tangent to a circle in this manner is based on the fact that the tangent to a circle is perpendicular to the radius at the point of tangency. From a *fixed* point, A, on the circle's circumference (where A is one of the 36 points), drop a perpendicular to meet t at P. Now construct tangents to all the remaining points (except through A), to each tangent repeating the preceding step of dropping a perpendicular from A

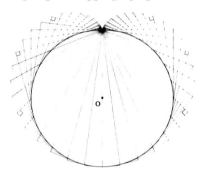

Figure 2

to t. The resulting figure will appear as shown in figure 2; the locus of all such points P is a cardioid. Point A is then the cardioid's *cusp*. In figure 2, certain construction lines from figure 1 were eliminated so as to enhance the final drawing. Also, 48 points were used along the base circle in figure 2 for a more compact appearing effect. Finally, note that the orientation of the cardioid in figure 2 differs from that in figure 1 by a 90° clockwise rotation of the cardioid about A.

Proof: In figure 1, let A be the fixed point on the circle 0. Let A also be the pole, and diameter $\overline{AB}$ the initial line, of a polar coordinate system. Draw $\overline{OT}$. Thus, $\overline{AP} \parallel \overline{OT}$. From 0, drop a perpendicular to meet $\overleftrightarrow{AP}$ at Q.
Then $\overline{OQ} \parallel \overleftrightarrow{TP}$ and OTPQ is a rectangle. Let OT = OP = a, r = AP and m $\angle$ BAP = θ. Then, from figure 1, r = AQ + QP.   (1)

In right $\triangle$ AQO, $\cos\theta = \dfrac{AQ}{a}$, so that

$\quad$ AQ = $a \cdot \cos\theta$.   (2)

With QP = a, and using (2), (1) becomes
$\quad r = a \cdot \cos\theta + a$, or
$\quad r = a(1 + \cos\theta)$,   (3)
which is the polar equation of a cardioid.

$\quad$ The procedure given above is an example of how a *pedal* curve to a given curve is generated (i.e., the cardioid is referred to as the *pedal* to circle O with respect to A). All pedal curves are obtained in this manner: Some arbitrary fixed point is chosen, often

on the curve itself, and from that point perpendiculars are dropped to various tangents to the particular curve. The locus of the intersection of the perpendiculars to each tangent from a fixed point defines the pedal curve. Though the tangent to a circle can easily be constructed, and hence a pedal curve drawn, further pedal constructions of a visual nature can prove challenging.

Method II. As in Method I, draw a base circle of diameter 3 inches, except that the circle should be placed about one inch left of center on a vertically-held 8½"x11" sheet (see figure 3). Divide the circle into 18 equally spaced points. Label the diameter AB =2a, with A once again a fixed point. Let M be one of these 18 points, distinct from A. Place the edge of a

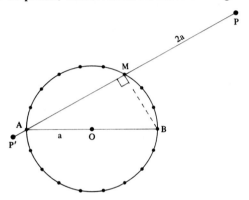

Figure 3

marked straightedge on M, being sure that the straightedge also passes through A. Locate two points of $\overleftrightarrow{AM}$, P and P′, on either side of M, at a distance of 2a units from M. Thus M is the midpoint of $\overline{PP'}$. Continue for all such points M, as M is allowed to move to each of the remaining points (of the originally selected 18 points) around the circumference. The locus of all such points P and P′ is a cardioid (see figure 4).

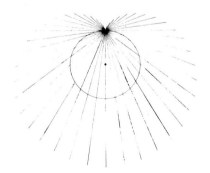

Figure 4

Proof: In figure 3, draw $\overline{MB}$, let AP = r, and let m $\angle$ BAM = θ. Since $\triangle$AMB is a right triangle,

$$AM = 2a \cdot \cos\theta. \tag{4}$$

But $r = AM + MP$, (5)

and by construction, $MP = 2a$. Substituting this, as well as (4), into (5), we get

$$r = 2a \cdot \cos\theta + 2a,$$

or $r = 2a(1 + \cos\theta)$, (6)

a form identical with (3) except for the constant $2a$. For $\theta + 180°$, we obtain P', so that $r = AP'$. Since $\cos(\theta + 180°) = -\cos\theta$, we would have obtained

$$r = 2a(1 - \cos\theta) \tag{7}$$

had we repeated the above steps.

The cardioid construction given here is an example of a *conchoid* curve. Using this technique with an ellipse, the choice of a fixed point could be an extremity of the major or minor axis. Varying the length of the line on either side of M to equal the major or minor axis creates several interesting combinations of conchoid curves for the ellipse.

Method III. The cardioid can also be generated as the locus of a point, P, on the circumference of a rolling circle which rolls, without slipping on a fixed circle of equal diameter.

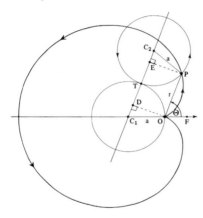

Figure 5

Proof: Let the fixed circle, C_1, of radius a, be centered at the pole of a polar coordinate system.

Let O be the intersection of circle C_1 with the initial line. Circle C_2, whose initial position was externally tangent to circle C_1 at O, has now rolled to the position shown in figure 5, carrying with it fixed point P. The locus of P is desired.

Circle C_2 is now tangent to circle C_1 at T. A line joining C_1 to C_2 will pass through T. Since $\overparen{PT} \cong \overparen{OT}$, $m \angle OC_1T = m \angle PC_2T$. If $C_2P = a$ is drawn, as well as $\overline{OP}$, we obtain isosceles trapezoid OC_1C_2P, and hence $m \angle POF = \theta$.

Drop perpendiculars from O and P to $\overleftrightarrow{C_1C_2}$, meeting $\overleftrightarrow{C_1C_2}$ at D and E, respectively. Immediately, $\triangle ODC_1 \cong \triangle PEC_2$, from which it follows that $C_1D = EC_2$ and $DE = OP$. In triangles ODC_1 and PEC_2,

$$C_1D = a \cdot \cos\theta, \tag{8}$$

and $C_2E = a \cdot \cos\theta$. (9)

Now $C_1C_2 = 2a = C_1D + DE + C_2E$. (10)

Substituting (8) and (9) into (10), and remembering that $DE = OP = r$,

$$2a = a \cdot \cos\theta + r + a \cdot \cos\theta, \tag{11}$$

which yields, upon simplification

$$r = 2a(1 - \cos\theta). \tag{12}$$

This is identical with (7).

The concept of a circle rolling smoothly on the circumference of another, fixed circle, has been well studied. The locus of a point on the circumference of the rolling circle gives rise to a curve called an *epicycloid,* of which the cardioid is a special case. Changing the ratio of the fixed circle's radius to that of the radius of the rolling circle results in a variety of well-known higher plane curves.

Postassessment

Refer to Method I for drawing the following two variations, and in so doing, possibly obtain equations similar to (3):

(a) choose the fixed point A *outside* the circle at a distance of $2a$ units from O;

(b) choose A *inside* the circle, at a distance of $\frac{a}{2}$ units from 0.

116 Complex Number Applications

The number system we presently use has taken a long time to develop. It proceeded according to the necessity of the time. To early man, counting numbers was sufficient to meet his needs. Simple fractions, such as the unit fractions employed by the Egyptians followed. While the early Greeks did not recognize irrational numbers, their necessity in geometric problems brought about their acceptance. Negative numbers, too, were used when their physical application became apparent, such as their use in temperature. Complex numbers, however, are studied because the real number system is not algebraically complete without them. Their application to the physical world is not explored by most mathematics students. This unit introduces students to some physical applications of complex numbers.

Performance Objectives
Students will be able to solve some physics problems involving complex numbers and vector quantities.

Preassessment
Students should be familiar with operations with complex numbers and vector analysis. A knowledge of basic physics is also recommended.

Teaching Strategies
In algebra, a complex plane is defined by two rectangular coordinate axes in which the real parts of the complex numbers are plotted along the horizontal axis and the imaginary parts are plotted along the vertical axis. This complex plane can be developed if we take an approach in which i is treated as the ''sign of perpendicularity'' as an operator functioning to rotate a vector through an angle of 90°.

To develop this idea we begin with any vector quantity, A, which is represented by a vector ⟶ whose length indicates the magnitude and whose arrow tip indicates sense. (To distinguish between vector and scalar quantities, a bar is placed over the symbol to indicate a vector quantity, $\overline{A}$, while a symbol without a bar indicates a scalar quantity, A). Now, if $\overline{A}$ is operated upon by -1 (multiplied by -1), we have $-\overline{A}$ whose graphical representation is ⟵. Thus, operating upon the vector $\overline{A}$ by -1 rotates it through 180° in the positive sense. Now, since $i^2 = -1$, i must represent rotating the vector through an angle of 90°, since two applications of 90° will result in a rotation of 180 °. Therefore, operating

upon a vector by i^3 rotates the vector through 270°, and so on. Similarly we can consider using as operators higher roots of -1, which will rotate the vector through a smaller angle. So $\sqrt[3]{-1} = (i^2)^{\frac{1}{3}} = i^{\frac{2}{3}}$ will rotate a vector through an angle of 60° since three applications of this operator is equivalent to operating by -1. We can show this in a vector diagram. Given a vector $\overline{A}$, with magnitude A, we operate upon it by $i^{\frac{2}{3}}$, i.e., we rotate the vector through 60°. This, of course,

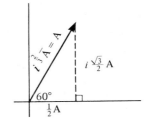

Figure 1

does not change its magnitude, A. Therefore, the real component is A cos 60° $= \frac{1}{2}$A and the imaginary component is A sin 60° $= \sqrt{\frac{3}{2}}$A. So $\sqrt[3]{-1}\,\overline{A} = i^{\frac{2}{3}}\,\overline{A} =$ A cos 60° $+ i$A sin 60°, which indicates the position of the vector. In this way $\sqrt[n]{-1}\,\overline{A} = i^{\frac{2}{n}}\,\overline{A} = \overline{A}\,\text{Cos}\,\frac{\pi}{n} + i\,\text{A Sin}\,\frac{\pi}{n}$. To generalize, to rotate a vector A through the angle Θ we use the operator cos $\Theta + i$ sin Θ.

Now, if we are given a vector $\overline{A}_1 = a + bi$, we can graph it on the complex plane. The position of the

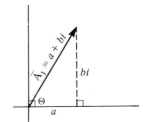

Figure 2

vector is given by $\Theta_1 = \text{arc tan}\,\frac{b}{a}$. Its magnitude is $A_1 = \sqrt{a^2 + b^2}$. Vector $\overline{A}_1$ is pictured in figure 2. Similarly vector $\overline{A}_2 = -a - bi$ has magnitude $A_2 = \sqrt{(-a)^2 + (-b)^2}$, the same as that of vector A_1. Its position is given by $\Theta_2 = \text{arc tan}\,\frac{-b}{-a}$ and is located in the third quadrant as pictured in Figure 3.

Now, we can explore a physical interpretation of these operators. In physics books $\sqrt{-1}$ is represented

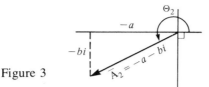

Figure 3

by the letter j and electrical current by the letter I. Since this paper is written for mathematics students, we used i to represent $\sqrt{-1}$ and, for the sake of clarity, we will use the letter J to represent the electrical current.

In the study of alternating currents, we have for the current the vector $\overline{J} = j_1 + ij_2$. The voltage $\overline{E}$ of this frequency can be represented by $E = \epsilon_1 + \epsilon_2 i$. The impedance (effective resistance of the current) of the circuit, *not* a vector, can be represented by $Z = r \pm ix$ where r is the ohmic resistance and x is the reactance. The angle between $\overline{E}$ and $\overline{J}$ is the phase angle (the angle by which the current lags behind the electromotive force, emf) and is represented by $\phi = $ arc tan $\frac{r}{x}$.

We can obtain mathematically the product of two impedances, but it has no physical meaning. The product of the voltage and the current, although it has no physical meaning, is referred to as apparent power. If, however, we take the product of the current and the impedance $Z\overline{J} = (r + ix)(j_1 + ij_2) = (rj_1 + xj_2) + i(rj_2 + xj_1)$, we have a voltage of the same frequency as the current, *the actual voltage*, i.e., $Z\overline{J} = \overline{E}$. This is Ohm's law in the complex form (recall that Ohm's law states that for direct currents the voltage is equal to the product of the resistance and the current). So, in direct currents one deals with scalar quantities while in alternating current circuits the quantities are vectors expressable as complex numbers obeying the laws of vector algebra. In the following diagrams for Ohm's law, the first diagram (Figure 4) has $\overline{J}$ on the real axis, the second diagram (Figure 5) does not.

Let us now try some problems.

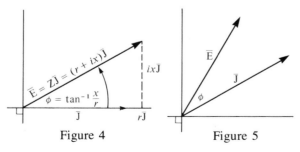

Figure 4   Figure 5

Example 1. Let $r = 5$ ohms, $x = 4$ ohms and the current J is 20 amperes. Take J on the real axis

Given this information we have the impedance, $Z = 5 + 4i$. The inductive circuit is $\overline{E} = \overline{J}Z = 20(5 + 4i) = 100 + 80i$. Therefore $E = \sqrt{100^2 + 80^2} = 128$ volts. The angle $\overline{E}$ makes with the real axis is $\Theta = $ arc tan $\frac{80}{100} =$

38°40′, which also happens to be the phase angle for this problem. The vector diagram is shown in Figure 6.

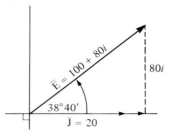

Figure 6

Example 2. Let us change the above example slightly by letting the angle that the current vector $\overline{J}$ makes with the real axis be 30°. We will let the remaining data be as before.

We still have $Z = 5 + 4i$. We now have $\overline{J} = 20(\cos 30° + i \sin 30°) = 20(.866 + .5i) = 17.32 + 10i$
$\overline{E} = \overline{J}Z = (17.32 + 10i) \cdot (5 + 4i) = 46.6 + 119.28i$
$E = \sqrt{(46.6)^2 + (119.28)^2} = 128$ volts, just as before
The angle E makes with the real axis is $\theta = $ arc tan $\frac{119.28}{46.6} = 68°40′$.
The phase angle ϕ remains the same, $\phi = $ arc tan $\frac{4}{5} = 38°40′$.
The vector diagram for this problem is:

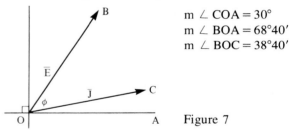

m ∠ COA = 30°
m ∠ BOA = 68°40′
m ∠ BOC = 38°40′

Figure 7

Students should now be able to solve similar physics problems involving complex numbers.

Postassessment

1. Let $r = 3$ ohms and $x = 4$ ohms. Take $\overline{J}$ on the real axis, $J = 3$. Find the impedance Z, the complex expression for $\overline{E}$ and the magnitude of E. What is Θ, the angle $\overline{E}$ makes with the real axis? What is ϕ, the phase angle? Draw a vector diagram for this problem.

2. Use the data for the above problem, letting $\overline{J}$ make an angle of 20° with the real axis. Recalculate all quantities, both the complex expressions and the magnitudes. Draw the vector diagram.

3. Let $\overline{E} = 4 + 14i$ and $\overline{J} = 2 + 3i$. Find the complex expression for Z and its magnitude. What is the phase angle? Draw a vector diagram.

Reference

Suydam, Vernon A. *Electricity and Electromagnetism*. New York: D. Van Nostrand Company, 1940.

117 Hindu Arithmetic

The mathematics curriculum may be enriched for students on many levels by the study of a number system and its arithmetic. An investigation into the mechanics of the system, its contribution to our own system, and other suitable tangents may be entered upon by a student on a high level. For other students it can serve as practice in basic skills with integers, as students check the answers they obtain in working out problems. This unit introduces students to the ancient Hindu numerical notation and system of adding, subtracting, multiplying and dividing (circa 900, India).

Performance Objectives

1. *Given an addition problem, students will find the answer using a Hindu method.*

2. *Given a subtraction problem, students will find the answer using a Hindu method.*

3. *Given a multiplication problem, students will find the answer using a Hindu method.*

4. *Given a division problem, students will find the answer using a Hindu method.*

Preassessment

Students need only be familiar with the basic operations of integers, i.e., addition, subtraction, multiplication and division.

Teaching Strategies

The symbols of the nine numerals used in Hindu reckoning in ascending order are: १ , २ , ३ , ४ , ५ , ६ , ७ , ८ , ९ , ० This system included a symbol for zero, ०. This, then, was a positional system, as in our own, as opposed to a grouping system such as that used by the ancient Egyptians. Therefore, similar to our modern system, 5639 would be represented as ५६३९ .

At this point we can discuss the importance of the Hindu symbol for zero. A comparison with the Egyptian numeral system might be instructive (see Unit 14 on Ancient Egyptian Arithmetic). The historical importance of zero could be investigated. Without a zero numbers were cumbersome, and intricate computations were difficult. In the Hindu system, record keeping and other computations necessary for commerce, astronomical computations, and mathematical tables were advanced, for with the existence of a placeholder numbers are easier to write and read, and can be manipulated with greater ease.

Hindu computation was generally written upon surfaces where corrections and erasures were easily done. For our purposes, instead of erasing numbers we will cross out numbers so that the methods discussed will be more easily followed.

Hindu addition, though set up vertically as in our method, was done from left to right. Consider the problem: 6537 + 886. The addition begins on the left with 8 being added to the 5. The 1 of this 13 is added to the numeral on the left, 6, changing it to 7, and the 5 is now changed to a 3. This process continues, from left to right. Thus, the solution would look like this:

```
7 4 2
7 3̶ 1̶ 3
6̶ 5̶ 3̶ 7̶      The result is 7423.
8 8 6
```

Subtraction was also done from left to right, the larger number being placed above the smaller one. To subtract 886 from 6537, we begin by subtracting 8 from 5. Since this is not possible, we subtract the 8 from 65, leaving 57. We put the 5 in place of the 6, and the 7 in place of the 5. We continue this process by subtracting 8 from 3 using the described method. The solution of the entire problem would look like this:

```
      6
5 7̶ 5 1
6̶ 5̶ 3̶ 7̶      The result is 5651.
8 8 6
```

To multiply as the Hindus did, we begin by placing the units' digit of the multiplier under the highest place of position of the multiplicand. To multiply 537 by 24 we begin this way:

```
    5 3 7
  2 4
```

We multiply 2 by 5 and place the resulting 0 above the 2, and the 1 to the left. We now multiply 4 by the 5, placing the resulting 0 in place of the 5 above the 4, and adding the 2 to the 0 we now have 2 in the next place:

```
  2 0
1 0̶ 5̶ 3 7
  2 4
```

Now that we have finished with the 5, we shift the multiplier one place to the right, the 4 now being below the 3, indicating 3 is the number we are now concerned with.

```
  2 0
1 0̶ 5̶ 3 7
    2 4
```

We multiply as before, first the 2 by the 3, then the 4, and when finished shift again to the right. When we have done the entire problem it will look like this:

```
          8
         7 8
         6 6
       2 0 2 8        The answer is 12,888.
     1 0 3 3 7
       2 4
         2 4
           2 4
```

It can be seen that crossing out, instead of erasing, requires space. As division is the most complex of the basic operations, the problem will be done step by step, instead of crossing out, substituting new results for the old numbers.

To divide, we place the divisor below the dividend, aligning them on the left. Thus, we begin the problem $5832 \div 253$ as $\begin{smallmatrix} 5 & 8 & 3 \\ 2 & 5 & 3 \end{smallmatrix} \, 2$. As 253 is below 583, we seek a number to multiply 253 by so that the product will be as close as possible to 583 without exceeding it. The number we seek here is 2, and it is placed thus:

```
        2
    5 8 3 2
    2 5 3
```

We now multiply 253 by 2 (as the Hindus did) and subtract the result from 583 (as the Hindus did). This gives us 77, which we put in the place of 583. So we now have:

```
          2
      7 7 2
    2 5 3
```

The divisor is shifted to the right to get:

```
          2
      7 7 2
      2 5 3
```

The process continues as above until we reach the results

```
       23
       13
      253
```

which shows the quotient to be 23 and the remainder 13.

Investigate these processes with your students to the extent you feel necessary. You will find instructive the similarity of these algorithms to ours.

Postassessment

1. Have students write the following numbers using Hindu numerals:
   a) 5342   b) 230796
2. Have students solve the following problems using Hindu methods:
   a) $3567 + 984$ b) $8734 - 6849$
   c) 596×37 d) $65478 \div 283$

Suggested References

Waerden, B. L. van der. *Science Awakening*. New York: John Wiley & Sons, 1963

Eves, Howard. *An Introduction to the History of Mathematics,* 4th ed. New York: Holt, Rinehart and Winston, 1976.

118 Proving Numbers Irrational

When high school students are introduced to irrational numbers, they are usually asked to accept the fact that certain numbers like $\sqrt{2}$, sin 10°, and so on are irrational. Many students wonder, however, how it could be proved that a given number is irrational. This unit presents a method to prove the irrationality of certain algebraic numbers.

Performance Objectives

1. Given certain algebraic numbers students will be able to prove their irrationality.

2. Students will find some specific patterns that will determine in advance whether a given algebraic number is irrational.

Preassessment

Students should be familiar with the concepts of irrational numbers and algebraic numbers. They should also have a general background in algebraic equations, radicals, trigonometry and logarithms.

Teaching Strategies

Begin the lesson by asking students to give examples of irrational numbers. Ask them how they are sure these numbers are irrational. Then have them define irrational numbers. Students will be curious enough at this point to want to investigate the following theorem.

Theorem:

Consider any polynomial equation with the integer coefficients, $a_n x^n + a_{n-1}x^{n-1} + \ldots + a_1 x + a_0 = 0$. If this equation has a rational root p/q, where p/q is in its lowest terms, then p is a divisor of a_0 and q is a divisor of a_n.

Proof:

Let p/q be a root of the given equation. Then it satisfies the equation and we have:

$a_n(p/q)^n + a_{n-1}(p/q)^{n-1} + \ldots + a_1(p/q) + a_0 = 0$ (I)

We now multiply (I) by q^n to obtain

$a_n p^n + a_{n-1}p^{n-1}q + \ldots + a_1 pq^{n-1} + a_0 q^n = 0$

This equation can be rewritten as

$a_n p^n = -a_{n-1}p^{n-1}q - \ldots - a_1 pq^{n-1} - a_0 q^n$

or

$a_n p^n = q(-a_{n-1}p^{n-1} - \ldots - a_1 pq^{n-2} - a_0 q^{n-1})$

This shows that q is a divisor of $a_n p^n$. But if p/q is in its lowest terms, then p and q are relatively prime and therefore q is a divisor of a_n. Likewise, if we rewrite equation (I) as

$a_0 q^n = p(-a_1 q^{n-1} - \ldots - a_{n-1}p^{n-2}q - a_n p^{n-1})$

we see that p is a divisor of $a_0 q^n$. Again, because p and q are relatively prime, we have that p is a divisor of a_0. This completes the proof of the theorem.

Example 1. Prove that $\sqrt{5}$ is irrational.

$\sqrt{5}$ is a root of $x^2 - 5 = 0$. Then according to the notation used for the theorem, $a_2 = 1$ and $a_0 = -5$. Now any rational root, p/q, of this equation will have to be of such a nature that p will have to divide -5, and q will have to divide 1. This is so because of the previous theorem. But the only divisors of 1 are $+1$ and -1. Thus q must be either $+1$ or -1, and the rational root of the equation must be an integer. This integer p, according to the theorem must divide -5, and the only divisors of -5 are: $-1, 1, 5$ and -5. However none of these is a root of the equation $x^2 - 5 = 0$, that is $(1)^2 - 5 = 0$; $(-1)^2 - 5 = 0$ $(5)^2 - 5 = 0$; and $(-5)^2 - 5 = 0$, are *all false*. Hence $x^2 - 5 = 0$ has no rational root, and $\sqrt{5}$ is therefore an irrational number.

Example 2. Prove that $\sqrt[3]{2}$ is irrational.

$\sqrt[3]{2}$ is a root of $x^3 - 2 = 0$. Then p must divide -2, and q must divide 1. Thus, if this equation has a rational root, this root must be an integer and a divisor of -2. Now the only divisors of -2 are: $2, -2, 1$, and -1. But none of these is a root of the equation $x^3 - 2 = 0$, because $(2)^2 - 2 = 0, (-2)^2 - 2 = 0, (1)^2 - 2 = 0$, and $(-1)^2 - 2 = 0$ are all false. Hence, $\sqrt[3]{2}$ is irrational.

Example 3. Prove that $\sqrt{2} + \sqrt{3}$ is irrational.

If we write $x = \sqrt{2} + \sqrt{3}$, we have that $x - \sqrt{2} = \sqrt{3}$. Now, square both sides and obtain $x^2 - 1 = 2x\sqrt{2}$

Squaring again gives us $x^4 - 2x^2 + 1 = 8x^2$ or $x^4 - 10x^2 + 1 = 0$.

This equation has been so constructed that $\sqrt{2} + \sqrt{3}$ is a root. But the only possible rational roots of this equation are those integers that are divisors of 1, that is, -1 and 1. But none of these is root of the equation because $(1)^4 - 10(1)^2 + 1 = 0$ and $(-1)^4 - 10(-1)^2 + 1 = 0$ are both false. Hence this equation has no rational roots and consequently $\sqrt{2} + \sqrt{3}$ is irrational.

Example 4. Prove the sin 10° is irrational.

We have the identity sin 3Θ = 3sinΘ − 4 sin $^3\Theta$. Now if we replace Θ by 10°, and notice that

$$\sin 30° = \frac{1}{2}, \text{ we get}$$

$$\frac{1}{2} = 3 \sin 10° - 4 \sin^3 10°.$$

If we now make sin 10° = x, we obtain

$$\frac{1}{2} = 3x - 4x^3 \quad \text{or}$$

$$8x^3 - 6x + 1 = 0.$$

According to the theorem, p must be a divisor of 1, and q must be a divisor of 8, thus the only possible rational roots are $\pm\frac{1}{8}$, $\pm\frac{1}{4}$, $\pm\frac{1}{2}$ and ± 1. But none of these eight possibilities is a root of the equation, as can be seen by substitution into the equation obtained. Therefore, this equation has no rational roots, and since sin 10° is a root of the equation, it must be irrational.

Students should now be able to prove irrational those numbers that occur most frequently in high school text books and that students are *told* are irrational. It is important to have students understand why a mathematical concept is true after they have comfortably worked with the concept. All too often students accept the irrationality of a number without question. This unit provides a method which should bring some true understanding to the average high school mathematics student. In addition to the problems posed in the *Postassessment,* students should be encouraged to use the technique presented here when the need arises.

Postassessment

Those students who have mastered the technique learned through the previous examples, should be able to complete the following exercises:
1. Prove that $\sqrt{2}$ is irrational.
2. Prove that $\sqrt[3]{6}$ is irrational.
3. Prove that $\sqrt[3]{3} + \sqrt{11}$ is irrational.
4. Prove that Cos 20° is irrational.
5. Prove that a number of the form $\sqrt[n]{m}$, where n and m are natural numbers, is either irrational or an integer.

119 How to Use a Computer Spreadsheet to Generate Solutions to Certain Mathematics Problems

This unit presents some simple examples of how spreadsheets, such as Multiplan and Visicalc, can be used to generate solutions to certain mathematics problems. A computer with an appropriate spreadsheet must be available and pupils should be familiar with its operation. Secondary school students of any grade should find this challenging as well as fascinating.

Performance Objectives
1. *Students will generate a Fibonacci sequence on a spreadsheet.*
2. *Students will create a Pascal triangle on a spreadsheet.*
3. *Students will list other mathematical problems appropriate for spreadsheet solution.*

Preassessment

Students need to review Enrichment Units 85 (Fibonacci sequence) and 99 (Pascal's pyramid — especially the first part, which discusses the Pascal triangle.) Students should also be familiar with basic operations on a microcomputer and electronic spreadsheets.

Teaching Strategies

An electronic spreadsheet is an array that appears on the screen of a microcomputer. Most spreadsheets have built-in mathematical functions so that elements in the ith row, j^{th} column can be easily accessed for any given i or j. For example, show students how maximum value, minimum value, average value, median, mode, standard deviation, and so on, can be determined for a set of numbers listed on a spreadsheet. Point out that other mathematical applications may be found for spreadsheets in addition to those already in the program.

One interesting application is to generate a Fibonacci sequence as well as a sequence of ratios of successive pairs of numbers. Pay special attention to the formula used to generate a Fibonacci sequence as it is listed in Enrichment Unit 85: $f(n) = f(n-1) + f(n-2)$.

One way this formula can be translated to "spreadsheet language" is, "For a given row, the number in the nth column is equal to the sum of the numbers in the two previous columns."

Together with the students, use "indirect addressing" to develop the formula that a given cell's contents should equal the sum of the entries of the two columns to its left in the same row. Thus, for a given cell,

$$entry = RC[-1] + RC[-2].$$

This technique may be used to write as many terms as will fit onto one row. Then, if you like, develop a variation of this formula that will permit continuation of the sequence to the next row for as many places as you want, considering the physical limitations of the computer.

A second sequence of ratios of successive pairs of terms, as indicated in the enrichment unit, may be generated with this formula:

$$entry = R[-1]C[+1]/R[-1]C.$$

The following sample was produced on an Apple IIe computer on a Multiplan spreadsheet.

	1	2	3	4	5	6	7	8	9	10
1										
2		FIBONACCI SEQUENCE								
3										
4										
5	1	1	2	3	5	8	13	21	34	55
6		2	1.5	1.667	1.6	1.625	1.615	1.619	1.618	

Now suggest a second application that might be of interest: the Pascal triangle. After some discussion of

Enrichment Unit 99, especially the rule for generating the triangle, suggest that the triangle be written as follows:

1	1				
1	2	1			
1	3	3	1		
1	4	6	4	1	
1	5	10	10	5	1

. . . .

Ask pupils to suggest an appropriate spreadsheet formula that would generate this triangle. Point out that the first and last entry of each row is 1 and that each of the other entries is the sum of the number in the row above and the number in that same row but one column to its left.

Postassessment

Ask the class to prepare a list of mathematical topics that might be appropriate for development via a spreadsheet, and solve some of them. You might suggest topics taken from the enrichment units in this book.

The following could prove to be challenging:

Magic squares
Palindromic numbers
The Sieve of Eratosthenes
Solving a quadratic equation
Pythagorean triples
Continued fractions

120 The Three Worlds of Geometry

It is the inquisitive nature of humans that causes them to probe deeply into that which troubles them. This unit presents the startling results achieved after twenty centuries of probing into a seemingly minor problem.

Many people throughout history were responsible for the geometry we know today. One man, however, stands above all others. That man is *Euclid,* the brilliant Greek mathematician of antiquity who developed and wrote the first geometry text, the *Elements,* ca. 300 B.C. The significance of this treatise was that it showed the capability of the human mind to arrive at nontrivial conclusions by reasoning power alone—a power that no other creature possesses.

In the *Elements,* Euclid developed geometry as a postulational system based on five postulates:

1. A straight line may be drawn from any point to any other point.
2. A line segment may be extended any length along a straight line.
3. A circle may be drawn from any center at any distance from that center.
4. All right angles are congruent to one another.
5. If a straight line intersects two other straight lines, and makes the sum of the interior angles on the same side less than two right angles, the straight lines, if extended indefinitely, will meet on that side on which are the angles whose sum is less than two right angles.

It was the length and relative complexity of this fifth postulate that led to its intensive investigation and analysis by scholars throughout the ages. Some of the fruits of these investigations are presented in this unit.

Performance Objectives

1. *Students will define the* Saccheri quadrilateral *and use it in formal proofs.*
2. *Students will compare and contrast the existence of parallel lines in the models of Euclid, Riemann, and Bolyai-Lobachevsky.*

3. *Students will learn how to prove that the sum of the measures of the angles of a triangle may be more than, less than, or equal to 180°.*

Preassessment

Students should be familiar with the traditional high school geometry course, especially the theorems related to parallel and perpendicular lines, the exterior angle of a triangle, geometric inequalities, and direct and indirect proofs.

Teaching Strategies

In the early part of the nineteenth century Playfair's postulate was shown to be a simpler, logical equivalent to Euclid's fifth postulate: *Through a point not on a given line, one and only one line can be drawn parallel to the given line. (When speaking of parallels in this unit, we use Euclid's definition: Parallel lines are straight lines that, being in the same plane and being extended indefinitely in both directions, do not meet one another in either direction.)*

An analysis of Euclid's fifth postulate yields three possible variations. We call them ''worlds'' and now compare them:

Euclid's postulate: Through a point not on a given line, one and only one line can be drawn parallel to the given line (Figure 1).

Riemann's postulate [in honor of Bernhard Riemann, German mathematician (1826–1866)]: Two straight lines always intersect one another (Figure 2).

Bolyai & Lobachevsky's postulate: In honor of mathematicians Janos Bolyai (1802–1860), Hungarian, and Nikolai Lobachevsky (1793–1856), Russian: Through a point not on a given line, more than one line can be drawn not intersecting the given line (Figure 3).

The Three Worlds. The teaching unit that you will present to your students will include some historical back-

One parallel
(Euclid)

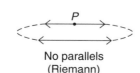

No parallels
(Riemann)

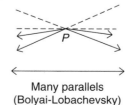

Many parallels
(Bolyai-Lobachevsky)

ground about Euclid's fifth postulate. Girolamo Saccheri (1667–1733) an Italian monk-mathematician, devised this quadrilateral to help him in his attempt to prove that Euclid's fifth postulate was in reality a theorem based on the other four postulates and thus not independent of them. He failed, but during the course of his efforts, he developed *other* perfectly consistent postulational systems and thus, without realizing it, other types of geometries—forerunners of what we now call non-Euclidean geometry.

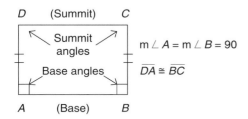

Now have the students use the following outline to complete the proof that the summit angles of a Saccheri quadrilateral are congruent.

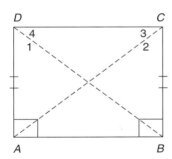

Given: Saccheri quadrilateral *ABCD*
Prove: $\angle D \cong \angle C$

1. Draw $\overline{BD}$ and $\overline{AC}$
2. Prove $\triangle ABD \cong \triangle ABC$
3. $\therefore \angle 1 \cong \angle 2$, and $\overline{BD} \cong \overline{AC}$
4. Now prove $\triangle DCA \cong \triangle DCB$
5. $\therefore \angle 4 \cong \angle 3$
6. $\therefore \angle D \cong \angle C$

Next have the students show, using only the reasons with which they are familiar from high school geometry, that in the world of Euclid, the summit angles of a Saccheri quadrilateral are *right*. However, they can also now show that the summit angles of a Saccheri quadrilateral are *obtuse* in the world of Riemann (where all lines meet)—*still using the same geometry they have been using all along:*
Given: Saccheri quadrilateral
          ABCD
Prove: $\angle 1$ and $\angle D$ are obtuse

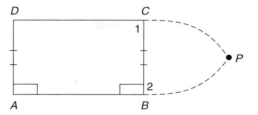

1. Extend $\overline{AB}$ and $\overline{DC}$ until they meet at point *P*. (Why can this be done? Remember that this is the world where all lines meet.)
2. m $\angle 2 = 90$
3. $m\angle 1 > m\angle 2$ (Recall a theorem about the exterior angle of a triangle.)
4. $\therefore \angle 1$ is obtuse
5. But $\angle 1 \cong \angle D$
6. $\therefore$ Both $\angle 1$ and $\angle D$ are obtuse.

At this point there can hardly be any doubt about the size of the summit angles of a Saccheri quadrilateral in the Bolyai-Lobachevsky world. Clearly they must be acute.

Next, show pupils how to develop a proof about the sum of the measures of the angles of a triangle as summarized in this chart:

Kind of world	Sum of the measures of the angles of a triangle
Riemann (no parallels)	Is more than 180°
Euclid (one parallel)	Is equal to 180°
Bolyai-Lobachevsky (many parallels)	Is less than 180°

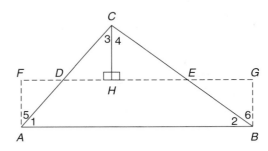

Given: $\triangle ABC$

1. Let *D* be the midpoint of $\overline{AC}$, and let *E* be the midpoint of $\overline{BC}$
2. Draw $\overline{DE}$
3. Draw $\overline{CH} \perp \overline{DE}$
4. Mark off $\overline{DF} \cong \overline{DH}$ and $\overline{EG} \cong \overline{HE}$
5. Draw $\overline{FA}$ and $\overline{BG}$
6. $\triangle FDA \cong \triangle CDH$ and $\triangle CHE \cong \triangle BGE$
7. Show that *FGBA* is a Saccheri quadrilateral with base $\overline{FG}$
8. $\angle 5 \cong \angle 3$ and $\angle 6 \cong \angle 4$

The sum of the measures of the angles of $\triangle ABC$

9. $= m\angle 1 + m\angle 2 + (m\angle 3 + m\angle 4)$
10. $= m\angle 1 + m\angle 2 + (m\angle 5 + m\angle 6)$
11. $= (m\angle 1 + m\angle 5) + (m\angle 2 + m\angle 6)$
12. $= m\angle FAB + m\angle GBA$
13. = the sum of the measures of the summit angles of Saccheri quadrilateral *FGBA*.

Your students will now appreciate why Saccheri felt he failed in what he had set out to do. He did, after all, prove theorems that appeared to arrive at contradictory conclusions. Instead, he turned out to be one of the unsung heroes of mathematics.

Postassessment

Show how residents of all three worlds can complete the following proofs:

1.
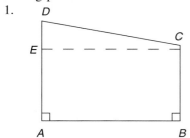

Given: $\overline{DA} \perp \overline{AB}; \overline{CB} \perp \overline{AB}; DA > CB$
Prove: $m\angle BCD > m\angle D$

2. The converse of (1) can also be proved by residents of each of the worlds. Show how this can be done by continuing the outlined proof:

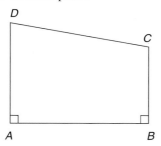

Given: $\overline{DA} \perp \overline{AB}; \overline{CB} \perp \overline{AB}; m\angle C > m\angle D$
Prove: $DA > CB$
Hint: Use *reductio ad absurdum*.

3. Complete the proof that the line joining the midpoints of the base and summit of a Saccheri quadrilateral (the *midline*) is perpendicular to both of them.
Given: Saccheri quadrilateral *ABCD; M* and *N* are midpoints; ($\overline{MN}$ is midline)
Prove: $\overline{MN} \perp \overline{AB}$ and $\overline{DC}$

1. Draw $\overline{DM}$ and $\overline{MC}$
2. Prove $\triangle AMD \cong \triangle BMC$ and $\triangle DNM \cong \triangle CNM$
3. To be completed by student

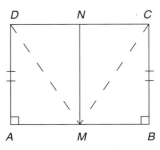

4. Only residents of Riemann's world (where the summit angles of a Saccheri quadrilateral are obtuse) can now prove this statement: The measure of the summit of a Saccheri quadrilateral is less than the measure of its base. An outline of the proof follows.

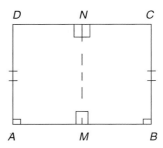

WORLD OF RIEMANN

Given: Saccheri quadrilateral *ABCD*
Prove: $DC < AB$

1. Draw the midline $\overline{MN}$
2. $m\angle BMN = m\angle MNC = 90$
3. $\angle C$ is obtuse (Why?)
4. In quadrilateral *MNCB* (with base $\overline{MN}$), $m\angle C > m\angle B$ (Why?)
5. $\therefore NC < MB$ (Why?)
6. $\therefore DC < AB$ (Why?)

5. Show how residents of the world of Bolyai-Lobachevsky (where the summit angles of a Saccheri quadrilateral are acute) can prove that the measure of the summit of a Saccheri quadrilateral is greater than the measure of the base.

6. Show how residents of the world of Euclid (where the summit angles of a Saccheri quadrilateral are right) can prove that the measure of the summit of a Saccheri quadrilateral is equal to the measure of the base.

Reference: Harold E. Wolfe, *Introduction to Non-Euclidean Geometry*. New York: Dryden Press, 1945.

121

πie mix

Leonhard Euler (1707–1783), a Swiss mathematician, startled the mathematical world when he discovered an expression that combined into a single formula theretofore seemingly unrelated numbers such as π, i, e, and 1. This unit demonstrates that formula and indicates how he might have developed it.

Performance Objectives

1. *Students will learn that* e^x, *sin x and cos x may be represented by means of a power series.*
2. *Students will see the consequences of probing into a previously uncharted course in mathematics.*
3. *Students will use Euler's formula to derive two trigonometric identities.*

Preassessment

Students should be able to evaluate powers of the imaginary number i. They should be familiar with factorial notation. Students must also be familiar with the natural logarithm base, e, and trigonometric identities for sine and cosine of the sum of two angles.

Teaching Strategies

Tell students that for any real x, it can be proved in calculus that certain functions, under given conditions, may be represented as infinite series of powers. For example,

$$\sin x = x - \frac{x^3}{3!} + \frac{x^5}{5!} - \frac{x^7}{7!} + \frac{x^9}{9!} - \frac{x^{11}}{11!} + \ldots$$

$$\cos x = 1 - \frac{x^2}{2!} + \frac{x^4}{4!} - \frac{x^6}{6!} + \frac{x^8}{8!} - \frac{x^{10}}{10!} + \ldots$$

and $$e^x = 1 + x + \frac{x^2}{2!} + \frac{x^3}{3!} + \frac{x^4}{4!} + \frac{x^5}{5!} + \frac{x^6}{6!} + \ldots$$

Euler took a bold step when he questioned the hypothesis that x must be real, because if we substitute for x the imaginary number $i\theta$, where θ is real and $i = \sqrt{-1}$, an interesting thing happens:

$$e^{i\theta} = 1 + i\theta + \frac{(i\theta)^2}{2!} + \frac{(i\theta)^3}{3!} + \frac{(i\theta)^4}{4!} + \frac{(i\theta)^5}{5!} + \frac{(i\theta)^6}{6!} + \ldots$$

Recalling that $i^2 = -1$, $i^3 = -i$, and $i^4 = 1$, we can simplify the terms of the series until we get:

$$e^{i\theta} = 1 + i\theta - \frac{(\theta)^2}{2!} - i\frac{(\theta)^3}{3!} + \frac{(\theta)^4}{4!} + i\frac{(\theta)^5}{5!} - \frac{(\theta)^6}{6!} - \ldots$$

$$= [1 - \frac{(\theta)^2}{2!} + \frac{(\theta)^4}{4!} - \frac{(\theta)^6}{6!} + \ldots]$$

$$+ i[\theta - \frac{(\theta)^3}{3!} + \frac{(\theta)^5}{5!} - \ldots]$$

$$= \cos\theta + i\sin\theta$$

Recalling again that $\cos 2\pi = 1$, and $\sin 2\pi = 0$, we may conclude that $e^{2\pi i} = 1$. It is *this* formula that caused a stir. We now turn to an unanticipated result.

Letting $\theta = x + y$ gives us

$$e^{i(x+y)} = \cos(x + y) + i\sin(x + y) \qquad [1]$$

But also,

$$e^{i(x+y)} = e^{ix}e^{iy}$$

$$= (\cos x + i\sin x)(\cos y + i\sin y)$$

$$= (\cos x\cos y - \sin x\sin y)$$

$$+ i(\sin x\cos y + \cos x\sin y) \qquad [2]$$

Equating the *real* and *imaginary* parts of [1] and [2], we get

$$\cos(x + y) = \cos x\cos y - \sin x\sin y$$

and $$\sin(x + y) = \sin x\cos y + \cos x\sin y$$

These are easily recognized as familiar trigonometric formulas.

Postassessment

1. Use the Maclaurin series approach to derive formulas for $\cos(x - y)$ and $\sin(x - y)$.
2. Show that $e^{\pi i} + 1 = 0$
3. Show how $e^{i\theta}$ may represent an operator that rotates a complex number counterclockwise through an angle θ along a unit circle.
4. Show the connection between Euler's formula and DeMoivre's theorem for finding powers and roots of a complex number.

Dr. Alfred S. Posamentier is a professor of mathematics education, Associate Dean of the School of Education, and former chairman of the Department of Secondary and Continuing Education at The City College of The City University of New York. Although he is intensely involved in the preparation and education of teachers of secondary school mathematics, both at the undergraduate and graduate levels, he is also very much involved with mathematics curriculum development for the secondary schools.

Dr. Posamentier has directed numerous development programs for teachers sponsored by the National Science Foundation (NSF). Some programs focused on using topics and concepts from higher mathematics to improve and enliven the instruction of mathematics at all secondary school levels.

Professor Posamentier has had extensive experience in several European countries in the field of mathematics teacher training. Among the many and varied activities was one designed to help teachers enrich their instruction by introducing them to topics generally considered "off the beaten path." Many of the topics presented in that program are found in Part 4 of this book. Refinements of this material resulted from the comments of many teachers who have been enrolled in this program over the years.

His extensive prior experience as both a secondary school mathematics teacher and supervisor is useful when he serves as a mathematics consultant to many school systems (both urban and suburban).

One of Dr. Posamentier's recent direct involvements with secondary school students has been through the Select Program in Science and Engineering (SPISE), which he developed at The City College in 1978, supported largely through corporate funds, and tax levy support from the New York City Board of Education and the City College. SPISE, which still continues to flourish, is designed to motivate and prepare about 700 disadvantaged high school sophomores annually for careers in science and engineering.

While teaching in secondary school he taught all mathematics courses and students at all levels of ability. During this time he also developed new courses for both enrichment and remediation.

Dr. Posamentier has received numerous awards both in the United States and abroad. These include the *Great Medal of Honor* from the Republic of Austria (1994), The City College Alumni Association's *Educator of the Year* (1993), combined with a citation from the President of the New York City Council, Fulbright Scholar (1990), and *Honorary Fellow* of the South Bank University, London, UK (1988).

In addition to articles which have appeared in professional journals and the many presentations he has made at mathematics teachers conferences, Dr. Posamentier has written several mathematics books for secondary school students as well as some for their teachers. This book ties together much of his earlier work.

Jay Stepelman has had over twenty-five years of experience as a mathematics teacher and supervisor at George Washington High School and Yeshiva University High School in New York City. He is directly involved with on-the-job teacher training and curriculum development in a practical rather than a theoretical setting. His experience ranges from planning, supervising, and teaching regular, honors, and remedial mathematics programs to developing a unique, individualized algebra program that has found special success with inner-city students, pupils with emotional handicaps, youngsters with limited reading ability, and bilingual students.

He is currently teaching at Baruch College and New York City Technical College of the City University of New York.

Dr. Stepelman is the author of *Milestones in Geometry* (Macmillan, 1970) and the *Algebra Tutor* series for the Apple II family of computers (Learning Well, 1985). In addition, he is the author of *Current Trends in Mathematics* and *State Mathematics Frameworks,* published by Kraus International Publications' *Curriculum Resource Handbook,* 1993 edition. He has lectured at professional meetings of the National Council of Teachers of Mathematics, the Association of Teachers of Mathematics of New York State, and the New York City Mathematics Chairmen's Association. He has received numerous awards, including Exemplary Supervisory Service Award (New York City Division of High Schools), and has been named as the person most influential in the success of several of Westinghouse Scholarship winners. He has also been honored by having many mathematics doctorate theses dedicated to him.

Dr. Stepelman has been called to evaluate mathematics programs and teachers at various private schools. He has served with the Board of Examiners of the City of New York in the area of teacher certification. His academic training includes mathematics and education work at the City College of New York, Courant Institute of Mathematics, New York University, and Adelphi University.

INDEX